Grünewald
Painter and Mystic
of the German Renaissance

This publications has been made possible
by CNSLAW® studio legale e notarile, Lugano, Switzerland

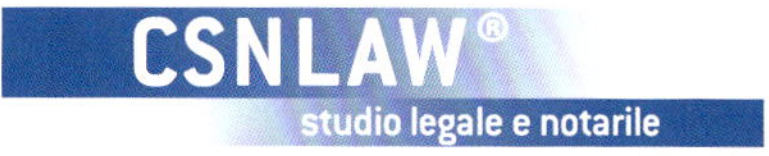

and by Alberto Savio Antichità, Trino (Vercelli), and CPM Manifold, Paitone (Brescia)

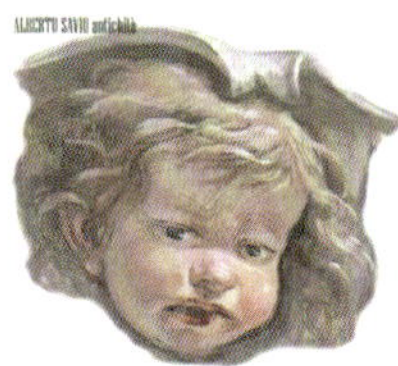

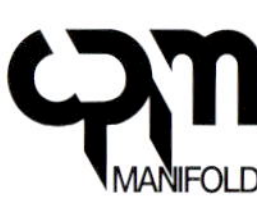

Art Director
Paola Gallerani

Designer
Elisabetta Mancini

Color Separation
Giorgio Canesin

Proofreading
Sandra Creaser

Printing
Intergrafica, Verona

Published by
Officina Libraria
Via dei Villini 10
00161 Rome, Italy

isbn 978-88-3367-334-9
www.officinalibraria.net

Printed in Italy

Edoardo Villata

Grünewald

PAINTER AND MYSTIC OF THE GERMAN RENAISSANCE

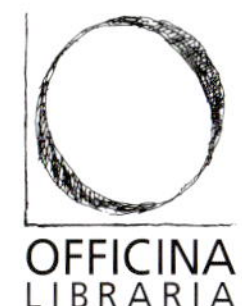

OFFICINA LIBRARIA

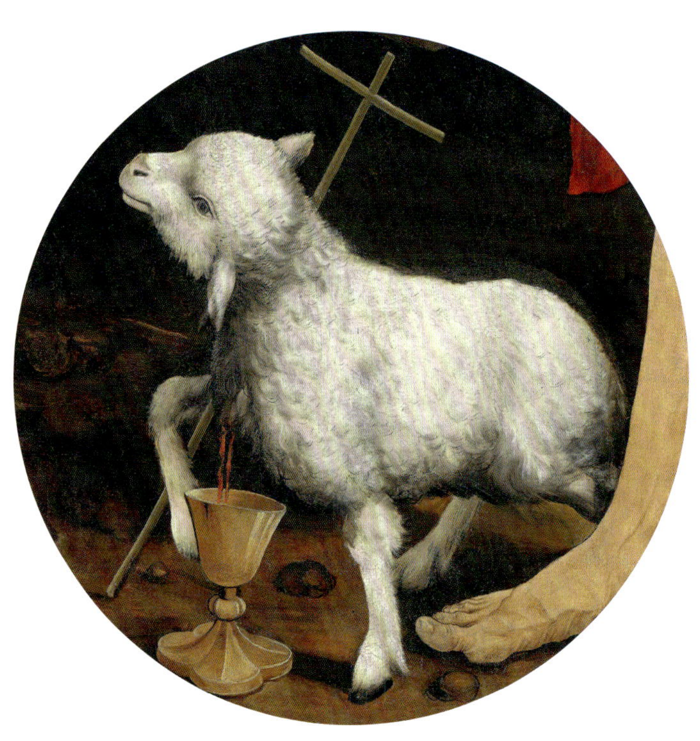

TABLE OF CONTENTS

Preface

After Heinrich Alfred Schmidt's seminal 1911 work, *Die Gemälde und Zeichnungen von Matthias Grünewald*, numerous authors have taken on the works of this artist. Some have explored the man himself, others the draftsman and others the painter, analysing his creations from a stylistic, historical or theological perspective. Previous exhibition curators have also attempted to bring together the works of Mathis Gothart Nithart in order to gain a better understanding of his style. The complementary events organized in Colmar, Karlsruhe and Berlin in 2007–2008 allowed all the drawings by the Master, or attributed to him, to be exhibited, along with some of his panels and the works of his contemporaries.[1] For conservation reasons, however, many of Grünewald's painted works were unable to travel.

Today, digital photography has allowed Edoardo Villata to have at his disposal the complete works of our artist. This is not a specific domain of the author, for currently, we can all have access to such data. Edoardo Villata, in addition to knowing how to use these digital tools, has traveled most of the world to see and study all of Grünewald's creations. The sixteen years of his life he devoted to studying the German painter – to get as close as possible to his works – and to understand them – are at the heart of this comprehensive work.

Of course, Villata bases his text on known sources and, above all, proposes new and intellectually exciting hypotheses about the painter's life, his training and the dates of his works. Not everyone will agree with some of his proposals, but isn't that the charm of art history when sources are lacking . . .?

The very structure of the book is based on chronology, but with chapters whose evocative titles show the author's singular approach: The Beginning; Early Maturity; Isenheim; Italy; Luther; the Revolt; Death.

Villata's in-depth knowledge of his subject, and his sensitivity to all the works he has come into contact with, enable him to put forward new ideas – and go into greater depth while analysing them – in conjunction with proposals pointed out by all the previous authors who have approached Grünewald's art. The bibliography of this work proves this author's desire to take into consideration all the texts directly or indirectly matching his favorite field.

The sources dedicated to the artist have all been analysed in detail by Villata. He also draws on the writings of mystics (St. Birgitta of Sweden, Ludolph of Saxony) and theologians. The personality and texts of Johann von Staupitz (1469–1524) are particularly well highlighted. This link with the written word goes so far that Villata does not hesitate to quote fragments of texts by the writer Joris-Karl Huysmans (1848–1907) or the philosopher Martin Buber (1878–1965). The same is true of the musical references in the book, the natural one being the opera *Mathis der Maler* by Paul Hindemith (1895–1963), and the more personal one, the *St Matthew Passion* by Johann Sebastian Bach (1685–1750). And in a unique perspective, he includes a cinematographic reference, comparing the face of St. Paul the Hermit – in the panel of the *Isenheim Altarpiece* [the encounter between Saint Anthony and Saint Paul the Hermit] – with the emaciated face of the actor Klaus Kinski . . .

On the difficult question of the painter's training, the author easily dismantles certain previously implausible hypotheses and proposes a strong link with sculpture.

Villata convincingly demonstrates – with the help of digital photographic equipment – the influence of the sculptures by Tilman Riemenschneider (1460–1531), who, like Grünewald, came from Würzburg. The author also makes numerous references to sculptors such as Veit Stoss (1447–1533), Hans Leinberger (1480–1531) and others from Italy, in his analysis of Grünewald's paintings and drawings. This detailed demonstration is fascinating. As are his comments on the light and color of the Master's works. He writes so aptly: "color does not 'receive' light and shade, it 'reacts' to them". This study of light in Grünewald's works led him to look for an Italian influence.

In fact, the chapter devoted to Italy goes much further than anything that has yet been written on the subject. Villata, himself Italian, has an in-depth knowledge of northern Italian painting from the late 15th and early 16th centuries. Using specific examples, he suggests that Grünewald traveled to northern Italy between September 1515 and August 1516. He shows the possible influences of Bernardo Zenale (1460–1526) or Bramantino (ca. 1460/65–1530) on his work, and conversely proposes an impact of Grünewald's art on Italian artists such as Amico Aspertini (1475–1552).

Finally, a major chapter is devoted to the *Isenheim Altarpiece*, a work that I have worked with for more than twenty-eight years as Curator of the Musée Unterlinden in Colmar. I do not agree with all of the author's proposals concerning this mythical work, but this art historian is also entitled to point out new hypotheses, especially as the contract between the commissioner and the artist(s) has never been found and no contemporary text provides us with information about the making of the altarpiece. Our main disagreement lies in the fact that Edoardo Villata explains the differences in style among the panels in terms of chronology, whereas I see them as the work of a team of several hands led by the great painter.

His analysis of the chronology of the panels is totally new, and offers some very interesting paths of research, particularly for the painted predella.

Readers will certainly want to immerse themselves in this work on the painter Mathis Gothart Nithart, very rich in references and offering a fine analysis of the chronology of his painted and drawn works.

Pantxika Béguerie-De Paepe
Honorary Curator of the Musée Unterlinden, Colmar

Preface to the English Edition

A mamma, con inesprimibile amore

The primary reason for advocating the publication of an English edition of this monograph, initially released in 2018, stems from the understanding that books originally published in Italian are not easily accessible to Grünewald scholars, who are mainly French and German (and obviously English) speakers. A secondary, not less important, reason is my desire to engage with my current students, whom I teach in English.

However, naturally, these two reasons—extremely compelling in their own right—also include a third: to continue, and in greater depth, the study of this great German painter, a scholarly pursuit I began in 2008. The ongoing research into Grünewald's style and the exploration of relevant literature, enriched by the publication of several critical books and essays (thanks, in particular, to Hanns Hubach, Giorgio Gualdrini and Wolfgang Minaty) and, above all, the spectacular restoration of the *Isenheim Altarpiece* (not to mention the major exhibitions held in Paris on Albrecht Altdorfer and in Karlsruhe on Hans Baldung Grien) commanded some key aspects be rethought.

What is presented here—in a language different from the one in which the book was originally conceived and written, translated into an English text that is strictly "academic" in its approach, organization and conclusions, and yet quite removed from certain stylistic conventions of Anglo-Saxon academic works, and should this departure provoke discontent among some, it may be that this book is not for them—is the true culmination of over sixteen years of study. Although this does not necessarily mean that I will never write about Grünewald again, it does signify that I will not approach this topic with the same aspirations for comprehensiveness and organic unity that characterized this work.

On a personal level, reflecting on the six years that separate the Italian edition from this one, I observe profound changes in my life, such as my marriage and my appointment at the university where I currently teach. On a general level, this new edition is also a product of the Covid-19 pandemic and bears witness to new wars. Our age is no less difficult or challenging than the one in which Grünewald painted his works, quite the opposite. On an intellectual, or even macrohistorical level, it is with a heightened urgency that I acknowledge, as compared to the first edition, that this book appears in the midst of a profound crisis afflicting our field. One that must be understood within the broader context of the end of Western civilization, the vestiges of which we must fight to preserve and transmit to future (not necessarily Western) generations, in the hope that the history of tomorrow will have its own new Lorenzo Valla, new Erasmus of Rotterdam, and even new Giovan Battista Cavalcaselle, Pietro Toesca and Roberto Longhi: three names that epitomize my epistemological fidelity.

It is my great pleasure to mention, once again, all those I thanked in the preface of the first edition: Roberto Contini, Marco Fratini, Hölger Jacob-Friesen, Francesca Pasut, Mauro Pavesi, Vilmos Tátrai and Stefano Zuffi, so important for the first edition, have lent their support again in this new one. Along with them, my utmost gratitude also goes to Svetlana Adaxina, Sandro Albini, Isabelle Artaud, Annika Baer, Markus

Beinrucker, Enilda Bekshiu, Hannes Bertram, Anne-Catherine Biedermann, Rosanna van den Bogaerde, Yvonne Brandt, Elizabeth Bray, Stefania Buganza, Jonas Burvall, Cecilia Cavalca, Olimpia Marini Clarelli, Dzifah Danso, Laurence Dereymez, Christoph Fichtner, Kirsten Fiege, Ulrike Fladerer, Marie-Claire Gander, Giulio Gipponi, Elisabeth Greil, Giorgio Gualdrini, Sandra Haupt, Marion Heisterberg, Lea Hughes, Melanie Krone, Florian Kugler, Michael Kummer, Anne Laffont, Marie Lionnet de Loitière, Mauro Magliani, Raphäel Mariani, Katharina Nittel, Theo Noll, Istek Peker, Delphine Petit, Gianluca Poldi, Erika Popova, Lucia Rinolfi, Mauro Salvatore, Sabrina Schauerhammer, Philippe Sénéchal, Mavia Severi, Corinne Sigrist, Serena Sogno, Fabian Steiner, Silvia Stenger, Federico Terzi, Frigyes Tikovics, Federico Troletti, Giovanni Valagussa, Barbara Van Kets, Kirsten Claudia Voigt, Sabrina Walz, Sabine Wölfel. Pantxika Béguerie-De Paepe not only offered me precious suggestions, precisions and corrections, but generously accepted my request to write the dense and positively dialectic preface that enhances this book.

Special mention also to Marco Jellinek who readily supported the idea of publishing this book, accompanying it with his usual and passionate accuracy, and the staff of Officina Libraria, whose guidance ensured its flawless publication. Naturally, my gratitude also goes to those who have made this project possible from an economic standpoint. Flavio Pozzallo and the CSN LAW studio in Lugano (thanks to lawyers Daniele Calvarese, Claudio Simonetti and Francesco Naef), who provided support for the Italian edition and also assured their generous support again this time, joined by Luca Tofanelli and C P M Manifold, Paitone and by Bo Sun, player of traditional Chinese instrument erhu and teacher at my own university, who supported this book with a great effort. The rest was financed by research funds granted by the College of Art of my university, the Northeastern University (NEU) of Shenyang. Moreover, I must thank Wan Xiuzeng, Zhang Yannan, Fan Qiangqiang and my students Li Ran and Yu Baitian, for their continuous efficiency, friendship and support.

Last, but certainly not least, my heartfelt congratulations to Pamela Cowdery Franceschetto for the skillful and sensitive translation of a difficult text, to Annita Brindani for her revision, to my former Italian student Elena Miserotti for her invaluable revision of the entire volume, and to Sandra Creaser for her precise proofreading.

Shenyang and Budapest, October 17, 2024

E.V.

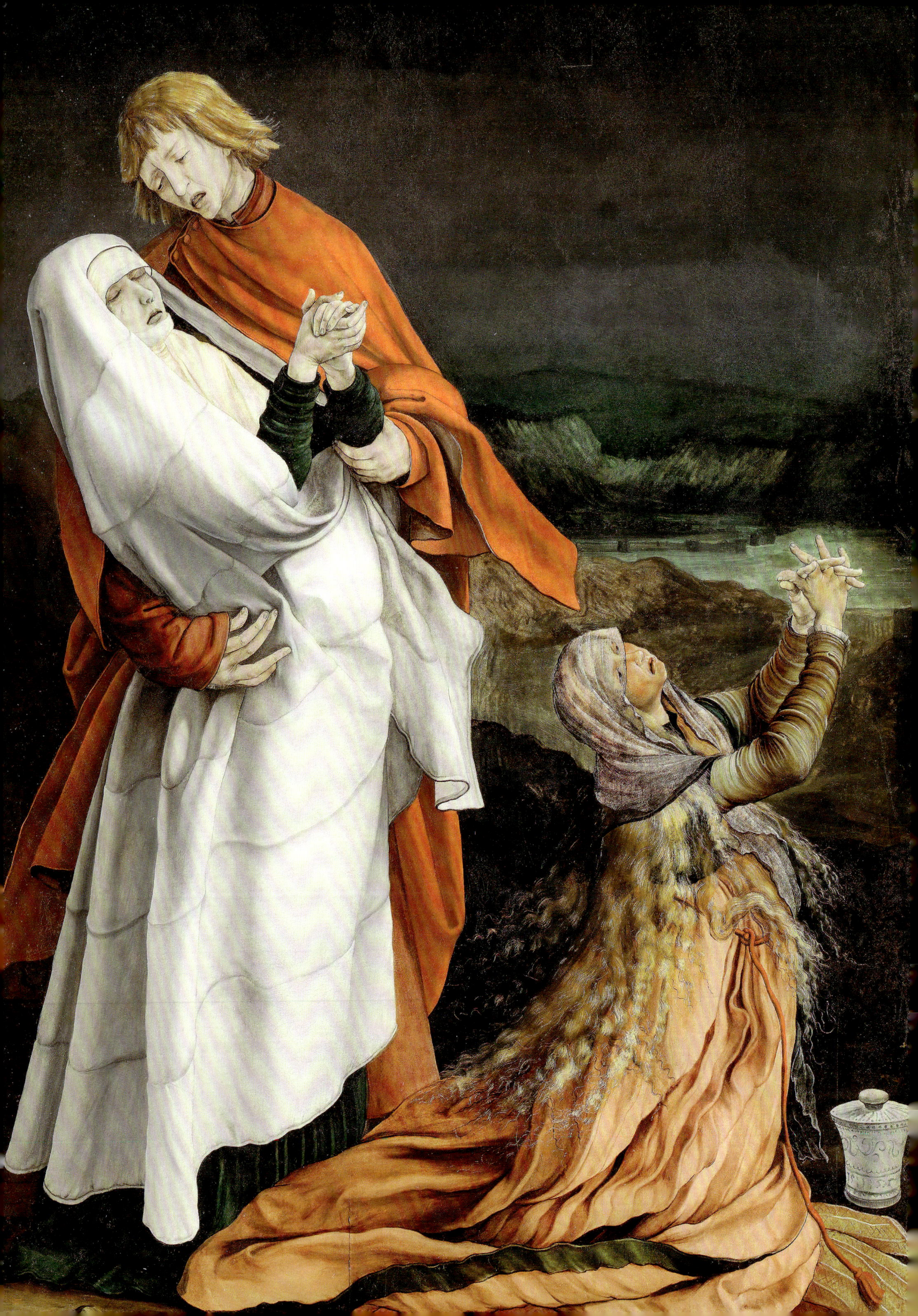

Introduction

Non enim hic tempus timendi, sed clamandi, ubi Dominus noster Ihesus Christus damnatur, exuitur et blasphematur. Unde quantum tu me ad humilitatem exhortaris, tantum ego te ad superbiam exhortor. Tibi adest nimis humilitatis, sicut mihi nimia superbia.
(Martin Luther to Johann von Staupitz, February 9, 1521)

A Berlino ci son stato con Bonetti
(Lucio Dalla, *Disperato erotico stomp*, 1977)

Between 2007 and 2008, three major exhibitions were held in Berlin, Colmar and Karlsruhe, showcasing the works of Mathis Grünewald, one of the most important German Renaissance painters (if not the most important), and one of the greatest in Western art, though much about him remains elusive. The historical and critical rediscovery of this artist dates from the 20th century, largely thanks to scholars including Alfred Heinrich Schmid, Louis Réau, Henrich Feurstein, Walter Karl Zülch, Lottlise Behling, Georg Scheja and Piero Bianconi, and more recently the important contributions of Pantxika Béguerie-De Paepe, Hanns Hubach, Reiner Marquard, Michael Roth, Pierre Vaisse and a few others. The painter's critical journey is anything but linear, and even after the three pivotal monographs published in the first half of the century (Schmid, 1911; Réau, 1920; Zülch, 1938), a number of divergent and sometimes misleading opinions persisted.

What little we do know—or what we think we can affirm with reasonable confidence—is that the painter we conventionally call Grünewald was named Mathis Gothart (at a certain point he adopted a second surname, Nithart). He was born in Würzburg and became a painter at the court of the archbishop of Mainz, Uriel von Gemmingen, primate of Germany and prince-elector of the Holy Roman Empire. The archbishop was succeeded by Albrecht Hohenzollern von Brandenburg, who, perhaps unwittingly, became a central figure in the emergence of the Protestant Reformation. Mathis left the court, and painting, in 1526, relocating first to Frankfurt and later to Halle, where he died suddenly it would seem, in 1528. Numerous indications suggest that in the last period of his life, he aligned himself, at least in principle, with Lutheranism, albeit with some contradictions.

This, in synthesis, is the scant information we possess about the man, remarkably little when compared with the wealth of documentation available on Albrecht Dürer or Lucas Cranach, for example.

Grünewald, however, is the author of a relatively limited corpus of works, which by scholars have centered around the altarpiece painted between 1512 and 1516 (more precisely, as detailed in the following pages, between 1513 and 1515, with a brief final phase the year after) for the main altar of the church of the Monastery of St. Anthony in Isenheim. This established catalog has preserved Grünewald's legacy not through bibliographical records, but through the power of the works themselves. Emperor Rudolf II, who yearned to own the altarpiece, did not know the author. Nor did Franz Christian Lerse, responsible for saving this masterpiece today in Colmar. Goethe barely knew his name, though years after he still remembered the paintings he found in Aschaffenburg and admired in his youth. Perhaps this obscurity explains why Grünewald does not enjoy the morbid mass appeal that surrounds others such as Leonardo, Caravaggio, Van Gogh, Modigliani, or now for different but no better reasons, Artemisia Gentileschi or Frida Kahlo. These artists have had their personal lives turned into a commercial phenomenon, overshadowing the understanding of their works, and have frequently had artworks unworthy of their greatness—or even forgeries—attributed to them, including in major exhibitions. Grünewald, thankfully, has been spared this fate and there is good reason to hope it will remain so.

The catalogues cited above are all admirable in their rigor and breadth of information, but they inevitably led me to question what could be discovered through an approach rooted in what I would define as an "Italian" historical-artistic method. This method emphasizes stylistic analysis aimed at identifying a credible path of development in the activity of the artist under examination, and it consistently sets their oeuvre in a dialectical relationship with that of their contemporaries, seeking to identify potential trends and evidence of mutual exchange. All this, while also naturally maintaining a strong connection to the historical and cultural milieu in which the painter lived and worked, broadening the scope of investigation by forcing oneself (and this is always the most difficult thing) to allow the works themselves to speak, rather than confining them within the constructs of our academic preconceptions. Therefore, the outcome of this method required broadening the field of observation to a wider spectrum of artists than those considered in recent studies and also extending it to sculpture—a domain where perhaps some of the most significant findings of this study emerged. Moreover, it required keeping quite separate the concepts of stylistic and iconographic comparison. At the cost of repeating myself, I must once again emphasize how deviating from the advice of the great Pietro Toesca—"first connoisseurs, then historians"—can only exacerbate the methodological crisis that our field has faced for years. We witness this daily in papers overflowing with bibliographies, often flaunted brazenly to compensate for the virtual absence of critical thinking, misguided iconographic adventures in religious or political garb, or fetishism for the written document, perhaps interpreted in arbitrary fashion to avoid having to come to grips with it. We are surrounded by the abandonment of historic profundity, the concept of art history and museums as money-making exhibition machines. Nothing new in this, but it is nonetheless painful to acknowledge. As I have previously stated, I believe that, in this bleak picture, research itself is an act of resistance. There is more revolution (if I may use this term, in an etymological sense) in patiently visiting big and small museums, churches in cities, towns and small villages, archives and libraries, with intellectual honesty and precise epistemological intent than gathering a few hundred people in an auditorium to proclaim stentorian shibboleths in a never-ending flow of mass-produced journalistic-style pamphlets.

And yet Grünewald is not only a painter for dispassionate connoisseurs. The emotional impact of his works is almost proverbially unsettling, and it is no coincidence that his 20th-century rediscovery was driven not only by scholars but also by writers, artists and musicians. For example, Émile Verhaeren and Joris-Karl Huysmans produced early exegeses that continue to amaze today for their subtlety; and the moving oratorio, *Mathis der Maler* by Paul Hindemith, representing a desperate disavowal of 1930s Germany, or the more recent Margherita Guidacci and Winifred Sebald. Many others could be cited here, as well as—in toto—the German Expressionists or Pablo Picasso.

It is an interesting coincidence that Grünewald's most famous work is found today in the church in which, in the 14th century, one of the great Rhenish mystics preached, Meister Eckhart. He belonged to a school of thought that would influence the young Augustinian monk and theology professor Martin Luther, as well as his teacher and mentor Johann von Staupitz. It is precisely the influence of Staupitz's thinking that perhaps emerges from the layers of meaning embedded in the *Isenheim Altarpiece*. Furthermore, the involvement of the court painter of Albrecht of Brandenburg (the person who, by promoting the vast system of indulgences, initiated a series of reactions that resulted in the birth of the Reformation) with Luther's theology is evident in the books he owned, as inventoried just after his death, and in the expressive and spiritual tone of his late works. In addition to Grünewald's lively curiosity about his fellow artists (including Italians, given that I believe it is virtually certain he briefly visited Lombardy in 1516), among the aspects that emerge from his art is his extraordinary religious tension that led him to create images of undeniable mystical significance. In fact, I would argue that Grünewald plays a major role not only in art history but also in Western mysticism, a role comparable to that of Hildegard of Bingen or Sebastian Franck.

However, one of the greatest challenges I faced was maintaining a critical distance from a subject in which I gradually found myself increasingly involved, even existentially. My initial foray into this research produced lecture notes for a course on this subject given at the Università Cattolica in Milan in 2009–2010, hastily written and entitled (perhaps too literarily) *I chiodi di Grünewald* [The nails of Grünewald]. I identified with those notes so deeply that I decided to make them the foundation for this book, though, upon reflection, this is actually a fundamentally different work. It includes footnotes, an extensively updated and expanded bibliography, reflecting eight years of further research and a significant amount of new material: figurative, documentary and literary. Some conclusions, particularly involving the chronology of the drawings, have been revised, new conclusions have been incorporated and, fortunately, a few errors have been corrected.

I am deeply indebted to the people I have encountered over such an extended period. I have been able to rely on a first revision of the text by Mons. Franco Buzzi, Federico Cavalieri, Marco Fratini and Stefano Zuffi. Among the numerous research trips made, the one in the spring of 2015 remains memorable, during which, while engaged in a different investigation, Francesca Pasut first drew my attention to the magnificent quality of the powerful *Portrait of an Ecclesiastic* in the Aschaffenburg Schlossmuseum. Additionally, I have been able to rely on, for purposes of comparison, exchange of ideas, comments during my conference presentations, critiques, bibliographical suggestions, material assistance and photography searches, the collaboration of Maria Grazia Albertini Ottolenghi, Pantxika Béguerie-De Paepe, Milvia Bollati, Marco Bona Castellotti, Chiara Cassinelli, Serenella Castri, Matteo Ceriana, Roberto Contini, Chrysa Damianaki, Glynn Davies, Erik Elsing, Ingrid Heeg-Engelhardt, Stephan Kemperdick, Hölger Jacob-Friesen, Claudia Gaggetta, Cecilia Ghibaudi, Katherine Lewis, Patrizia Mancinelli, Rodolfo Martini, Dora Merai, Christof Metzger, Vittorio Natale, Mauro Pavesi, Cristina Quattrini, Mons. Alberto Rocca, Jochen Sander, Federica Sesana, Béla Zsolt Szakács, Katalin Szende, Vilmos Tátrai, Pierre Vaisse, Giovanna Virgilio, Thomas Wehner and Fabian Wolf.

It has not been easy to reach port during these tempestuous times for art publications and without being able to rely on institutional funding. Because of this, and on the excellent suggestion of Alia Regli, I decided to launch a crowdfunding campaign on the Ulule online platform (where I was superlatively aided by Francesco Natale), along with other contributions. My warmest thanks go to those who have taken part in this adventure, found in the tabula gratulatoria [not present in this edition—eds.], and in particular to Francesco Alberti Lamarmora, Associazione ex Alunni del Liceo Classico di Lecco, Ezio Benappi, Maurizio Canesso, Cesare, Ester and Manuela Concina, Mario Romano Negri, Flavio Pozzallo, Massimo Rossi and Caterina Sella. A special mention goes to Riccardo Lorenzino and Hapax Editore for the enthusiasm they have brought to this project and for the superb quality of their work. Particularly gratifying is the fact that this volume marks the renewed publication of the "La Galeria" series founded in 2012 by Ennerre Editors in Milan, which, in the meantime, has experienced an extended hiatus. Our hope is that they can now continue their journey with greater serenity.

While this book does not have a dedication, it bears, in a different way and for different reasons, the mark of Mamma, Carlo and Zsófia who I want here beside me at the conclusion of a work that is the dearest to me of all those I have written to date.

Vercelli, February 9, 2018
Edoardo Villata

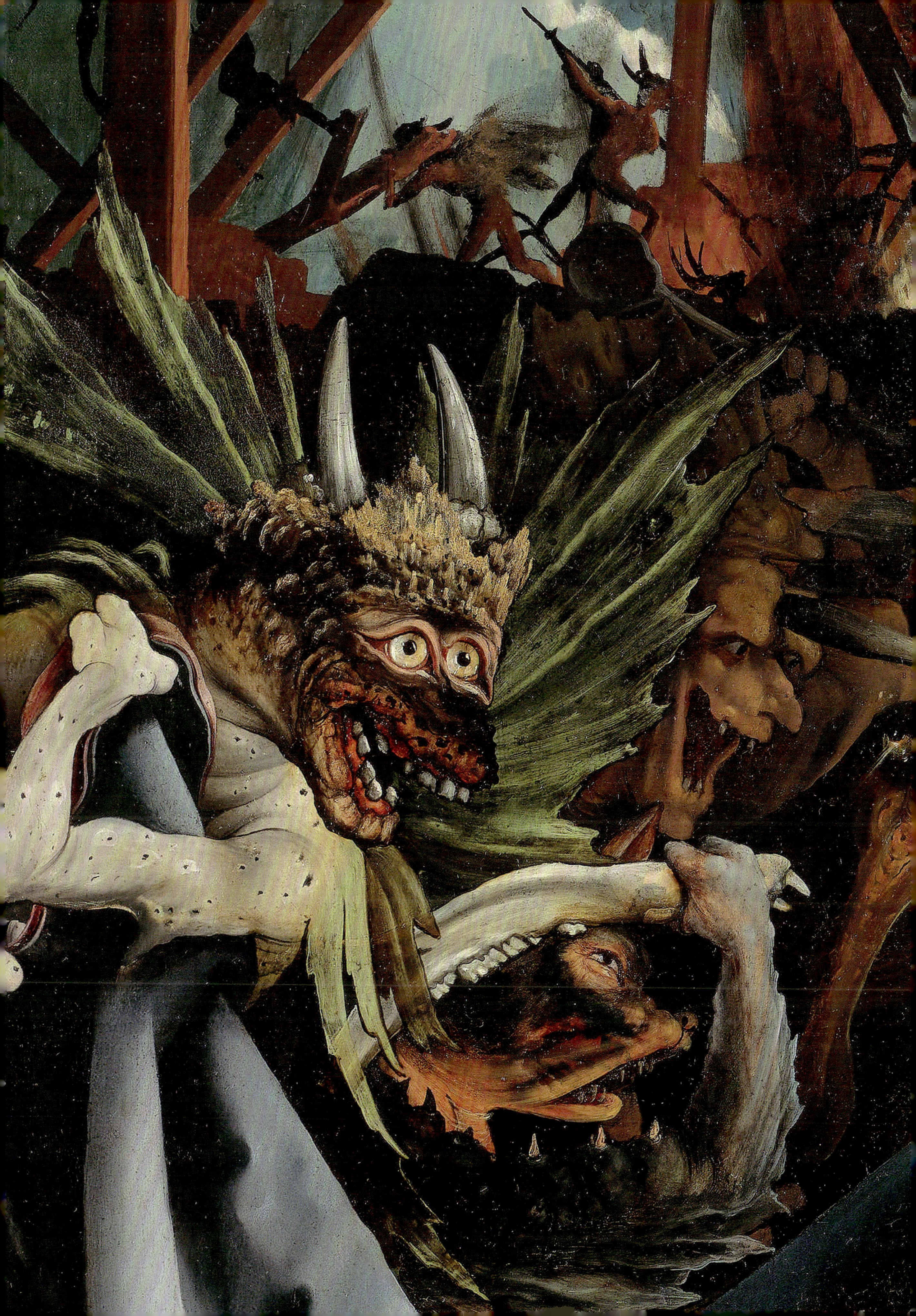

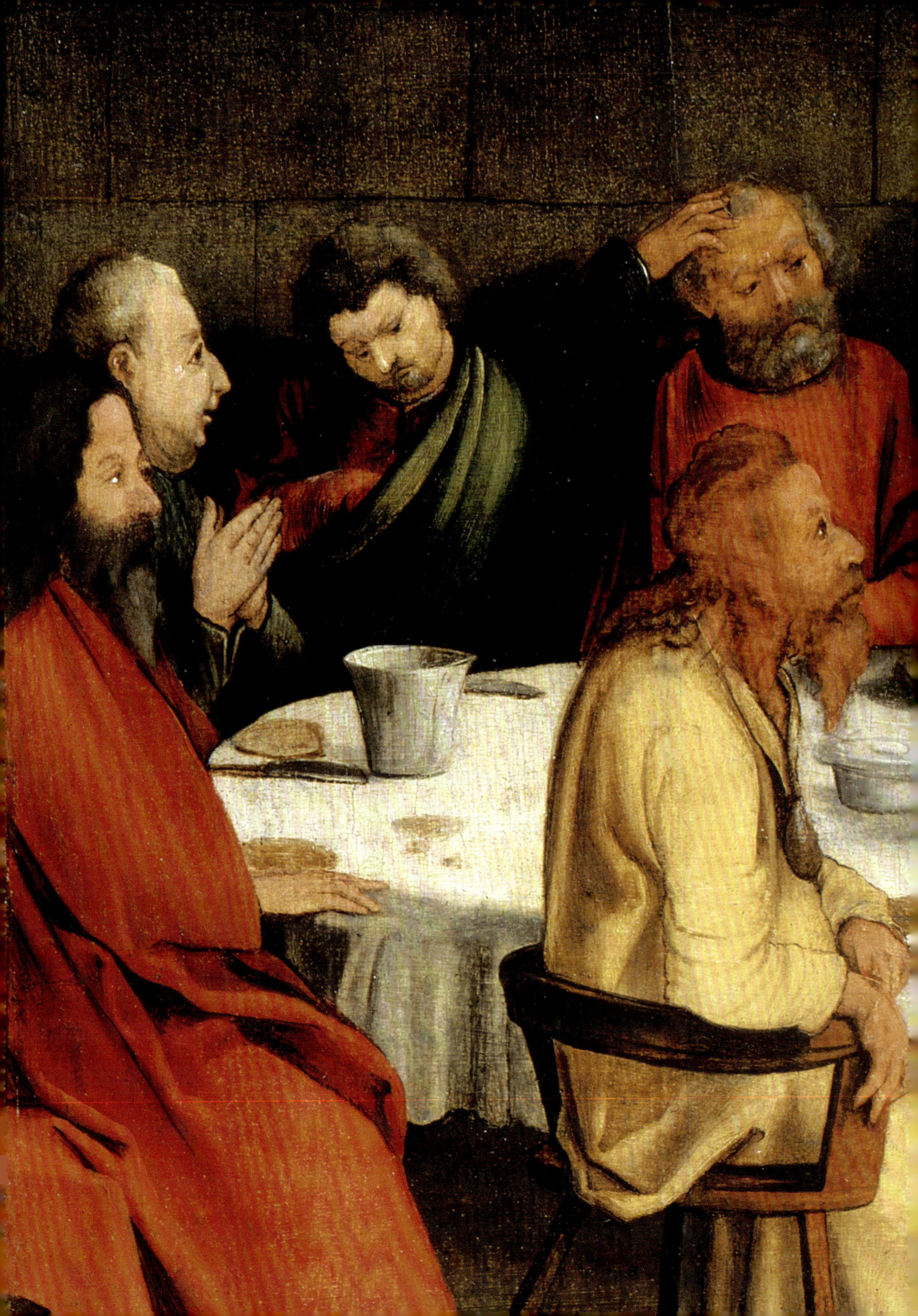

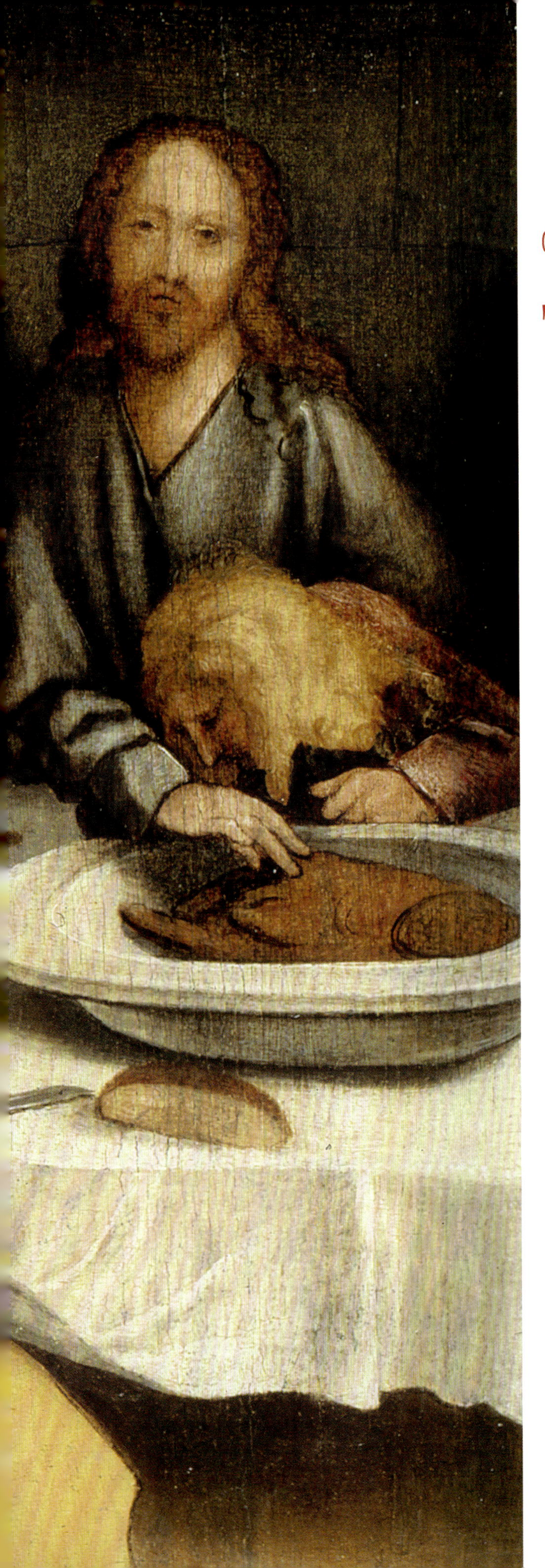

CHAPTER I

The Beginning

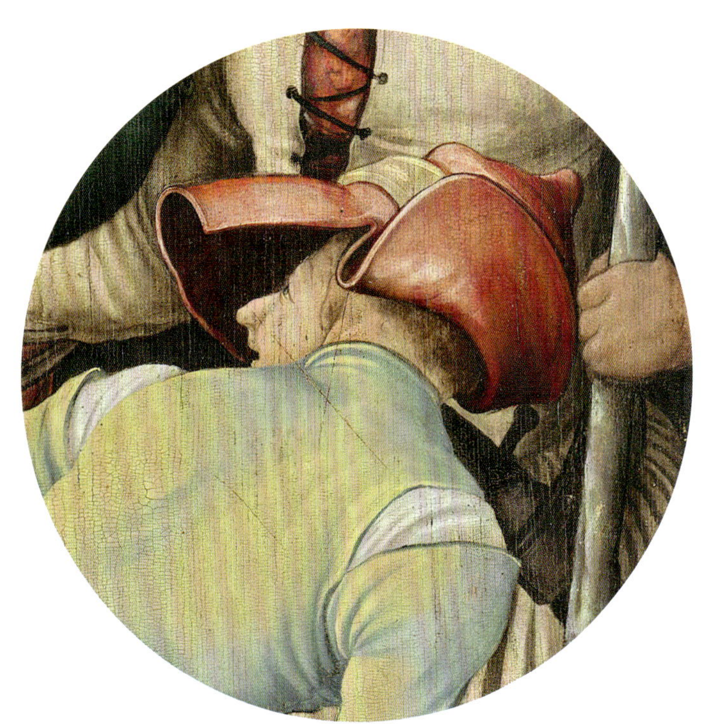

The name of "Matthias Grünewald" appears in this form only at a quite advanced date, in the *Teutsche Akademie*, published in 1675 by painter and sculptor Joachim von Sandrart.[1] Sandrart also notes that this artist is also known as "Mathis of Aschaffenburg" to underscore the identity of a master painter whose memory, although obfuscated, had not been totally lost. Also in 1573, in the German edition of the *Accuratae Effigies Pontificorum Maximorum* by Octavius Panvinius, preface authors Bernhart Jobin and Johann Fischart note, apparently based on hearsay (as the vague spelling of place names would seem to indicate), "Mathis of Oschnaburg, whose excellent paintings are seen in Issna [Isenheim]".[2] Before Sandrart, in 1620,[3] Vicenz Steinmeyer, as well as other collection inventories, mentioned in a fairly generic way Mathis of Aschaffenburg, although sometimes giving him the surname Grün, which in some ways was significant, but also the source of some confusion.[4] French *savant* Balthazar de Monconys saw an album of his drawings in 1664 and, writing about them a few years later, said that the painter, whose name was further distorted as "Martin of Aschaffenburg", is "bien plus estimé qu'Albert Dure, mais peu connu en France".[5] That this was Grünewald, and not some other painter named Martin, is confirmed through comparison with the information offered by Sandrart, which will be spoken of again. The latter tells us that an album of Mathis's drawings was in the possession of his student Hans Grimmer, who had given it to the painter Philipp Uffenbach, whose widow had then sold it to the Frankfurt bibliophile Abraham Schelkens, where, on January 5, 1664, the drawings were seen by Monconys (Schelkens obviously being the "M. Chelexens" who showed the album to the French visitor). Schelkens died in 1684 and the fate of the Grünewald album is unknown.[6] This information is confirmed by what can be deduced from a letter of Emperor Rudolph II to Count Albrecht von Fürstemberg, dated July 15, 1597: "We have been informed that in Isenheim, in a church of the Antonite monks, there is a lovely painted panel, done with great artistry by an excellent master artist."[7] Rudolph II was aware of the masterpiece held by the Antonite monks in Isenheim, which he tried to take possession of, as was also the case with the altarpiece of the main altar in the Freiburg Cathedral, painted by Hans Baldung Grien. Rudolph's interest in major German artists of the early 16th century is very striking, as well as his offer to replace them *in situ* with works by his "best painter". This was fairly standard practice in situations of this type, but it is intriguing to think that a copy of the *Isenheim Altarpiece* would have appeared painted by Hendrik Goltzius, Bartholomaeus Spranger, Joseph Heintz or Hans van Aachen (with the impact that knowledge of the *Isenheim Altarpiece* would have had on Rudolfine, and therefore European, Mannerism), even to the point of regretting that this copy was never painted. What a challenge it would have been to translate their ultra-refined cerebralism into the horrors of the Crucifixion, the indescribable glory of the Resurrection, or the violent formal shipwreck! But we must also note that while the renown of the altarpiece reached as far as Prague, even a connoisseur like Rudolph II does not seem to have known the name of its creator. The altarpiece's fame remained strong, at least locally, attracting illustrious visitors throughout the 17th century, both as an anonymous work or attributed to Dürer.[8] In other words, a split was created. Some of the works of Grünewald (as we will continue to refer to him) continued to be appreciated, albeit under a false name (before being traced to Matthias by Jakob Burckhardt in 1844,[9] the *Isenheim Altarpiece* would be attributed to Dürer and Hans Baldung Grien), while the memory of the artist would survive,

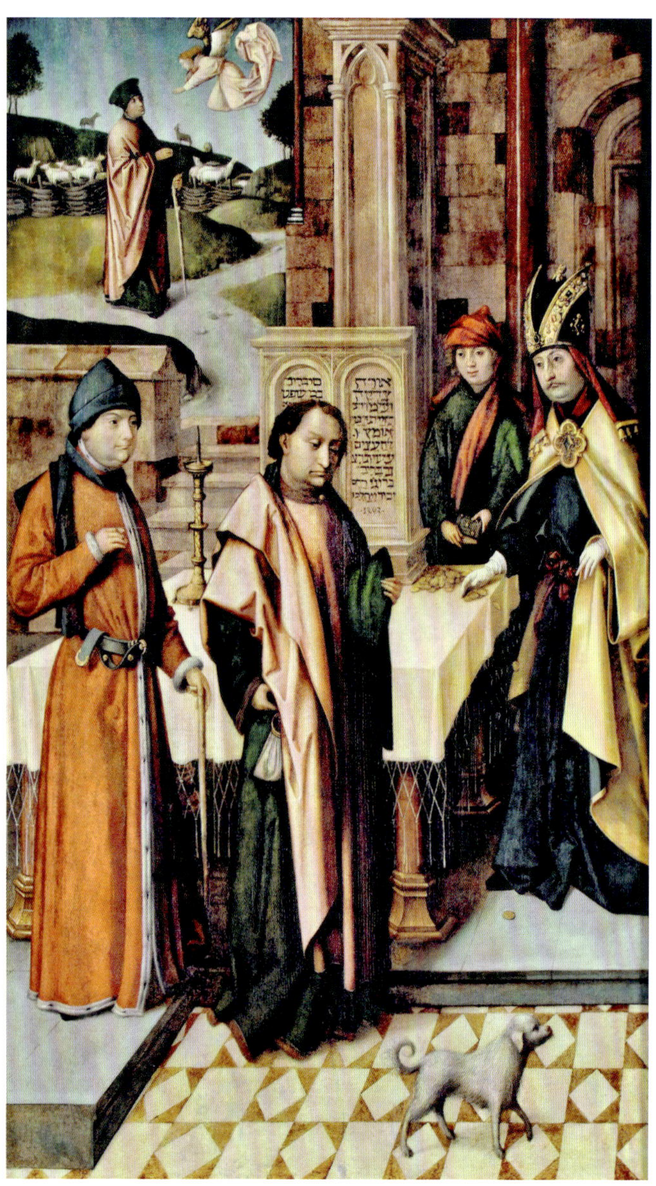

1 | Hans Holbein the Elder, *Saint Joachim expelled from the Temple* (detail from a polyptych), 1493. Augsburg, Cathedral.

but detached from his works or tied to *corpora* that, in reality, were not relevant.

And yet the critical fortunes of "Matthias Grünewald" began fairly early and in a prestigious manner. The first literary mention of the artist appeared in the *Elementorum rethorices libri duo* (Wittenberg, 1531), by the great humanist, friend and collaborator of Luther, Philipp Melanchton, in which the painter "Mathis" is mentioned alongside Dürer and Cranach.

We will return to this extremely important evidence, despite which, however, Grünewald's fame would decline in the centuries to follow, only to slowly bloom once again in the 19th century, yet not without difficulty and contradictions. However, mention must be made at least of the Aschaffenburg memory of Goethe (whose old school companion Franz Christian Lerse played a fundamental role in salvaging the altarpiece today in Colmar[10]) in 1814: "Hier befinden sich altdeutsche Gemälde aus aufgehobenen Klöstern: von Grünewald und andern, vielleicht auch von Dürer".[11] This is not the place to review the historical trials and tribulations of rediscovering the "Grünewald" identity. Having rejected the earlier hypothesis in favor of the sculptor Mathis Grün of Aschaffenburg, of a "Meister Mathiss" of the same city, documented between 1486 and 1490, and others as well, today scholars are in general agreement—thanks above all to the ground-breaking research by Schmid (1911) and Zülch (1938)—in identifying our artist with Mathis Neithard (Nithardt, Neidhardt) Gothart (Gothardt). Originally from, or at least a native of, Würzburg, he is documented starting in 1505. From at least 1511, he became court painter of the archbishop of Mainz (home of one of the most important German archdioceses whose archbishop was also prince elector of the Holy Roman Empire), and later worked in the Antonite monastery in Isenheim and subsequently in Halle, where he died in 1528.[12]

Of scarce significance is the divergent opinion of Giovanni Reale who, it could be said, for religious reasons that are no longer pertinent, would like to resurrect the outdated identification of Grünewald (also revived in modern times by Rieckenberg)[13] with Mathis Grün, who remained faithful to Roman Catholicism, unlike Mathis Gothart, who perhaps embraced the Reformation, or at least was certainly very interested in it. This hypothesis is challenged by a number of contradictions, some of which—and not even the most serious—we will examine later.[14]

However, to understand Grünewald, it is necessary to try to identify the stylistic possibilities a young painter could encounter, starting from Würzburg and surrounding areas. The years that interest us should not go beyond the last decade of the 15th century. That Mathis's early works, as we will see, do not pre-date 1502–1503 and still have that raw appearance typical of young talent, certainly indicates that he must have been born between 1480 and 1485 (unlikely before and certainly not after). His artistic education, whatever it was, occurred, therefore, in the 1490s.

In any case, the identification of "master painter" Grünewald remains one of the most frustrating exercises among those undertaken by scholars of this great artist. First of all, it should be remembered that the city of Nuremberg was home to one of the most important German workshops, that of Michael Wolgemut in which Dürer (born in 1471) would also train during the 1480s. In the crucial decade for Mathis, his younger student would seem to have been an influence on Wolgemut himself. However, it seems we can exclude that Dürer's teacher was also the first model for Mathis. As we will see, there is very little to be found in Grünewald's youthful works of Wolgemut's steady, compact and minutely descriptive style, which means we must turn our attention elsewhere.

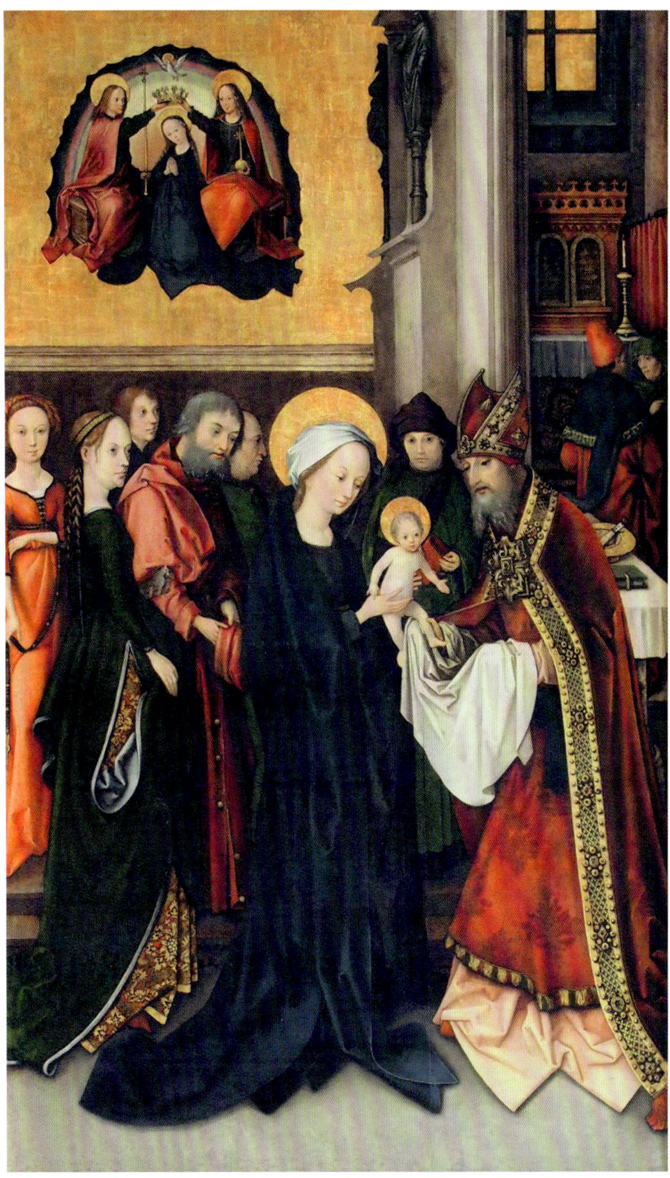

2 | Hans Holbein the Elder, *Jesus presented in the Temple* (detail from a polyptych), 1493. Augsburg, Cathedral.

A potential teacher has been seen several times in Hans Holbein the Elder, who worked predominantly in Augsburg.[15] The altarpiece in Augsburg Cathedral, dated 1493 [figs. 1–2], that is, when Mathis must have been a young teenager, shows a Flemish painting style whose point of reference is no longer Jan Van Eyck (as was the case in Köln in the '40s for Stephan Lochner), but Rogier Van der Weyden, through whom Holbein interpreted Wolgemut in a visually more synthetic way.

A decade later, around 1502, his painting is more dramatic (for example in the altarpiece in Munich or the panels at the Bayerische Staatsgemäldesammlungen in Augsburg, (namely the epitaph of the Vetter Cousins, 1499, inv. 4669, or the triptych of the Crucifixion, inv. 4531–4533), but the painting style and, above all, experimentation with light and space remain the same, despite the fact that his palette has become more fluid and reinforced with deeper hues. As I think will be clear shortly, this discourages the hypothesis that Mathis's teacher is to be seen in Holbein.[16]

Not even the most effusive pictorialism of Martin Schongauer offers itself as a real model for our artist. It is true that in certain works by Grünewald, we sometimes see the emergence of aspects reminiscent of Schongauer's work, especially

3 | Martin Schongauer, *Madonna of the Rose Bower*, before 1473. Colmar, Dominican Church.

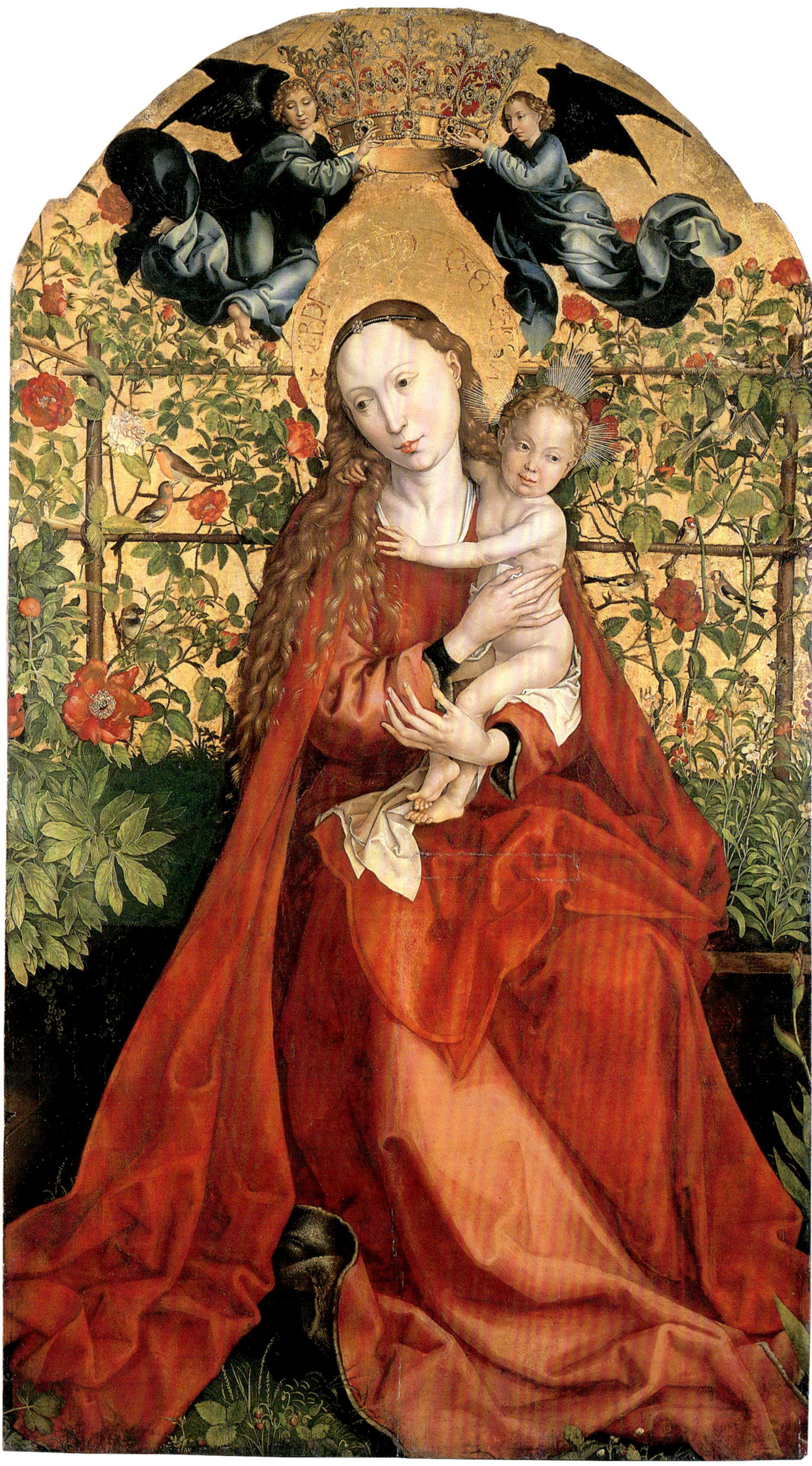

his etchings, which were, in fact, widely distributed.[17] But his biography itself contradicts this hypothesis: Schongauer died young in 1491, making it impossible for Dürer to know him personally as he would have liked, and *a fortiori* for Mathis to have been trained by him.[18] However, having mentioned the great master painter of Colmar, it is worth familiarizing ourselves with one of his youthful masterpieces, the *Madonna of the Rose Bower*, painted no later than 1473 [fig. 3], housed in the Dominican church in that Alsatian city. An image in which various shades of red predominate, flowing with extraordinary mastery over the draped fabric of great optical clarity. Also noteworthy is the virtuosity shown by Martin Schongauer in the edges of the drapery, painting with utmost freedom the interior of the garment in minute detail. Behind the Virgin is a magnificent rose garden that characterizes the painting and is explored with a botanical eye.

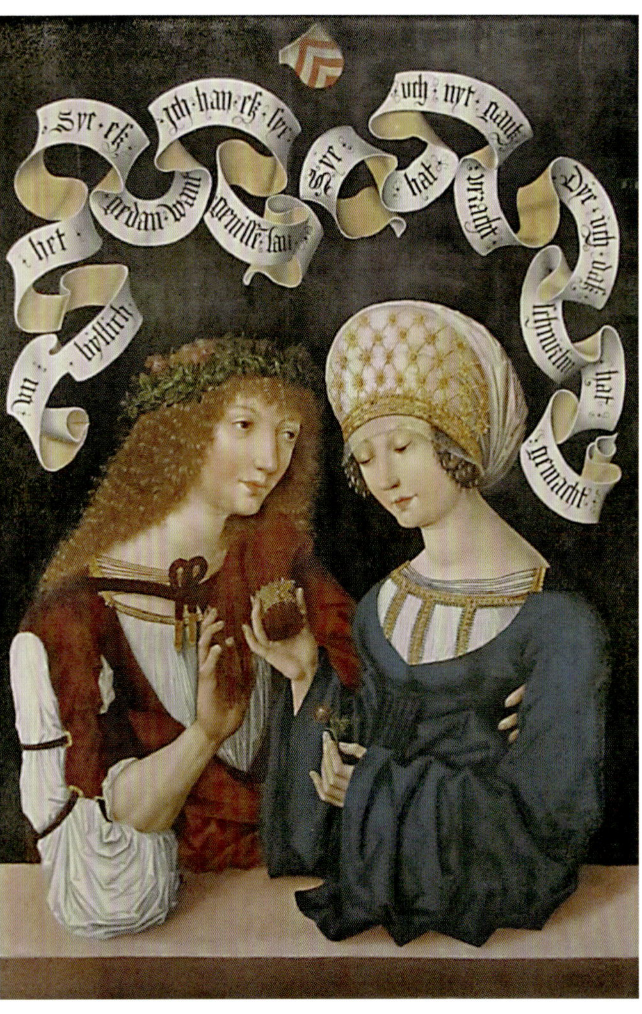

4 | Master of the Housebook (or of the Amsterdam Cabinet), *Couple of Lovers*. Gotha Herzoglisches Museum, inv. SG 703.

The hypothesis that Grünewald was a very young collaborator or student of Albrecht Dürer in person was also short-lived.[19] Contact with the latter is perceptible in a specific moment of our artist's career, as we will see, and the time frame is fairly easy to set: a significant influence from the Nuremberg painter cannot be considered. Nor is there any significant role to be mentioned from other examples more removed in time and distance, as is the case with Dürer's indomitable curiosity. There is no sign of the courtly culture of Stephan Lochner, refined by Eyckian luminosity, nor, from the south, of an interest in the "perspective synthesis of form-color" of Piero della Francesca, precociously detectable in Michael Pacher.[20]

In areas that partially coincide with those in which Grünewald worked, we should not forget primarily the etchings, but also the paintings, by the Master of the Housebook (also known as the Amsterdam Cabinet), sometimes considered a true antecedent of our artist because of his great inventive freedom. A panel formerly attributed to Mathis, now at the Gotha Herzoglisches Museum, inv. SG 703 [fig. 4], depicting a *Pair of Lovers* (identified as Count Philipp von Hanau-Münzenberg the Younger and his mistress, Margarethe Weisskircher), was later included in the Master of the Housebook catalogue.[21] But once again, I find it difficult to see analogies between the two artists that go beyond anything but an obvious generic resemblance.[22] Naturally in Franconia, where Mathis was born and predominantly worked, there was no dearth of painters and one of these must have actually been his teacher. But what should be noted is that none of the various stylistic alternatives found in the Middle Rhine region and its environs seems to have played a truly determinant role in his development. It seems to me no accident that when reasonable attempts were

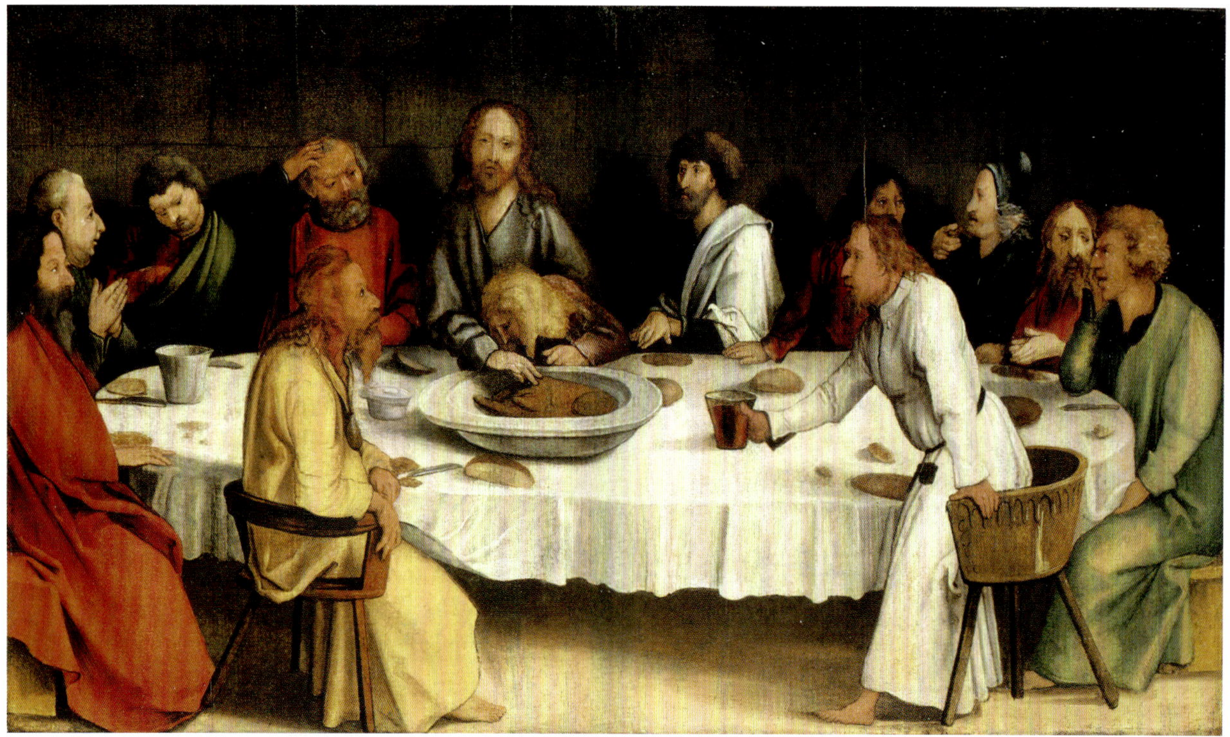

5 | Mathis Grünewald, *Last Supper*, Coburg, Kunstsammlungen der Veste Coburg, inv. M 421.

made to identify potential initial stimuli for Mathis in Würzburg, in the end, what were noted were works dating from the late Gothic to about 1480. At best, these represent precedents from an iconographic (but not even compositional) standpoint, and without any real stylistic connection—the only aspect that interests us in this phase.[23] This attempt, for which we should nonetheless be grateful, ends by demonstrating the opposite of what was intended: in essence, Grünewald's break from the traditional painting context in Würzburg and Franconia.

Once having briefly reviewed the main figurative options available in the area, we must examine what has been identified as Grünewald's earliest work in order to offer concrete hypotheses about the painter's training.

The first work that can be attributed to him with certainty is a hinged painting (Coburg, Kunstsammlungen der Veste Coburg, inv. M 421), created for private prayer or, more likely, as a fairly small predella of an altar, measuring 49 cm in height and 86 cm in width. With the panels closed, there is a *Last Supper* [fig. 5] and with them open, we see, respectively, *Saint Agnes* and *Saint Dorothy* [fig. 6]. It is probable that between them there would have been a wooden statue, perhaps of the Virgin and Child—or if it is a predella—Christ with the Apostles.[24]

The first thing we notice looking at the *Last Supper* is that, surprisingly, it represents a break from what we have seen until now. The work is characterized by a presence of shadow and a lack of glazed colors. The features of the apostles are less noble than those seen in the paintings by the artists previously mentioned and they appear almost grotesque and caricatural, but without the exaggerated expressiveness typical of 15th-century German painters. The apostle who slips his hand into his cloak as if to scratch himself, or a stumpy and ungainly Judas—as unquestionably "comic" as they appear, they also seem perfectly credible and natural and in no way exaggerated.

What is most striking is the different way Grünewald uses light: mutable, able

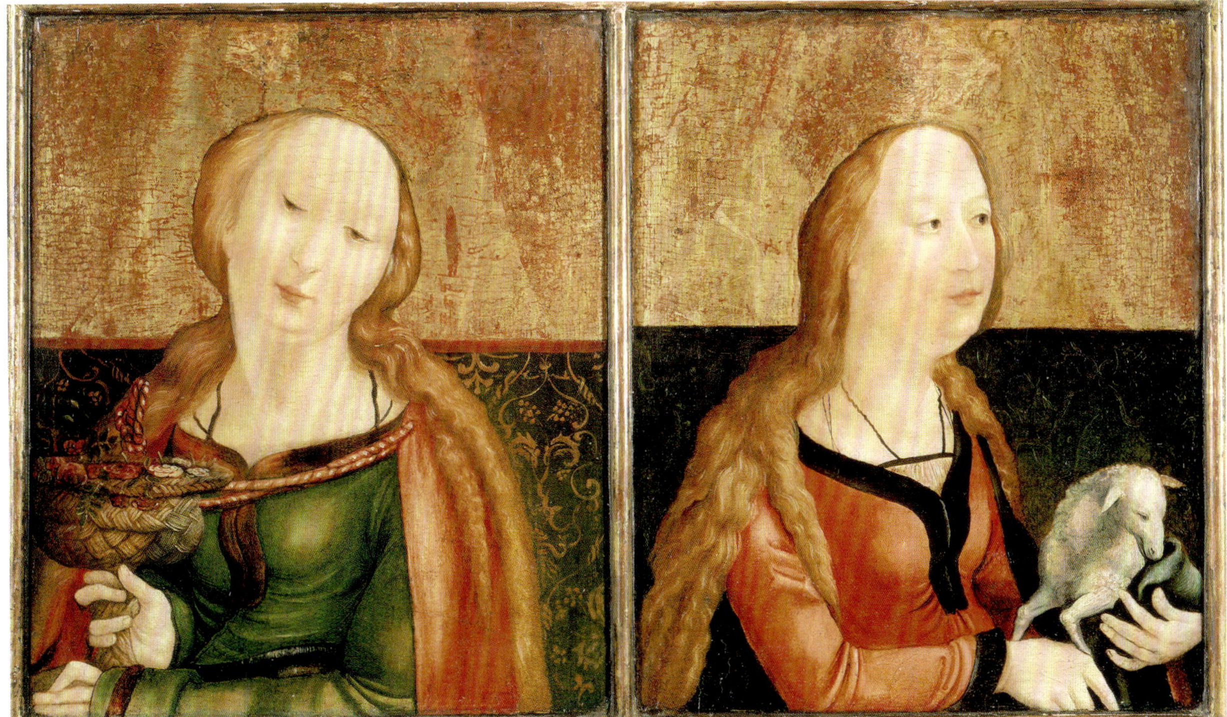

6 | Mathis Grünewald, *Saint Agnes and Saint Dorothy*, ca. 1502–1503. Coburg, Kunstsammlungen der Veste Coburg, inv. M 421.

to adapt itself differently to each body, as if light and color and the surfaces were totally inseparable.

This work, which has been in Coburg since 1986, and permanently held by Veste Coburg since 2003 after having been part of a number of private collections, is usually dated between 1500 and 1505. The model for it is sometimes traced to a drawing by Albrecht Dürer at the Berlin Kupferstichkabinett, which depicts a *Last Supper* dated ca. 1495–1500 (inv. KdZ 11715)[25] [fig. 7], or also, less implausibly, to a woodcut from the workshop of Michael Wolgemut found in the chivalric novel, *Schatzbehalter*, by Stephan Fridolin, published in 1491 [fig. 8].[26]

I struggle, however, to find any particular link with these works. Yet, as we shall see, I think a prototype does actually exist, though it is to be found elsewhere, and it will also provide us with a good chronological reference point. But first, we should take a close look at this work.

The *Last Supper* already contains some aspects that will remain characteristic of Mathis's work, first and foremost his attention to color. This means that color is not used in a volumetric sense, and it is not, let's say, passive in terms of light that silhouettes and highlights it. Rather, color and light fuse to become one.

It should be noted that the chromatic range of the garments of the apostles and Christ himself is fairly limited. However, thanks to a difference in modulation depending on the reaction to light, Grünewald is able to create both a perfect balance between the chromatic "islands" represented by each figure and, above all, a delicate chromatic balance that does not flatten the scene but expresses a concept of the relationship between light and color as if they were united in a sort of chemical reaction. Every figure, and even every part of the figure (a face, a sleeve, the tablecloth, a glass, the wall in the background) represents a different situation, like an optical dissection of the visible world in which a different dosage of the light-color ingredients create effects—or better, physical realities—that are always different

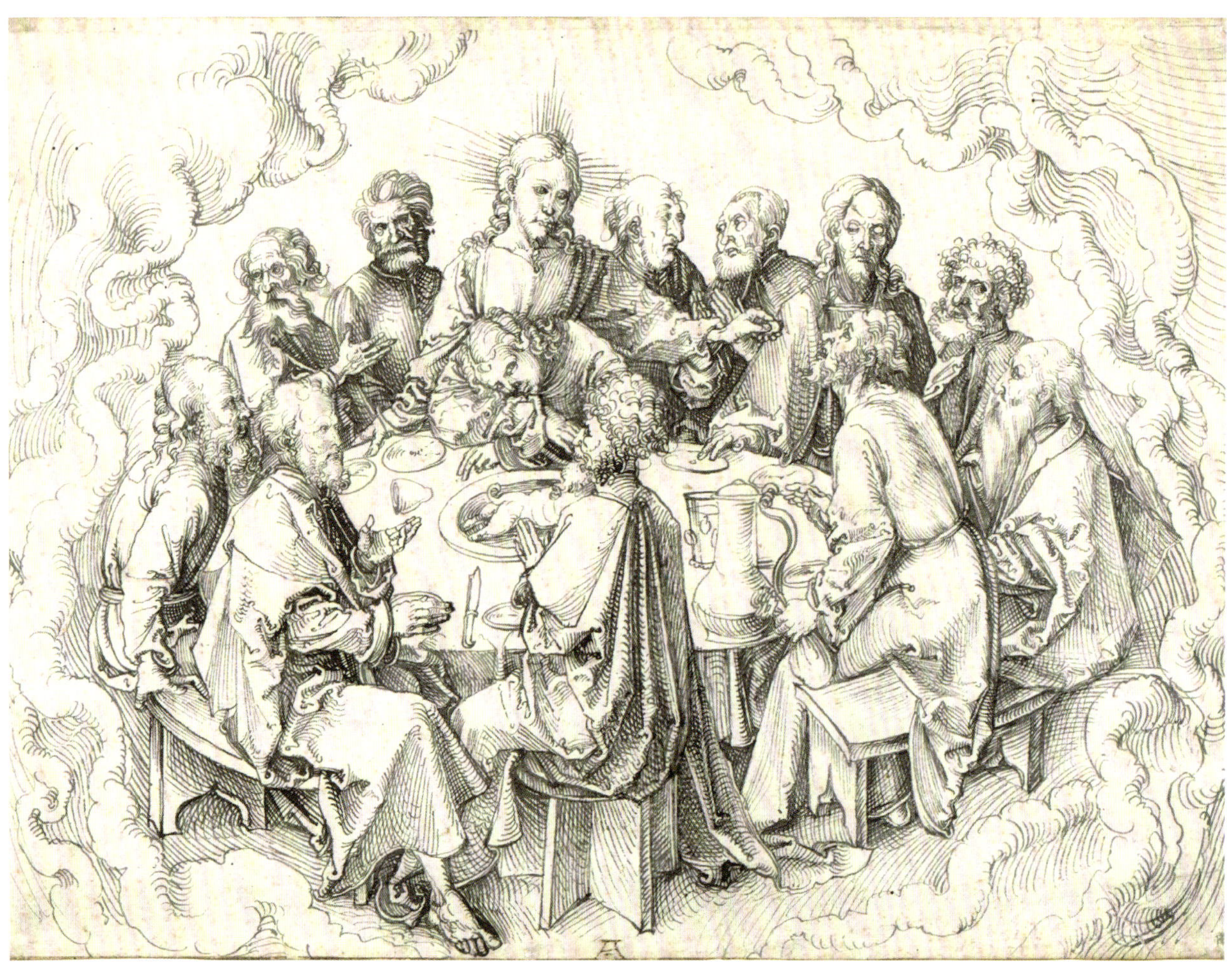

7 | Albrecht Dürer, *Last Supper*. Berlin, Staatliche Museen, Kupferstichkabinett, inv. KdZ 11715.

(I insist so strongly on this aspect because I feel it is essential to understand the entire *oeuvre* of this artist). To reiterate: Grünewald's optic conception, at this time, shuns large-scale chromatically homogeneous surfaces in favor of a more dynamic approach. As a result, each detail reacts autonomously to every change in luminosity with an interaction between light and color, like the tonal color of Giorgione, to cite an Italian example.

Another example of Grünewald's style that is already evident in this first painting is his attention to optical rendering. It is closer to a Flemish, rather than a German, concept and is well-expressed in the almost epidermic rendering of the hands and arms with very sophisticated light play on the same color.

Regarding the quest for a model other than that of Dürer, it is worth noting the significant similarities with Tilman Riemenschneider's *Last Supper* scene, carved as the central scene of the Holy Blood altarpiece in the Sankt Jakobskirche in Rothenburg [fig. 9].

Both works share the use of a lowered perspective point to portray the scene, have Christ seated off-center, and feature Judas as the only person standing. In the Coburg panel, Judas is dressed in the same white as the tablecloth, almost as if he were part of it.

It should be stressed that the reference to the sculptor would seem extremely plausible, both in terms of the time frame and geographical location. In fact, Tilman Riemenschneider, born in the 1460s, was the court sculptor of the prince-bishop of

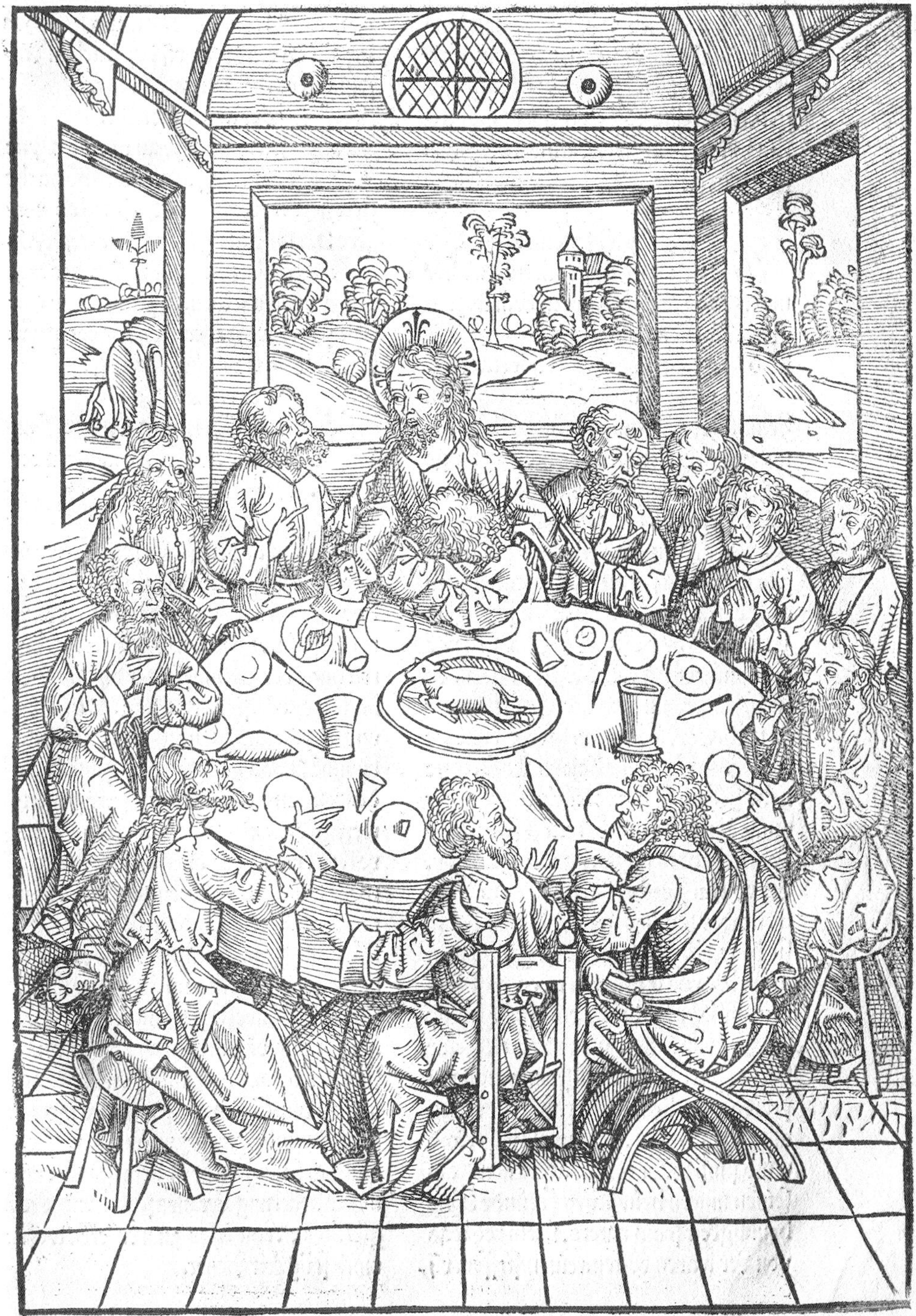

8 | Workshop of Michael Wolgemut, *Last Supper*, from Stephan Fridolin, *Schatzbehalter oder Schrein der wahren Reichtümer des Heils und ewigen Seligkeit* (Nuremberg: Anton Koberger, 1491), f. q iii.

Würzburg, the city in which his presence is documented from 1483 onwards (operating as an independent artist from 1485), and where he also had a studio. Mathis grew up in Würzburg surrounded by the works of Riemenschneider, by far the most esteemed and prestigious artist in the city and its environs.[27]

This close connection to wood sculpture,[28] not just an isolated episode as we will discover, brings us to a *Fassmaler* studio—literally a decorative painter—where daily activity as a painter included, among other things, painting statues. It should be noted that in Aschaffenburg, a Meister Mathis, a *Fassmaler*, is documented from

9 | Tilman Riemenschneider, *Last Supper* (detail from a carved altarpiece), ca. 1502. Rothenburg am See, Sankt Jacobskirche.

1480 to 1489,[29] who, according to Wolf Lücking, would actually be Grünewald's father.[30] This hypothesis must be formulated within the context of different appurtenance of our painter. If we consider that registry documents indicate that Mathis Gothart was a native of Würzburg, yet 17th-century sources also state him to be from Aschaffenburg, we could suggest that the latter was not his birth place, but rather where his family was from, or had lived for a period of time. In this case, the hypothesis of recognizing this Mathis of Aschaffenburg, known until 1489, as the father (or, perhaps better, grandfather) of Grünewald might even regain some credibility. However, we will revisit the topic of the painter's family later on.

The idea that emerges from the analysis of the Coburg *Last Supper*—Grünewald's training within a milieu of artists who paint wood—explains some aspects of our artist's personality. On one hand, it underscores the critical difficulty of identifying in the young Mathis a single pictorial reference (which painter could be indicated as his probable teacher? Plus, let us not forget that Grünewald always maintained enormous freedom in his choice of models in his various works.). On the other hand, it would explain the use of color conceived in such a local manner and such an extraordinary sensibility to the transition of light, reminiscent of a painted sculpture where perception changes as the light and point-of-observation change.

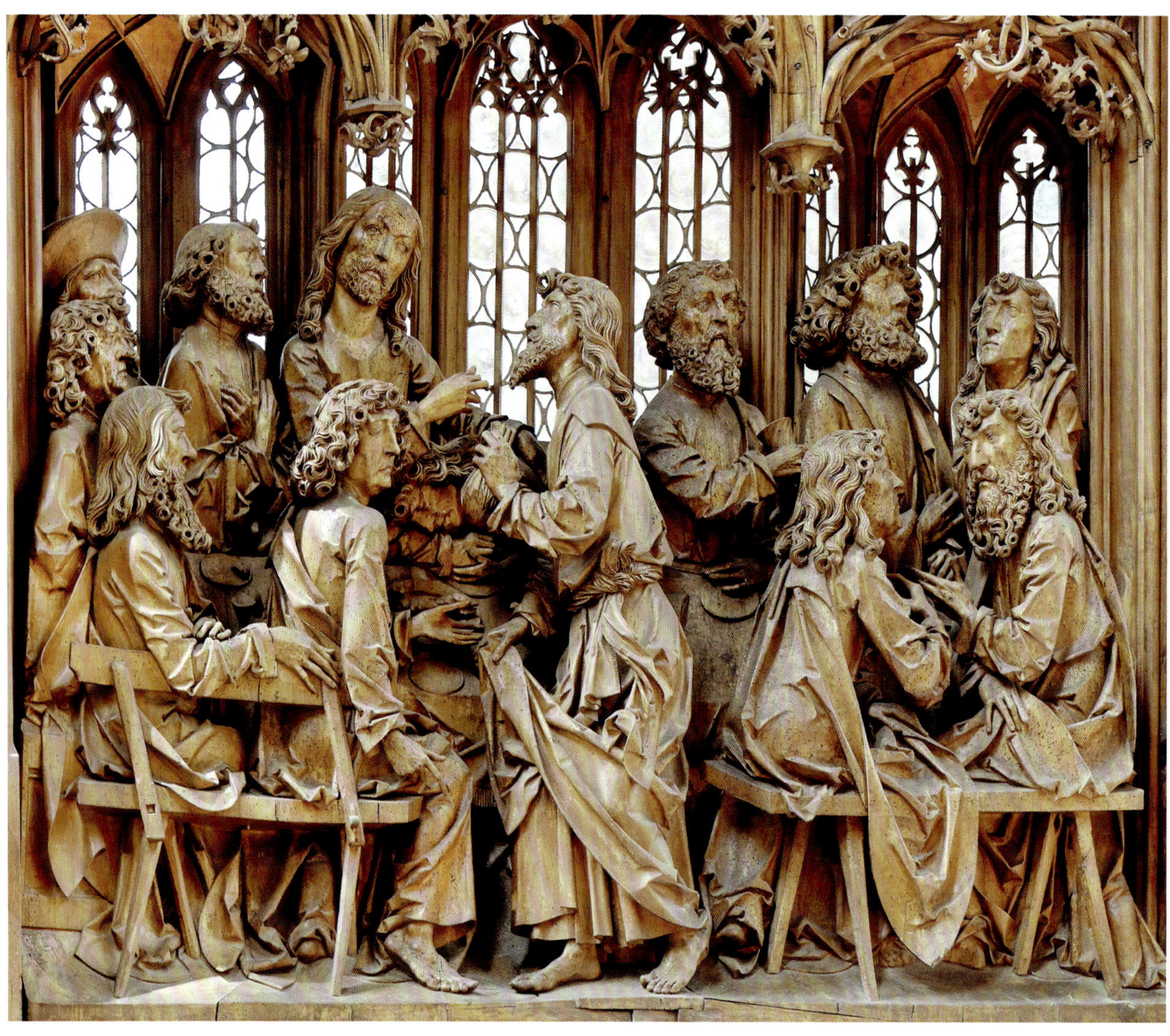

However, it could be objected that the Holy Blood altarpiece in Rothenburg lacks color entirely. In fact, Riemenschneider was one of the first to sometimes forgo color in his statues (here, the work is only varnished, which mitigates the roughness of the wood and softens the image).[31] Nevertheless, considering this altarpiece was created shortly after our painter's training, the absence of color is not incoherent with the process we have tried to delineate thus far.

In fact, documentation shows that the woodworking on the altar was commissioned by the city council to local carpenter Erhart Harschner, who provided the structure in 1502. In the meantime, the sculptures were assigned to Riemenschneider on April 15, 1501, and he began work immediately, delivering the figures for the altar in batches between 1502 and 1505. If the Rothenburg altarpiece is really the model, then Grünewald's *Last Supper* could not have been painted before late 1502. The depiction of the two saints painted on the inner panels further confirms the setting of the date in the early years of the century. One point of comparison could be the two panels by Hans Baldung Grien preserved in the Lutheran church of San Martin in Schwabach, part of what is known as the Paumgarten altar[32] [figs. 10–11], dated ca. 1503–1504, which seem, in some way, related to ours, although a direct connection between the two works is not essential. Moreover, by transcending the conventional tendency to compare painting solely to painting and sculpture solely to sculpture (a process that will prove useful more than once in this study), we can easily see that Grünewald's two saints can be compared to Riemenschneider's female figures dating from the 1480s to the 1490s or precisely the turn of the century: for example the damaged wooden *Virgin with Child* or the alabaster *Saint Barbara* in a private collection, and even more so to the alabaster *Our Lady of the Annunciation* in the Louvre (inv. RF 1384), particularly similar in the rendering of the slender, very mobile hands [fig. 12].[33]

This early dating is also confirmed by some consistently recurring stylistic characteristics, observable up to the *Isenheim Altarpiece*. For example, the agitated, virtually boneless hands, where the virtuosity of the skin fold on St. Dorothy's right palm does not fully achieve physical credibility. It is almost as if the artist were still reluctant to depict the fullness of the form through drawing and not just pictorially—a defect that would be understandable if we are looking at the early panel paintings of an artist educated in the use of color starting from a predetermined formal structure (sculpture).

Examining the two saints we see a cultural divergence with the scene of the *Last Supper*. Unlike the former, which seems more closely tied to the culture of Upper Germany, the latter retains a surprising formal affinity with the works of Hieronymus Bosch, and in particular with *The Conjurer*, also called *The Magician* (ca. 1475–1480, my reference is the copy at the Musée Municipal in Saint-Germain-en-Laye, inv. 872.1.87 [fig. 13][34]), as evident both in the caricatural depiction of the faces of the apostles and the radiance of the surfaces, especially the garments. Aside from the human figures, which are not dissimilar, and also the awkward apostle with clumsy mechanical movements dressed in white [fig. 14], reminiscent of Bosch's conjurer, what stands out above all is the overlapping of white-on-white of the clothing of the disciple himself and the tablecloth that, along with the stiff folds of the cloth, are so similar to the headscarf of the conjurer's victim in the painting by the Dutch artist. Additionally, the darkening of the shadow on the wall in the background of the *Last Supper* in Coburg seems to correspond to the same, unusual optical laws of the low wall covering the horizon in the Bosch painting. Even the bravura shown by Grünewald in the wine seen through the glass offered by the disciple dressed in white, to Judas (identifyable by the money purse and the yellow garment),[35] is, if I am not mistaken, more reminiscent of Flemish, rather than German, style. How could Mathis have known this, or other analogous works by Bosch?

We have already mentioned the extreme freedom, perhaps aided by the type of training he received, our painter was able to maintain from the very beginning with the figurative examples around him. But, above all, it is probable that Mathis also spent his period of apprenticeship outside his city as normally provided for in guild statutes.[36] This could explain the influence of Bosch. Bosch's *Conjurer* was

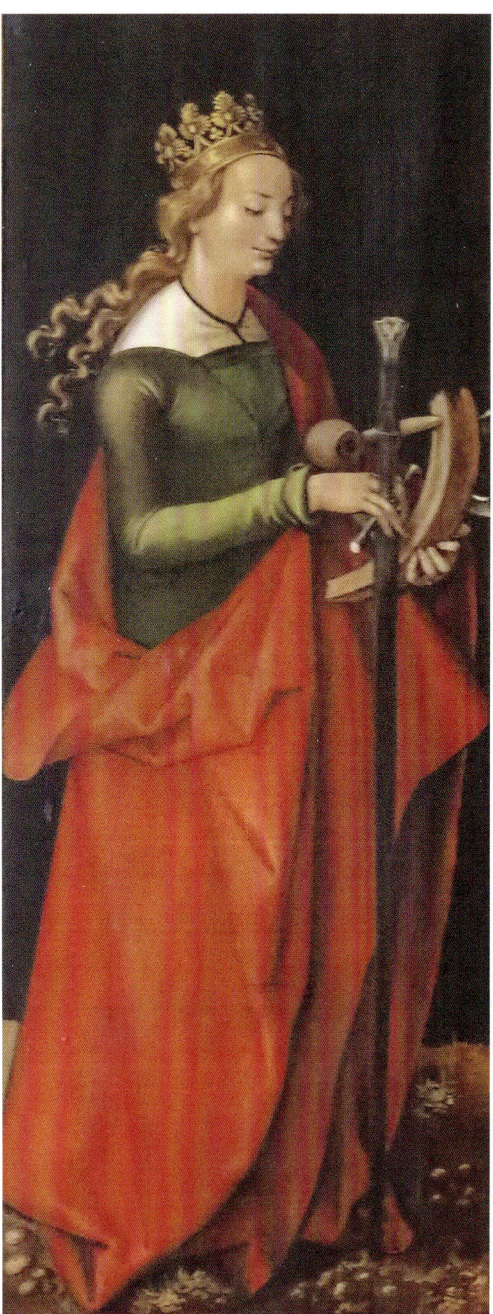

10 | Hans Baldung Grien, *Saint Catherine* (from the former Paumgarten altar). Schwabach, Lutheran church of Saint Martin.

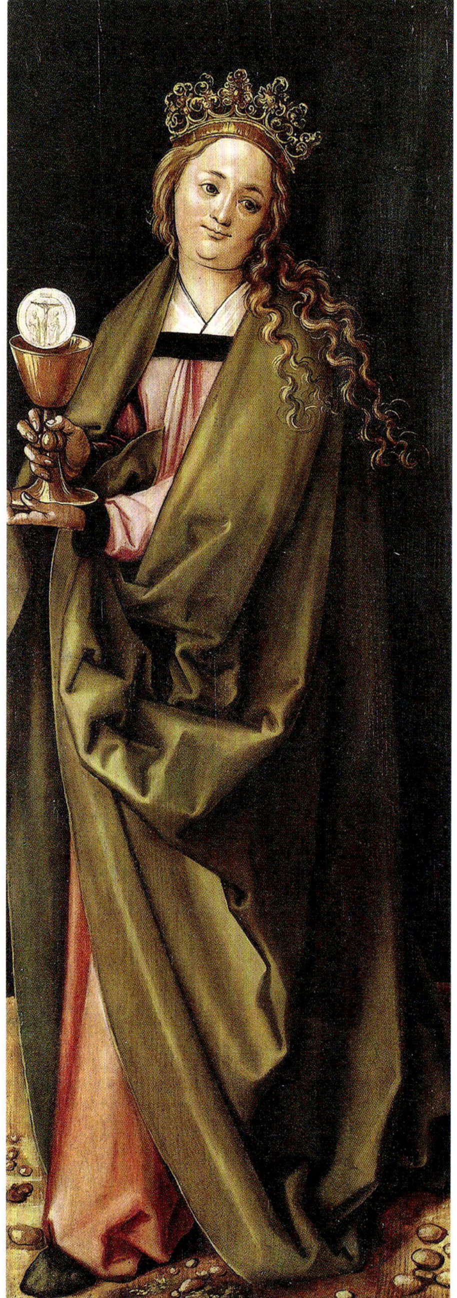

11 | Hans Baldung Grien, *Saint Agnes* (from the former Paumgarten altar). Schwabach, Lutheran church of Saint Martin.

12 | Tilman Riemenschneider, *Madonna of the Annunciation.* Paris, Musée du Louvre, inv. RF 1384.

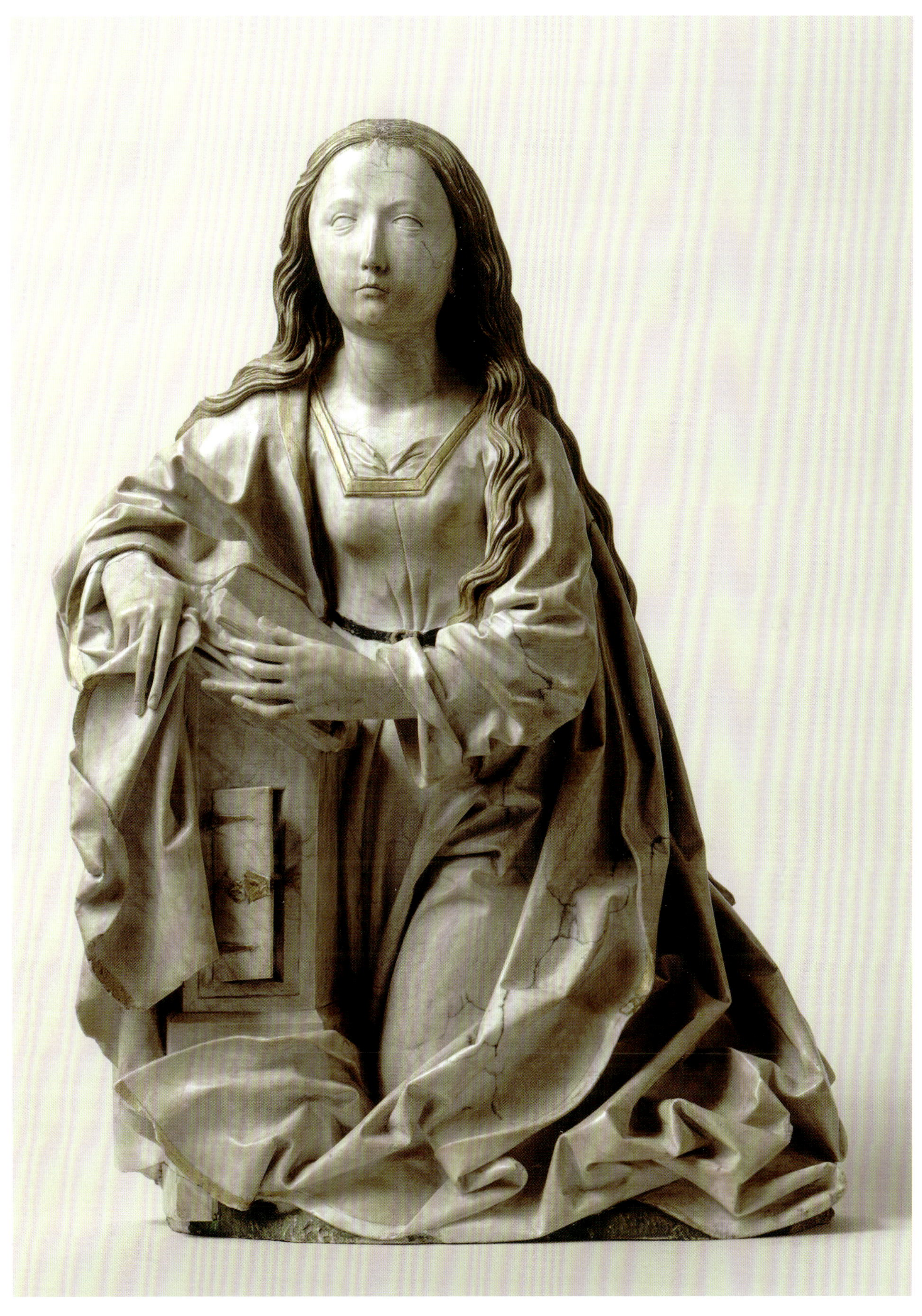

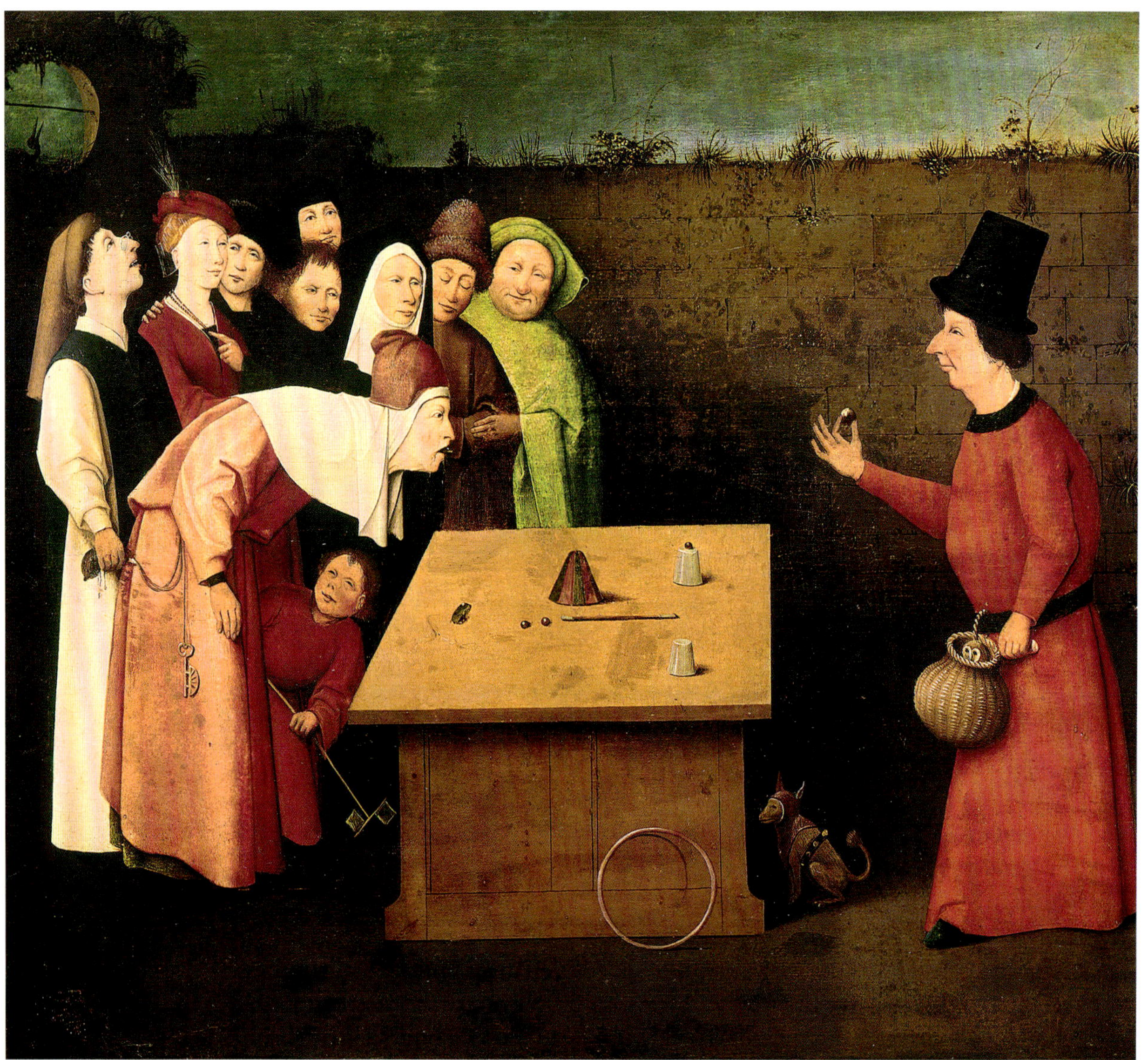

13 | Attributed to Gielis Panhedel, *The Conjurer* (after Hieronymus Bosch). Saint Germain-en-Laye, Musée municipal, inv. 872.1.87.

14 | Mathis Grünewald, *Last Supper*, Coburg, Kunstsammlungen der Veste Coburg, inv. M 421 (detail).

quite popular, as proved by the surviving copies, and so it would not be surprising if Mathis had known it, directly from the original (now considered lost, due to doubts about the copy in Saint-Germain-en-Laye) or at least a copy. It is of extreme importance to note that at least two works by Bosch, today lost, were placed in the Bonn cathedral (a triptych with Stories of Jesus and Christ Bearing the Cross), one acquired in 1518 and the other mentioned in 1584. Therefore, it is not necessarily true that Grünewald would have seen them in his youth. However, they indicate the early popularity of Bosch's works in areas not distant from where Mathis was. Moreover, we should not forget that the works of this great Dutch painter could, and still can, be seen in Venice, and this is where Albrecht Dürer encountered them during his hypothetical first voyage in Italy. In short, information about him was not lacking in Germany.

Among Bosch's works in Venice is the *St. Liberata Triptych* (today in the Palazzo Ducale collection, cat. 2045) [fig. 15], dated ca. 1500.[37] Compared to *The Conjurer* (confirmed to be an earlier work), Bosch has profoundly innovated both the luminist timbre, here more delicate and mellow, and the drawing, which became more

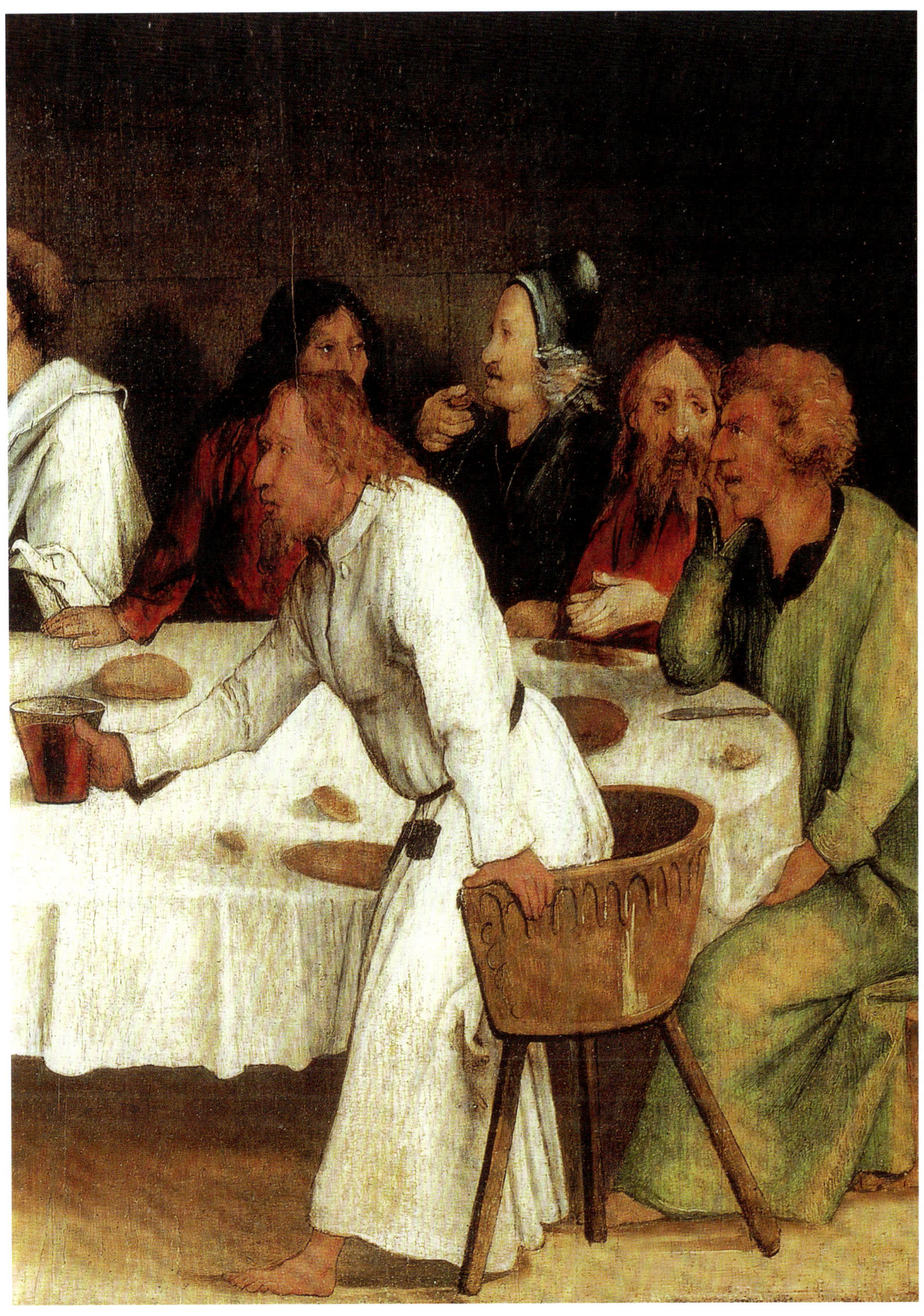

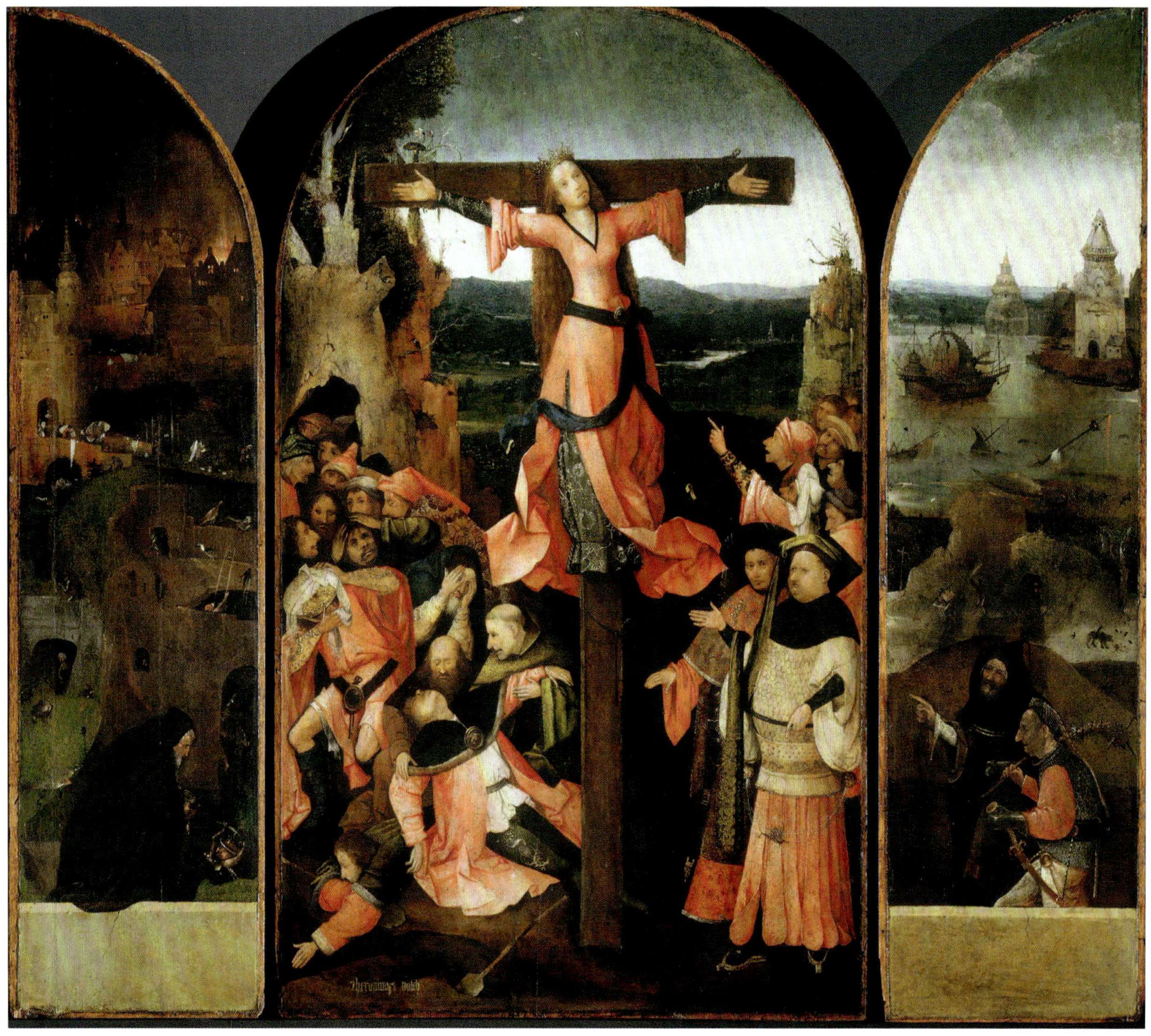

15 | Hieronymus Bosch, *Saint Liberata tryptich*. Venezia, Palazzo Ducale, cat. 2045.

16 | **a** Mathis Grünewald, *Saint George and other six Holy Helpers*, 1503. Lindenhardt, Parish church.
b Mathis Grünewald, *Saint Denys and other six Holy Helpers*, 1503. Lindenhardt, Parish church.

fluid and sophisticated. That Grünewald demonstrated familiarity with this phase of Bosch's painting in the later Coburg altarpiece indicates that, by 1500–1502, he had a comprehensive and precise knowledge of Bosch's oeuvre, encompassing to both past and very recent works of the Dutch master, and that he had studied them closely and avidly.

This conclusion is supported by the second work definitely attributed to Mathis (unless, originally, the two works were part of a single group): a small winged altar found in deplorable condition in the parish church of Lindenhardt, in northern Franconia.[38] It consists of winged panels (159 × 68.5 cm each) [figs. 16a-b], painted on the exterior of a sculpted triptych altar with hinged wings [fig. 17] by a sculptor identified alternately as Arnold Rücker, Hans Nussbaum of Nuremberg, or a member of Michael Wolgemut's workshop, and in any case not far removed from Michel Erhart (the sculptor of the Blaubeuren altarpiece, which Maria Lanckoronska attributed to Mathis himself).[39] The work comes from the church of the nearby town of Bindlach, near Bayreuth, where it remained until 1685. What is more important is that this work bears the date of 1503 on the front of the left panel. It depicts the *Fourteen Holy Helpers*: on the left, *St. George surrounded by saints*, on the right *St.*

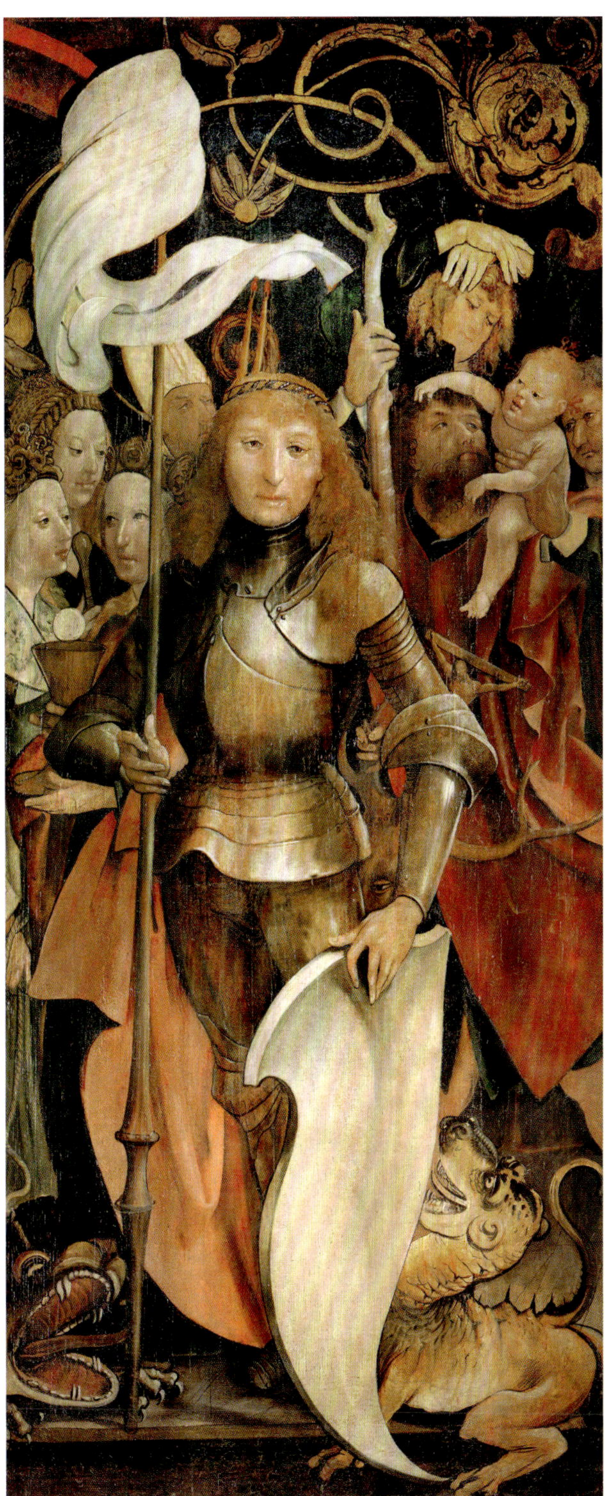
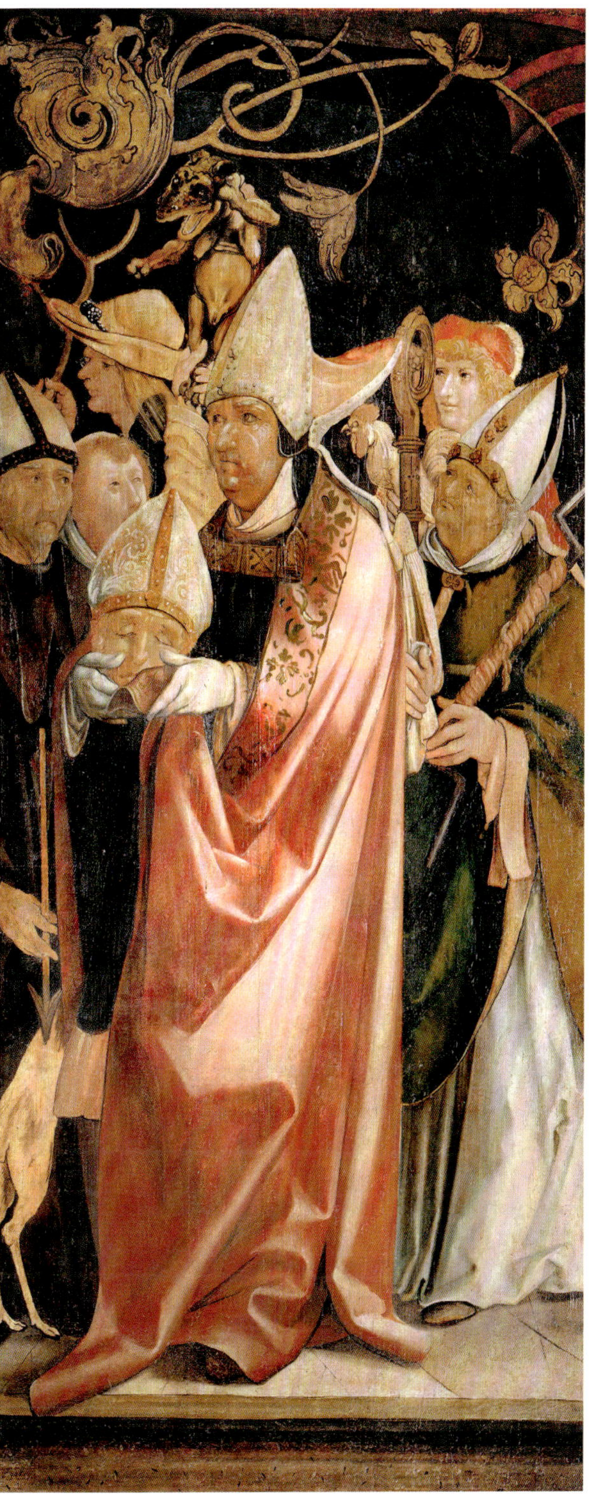

Denys with the Bishop Saints, and painted on the back of the cabinet is the image of the *Man of Sorrows* [fig. 18]. Despite its poor state of preservation (which led some scholars, including Ziermann, to exclude the work from Grünewald's autograph works,[40] and Italo Bacigalupo to even attribute it to Hans von Kulmbach[41]), the Lindenhardt altar is indispensable to reconstructing Mathis's beginnings.

The faces of the saints retain a caricatural style with penetrating gazes, as do

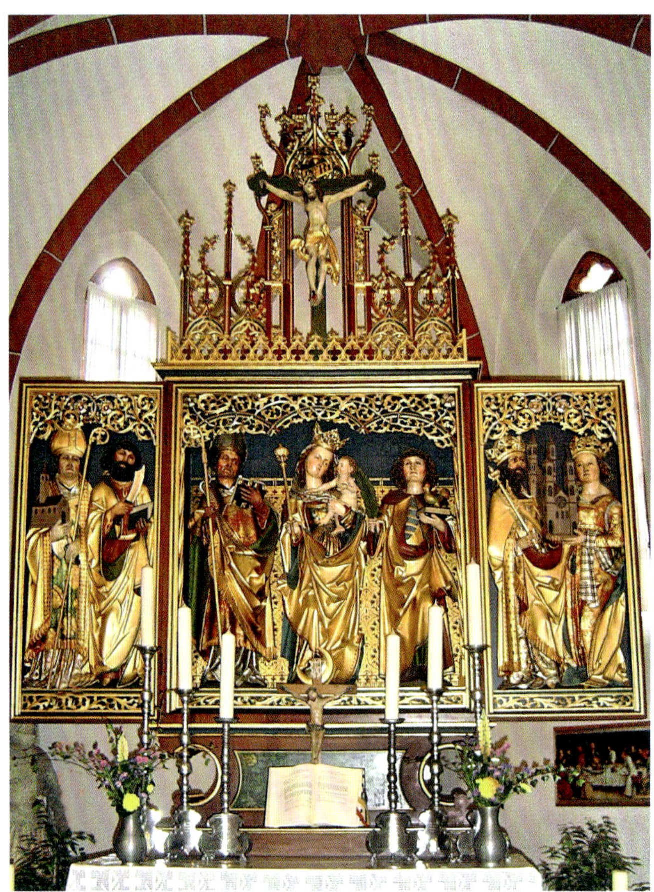

17 | Franconian Sculptor, *Madonna with Child and Saints*, 1503. Lindenhardt, Parish church.

the apostles in the *Last Supper* in Coburg, and the extremely mobile and almost disjointed hands are those we have already familiarized with. Concurrently, the work is compositionally more complex and bolder in depicting the garments, which, as has already been mentioned, seem to draw on Bosch once again, reminiscent of Bosch's influence, albeit with a more contemporary flavor. As far as it can be ascertained given the condition of the panels, the colors still exhibit the same sensitivity to the minutest variation in light as in the Coburg work, but appear somewhat softer and mellower. The single color variation exercises (for example the iridescent shadings of St. George's armor on the left and St. Christopher's cape on his shoulders, or St. Denys's cape in the foreground on the right panel and the white stole of Bishop Saint behind him) seem to be less vitreous.

This work, on display in a church, marks Mathis's first-known public exhibition, as far as we know. It is also subject to a constraint that is anything but easy: having to depict a large number of saints in two panels in a complicated vertical format. The compositional approach, which involves gathering many figures behind the main ones (respectively, St. George and St. Denys), reveals a sort of pictorial translation from the bas-relief technique, once again suggesting a profound connection between Grünewald's beginnings and the world of sculpture. Moreover, despite the efficacy of some foreshortenings (especially the view from below St. Christopher's face, a solution which, lo and behold, also often appears in Bosch), we can see a certain difficulty in representing depth, where the painting quality is very high in rendering the luminous and physical texture of the surfaces. In fact, the figures further to the back on the left panel seem little more than two-dimensional silhouettes.

The breathtaking realism of the old, drooping, decapitated head of St. Denys [fig. 19] provides the definitive confirmation of young Mathis's debt to sculpture, and in particular to Tilman Riemenschneider. In fact, it would be unthinkable without the precedent of an artwork the painter certainly knew very well: the tombstone of the prince-bishop of Würzburg, Rudolph von Scherenberg, carved by Riemenschneider in the city's cathedral between 1496 and 1499[42] [fig. 20]. Even more immediate is the comparison with a minor work, but one of extraordinary quality, such as the wooden *Bishop Saint* at the Metropolitan Museum in New York, inv. 1970.137.1 [fig. 21], dating from the same years (sometimes identified as one of the Holy Helpers commissioned from Riemenschneider for the hospital chapel in Würzburg in 1494), whose face seems to have been literally copied by Grünewald.[43] For anyone still not convinced, I have one more card up my sleeve, and perhaps the most convincing one. There can be no doubt, in fact, about the explicit—and

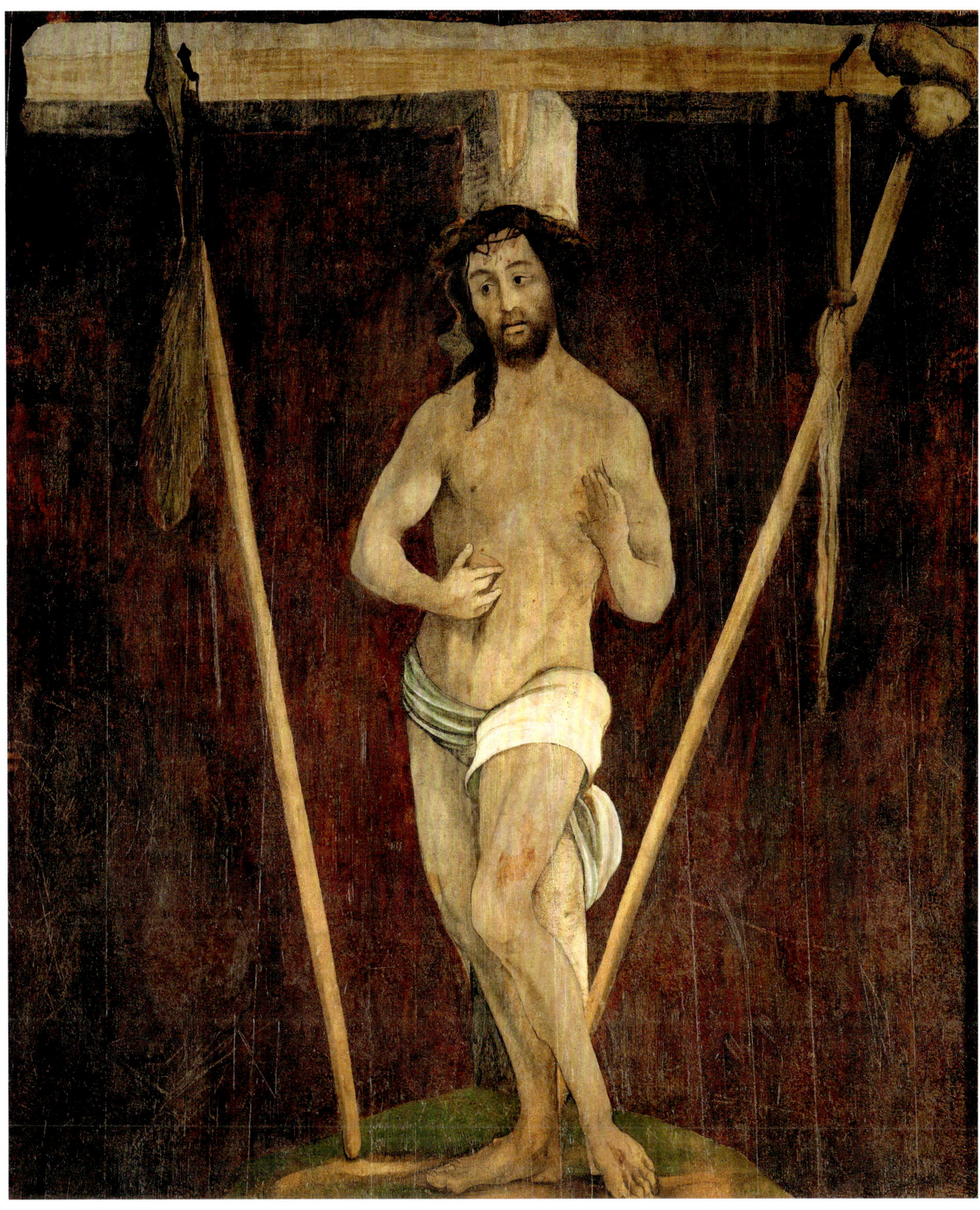

18 | Mathis Grünewald, *Man of Sorrows* 1503. Lindenhardt, Parish church.

proudly proclaimed—dependence of Grünewald for his St. George [fig. 22] on the tombstone of Konrad von Schaumberg who died in the Holy Land in 1499, carved in stone by Riemenschneider around 1500 and placed in the Chapel of the Virgin in Würzburg[44] [fig. 23]. The pose, the armor, the way the effigy occupies the space and looks at us are perfectly identical in the two works. The most surprising thing is that the comparison between Grünewald's panel and the von Schaumberg tomb

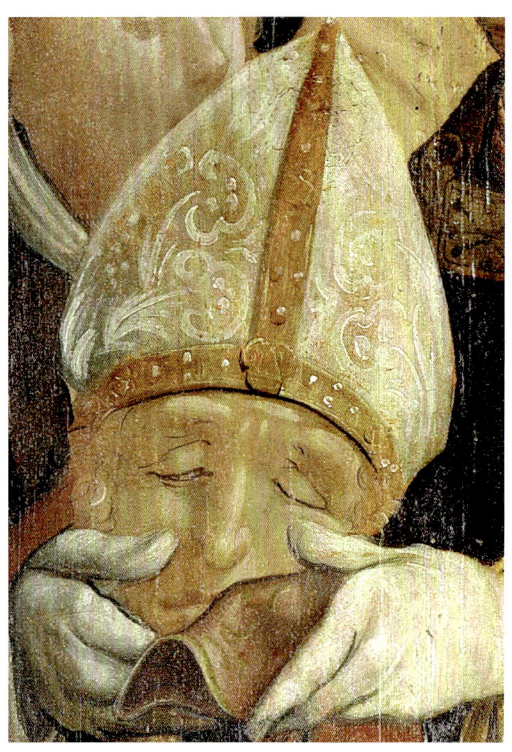

19 | Mathis Grünewald, *Saint Denys and other six Holy Helpers* (detail), 1503. Lindenhardt, Parish church.

has already been pointed out in studies, but without any real consequences.[45]

The *Man of Sorrows* painted on the back of the cabinet is in an even worse state of conservation: the overall shape has almost completely disappeared. What survived is the silhouette, in which can still be seen the subtle play of contrasts that governs the figure of Christ. We are no longer surprised to see that this theme so dear to medieval iconography is represented according to a formal conception not that distant from that in Riemenschneider's sculptures. The rhythmic movement is unquestionably reminiscent of the famous *Eve* he sculpted between 1491 and 1493 for the façade of the Chapel of the Virgin (today at the Museum für Fränken in Würzburg [fig. 24]). In fact, Riemenschneider dealt with the same theme a number of times, and the comparison of some versions of the *Vir Dolorum* carved by Tilman or his studio (for example, the pieces in the Rosenberg Fortress in Kronach, ca. 1495–1500,[46] or even more so the Holy Blood altarpiece in Rothenburg, a work which Mathis studied in detail [fig. 25]) with the painted one in Lindenhardt is so close that it not only touches the iconographic aspect, but the concept of the figure itself. Grünewald's connection to Riemenschneider and Würzburg's artistic output, especially sculpture, is now a given.

It should also be noted that Riemenschneider often collaborated with painters (the most-studied instance is probably that of Martinus Schwarz of Rothenburg),[47] and that his son, Bartlmä Dill, as a painter, was anything but insignificant.[48] Nor should we forget that, as revealed by examining the back of one of his wood reliefs which bears the elegant, yet quickly executed life-size sketch of a dancer (?) (part of an altar dedicated to Christ with the Apostles created in 1509, previously at Windsheim and now in the Kurpfälzisches Museum in Heidelberg), drawing was part of the activity in his studio,[49] a significant point for an outstanding artist such as Grünewald, as we will see later. And we will also see that, in a 1511 document, Mathis is identified as "Maler und Steinmetz", indicating that his training also included working in stone, a material with which Riemenschneider was familiar.

Therefore, can we be so daring as to imagine young Mathis learning his trade in Riemenschneider's studio? In documents relating to the Guild of St. Luke in Würzburg, published by Paulus Weissenberger in 1936, the name of Mathis does not appear, neither as a master artist nor apprentice. The documentation is in no way exhaustive, but it is an important starting point. However, I would place a small bet on the studio of Meister Simon, a painter documented starting in 1470 and who died in 1501. He was married to "Anna Riemenschneiderin",[50] and a woman of the same name is found in the sculptor's "family"[51]—not a local family, given that the young Tilman did not arrive in Würzburg until 1483. Therefore, in all probability, a painter, perhaps even a *Fassmaler*, related to Tilman Riemenschneider and very likely in active collaboration with him.

Finally, it is worth exploring a small, but intriguing, aspect for research: Grünewald's possible education in the city in which he was born, where, a few years later, around 1523, a "Paulus Gothart von Würzburg" appears as a student of

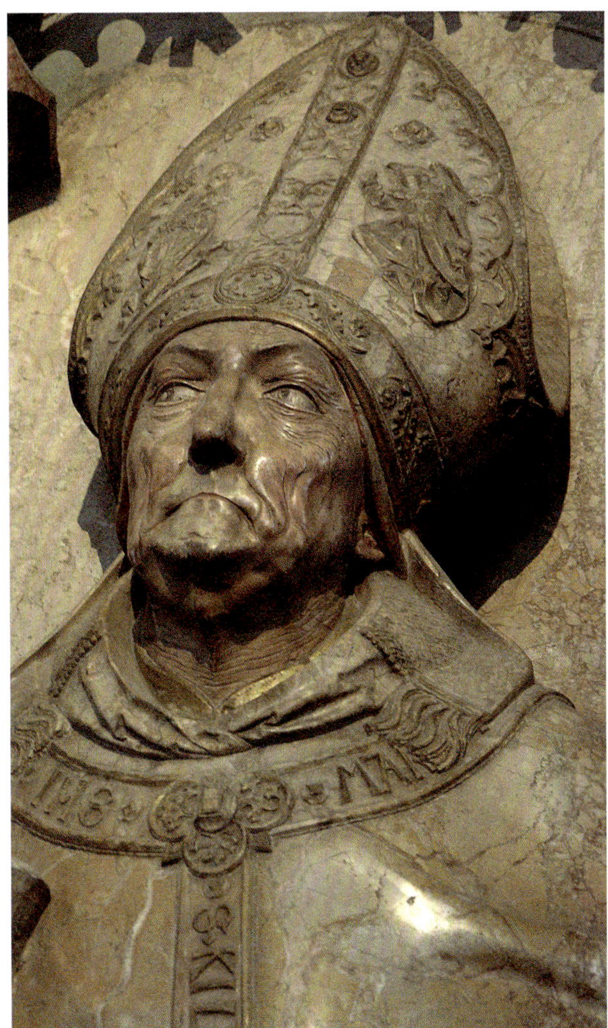

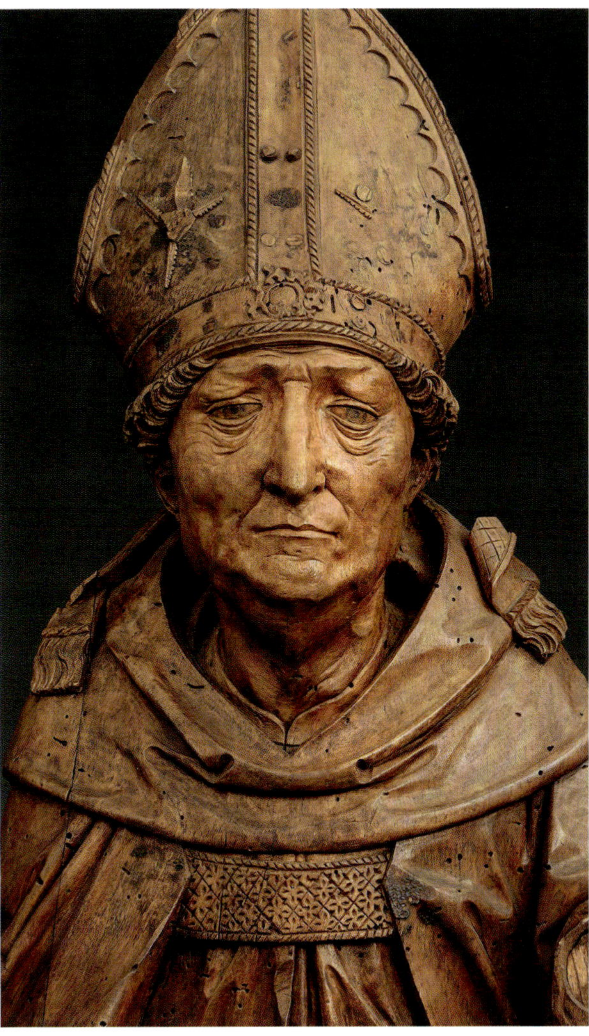

20 | Tilman Riemenschneider, *Tombstone of bishop Rudolph von Scherenberg*, 1496–1499. Würzburg, Cathedral.

21 | Tilman Riemenschneider, *Saint Bishop* (detail), ca. 1495. New York, The Metropolitan Museum of Art (inv. 1970–137.1).

glass-maker Anton Stang.[52] Most likely he is a relative of the homonymous Paulus Gothart who took part as a representative of "eines erbahren raths" in the laying of the cornerstone of the city's mill on August 19, 1512, and appears as "derzeit bawmeister" in 1515,[53] all professions related to those practiced by Mathis and an indication of a homogenous social environment.

In the Aschaffenburg Staatsgalerie im Schloss Johannisburg, there is a little-known predella (38.8 × 116.5 cm, inv. 9874) depicting the *Fourteen Holy Helpers*, very similar, including its poor conservation, to the Lindenhardt altar [fig. 26].[54] In many places, the color has been rubbed away to reveal to the naked eye the outlines traced by the brush to create edgy shapes, gawky faces (often overloaded by old repainting), and drapery struggling to maintain substance and becoming rigid. The quality of this predella, which could perhaps benefit from restoration, seems rather inferior to that of the Lindenhardt altar, raising the suspicion that it could be the work of a very young follower. In fact, in 1505 Grünewald already had at least one assistant. But I would not rule out the possibility that this predella could provide us with a very early glimpse of Mathis's activity, or at least shed some light on his actual "master". Perhaps it is no accident that the almost-caricatural features and drapery still quite removed from the fine graphism of the Lindenhardt work bring to mind the paintings of Veit Stoss, in particular a grouping chronologically

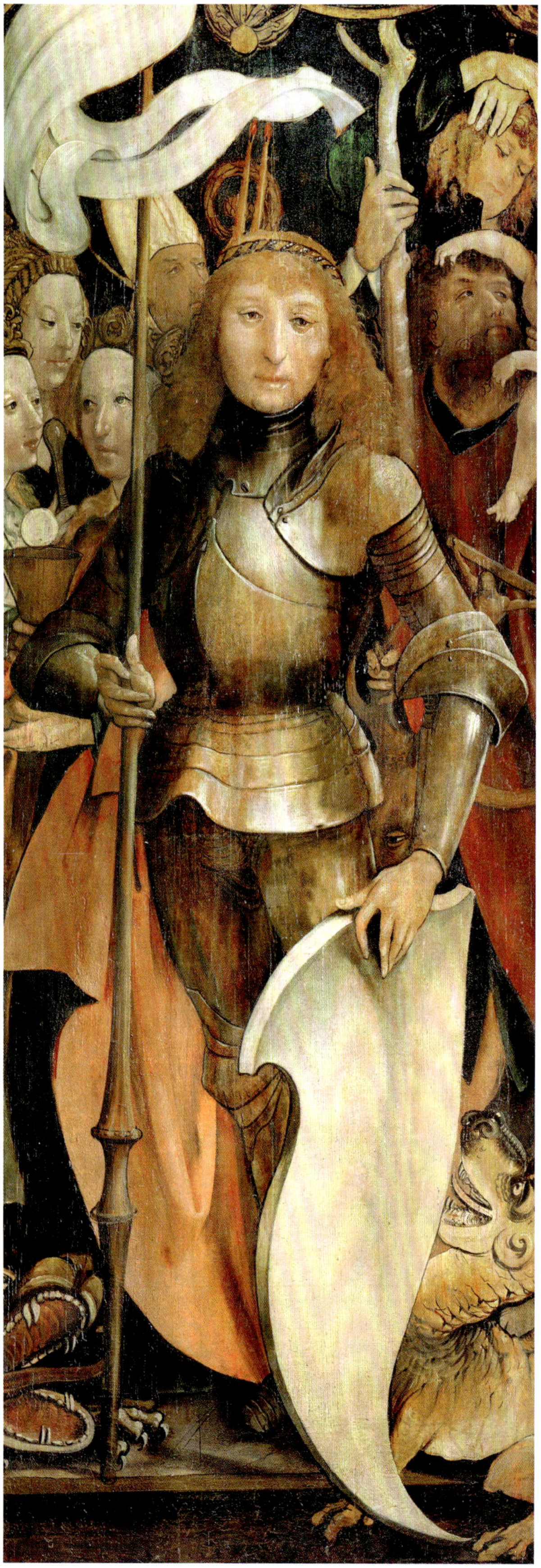

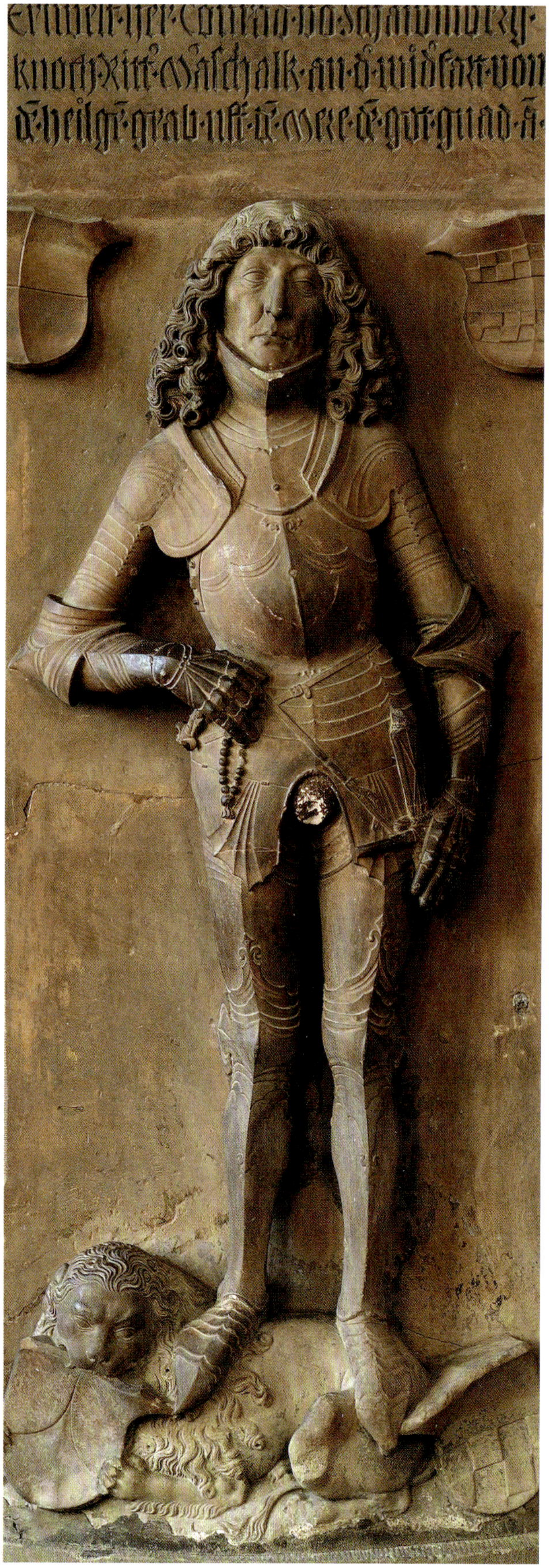

close to the painting currently in Aschaffenburg: the wings painted in 1504 for the wooden altar in Münnerstadt that was carved in 1491 by none other than Tilman Riemenschneider.[55] It is plausible that Grünewald might have focused some attention on a major center such as Nuremberg, not on the studio of Albrecht Dürer as Hans Baldung, more or less his contemporary, did, but on a great sculptor like Stoss, who, unlike Riemenschneider, also painted.

However, the most noteworthy aspect of the Aschaffenburg predella is its extreme similarity with the painted part of the Gerolzhofen altarpiece (now at the Munich Bayerisches Nationalmuseum, inv. MA 1963), a work produced by the Riemenschneider workshop between 1513 and 1519 [fig. 27].[56] The drapery is similar, as are the design of the hands and the large-nosed visages; the similarities are even closer in the severely damaged angels on the back. Currently, it is not feasible

22 | Mathis Grünewald, *Saint George and other six Holy Helpers*, 1503. Lindenhardt, Parish church.

23 | Tilman Riemenschneider, *Tombstone of Konrad von Schaumberg*, ca. 1500. Würzburg, Marienkapelle.

24 | Tilman Riemenschneider, *Eve*, 1491–1493. Würzburg. Museum fűr Fränken.

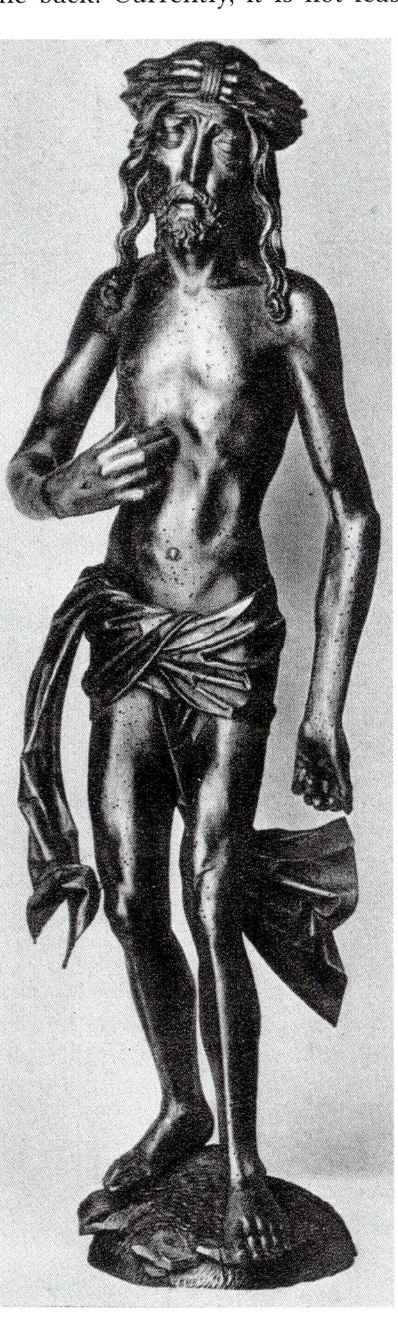

25 | Tilman Riemenschneider, *Man of Sorrow* (detail from a carved altarpiece), ca. 1502. Rothenburg am See, Sankt Jacobskirche.

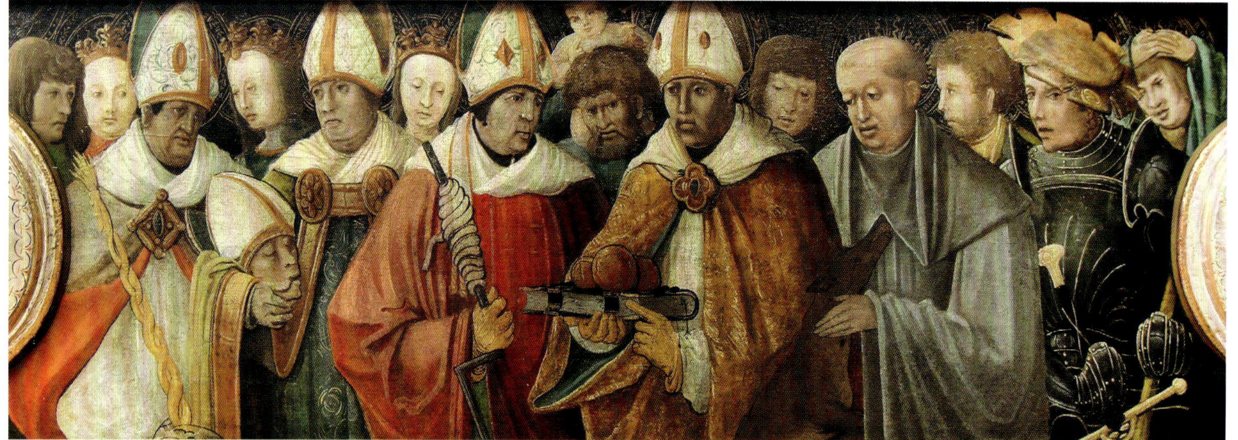

26 | Collaborator of (?) Mathis Grünewald, *The Fourteen Holy Helpers*. Aschaffenburg, Staatsgalerie im Schloss Johannisburg, inv. 9874.

to attribute the generally modest paintings of the Gerolzhofen altar to Mathis. However, the numerous similarities between the work of a collaborator of Riemenschneider and a predella also very close to one of Grünewald's early works (the Lindenhardt triptych), represents, I believe, the definitive confirmation of the reconstruction of Mathis's training presented here.

1503, the year indicated on the Lindenhardt triptych, is the same as the one once seen on a painting which, for us, is a fairly fixed point in the reconstruction of our painter's career: the *Mocking of Christ*, today at the Munich Alte Pinakothek (inv. 10352) [fig. 28], approximately 109 × 76 cm and with a cut several centimeters long on the lower edge. During its restoration in the 1930s, the fragment of an inscription was discovered on the lower edge, "Anno MDIII Die XXIII Decem", which was certainly not authentic and overlapped another inscription, equally as spurious, that repeated the same words. It is virtually certain that these two inscriptions must have retraced the original, likely located in the now-missing part of the painting.

A 19th-century inventory of the Munich Gallery recorded the original dimensions of the painting which were larger than the current ones, as well as the presence of the date 1503, placing the work either contemporary with or immediately after the Lindenhardt triptych.

We are also aware of a number of copies of the work, which therefore enjoyed significant public viewing, in the Hanau, Hermannstadt and Aschaffenburg museums. The Aschaffenburg copy, a work of Johann von Gulchen and dated 1603,[57] is especially important, despite its poor quality, because it has four coats of arms of the von Cronberg, von Dehrn, von Schönborn and von Landsberg families, and an inscription on the back giving the occasion for which it was made: the wedding of Hartmut von Cronberg and Anna Kunigunde von Dehrn. Zülch (1938), researching the families to which the coats of arms painted on the von Gulchen copy belonged, discovered the news of the death on December 23, 1503, of Apollonia von Frankenstein, the sister of Johann von Cronberg. Thus, the painting would have been commissioned in memory of Apollonia. Therefore, the end of 1503 represents only a *post quem*. But there is much more. Johann von Cronberg was the vicar in Aschaffenburg (for whose church the painting was realized) of the archbishop of Mainz, Uriel von Gemmingen, in whose service Mathis would be documented in a few years' time. This work thus represents the first indication of Grünewald's entry into the orbit of the prestigious court of the archbishop of Mainz, an extremely important piece of information. That the work enjoyed significant prestige is shown not only by the existence of early copies but also the probable acquisition, already in 1613, by Wilhelm V, Duke of Bavaria, for his collection.

Another aspect to consider is that Johann von Cronberg died in 1506, and therefore it is quite probable that the painting of the Munich *Mocking of Christ* occurred before that event in 1504–1505. Continuing along this point, we might be able to be more precise. Following Würzburg being indicated as Mathis's city in various documents, the case for Aschaffenburg also begins to take shape, being cited as his home town in literary sources from the late 1500s and early 1600s, as mentioned in the opening pages of this book. Moreover, the current dating for the Munich painting addresses the reluctance of some critics, particularly Ruhmer, to accept the Lindenhardt altarpiece among his autograph works.

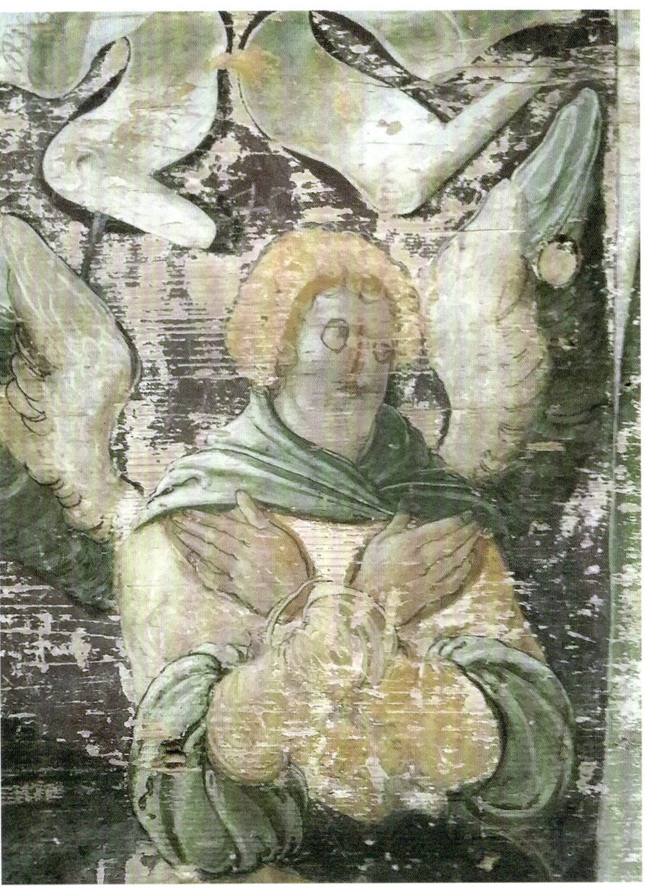

27 | Collaborator of Tilman Riemenschneider, *Angel in adoration* (detail from a polyptych), 1513–1519. Munich, Bayerisches Nationalmuseum, inv. MA 1963.

From a compositional standpoint, the Munich work is much more complex than the Lindenhardt triptych, where the figures are essentially posed and static, while here they are in rapid movement. The lighting approach is sharp, likely developed by taking into account the lighting conditions of the original setting. The source of light comes from outside the painting, from the left, perhaps a door that opens on the large, crowded room, like a ray of light falling perpendicularly to the bottom on the right. Similar to the Lindenhardt triptych, there is little attention to the aspect of perspective depth. Once again, following a sculptural approach, the spatial retreat is represented through the greater amount of shadow that envelops the figures in the background and their lesser focus. The difficulty in rendering the foreshortening is still evident, for example in the drummer on the left, suggesting that the work should be dated close to the Lindenhardt, therefore around 1504 rather than 1505. The faces in the shadows and the extremely fine weaving of color reflect a strong interest in Bosch's recent works, now mastered and transformed into something distinctive by Grünewald. The iridescence of the yellow jacket of the villain with the knotted cord and the infinite layering of purple on that of the thug, are all uniquely Grünewald's.

According to a fascinating and quite plausible hypothesis by Howard Collinson, the painting would have been the central part, the only figurative one, of an epitaph that followed a layout common in Germany in that period.[58]

Looking at the work, one can clearly see an "X"-shaped compositional layout, centered on the dark area above the head of Christ.[59] The diagonal descending from left to right passes through the jacket of the thug who is about to land a punch, through the top of the blindfolded head of Jesus, then through the lower part of the vest and the right forearm of the other villain with the cord. The opposite diagonal is seen rising from the left forearm of the said villain to the shoulder of the fat

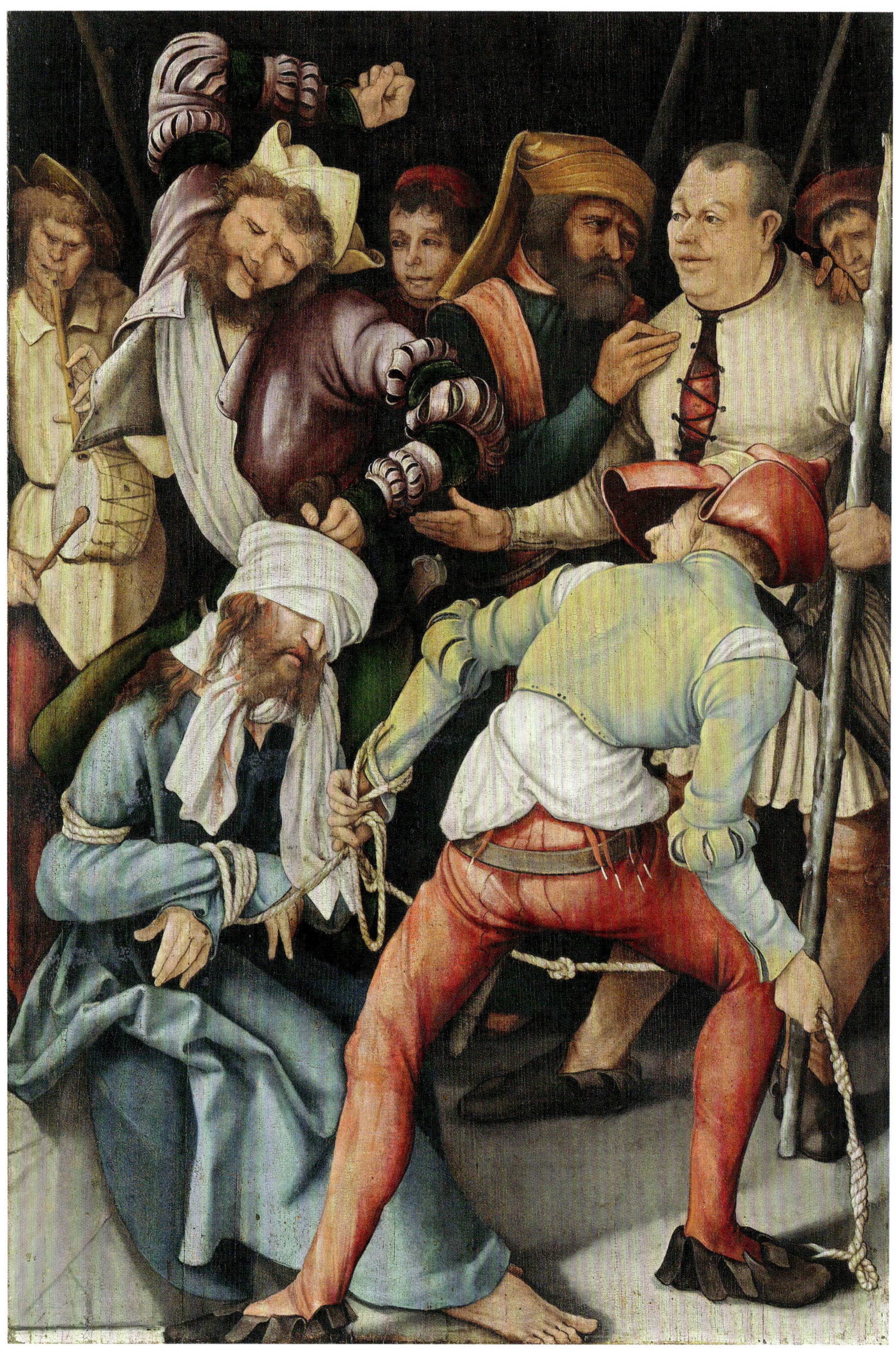

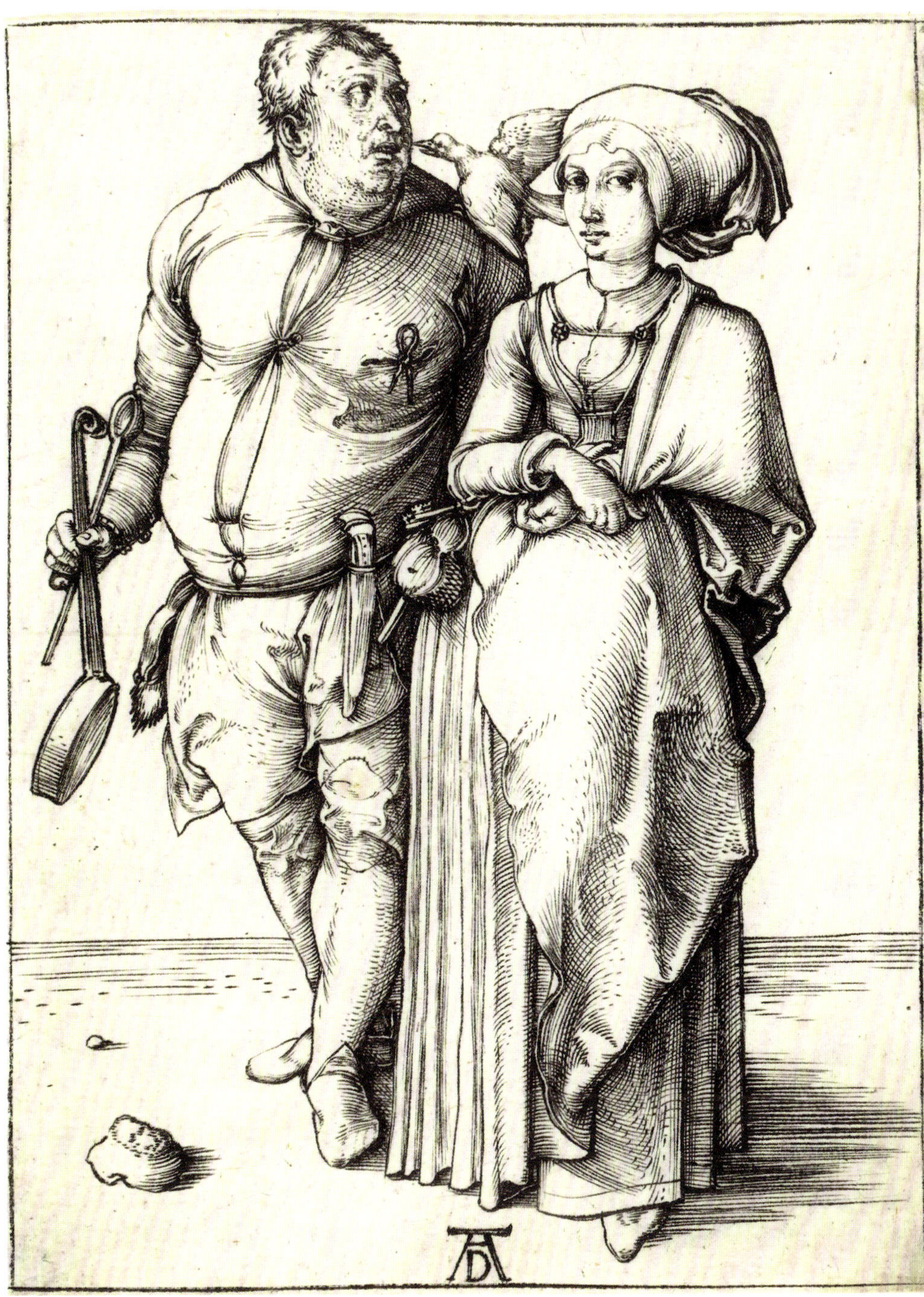

28 | Mathis Grünewald, *Mocking of Christ*, ca. 1504. Munich, Alte Pinakothek, inv. 10352.

29 | Albrecht Dürer, *The Cook and His Wife*, ca. 1496–1497, woodcut.

guard, whom Zülch believed was inspired by Dürer's etching of *The Cook and His Wife*[60] [fig. 29]. Other secondary axes orchestrate the scene: two diagonals parallel to the main ones, the equivalent of rhyme in poetry (a comparison between poetry and figuration previously employed by Baxandall in reference to wooden sculpture[61]). One passes through the shoulders of the two main tormentors, the other from the right leg of Jesus, and a horizontal one from the lower edge of the drum and the extended arm barring the way of the guard noted above. In the seemingly frenzied—and actually highly calculated—explosion of violence, the figure of Jesus seems even more isolated: fully lit, chromatically different from all the others in his light blue robe, static and resigned in his role of sacrificial lamb, and totally

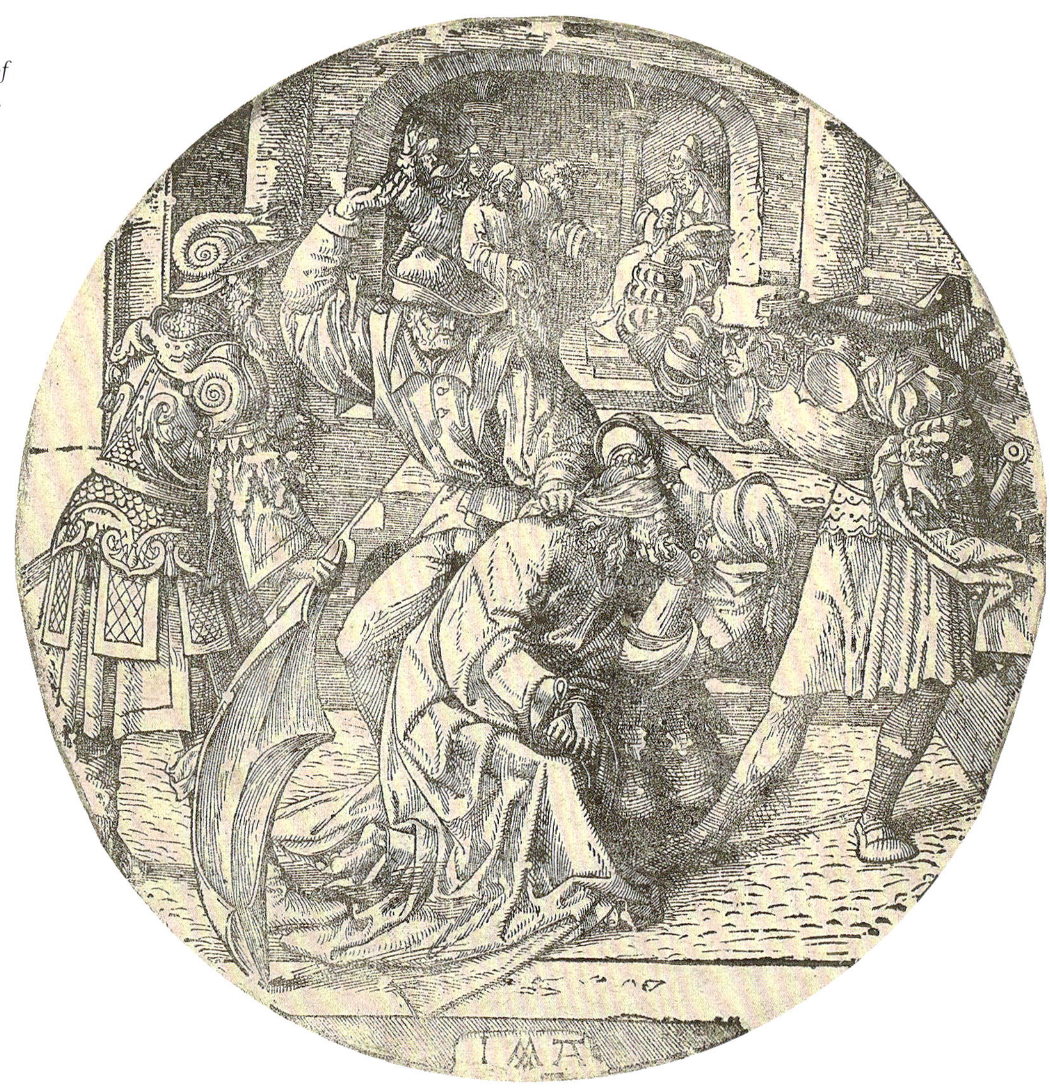

30 | Jacob van Oostanen, *Mocking of Christ*, 1511, woodcut.

passive. The only sign of life in this desolate figure is the almost-electrical, galvanic spasm of his fingers, the only perceptible reaction to the pain from the blows and lashings. An extraordinarily poetic expedient which, alone, is enough to indicate the degree to which the painter was emotionally involved in his subject.

More than in earlier representations of Christ being mocked, in which Jesus is placed in the center of the scene (as seen in a 1511 woodcut of the same subject by Jacob van Oostanen[62] [fig. 30], that borrows quite a few elements from Grünewald's painting, perhaps making it the earliest indication of its visual success), Mathis's compositional approach chosen seems to harken back to the iconographic tradition of the Capture. Here it is not difficult to identify an authoritative model and one, it seems to me, certainly known to our painter: the scene of the Capture of Christ carved in sandstone by Veit Stoss as part of the memorial for Paul Volckamer (1499) in the Sankt Sebaldskirche in Nuremberg[63] [fig. 31]. Once again, preference is given to sculpture, but Mathis's horizons have expanded beyond Riemenschneider toward the other protagonist of German Renaissance sculpture, confirmation of what has already been said about the relationship between our painter and Stoss. There is a clear kinship between the two main thugs in Grünewald's painting and the two figures at the edges of Stoss's relief: St. Peter striking a blow against poor

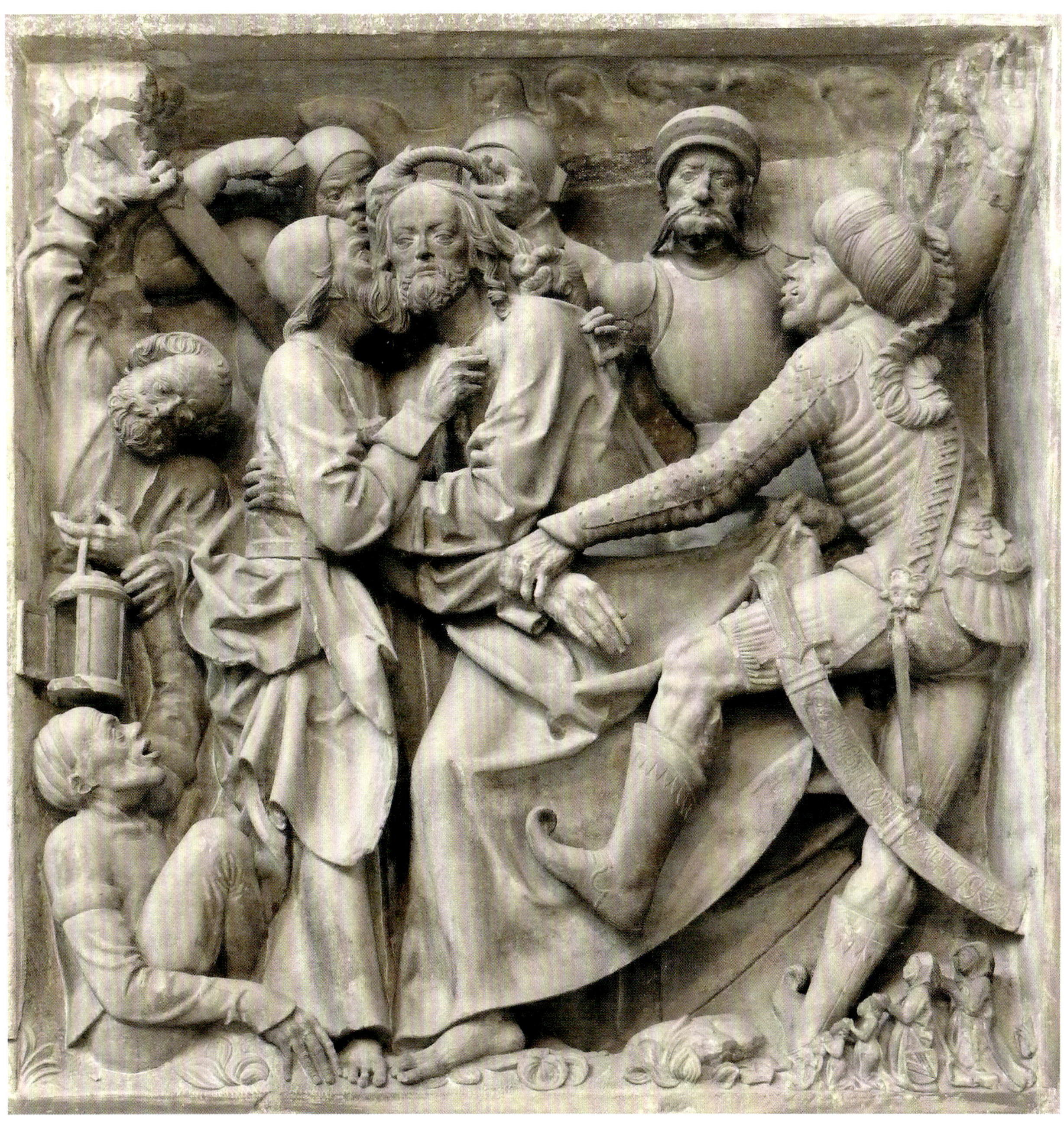

31 | Veit Stoss, *Capture of Christ*, detail from the Paul Volckamer memorial, ca. 1499. Nuremberg, Sankt Sebaldskirche.

Malchus and the big, grotesque soldier grabbing Jesus. The scene orchestrated by Stoss is also constructed on the basis of intersecting diagonals. It could be argued that St. Peter with a raised arm can also be found in other representations of the capture of Christ. This is true, of course, but only in Stoss's image do we find so many close analogies with Mathis's painting found today in Munich. And yet, precisely when we become aware of this derivation, we cannot help but notice how freely our painter has been able to reinterpret his model, to the point that it becomes something completely different. The rhythm is more intense, convulsive and suffocating than Stoss's dramatic, but more narrative scene, almost as if driven by some infernal timepiece.

Therefore, having acquired a presence in Nuremberg, it is curious that he was so little impressed by Dürer's paintings which he could have studied in this city.[64]

32 | Mathis Grünewald, *Crucifixion*, ca. 1505–1506, Basilea, Öffentliche Kunstsammlungen, inv. 269.

However, the question arises whether the greater precision in drawing the drapery, the idea of inserting a "cold" area (Jesus's garment) at the edge of the painting, and the extremely close relationship between the faces and expressions might suggest, at least, close attention to the Deposition, also today at the Munich Alte Pinakothek, painted by Dürer around the year 1500 for the Grimm family.

Another possible connection with Dürer, albeit slight, could be offered by the iconography. Following an intuition by Gert Von der Osten,[65] James H. Marrow suggests interpreting the pose of Christ and the presence of the piper and drummer as an allusion to the figure of Job, the just who patiently accepts misfortune, with particular reference to Job 30:9: "I am become their song, and am become their by-word".[66] It should be recalled that a similar musical ensemble was depicted by Dürer in a panel of the Jabach altar (Cologne, Wallraf-Richartz Museum, inv. WRM 0369), precisely in the period 1503–1504, probably for the chapel in Wittenberg Castle, the church that would receive Luther's 95 Theses.[67]

One of the visages in the Munich painting, that of the bearded man with the sorrowful expression who seems to implore the guard to stop the slaughter, on one hand, is related once again to the humanity of the Coburg *Last Supper* and, on the other, and even more so, seems to be the brother of Longinus in the *Crucifixion* in the Öffentliche Kunstsammlungen in Basel (inv. 269), the next work we will examine [fig. 32].

It is a linden wood panel measuring 74.8 × 54.3 cm, and it is generally believed to have been part of a larger structure that has not survived, as suggested by marks that may be attachment points on the lower edge. However, this hypothesis has recently been seriously questioned, preferring to see the painting as a small altarpiece probably created for the private devotions of a wealthy client.[68]

As has been said, it is a youthful work (even though Ruhmer, with no follow-up in subsequent studies, dates it to "before 1515", just prior to the *Isenheim Altarpiece*[69]) given the fact that the figures still exhibit a certain weakness and spatial inconsistency.

Longinus again exhibits a resemblance to the expressions of the apostles in the Coburg *Last Supper* and, even more so, to the bearded and compassionate figure in the *Mocking of Christ*. The same is true of St. John, who bears a similarity to the expressions of the saints in the Lindenhardt triptych: the prominent jaw and the shiny, penetrating eyes of the suffering disciple we have already seen in the Lindenhardt saints, and even in the Aschaffenburg predella. The extremely flowing draperies are reminiscent once again of the experiences of Bosch, who played such an important part in the 1503 altarpiece (look, once again, at the wind playing with the fringed drapery of Bosch's St. Liberata and turbulent whirling of St. John's garments).

These observations have led to dating the *Crucifixion* to 1504–1505. Before undertaking a formal analysis of the painting, I believe this view to be substantially correct, but it could be more precise. The work is probably slightly later than the Munich painting, from a period indicatively around 1505–1506.

The *Crucifixion* is an impetuous work with numerous *pentimenti*, something destined to become typical throughout Mathis's career. For example, it can be seen that the pious St. Veronica hugging the cross must have been inserted, or at least enlarged, later (the x-ray radiography, published by Kemperdick, does not seem decisive in clarifying this question). From direct examination, we see the landscape

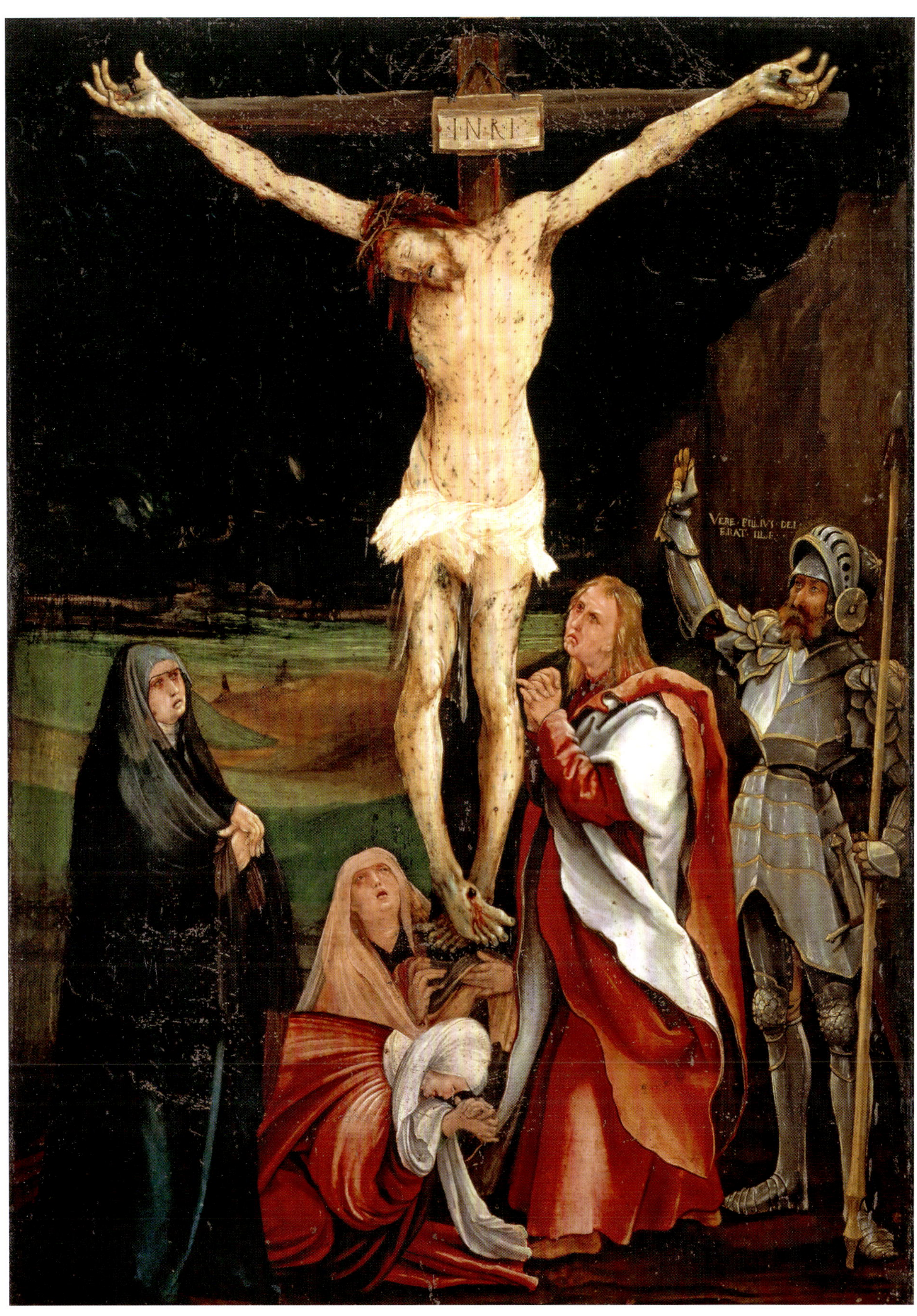
I·N·R·I
VERE·FILIVS·DEI
ERAT·ILLE

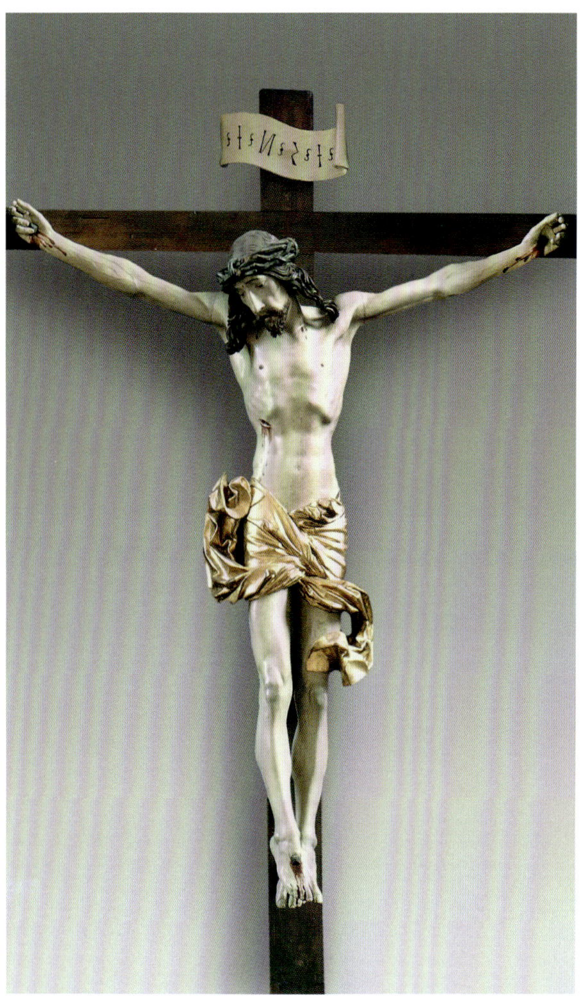

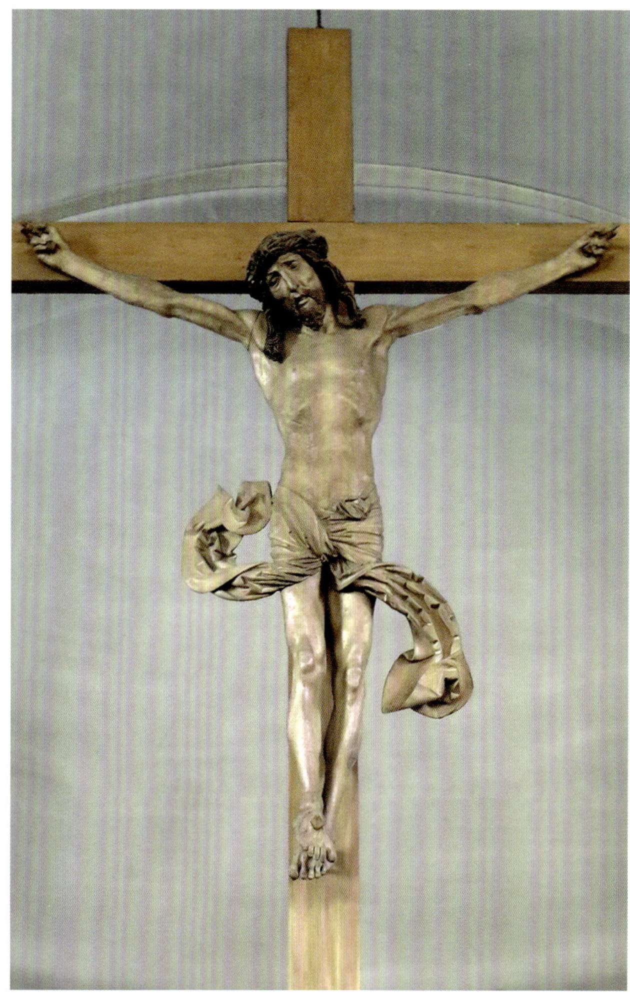

33 | Tilman Riemenschneider, *Crucifix*. Heroldsberg bei Nürnberg, Evangelic church of Saint Matthew.

34 | Tilman Riemenschneider, *Crucifix*. Gerolzhofen, Catholic church of Maria vom Rosenkranz.

continues below the part external to the woman's yellow veil, the transparent areas of Mary Magdalene's mantle do not match up well with St. Veronica's garments, and Christ's loincloth must originally have been smaller.

The work shows once again a painter unable to dominate the space—therefore, a youthful work—and the insertion, or at least the enlargement, of the "Woman in Yellow" at the foot of the cross would seem intended as an element of compositional rebalancing, at the risk of revealing contradictions in the realization of spatial depth.

The landscape behind the cross is abstract and generic, the shadows are broken by artificial light that gives the work an anguished, almost haunted, unnaturalistic atmosphere.The primary light source seems to be the body of Christ itself, with the numerous wounds standing out against its whiteness. According to the medieval iconographic hierarchy, the Savior is shown slightly larger than the other figures (as will always be the case in *Crucifixions* painted by Grünewald). His figure offers clear, deliberate anatomical straining: the very long arms seem terribly stretched in the spasms of agony that have twisted his fingers. Against this base of extremely violent emotional impact, his head dangling against his chest takes on almost unbearable force, with his stiffened mouth open in a final scream and his hair caked with blood. The red, illuminated mantle of St. John seems to echo the blood of Christ which has begun to become encrusted on the wounds. We can never forget the terrible pictorial invention that uses the Flemish lenticular of realism to turn it into pure, too real, pain, with bruised, almost necrotic flesh, a cold light coalescing around the heads of the nails, the same light a Flemish painter would have had dance off a vase or some precious object. The physical structure of the crucified Christ has slim hips and a broad chest, which reflects a white, dull light that breaks against all the edges of the sternum to give them total plasticity, a plasticity that reveals the profound, systematic meditation on the numerous *Crucifixions* produced by Riemenschneider and his workshop, and together their intense distortion (for example, those of Heroldsberg, Aub, Insingen, Bibra, Gerolzhofen, Würzburg and Graz[70] [figs. 33–34]). Above and beyond the expressive tension, it must be noted that this early Grünewald Christ is based on a formal, anatomic conception fed precisely by these examples.

From the minute *craquelures* seen on the ghostly greenish angels above Jesus's right hand, we get a hint of a red preparation which also takes on aesthetic importance in that Grünewald is able to obtain a deep hue which on the chromatic scale is particularly dark and opaque. It is all emphasized by a heightened richness in the intensity of the colors compared with the earlier works.

As recent studies have noted, the painting technique adopted by Grünewald is quite different from that of his contemporaries, such as Dürer and Cranach, who, being both painters and engravers, transferred the etching technique to their paintings, accurately delineating the *chiaroscuro* and very precisely filling the detailed parts of the drawing with color. Grünewald, however, employs an almost opposite process. With the brush dipped in the paint—black or less-frequently red—he sketches out the composition which is subject to change and *pentimenti*. The act of painting is not conceived as starting from a solid drawing to be painted in with color but rather creating the painting starting from color. The drawing serves merely as an outline before painting: it is the color that literally models the figure.

Iconographically, the "nocturnal" scene is explained by referencing the Gospels of Luke and, especially, John, which state that at the crucifixion of Jesus, "from the sixth houre there was darknesse over all the land unto the ninth houre" (Mt 27:45). For Grünewald it is perhaps not yet a question of evangelic tension (although it cannot be denied that there is intense involvement, almost a sense of identification?), but rather the wish of his patron, perhaps a religious person, which would also explain the presence of the Latin phrase next to Longinus "*Vere fillius* [sic] *Dei erat Ille*" (Mt 27:54).

The armor worn by the centurion makes his figure a bit cramped in his allotted space: long-limbed and elongated, almost neo-Gothic. This type of armor actually existed, but it is neither Roman nor contemporary to Grünewald. The same model is found in an etching at the British Museum (inv. 1920.1113.1), formerly in Cassiano del Pozzo's collection in Rome, by an anonymous Netherlandish artist, conventionally known as Master of Calvary, dated around 1440–1450 [fig. 35].[71]

The use of this type of armor could be explained by the desireo to place the scene outside of any set time period and only generically tied to a more or less remote era. The decision not to use Roman-style armor could indicate the basic disinterest of Grünewald and his client in a philological recreation of antiquity. But it could also simply mean that Mathis had in his mind's eye the memory of a *Crucifixion* with a Longinus similarly equipped, something similar to the pen-and-ink drawing in the Fine Arts Museum in Budapest (inv. no. 4 [fig. 36]),[72] correctly

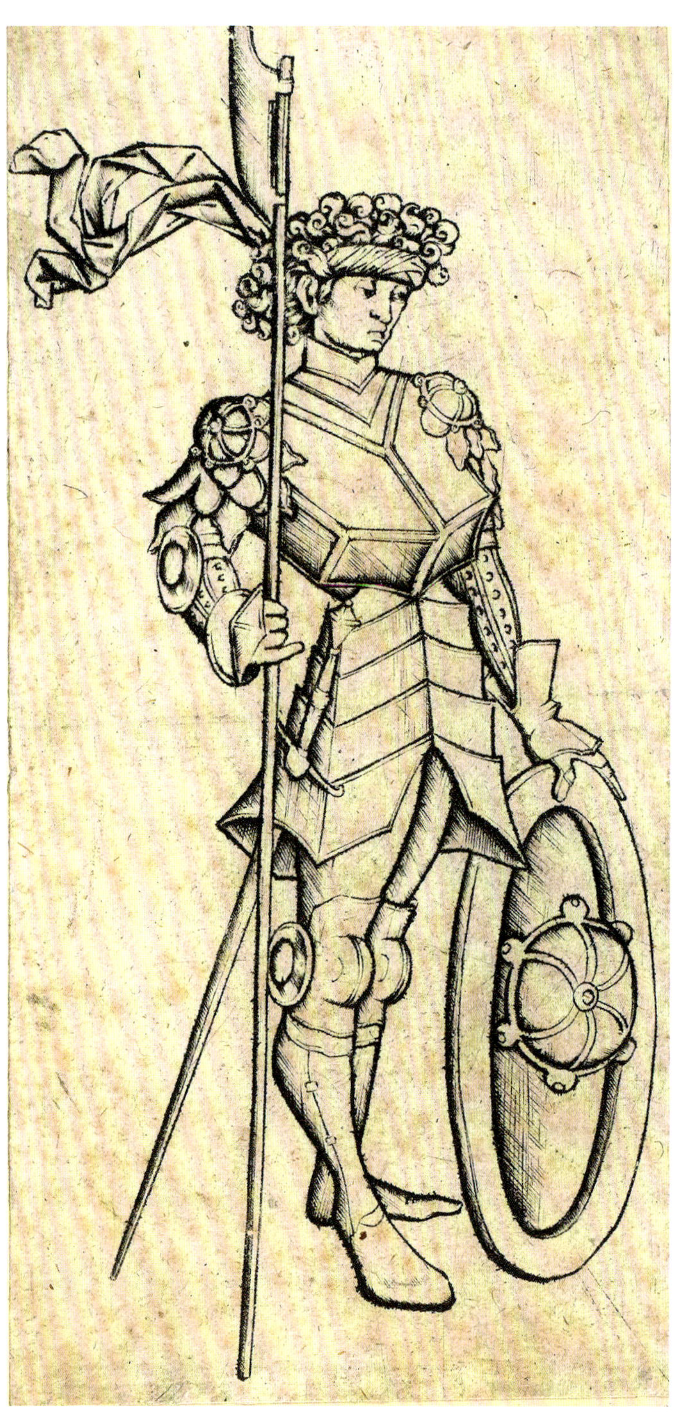

35 | Master of Calvary, *A Warrior in armour*, etching. London, The British Museum, inv. 1920.1113.1.

36 | Workshop of Hans Pleydenwurff. *Crucifixion with Longinus*. Budapest, Szépművészeti Múzeum.

attributed to the workshop of Hans Pleydenwurff, an artist active for most of his career in Nuremberg, where he died in 1472. It is a drawing in which Longinus's gesture, also characterized by a phylactery destined to contain his recognition of the divinity of Jesus, is very similar to that in the small panel by Grünewald. We have already seen Nuremberg's role in Grünewald's artistic development, and this point seems to be an important confirmation.

In comparing paintings contemporary with Grünewald's, in particular two *Crucifixions* by Lucas Cranach—the first dated 1500 and now at the Kunsthistorisches Museum, Vienna (inv. Gemäldegalerie, 6905), and the second three years later and today in Munich, at the Alte Pinakothek (inv. 1416) [fig. 37]—a lesser expressive freedom is seen compared to Mathis, despite the three paintings' similar disarticulated treatment of the hands. This comparison marks the beginning of a low-key dialogue between the two painters, which, although never profound, nonetheless continues. While in Cranach expressionism is only transmitted through the pose of the hands, in Grünewald it permeates everything. The perspective in the Munich *Crucifixion* by Lucas, characterized by a framing in which the cross is placed off-center, cannot be considered an expressionistic trait as it is not uncommon in German painting. In the background, barely outlined with the tip of the brush, we see the pious women at the sepulcher on the left and the soldiers returning to Jerusalem after the execution. An almost miniature-like treatment that confirms the refined execution of the work and the exacting preferences of the client, whose identity is still unknown.

In 1773, Grünewald's painting appeared in a Basel collection, but no traces regarding who commissioned it remain. It is hypothesized that it comes from the Antonite monastery in Basel, an order named after St. Anthony the Hermit which followed the Rule of St. Augustine and had numerous contacts with Mathis Grünewald during his lifetime, although, as far as we know, he never worked for those in Basel.

It is speculated that Heinrich Reitzmann, canon of Aschaffenburg, and a figure who would accompany Grünewald for an extended period of his life, might have

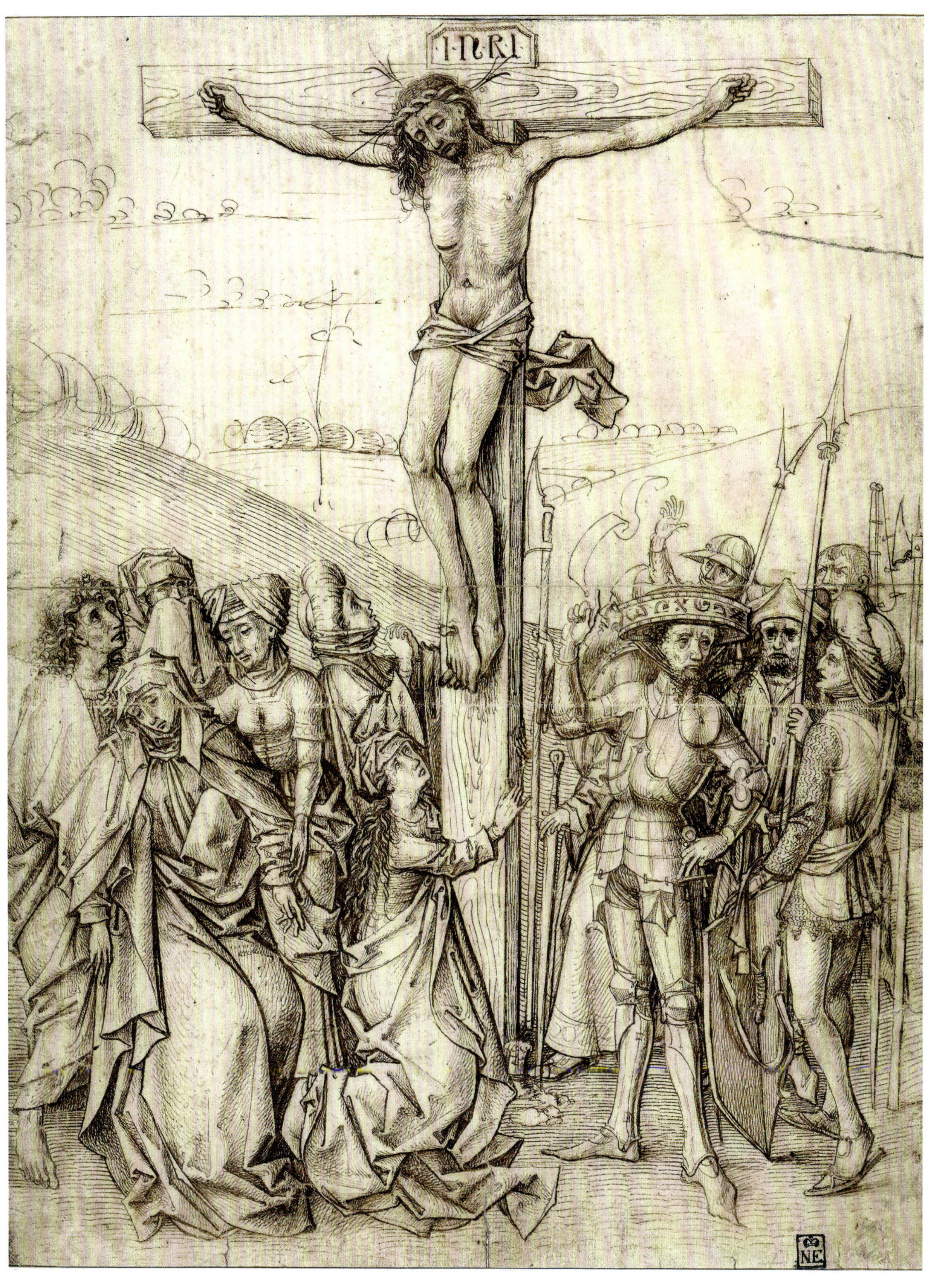
I·N·R·I

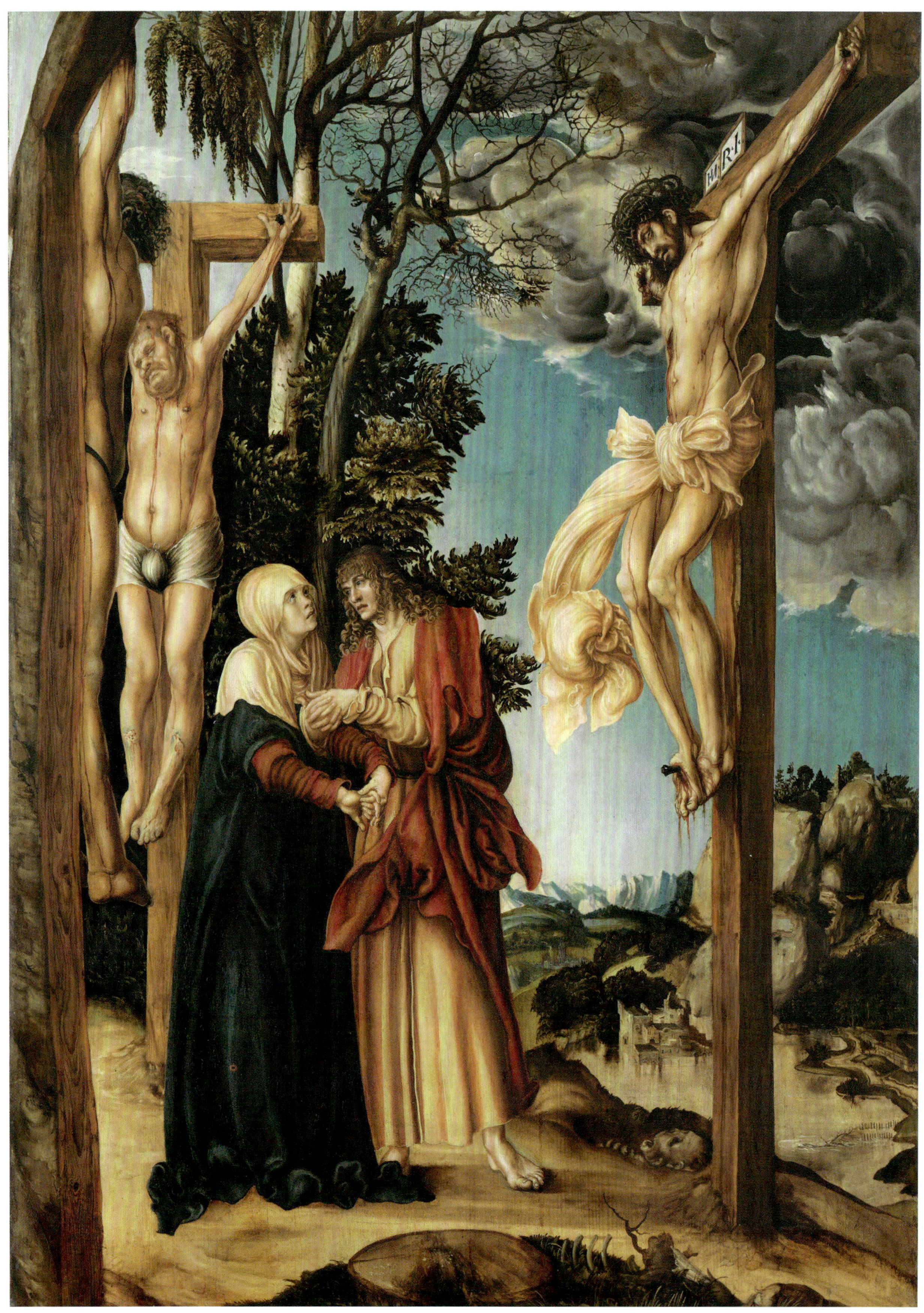
I·N·R·I·

commissioned it. A learned canon, connoisseur of Italy and, we imagine, a collector of prints (sometimes thought by scholars to be by Andrea Mantegna), Reitzmann first appeared in relation to Mathis on November 30, 1505, when he paid a small sum to a "famulo meister Mathis ad pingendam et scribendam tabulam epitaphii" in commemoration of his brother, vicar Jacob Reitzmann.

This document provides two fundamental pieces of information: confirmation of the relations between the two men starting at least in 1505, and that—in that year—Mathis could already count on the help of an assistant and probably, therefore, a small workshop.

Heinrich Reitzmann owned, but had not commissioned, another small *Crucifixion* by our painter, which we will discuss later, discouraging the fascinating hypothesis of his direct involvement in the Basel panel's realization. Or perhaps, on the contrary, it makes it more likely? This immediately raises the question of whether he had not participated in the epitaph (in the form of a triptych, according to the traditional style noted in relation to the *Mocking of Christ* in Munich) in memory of Jacob Reitzmann, which could be dated to the year 1505.

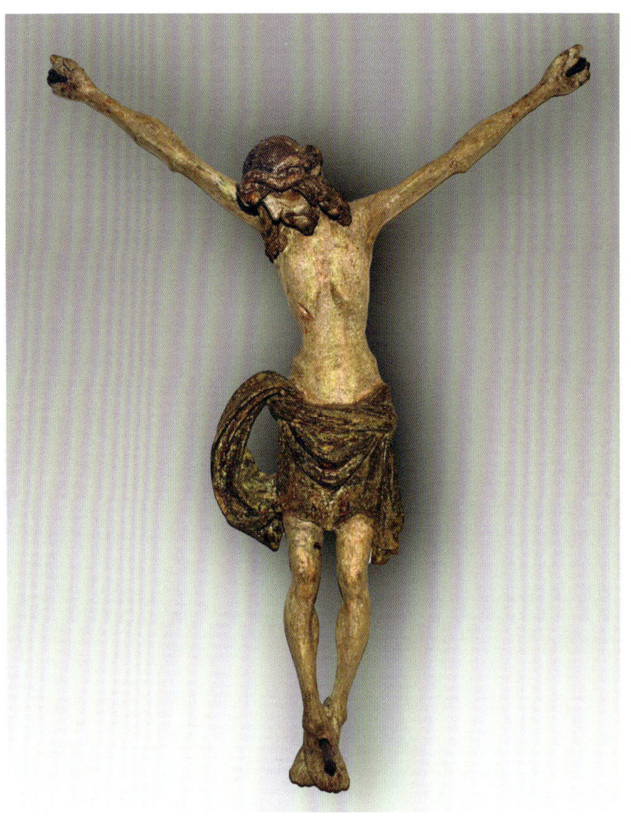

37 | Lucas Cranach, *Crucifixion*, ca. 1503. Munich, Alte Pinakothek, inv. 1416.

38 | Hans Geiler, *Crucifix*. Private collection.

Here I would like to make a brief digression to mention a small but very remarkable wooden *Crucifix* in a private collection (56 × 40 × 12 cm). The arms are very long, and the focus on the chest's structure and the alarmingly twisted feet are very similar to Grünewald's Basel painting [fig. 38]. Of course, it could not be a sculpture by Mathis because the work appears to have come definitively from Hans Geiler's workshop in Freiburg, around 1520.[73] However, it does suggest that the work (probably for an important client, given the traces of gilding on the loincloth) reveals a certain authoritativeness of our artist among carvers well beyond the confines of Würzburg, and even beyond Germany.[74]

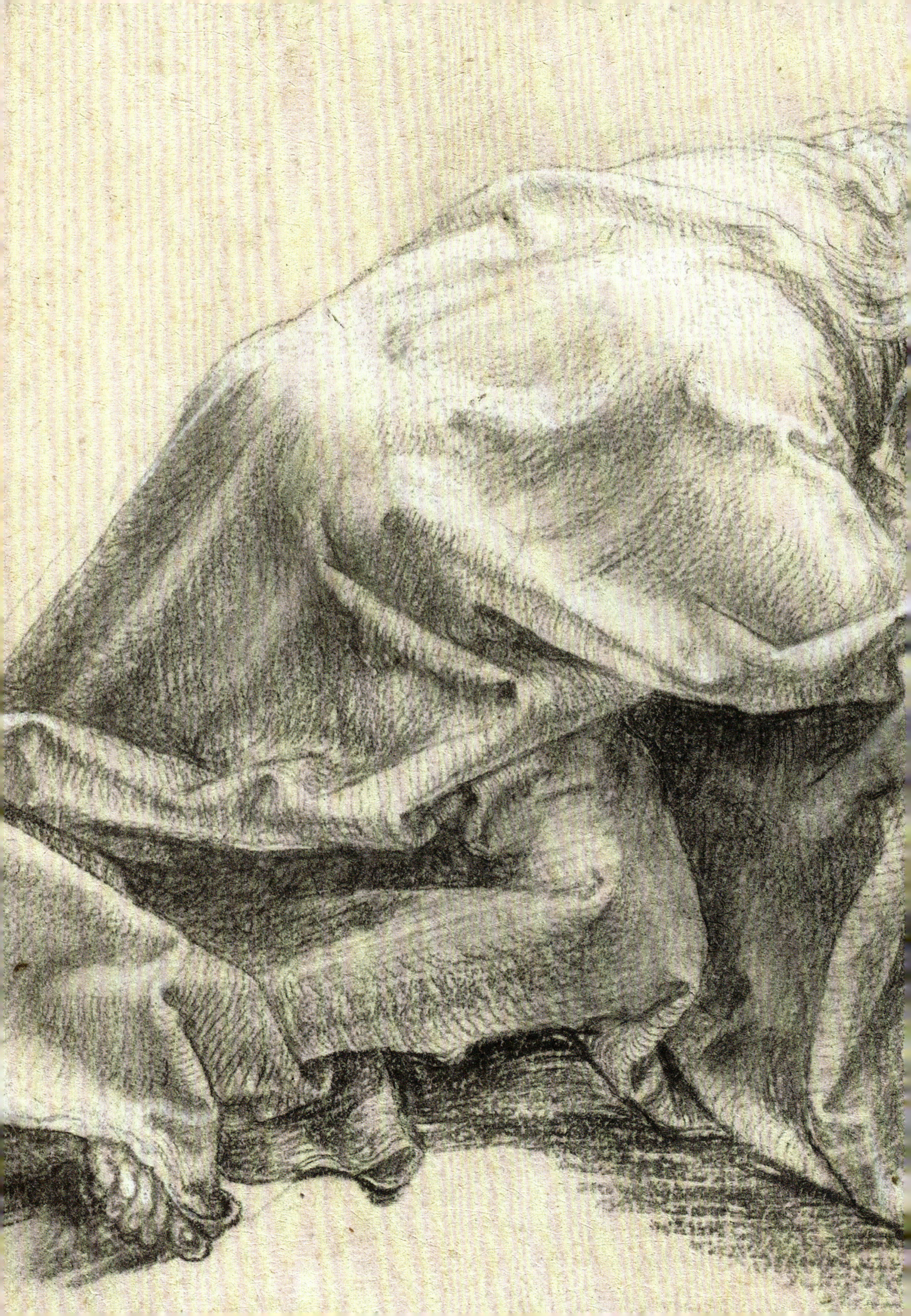

CHAPTER II

Early Maturity

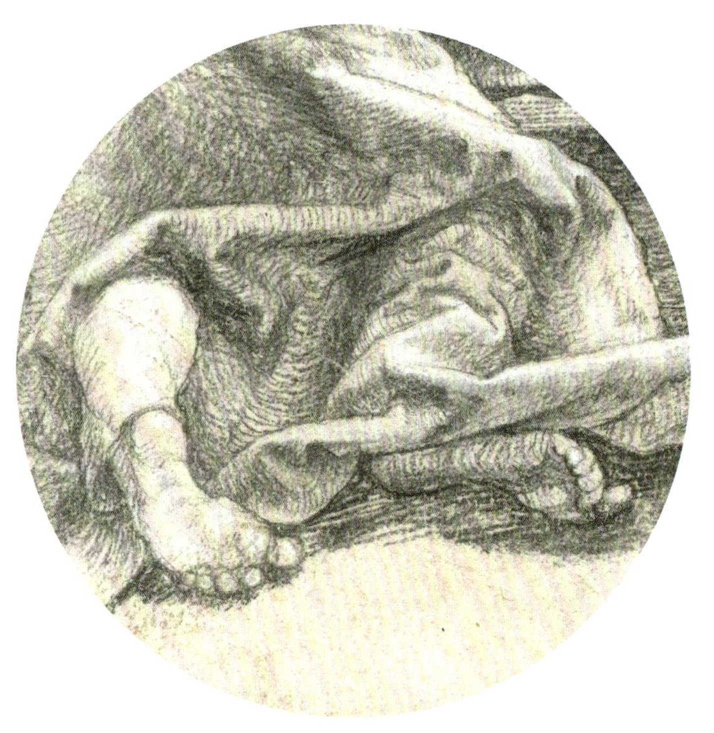

We have already emphasized the wealth of *pentimenti* in Grünewald's paintings and the extreme attention to color in them (aspects we will revisit). Perhaps it is no accident that he is, in fact, the only great German Renaissance painter not to have done any etching. Dürer or Cranach (to name just two major examples) took great care in the outlining of their images, shading them with very precise cross-hatching—a technique borrowed, in fact, from etching—to create volume, then applying color to these detailed monochrome figures, and finally retouching with a brush those areas intended for shading. Mathis, on the other hand, only sketches the outlines on the panel in black or, later and rarely, in red, giving himself absolute freedom to make modifications, but, above all, entrusting the shading to the addition of color.[1] This may seem only a technical distinction, but it actually represents a different conception of the natural world. Light and shade are not something to be layered onto plain surfaces in a greater or lesser amount, but rather an element intrinsically connected to color. Color does not "receive" light and shade, it "reacts" with them—chemically, it could be said—absorbing and subsuming them into itself, in a state of constant change. Grünewald's lack of etching experience thus becomes a demonstration of extreme, implacable coherence, even more significant given that the twenty-odd drawings positively attributed to Mathis reveal him to be very gifted in sketching. Having said this, we must begin to examine Mathis's first-known graphic works, their formal and stylistic characteristics and their function.[2]

The oldest-known drawing by Mathis is a sheet at the Kupferstichkabinett at the Staatliche Museen in Berlin (KdZ 12038). It measures 324 × 216 mm, drawn in black chalk with white highlighting, and is dated to the first decade of the 16th century. On the recto is St. Catherine of Alexandria [fig. 39] and on the verso, a female figure, lightly sketched, also probably a saint.[3] The latter is holding a ring and, in all probability, is an alternate version of St. Catherine, depicted in this case during her mystic marriage to Christ.

St. Catherine is quite slender and, as Roth observes, is reminiscent once again of the extremely bent head, unnaturally stylized proportions and very slim waist of the female saints in the internal panels of the Coburg altarpiece. This female silhouette feels similar to many works from the Riemenschneider workshop. The pose of the figure seems to be borrowed from an already old-fashioned etching of the same subject by Martin Schongauer [fig. 40].[4] Additionally, if I am not mistaken, there seems to be a close affinity with Cranach's painting style, in particular the tiny, sprightly eyes and childish, round faces, but also the clear pursuit of expressive delicacy in the gently slanted gaze.

Let's compare the Berlin drawing with Cranach's paintings, such as the *Madonna with Child* (Madrid, Museo Nacional Thyssen-Bornemisza, inv. 114, ca. 1508–1510), or the famous woodcut of *Venus and Cupid*, dated 1506 but perhaps slightly later[5] [fig. 41]. These are fairly youthful works from the period 1505–1510 when Cranach, coming from Vienna, had just settled in the fateful Wittenberg, and are therefore chronologically close to our drawing. We see precisely this type of physiognomy which Cranach, soon to achieve his figurative maturity, maintained throughout his life, while Grünewald would soon, almost immediately, abandon it. This interest seems to indicate renewed curiosity in contemporary painting. In comparing the two works, the difference in sense of security can be attributed to Cranach's ability to find almost immediately, as was said, his mature style, unlike Mathis who still appears to be searching for his own, unmistakable stylistic imprint.

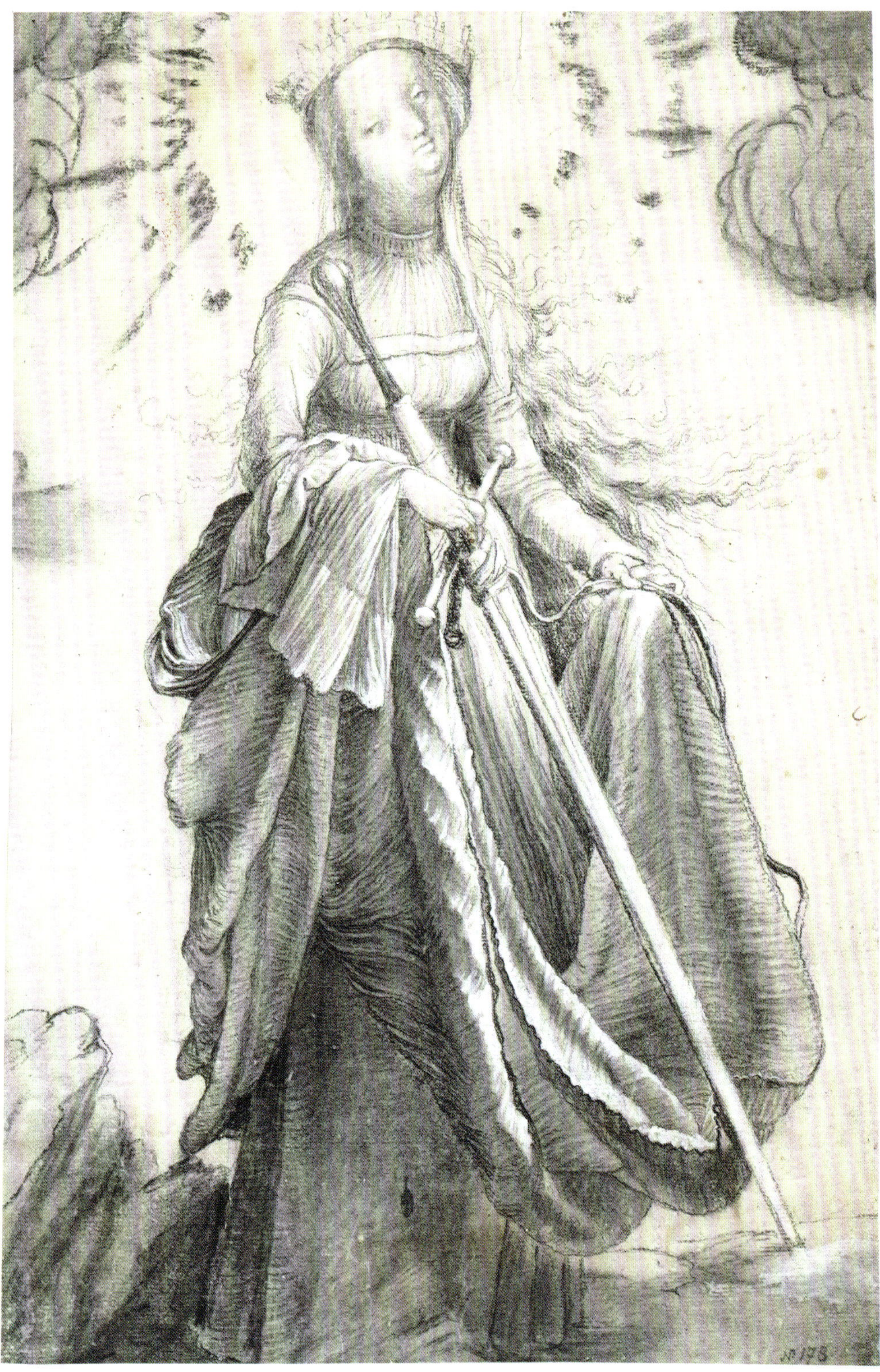

39 | Mathis Grünewald, *Saint Catherine*, ca. 1508–1509. Berlin, Staatliche Museen, Kupferstichkabinett, inv. KdZ 12038 recto.

However, the greatest contrast between Mathis and Lucas is in the drapery, where Grünewald demonstrates his special skill in the use of black pencil and different treatment of the tactile, woolly texture of the fabric. The light is unidirectional, homogeneously arriving from the right. It is reflected in the very long blade of the sword, the main axis of the image. From there it reverberates off the folds of the

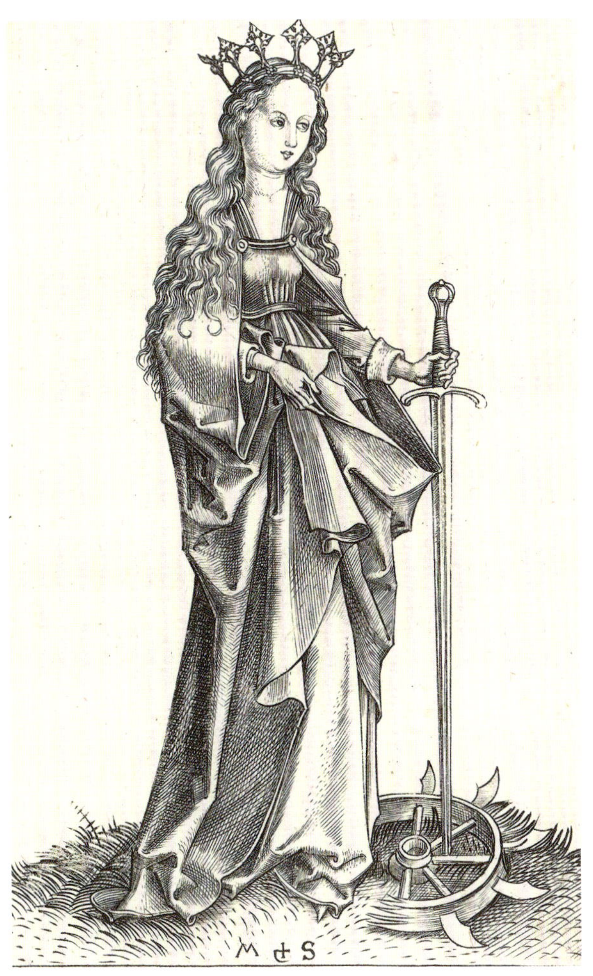

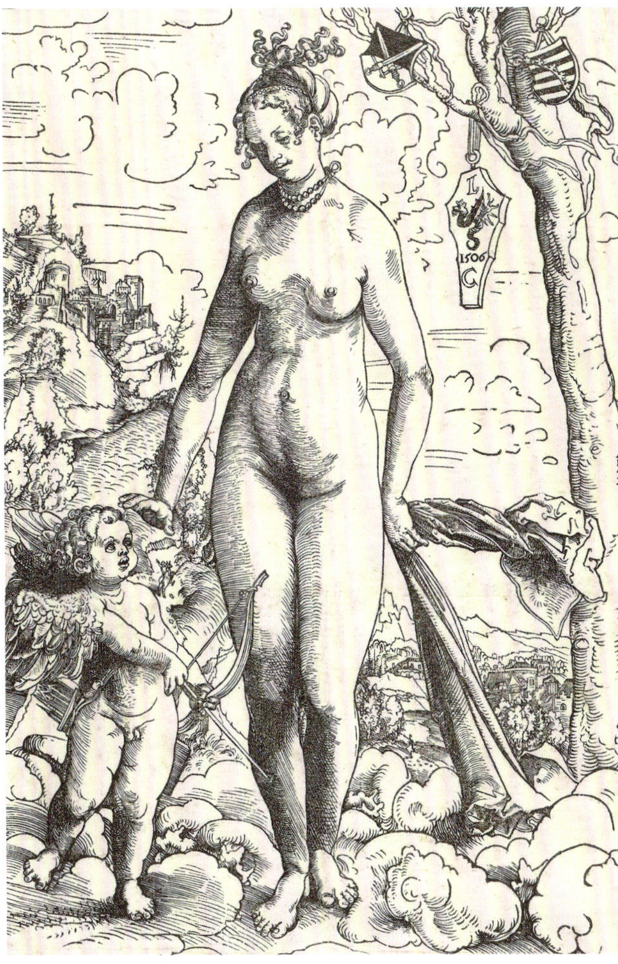

chalky and silvery fabric to insinuate itself into the minuscule pleats of the garment behind the right arm of the saint. Despite the fact that the face is less secure than that of Cranach's women, with the simple technique of black pencil and white chalk, Mathis displays a more profound ability to conceive and manage light. His drawings also reflect this type of pictorial approach: the figure is constructed by the way the light interacts with it to reveal its form.

40 | Martin Schongauer, *Saint Catherine*, etching.

41 | Lucas Cranach, *Venus*, ca. 1505, woodcut.

What date can we assign to this drawing? Unquestionably later than the works we have seen until now and which extend to 1506, where this interest in Cranach never appears. This is only logical, given that Cranach's move from Vienna to Wittenberg occurred in 1505, the date from which Lucas began to be a painter known throughout central-southern Germany. In fact, Grünewald's interest in him, albeit superficial, is especially precocious. We are probably somewhat before the monochromes today in Karlsruhe, which we will discuss shortly, datable to 1509–1510, in which the overall rendering of the figure is quite a bit more advanced. This leaves a three-year gap in his works that could offer a clue to his updated interest in the art of his contemporaries. Precisely for the technical characteristics mentioned above, for Grünewald, drawing is an essential stage in the elaboration of a painting. One in which, even before the actual phase of painting, he studies not only the composition but the overall relationship of light and shade. Considering this, and that virtually all his drawings were preparatory studies for paintings, it is quite probable that the Berlin *St. Catherine* is none other than the finished study for a painting of this subject. A work conceived

42 | Master of Saint Bartholomew Altar, *The Saints Andrew and Columba*. Mainz, Landesmuseum, inv. 441.

43 | **a-b** Hans Baldung Grien, *Saint Catherine. Saint Agnes* (details from a triptych), ca. 1506–1507. Berlin, Staatliche Museen, Gemäldegalerie, inv. 603A.

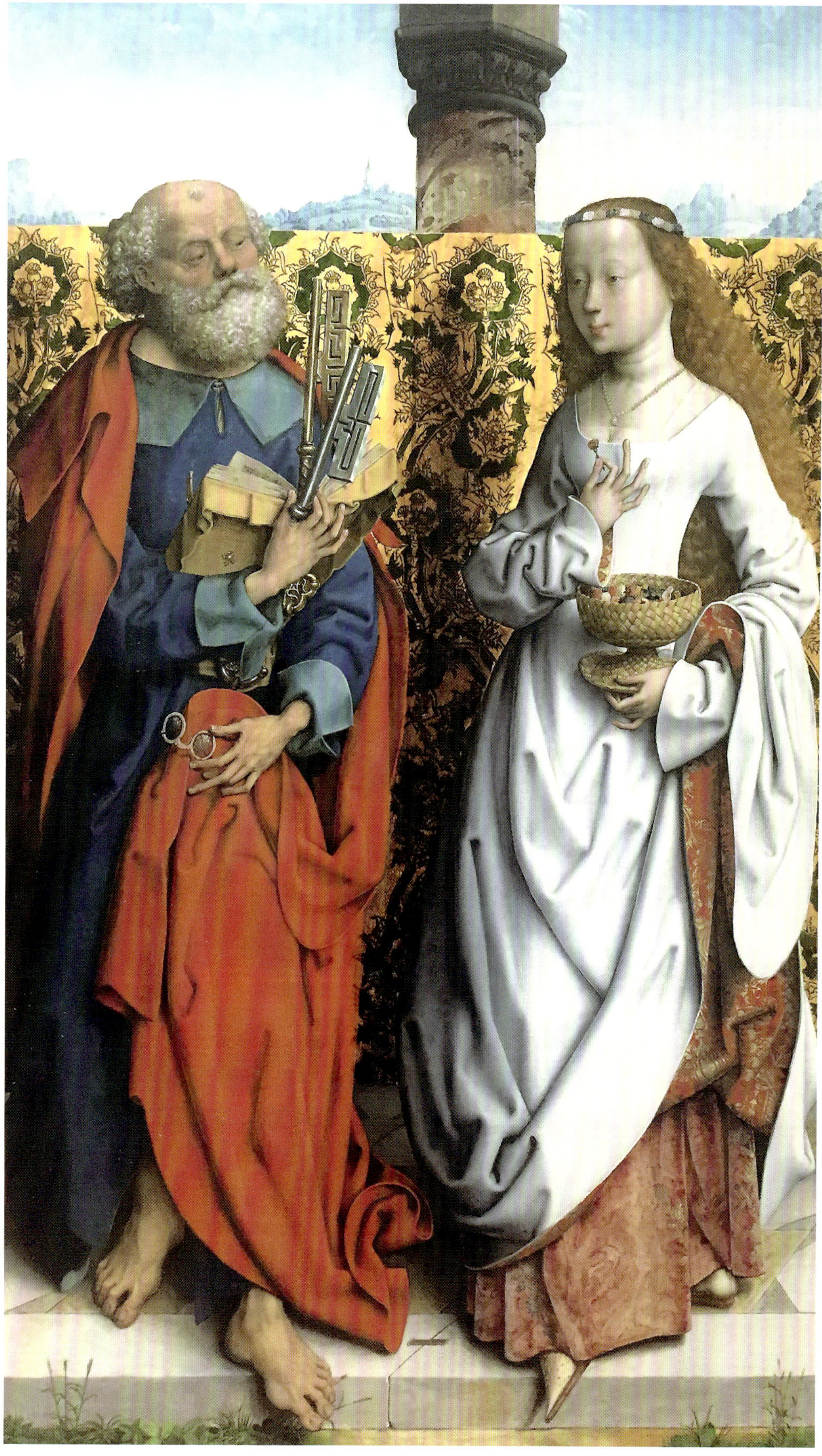

with strong illumination from the right and, perhaps, given the three-quarter stance of the saint, the left panel of a triptych or, even better, perhaps the panel of a hinged altarpiece. We know nothing about it except, thanks to the previous analysis, its probable chronology, and possibly the fact that its author was familiar to the artist conventionally called the Master of the St. Bartholomew Altarpiece. This Master, whose style was influenced by Holbein the Elder with some discreet Dürerian input, would seem to cite it as a counterpart in the *Saint Columba* (next to *Saint Andrew*), at Mainz Landesmuseum (inv. 340), part of an altarpiece dated to ca. 1510 and now divided between that museum and the National Gallery, London [fig. 42].[6] Though at the same time, this image belongs to a precise typological tradition, to which also belongs, quite close in time, the upper part of the external views of the two side panels of the *Three Kings Altarpiece*, depicting *St. Catherine* and *St. Agnes* by Hans Baldung, dated 1506–1507, today at the Berlin Gemäldegalerie (inv. 603A) [figs. 43a-b].[7]

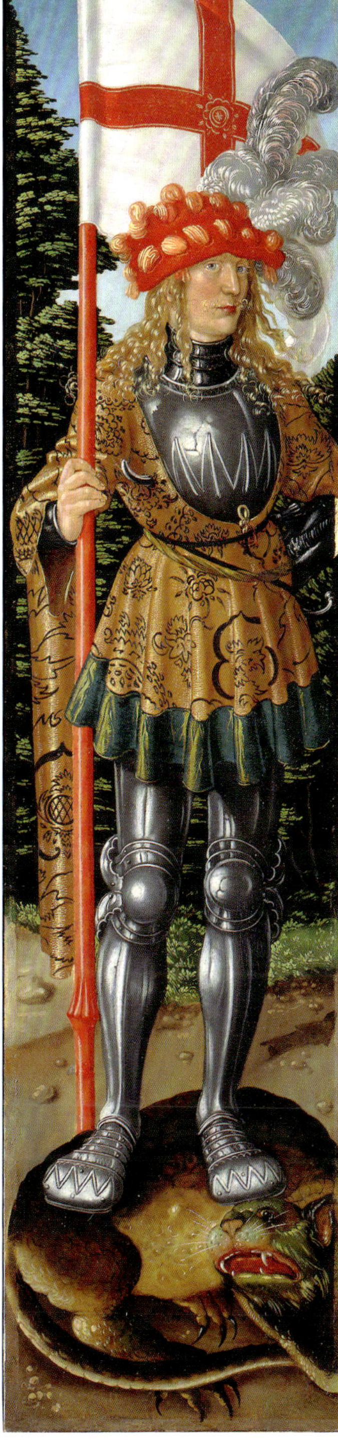

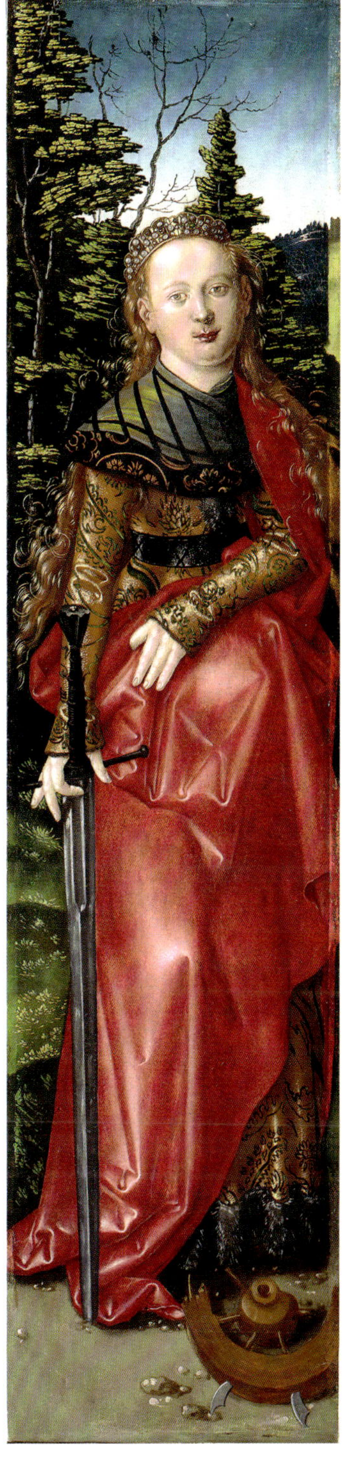

One piece of information that could contribute in part to explaining this strange chronological hiatus is the fact that, as we have already seen, from at least 1505, Grünewald had entered into the circle of the Mainz court. On June 13, 1510, the chapterhouse of the Mainz cathedral sent "Meister Mathis meler" ("master painter Mathis", without further information, which would identify him as someone who was well-known or even someone on the payroll) to Bingen as a hydraulic engineer to work on the castle fountain. The following year, as we know from the proceedings of a trial in 1514–1516, Mathis was certainly in the employ of the learned archbishop of Mainz, Uriel von Gemmingen, for whom he designed a fireplace in the Aschaffenburg castle.[8] As we can see, Grünewald's life began to fill with commitments that were not only pictorial. One of these legal documents, dated June 9, 1514 (mentioned briefly above), mentions the artist "Meister Mathis Maler und Steinmetz zu Aschaffenburgk am Schloss" ("Master painter and stonecutter Mathis in the Aschaffenburg castle"). For the moment, it is an isolated bit of proof of Grünewald's sculpting skills, but it is something, nonetheless.

After what has been said about his training, it is not surprising. These different skills could explain, in part, the lack of painted works during the years 1506–1508, but we will see that this hypothesis could be misleading. If anything, this new and illustrious professional role could have given Mathis greater opportunity to learn about contemporary painting trends.

Fate would have it that the Aschaffenburg castle was partially destroyed back in 1552 and, in any case, nothing of Grünewald's work there has remained.

As noted, the next work by Grünewald that we encounter comprises four monochrome panels, originally the two wings of a vertical altarpiece. These are found, in part, at the Städel Museum in Frankfurt, *Saint Cyriacus* and *Saint Lawrence* /(respectively, inv. HM 37 and 36; 99.2 × 40.8 and 99.2 × 43 cm),[9] which originally must have been placed in the upper section, and in part at the Staatliche Kunsthalle in Karlsruhe, *Saint Elizabeth* and *Saint Lucy* (?) (respectively, inv. 2604 and 2605; 95.8 × 42.8 and 101.2 × 43.7 cm),[10] in the lower section. All these paintings include on the back the monochrome image of a column [figs. 44a-b-c-d]. Generally, they are considered to be fixed external panels added to a large altarpiece commissioned by the merchant

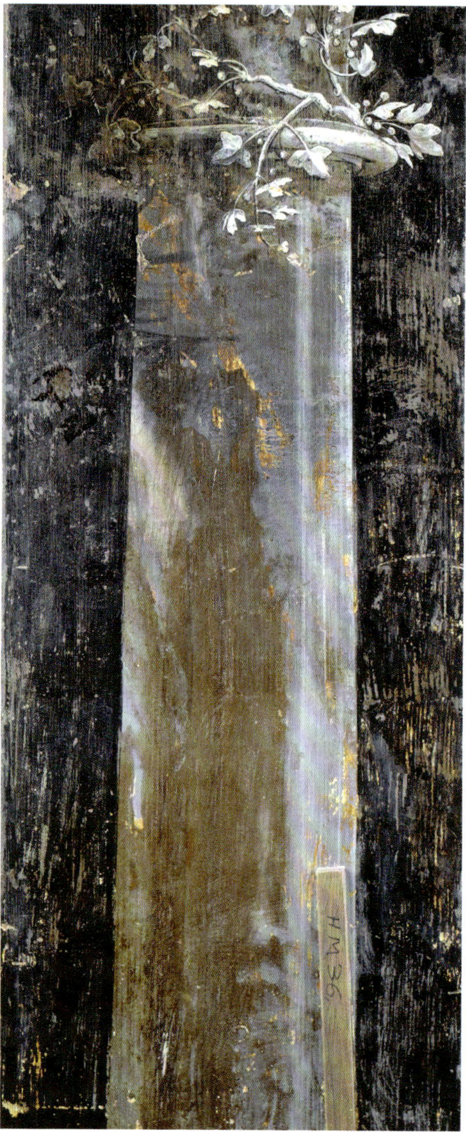

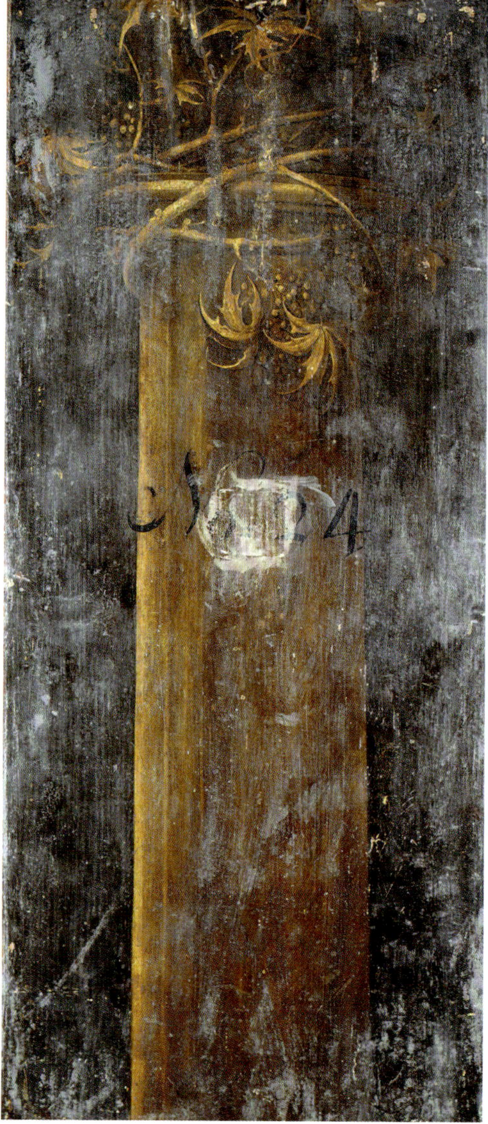

44 | **a-b-c-d** Mathis Grünewald, *Columns*, ca. 1509–1510 (back of the panels from the Heller altarpiece. Karlsruhe, Staatliche Kunsthalle, inv. 264–265, and Frankfurt am Main, Städel Museum, inv. 2604–2605.

Jacob Heller from Albrecht Dürer for the church of the Dominican Order in Frankfurt.[11] The source is the description provided by Sandrart in 1675:

> This artist lived during the era of Albrecht Dürer, around 1505, seen at the altar of the *Assumption of Mary*, created by Dürer in the church of the Preachers friars in Frankfurt, for which Mathis painted finely, although closed, four monochrome panels. These depict Saint Lawrence with the gridiron, Saint Elizabeth, Saint Stephen [sic, instead of Saint Cyriacus] and a fourth, similar, image; all can be seen in Frankfurt.[12]

We also have another document from 1511 that informs us of an unidentified activity of Grünewald for the Dominicans in Frankfurt, but we will come back to this later.

Dürer's altarpiece has been lost (apart from three of the four external monochrome wings created by the painter's assistants in Nuremberg and today at the Historisches Museum in Frankfurt, inv. B0265), but a faithful copy by Jobst Harrich remains, painted in 1614 [fig. 45].

Prior to 1743, the wings were detached and removed. *Saints Cyriacus* and *Lawrence*

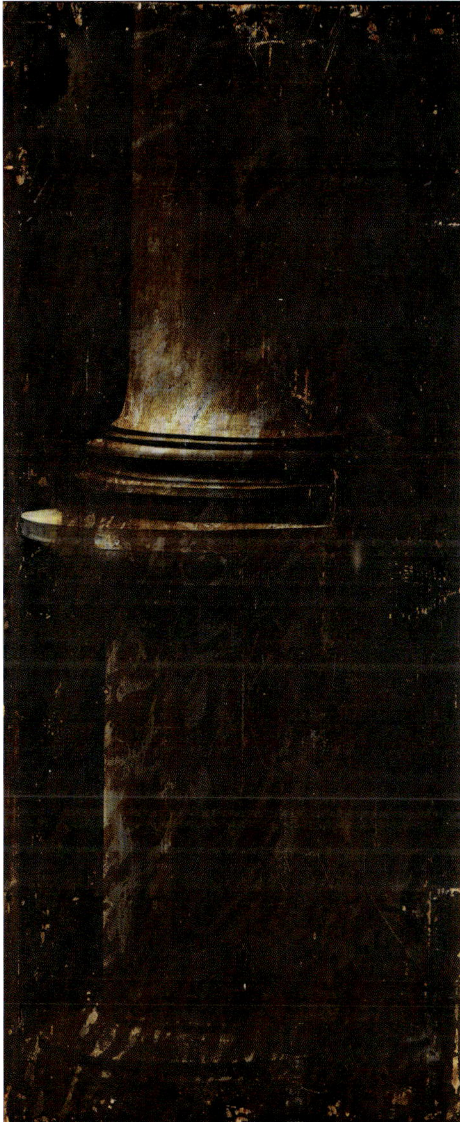

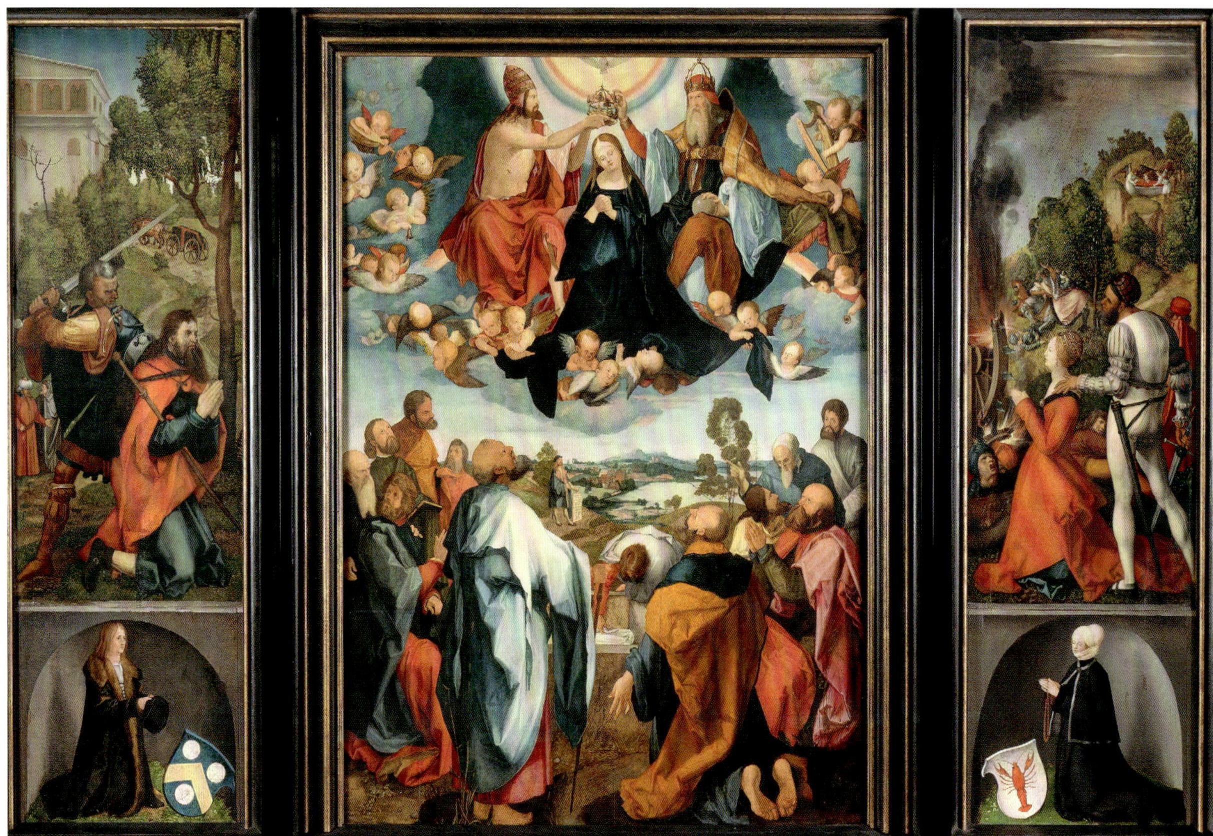

45 | Jobst Harrich, *Assumption of the Virgin Mary, Martyrdom of Saint James, Martyrdom of Saint Catherine, Jakob and Katharina Heller in prayer*, 1614 (after Albrecht Dürer). Frankfurt am Main, Historisches Museum, inv. B0265.

remained in Frankfurt (today one of the treasures of the Städel Museum), while all trace was lost of the two female saints until they reappeared in a private collection in 1950, and were finally purchased by the Karlsruhe Staatliche Kunsthalle in 1971.[13]

The altarpiece commissioned by Jacob Heller was delivered by Albrecht Dürer in August 1509, following a tension-fraught relationship between the artist and his patron. Later, on October 12, the artist provided instructions about the frame.[14]

The copy by Harrich provides us with the image of the central panel. When open, the center of the altarpiece contained the grand scene of the *Assumption of the Virgin* and, on either side, the *Martyrdom of St. Catherine of Alexandria* and the *Martyrdom of St. James* above the two sections with *Jacob Heller and his wife kneeling in prayer*. When closed, there was a series of monochrome saints that could have been flanked, precisely, by Grünewald's [fig. 46].

It is unclear why Heller decided to entrust completion of the work to Grünewald and not Dürer (to streamline the operation and make use of a painter who probably cost less?). It is not impossible that the impulse that pushed Jacob Heller to create further protection for the altarpiece could have been advice he received from Dürer himself, given in a letter sent to the Frankfurt merchant on August 26, 1509:

> I'm sure you will keep it clean, so that it will stay fresh and unmarked for five hundred years. For it is not painted as people usually paint. So make sure it is kept clean, and it is not fingered and doesn't have holy water splashed on it.[15]

In any case, Heller was a rich and demanding patron, and so his going to Mathis would be an indication that the young painter had already achieved a certain fame.

Another explanation could be Heller's strong propensity toward the court of the archbishop of Mainz, given that in 1509 he commissioned a *Crucifix* from the sculptor Hans Backoffen who, like Mathis, was employed by Uriel von Gemmingen.

However, considering Grünewald's monochromes as part of the Heller altarpiece does potentially create some difficulties. In fact, this hypothesis is only supported by Sandrart's later testimony which, theoretically, could also describe a situation that had changed during the over 150 years that separate the creation of the works and their appearance in his text, as well as the compatibility of their height with the rest of the Dürer altarpiece. However, it should be noted that a small group of scholars considered them to be separate works, perhaps wings for a *Transfiguration* (probably dated 1511), once again painted for the Frankfurt Dominicans.[16] In any case, the chronology of the two female saints should be around 1510–1511, and preferably, for stylistic reasons which will be discussed shortly, the earlier date. I propose this dating uniquely to the Karlsruhe panels since, observing the four monochromes, a significant distance can be seen between the two women, St. Elizabeth of Hungary and St. Lucy (?) [figs. 47–48], and the two men, St. Lawrence and St. Cyriacus.

In fact, the figures of the two male saints are monumental and almost geometrized, the drapery extremely sharp, the vegetation very realistically rendered, and permeated with a pearly light that is unstable, extremely mobile and accentuated by the use of gilded paint in some places.

The foreshortened views of the figures remaining in Frankfurt are much more convincing. For example, with St. Lawrence: the hand holding the book takes on a

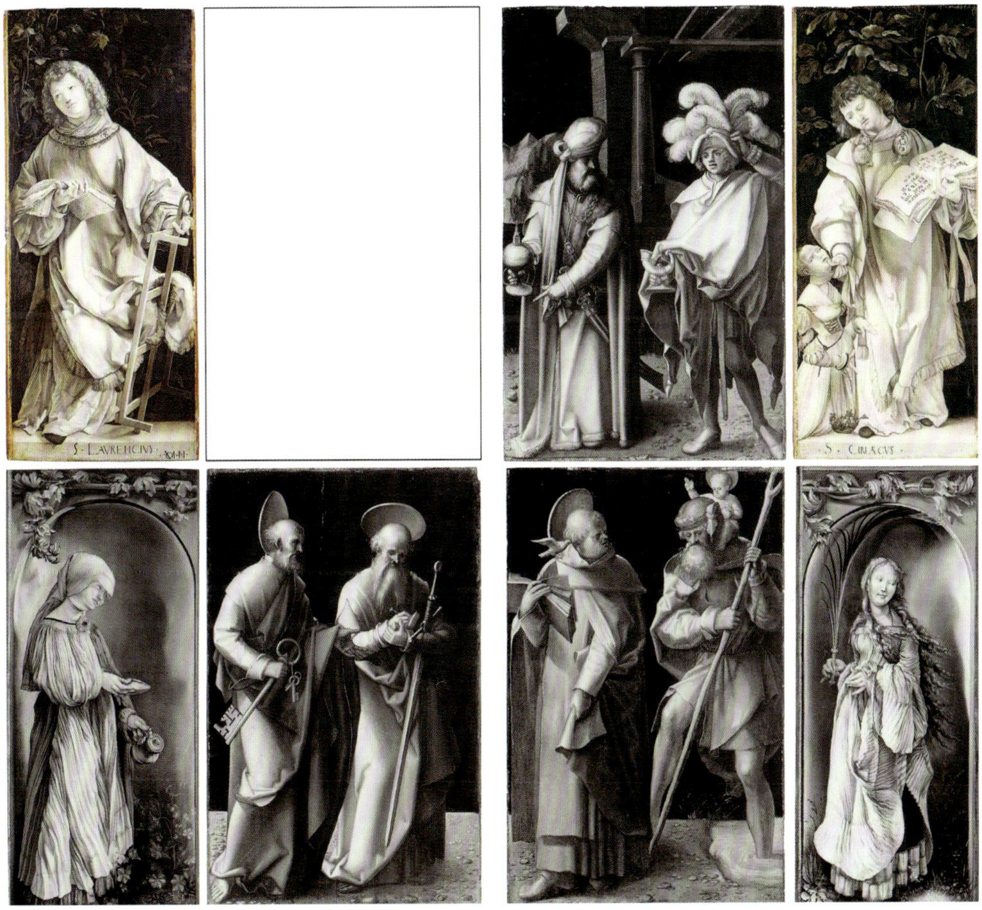

46 | Albrecht Dürer's Workshop, Grisailles of the Heller altarpiece (flanked by Grünewald's ones), ca. 1510–1512 Frankfurt am Main, Historisches Museum.

perspective force that is quite removed from the prehensile, almost plant-like hands still seen, to a certain extent, in the Karlsruhe panels.

The female saints are presented differently: the proportions are varied and slimmer than those of the male saints, the vegetation has a calligraphic, decorative flow, and the light still has a totally volumetric and sculptural consistency, similar to the drawing of *St. Catherine* in Berlin, particularly in the rendering of the garment's textures and proportions.

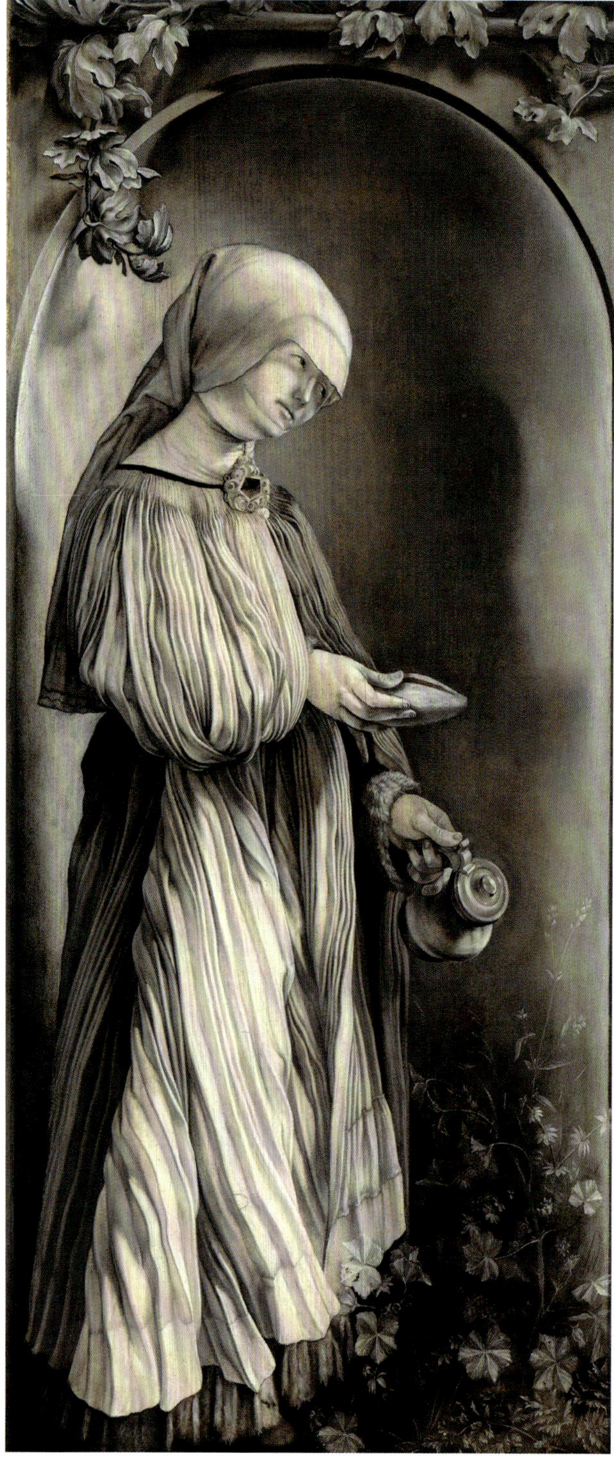

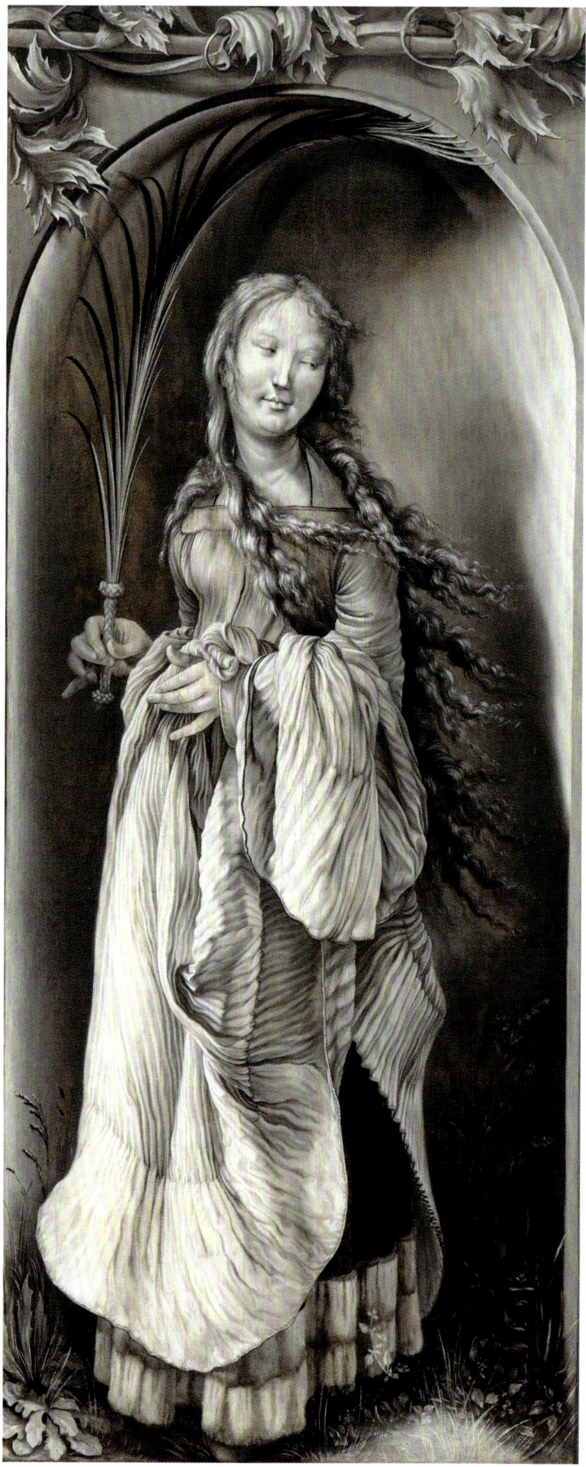

Thus, the four monochromes belong to two distinct moments in Grünewald's career. This conclusion would seem to be utterly contradicted by the results of the scientific analysis which showed that the four panels were made from the same wood, even from the same tree, in fact. Unfortunately, 5 cm have been cut from the upper edge of the Karlsruhe panels (the panels vary in height from 95.8 cm for the *Saint Elizabeth*, to 101.2 cm for the presumed *Saint Lucy*, with a width of 43 cm). It is difficult to determine whether there were originally only two very long panels (which would complicate the current hypothesis), or if from the very beginning, Grünewald was given four panels. The trimming of the upper edge of the Karlsruhe female saints makes it impossible to assess the cut and join compared with the two male saints in Frankfurt. The idea of four smaller panels rather than two large ones of 45 cm in width and over two meters in length—which would certainly simplify explaining their creation in two different time periods—seems more logical from an operational standpoint because it would be easier to work with, transport and store four smaller panels rather than two larger ones.

However, as has been said, style—inevitably—forces us to think that, for some reason, the rendering of the female saints today in Karlsruhe pre-date the Frankfurt panels. Therefore, for the moment, we will only focus on the first two.

The idea of featuring the two female saints in a niche with a convex surface covered in dense shadow would seem to mirror a similar solution Dürer adopts for the effigies of the Heller husband and wife [fig. 49a-b]. This inference does not impact the actual figurative language (as no concrete Dürerian element can be seen in the two female saints), which suggests that Mathis painted the two saints only after the altarpiece arrived in Frankfurt, but without having absorbed, for the moment, anything of the pictorial idiom seen in the Heller altarpiece. So, we have a *post quem* of late August, or even October 1509. If we also take into consideration the assignment in Bingen in June 1510, of which we do not know the duration, we arrive quite near to the already-recorded presence of Grünewald in Frankfurt in 1511, which we will return to shortly.

47 | Mathis Grünewald, *Saint Elizabeth of Hungary* (from the Heller altarpiece), ca. 1509–1510. Karlsruhe, Staatliche Kunsthalle, inv. 264.

48 | Mathis Grünewald, *Saint Martyr* (Saint Lucy? from the Heller altarpiece), ca. 1509–1510. Karlsruhe, Staatliche Kunsthalle, inv. 265.

49 | a-b Jobst Harrich, *Jakob and Katharina Heller in prayer*, 1614 (after Albrecht Dürer). Frankfurt am Main, Historisches Museum, inv. B0265.

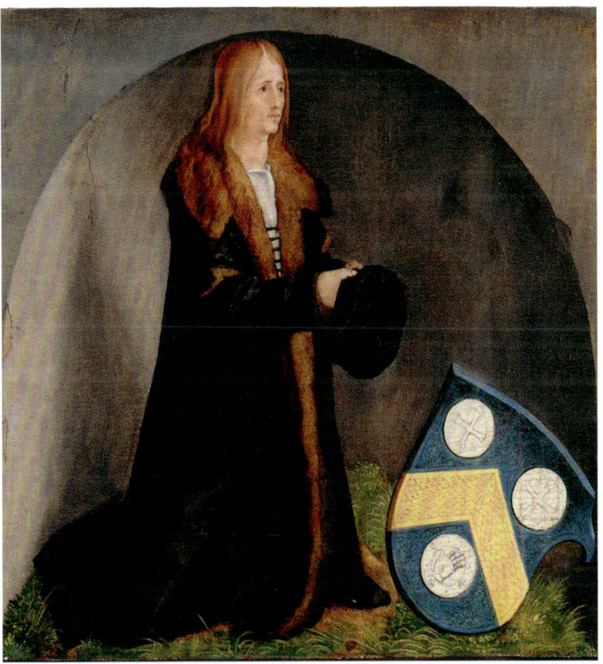

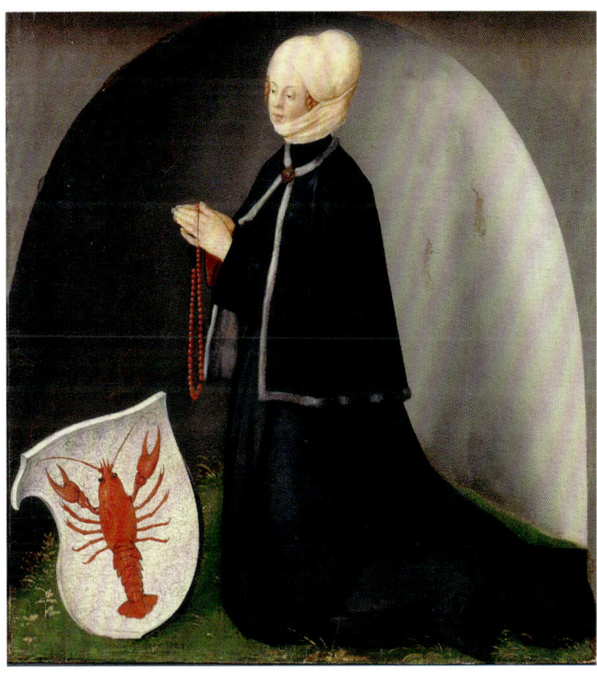

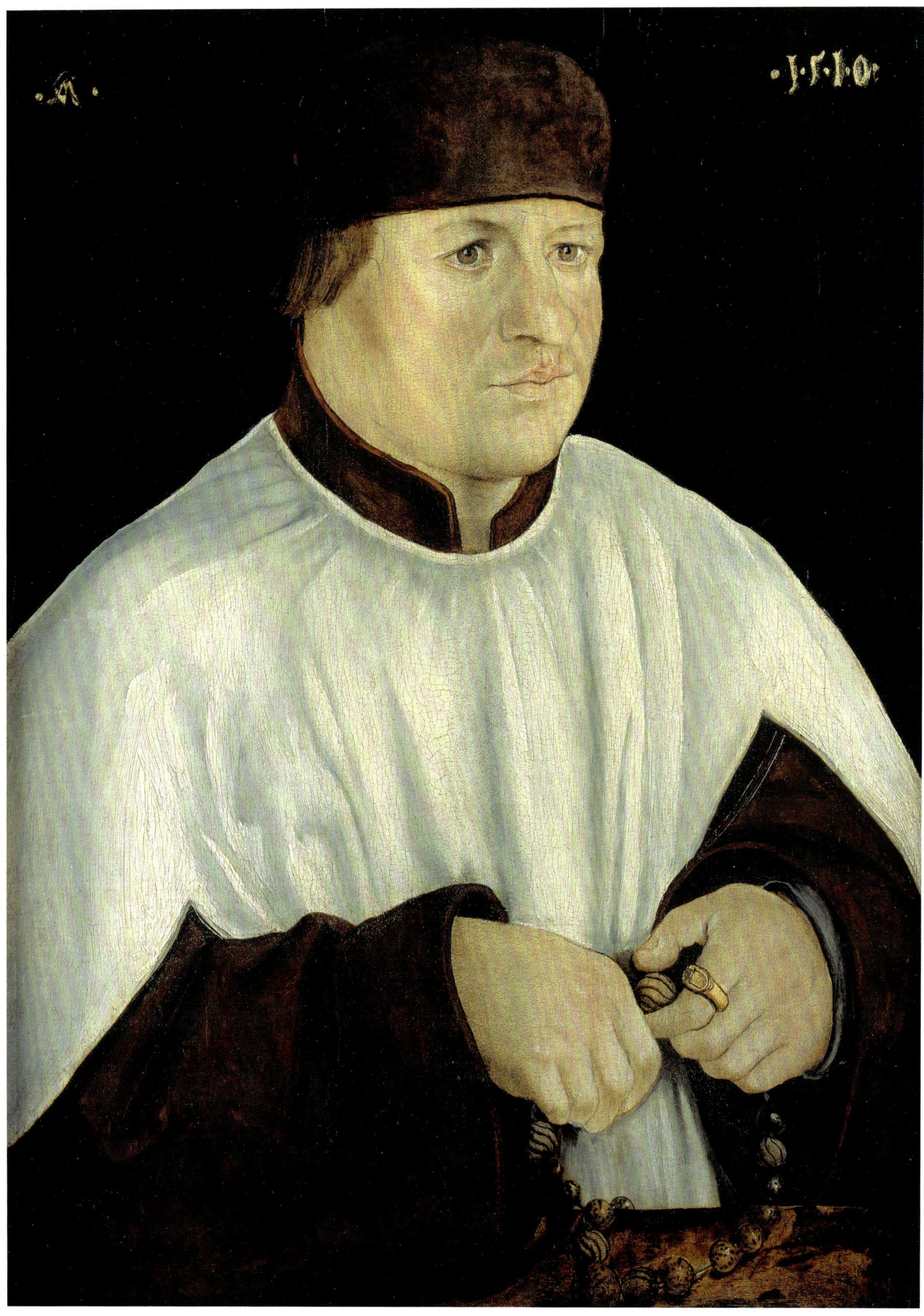
·1·5·1·0·

We also notice that the attention given to Cranach, as seen in the drawing of *St. Catherine*, is substantially over, thus confirming that it came earlier, even if only slightly (for the resemblances that have already been listed), placing it chronologically around 1509.

As with the previous works, we see here once again a close correspondence with sculpture, even if with positions in no way subordinate. The *chiaroscuro* shading of the edges is used to create a three-dimensional sense that clearly differentiates Grünewald's work from that of the workshop of Dürer, whose monochromes in the Heller altarpiece "just" seem to be paintings left uncolored, not figures that invite the viewer to look around them, creating an illusion of depth.

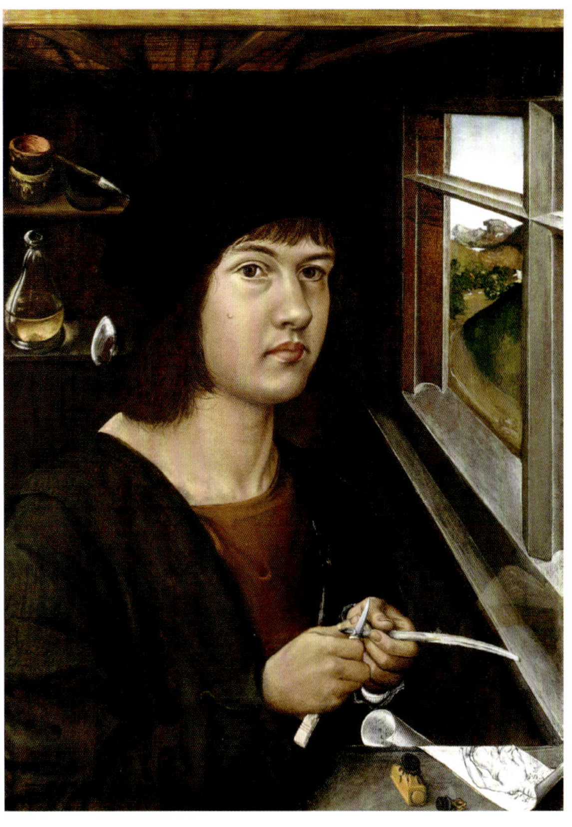

A *Portrait of a Priest* dated 1510 is currently preserved at the Staatsgalerie im Schloss Johannisburg in Aschaffenburg, where it arrived after having been purchased on the English antique art market in 1938 (inv. 10643, 55.2 × 41.5 cm) [fig. 50].[17] In addition to the year, there is also a monogram that could be read as either M G or M C. This inscription has given rise to much uncertainty and questioning, but, as verified during restoration of the painting, it is to be considered authentic. However, we cannot deny that the interpretation is anything but simple, and, in any case, it should be put aside for the moment to concentrate on a stylistic examination of the work. I think everyone would agree that it is a masterpiece, one that stands up to comparison with Dürer's most celebrated portraits. The sitter commands the entire space of the painting, which is dominated by the dazzling symphony of white of his vestment. There is no idealization of the subject: he is corpulent with rough, irregular features. And yet, how much humanity, how much life in his face where the blush on his cheeks appears and disappears, in which the light flickers and sets in his seemingly anxious eyes. The image appears static, but there is a latent uneasiness that vibrates in the movement of his eyes and in the hands holding a rosary in which the grooved beads seem to yield under the energetic pressure of his fingers. Fingers that seem to lie somewhere between those of the torturers in the *Mocking of Christ* (1504) and those of *St. Anthony* in the *Isenheim Altarpiece* (1513–1514). This similarity is also evident in the early Grünewald palette, which is warm but continuously rippled with bits of light. This highlighting, as if rising from inside the figure, to define the eyes, the mouth, and the knuckles, is comparable to the technique used in the *Saint Erasmus* painted many years later for the collegiate church in Halle, a portrait of Archbishop Albrecht von Brandenburg. Additionally, the rendering of the tuft of hair emerging from his cap is quite similar to that in the two St. Johns in the Isenheim *Crucifixion*.

50 | Mathis Grünewald, *Portrait of a Priest*, 1510. Aschaffenburg, Staatsgalerie im Schloss Johannisburg, inv. 10643.

51 | Forger of the first half of XX century (?), *Portrait of a Young Artist*. Chicago, The Art Institute, inv. 1947.77.

The attribution to Mathis, cautiously suggested by Ernst Buchner and repeated equally as guardedly by Weixlgärtner, was again mentioned by Bianconi but later became less prominent in subsequent Grünewaldian literature.[18]

Stephan Kemperdick, whom I thank for his opinion, expressed skepticism about this attribution (I believe it is clear that I am explicitly claiming the Aschaffenburg portrait as an autograph masterpiece by Grünewald). Kemperdick suggests

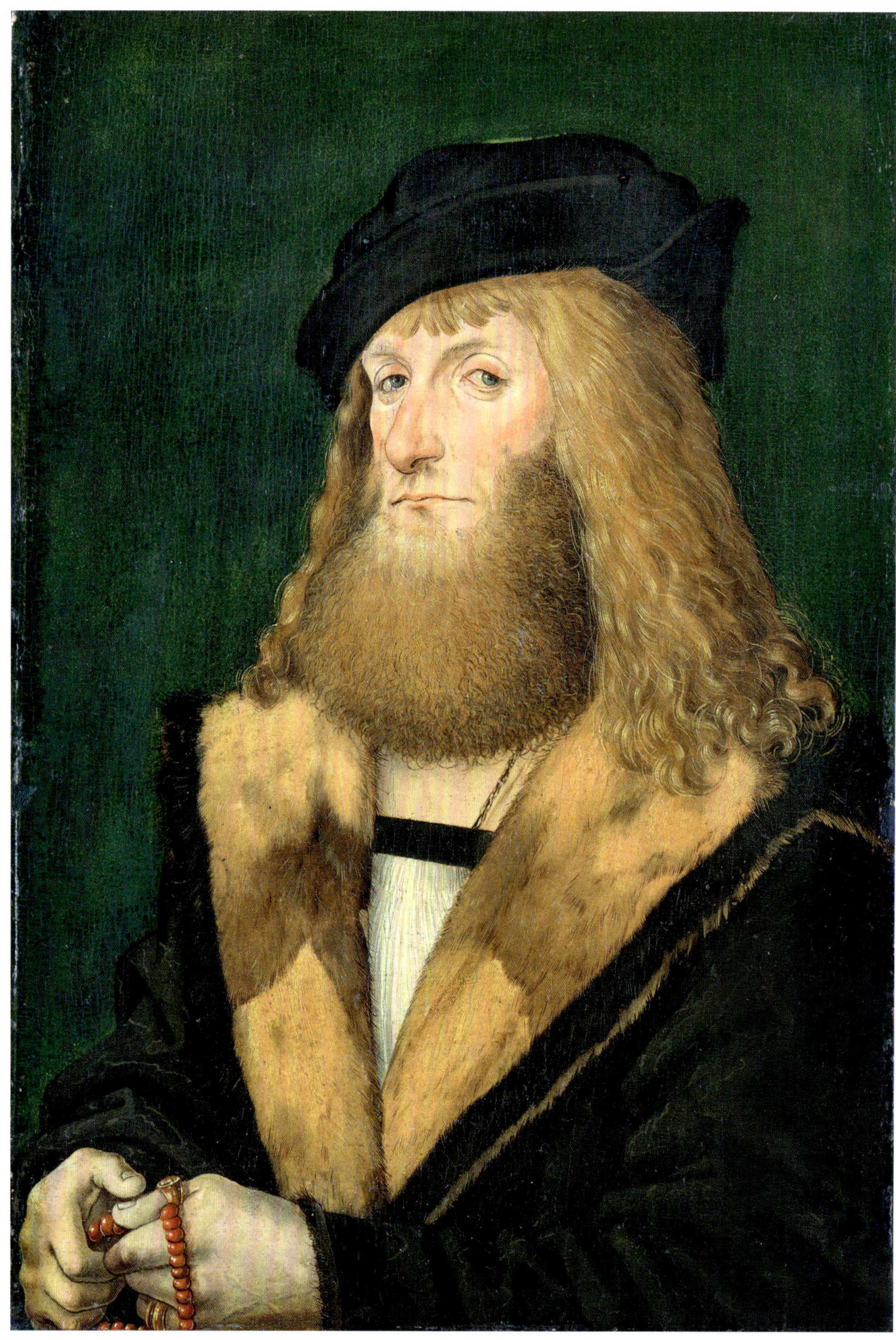

52 | Martin Caldenbach, *Portrait of Jakob Stralenberger*, 1506. Frankfurt am Main, Städel Museum, inv. 1739.

considering Martin Caldenbach (or Kaldenbach) as a hypothetical candidate, alongside the painter from Ulma, Conrad Merkel, if the monogram were interpreted as M C. He cites the *Portrait of Jakob Stralenberger* at the Städel Museum in Frankfurt (inv. 1739), dated 1506 [fig. 52],[19] because of the position of the hands and the presence of a rosary. However, despite the unquestionable compositional similarities, Caldenbach's painting style does not seem to reflect this analogy. Caldenbach's admittedly magnificent *Portrait* lacks the monumental presence, the exceptional sensitivity in

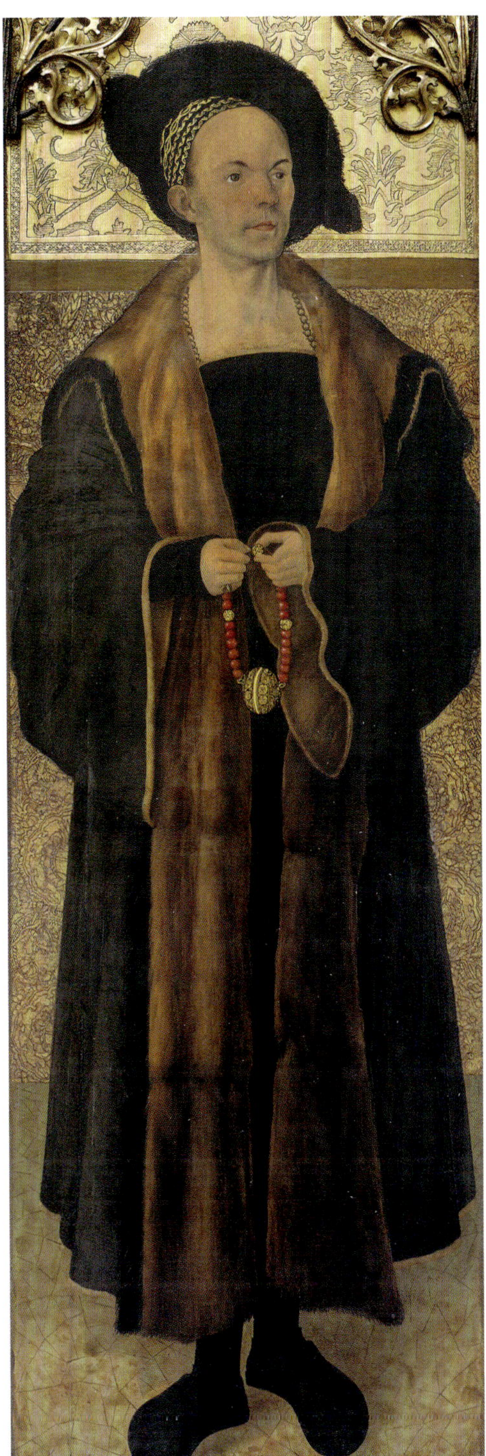
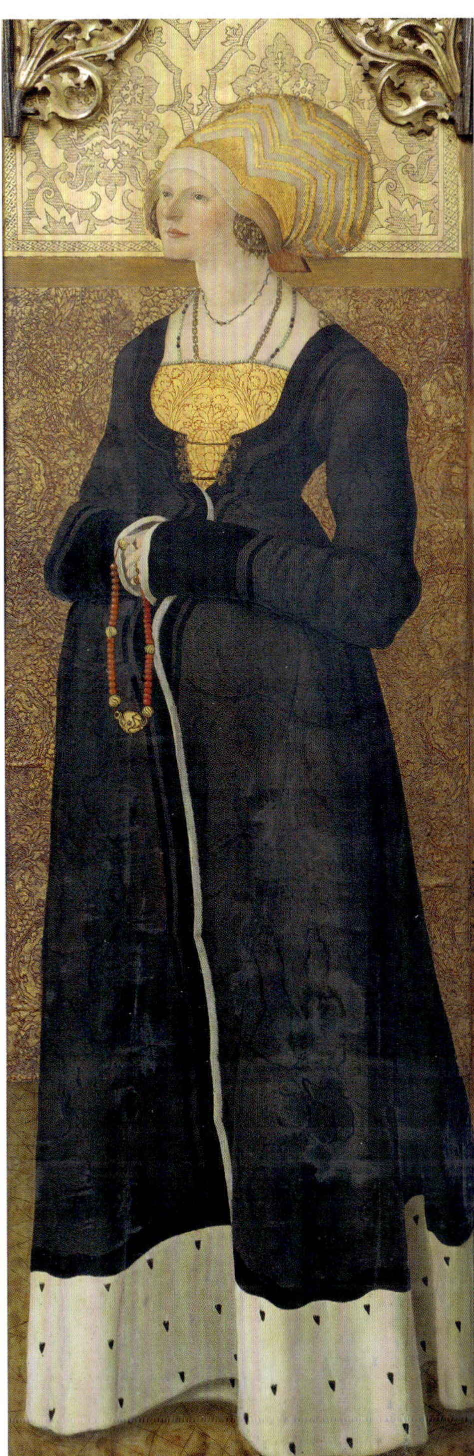

53 | **a-b** Master of the Stalburg Altar, *Portrait of Claus Stalburg and his Wife.* 1504. Frankfurt am Main, Städel Museum, inv. 845–846.

the play of light, and the moral vigor that characterizes the Aschaffenburg priest.

In contrast, greater similarity can be seen in the panels of the Stalburg altar in the same museum, painted for Frankfurt in 1504 (inv. 845–846) [fig. 53a-b].[20] Design and color, such as the rosary held by Claus Stalburg, seem similar to those we saw in Grünewald's work, although they are more traditional and lack the play of light and excesses we have come to know in Mathis. The Stalburg panels are attributed to an anonymous painter active in the workshop of Martin Caldenbach and, more

54 | Martin Caldenbach, *Saint Catherine*, 1506. Frankfurt am Main, Städel Museum, Graphische Sammlung, inv. 15179Z.

importantly, to his father Hans. If we add to this that another model—even closer to the Schongauer etching, taken into consideration by Grünewald for the Berlin drawing of *St. Catherine*—is a youthful drawing by Martin Caldenbach dated 1506, of the same subject (today part of the Graphische Sammlung at the same Frankfurt museum, inv. 15179Z [fig. 54]), it is enough to suppose (and more will be said about this later) that there was significant contact between Mathis and the Caldenbach workshop in the period 1505–1510.[21] This could contribute to explaining the early connection of our artist with Frankfurt.

At this point, the monogram that appears in the upper left, though not definitive for attribution purposes, must necessarily be M G, Mathis Gothart. Examining the documents and chronicles, it is evident that in Würzburg he is always referred to by the surname Gothart, indicating his status as a member of the city's upper middle

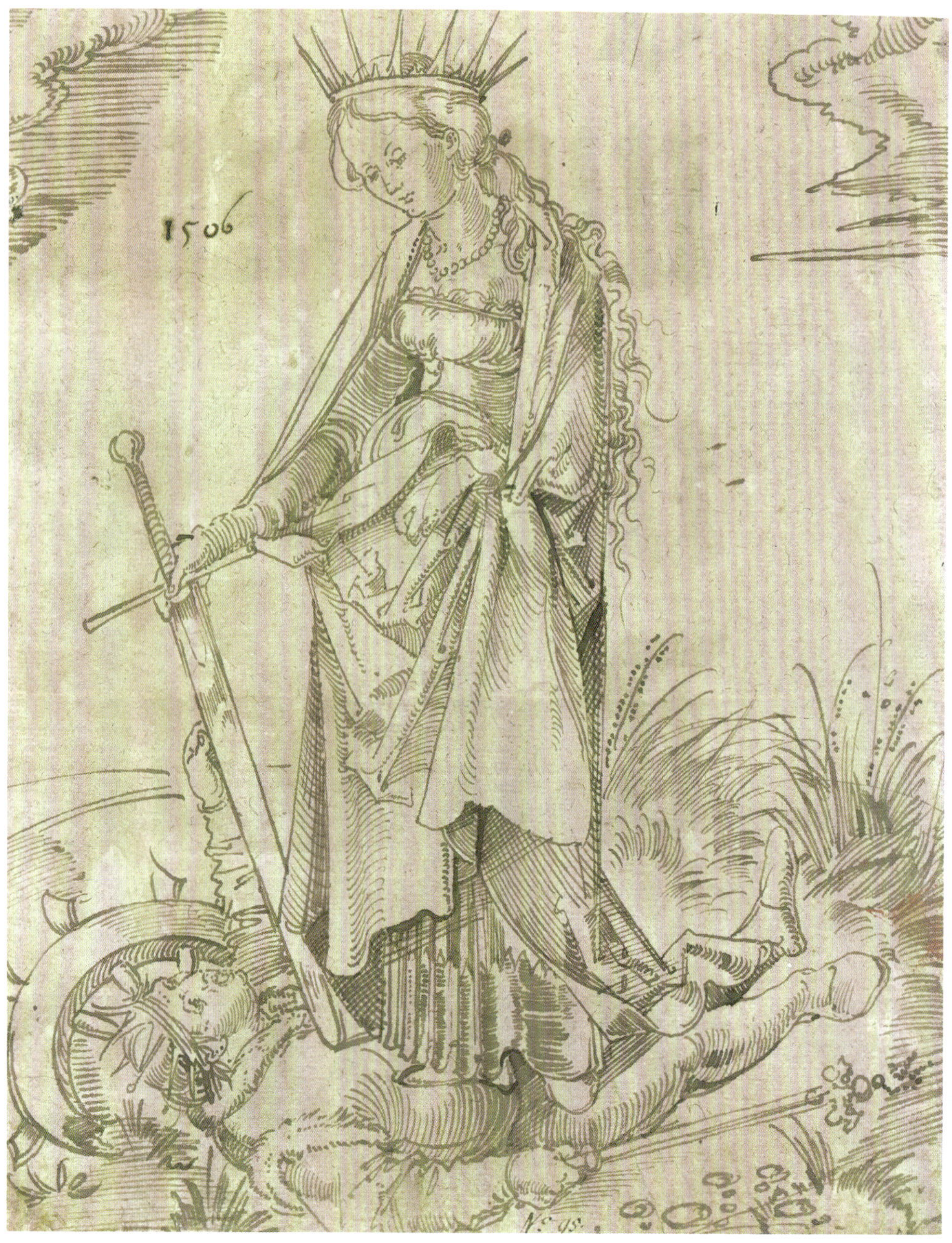

class. Conversely, the surname Nithart only appears in Mainz documents, and once again the family is of the same social class. For example, a Johannes Nythart is the chancellor in Geismar in December 1518 and again in December 1527, and an Ottilie Neithart is mentioned on March 18, 1534.[22] This suggests the working hypothesis (in the absence of more certain information for the moment), that Mathis, born Gothart, added the surname Nithart in Mainz, upon entering the service of the archbishop, to reinforce his social standing. Where he got it from is difficult to ascertain. We can only hypothesize, for example, that Nithart was the family name of his mother, or perhaps his wife. A clue supporting the latter supposition could be the fact that the documentation regarding Mathis's adopted son, Endres, refers to him with the surname Neithart.[23]

Given the very close ties between Mathis and Heinrich Reitzmann, it is tempting to consider the latter as the sitter of the Aschaffenburg portrait. A likeness of Reitzmann is known from his tombstone at the Stiftkirche in Aschaffenburg, dated 1528, a fairly modest work from the workshop of Tilman Riemenschneider (or, more precisely, of Meister Wendel) [fig. 55].[24] Despite the significant differences between the two works (one is a painting, the other a sculpture; one is a masterpiece, the other is not; one is dated 1510, the other 1528), the features on the tombstone do not seem to me to be at all incompatible with those of the Schlossmuseum portrait. From the tombstone we learn that Reitzmann died at the age of sixty-six and, therefore, in 1510 he would have been forty-seven, an age close to that depicted in the painting.[25] It is a tempting hypothesis, but it should be noted that the painting does not appear among those hung on the walls of the presbytery in Aschaffenburg, which were inventoried in 1511, explicitly described as canvases ("gemalt Lynen-ducher").[26] Two are hung "an der want" in the "aula", and one "in cubile meo". Only for one painting "de passione domini" (a *Crucifixion*? Perhaps the one today in Basel?), located "in stuba parva", is the subject indicated, but nothing is said about its support, which could have been a panel.

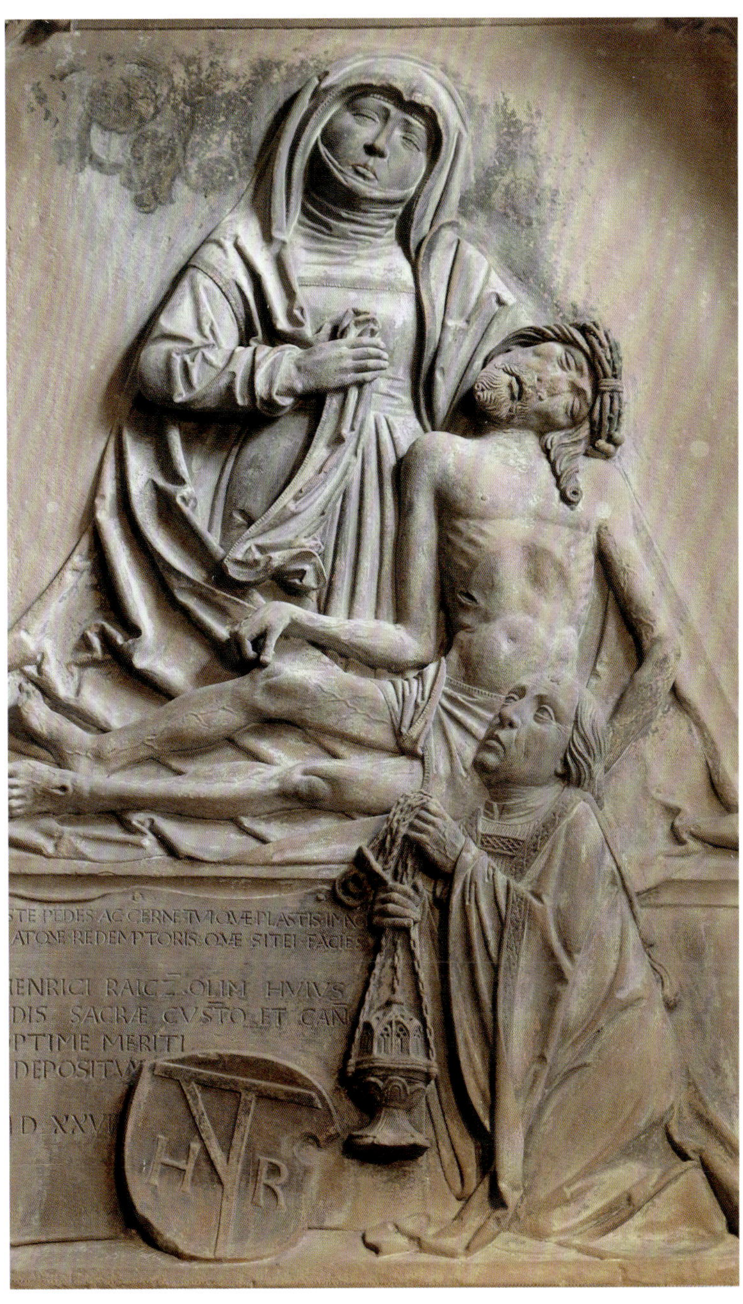

55 | Meister Wendel, *Tombstone of Heinrich Reitzmann*, 1528. Aschaffenburg, Collegiate church.

As has been noted, on the verso of the *St. Catherine* in Berlin is another

56 | Mathis Grünewald, *Study of a female figure*, ca. 1510. Berlin, Staatliche Museen, Kupferstichkabinett, inv. KdZ 12038 verso.

57 | Mathis Grünewald, *Vergin Mary in Glory*, ca. 1510. Rotterdam, Museum Boijmans van Beuningen. inv. MB 1958/T29.

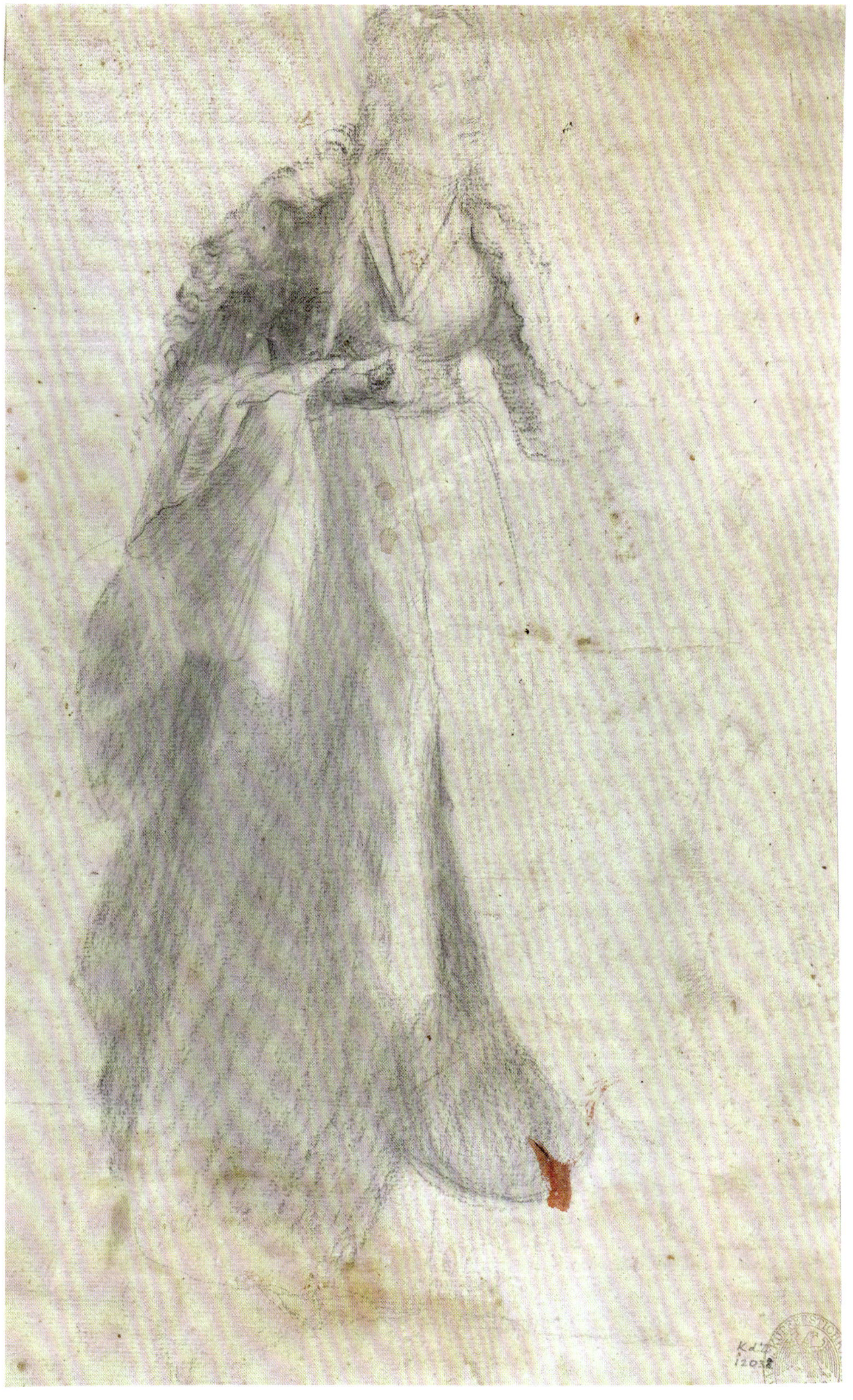

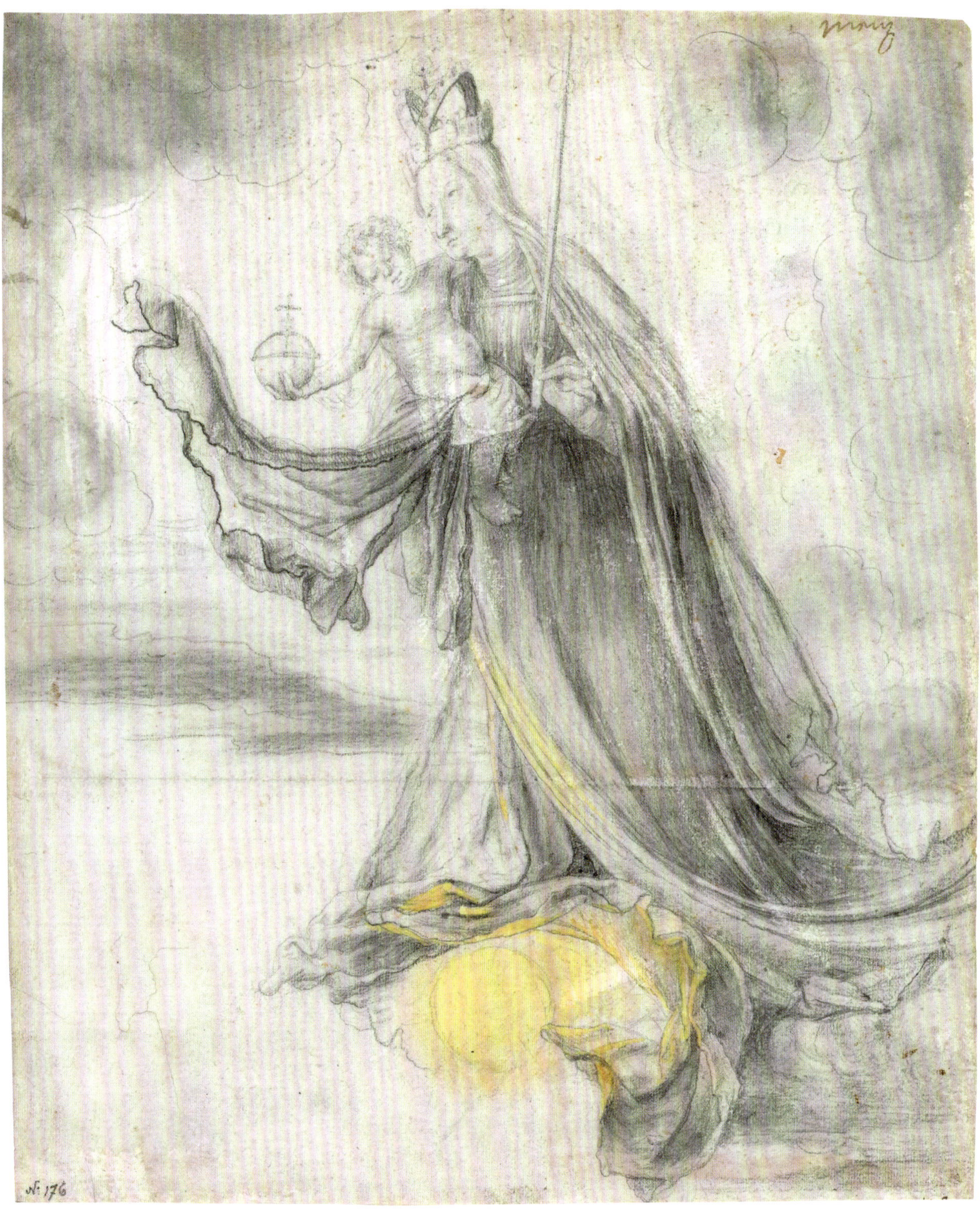

unfinished drawing of a female figure, whose rendering is somewhat different [fig. 56]. The face is less childlike and actually has some fairly heavy features, and her garment, which is not as detailed, emphasizes the overall volume, only through the use of black chalk. The same characteristics, although more finished, can be seen in a drawing of the *Vergin Mary in Glory* (Rotterdam, Boijmans van Beuningen Museum, inv. MB 1958/T29, 322 × 268 mm) [fig. 57] in black chalk and yellow watercolor, where

58 | Mathis Grünewald, *Saint Dorothy*, ca. 1511–1512. Berlin, Staatliche Museen, Kupferstichkabinett, inv. KdZ 12035.

in the upper right corner is the old inscription "Menz", i.e., Mainz. Scholars have suggested that this is a preparatory drawing for a now-lost work for the city of Mainz, datable to 1516–1520. However, this seems extremely unlikely given that Grünewald's graphic style in that period appears to be quite different.[27]

Naturally, as noted by Ruhmer,[28] the chronology of the *St. Catherine* in Berlin does not necessarily have to be the same as the sketch on the verso which, in turn, is stylistically very similar to the Rotterdam drawing. Yet, iconographically, the two images of the Berlin sheet seem coherent, and so even the dating of the Boijmans van Beuningen drawing should not be all that different from that for *St. Catherine.*

Therefore, we can tentatively date the Rotterdam *Madonna* to around 1510 or immediately after. The flourishes of the *Madonna*, with their re-traced borders, already hint at the harmonic flow of the drapery in Dürer's Heller *Assumption*, and both certainly anticipate the same detailing in the *Annunciation* of the *Isenheim Altarpiece* (ca. 1513). This dating would not conflict with a destination for a work in Mainz.

Sandrart (1675) describes three works in the city's cathedral:

> Finally of this noble hand [of Grünewald] there were in the Mainz Cathedral, to the left of the choir in three different chapels, three altarpieces, each with two panels painted front and back. The first is the Madonna in the Clouds. Underneath, on the ground are a number of ornate female saints, Catherine, Barbara, Cecilia, Elizabeth, Apollonia and Ursula, all so very noble, natural, elegant and correctly drawn, that they seem to be in the sky, rather than on Earth. Depicted in another altarpiece is a blind hermit guided by a young boy who steps onto the frozen-over Rhein. On the ice, he is attacked by two assassins and killed, and he falls on the boy who is screaming, painted with natural and true emotion and intent, extremely admirable. The third altarpiece is more imperfect than the other two, and all three were stolen around 1631 or 1632 in the terrible war and sent off in a ship to Sweden, but, along with many other works of art, they were shipwrecked and finished at the bottom of the sea[29]

According to Sandrart, the Rotterdam drawing as a study for Mainz Cathedral's *Madonna of the Clouds*, with whose chapterhouse, it should be remembered, Grünewald was working in 1510, if not earlier. The Berlin drawing has also been seen as related to the works created for the cathedral in Mainz, because of the "noble, natural, elegant and correctly drawn" St. Catherine. Yet, the posed saint looking directly at us would not seem to be taking part in any action, even supernatural, and as has already been said, she might be better suited to a section of an altarpiece or external panel.

From clues we will be examining elsewhere, it can be presumed that the altarpiece with the murdered hermit belongs to a later period in Mathis's career, while for the third work, it needs to be understood that if by "more imperfect" Sandrart means unfinished or less beautiful. In any case, even if only one altarpiece is from 1510, we should remember that we are talking about an altarpiece with hinged wings, therefore with multiple images.

Another drawing, dating to the first decade and representing *Saint Dorothy* (Berlin, Kupferstichkabinett, inv. KdZ 12035, 359 × 259 mm)[30] [fig. 58] depicts a robust figure with many of Grünewald's signature elements: the woolly texture of the fabric; the hands, with some uncertainty, continue the search for a sense of depth already seen in the Rotterdam *Madonna*; and once again, there is the serpentine pose so splendidly commented by Michael Baxandall, typical of the wood sculptures of

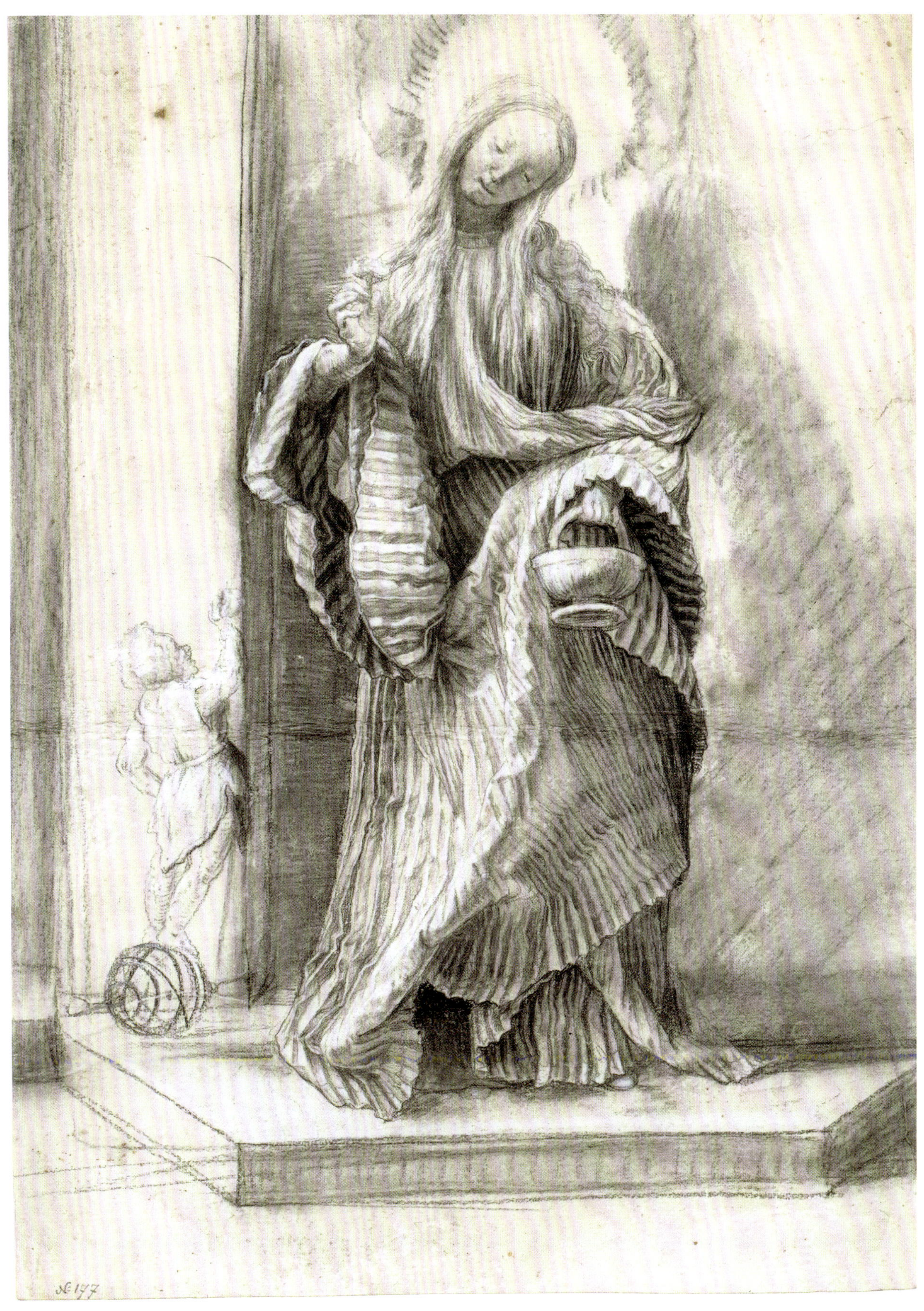

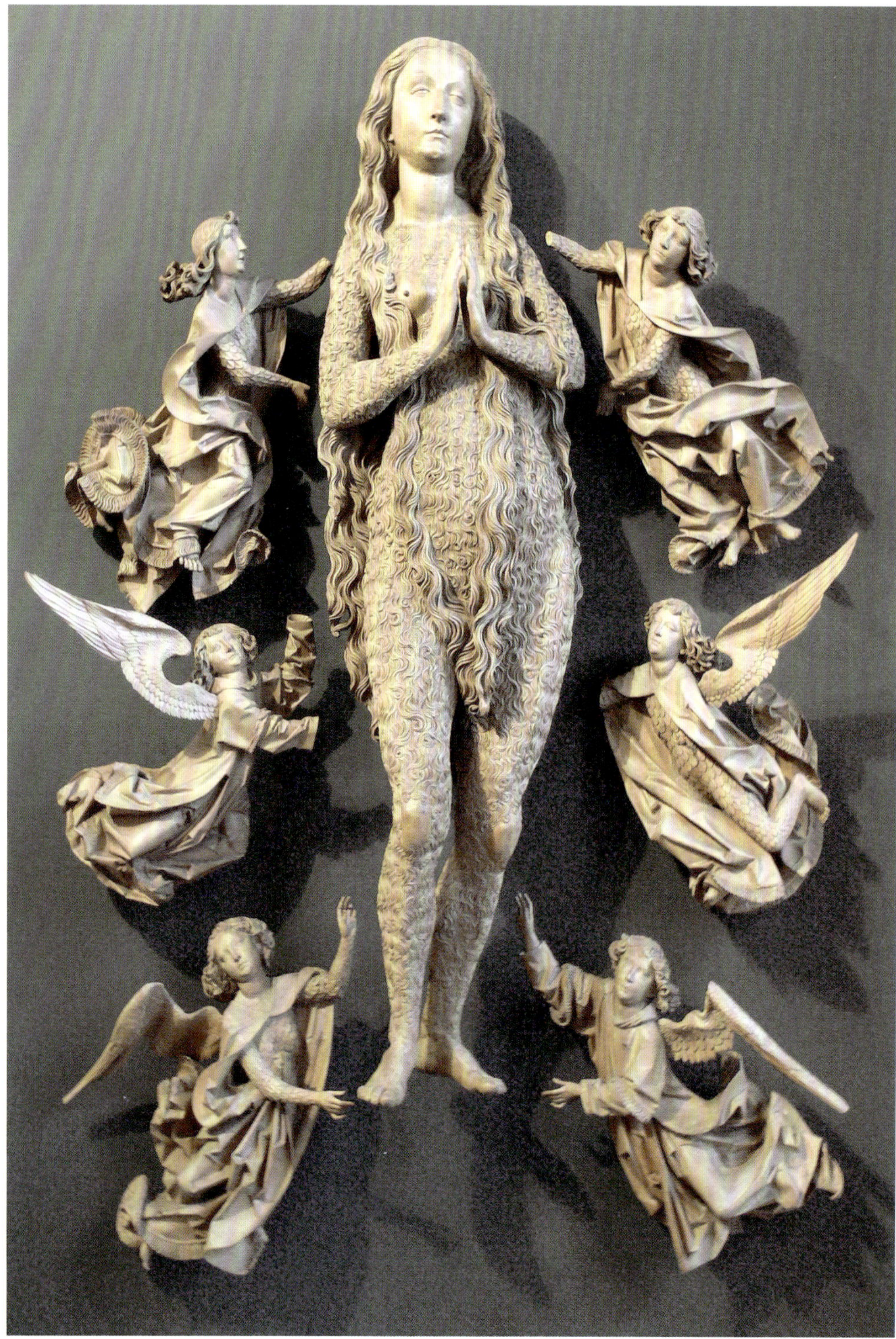

59 | Tilman Riemenschneider, *Glory of Saint Mary Magdalene*, ca. 1490–1492. Munich, Bayerisches Nationalmuseum, inv. 4094.

Riemenschneider and Erhart, but with an incomparable richness of the carved layers with an almost contrapuntal play in the draping. There is the intimation of the right leg gracefully bent in a pose which, although more emphasized, brings to mind once again Riemenschneider's style, as in the *Mary Magadelene* now at the Bayerisches Nationalmuseum in Munich (inv. 4094, formerly at Münnerstadt, ca. 1490–1492) [fig. 59].[31] Grünewald's reinterpretation of sculptural models becomes increasingly free; he reinvents and transposes them autonomously through the graphic medium.

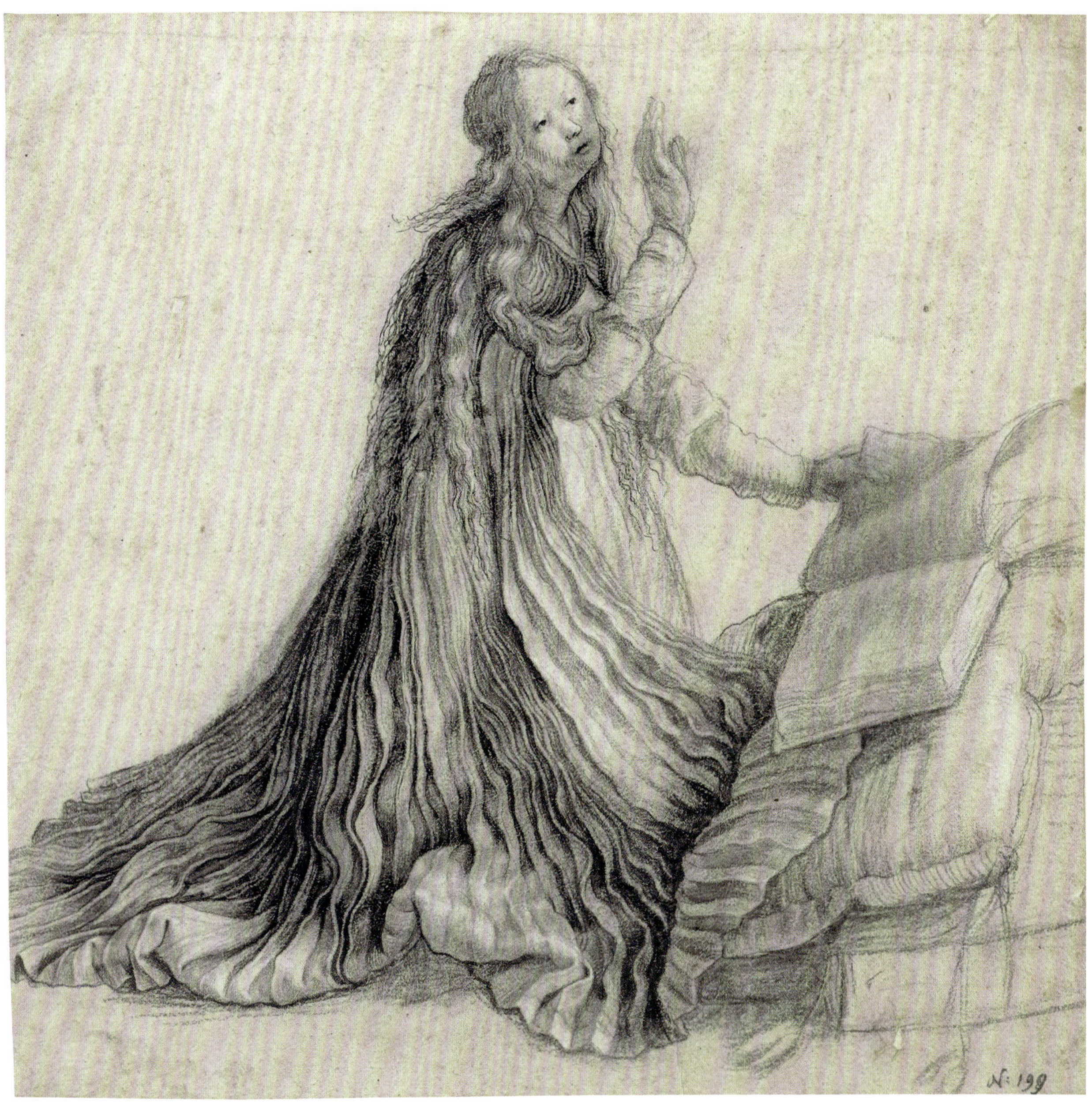

60 | Mathis Grünewald, *Virgin of the Annunciation*, ca. 1511–1512. Berlin, Staatliche Museen, Kupferstichkabinett, inv. KdZ 12040.

The *Saint Dorothy* reflects onto the wall the same shadow of the Heller female saints in Karlsruhe, and also similar and comparable is the study drapery layers, resulting in an extremely decorative effect, and the playful flow of the garment. Therefore, the dates must be fairly close. However, I believe the drawing dates to the early years of the second decade, rather than precisely 1510. Therefore, slightly later than the Karlsruhe female saints due to the more monumental treatment of the figure. This image could also be easily conceived as a hinged wing, just like the *Annunciation* in another drawing, also in Berlin (inv. KdZ 12040, black chalk and white lead, 206 × 212 mm) [fig. 60], congruent in every aspect with the *Saint Dorothy*. Normally, this drawing is considered preparatory to the *Annunciation* in the *Isenheim Altarpiece*. But Roth, with good reason, links it to *Saint Dorothy*, indicating an "ante Isenheim" chronology.[32] Compared to previous works seen so far, this *Annunciation* shows a greater search for movement, to seize the moment in which

61 | Albrecht Dürer, *Adoration of the Holy Trinity*, 1511. Vienna, Kunsthistorisches Museum, inv. Gemäldegalerie, 838.

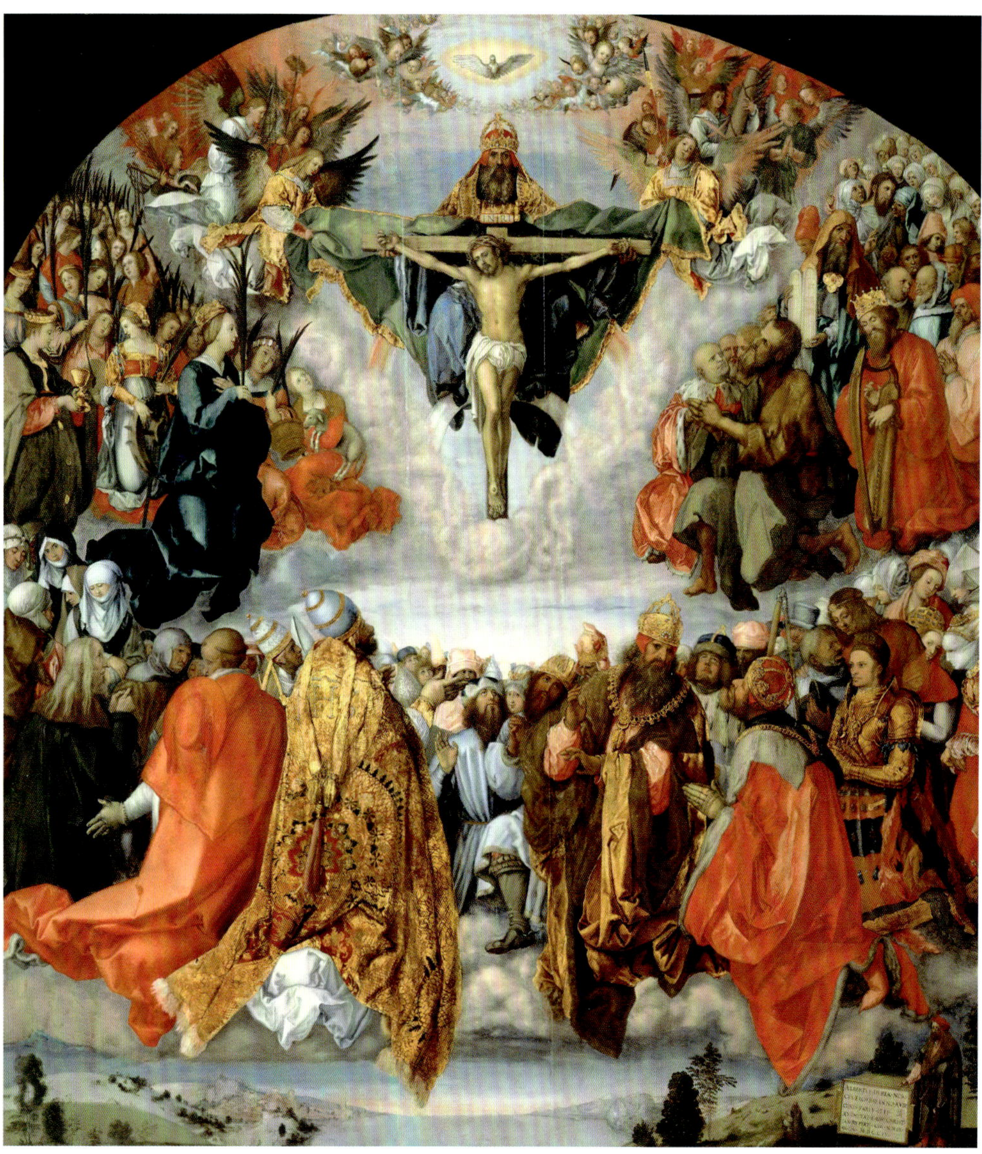

the sudden appearance of the angel freezes the Madonna just as she is turning the page of the book, forcing her to shield herself with her right hand, thus creating a sophisticated and stunning play of shadow on her face. The composition has been planned down to the last detail and, therefore, seems preparatory to the creation of an actual painted work. For example, details like the tassel falling on the floor and the cushion used as a bookrest for the massive *in folio* (not a book of hours!) which receives and actually reflects the light that we must imagine emanating from the unseen angel, illuminating Mary's face, adding symbolic importance.

At this point in our analysis, a question arises: given the close physical proximity to Albrecht Dürer's works, why did Grünewald, usually attentive to his surroundings, not assimilate more pictorial elements from Nuremberg's most celebrated artist?

First of all, we must imagine what Grünewald actually saw of Dürer's work: in other words, how the Heller altarpiece was presented.

While the Harrich copy is fundamental for us, it does not fully convey what colors Mathis actually had before his eyes. To bridge this gap, we must look at an autograph work by Dürer as analogous as possible in terms of chronology and execution, such as the *Adoration of the Trinity*, now at the Kunsthistorisches Museum in Vienna (inv. Gemäldegalerie, 838), but painted for Nuremberg in 1511 [fig. 61]. We can imagine in the kneeling apostle behind the lost *Assumption* the same red cape with orange highlights which in the Vienna work we see in the saint with his back turned to us in the foreground. He is harmonically counterposed to the apostle with the light-colored tunic that we can "see" to be analogous to that worn by the man in the center of the composition of the Vienna altarpiece, below the Crucifix.

In contrast, Mathis's female saints, both painted and drawn, do not echo the piece Grünewald was working alongside or completing. At most, the meticulousness of the drawing technique depicting the *Annunciation*, commented above, may reflect the acute desire for visual and mental precision in the Dürerian drawing—more than painting—style.

Two particular drawings are fully akin to both Dürer and what Sandrart wrote in 1675:

> Remarkable above all is the rendering in water colors of the Transfiguration of Christ on Mount Tabor, and especially marvelous the cloud in which Moses and Elijah appear, and with them the apostles kneeling on the ground; so stupendously depicted in terms of conception, coloring and ornamentation that nothing could surpass it, as incomparable as it is in style and originality.[33]

There has been much debate over what Sandrart meant by "water colors". I think it simply means that the work he is describing was painted in tempera.

A 1514 document (a summons to testify at a trial, which we will discuss later) informs us that in 1511 Grünewald was painting a panel for the Dominicans in Frankfurt ("Als Mayster Mathys nach folgens hie zu den predigern eyn tafel gemoelet hat"[34]). In light of the observations made to this point, it is unlikely that they are the so-called Heller monochromes, and therefore it is highly probable that the reference is to another work, almost certainly the *Transfiguration* for which we have the preparatory drawings.

Two such drawings—both at the Kupferstichkabinett, Dresden Staatliche Kunstsammlungen, which acquired them in 1910 from the Winkler collection in Leipzig—depict two men in antique robes, engaged in an act of adoration or terror, very likely the apostles Peter (black chalk with white lead highlighting, inv. C 1910–41, 147 × 266 mm) [fig. 62] and John (black chalk and white lead, inv. C 1910–42, 144 × 208 mm)[35] [fig. 63]. In the upper left of the latter is the inscription "Frankfurt", which confirms the connection of the two drawings to the Frankfurt *Transfiguration*. The apostles' scared and kneeling poses fit that subject; thus we can date them to around 1511, gaining another reference point to orient ourselves in the evolution of Mathis's drawing style.

In terms of the evidence already examined, here we observe a renewed richness and conciseness in the drapery which almost seems sculpted, although lost is the obsession with the nature of the material that marked the drawings of the female saints we saw earlier. The bodies are delineated by the relationship the painter creates between the areas of light and shadow through the use of *chiaroscuro*. The weight of the body under the drapery can be seen, but still with some residual difficulty in portraying the foreshortening.

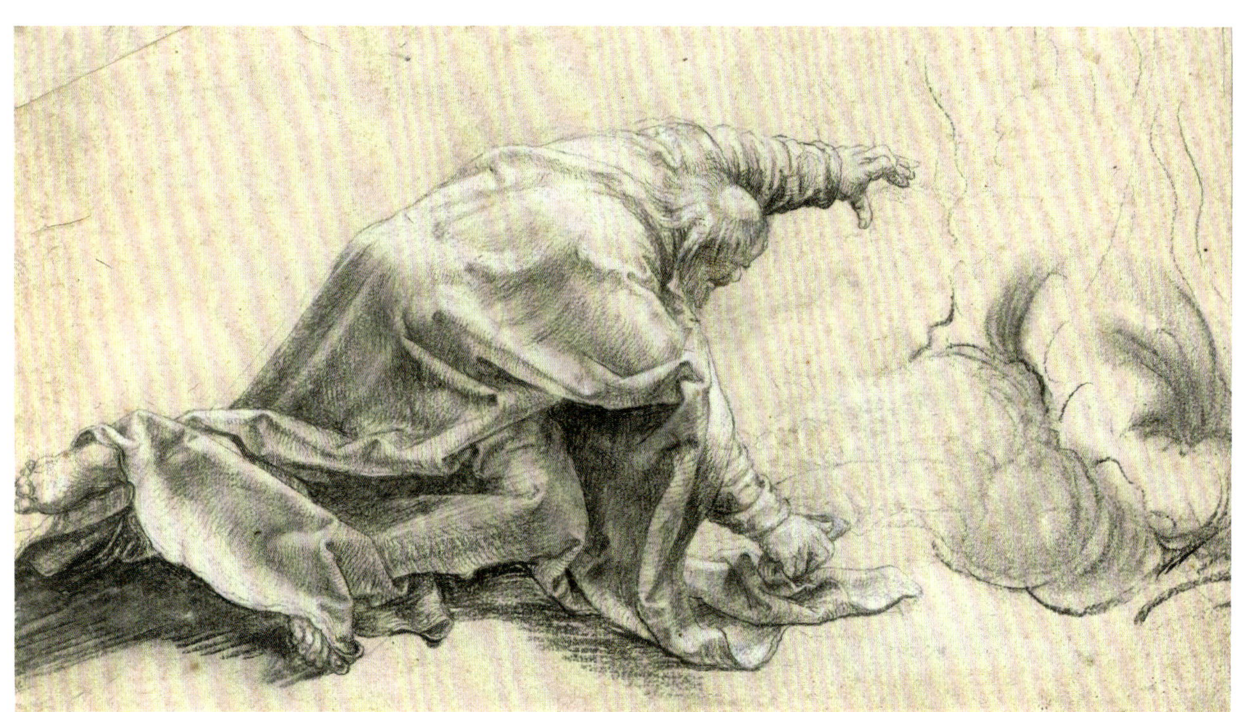

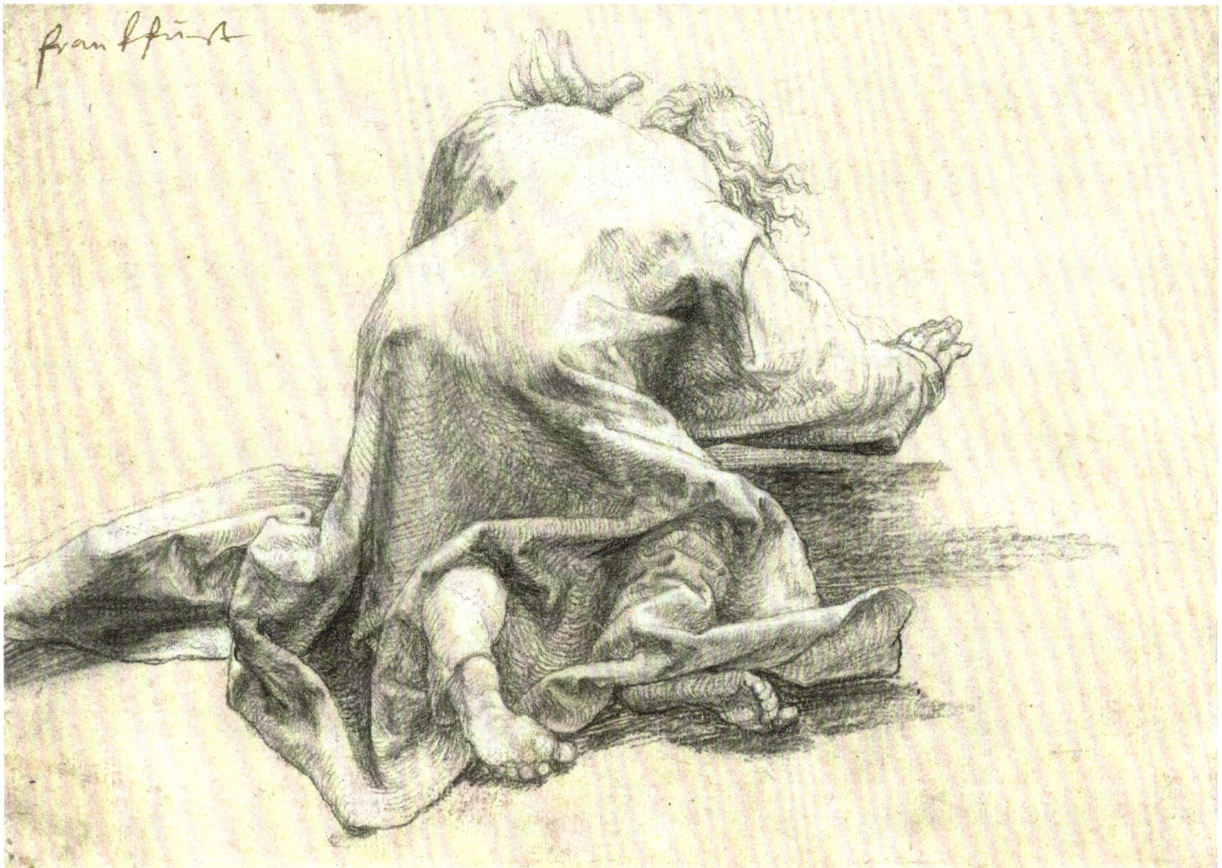

Of special interest is the new approach to the drapery, which now serves as a means to measure the depth of the space. This is accompanied by a different dramatic sense, greater pathos than in the previous works, although less imbued with expressive violence, something that had already been alluded to by the decision to depict the Virgin at the dramatic peak of the scene in which she is the protagonist.

These two Dresden drawings seem to be the works by Grünewald closest to the contemporary activity of Dürer, and this can be shown in the comparison of the poses of the two saints in the drawings in Dresden and the saints in the foreground in the panel by Jobst Harrich. The pose of St. John with an exposed foot in the immediate foreground appears to be a direct re-elaboration of the Heller saint with the close-up of his feet, and St. Peter brings to mind the same volumetric placement of the standing saint in profile in the Heller panel, as noted unfailingly once again by Roth.

The two drawings, along with the *Transfiguration*, offer the most complete answer, in volumetric terms, to the Dürer work. The approach to sketching the shadows with heavy pencil strokes seems very similar, parallel to the results obtained on the back of the Berlin drawing as well as that of Rotterdam, although with greater study of the depth and cubic space than in the previous ones. This evolution also marks greater mastery of the graphic medium by Mathis. From these observations we can also draw another—and not insignificant—conclusion. If the Karlsruhe monochromes (excluding the Frankfurt ones because I believe they were executed several years later) still appear untouched by Dürer's influence, while this influence can be seen, on the other hand, in the preparatory drawings for the *Transfiguration*, we must conclude that the two works, although close in time, belong to different moments in the artistic journey of our painter. Therefore, they do not form a unified group. Detached from the lost *Transfiguration*, the Karlsruhe and Frankfurt monochromes must necessarily be connected with the Heller altarpiece.

Revisiting the drawings with *Saint Dorothy* and the *Annunciation*, there is a noticeable distance between them and the two Dresden drawings, given that the former still have a more decorative quality. If the Dresden drawings date to 1511, thus reconnecting them to the lost *Transfiguration*, we can confirm a dating of around 1510 for the drawings we saw above. If what has been hypothesized to this point is true, between 1509 and 1511 Grünewald was involved in at least one altarpiece with hinged wings for Mainz Cathedral, with the presumed addition to the Heller altarpiece and the creation of the *Transfiguration* for the Frankfurt Dominicans, as well as his work as a hydraulic engineer, architect and perhaps even sculptor in the Bingen and Aschaffenburg castles. A tireless whirlwind of activity that could, perhaps, explain the reason for the temporarily unfinished state of the Heller monochromes (as well as the fact that the Dürerian altarpiece could easily fulfill its purpose even without being completed by the Grünewald monochromes).

Looking more closely, three of the four drawings representing *The three prophets* (?) act as a sort of hinge [figs. 64–66]. Today, these are also at the Kupferstichkabinett in Berlin, but originally they were glued into the pages of his German Bible by Hans Plock, a tailor from Halle who was an early adherent of the Reformation and would be one of the executors of Mathis's will (inv. KdZ 4190, inv. AM 23-1953, inv. AM 21-1953; they measure, respectively, 324 × 208 mm, 283 × 129 mm, 244 × 127 mm).[36] They share a similar technique (black chalk), with some coloring added later.

Drawings 4190 and AM 21–1953 feature a complex treatment of the drapery, once again reminiscent of the Riemenschneider cedillas and, at the same time, quite close

62 | Mathis Grünewald, *Study of Saint Peter (?)*, ca. 1511. Dresden, Staatliche Kunstsammlungen, Kupferstichkabinett, inv. C 1910-41.

63 | Mathis Grünewald, *Study of Saint John*, ca. 1511. Dresden, Staatliche Kunstsammlungen, Kupferstichkabinett, inv. C 1910-42.

64 | Mathis Grünewald, *Prophet (?)*, ca. 1511. Berlin, Staatliche Museen, Kupferstichkabinett, inv. AM 23-1953.

65 | Mathis Grünewald, *Prophet (?)*, ca. 1511. Berlin, Staatliche Museen, Kupferstichkabinett, inv. KdZ 4190.

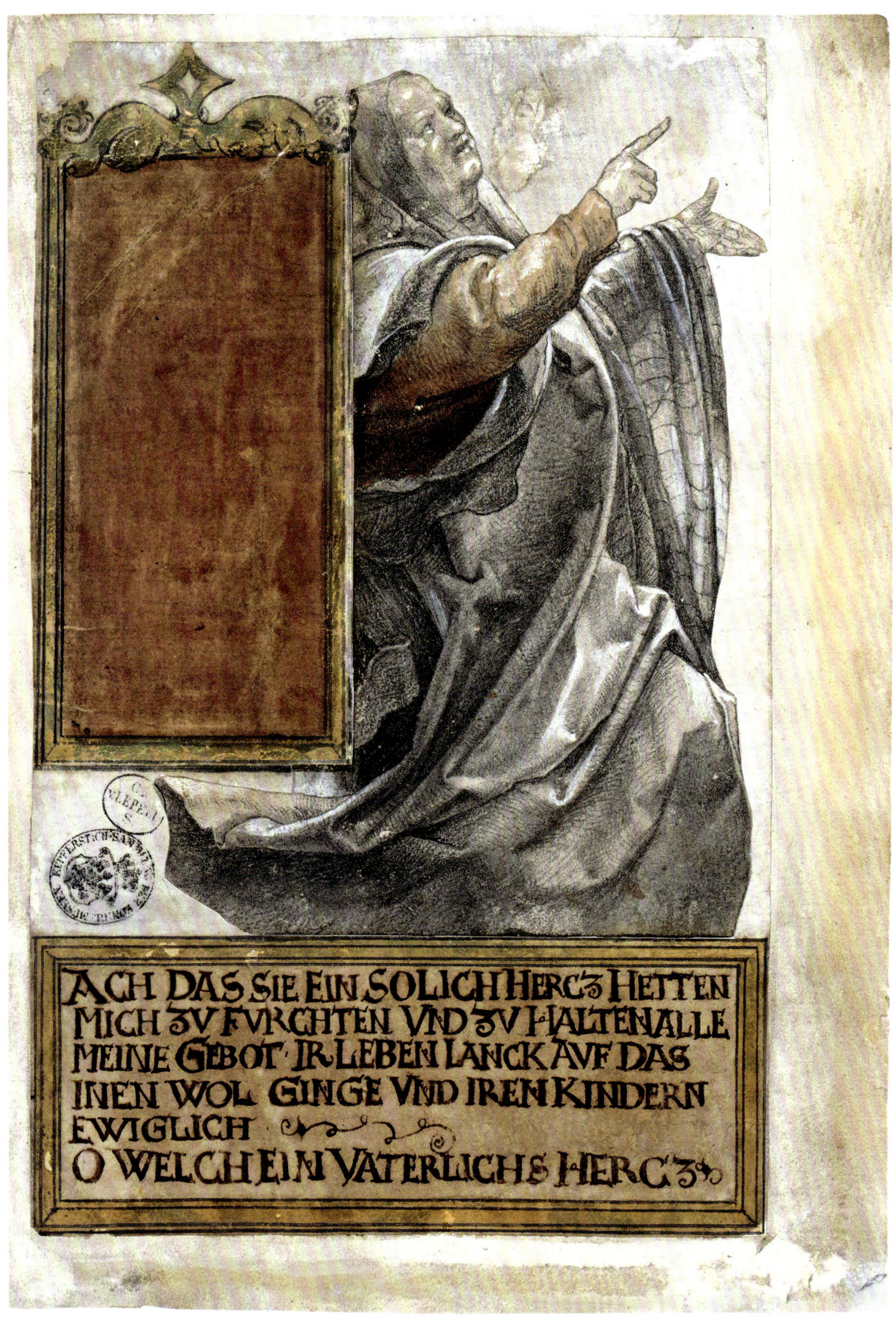
ACH DAS SIE EIN SOLICH HERCZ HETTEN
MICH ZV FVRCHTEN VND ZV HALTEN ALLE
MEINE GEBOT IR LEBEN LANCK AVF DAS
INEN WOL GINGE VND IREN KINDERN
EWIGLICH
O WELCH EIN VATERLICHS HERCZ

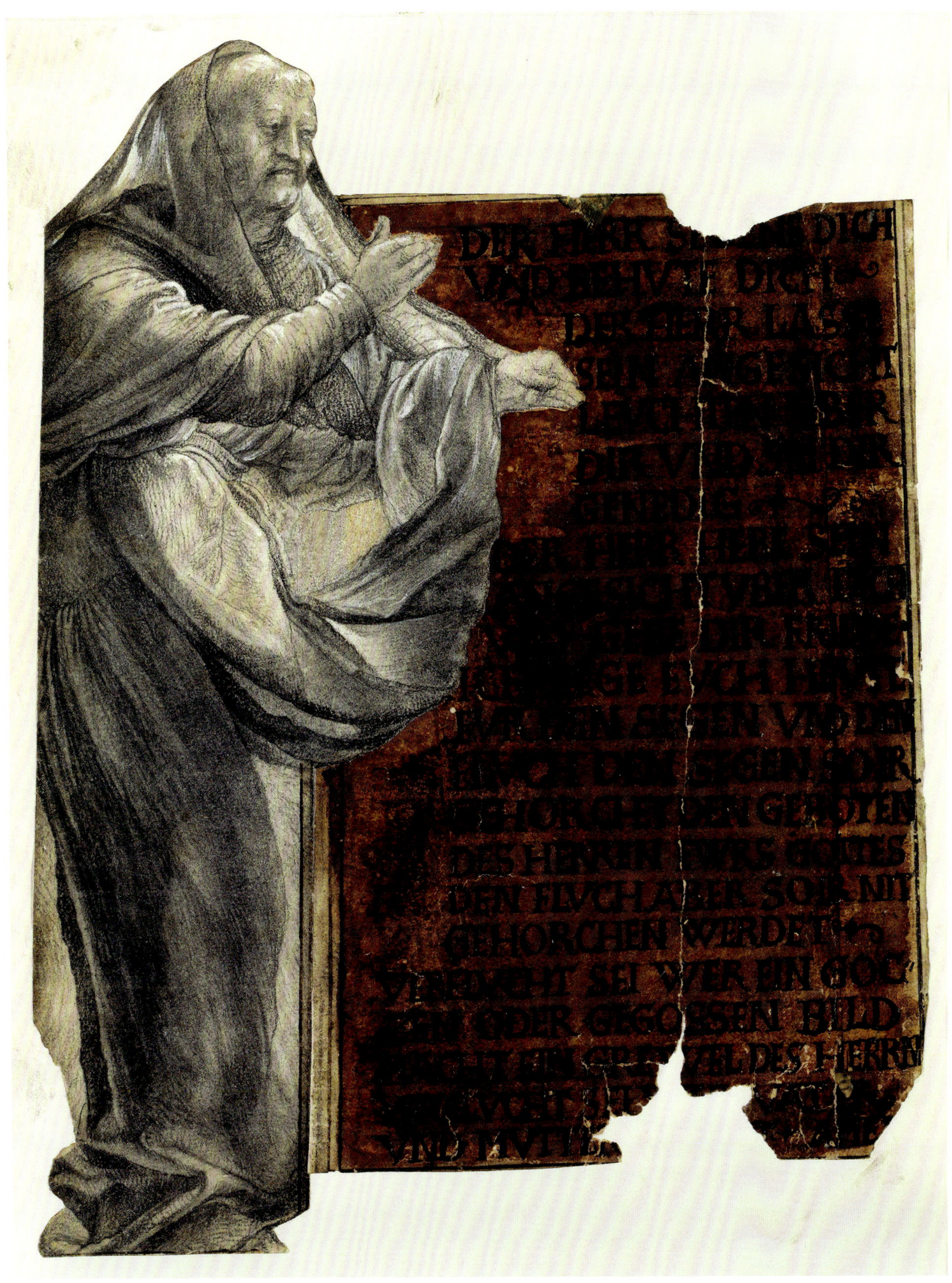
DES HERREN
GEHORCHEN WERDET
ODER GEGOSSEN BILD

66 | Mathis Grünewald, *Prophet (?)*, ca. 1511. Berlin, Staatliche Museen, Kupferstichkabinett, inv. AM 21-1953.

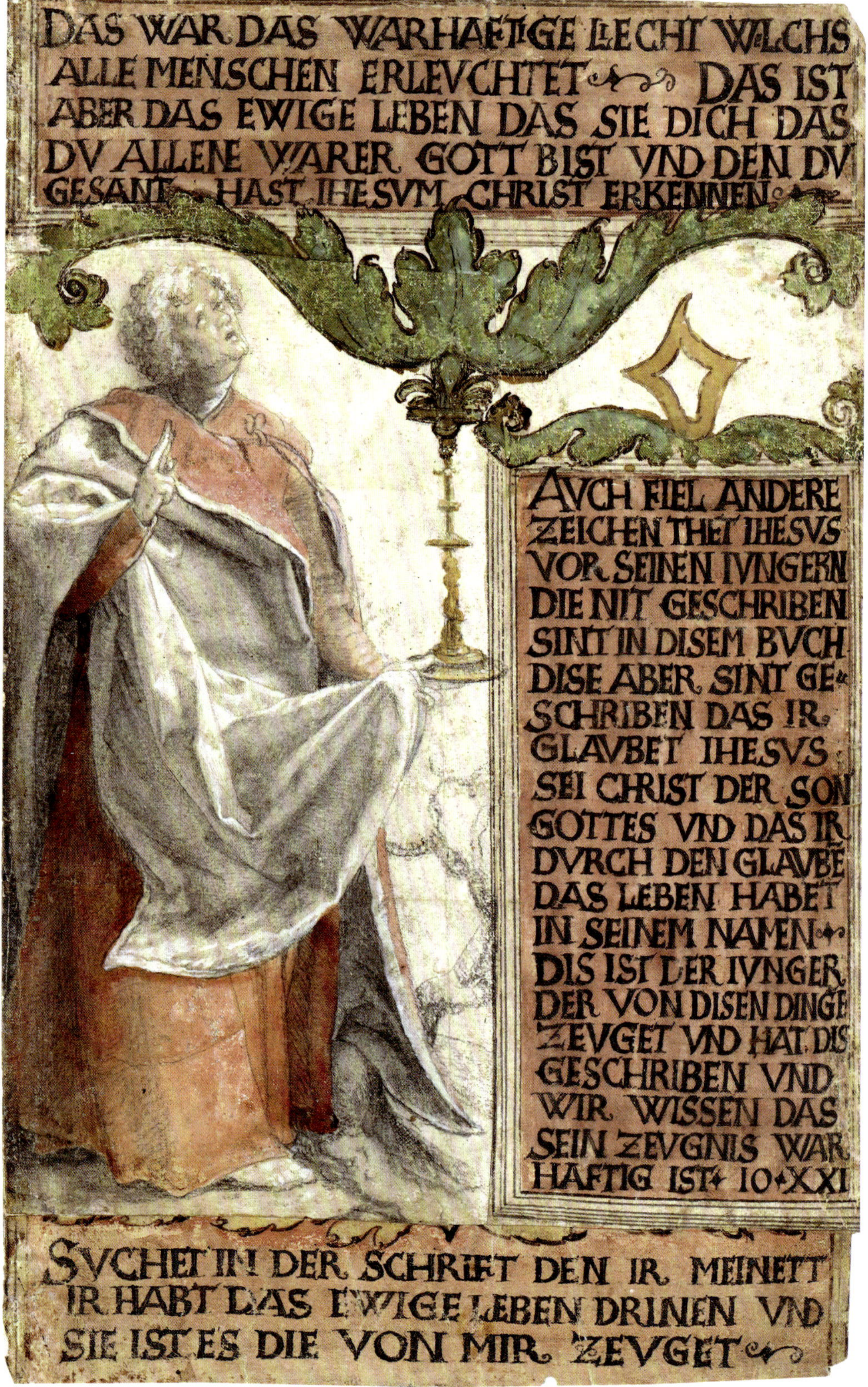

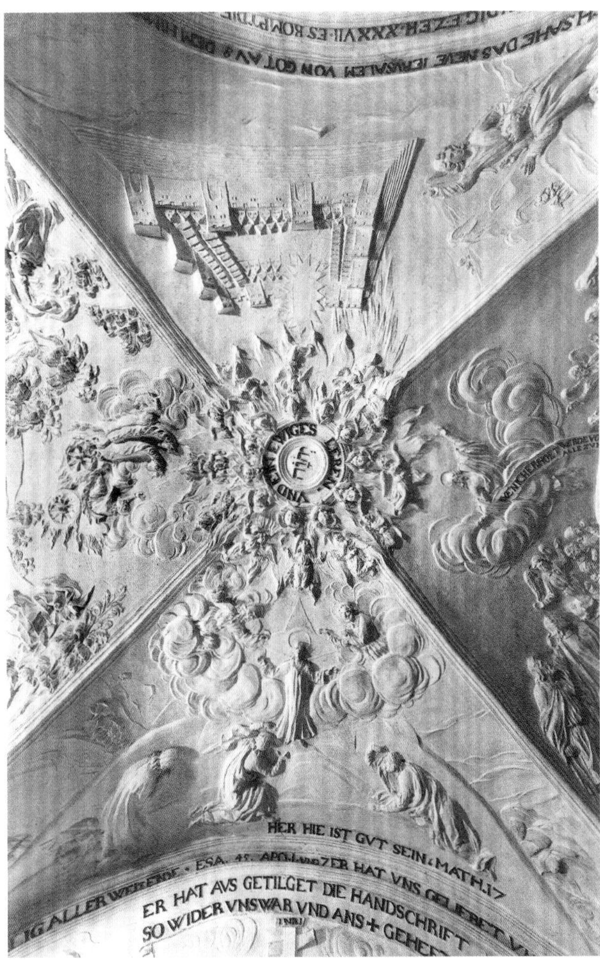

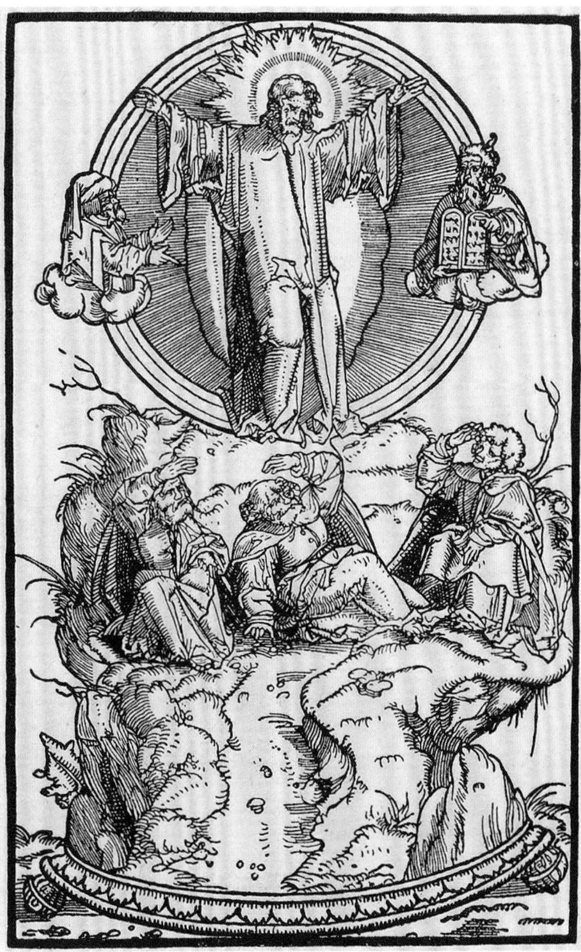

67 | Christian Steffan, *Transfiguration*, 1624. Butzbach, Parish church, crypt.

68 | Nuremberg Artist, *Reliquary*, woodcut, from *Halle'sche Heiltumsbuch*, Nuremberg, P. Vischer, December 1524.

to the already-commented study for the *Annunciation*. They also share the gaze and gestures of the figures turned upwards, as if they were also part of the group of saints in adoration of the Virgin Mary in the clouds in one of the altarpieces already in Mainz Cathedral (despite Sandrart referring only to female saints).

Slightly more organic and compact, yet still virtuosic is AM 23–1953, closely related to the studies for the *Transfiguration*, a connection also justified by the iconography. The elderly figure, dressed in the style of an Old Testament prophet, unlike the two figures commented on above, is looking ahead and not upwards, and appears to be engaged in a discussion. He could be a heavenly interlocutor of Jesus in a *Transfiguration*, in particular given the absence of the flame on his forehead that characterizes Moses and Elijah. And, coincidentally, the same gesturing pose of the prophet Elijah is also seen in other renderings of this New Testament event, all already connected with the lost Grünewald painting: the fresco painted by Jerg Ratgeb for the Carmelites in Frankfurt between 1514 and 1518; the stucco decoration of the crypt vault in the parish church of Butzbach, realized in 1621 by Christian Steffan, depicting a *Transfiguration* in which the apostles are quite similar to those in the Dresden drawings [fig. 67]; and a woodcut in the Halle *Heiltumsbuch* [fig. 68].[37]

Another work by Grünewald that potentially relates to Dürer is the *Crucifixion* at the National Gallery in Washington (inv. 1961.919) [fig. 69], from the Samuel Kress Collection.[38] The 61.3 × 46 cm oil panel at first glance seems akin to the Basel painting that we have already examined.

69 | Mathis Grünewald, *Crucifixion*, ca. 1512. Washington, National Gallery of Art, Kress Collection, inv. 1961.919.

Yet, there are substantial differences. The rendering of the scene and bodies seems more resolved, the chromatic scale is sharper and with greater contrast and, finally, the figure of Christ is also more expressive.

Its size would indicate that it was meant for private worship. To be precise, we know that in 1526 it belonged to a canon in Aschaffenburg, Caspar Schantz, whom we will meet again, and who on that occasion presented it to none other than Heinrich Reitzmann, who mentions it in his will on August 5, 1528.[39] Through various changes of hand, it reached the Duke Wilhelm V of Bavaria, called the Pious, who had it copied as an etching by Raphael Sadeler in 1605 (the most copied of all Grünewald's works) and where Sandrart would see it, until its final purchase by Samuel Kress in 1940. The dating is quite controversial, with some critics placing it around 1502, the year in which, on October 1, there was a lunar eclipse likely witnessed by the painter of the Washington *Crucifixion*.[40] Others date it to 1517–1520 for its presumed similarity with the Miracle of the Snow that we will examine below,[41] and still, others see the panel as essentially contemporaneous with the *Isenheim Altarpiece*. Recently, a fairly broad dating seems to have prevailed: 1511–1520;[42] so wide that it becomes meaningless.

However, a more plausible dating is mid-way between the two extremes proposed by scholars. In fact, the figure of Christ in Washington seems to pre-date and not follow that of the *Isenheim Altarpiece*, showing some indecision in defining the weight of the figures, presented almost as outlines, a trait absent in the Colmar painting. Moreover, the scene echoes Dürer's work, not present in the two Karlsruhe monochrome female saints, but detectable in the Dresden drawings, which act, therefore, as a chronological anchor also for the small Kress panel.

The points of consonance with Dürer's altarpiece in Frankfurt can be seen in the high-contrast use of yellow and red in nearly pure form[43] and in the torn drapery full of cascading tongues of fabric. These are more closely related to Dürer's preparatory drawings than to the 17th-century copy (demonstrating that Grünewald was studying with strong attention Dürer's style, not only his iconographies), especially in the famous preparatory drawing of the apostle standing next to the sarcophagus (Berlin, Kupferstichkabinett, inv. KdZ 12) [fig. 70].[44]

The most plausible dating for the *Crucifixion* is 1512, close to the time of the lost Frankfurt *Transfiguration* and before Mathis began to work on the *Isenheim Altarpiece*, likely in 1513.

As in the previous version in Basel and as will also be the case in Isenheim, the night scene is somber and unearthly, following the accounts in the Gospels of Mark and Matthew. On the other hand, here the connection of the *Crucifix* with the sculpture of Riemenschneider is much looser, whereas in the older version of this theme, it was obligatory. The depiction of Christ shows even greater stress, especially his hands and body, which are emphasized in an unnatural way, with the limbs so lean that the rib cage emerges forcefully. Paradoxically, this convulsive deformation is achieved thanks to the painter's enhanced anatomical awareness. The corpse of Christ is no longer erect as in a sculpture, but yields under its own weight with a truthfulness and visionary approach unknown up to this point not only in Grünewald, but in all of German, and perhaps European, painting.

The scene is terrifying: Christ's skeletal body hangs from the cross, maimed with bruises and wounds. Compared to the Basel version, the feet are even more twisted, almost at right angles, based on an iconography borrowed from the *Revelations*

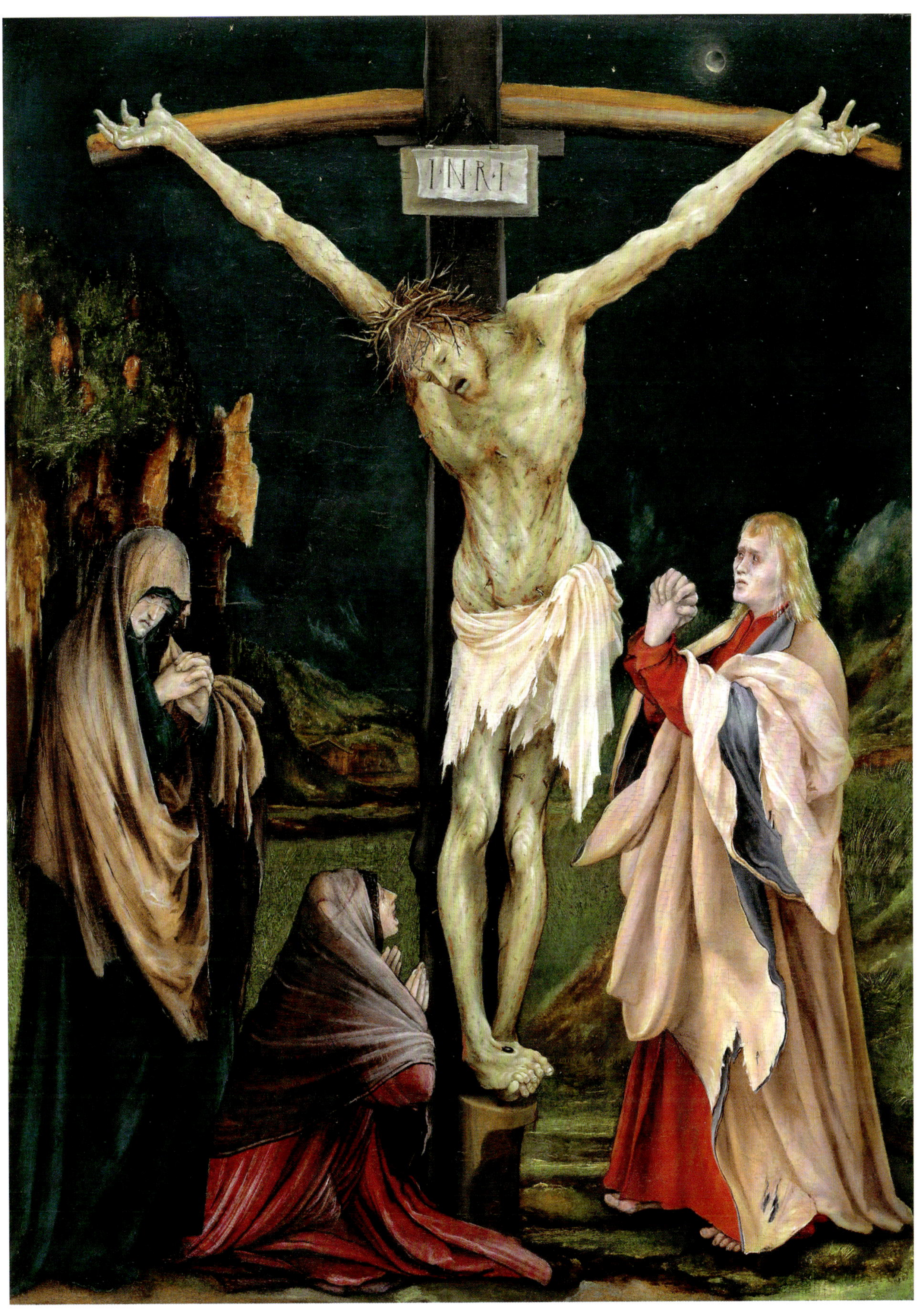
I·N·R·I

of St. Birgitta (IV, 70), a well-known source, with a German edition, published in Nuremberg in 1502:

> Now the color of death appeared in those parts of his body that were visible beneath the blood. His cheeks cleaved to his teeth. You could count his thin, naked ribs. His stomach, emptied now of all its juices, was sucked in toward his back, and even his nostrils looked thin now. When his heart was near to breaking, his whole body shook and his beard fell toward his chest. Right then, I collapsed lifeless to the ground. His mouth remained open, as he had already breathed his last. His tongue and teeth and the blood in his mouth were visible to onlookers. His half-closed eyes had rolled backward. His now dead body sagged downward, with his knees bent to either side, and his feet bending on the nails like hinges.[45]

In terms of the light, Christ is no longer the source. Instead, light comes from the right of the painting illuminating St. John and casting shadows on Mary Magdalene and the Virgin Mary. It is probable that the direction of the light was developed on the basis of the work's original placement.

Grünewald demonstrates again an incredible and masterful ability to play with contrasting colors, moiré effects and colored shadows. Like the *Mocking of Christ* in Munich, we see again the color red reflected this time by Mary Magdalene's mantle onto the feet of Christ.

Precisely observing Mary Magdalene, we find a significant executive subtlety: after painting the whole garment red, Grünewald added another, unevenly applied layer of dark paint to create the transparency of the shawl, under which, again unevenly, the strong hue of the dress can be glimpsed, with a marvelous effect of sculpted softness and chromatic vibrancy.

The Virgin Mary, with her dark dress and yellow veil with green shadows covering its top, conveys to the viewer a sense of bleakness and resigned and indescribable pain. This is even more profound than the expressions of St. John the Baptist (whose alleged dependency on Mantegna's burin depicting the *Deposition of Christ* in the sepulcher would seem a fact to be excluded[46]), with clasped hands, partially open mouth and reddened eyes, and the kneeling Mary Magdalene, who seems to scream out in agony.

Mary Magdalene is shown from a challenging angle, in *profil perdu* and slightly from below, conceived almost identically to that of what is likely St. Peter in the Dresden drawing: another aspect which confirms the dating between 1511 and 1512.

A later dating is to be excluded when considering the step on which Christ's feet rest. This element, found both in Basel and Karlsruhe, differs significantly in terms of spatial placement and lighting in the latter, causing it to appear less solid and three-dimensional. Furthermore, on the upper part of the cross was found, in lower-case gothic lettering, the monogram m g, as was the praxis for works created for Aschaffenburg and not for Mainz, while the three-letter version, M G N, appears only in works subsequent to the *Isenheim Altarpiece.* Although this monogram does not seem to be original, it might reflect the memory of a signature, perhaps on the frame.

Finally, let's consider the lunar eclipse depicted in the painting. Why would a celestial phenomenon observed—perhaps personally—in 1502 wait ten years to be reproduced in a painting? Probably because it was only then that Mathis had the occasion to do so, probably at the request of his patron. In fact, the eclipse is an iconographic

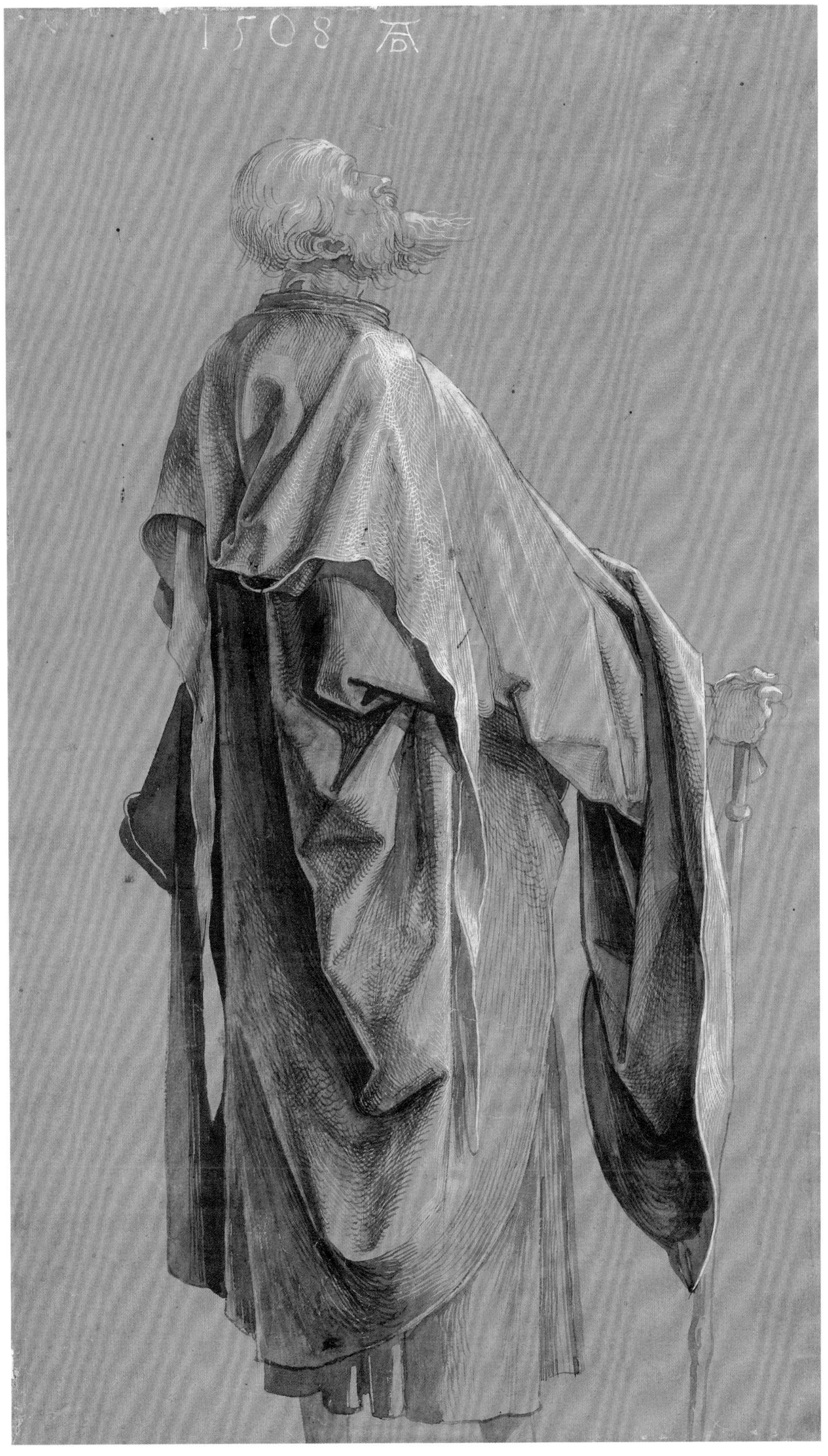

70 | Albrecht Dürer, *Study of an Apostle*, 1508. Berlin, Staatliche Museen, Kupferstichkabinett, inv. KdZ 12.

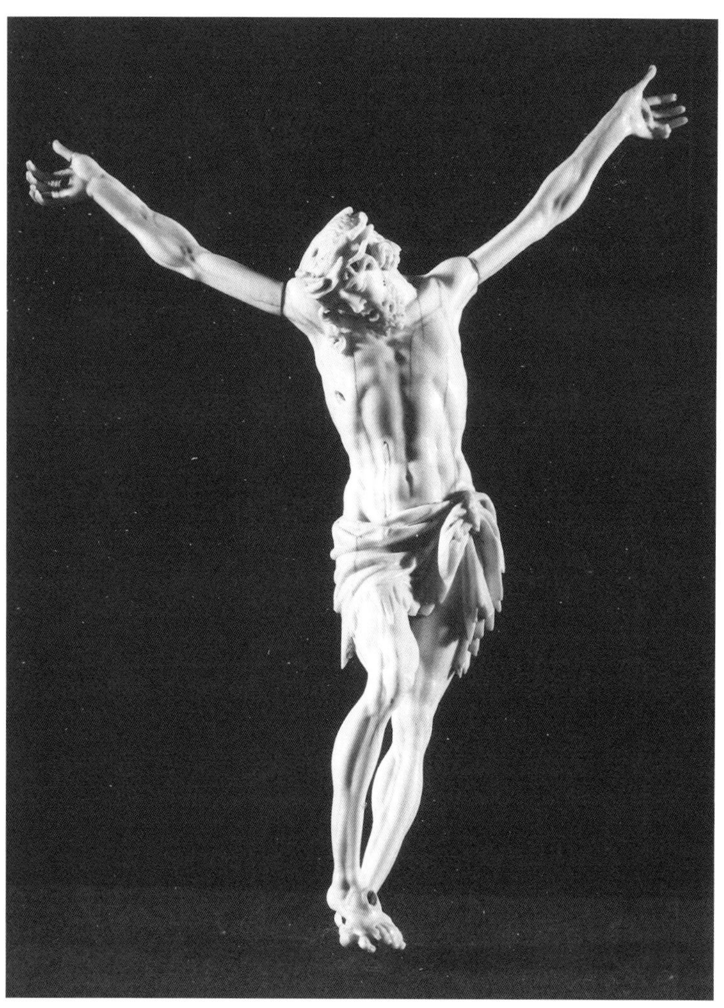

71 | XVII century German Sculptor, *Crucifix*. Paris, Galerie Charles Ratton & Guy Ladrière.

element that is not infrequent, although usually accompanied by the mirror image of the sun, which in the *Small Crucifixion* in Washington does not appear.

As previously mentioned, the *Small Crucifixion* is the most copied of Grünewald's works, especially during the 17th century,[47] a fact that is unquestionably rather surprising, and even more so considering the existence of highly refined three-dimensional copies. Notable examples include one in hollow metal, dated 1620–1630, and preserved at the Museum für Angewandte Kunst in Frankfurt (inv. 6817, 47.5 × 36 cm),[48] one from the same period, in wood, at the Museum der Stadt Aschaffenburg (inv. 157/61, 70 × 15 cm, but it is missing its arms and feet)[49] and an unusual one in ivory in the Guy Ladrière collection in Paris, of especially fine quality (22 × 16.5 × 6 cm, with a shortened right arm due to damage; the work, therefore, would have been even closer to that of the original painting) [fig. 71]. This would lead us to think that there was a special appreciation and perhaps even a specific type of devotion connected with this image. If this is truly, as would seem likely, the "tefflin mit en Crucifix" owned by the Aschaffenburg canon Caspar Schantz, inherited by Reitzmann in 1526, as suggested by Weixlgärtner,[50] and it could have been the Aschaffenburg priest who, in some way, championed the fame of this image.

It is possible that the Washington panel was not the second, but the third, opportunity for Grünewald to return to the subject that so moved him: the Crucifixion. I believe that the problematic drawing, today just a fragment pasted on a piece of paper which also depicts the crucified Christ, at the Staatliche Kunsthalle in Karlsruhe (black chalk, 539 × 328 mm, inv. VIII 1500 [fig. 72])[51] could be considered an intermediate version between the two paintings examined so far. The drooping of the lifeless torso, a motif conceived from St. Birgitta's description to which Mathis would remain faithful in his subsequent exploration of this theme, foreshadows the much-later panel of the same subject, today at the Karlsruhe Museum. This indicates that Grünewald had intuited a motif that would reach full maturity only in his future work.

The steady, confident stroke indicates a mature hand, and perhaps it is a presentation drawing, already in the format proposed for the final painting. Certainly, the visionary force of the Washington panel is not yet visible, nor does there seem to be any reference to Dürer, which would place the drawing in a chronology around 1510, separating it from the paintings considered thus far.[52]

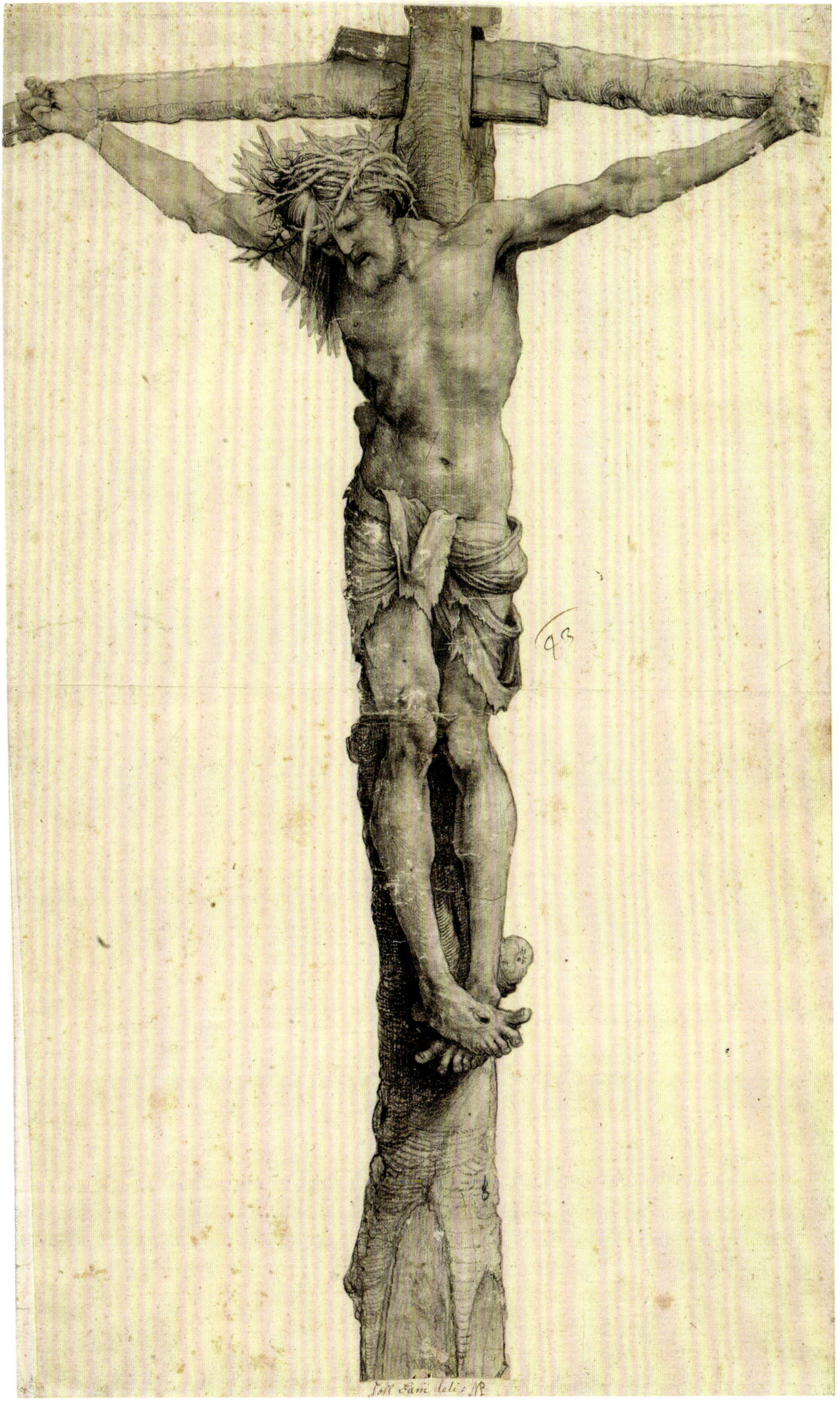

72 | Mathis Grünewald, *Crucifix*, ca. 1510. Karlsruhe, Staatliche Kunsthalle, inv. VIII 1500.

A strong, confident stroke, similar to that of the Karlsruhe fragment, is seen in another drawing, often compared with the Frankfurt *Transfiguration* at the Smith College Museum of Art in Northampton, Massachusetts (black chalk, 131 × 181 mm, inv. SC 1958.3) [fig. 73], which tends to be interpreted by scholars as a study of drapery falling on the legs of a seated man,[53] If this interpretation is correct,[54] seeing the image as the depiction of an apostle who, before the figure of Christ transfigured, completely covers himself with his cloak, it would reveal extraordinary lyricism and imaginative ability. However, I find this hypothesis complicated.

Regardless, the depiction of the tattered drapery, skillfully explored in the heavy folds and pointed, metallic turn-ups, seems consonant with the Washington *Crucifixion* and, therefore at the height of Grünewald's proximity to Dürer. It also seems to me that, if the idea of a study of drapery covering the legs of a seated individual is convincing, it could easily be a Madonna. A certain similarity could perhaps also be seen in an analogous detail of the woodcut by Dürer depicting the *Holy Family with two angels in a portico*, datable to ca. 1503–1504 [fig. 74].[55]

So, should we believe that around 1512 Grünewald painted a Madonna which we know nothing about? There would be nothing strange about this and, in any case, a drawing with different interpretations is too weak a foundation on which to base a hypothesis. However, I think there is another clue to Grünewaldian works in this precise time period: a painting I believe can be attributed to Christoph Krafft, an artist we will meet again, who is apparently a specialist in making copies of Mathis's works. This painting, a panel representing *St. James the Elder* (94.6 × 56 cm) [fig. 75]

73 | Mathis Grünewald, *Study of Drapery*, ca. 1511 (?). Northampton (Mass.), Smith College Museum of Art, inv. SC 1958.3.

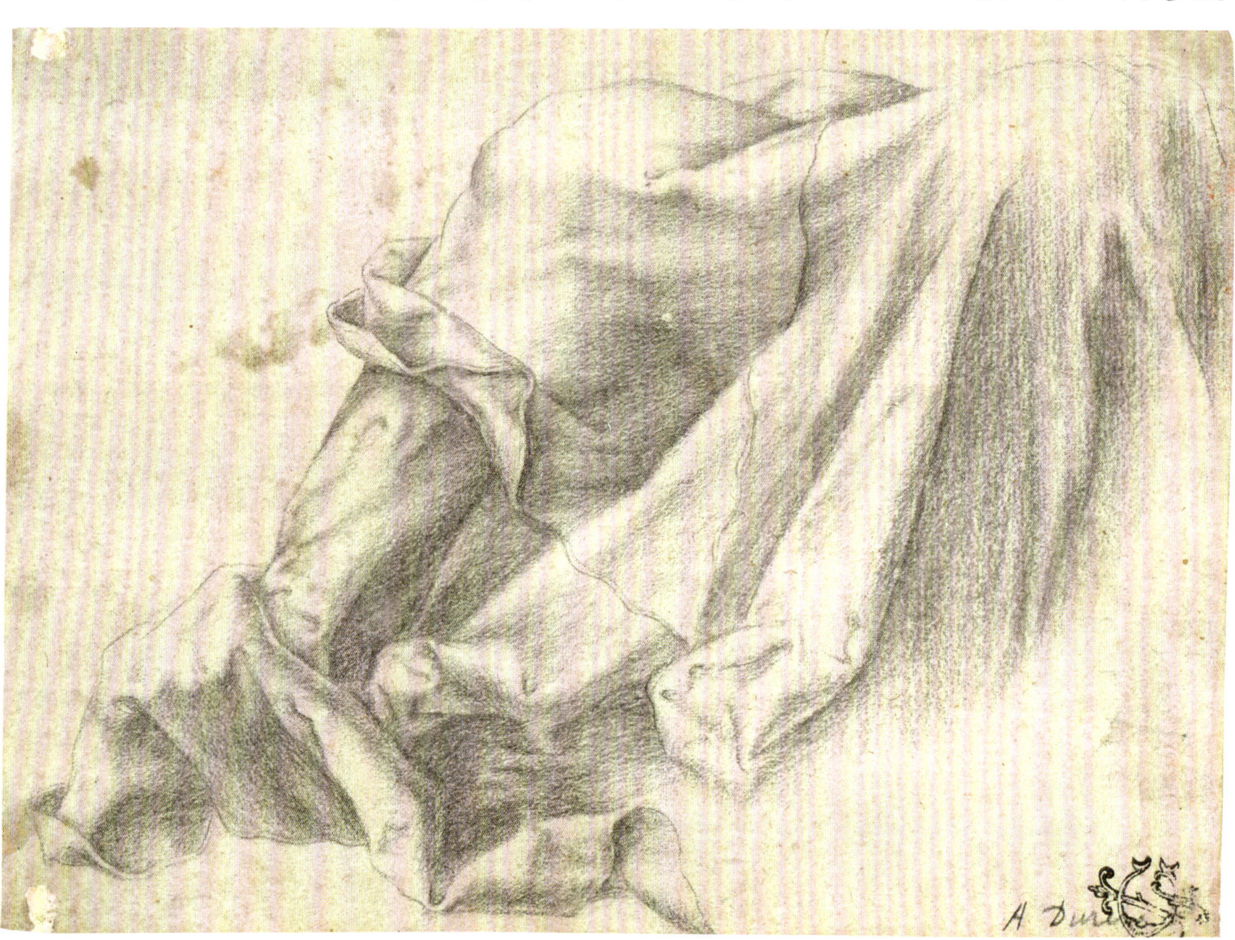

is today in an Italian private collection, though it came from a German collection (evidenced by some fragments of German parish notices preserved on its back and glued over traces of faux marble decorations; the work was, therefore, the wing of a small hinged altarpiece).[56] If my attribution is correct, the painting is extremely important, not so much because it is an additional piece in the Krafft catalogue but because it provides a visual memory of a work by Mathis previously unknown. Despite the 17th-century transposition, the formal aspects of the image unquestionably lead back to Grünewald between the drawing of *St. Catherine* in Berlin (for example,

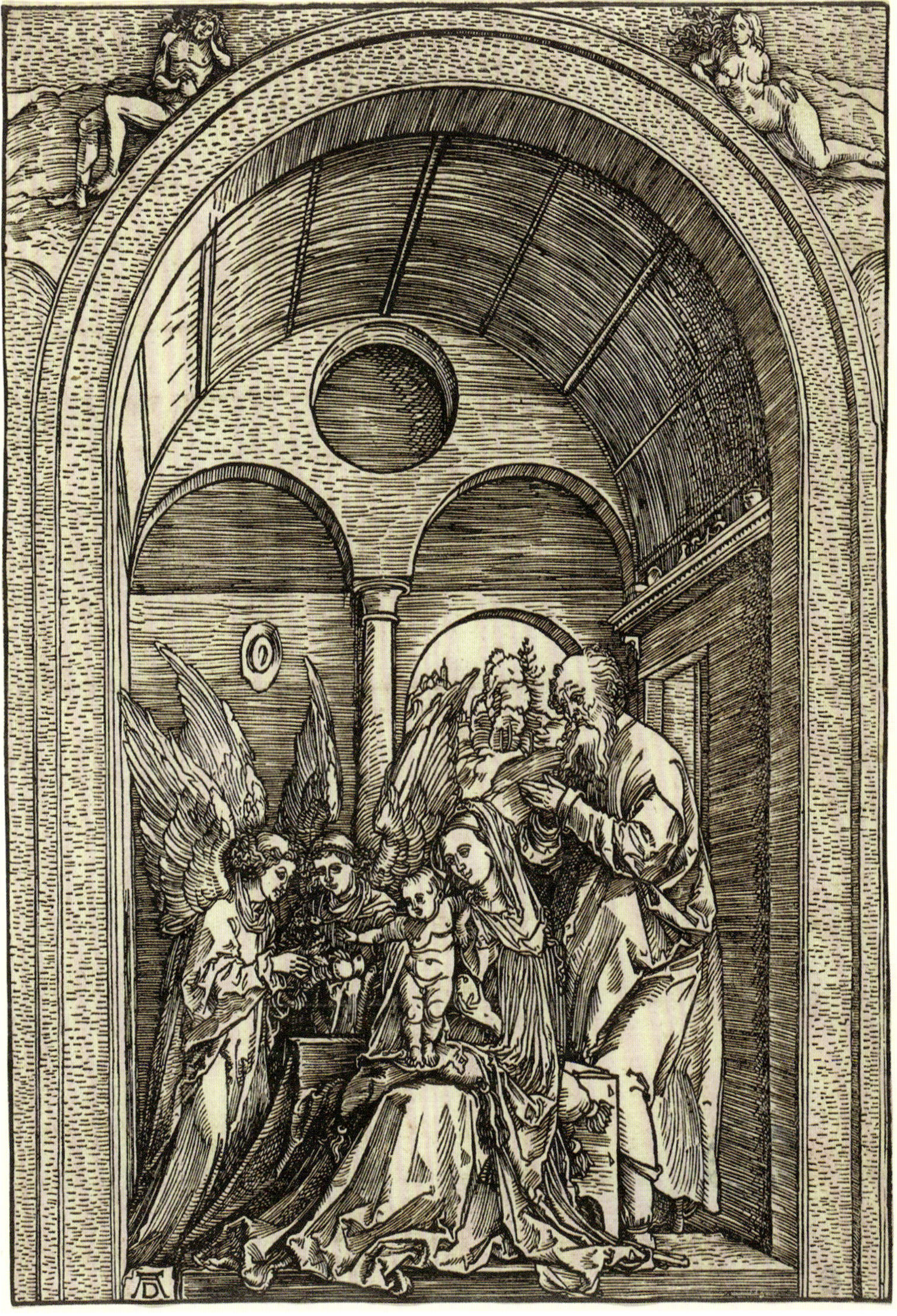

74 | Albrecht Dürer, *The Holy Family with two Angels in a portico*, ca. 1500, woodcut.

75 | Christoph Krafft, *Saint James the Elder* (after Mathis Grünewald?). Private collection.

76 | Mathis Grünewald, *Head of an aged bearded Man*, ca. 1512. Weimar, Kunstsammlungen, Graphische Sammlung, inv. KK 118.

the stereotypical rendering of the rocks to suggest a generic setting) and the Washington *Crucifixion*. The timid rotation of the pose is also not conceptually removed from that of the presumed *Saint Lucy* today in Karlsruhe.

The secure, almost sharp-edged stroke that is unquestionably coherent with Dürer, suggests that the study of an old man with a long, parted beard (black pencil, 342 × 254 mm: Weimar, Kunstsammlungen, Graphische Sammlung, inv. KK 118[57]) [fig. 76] of extraordinary graphic power, belongs to the same period. Usually, this drawing is connected with the depiction of *St. Anthony* in the *Isenheim Altarpiece* but, as we shall see, Grünewald's drawing style in that period will have noticeably different characteristics. Ruhmer's observation seems accurate: "This masterly drawing seems to me to have been influenced by Dürer and to belong to the early part of the second decade".[58] Of some relevance is the presence of a watermark on the paper attributable to Mainz between 1506 and 1516.[59] This is not a reason why the drawing's connection to Isenheim should be denied (Grünewald could easily have

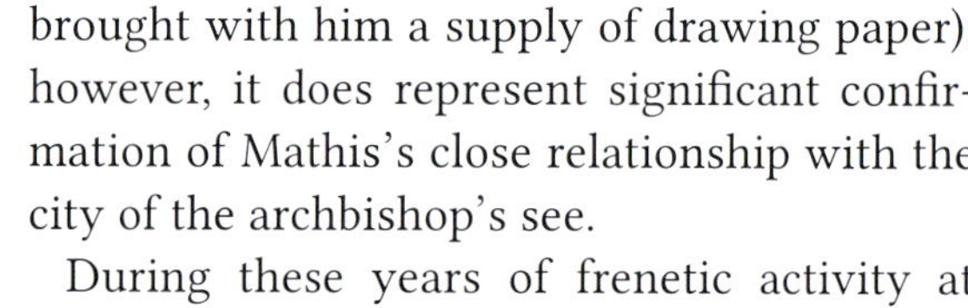

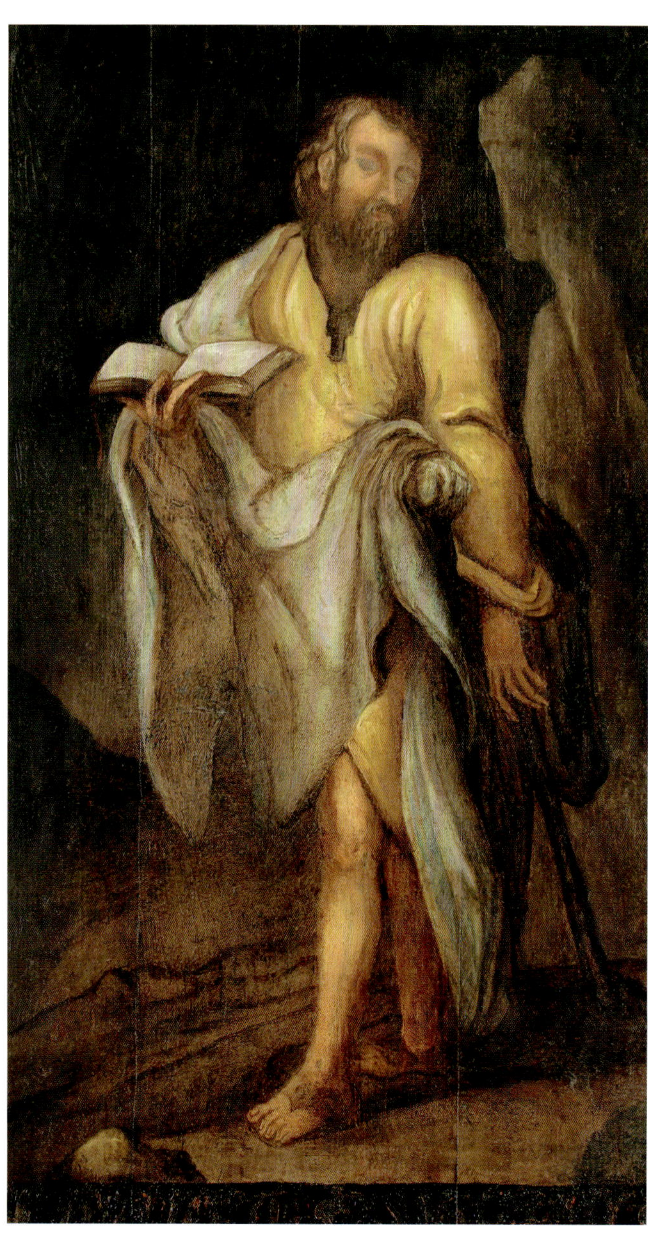

brought with him a supply of drawing paper); however, it does represent significant confirmation of Mathis's close relationship with the city of the archbishop's see.

During these years of frenetic activity at the beginning of the decade, Grünewald, employed at the Mainz court and well-introduced into Frankfurt, maintained close ties with the city of Aschaffenburg and particularly, as we have seen, with canons Caspar Schantz and Heinrich Reitzmann. One wonders, is it likely that the latter, who had a fairly good knowledge of Italy, never showed Mathis his copy of the "Triumpha [sic] Cesaris"—a print based on Mantegna?[60] Specifically, according to the inventory of his possessions prepared in 1511, Reitzmann's collection included two paintings on canvas (evidently a pair) hung on the wall, another painting on canvas hung on the wall, and a painting "de passione Domini, Triumpha Cesaris" hung on the wall. Due to the use of the plural (though incorrect), *Triumpha*, it could be argued that there was more than one of these Victories, and it is very likely that they were really prints. I would like to think that they were pieces that came directly from Mantegna's workshop, or were more or less authorized copies.[61] However, it seems likely that Reitzmann possessed the most available wood engravings of the series, "Triumphus Caesaris", etched in 1504 by Iacobus Argentoratensis (Jakob von Strassburg) from the drawing by the Paduan artist Benedetto Bordone.[62] This information likely represented the first

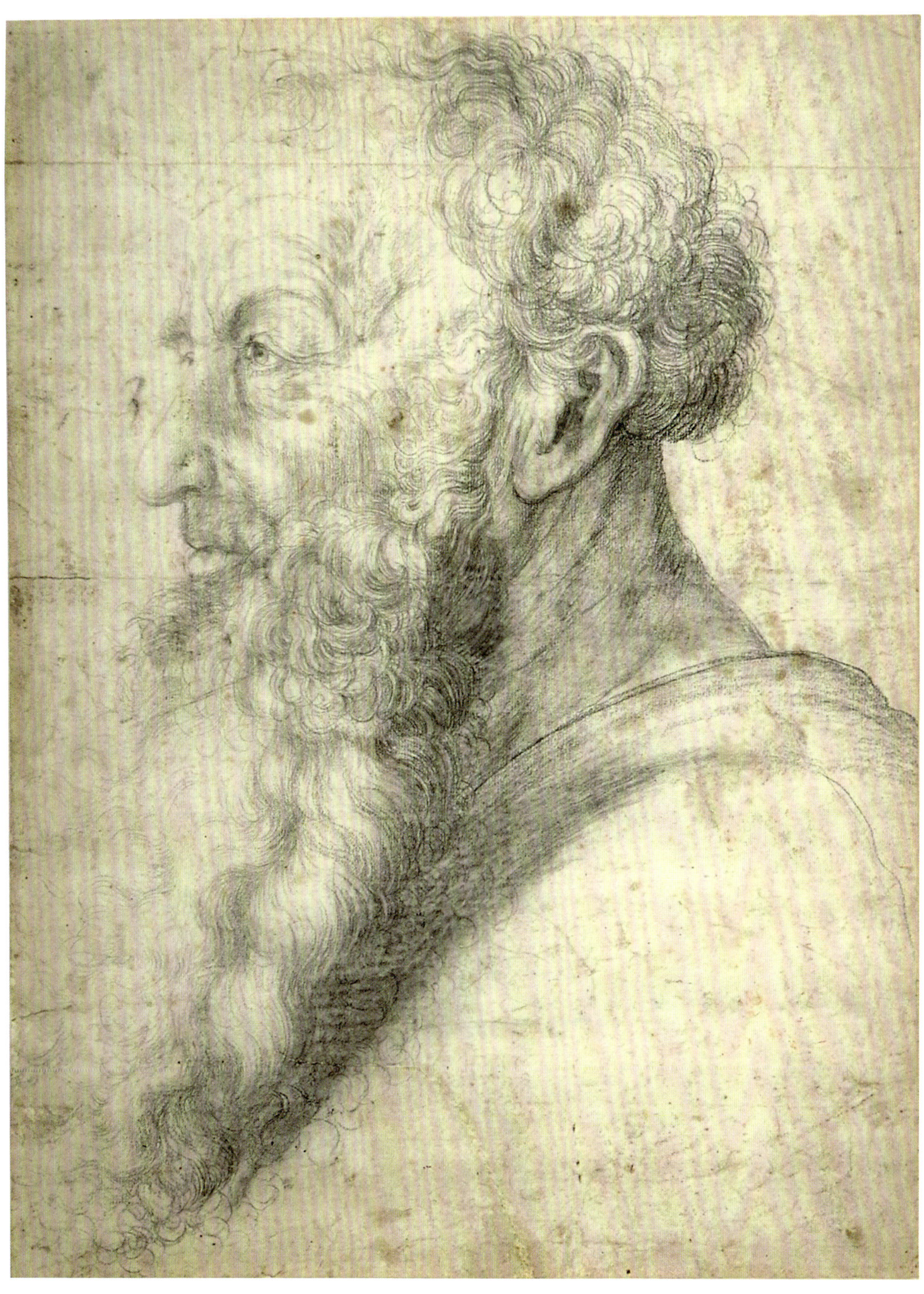

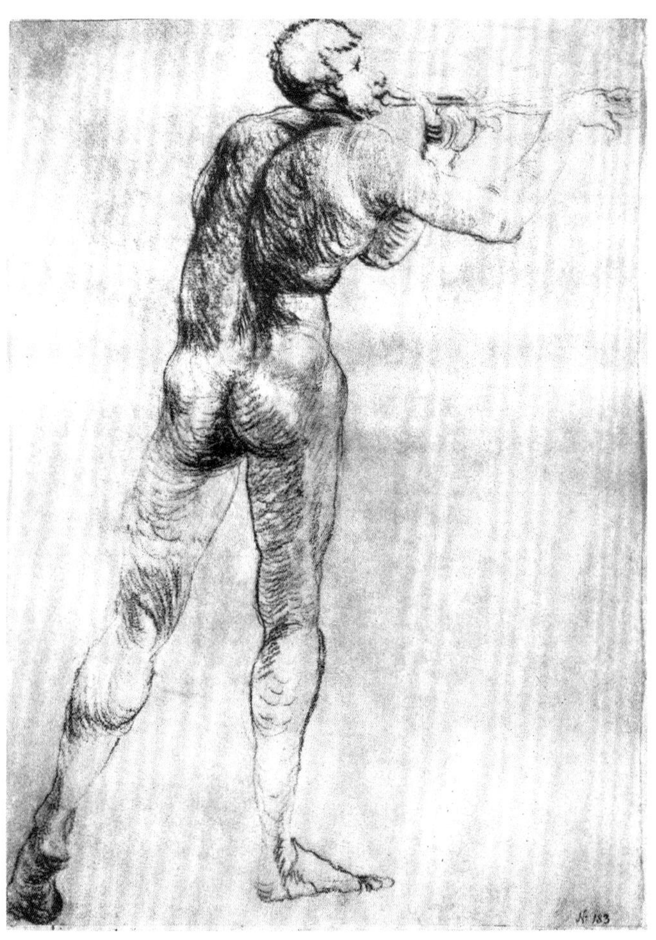

77 | Attributed to Mathis Grünewald, *Naked Trumpeter*, ca. 1512. Formerly Rotterdam, Museum Boijmans van Beuningen, inv. D I 43.

direct contact of our painter with Italian art, supporting the previously questionable attribution of the drawing formerly in Rotterdam (Museum Boijmans van Beuningen, inv. D I 43) depicting a *Naked trumpeter seen from the back* [fig. 77]. This subject, unusual for Grünewald, was done using his usual black pencil technique, although with a bit more *chiaroscuro* (the "Morellian" characteristics, the rendering of the hands and feet, the stroke and the high quality of the drawing, all suggesting it is indeed an autograph by our painter). It would be tempting to interpret this drawing in relation to one of the existing prints of the scene of the *Elephants* [fig. 78], in which the last trumpeter on the left, marching, with his foot raised and calf muscle contracted, could have suggested much to the creator of the Rotterdam drawing. And it would be nice to think that the latter was familiar with the vibrant exemplar attributed to Giulio Campagnola, dated ca. 1498–1499.[63] However the figures of naked trumpeters, though less sophisticated but dissimilar, are also seen in one of the etchings by Jacobus Argentoratensis (plate H [fig. 79]), and this would have been sufficient to trigger Grünewald's imagination. The undeniable resemblance, not only in composition but also the lighting, with the *Two musicians* in Cologne, Wallraf-Richartz Museum (inv. WRM 0369), part of an altarpiece painted by Dürer for the Schlosskirche in Wittenberg, commissioned by Frederick the Wise around 1504 [fig. 80], demonstrates that the dialogue with the great master from Nuremberg continued, according to a logic that will be better clarified further on.

Heinrich Reitzmann likely commissioned a painting from Mathis in his lost will, drafted on August 5, 1513. However, this painting would only be realized several years later, confirming the strong bond between the artist and the canon during this period.

It seems to me that this also period includes the creation of the pitiless, though not harsh, *Portrait of a cleric* in black chalk on paper at the Nationalmuseum in Stockholm (inv. NM 1853/1863, 254 × 189 mm) [fig. 81].[64] Once again Flemish-like the lenticular study of the elderly man's face, the drawing style alternates between the delicate strokes of the face and the more energetic ones of his cap.

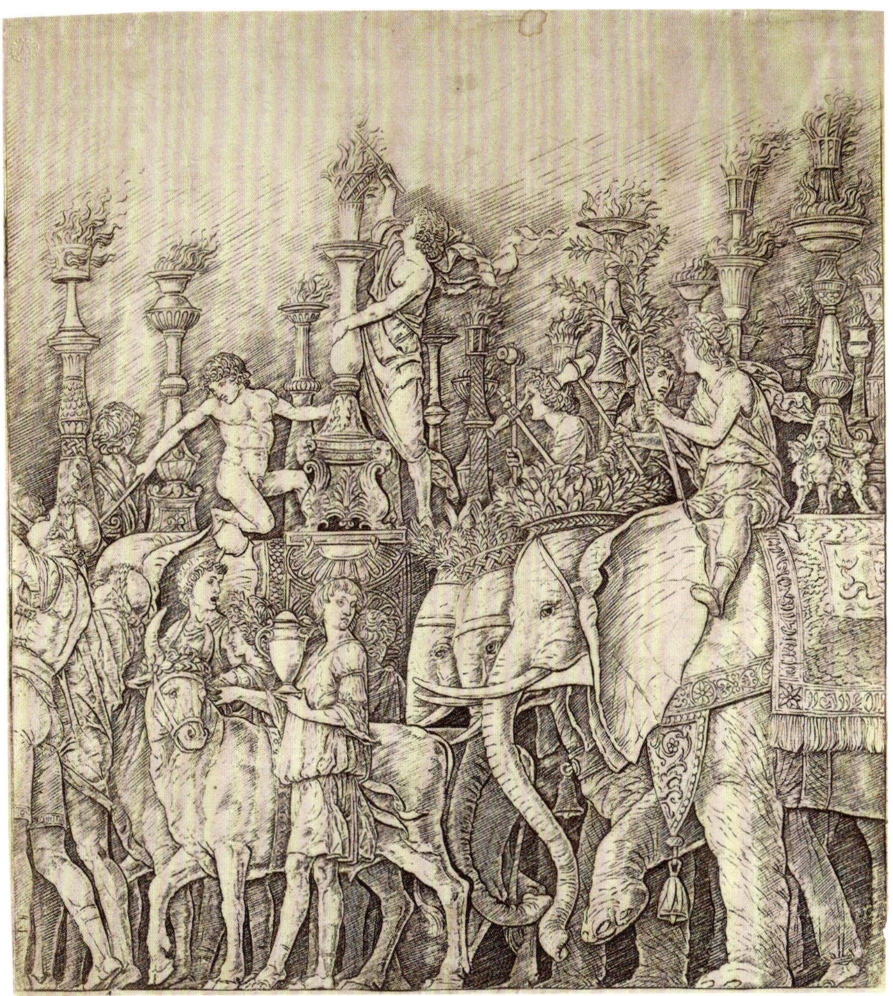

78 | Giulio Campagnola after Andrea Mantegna, *The Elephants* (from the series of the Triumphs of Julius Caesar), 1498–1499, burin. Pavia, Musei Civici.

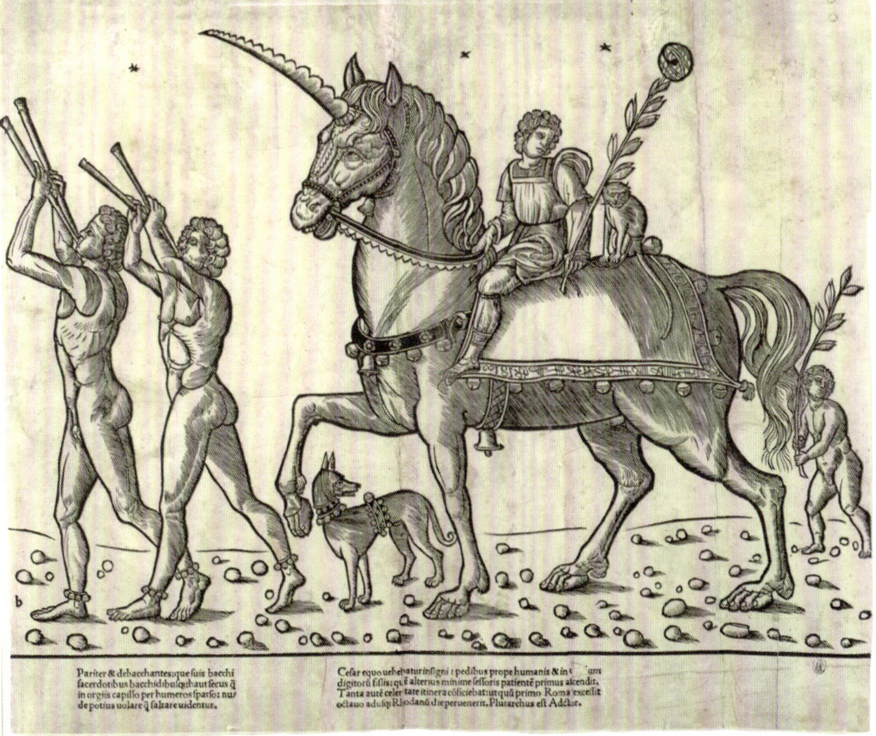

79 | Jacobus Argentoratensis, *The Triumphs of Julius Caesar*, plate H, etching.

80 | Albrecht Dürer, *Two Musicians* (from a polyptych in Wittenberg), ca. 1504. Cologne, Wallraf Richartz Museum, inv. WRM 0369.

81 | Mathis Grünewald, *Head of an old Priest*, ca. 1512–1513. Stoccolma, Nationalmuseum, inv. NM 1853/1863.

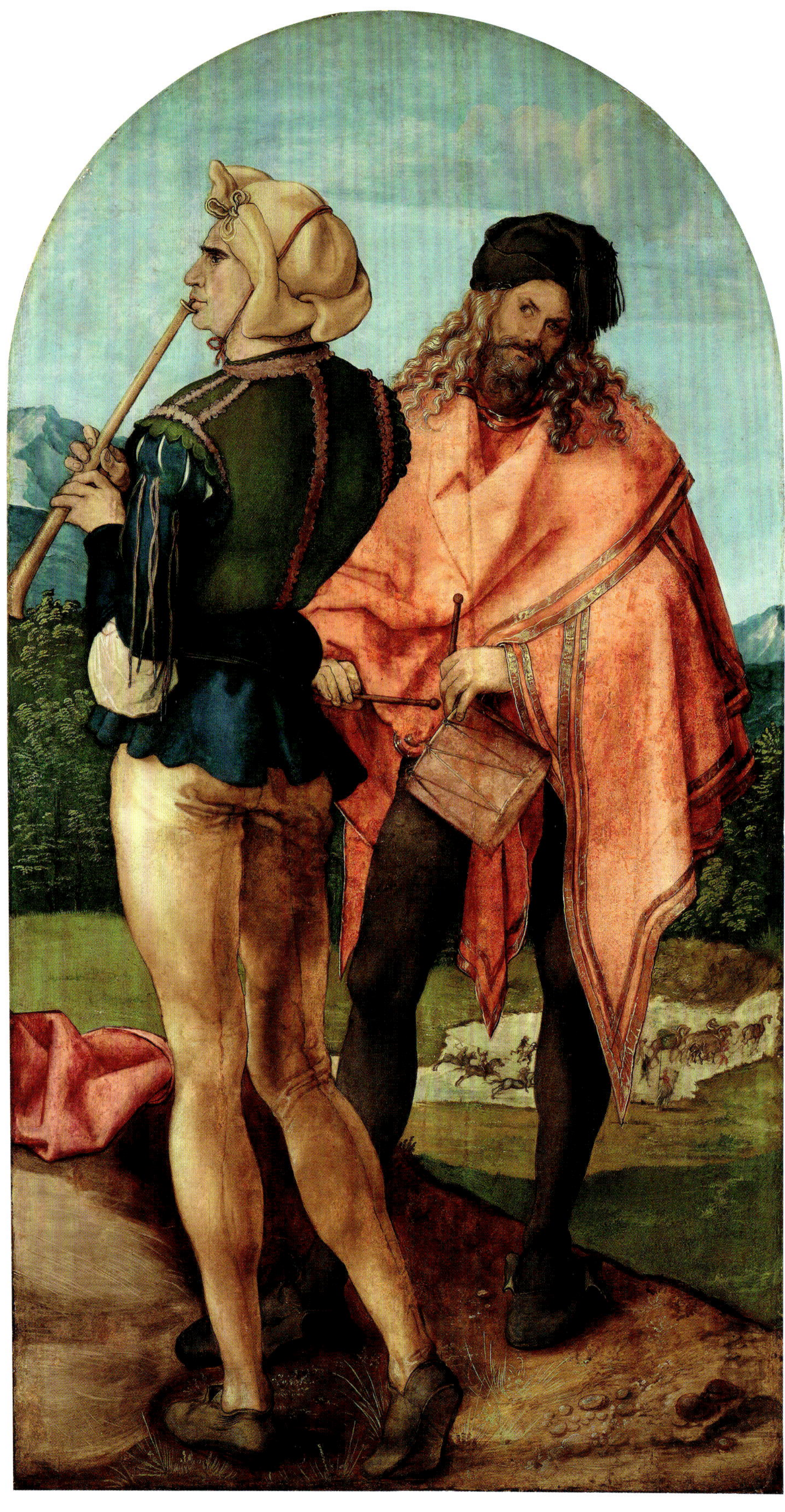

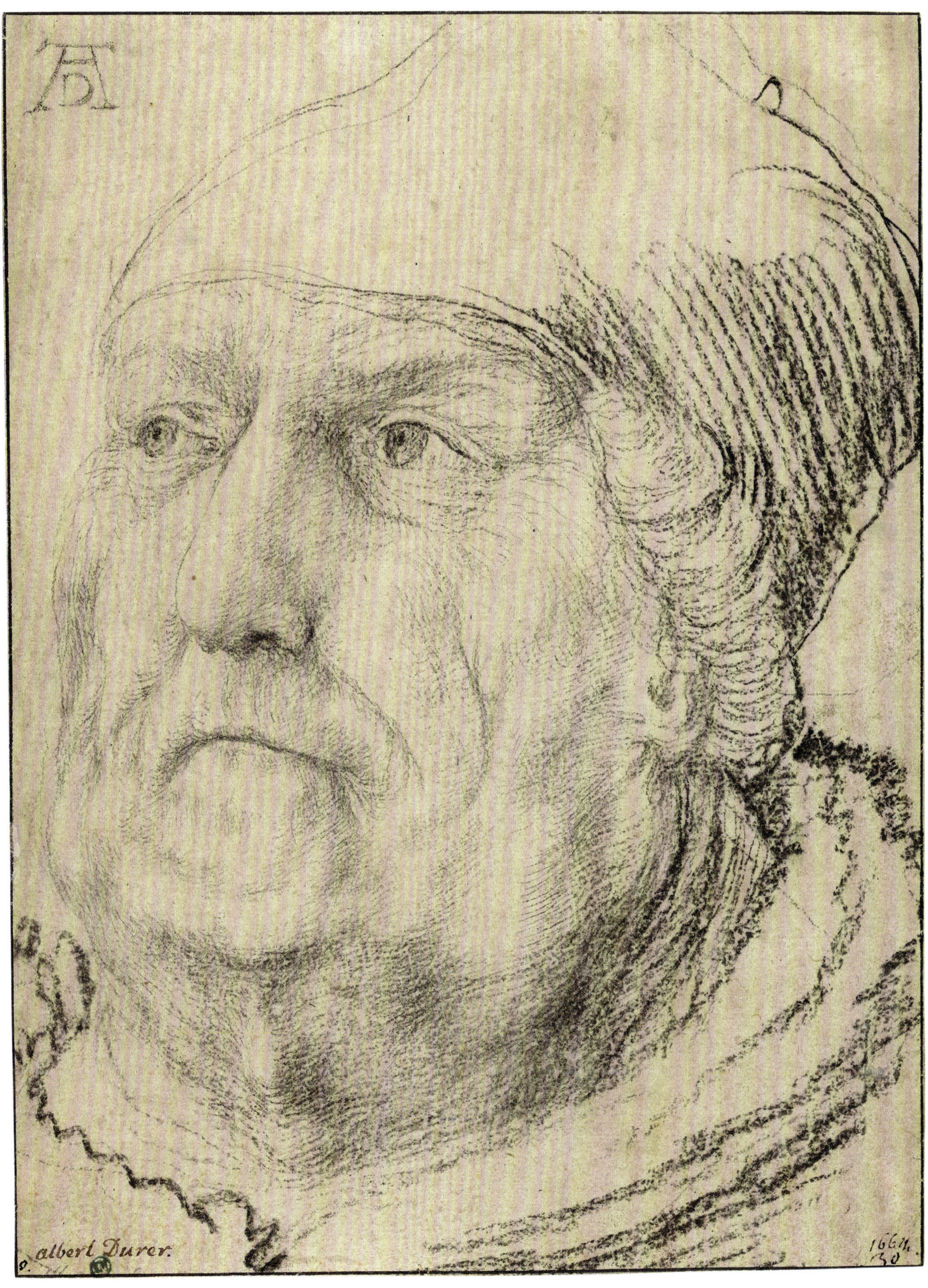

albert Durer.

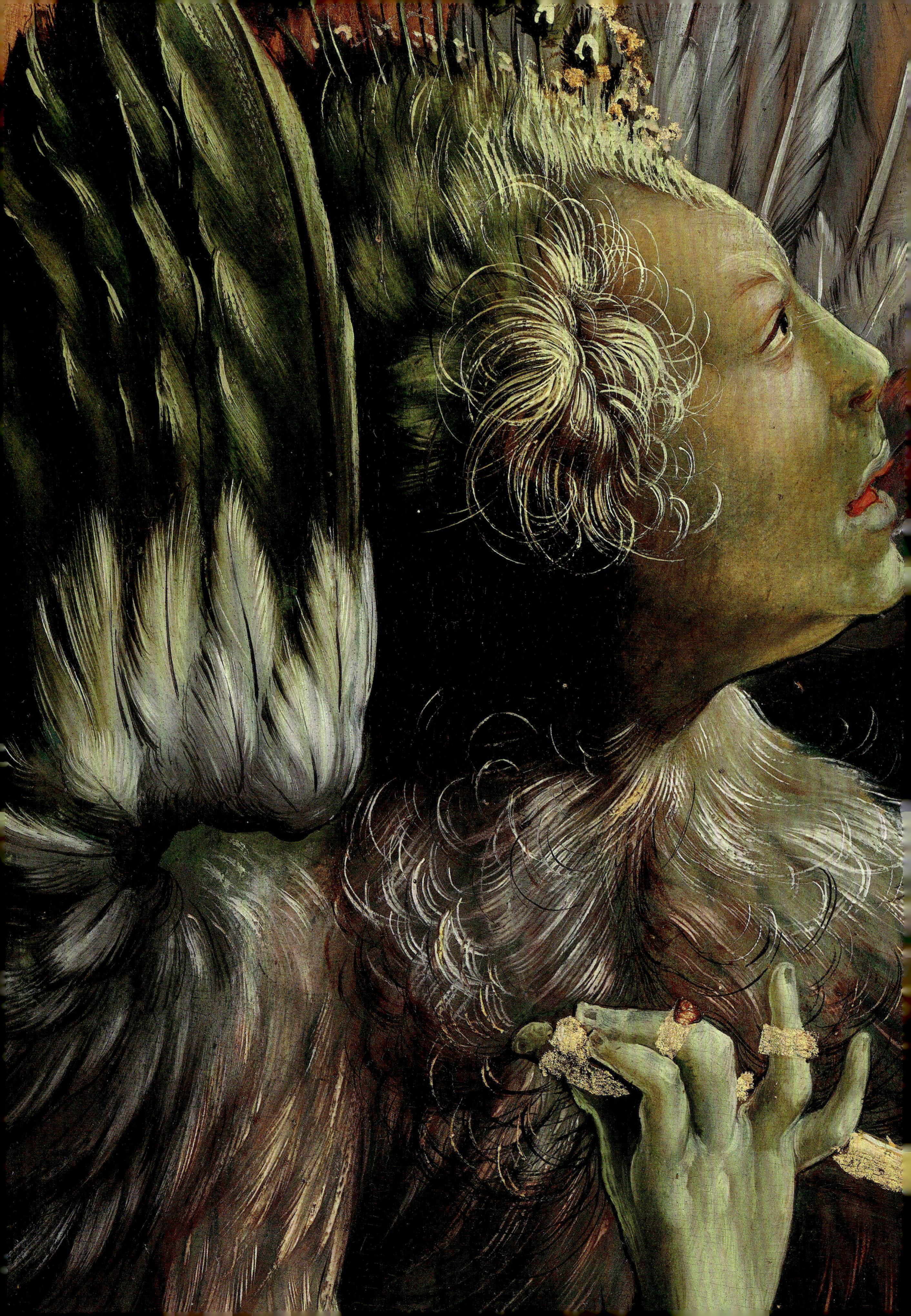

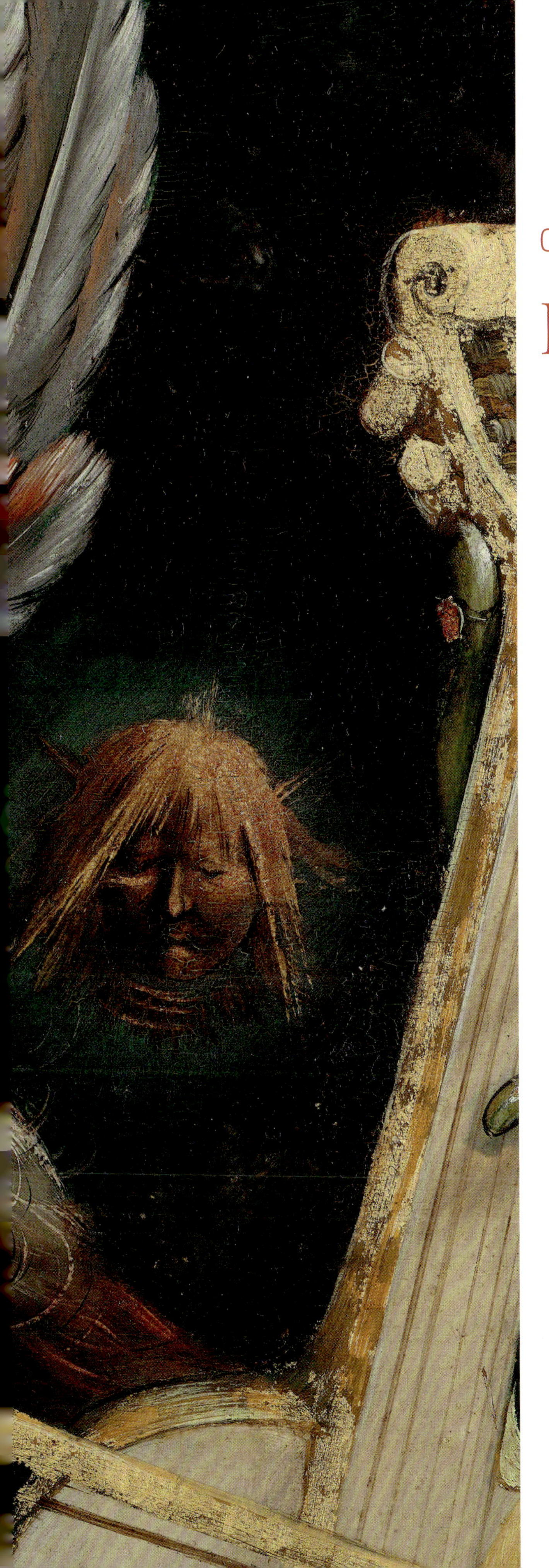

CHAPTER III

Isenheim

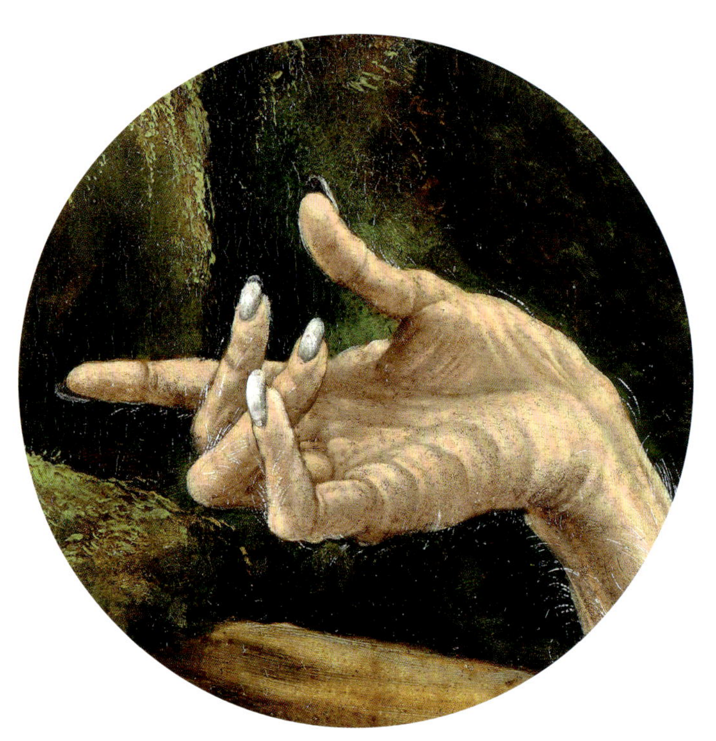

Usually considered Grünewald's most famous work and one of the most renowned masterpieces of European painting, this piece is dated to the years 1512–1516. The exact period can be further narrowed through documentation.

The work in question is a very large, hinged-shutter altarpiece created for the main altar in the church of the Antonite monastery in Isenheim, a village in Alsace between Strasbourg and Colmar, where it is now located, the pride of the Musée d'Unterlinden.

Today, fully opened, it measures about 340 × 420 cm overall, but it must be considered that the original frame, most certainly surmounted by a large, sculpted fastigium, is completely missing.[1]

The Antonites were a large and powerful religious family who wore the habit and followed the Rule of the Augustinian Order.[2] In Renaissance Germany, the Order of St. Augustine was one of the most morally strict and, above all, the most prestigious from a cultural point of view. In fact, Johann von Staupitz, the vicar general of the German Congregation of Augustinians, was Martin Luther's mentor, and Luther began teaching at Wittenberg University precisely during the years Mathis was working on the altarpiece.[3]

The Antonites do not correspond *tout court* to the Augustinian Order, but there is no question that the religious brothers of Staupitz and Luther—the most forward-looking from a humanistic standpoint among German religious orders—were the ones who could have influenced their spirituality most. The fact that the preceptor at the Isenheim monastery (whose identity will be discussed later) is depicted in the altarpiece kneeling at the feet of St. Augustine is an eloquent declaration of the importance of the Augustinian Order for the Antonites. Moreover, precisely during the altarpiece creation, Staupitz's influence extended well beyond the strict confines of the Augustinian Order, including, for example, creating in Nuremberg a true *sodalitas Staupiciana* to which Dürer also belonged.[4]

In particular, the Antonites, who also possessed houses in Würzburg and Aschaffenburg, were dedicated to caring for victims of the plague, syphilis and, especially, shingles (also called St. Anthony's fire) which at that time, was a serious, even dramatic disease. The Isenheim preceptory was also very respected for the care it provided.[5]

One of the altarpiece panels, the *Meeting of Saints Anthony the Abbot and Paul the Hermit*, features the coat of arms of Preceptor Guy Guers, native of the Dauphiné [fig. 82],[6] who governed the Isenheim preceptory from 1490 to his death in 1516, which would likely be the latest date for the completion of the work.

The innermost side contains painted sculptures, carved by Strasbourg sculptor Niclaus Hagnower (also called Nicolas de Haguenau) [figs. 83–86].[7] Until the perceptive observations of Pantxika Béguerie-De Paepe, it was thought (and some still think[8]) that these were made under the previous prior, Jean d'Orlier (or d'Orliac), who commissioned Martin Schongauer's large altarpiece, also now at the Musée d'Unterlinden (inv. 88BP452).[9] This belief arose because d'Orlier's likeness was seen as the donor kneeling beside the enthroned St. Anthony. However, irrespective of the physiognomical aspect—comparison with the portrait of Jean d'Orlier by Schongauer in the above-mentioned altarpiece, although not decisive, could stand; but it could also be a *post mortem* homage to the preceptor who did so much to complete the monastery church, based on Schongauer's painting, or even an effigy of Guers—the observations of Béguerie-De Paepe are valid: it is improbable that a sculpted

82 | Mathis Grünewald, *Temptations of Saint Anthony* (detail, from the Isenheim altarpiece), ca. 1515. Colmar, Musée d'Unterlinden.

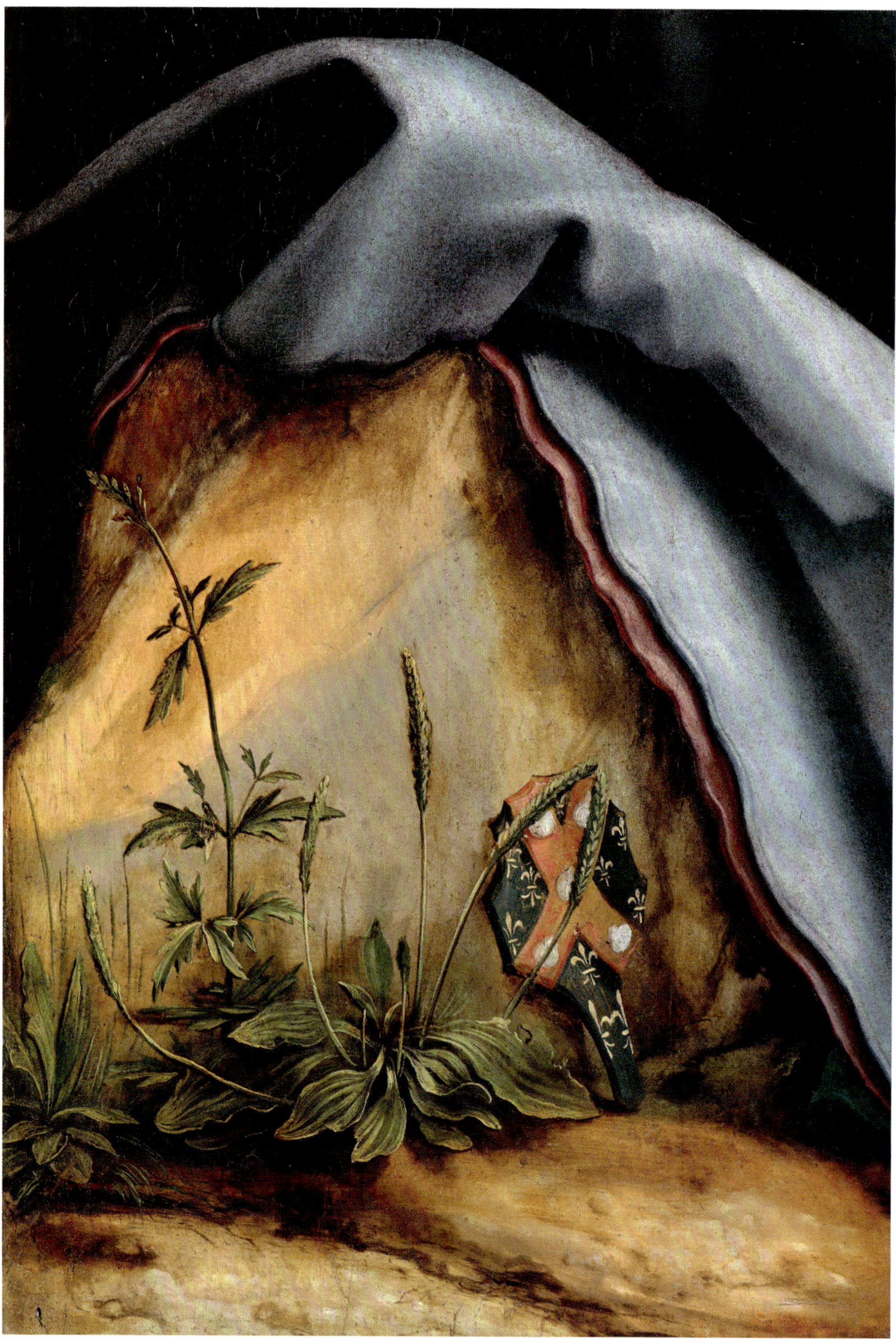

altarpiece would have to wait so many years for the painted panels, and the fact that the sculptures are stylistically closer to the development of Niclaus Hagnower around the years 1510–1515 than earlier.[10]

Additionally, the sculptor may also be responsible for the misunderstanding around the surname Grünewald which, as has been said, Sandrart used in 1675 but does not appear in any document or source prior to the 1630s.[11] It seems to me that the document dated 1429, found in the Strasbourg city archives, has been overlooked. It attests

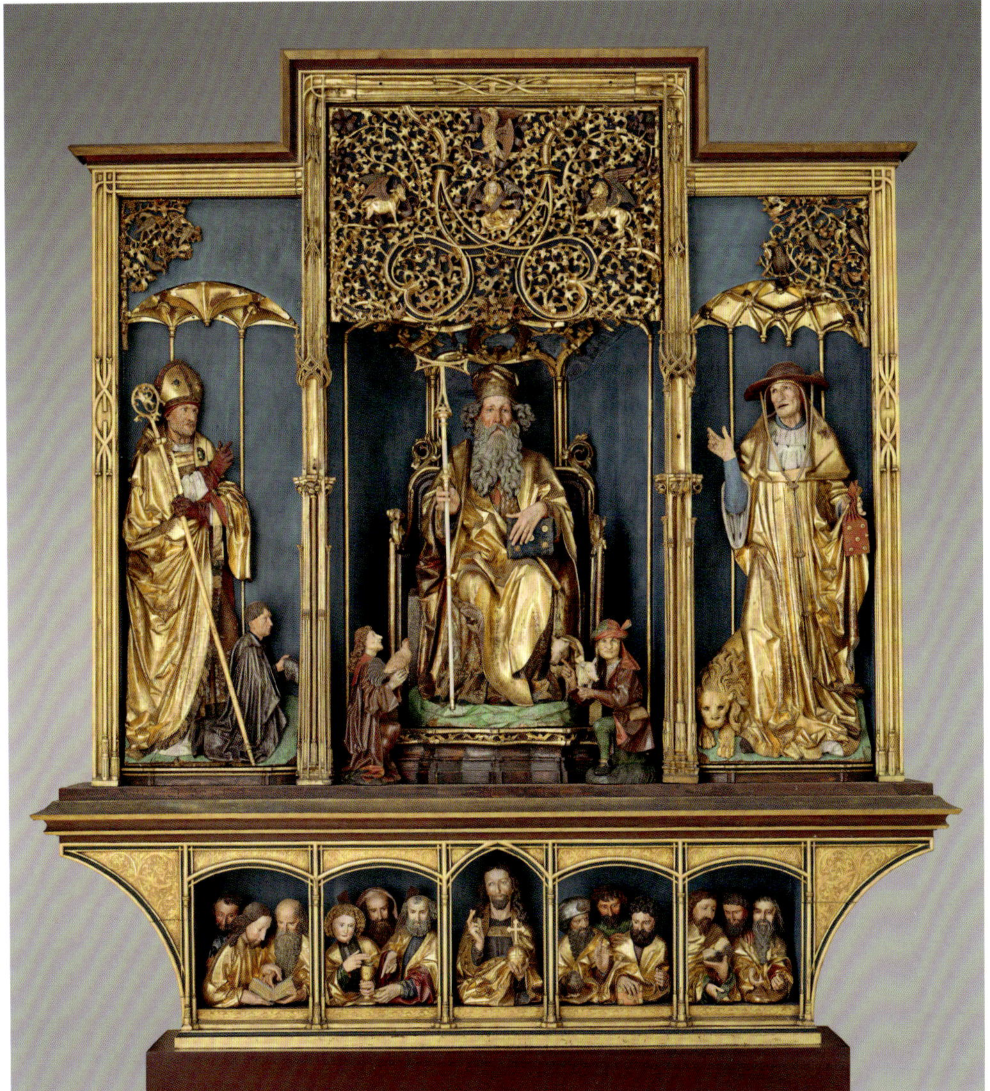

83 | Niclaus Hagnower (and Mathis Grünewald?), *The Saints Anthony the Abbott, Augustine, Jerome with the preceptor Guy Guers (or Jean d'Orlier) and a peasant*, and *Jesus with the Twelve Apostles* (from the Isenheim altarpiece), ca. 1513. Colmar, Musée d'Unterlinden.

to the presence in the city of a Nicolas von Rhine de Haguenau "dit Grünwalt", who purchased land in Hochfeld.[12] The city and the name are the same as the sculptor of the statues in the *Isenheim Altarpiece*, but it should be clarified whether the Nicolas de Haguenau documented in 1429 is the grandfather or other relative of the sculptor, and if there is proof that the surname Grünwalt is also linked to the Hagnower family. It should be said that in the signatures left by Niklaus on his works, this name never appears, and that he, himself, had to acquire Strasbourg citizenship, suggesting that he arrived there from some other place. But if it were the case, however, a plausible hypothesis could be that the now-lost frame of the *Isenheim Altarpiece* bore the signature of the sculptor, whose surname would later be transferred to the sculptor of the more famous painted panels.[13] The not-infrequent presence of the surname Grünewald or Grünwalt in Strasbourg and Aschaffenburg may have contributed to Sandrart's error.[14]

The probable, though not definite, consequence deriving from the logic of the altar's construction, is that Grünewald had not painted the enormous panels in Mainz and then transported them to Isenheim, but rather produced them directly on-site. Or, as Béguerie-De Paepe suggests, in Strasbourg in the workshop of Niclaus, whose

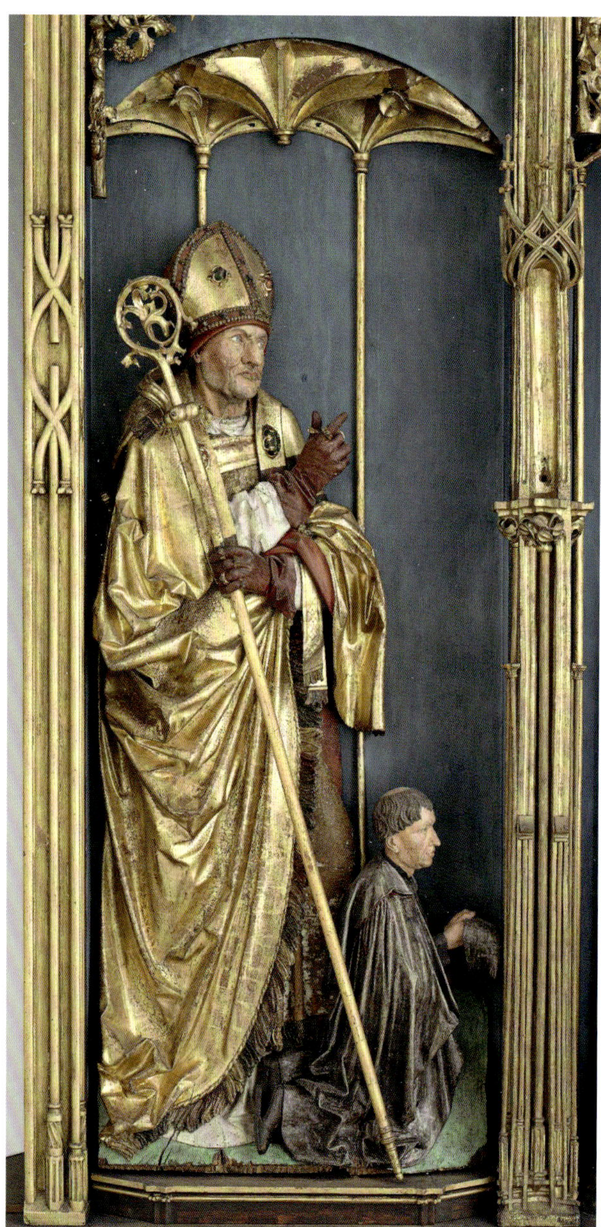

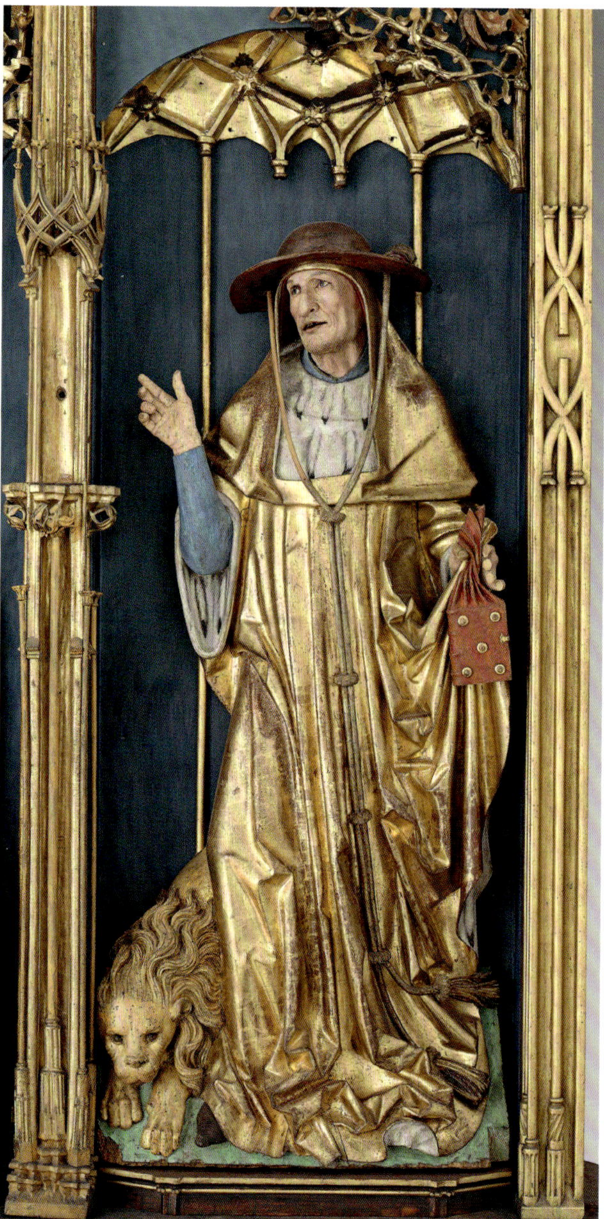

statues, it is then possible, could have been painted by Mathis personally.[15] In fact, as Pantxika Béguerie-De Paepe so kindly informs me, the recent restoration of the altarpiece has shown that stibine had been detected in the polychromy of the sculptures. Stibine is a rare antimony sulfide-based pigment, which is also found in the chain mail of the soldier in the foreground in the altarpiece panel depicting the *Resurrection*. The restoration, which results, when published, will significantly enhance our knowledge of this painter, has revealed a very high-quality color scheme, filled with detailing and chromatic innovation, that has even led to discussion about a "Grünewald workshop". However, there is no evidence of the existence of such a workshop and, in fact, works by Mathis appear to have been solely managed by him, supporting my hypothesis about Grünewald's artistic training with a *Fassmaler*.[16]

To further confirm whether the panels were done in Isenheim or Strasbourg, we can consider the similar case of the large altarpiece for the main altar in the Freiburg

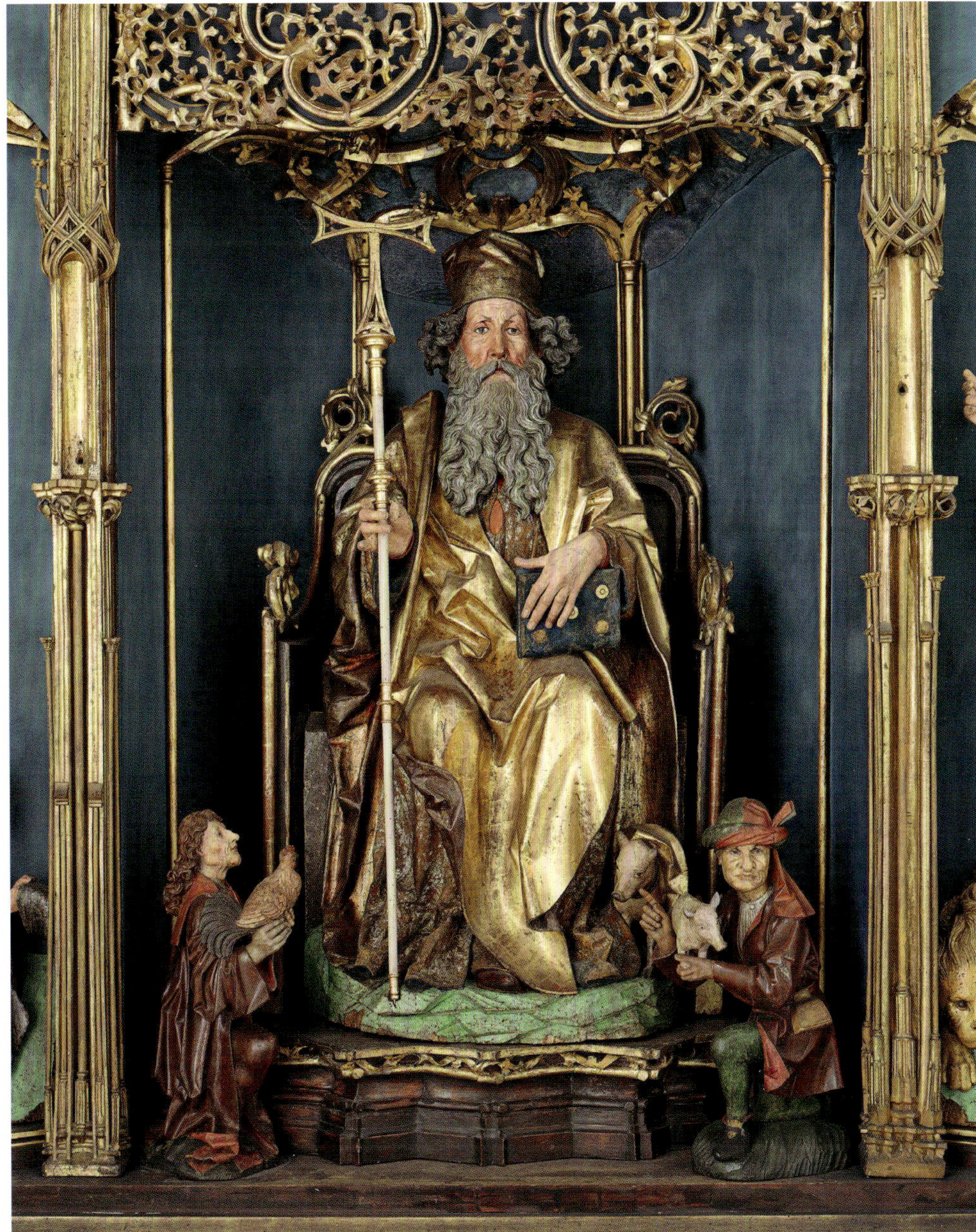

84 | Niclaus Hagnower (and Mathis Grünewald?), *Saint Augustine and the preceptor Guy Guers (or Jean d'Orliac)*, from the Isenheim altarpiece, ca. 1513. Colmar, Musée d'Unterlinden.

86 | Niclaus Hagnower (and Mathis Grünewald?), *Saint Jerome* (from the Isenheim altarpiece), ca. 1513. Colmar, Musée d'Unterlinden.

85 | Niclaus Hagnower (and Mathis Grünewald?), *Saint Anthony the Abbott* (from the Isenheim altarpiece), ca. 1513. Colmar, Musée d'Unterlinden.

cathedral, painted by Strasbourg native Hans Baldung Grien [fig. 87], who for the period he was working on it, from 1512 to 1516 (and so nearly perfectly coinciding with that of Mathis in Isenheim) also lived in Freiburg.[17]

Therefore, we must think in terms of a prolonged absence, which though, I am sure, does not mean he was unable to travel. A prolonged absence which, for the court painter of the Mainz archbishop, would certainly have required special permission. Therefore, it only seems right to reconsider the hypothesis developed by Weixlgärtner, that the arrival of Mathis in Isenheim was mediated by Goswin von Orsoy de Wesalia, the powerful Head Preceptor of the Antonites, who had close ties with the Mainz court and whom we will be meeting again.[18]

It should also be recalled that the Isenheim preceptory had a number of other houses, including one in Würzburg, Grünewald's home city.[19] Personally, however, I do not think this fact played a particular role in him being summoned by Guy Guers.

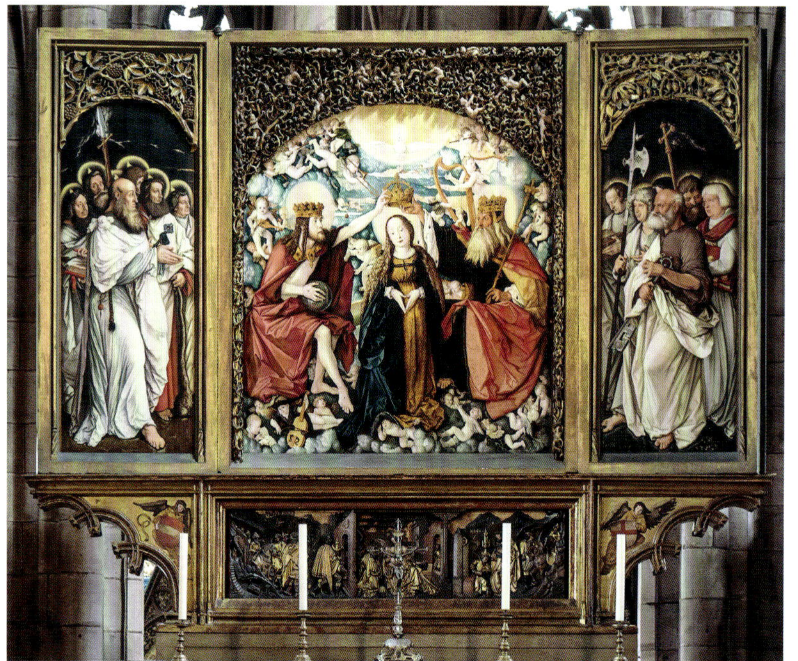

87 | Hans Baldung Grien, Polyptych of the main altar with open wings, 1512–1516. Freiburg im Breisgau, Cathedral.

Reviewing the limited known dates, besides Guers's death in 1516, we know of two contracts in Mathis's *post mortem* inventory with carpenter Michael von Altkirch in 1513 and Michael Wesser in 1515, almost certainly the same person. If Grünewald safeguarded these documents, it means they were important to him. Almost certainly he was personally involved in maintaining for a certain number of years something which, in turn, required him to subcontract a part to this Michael Wesser.[20] For those who have some experience with notarial documents from the early 1500s (even, as in my case, more Italian than German), it does not seem at all strange that a major altarpiece would be entrusted entirely to a painter who would personally have to see to its installation and maintenance and, in turn, would have to assign the woodworking to a carpenter he trusted, from whom he would require similar guarantees. This is probably why Mathis retained these documents that were so important to him, and it is difficult to think that in the period 1513–1515, these could have pertained to anything but the *Isenheim Altarpiece*.[21] Unfortunately, the inventory does not provide a summary of the two contracts, but it would seem probable that in 1513 Mathis had ordered the panels he was to paint (it should be recalled that the strict regulations of the German guilds required the separation of the work of sculptors and painters, thus Niclaus Hagnower could not have prepared them), and the 1515 contract could be for the installation of the painted panels. In addition—and this seems to me to be a decisive point—Altkirch is a city in Upper Alsace not far from Isenheim. It is hard to see in what other context Mathis could have contacted a master carpenter in that area. This would give us a chronology of 1513–1515, a 2 to 3-year period essentially compatible with the requirements of a work of that size, with the date of "1515" seemingly inscribed on Mary Magdalene's ointment jar in the *Crucifixion*. If, as will be seen, there was a short extension in this period, it was not long enough to impact the time frame we are proposing at all.

In addition, as has been noted a number of times, there were hearings in Frankfurt in 1514 in the trial regarding work on the Aschaffenburg castle fireplace, and from these acts, we gather, among other things, news about activities of the Dominicans in 1511. Mathis is mentioned several times as a key witness, but he never appeared, evidently because he was away or perhaps he never even received the summons.

Dcviating somcwhat from the process used to this point, I suggest a different approach for the altar: first, examine it as a liturgical object, attempting to indicate, in a general way, the iconography. Then, analyse in detail the scenes individually from the perspective of style and materials used, no longer following the iconographical order, but rather the most likely internal chronology.

The altarpiece was the visual culmination of a quite exceptional decorative effort.

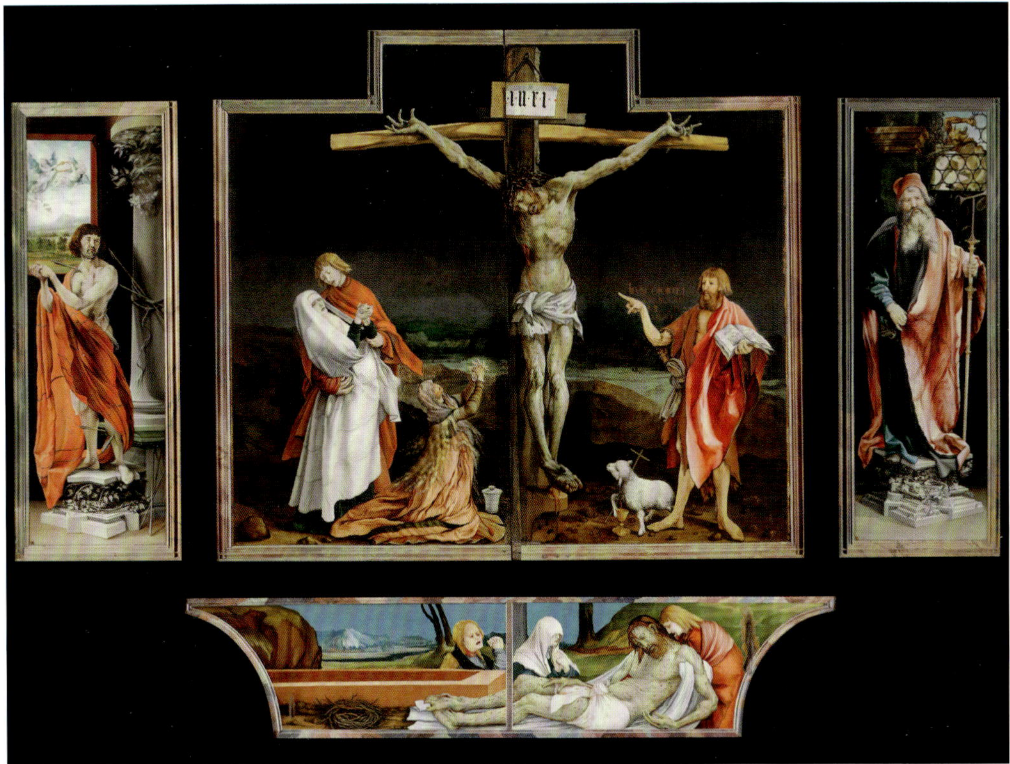

88 | Mathis Grünewald, Isenheim altarpiece, first opening, ca. 1513–1516. Colmar, Musée d'Unterlinden.

Although late (September 25, 1650), the description of a previously mentioned unnamed visitor within the Order gives a good idea of the magnificence of the Church of St. Anthony in Isenheim:

> Par une merveille tenant du miracle, l'argenterie et ornements de l'église, les figures et dorures des autels, la plupart des vitres, les meubles, linges et livres ont estés conservés, et tous les bastiments de la maison en gros. Je n'ay veu aucune maison de l'Ordre en laquelle il y eust tant et de si bons livres qu'icy, excepté Saint-Antoine et Paris, ny aucune de nos églises si belle en sa structure, avec ses voultes bien peintes, les vitres aussi riches que celles de la Sainte Chapelle du Palais à Paris, et les dix autels garnis de leurs petits retables antiques, pleins de figures bien faictes, dorés admirablement bien. Le choeur est tout entire travaillé à jour, avec des petites figures d'une menuyserie aprochant de celle des Dominicains de Troyes, le jubé fort bien faict, avec ses petites voultes et les fusts des deux orgues, mais sans tuyaux.[22]

During ordinary times in the liturgical year, worshippers were faced by the large *Crucifixion* flanked by the images of *St. Anthony the Abbot*, the saint after whom the Order was named and protector against "St. Anthony's fire" (shingles), and *St. Sebastian*, traditionally called upon against the plague [fig. 88].

During festivities (probably including Christmas, Easter and others such as Corpus Christi, Epiphany and the even more solemn feast of Pentecost[23]) the two wings on which the *Crucifixion* is painted were opened to display the glorious scenes of the *Annunciation* and the *Resurrection* which flanked the *Allegory of the Incarnation* [fig. 89]. Perhaps on the feast day of St. Anthony, and maybe also of St. Augustine and St. Jerome (sculpted by Niclaus Hagnower), the panels were opened yet again to reveal the radiant sculpted section flanked. by the painted images of the *Meeting of*

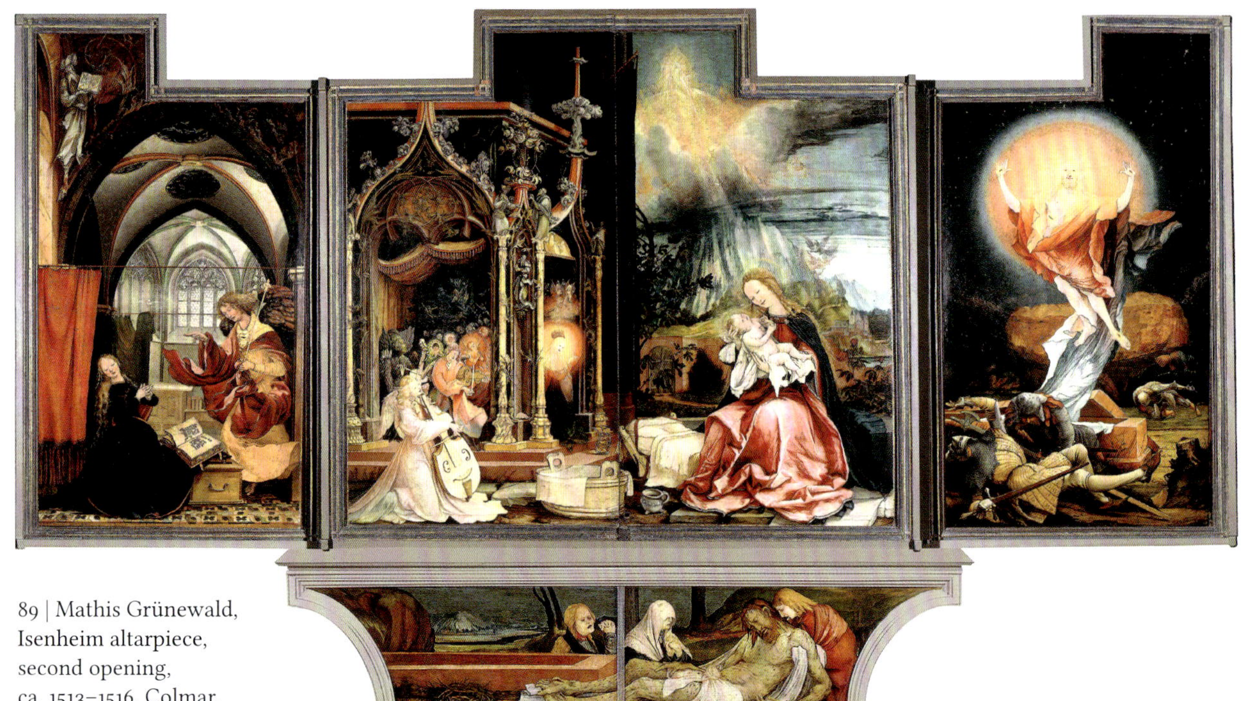

89 | Mathis Grünewald, Isenheim altarpiece, second opening, ca. 1513–1516. Colmar, Musée d'Unterlinden.

90 | Niclaus Hagnower and Mathis Grünewald, Isenheim altarpiece, third opening, ca. 1513–1516. Colmar, Musée d'Unterlinden.

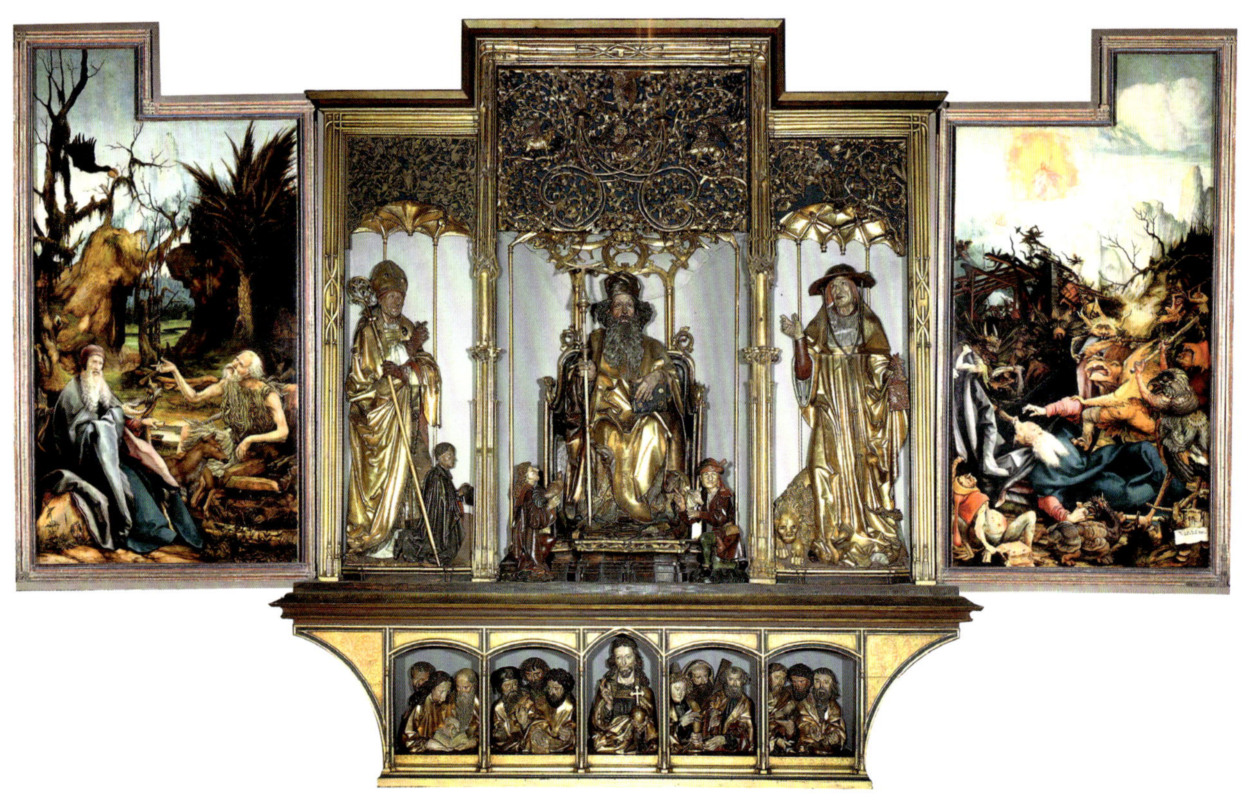

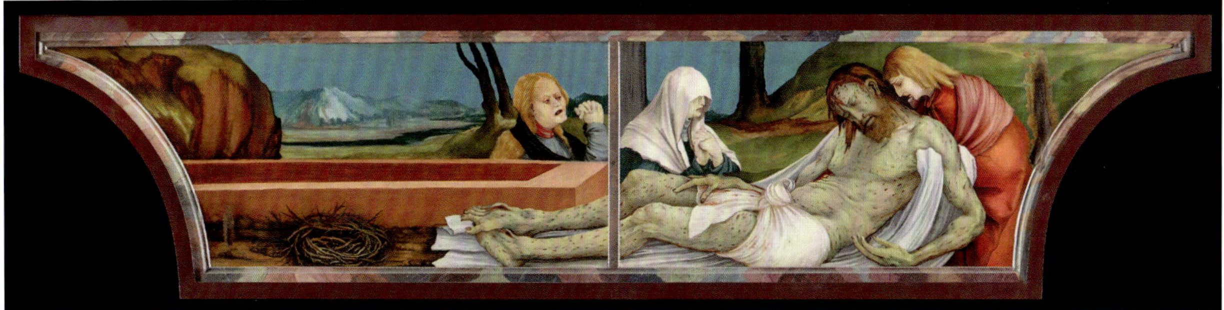

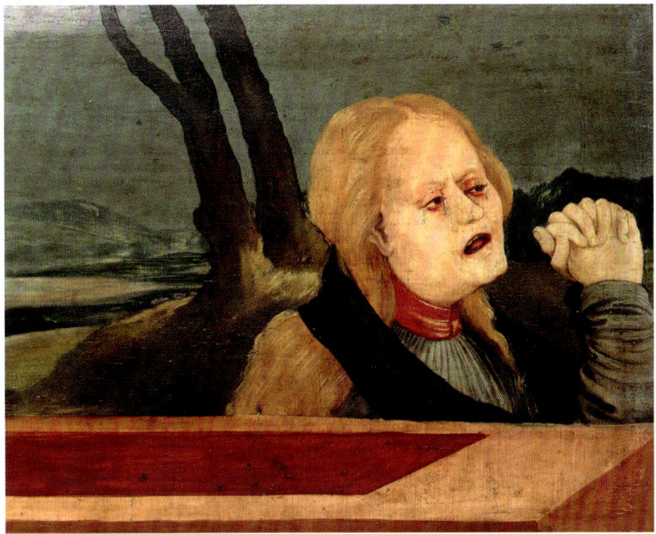

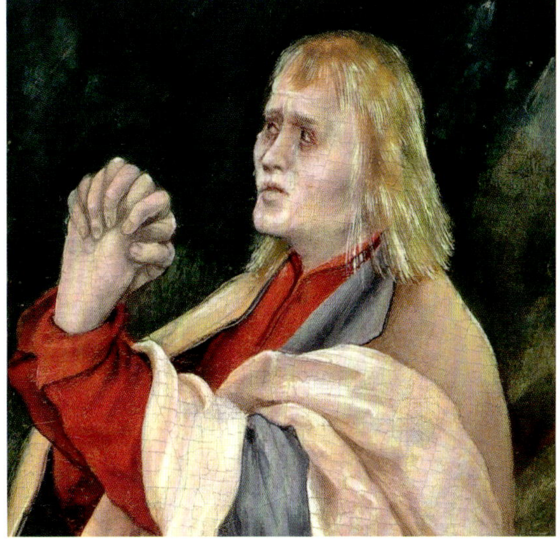

Saints Anthony the Abbot and Paul the Hermit, as well as the *Temptation of St. Anthony* [fig. 90].

Grünewald's expressive apex is taken here to the extreme, with almost unbearable moments of cruelty, tenderness, glory and anguish: these moments serve not only for the artist's pictorial needs but also aim for an emotional impact on pilgrims and the sick.

Having explained how the altarpiece was presented in the church of the Antonites in Isenheim (something the reader must always keep in mind), we now turn to the stylistic, and when appropriate, iconographic, examination of the individual paintings.

I dare say no one could doubt that the oldest scene, still closely tied to previous experiences, is the hinged predella depicting the *Lamentation of Christ* (overall 67 × 341 cm) [fig. 91]. It is a work often underrated compared with the other panels of the altarpiece, even to the point of being considered the work of a collaborator.[24] Once again, it shows itself to be completely tied to the expressive style of the Kress *Small Crucifixion*: the same colors and the same draping. Even the face of Mary Magdalene [fig. 92] is disfigured by the same pallor and the same swollen, red eyes of the *St. John* from the Washington *Crucifixion* [fig. 93], and she wrings her hands in the same way. We also see a more monumental Christ, despite being in the throes of martyrdom, and an immensely desolate and bleak landscape. As if having dispersed the thick shadows of the *Crucifixion* to be replaced by a flat, oppressive sky, the world has reawakened bare and deserted, only faintly illuminated by a dark, muted glimmer that is more distressing than the dead of the night. The compositional design, with Christ

91 | Mathis Grünewald, *Lamentation of Christ* (from the Isenheim altarpiece), ca. 1513. Colmar, Musée d'Unterlinden.

92 | Mathis Grünewald, *Lamentation of Christ* (detail, from the Isenheim altarpiece), ca. 1513. Colmar, Musée d'Unterlinden.

93 | Mathis Grünewald, *Crucifixion* (detail), ca. 1512. Washington, National Gallery of Art, Kress Collection, inv. 1961.919.

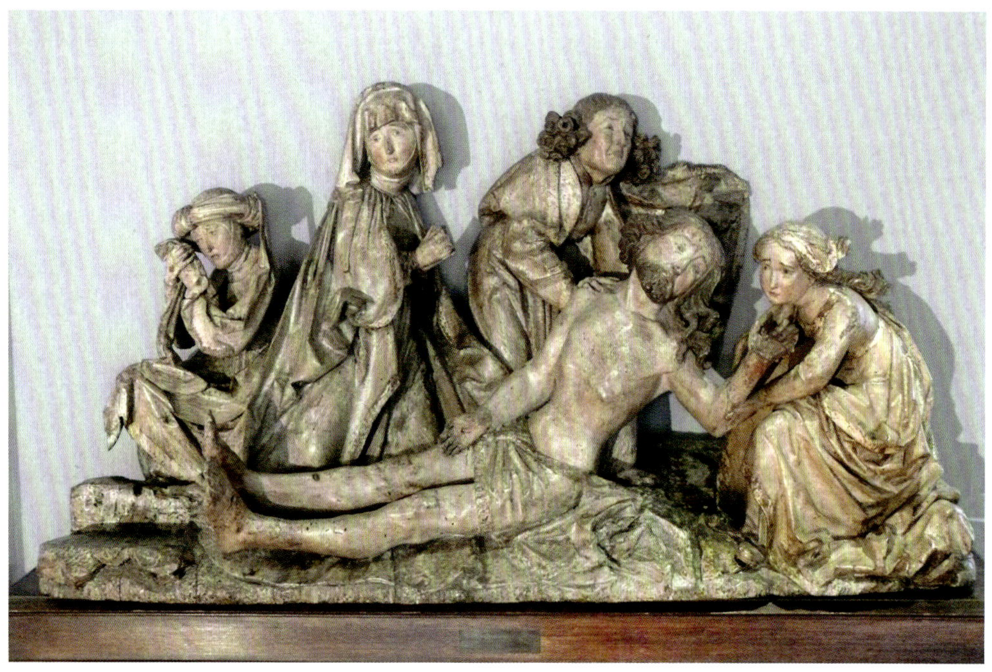

94 | Niclaus Hagnower, *Lamentation of Christ*, ca. 1501. Strasbourg, College Episcopal Saint Étienne.

lying towards the right and his chest raised, is fairly common in Germany, both in painting (for example, the *Lamentation* of the same period by Hans Baldung Grien, dated 1513, at the Tiroler Landesmuseum in Innsbruck, inv. Gem 899),[25] or, even closer to our altar, the sculpture of the same subject by Niclaus Hagnower in 1501 (today at the College Episcopal Saint Étienne, Strasbourg) [fig. 94], which was also created as the predella of a large altarpiece for the main altar of the Strasbourg cathedral.[26]

Although this could be a rash hypothesis given the lack of documentary proof, the fact that Grünewald began work on a relatively minor element could perhaps be seen as a "test" for the client from a painter who had a number of prestigious works to his credit, but was perhaps less-known in Alsace, where, over twenty years after the death of Schongauer, the more famous painter was Baldung Grien. But Baldung Grien was absent from Strasbourg since 1511, and succeeded in making a name for himself in France (he is cited as "Hans Grun", among many other painters, including Perugino, Mantegna, Leonardo, Michelangelo, Hugo van der Goes, a "Lucas" who could be Cranach or van Leiden, Dürer—but not Grünewald—by Jean Pelerin Viator in *De Artificiali Perspectiva*, Toul 1521).[27]

The second scene to be painted was probably that of the *Annunciation* [fig. 95].

To a certain extent, the layout is once again that of the Virgin Mary in the Berlin drawing we have already seen, but here Mathis accentuates the dramatic turning aside. With the appearance of the angel, Mary does not merely shield herself with her hand, just somewhat surprised, but rather turns away quickly, almost in horror ("as if to the news of an incurable disease", wrote John Berger;[28] and even better, as a poem, Margherita Guidacci: "The hawk, not the dove, falls from the sky—she is the dove, frightened, / who averts her gaze and would like to hide / and joins, trembling, almost in defense, her hands").[29] As the work progressed, Mathis seems to have made decisions rather than planning everything in advance. This appears evidently in the preparatory drawing in black chalk, also in Berlin (Staatliche Museen, Kupferstichkabinett, inv. KdZ 12037, 160 × 148 mm) [fig. 96].[30] This drawing offers an approach similar to those for the *Transfiguration*, but simplified, without the use

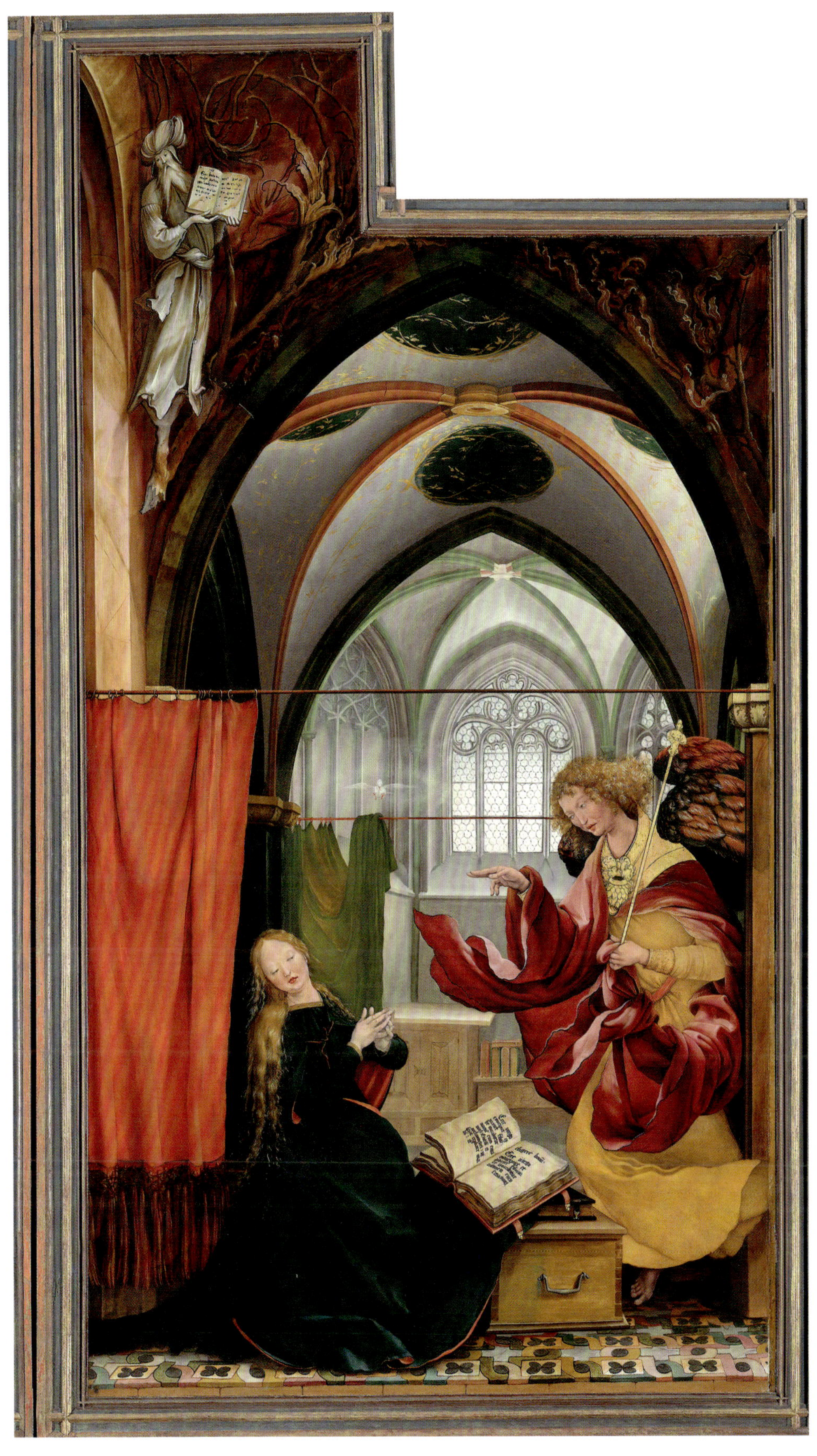

95 | Mathis Grünewald, *Annunciation* (from the Isenheim altarpiece), ca. 1513. Colmar, Musée d'Unterlinden.

96 | Mathis Grünewald, *Annunciation*, ca. 1513. Berlin, Staatliche Museen, Kupferstichkabinett, inv. KdZ 12037.

97 | Mathis Grünewald, *Annunciation* (detail from the IR-photograph), from the Isenheim altarpiece, ca. 1513. Colmar, Musée d'Unterlinden.

98 | Mathis Grünewald, *Annunciation* (detail from the IR-photograph), from the Isenheim altarpiece, ca. 1513. Colmar, Musée d'Unterlinden.

99 | Jean Pelerin Viator, *De Artificiali Perspectiva*, Toul 1505, c. E 1 verso.

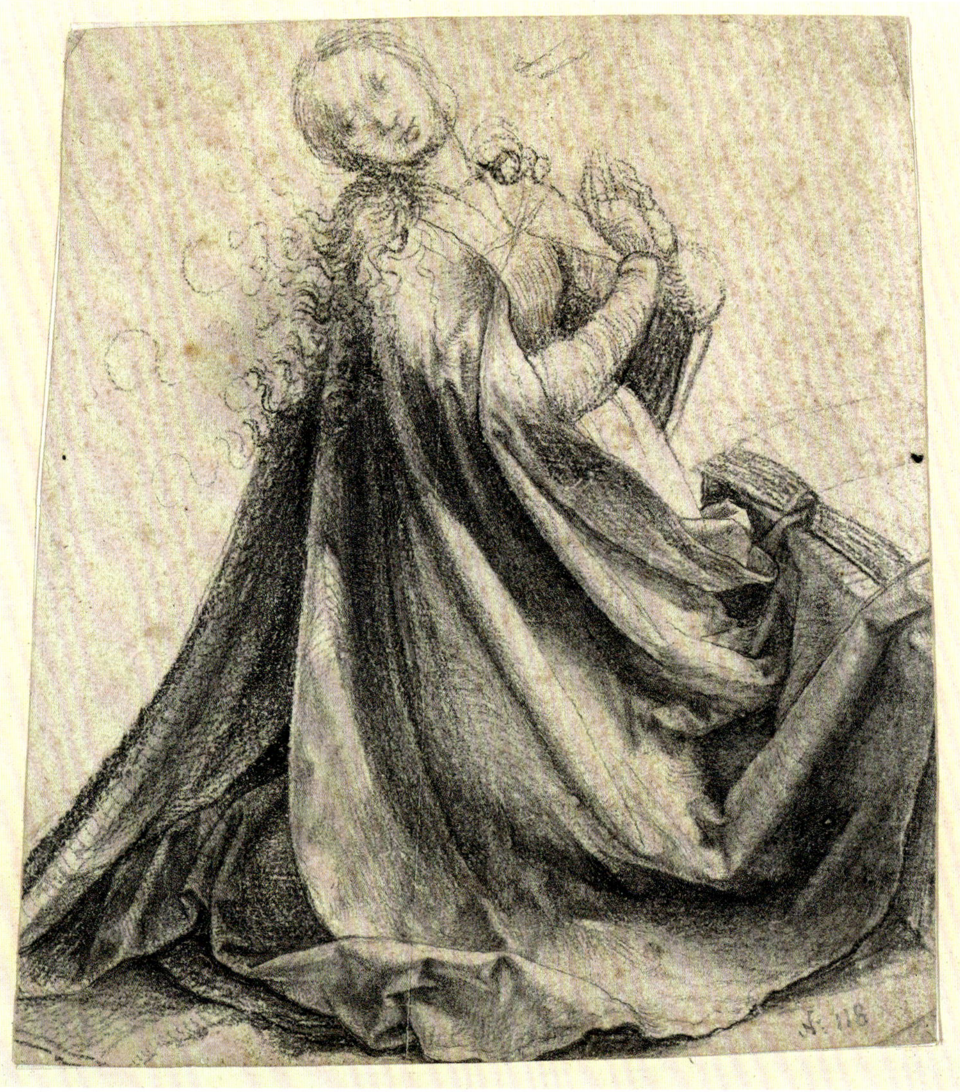

of white highlighting. Compared with the other drawing of the same subject, this Mary appears more dynamic in the twisting of her torso, and more monumental given the volume of her gown with its drapery in parallel folds. But we can see that in the painting, Mathis only followed this approach in part. The hands of the Virgin Mary were initially posed in a more forward position, as scientific examination of the altarpiece has revealed [fig. 97],[31] similarly to the concept presented in the Berlin drawing, then brought back closer to her chest but more angled towards the outside. This creates a more contracted pose, as if the Virgin Mary were trying to make herself smaller and disappear, and in which the chiasmus with the sudden movement of the head becomes more evident. The interlacing of the fingers, which also reveal a *pentimento* that has greatly elongated the index figure of the right hand, provides a sense of greater tension, as does her grimace which deforms her florid, childlike face (again similar, including the hair being blown by the wind, to the *St. Lucy* today in Karlsruhe, thus confirming the early dating of this scene). The detailed drapery studied in chalk in the Berlin drawing has been maintained in the painted version, but the intense, rich blue softens the deep folds. On the other side, the angel breaks in, his garments displaying unusual combinations of richly shaded gold in his robes and

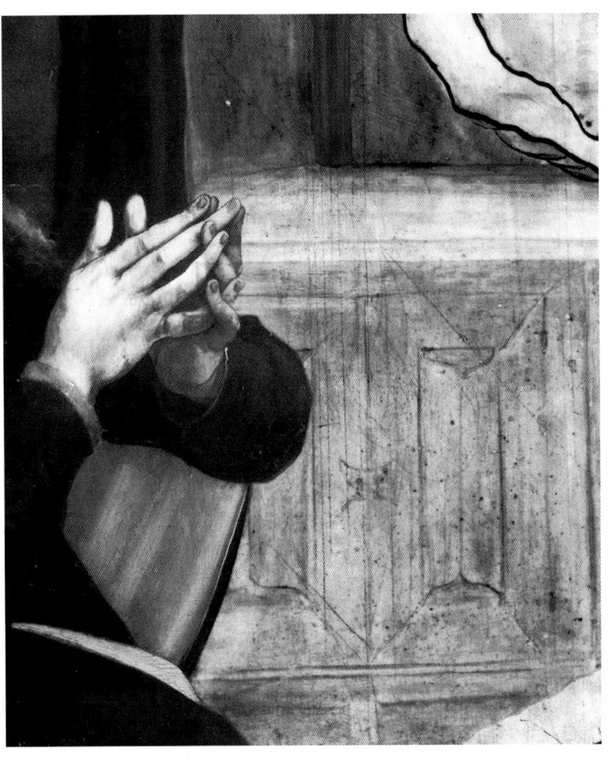

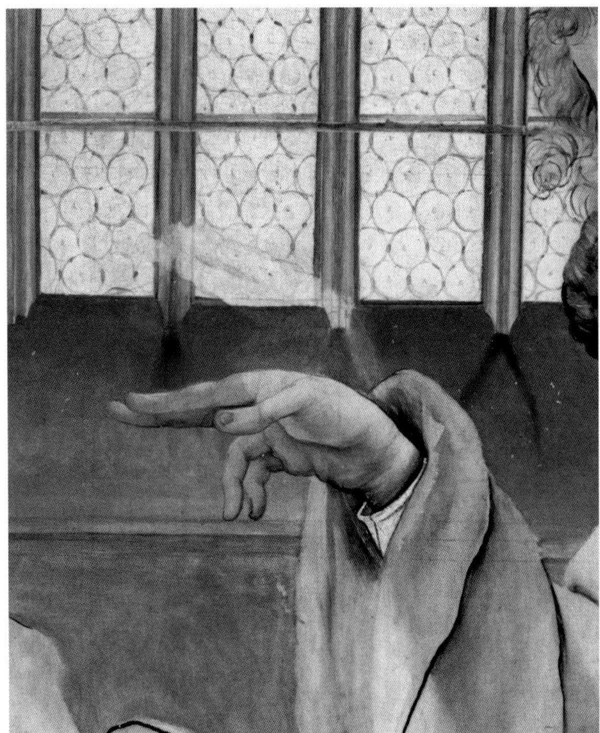

the bright red of his cape. The latter, in turn, like the flourish of the cape in the Virgin Mary in the Rotterdam drawing, breaks into a striking variety of halftones, playing with the intense light of the room filtered by the window at the back, which strikes it in full. We begin to witness Grünewald's complete mastery of color. In modifying the pose of the Virgin Mary, Mathis also reworked that of the angel, lowering his annunciating hand. The familiar gesture of benediction has become a direct, unappealable call, whose dramatic import is well-described by Gertrud Schiller: "The divine power is embodied in the angel with the billowing garment who descends upon Mary in so bewildering a manner that she takes fright and at the same time draws back in ecstasy"[32] [fig. 98]. The definition of the space—a room much like a Gothic chapel in Flemish iconography (the very young Mary lived inside the temple)—although it does not follow to the letter the rules of central perspective, is much more complex than anything attempted by Mathis to this point. I also believe it is probable that the artist sketched the perspective following the example of the plate in c. E 1 verso of the *De artificiali perspectiva* by Jean Pelerin Viator, present only in the first edition, published in Toul in 1505 [fig. 99].[33] It seems very likely that Mathis owned this book, which, while written

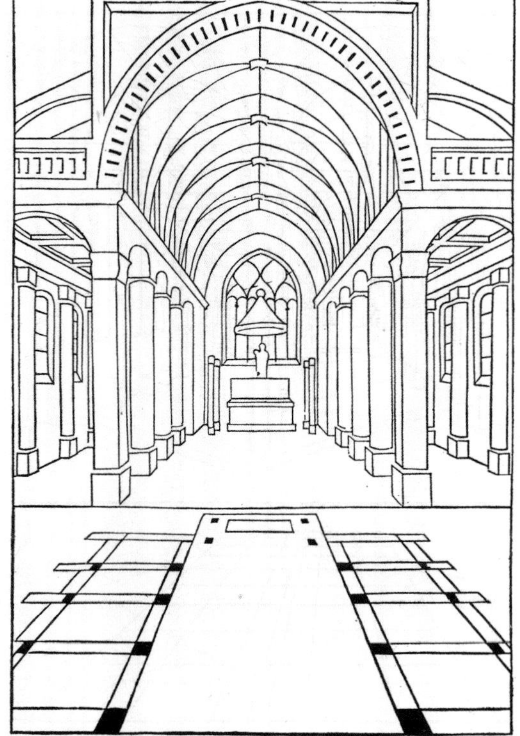

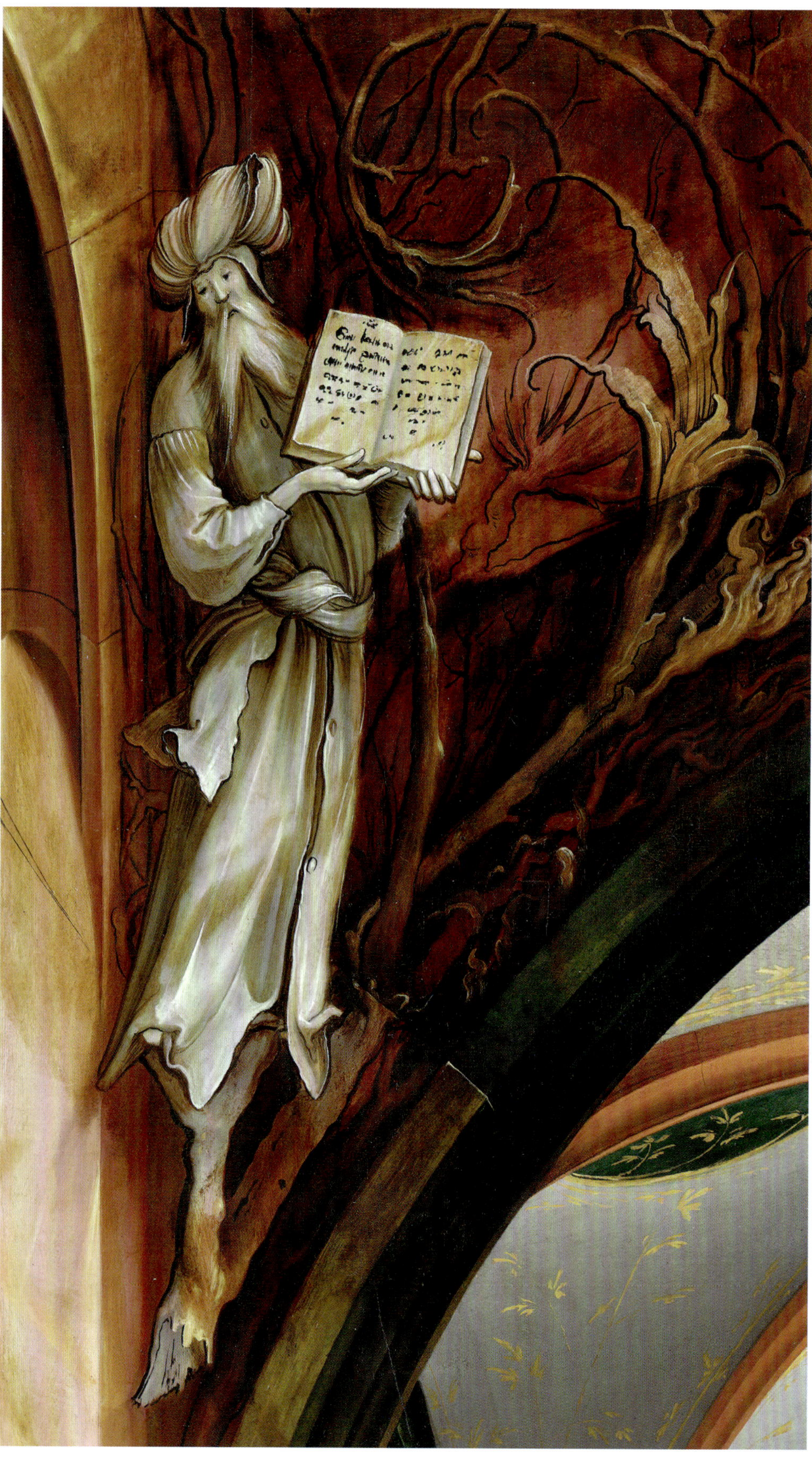

100 | Mathis Grünewald, *Annunciation* (detail, from the Isenheim altarpiece), ca. 1513. Colmar, Musée d'Unterlinden.

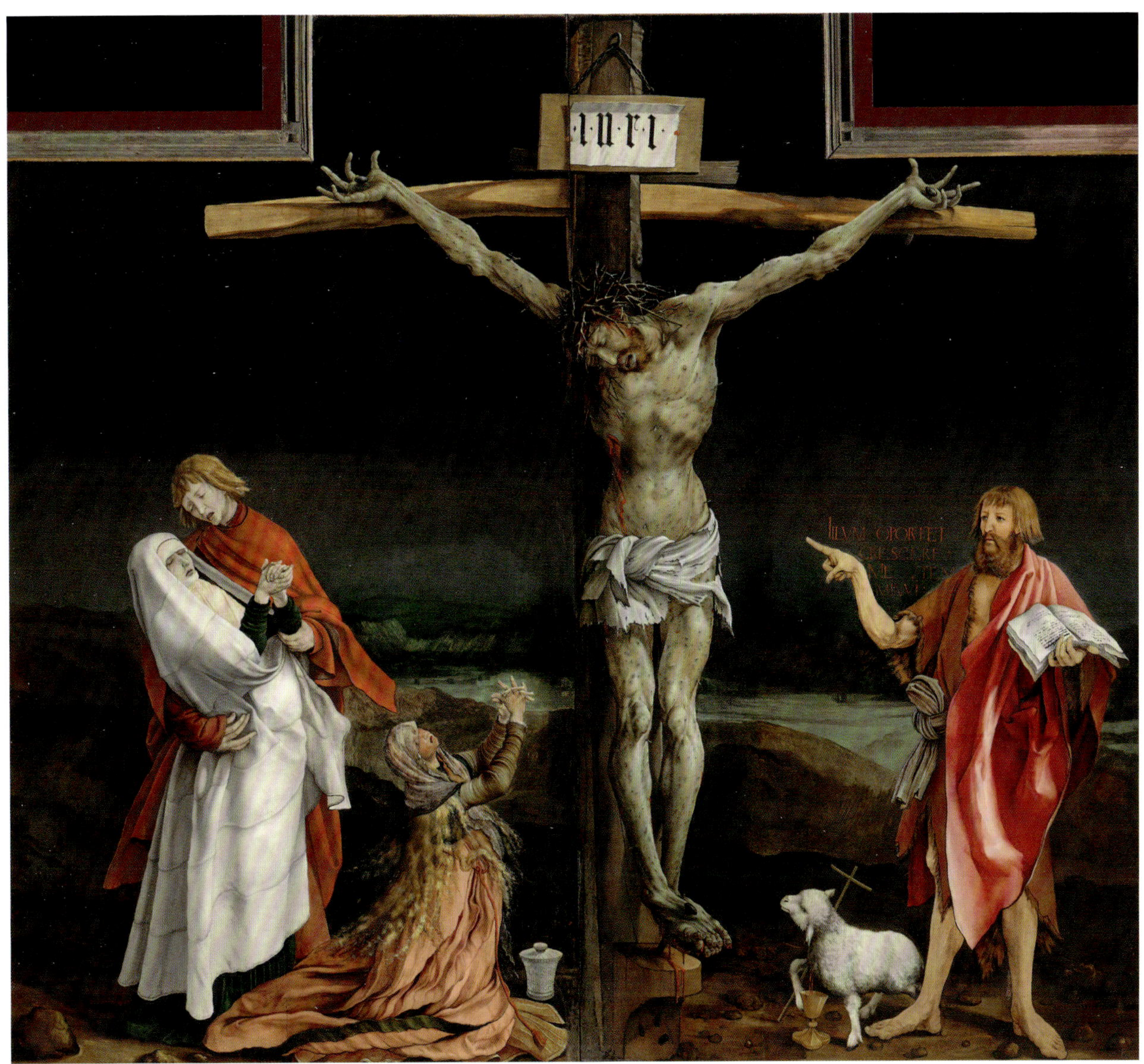

101 | Mathis Grünewald, *Crucifixion* (from the Isenheim altarpiece), ca. 1513–1514. Colmar, Musée d'Unterlinden.

in Latin, featured plates he would have understood at sight. Alternatively, he might have found it in the library of the Isenheim monastery.

However, the real spatial indicator is color, even in its internal references: the red of the angel and of the taut curtain against the blue of the Virgin Mary and the darkness of the shadowed sections of the wall and the vaulting. As well as the elements of virtuosity, such as the unstable dancing of the light on the high Gothic sculpture of the Prophet Isaiah (who, according to the Christian interpretation, foretold in his book the incarnation of the Messiah in a virgin: Isaiah, 7:14, the excerpt also seen in tiny Gothic characters in the book Mary is reading, in which it is also repeated twice)[34] [fig. 100].

After completing this image, Mathis certainly began work on the other side of the panel and, together with another of similar size, conceived his grand and terrifying *Crucifixion* (overall, 258 × 307 cm) [fig. 101].

This is what the faithful, pilgrims, the sick waiting to be cured (often attained, or only hoped for, through devastating amputations),[35] and the dying, saw before them for the greater part of the year as they prayed in church. An imposing Christ,

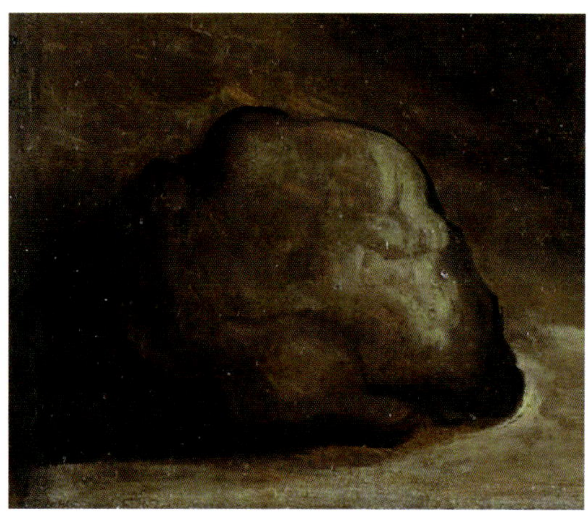

102 | Mathis Grünewald, *Crucifixion* (detail, from the Isenheim altarpiece), ca. 1513–1514. Colmar, Musée d'Unterlinden.

103 | Mathis Grünewald, *Crucifixion* (detail, from the Isenheim altarpiece). ca. 1513–1514. Colmar, Musée d'Unterlinden.

proportionally larger than the other figures, who also stands out for the ashen pallor of his body already almost in decomposition against the fuliginous darkness of the background. This background, whose magnificent restoration was carried out by the team of Anthony Pontabry between 2018 and 2022, can now be examined in more detail.

Behind the Crucifix is a landscape characterized by an unnatural light, providing depth and contributing to rendering this image literally frightening (how many other works in the history of art are *really* scary?). The ethereal gray-green rocks on the left form a series interrupted only by a muted and mysterious reddish light, as if caused by an explosion or, even better, by a lugubrious and silent lava flow. On the right, behind John the Baptist, is a short, intense strip of light, but it is also leaden, like a forgotten neon light left on in the desert. Following the restoration work, the sky is once again variegated. It is not uniformly dark, but loses color towards the top, becoming increasingly somber, as if the bleak light running through it were nothing more than some bizarre dust deposited on the already-deformed bar of the cross.

In the lower-left corner, we see a strange object. It is hard to say if it is an unusual, anthropomorphically shaped rock or a gruesome human skull (perhaps Adam's, often depicted at the foot of the cross), which has become petrified before decomposing completely [fig. 102].

Grünewald revisits and fully develops to their extreme the premises on which his previous, small works on this theme (it would seem, for him, of existential importance) were based. The corpse hangs heavily from the rough wooden cross, a heaviness that is both physical and theological given that this body also bears the weight of our sins according to an image dating back to a text that had circulated widely, the *Cur Deus homo* dialogue by Anselm of Canterbury.[36] By now, it is no longer a question of identifying sculptural or any other type of model. The painter's personality has found its true dimension, and no model could truly be adequate. The head falls forward in a torment of thorns,[37] blood dripping from his forehead, temples and nose. What stands out most are the still-delicate folds of his neck, the final, distant remnant of his human gentleness, the blackened eyelids, and the cyanotic mouth hardened by the effort of a final scream ("when hee had cried againe with a loud voice, yeelded up the ghost"), as shocking as one of Bosch's anthropofish-like monsters [fig. 103]. The extremities of the crucified figure graphically portray the torment and agony. The feet, again overlapped in the description of St. Birgitta, have become a formless, ulcerated mass, from which oozes on the cross and the ground, in two rivulets, blood so horrifyingly dense and thick that it projects its shadow on the wood [fig. 104] (a detail which, alone, is enough to indicate this as a masterpiece).[38] The hands have been surprised by death in a moment of maximum torment, torn by nails where, once again, the light is reflected (the same light external to the painting that illuminates the protagonists), with an unrelenting optical exactitude of Flemish origin [fig. 105].[39] The cold light flows with unexpected softness over even the smallest wounds, the tiniest protrusions of ravaged human tissue. Each traumatic irregularity becomes the occasion for delicate, luminous reflections. We are able to analyse the crumpling of the precociously shriveled skin on the wrists and hands, or the unnatural

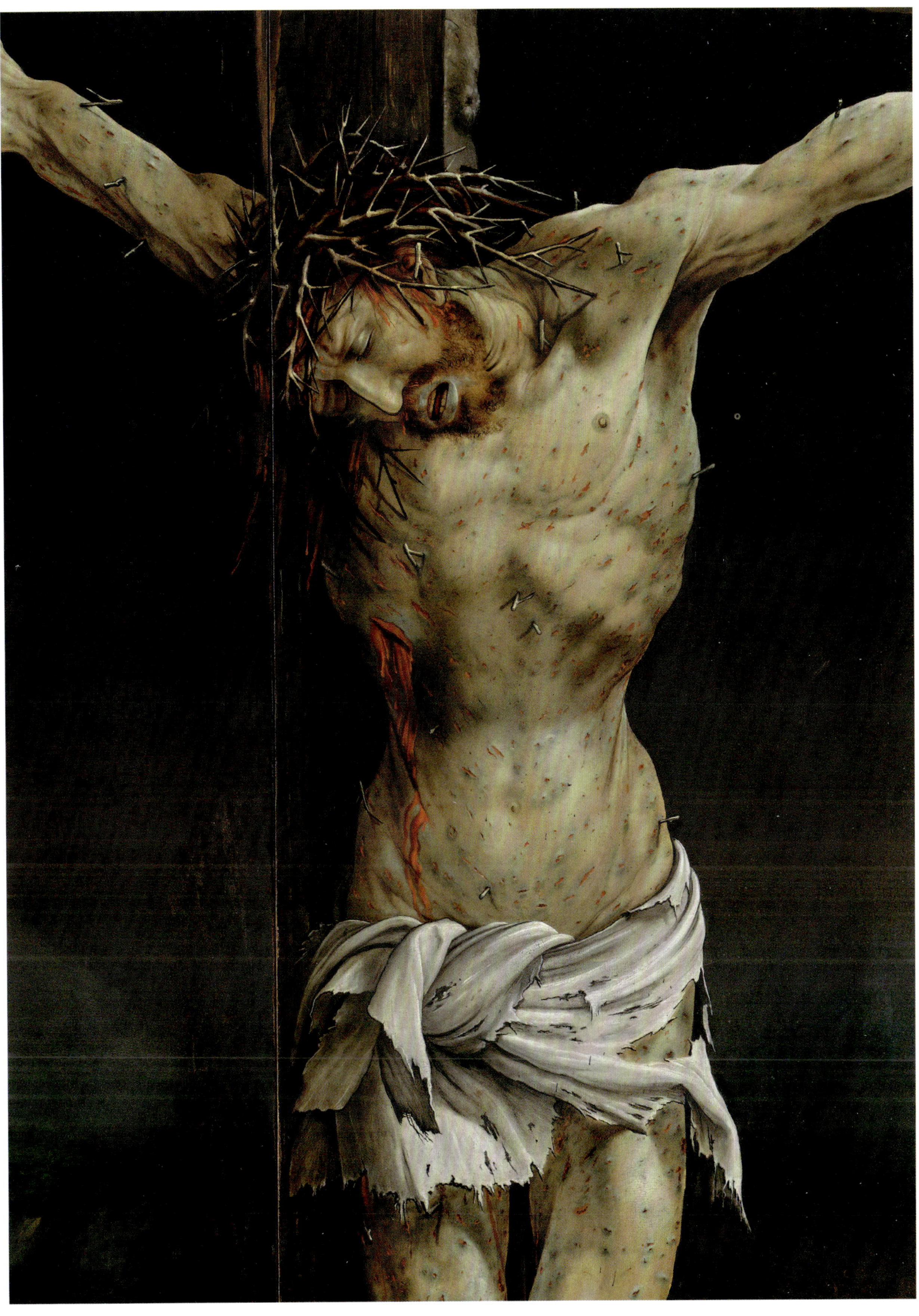

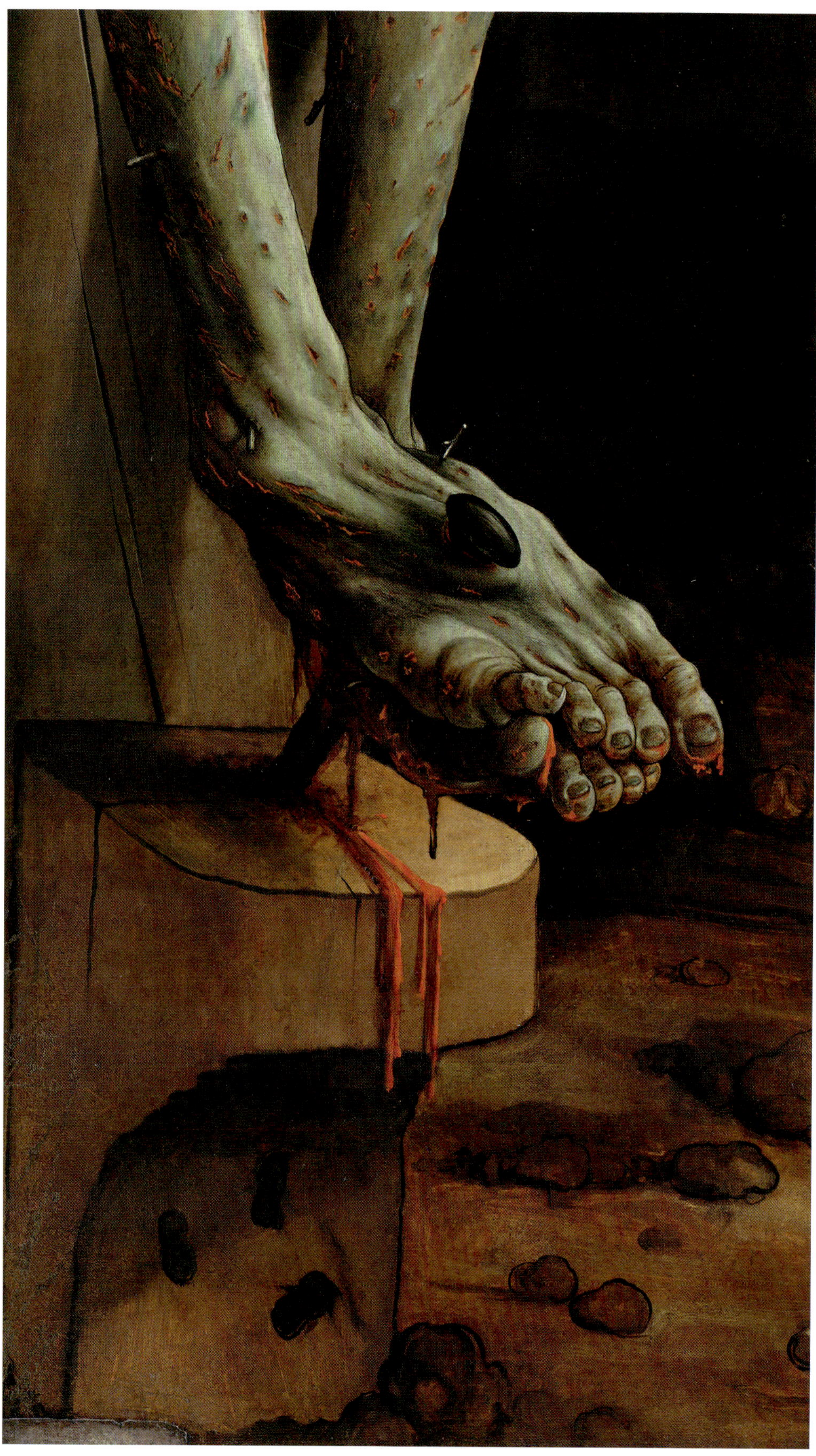

104 | Mathis Grünewald, *Crucifixion* (detail, from the Isenheim altarpiece). ca. 1513–1514. Colmar, Musée d'Unterlinden.

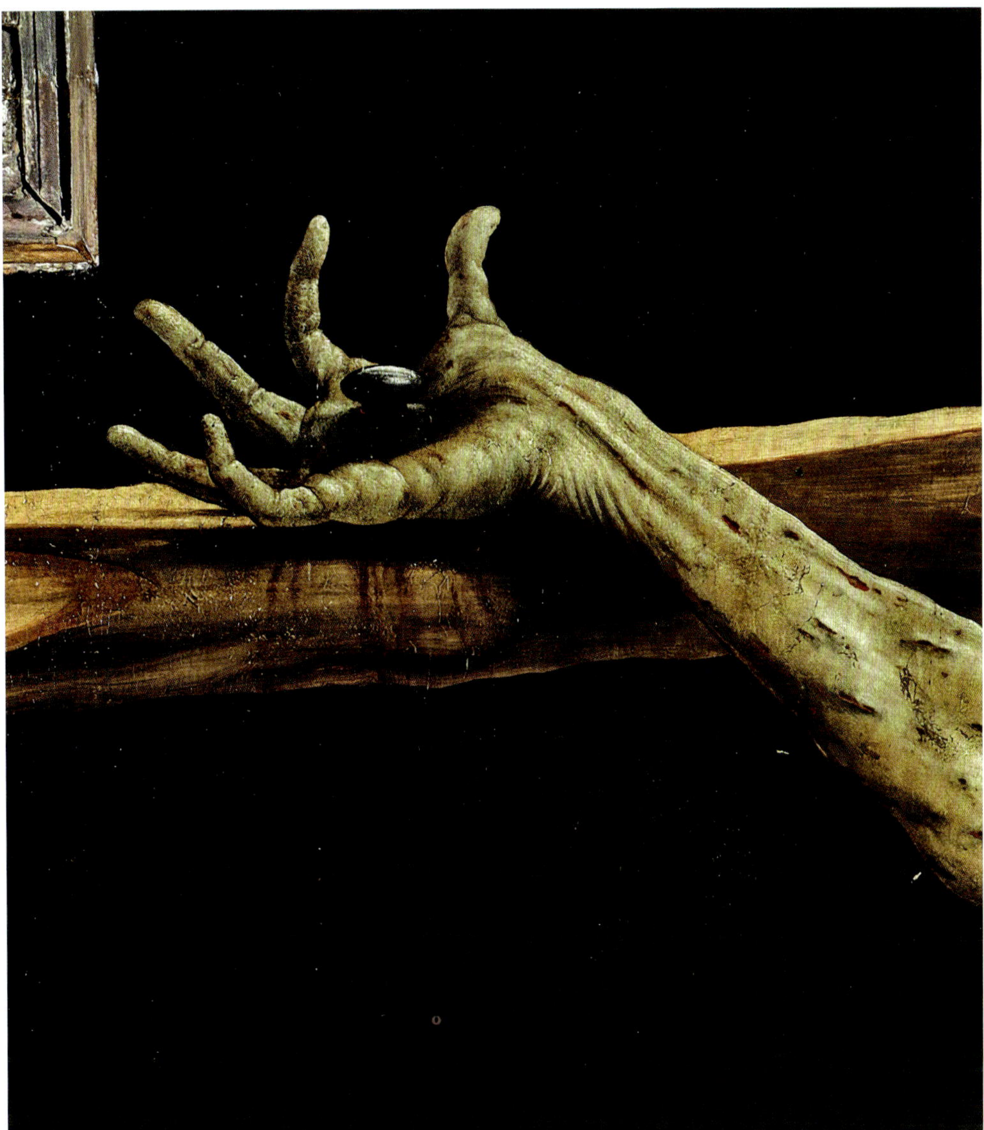

105 | Mathis Grünewald, *Crucifixion* (detail, from the Isenheim altarpiece), ca. 1513–1514. Colmar, Musée d'Unterlinden.

overlapping of the muscles and nerves on the feet, almost bound by the oval nail: the sooty shadow measures the hollows and depressions with a cartographer's precision.

We may also get an initial glimpse of Johann Staupitz's thoughts, particularly evident in the popular and influential sermons given in Salzburg in 1512, just prior to when Mathis began painting the Isenheim panels.[40] Staupitz emphasizes the importance of contemplating Christ's suffering, first externally and then internally, as the key to being able to savor God's "sweetness". He dwells (sermon 11) on horrific aspects, such as the extreme tension in Jesus's crucified body which even leads to the fracturing of his bones,[41] or the decomposition of his flesh, but then immediately interprets this from a metaphysical point of view (sermon 7):

> From all [of Christ's] veins and bones his divine blood, which has the taste of the divine mercy, flows out. Nowhere [on his body] is there any wound or opening that would be too small to enter. So enter in and advance to the soul [of Christ] and through his soul to his divinity. There you shall taste and try his most sweet mercy. God may grant this to me and to you. Amen.[42]

But, above all, it is the skeletal, pustule- and wound-lacerated body that leaves us dumbfounded. Yet I think we can fully agree with the very early interpretation of the great writer Joris-Karl Huysmans (*Trois primitifs*, Paris, 1905), who, even before any real study of Grünewald appeared, had already intuited the correct iconographic interpretation of the work:

> That awful Christ who hung dying over the altar of the Isenheim hospital would seem to have been made in the image of the ergotics who prayed to him; they must surely have found consolation in the thought that this God they invoked had suffered the same torments as themselves, and had become flesh in a form as repulsive as their own; and they must have felt less forsaken, less contemptible. [. . .] His pestiferous Christ would have offended the taste of the courts; he could only be understood by the sick, the unhappy and the monks, by the suffering members of Christ.[43]

This is a Christ who has subsumed into himself the diseases of the sick who made their way to the Antonites in Isenheim. A Christ who died not only from the torment of the cross but also the plague and shingles. According to the poetic interpretation of Ivan Illich, illness was seen as a calling to be answered through the Antonite congregation:

> This affliction was taken as a bodily sign from God, which opened to the sufferer a very special and glorious way of caring for the dying and then dying himself in the community bodily established through this most painful drying off and withering away of the limbs.[44]

Despite the painter's savage *cupio dissolvi*, I think it is possible to see here, as already proposed by Hayum, an Augustinian theme, that of *Christus medicus*, expressed, for example in sermon 38 of the New Testament:

> But he bore with His revilers, because He accepted the cross not as a test of power but as an example of patience. There He healed your wounds where He long bore His own. There He healed you of an eternal death where He deigned to die a temporal death.[45]

Nor would I exclude that the river of blood that flows from the body of Christ could also have, among others, a therapeutic significance in line with a theme common to popular belief in southern Germany since the 14th century.[46] A similar interpretation seems supported by another text, very close chronologically to the *Isenheim Altarpiece* and which was well-known in early 16th-century Germany, la *Viola animae* by Pierre Dorlant, published in 1499: "He [Christ] wished to be wounded that he might repair our wound and poured out his blood that he might by grace revive to life those only half alive."[47] The sick, who as an integral part of their "treatment", prayed before this work, faced a Christ who bore on his body the same wounds they did and they, in turn, shared in his suffering. However, we do not know how these prayers took place because it seems that the Antonite church in Isenheim had a partition. In that case, the altarpiece would normally have been viewed by the faithful only from a distance, and perhaps through a grille,[48] but it is likely that patients, dressed in the Antonite habit, were granted special access.

Once again, we can draw on Staupitz's Salzburg sermons to have a better idea of this practice.

In his first sermon, he writes:

> But, as soon as you are enkindled in your contemplation, close your eyes, but do not remain there. The external picture of the [tortured] body only shows you Christ's suffering in the body, while contemplation of the soul [of Christ] makes this suffering fruitful to you, and it is in the divinity [of Christ] where one finds hidden the kernel of sweetness.[49]

In this ambiance, even if they were not cured, the sick could at least find a reason for their suffering: "It is more pleasing to God if you patiently bear what He sends you, rather than carry out what He commands you to do. Today, suffering is noble and honorable."[50] And it continues to intensify: "Remember these three things: the aftermath of suffering is in the body; discipleship is in the soul; joy is in divinity."[51] Or, as Elias Canetti wrote in reference to his experience in front of the Isenheim Crucifix, in the spring of 1927: "Salvation consists in NOT turning your head away."[52]

Given this context, I find convincing the proposal by Marrow who links the Grünewald Crucifix with the Man of Sorrows in Isaiah 54:4–5:

> vere languores nostros ipse tulit et dolores nostros ipse portavit et nos putavimus eum quasi leprosum et percussum a Deo et humiliatum, ipse autem vulneratus est propter iniquitates nostras, adtritus est propter scelera nostra, disciplina pacis nostrae super eum et livore eius sanati sumus,

and the very popular *Vita Christi* by Ludolph of Saxony:

> Et tunc sanguinis per aculeos coronae de capite extractus, et largiter fluens, tinxit caput et genas ejus, ita ut appareret quasi leprosus, quia sanguis et sputa apposita faciebant eum leproso similem.

In Isenheim, Christ *quasi leprosus* becomes *vere leprosus*, creating an iconographic and emotional short-circuit which, at that time, would probably have been evident to viewers and, above all, those praying.[53]

The group with the Madonna and St. John the Evangelist is equally dramatic: Jesus's mother, pain-stricken, collapses backwards with her hands stiffened in the typical gesture of desolation [fig. 106]. Perhaps here Mathis drew inspiration from a famous passage in Lamentations (1:12) which is traditionally attributed to the prophet Jeremiah, which Christian exegesis connects to the Virgin Mary at the foot of the cross:

> de excelso misit [Deus] ignem in ossibus meis et erudivit me, expandit rete pedibus meis, convertit me retrorsum, posuit me desolatam tota die maerore confectum.[54]

However, the artist does not make use of exaggerated pathos, preferring the cold objectivity of a documentarist, as if leaving the Madonna at the mercy of her own desperation. St. John unnaturally extends his right arm to support her, while his left holds her elbow, creating a sort of paradoxical dance step. Once again, the use of color is masterful. The contrast between the white of the Madonna and the red of St. John not only powerfully strengthens the plastic effect but also accentuates both the prominence of her corpse-like pallor and his frantic encumbrance.

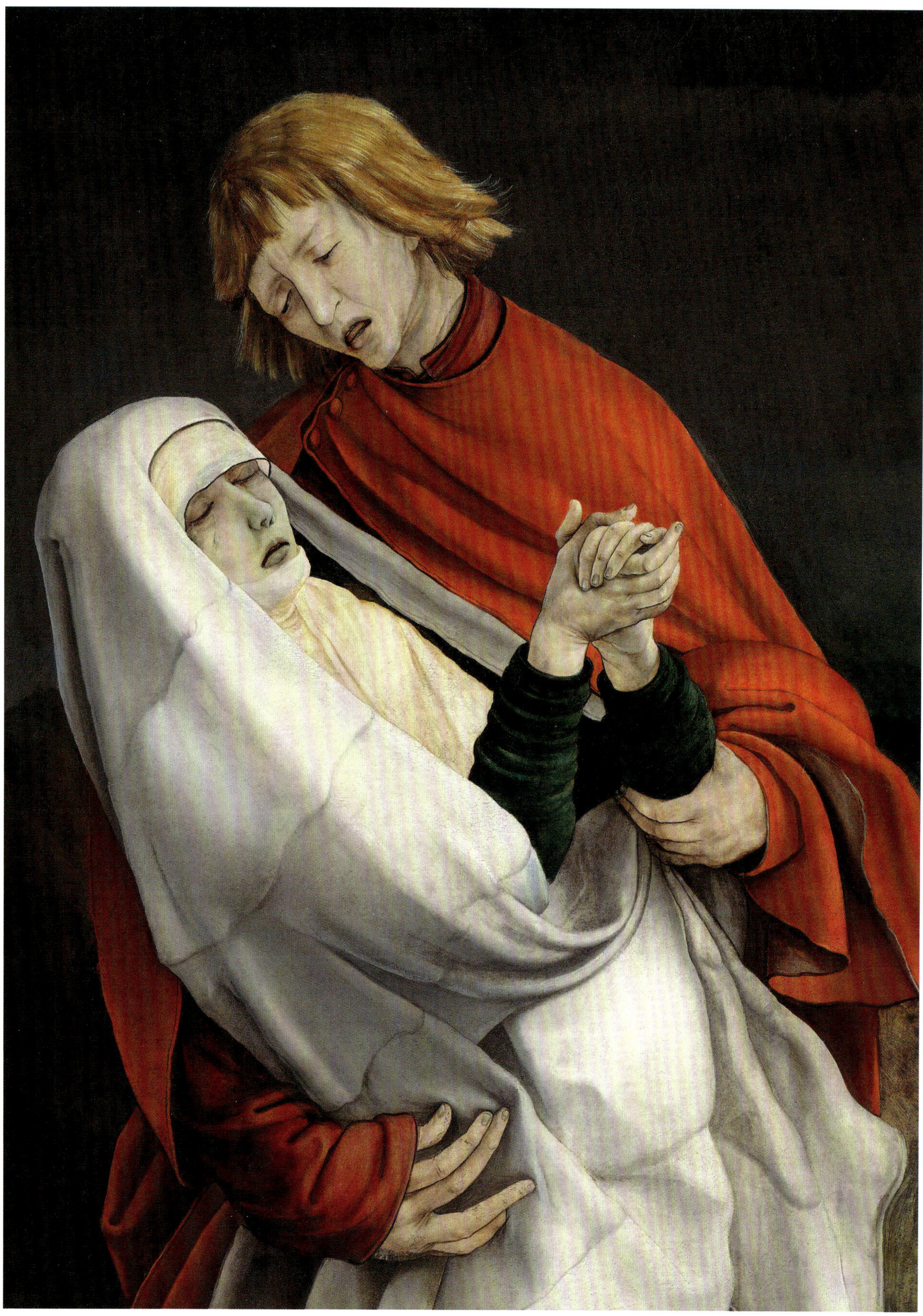

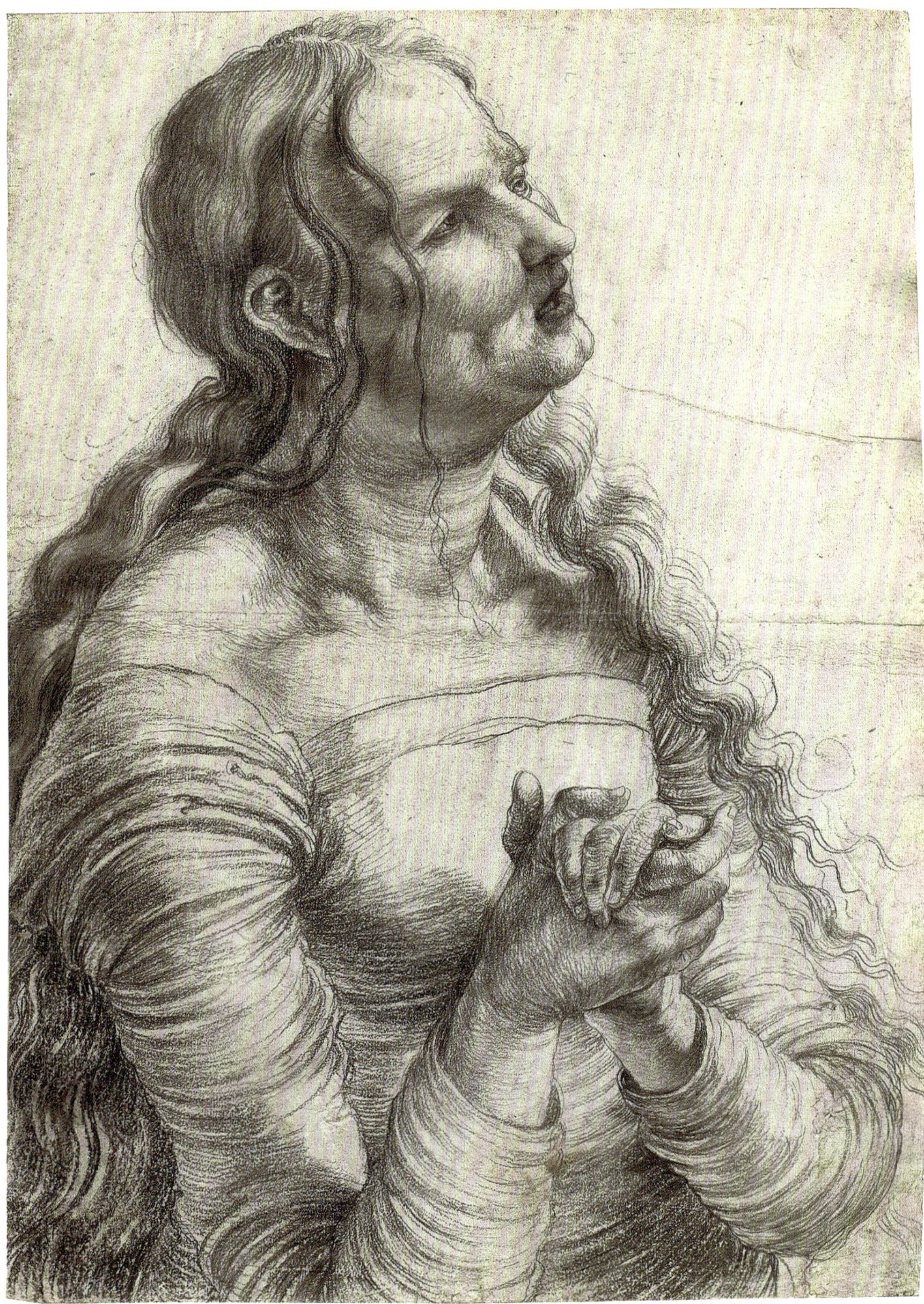

106 | Mathis Grünewald, *Crucifixion* (detail, from the Isenheim altarpiece), ca. 1513–1514. Colmar, Musée d'Unterlinden.

107 | Mathis Grünewald, *Study for a Saint Mary Magdalene*, ca. 1513–1514. Winterthur, Oskar Reinhardt Stiftung, inv. 1926.1.

Evidence suggests that Mathis had originally conceived the scene somewhat differently. Roth notes the correspondence between a drawing with the image of the suffering Mary Magdalene (black chalk, 413 × 302 mm: Winterthur, Oskar Reinhardt Stiftung, inv. 1926.1) [fig. 107] and this painting, particularly in the treatment of the hands.[55] It is worth noting how Mathis's drawing technique has evolved quickly. The shading of the hair and full bodice is still rendered in the way we already know, but we see that the *chiaroscuro* cross-hatching—which is somewhat heavy, perhaps to add to the pathos—tends to follow the body's, although in a non-systematic manner. The result is intense and vibrant and, once again, would seem a response to

108 | Albrecht Dürer, *Christ among the Doctors*, 1506. Madrid, Museo Nacional Thyssen Bornemisza, inv. 134.

109 | Mathis Grünewald, *Crucifixion* (detail, from the Isenheim altarpiece), ca. 1513–1514. Colmar, Musée d'Unterlinden.

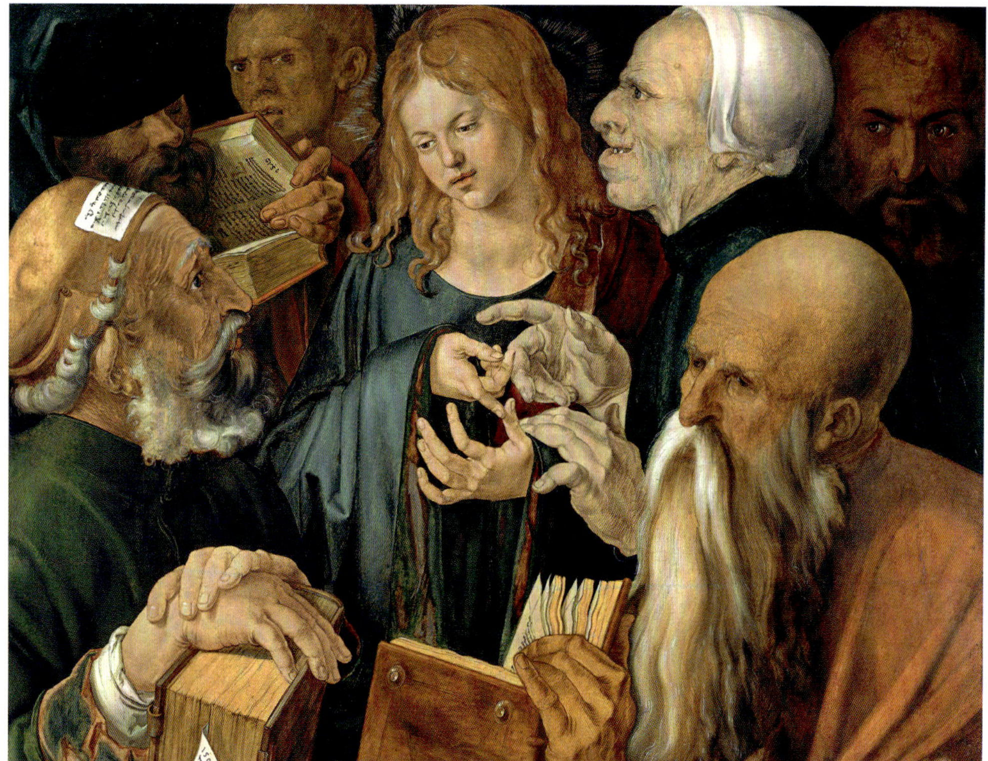

Dürer, in particular to his "Italian" works, such as *Christ Among the Doctors* today at the Thyssen-Bornemisza Museum in Madrid (inv. 134), but painted in 1506 (in Rome, according to some scholars), during the Nuremberg artist's second visit to Italy [fig. 108].[56] This is seen especially in the reference and position of the intertwined hands which corresponds to that of the hands of Christ and the Doctors. In all probability, Grünewald did not have the opportunity to see *this* painting, but the analogy is so strong that it removes any doubt about the fact that, once again, Dürer was a point of reference, both to be respected and contradicted, at the time of the Isenheim works. There are, however, substantial differences. In contrast, Dürer extends irregular cross-hatching across the color, while Grünewald, despite using a similar approach in his drawings, replaces in his paintings the *chiaroscuro* with tonal changes, with unmistakably gentle effects. We have already had the chance to comment on this, but it is worth repeating: this is a methodological difference that is also an indication of a different conception of the relationship between material and light. In Dürer, light rests on the material according to an approach in which they are distinct aspects, while for Grünewald there is no separation: material and light merge to form an indivisible whole. The magnificent hands of the "molded" Madonna, which are both so plastic and so responsive to the shadows reflected from one to the other, are enough to confirm this thesis.

Originally, Mathis probably had in mind an upright Mary Magdalene (perhaps kneeling at the foot of the cross), with her hands intertwined, which he then decided to attribute to the Madonna. Again, here scientific analysis (and even earlier, the extraordinarily good intuition of Schmid)[57] indicates that the first version sketched onto the panel saw the Madonna still standing upright and vigilant, discreetly held by St. John. However, as work progressed, Grünewald decided to portray the moment the Madonna faints, when she falls back, as if turned to stone. As a result, the

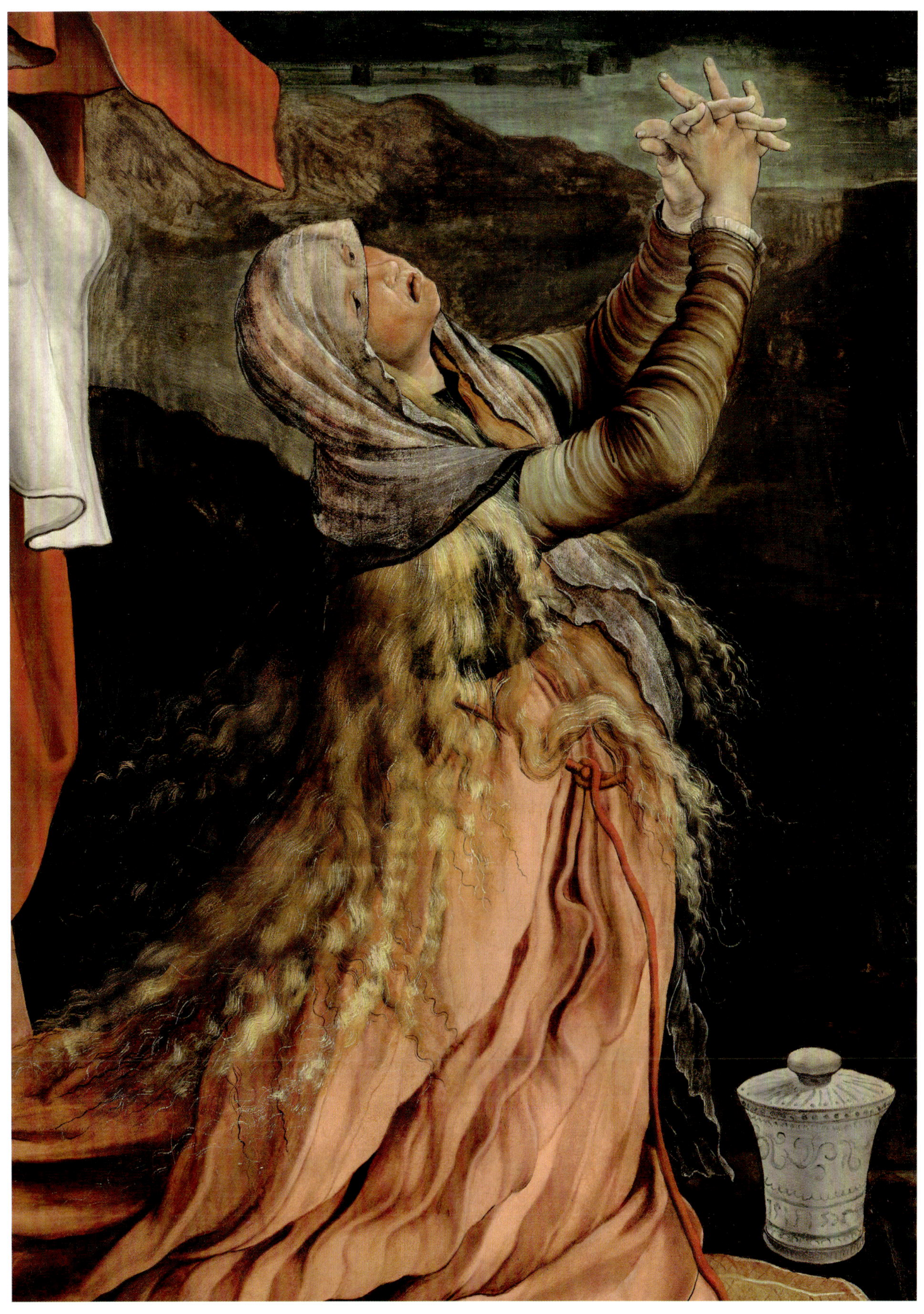

Evangelist's arm was elongated unnaturally, but evidently intentionally, to accentuate the impression of a sudden movement, and with it the drama of the image (it would not have been difficult for the artist to modify the group pose).

As previously mentioned, there is also a resemblance between the face in the Winterthur drawing and the figure of Mary Magdalene in the painting [fig. 109], but the somewhat heavy pathetic tone of the drawing is far and away surpassed by the sense of tragic abandon in the finished painting. She is even smaller than the other mourners, in line with medieval hierarchy, but the memory of her is perhaps even more forceful. Her body is essentially hidden by the infinite cascading folds of her pink dress, into which are commingled her long, blonde tresses. Only her arms and intertwined hands—thin and straight as a wild shrub, resalting on the background of a Jerusalem imagined as an oversized military fortress protruding on a large, desolated green-bluish plateau—restore life to that bundle of clothing and hair. Once again, Mathis makes use of the transparent veil that covers without covering. But here he has it fall over the saint's eyes which become marvelously obfuscated, thus highlighting the pained downward grimace of her mouth.[58]

In comparison, the priestly John the Baptist, who stands alone on the right [fig. 110], counter-balances the unbearable tension of the scene with his immobile symbolism. Removed from time and space, he indicates Christ, accompanied by the verse from the Gospel of John "illum oportet crescere me autem minui", and the symbolic mystic lamb whose blood flows into the chalice.[59] As noted by Marco Fratini, the solitary figure of John the Baptist, intent on indicating to the faithful the Crucifix as a source of grace, will have a long history, specifically in the Lutheran church, in the works of Lucas Cranach the Younger. But here it seems to make one of its first appearances as an iconographic element of special importance, as a meditative pause within this unbearably violent scene.[60] Finding in Isenheim the incunabulum of a theme typical of the Lutheran figurative tradition would seem to confirm that the iconography of the altarpiece was quite linked to the premises of the thinking of Luther, thus reinforcing the connection with Johann von Staupitz suggested here.[61] And yet, as accurately noted by Schiller, the pathos here experienced is quite different from the didacticism of subsequent Lutheran iconography:

> Grünewald did not invent the figure of John the Baptist accompanied by the bleeding Lamb of God pointing at the crucified Christ, but he has given it a degree of significance that it had not previously had in the Crucifixion image. The *Agnus Dei* gives the Death of the martyred Christ on the Cross the sense of a sacrificial and expiatory Death; The last of the prophets, who testified that Christ was 'the Lamb that bears the sins of the world', points to the dead Christ with the words from John [. . .]. Although mysticism of the Passion lies at the root of Grünewald's Crucifixion image, a strength of witness outshines the emotional content. Specifically Protestant art never achieved this intensity of artistic statement, because—in a new age—instead of symbols, it created didactic images designed to demonstrate the doctrine of Reformation.[62]

Behind John the Baptist ends the grass plateau, sometimes interpreted as a rivulet, probably the Jordan, with a baptismal reference.[63] This single figure balances the composition with all the colors distributed among the three grieving figures on the left. The intense white of the Virgin Mary is found in the book and the lamb, the red of John the Evangelist's cloak is essentially that of John the Baptist's, whose shadows

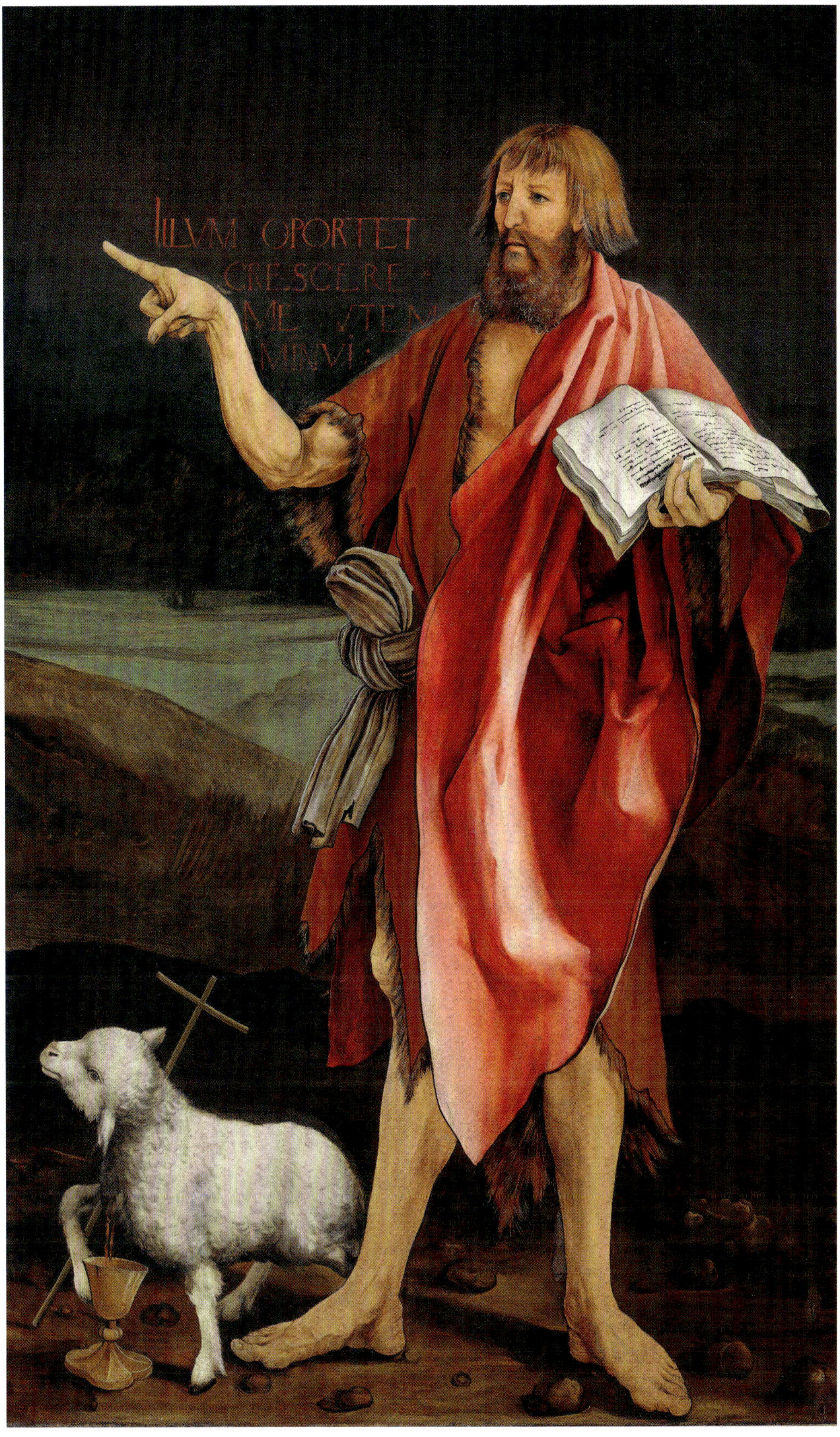

110 | Mathis Grünewald, *Crucifixion* (detail, from the Isenheim altarpiece), ca. 1513–1514. Colmar, Musée d'Unterlinden.

111 | Mathis Grünewald, *Resurrection of Christ* (from the Isenheim altarpiece), ca. 1514. Colmar, Musée d'Unterlinden.

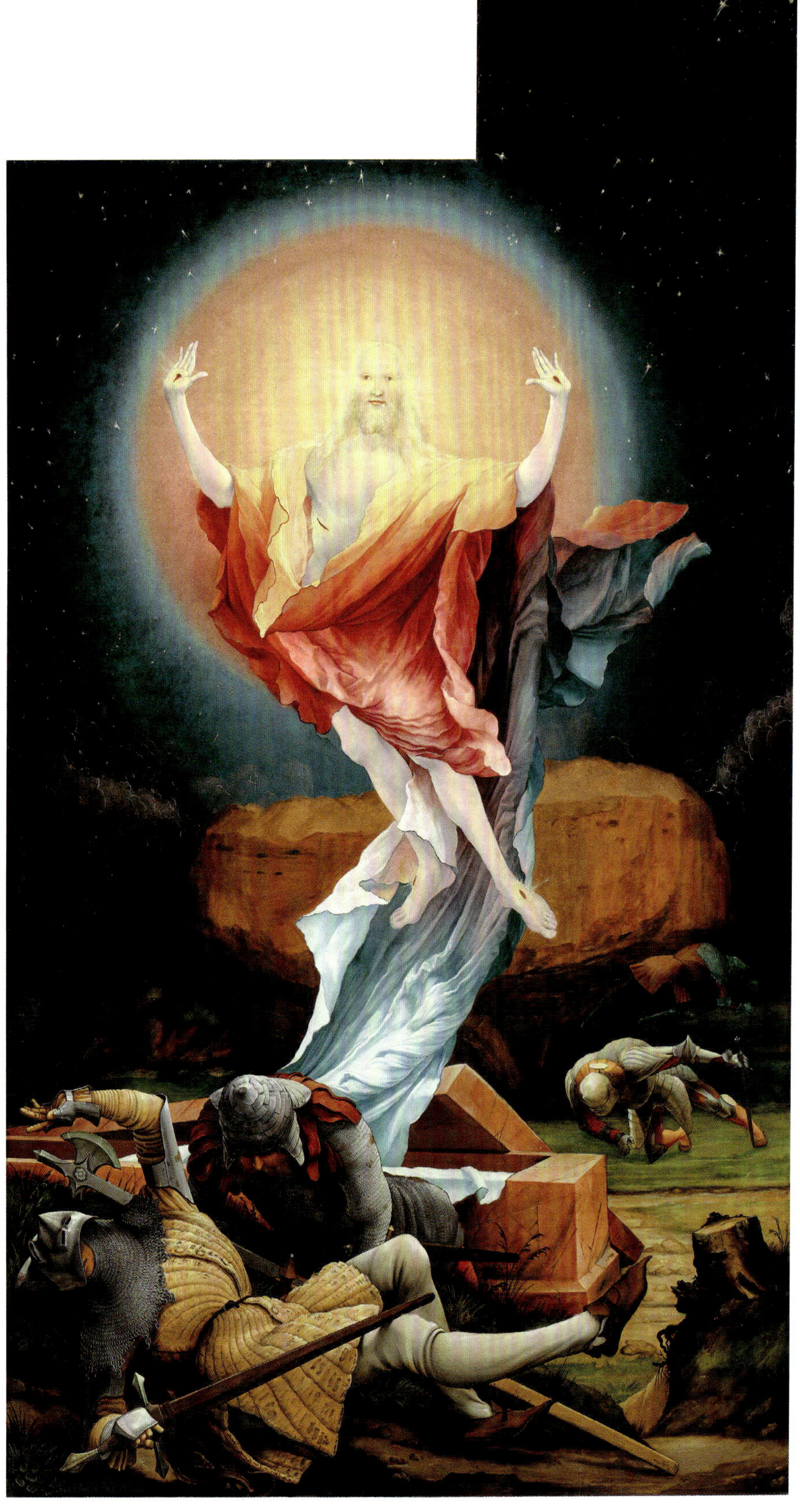

have the same pink hue as Mary Magdalene's long dress and her hair is golden like the chalice that receives the blood of the Apocalyptic Lamb. We also see that John the Baptist's arms and legs are so vigorous and sculpted in the folds of the skin and outlining of the veins that they seem to be the result of detailed anatomical study.

Logically, Mathis must have been facing the last side of these two double-sided panels, the one dedicated to the Resurrection of Christ (269 × 143 cm) [fig. 111].

Discussing this painting risks diverging from art history into mysticism. However, I believe this is the only *real* Resurrection that has ever been painted and would perhaps deserve greater prestige in the cultural series (which, in this context, does not interest us) of Christian theology and mysticism than the myriad written "revelations", often of an embarrassingly poor cultural and even moral plane, on the same level and with at least the same authoritativeness of a Meister Eckhart or a Sebastian Franck (but lacking their eventual obscurity). Or, for example, in the wake of the Rheinland mystic tradition of the 14th century, linked to Heinrich Suso and Meister Eckhart, of which, in a certain way, Staupitz could be considered a later exponent.[64] Once again, this aspect was grasped with amazing clarity by Huysmans:

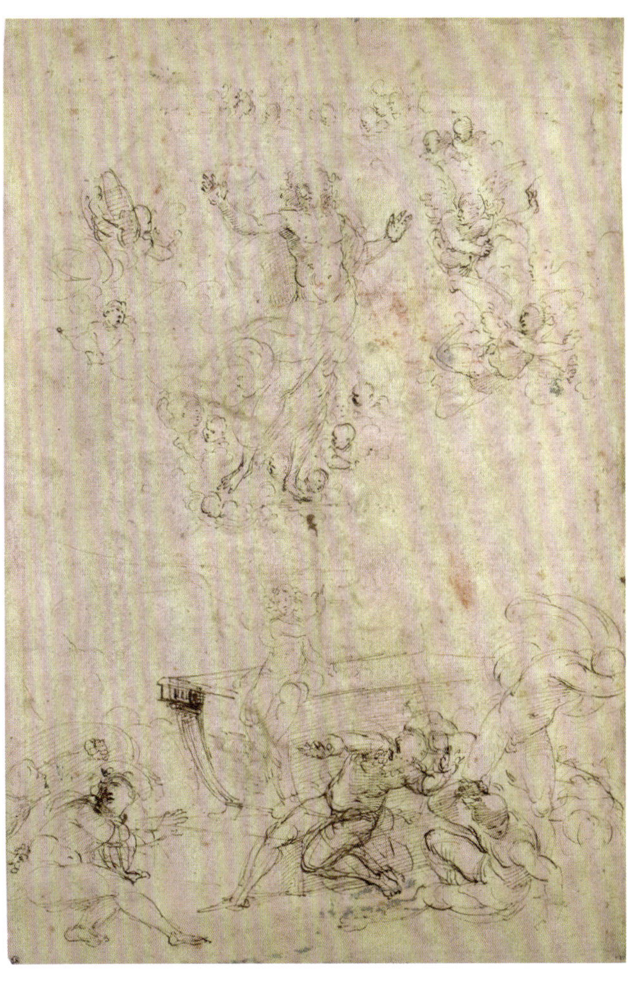

112 | Raphael, *Study for a Resurrection of Christ*, ca. 1513–1514. Bayonne, Musée Bonnat, inv. 635.

> In it Grünewald shows himself to be the boldest painter who has ever lived, the first artist who has tried to convey, through the wretched colours of this earth, a vision of the Godhead in abeyance on the cross and then renewed, visible to the naked eye, on rising from the tomb. With him we are, mystically speaking, in at the death, contemplating an art with its back to the wall and forced further into the beyond, this time, than any theologian could have instructed the artist to go.[65]

And, of course, we must stress the courage the artist—and his patron—had in openly showing what St. Paul says we see only "per speculum et in aenigmate" (I Cor. 13:12): a body resurrected and glorified, whose reacquired divinity does not repudiate the ascertainable physical reality.

Perhaps the only painted examples that could serve as a comparison, for their intense creativity and complexity of the light play, are by Raphael: the *Liberation of St. Peter* in the Stanza of Heliodorus in the Vatican, and the *Transfiguration* at the Vatican Gallery (cat. 40333). For reasons, above all chronological, it is impossible that Mathis and Raphael (one working in Isenheim and the other in the Vatican) could have had news of each other. In theory, even if currently there is no concrete proof, it could be possible that around the year 1519, Raphael could have had some indirect knowledge of the work of his German colleague. And yet, we cannot help but be

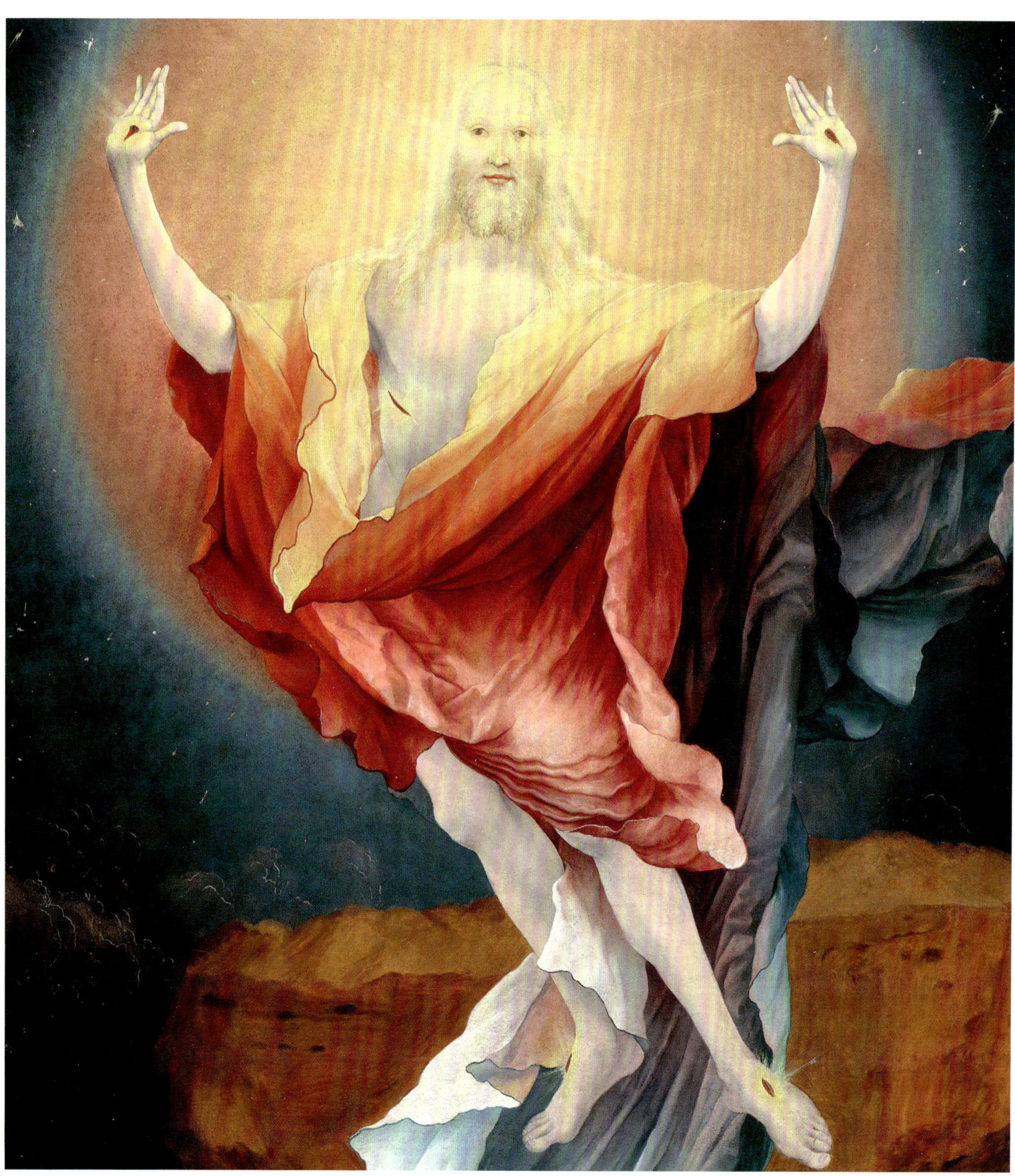

113 | Mathis Grünewald, *Resurrection of Christ* (detail, from the Isenheim altarpiece), ca. 1514. Colmar, Musée d'Unterlinden.

amazed thinking that at the same moment in which Grünewald was painting the *Resurrection* in Isenheim, Raphael was also planning one that was never realized, but whose preparatory drawing (Bayonne, Musèe Bonnat, inv. 635 [fig. 112]) is filled with ideas in certain ways parallel to those of Grünewald, and later partially included in the *Transfiguration.*[66] Suffice it to say that these two painters, extreme opposites from an aesthetic point of view, were the most profound interpreters, from Germany and Rome, of their era. In essence, this was already said by Roberto Longhi in a passage memorable in a number of ways in *Arte italiana e arte tedesca* (1941):

Once again, the ostentatious opposition ready to become local myth and ritual (the presumably insuperable antinomy), was nothing more than a range of simply human possibilities, the right to expression based on a constantly-changing culture that is always a condition of freedom. So, it was not Grünewald or Raphael who represented all of Germany or all of Italy, it was Germany and Italy which, in that moment, were represented by them.

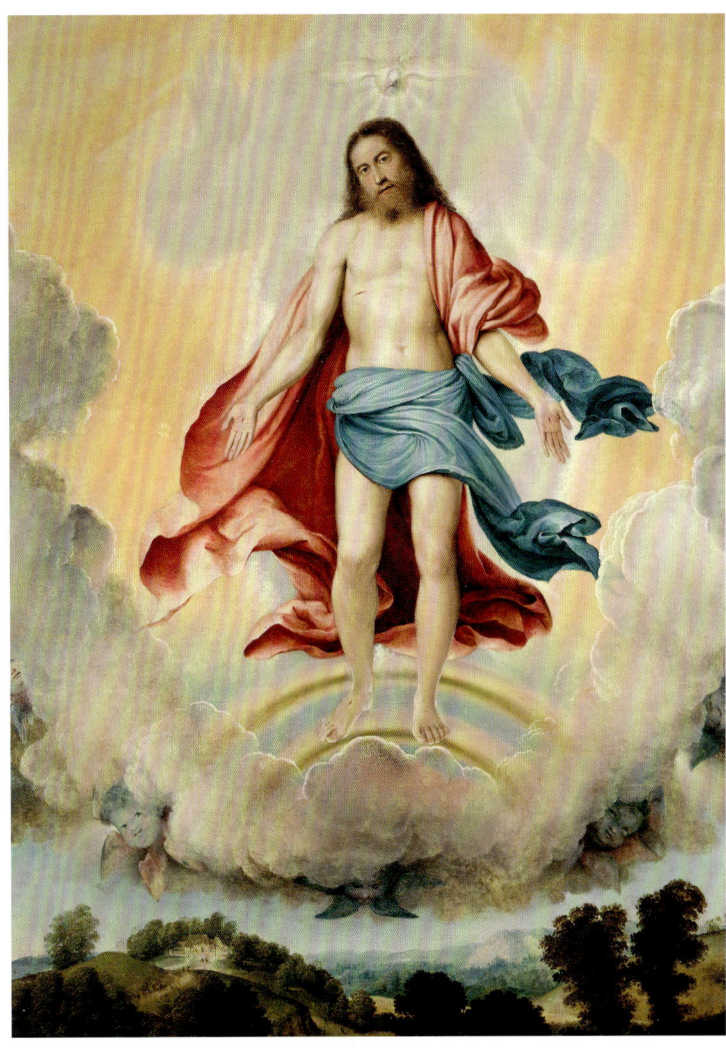

114 | Lorenzo Lotto, *The Holy Trinity*, ca. 1523–1524. Bergamo, Museo Diocesano "Alessandro Bernareggi", inv. 3000.

And we must admit that Grünewald was also the one who dreamed more deeply than anyone else. This is the unique and unreproducible magnitude of his genius. But it also remains for us that the remote Thule of a dramatic, roving and irrational sentiment was not at all unknown territory.[67]

In the Isenheim *Resurrection*, Christ's horridly disfigured form from the Crucifixion transforms into immaculate perfection. His skin is as white as snow (as it appeared to Peter, John and James in the Transfiguration, and it should not be excluded that the Isenheim panel retains some aspects of the lost Frankfurt *Transfiguration*), his face seems a unified whole with the rising sun behind him [fig. 113], or even the incandescent source, and the gangrenous wounds, now precious embellishments, emit golden rays. And yet, as has already been said, despite being transfigured and glorified, it is not a disembodied corpse, but a real body, that emits and receives shadow, and it is indeed shadow that seems to dissipate immediately on contact with such a gleaming body. It is probably no accident that the most insightful comment about the *Resurrection* panel in Isenheim was offered not by an art historian but by a scholar of mysticism, Martin Buber:

> He includes all hues of being in his unique tonality, each tone pure and intensified. All fused under the law of the person who ties the world together. The shades are not iridescent, they shine in themselves, ranged around a higher self that has received them all, and bears them upward—all colors and angels and beings.[68]

Perhaps, from a Pauline and Augustinian perspective, Grünewald (with his patrons) conceives the *Resurrection* as a veritable second creation. The moment in which he emerges from the tomb, Jesus takes on old medieval iconography to (literally) create the sun and star-studded sky:[69] "a new heaven and a new earth" as announced in Apocalypse (21:1) already exist in that moment.[70]

This interpretation is enriched by Berta Reichenauer's reference to a passage by Hildegard von Bingen, whose works were very likely owned by the library of the Antonite monastery, especially those involving medicine and botany,[71] and whose *Liber Scivias* had been published in 1513, in Paris, by Jacques Le Fèvre d'Ètaples, the French humanist and admirer of Luther:

> Deinde vidi serenissimam lucem et in ipsa sapphirini coloris speciem hominis, quae tota suavissimo rutilante igne flagrabat. Et illa serena lux perfudit totum illum rutilantem ignem, et ille rutilans ignis totam illam serenam lucem, ac eadem serena lux et idem rutilans ignis totam speciem eiusdem hominis, ita lumen unum in una vi possibilitatis existentis.[72]

I also wonder, without knowing how to answer (if anything, soliciting a response from scholars of the mystical and alchemic literature), whether the analogies between when Grünewald was painting and what the "illiterate" mystic Jakob Böhme would write over a century later, are casual:

> Like as the candle dies in the fire, and out of that death the light and power proceed, viz. the great painless life; so out of Christ's dying and death the eternal divine sun should and must arise in the human property [. . .]. And as Adam changed the likeness of God into the dark death's form, so God did again change the likeness through his fire-wrath out of death into the light; he drew forth the likeness again out of death, as a blossom grows from the harsh earth. [. . .] The death arises in a new body out of the darkness of death, in a white fair colour, but as an hidden lustre, wherein the colour is not rightly and distinctly known, till it dissolves itself, and the materia becomes desiring; then the sun arises in the centre, and Saturn in the property of Jupiter and Venus in all the seven forms (that is in the verbum fiat) as a new creation, and the desire of all the seven forms tend to Sol's lustre, viz. to the white and red colour from the fire and light, which is the majestical [colour, lustre, or glory].[73]

Perhaps this is the hidden key to the relationship between Grünewald and Lotto sensed by Alessandro Ballarin.[74] The visionary power of this work is certainly linked to the *Trinity* by Lorenzo Lotto at Sant'Alessandro della Croce in Bergamo (currently in storage at the local Museum Adriano Bernareggi, inv. 3000), ca. 1519–1520 [fig. 114]. How the Venetian painter, who was always open to Nordic influence, could have known about Grünewald's innovations will perhaps become clearer as our journey progresses.

Jesus's clothes are bathed in light, and they display a richness of tonal variation that we have not seen before, with points of virtuosity pushed to the extreme in the iridescence of the fluttering drapery on the right. The shadows bounce the colors off each other, even the edge of the shroud still entangled between Jesus's legs is discolored by the petrol blue of his cape and the red of his garments. Also hit by varying degrees of light are the unfortunate guards who fall to earth like puppets whose strings have been cut.

Here, Grünewald is decidedly saying something new in German painting and, to tell the truth, something that will struggle to be understood (we will realize this soon while examining another *Resurrection*, painted by Jerg Ratgeb, which is perhaps the painting most directly influenced by this masterpiece by Mathis). The

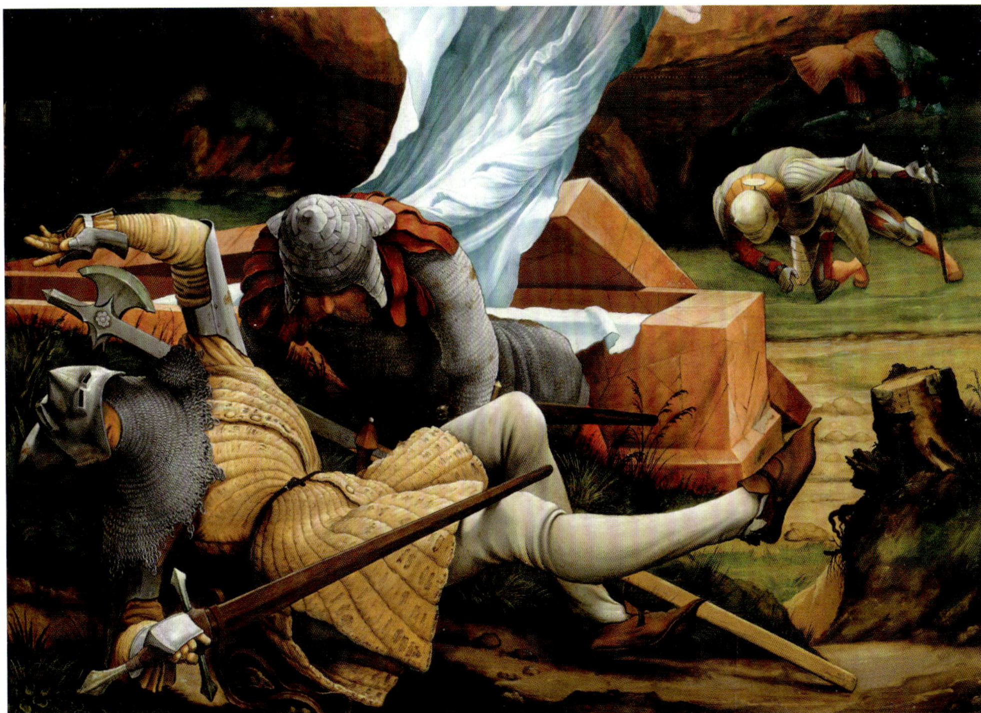

115 | Mathis Grünewald, *Resurrection of Christ* (detail, from the Isenheim altarpiece), ca. 1514. Colmar, Musée d'Unterlinden.

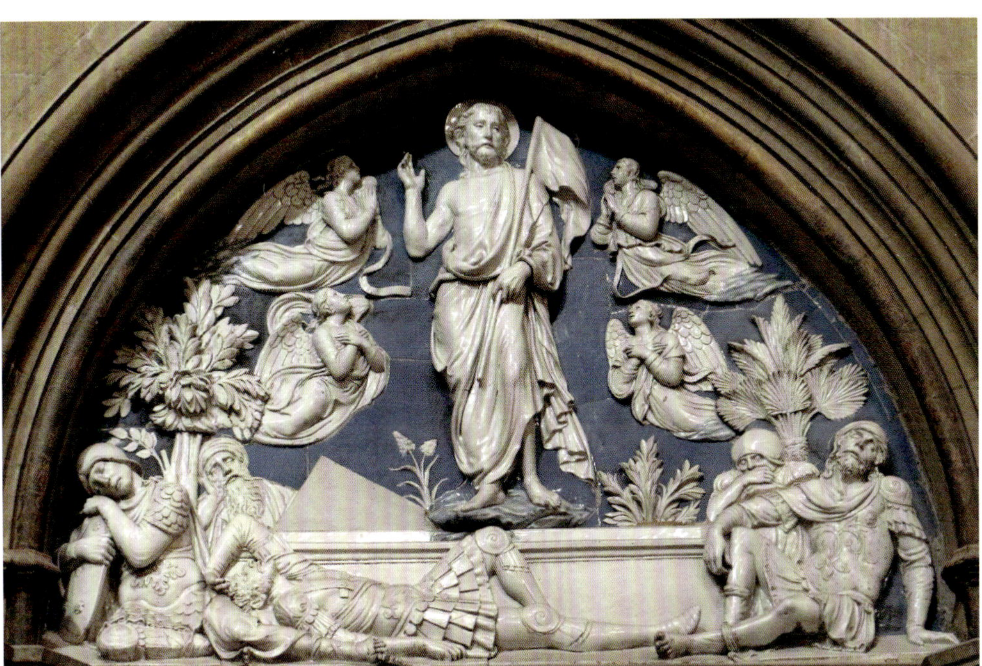

116 | Luca della Robbia, *Resurrection of Christ*, ca. 1442–1448. Florence, Santa Maria del Fiore, sacristy.

daring, inventive, experimental and even poetic use of light and color reaches full maturity here, and it is not even worth stopping to describe some of the numerous episodes, both large and small, with which the painter embellishes his work. We only note that it is not at all necessary to compare the soldier in the foreground [fig. 115] with the analogous one shaped by Luca della Robbia on the exterior of the sacristy of Santa Maria del Fiore in Florence [fig. 116] (ca. 1442–1446).[75] For someone like Mathis, in this creative explosion, the inspiration of the Malchus in *The Capture of Christ* (ca. 1480) by Martin Schongauer [fig. 117] (an artist, it should be recalled, whose important altarpiece was displayed in the Church of St. Anthony in Isenheim

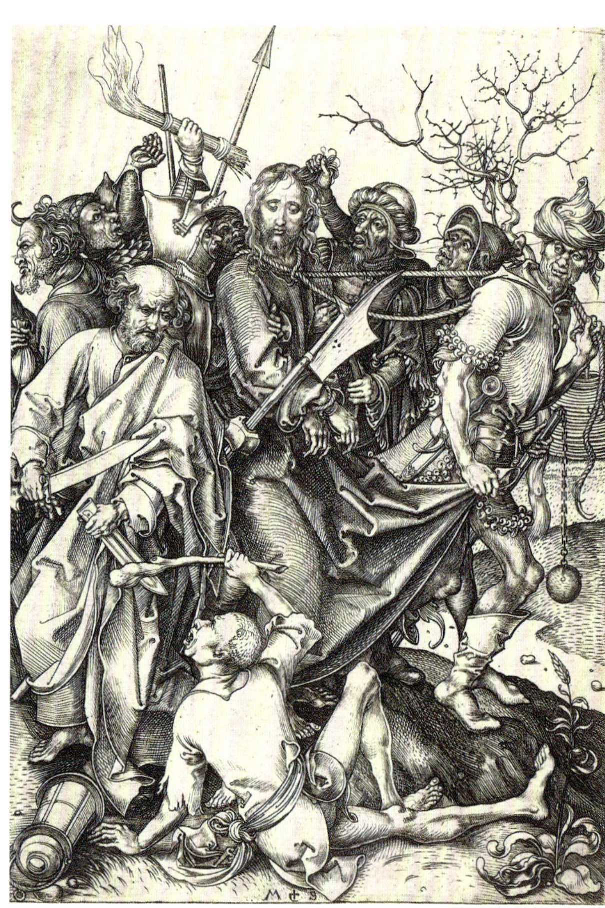

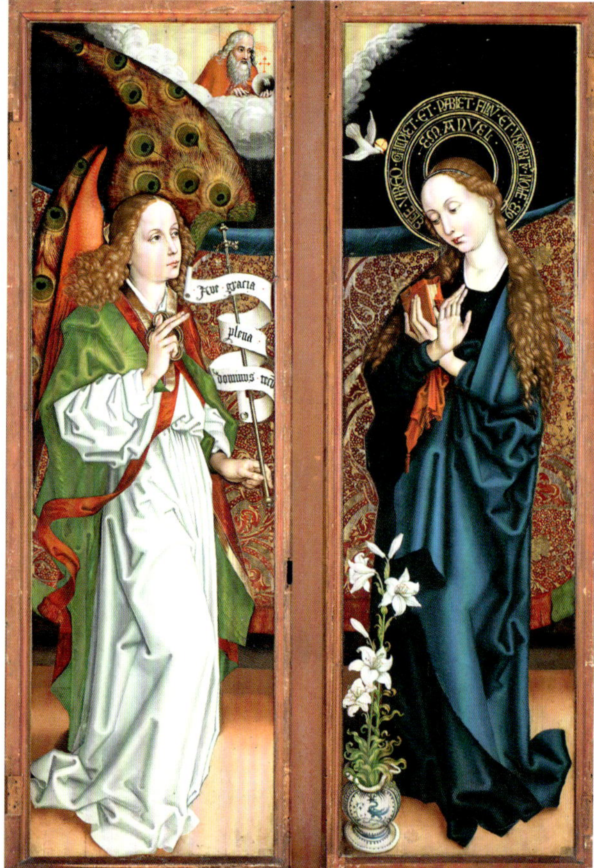
Ave gracia
plena
dominus

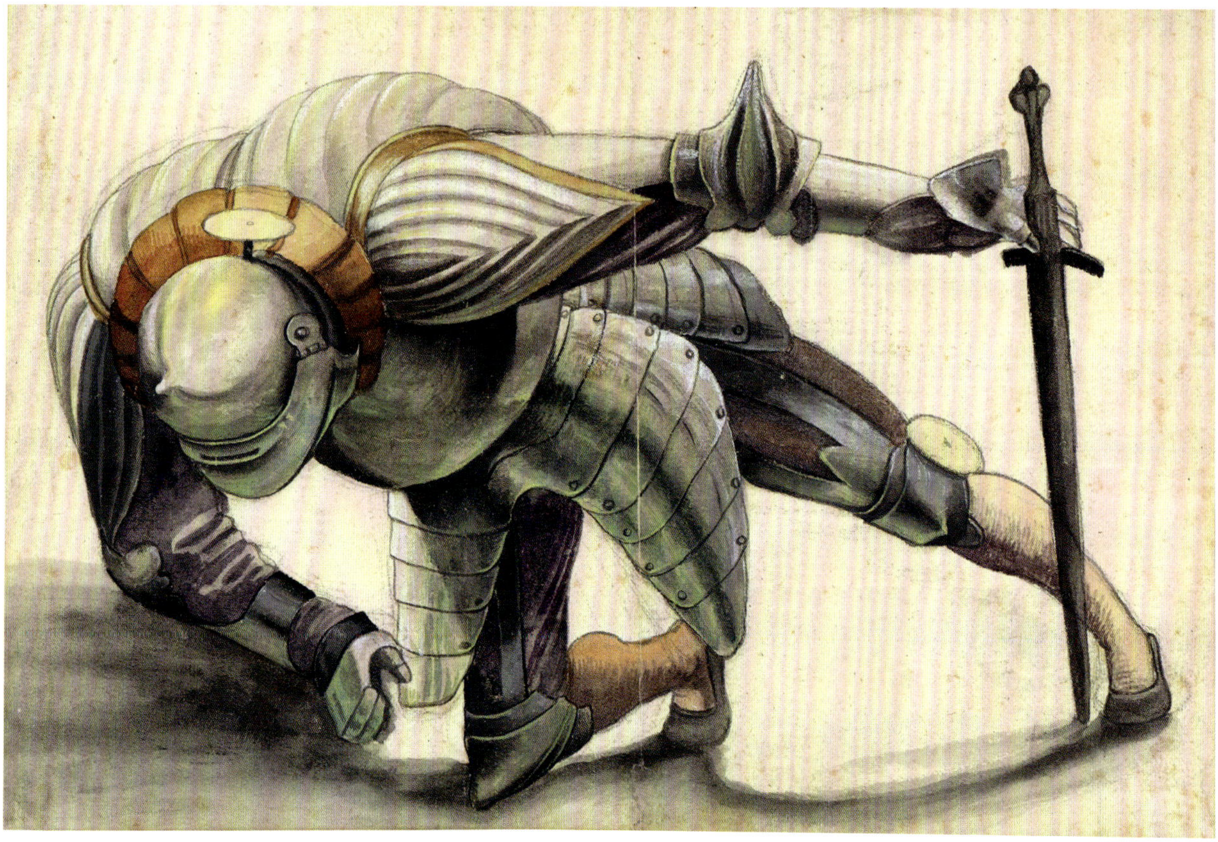

(today at the Musée d'Unterlinden) [fig. 118]) was more than sufficient.

One of the soldiers (which, like the Basel Longinus are wearing out-of-date, but certainly not "ancient" armor) was used as a model by an anonymous but very scrupulous copyist who, in a drawing now at the Staatliche Kunsthalle, Karlsruhe (inv. VIII 1499), reproduced the guard that, in the background, falls face-down on the ground.[76] [fig. 119]

I believe the next step for Mathis was the creation of the two fixed panels depicting *St. Anthony the Abbot* (232 × 75 cm) and *St. Sebastian* (232 × 76.5 cm) [figs. 120–121].[77]

Until 1965, these were located, respectively, on the right and left of the person

117 | Martin Schongauer, *Capture of Christ*, woodcut, ca. 1480.

118 | Martin Schongauer, *Annunciation* (detail from a polyptych), ca. 1490. Colmar, Musée d'Unterlinden.

119 | After Mathis Grünewald, *Soldier falling face-down*. Karlsruhe, Staatliche Kunsthalle, inv. VIII 1499.

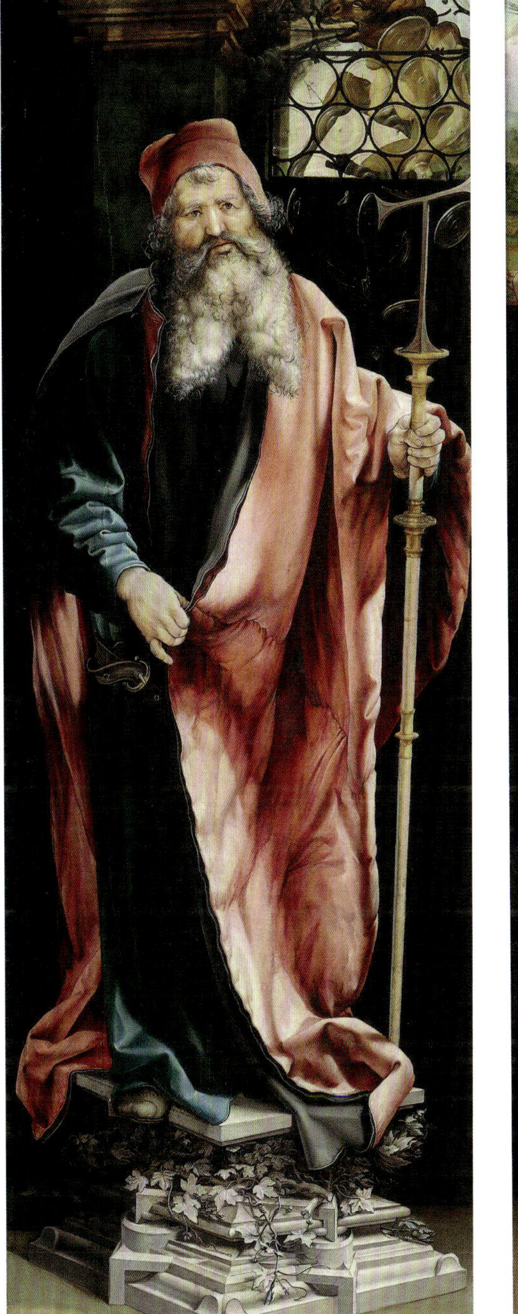

120 | Mathis Grünewald, *Saint Anthony the Abbott* (from the Isenheim altarpiece), ca. 1514. Colmar, Musée d'Unterlinden.

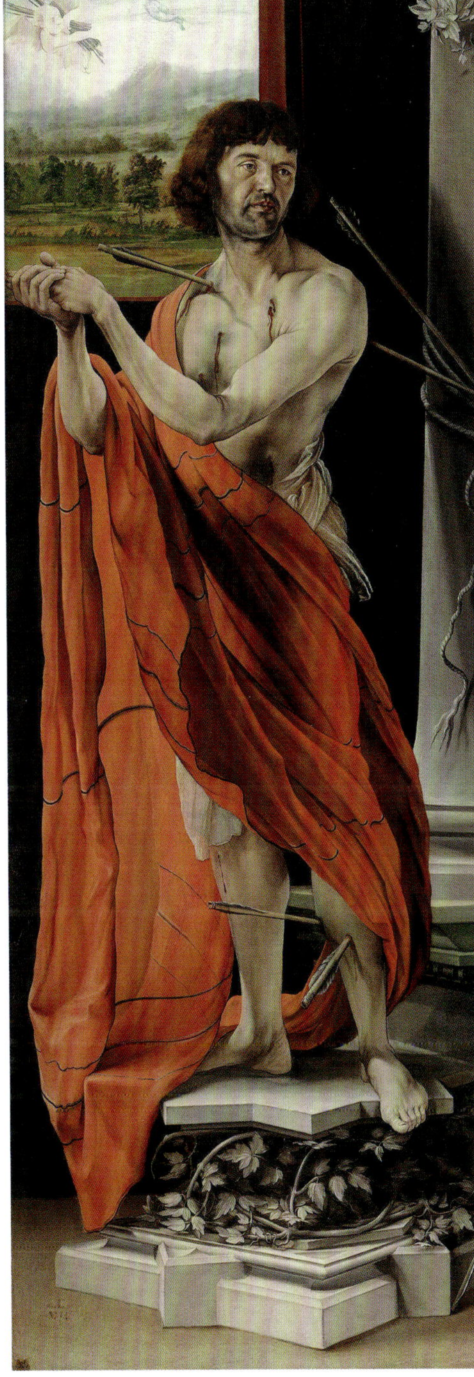

121 | Mathis Grünewald, *Saint Sebastian* (from the Isenheim altarpiece), ca. 1514. Colmar, Musée d'Unterlinden.

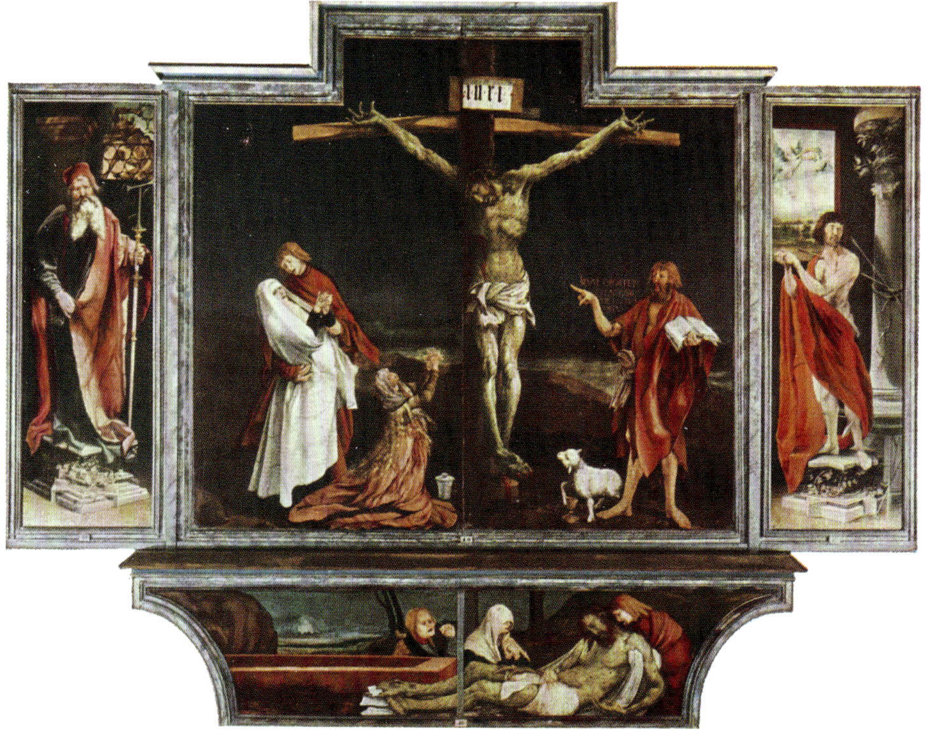

122 | Mathis Grünewald, Isenheim altarpiece, ca. 1513–1516, first face before the inversion of the side panels.

looking at the *Crucifixion*. Then, in that year, their positions were exchanged on the suggestion of the interpretation given by Sarwey of the description of the altarpiece provided at the end of the 18th century by Franz Christian Lerse. This new arrangement was approved by virtually all subsequent critics.[78]

However, according to Pierre Vaisse, Hans Reinhardt, Lottlise Behling, Charles D. Cuttler, Rainer Marquard and Giorgio Gualdrini,[79] with whom I concur, the old arrangement appears most satisfactory for a number of simple reasons that I will elucidate prior to the stylistic analysis. We will follow this reasoning with the aid of an old photograph, taken before the two side panels were inverted [fig. 122]. First of all, the position to the right of Christ (and the left of the viewer) is traditionally the place of honor in the iconographic organization of an altarpiece. So, it would seem logical to expect that, in an Antonite church, this would be occupied by *St. Anthony* rather than *St. Sebastian*. Secondly, the corners of bases similar to the overturned capitals (resembling the platform on which the *St. Anthony* carved by Niclaus Hagnower is seated) are placed to close visually on the right below Sebastian and on the left below Anthony. Examining the light direction, which comes from the right, reveals an illogical light effect: it appears to illuminate St. Sebastian, further away from the light source, and only partially St. Anthony, who is closer. In addition, in this placement of the panels two diagonals are visible: one from the upper left to the bottom right, delimited by the left shoulder of St. Anthony, the right arm of St. John and terminating at the foot of the cross; the other, a mirror image, delimited by the hands of St. Sebastian, the crooked neck of the lamb and, again, terminating at the foot of the cross. Most importantly, consider St. Sebastian's gesture: what can his joined hands signify, if not being in prayer? However, currently, St. Sebastian prays into the void, turning his head towards the cruel scene of the Crucifixion. If repositioned ideally on the right, instead his gesture would regain its logical coherence. The saint prays, beseeching the crucified Christ on behalf of the faithful

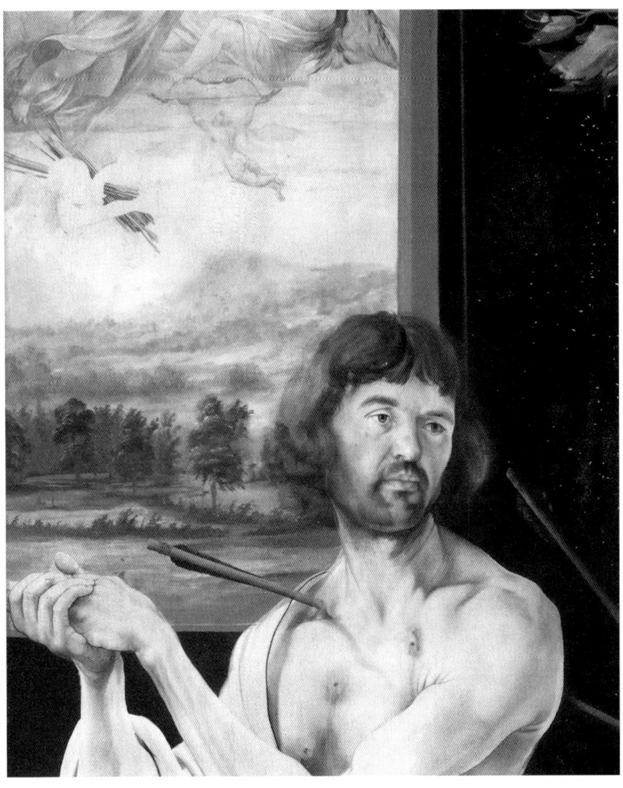

123 | Mathis Grünewald, *Saint Sebastian* (detail of the IR-image), from the Isenheim altarpiece, ca. 1514. Colmar, Musée d'Unterlinden.

and sick of Isenheim, turning towards them perhaps to indicate them to Christ, or, even better, to invite them to pray with him. It would explain why Mathis, initially, as the infrared images reveal [fig. 123], conceived St. Sebastian as looking straight in front of himself (a logical behavior if turned towards the Crucifix and not towards the void), subsequently directing him to pray not only for himself but for the Isenheim's afflicted.[80]

However, the physical and technical examinations of the panels seem to confirm the historical correctness of the current arrangement.[81] In fact, this is further corroborated by recent studies conducted during restoration, as Pantxika Béguerie-De Paepe has kindly informed me. A strange short-circuit that could perhaps be explained either by the decision to invert the two saints while the altarpiece was still being completed (this would explain the change in direction of St. Sebastian's head imposed by Grünewald), or by an early inversion made shortly after this monumental work's completion. It is also important to note that the scientific examinations have definitively disproved the bizarre hypothesis of Schmid[82] who thought that the two saints were originally monochrome paintings, like the Heller panels.

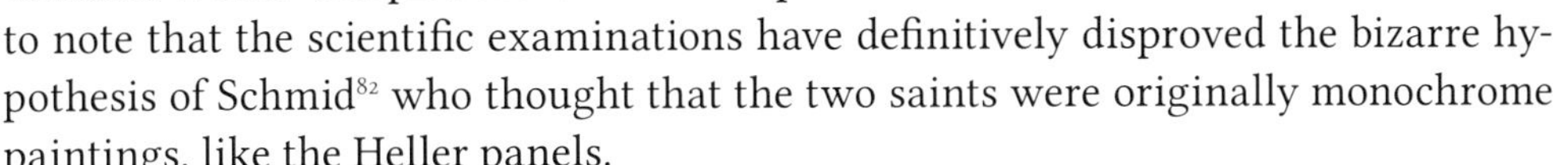

The anomalous discrepancy in the dimensions of the two saints is apparent to all observers. I confess that I am unable to offer a satisfactory explanation for this. The only one I can suggest—the desire to give greater importance to St. Anthony's priestly image—could be true, but, overall, it is not fully adequate.[83] What is certain is that *St. Anthony the Abbot* marks a culminating point to-date in the monumentality of Grünewald's work. His mass occupies nearly the entire space in the panel, and he remains oblivious to the presence of the demon—actually, the she-devil[84]—behind him who is tearing apart the leaded glass windows (a clear and perhaps ironic homage to Flemish painting). His sober magnitude is accentuated by the decision to play with only a few colors, the petrol blue of his garment and the magnificent pink-red of his cloak.

In comparison, St. Sebastian seems excessively minute, standing in a workshop-style pose rather than being martyred. If Mathis had portrayed him as suffering, Jesus's sacrifice would have been less all-consuming, and it is, therefore, a very sophisticated rhetorical device.

To compensate—and perhaps this is the key to addressing the perceived aporia—this panel is extremely dynamic and varied in terms of its use of color.

The apparent Italianate quality of this image can actually be interpreted as an in-depth study of reality by Grünewald. His care in realistically depicting the nude body, leaving aside sculptural models, could have been abetted to some extent by the example of Dürer, whom we have already seen becoming relevant once again in the Winterthur drawing, the aspect that confirms the chronological proximity between the Crucifixion and saints in the fixed panels. The precision of his study is

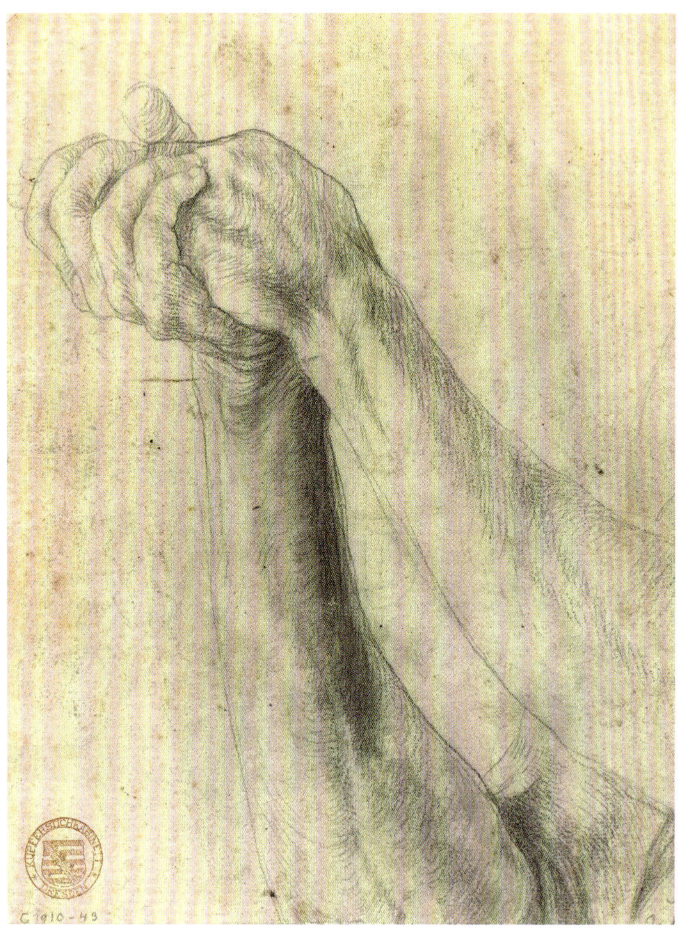

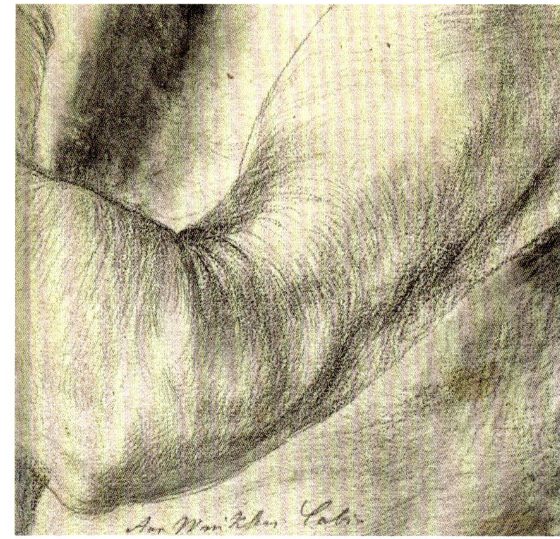

124 | Mathis Grünewald, *Fragment of a study of male arms*, ca. 1514. Dresden, Staatliche Kunstsammlungen, Kupferstichkabinett, inv. C 1919-43 recto.

125 | Mathis Grünewald, *Fragment of a study of male arms*, ca. 1514. Berlin, Staatliche Museen, Kupferstichkabinett, inv. KdZ 17659 recto.

126 | Mathis Grünewald, *Saint Sebastian* (detail), ca. 1514. Colmar, Musée d'Unterlinden.

seen in a remarkable preparatory black chalk drawing of the saint's arm, today divided into two parts preserved, respectively, at the Staatliche Museen, Kupferstichkabinett of Dresden (236 × 188 mm, inv. C 1919–43), and of Berlin (289 × 203 mm, inv. KdZ 17659)[85] [figs. 124–125]. We can appreciate the effort behind this study from life, unrelentingly pursued down to the first signs of slagging skin, but also, and above all, the similarity with the study of *Mary Magdalene*. Grünewald confirms to have understood, completely on his own, something like the curved stroke "following the form" which characterized Leonardo's drawing in the same period (a way of conceiving the form which was seen first in the early Berlin drawing of *St. Catherine*). Unlike the Italian master, however, his interest lies more in the figure's reaction to light rather than the three-dimensional curve of the drawn figure. We can also see that, compared with the Winterthur drawing, the stroke is more secure and relaxed.

In the background, from an open window, we see a realistic, clear and even serene landscape [fig. 126], vaguely Italianate in the style of Bellini.[86] This, however, is likely driven by examples by Dürer, a true master of this genre. Above this landscape, holding the martyr's crown, are two angels of indeterminate physical consistency (the reference to Raphael suggested by Ziermann[87] seems totally out of the question, just as the reference to the saint's pose to the Judith by Mantegna seems debatable to me, a reference offered by Vogt in 1958 and repeated by Ziermann).[88]

On the verso of the two sheet fragments in Berlin and Dresden, which feature the study of the *Chest and arms of St. Sebastian*, are two quite finished drawings [figs. 127–128] for another panel of the *Isenheim Altarpiece*: the St. Anthony of the

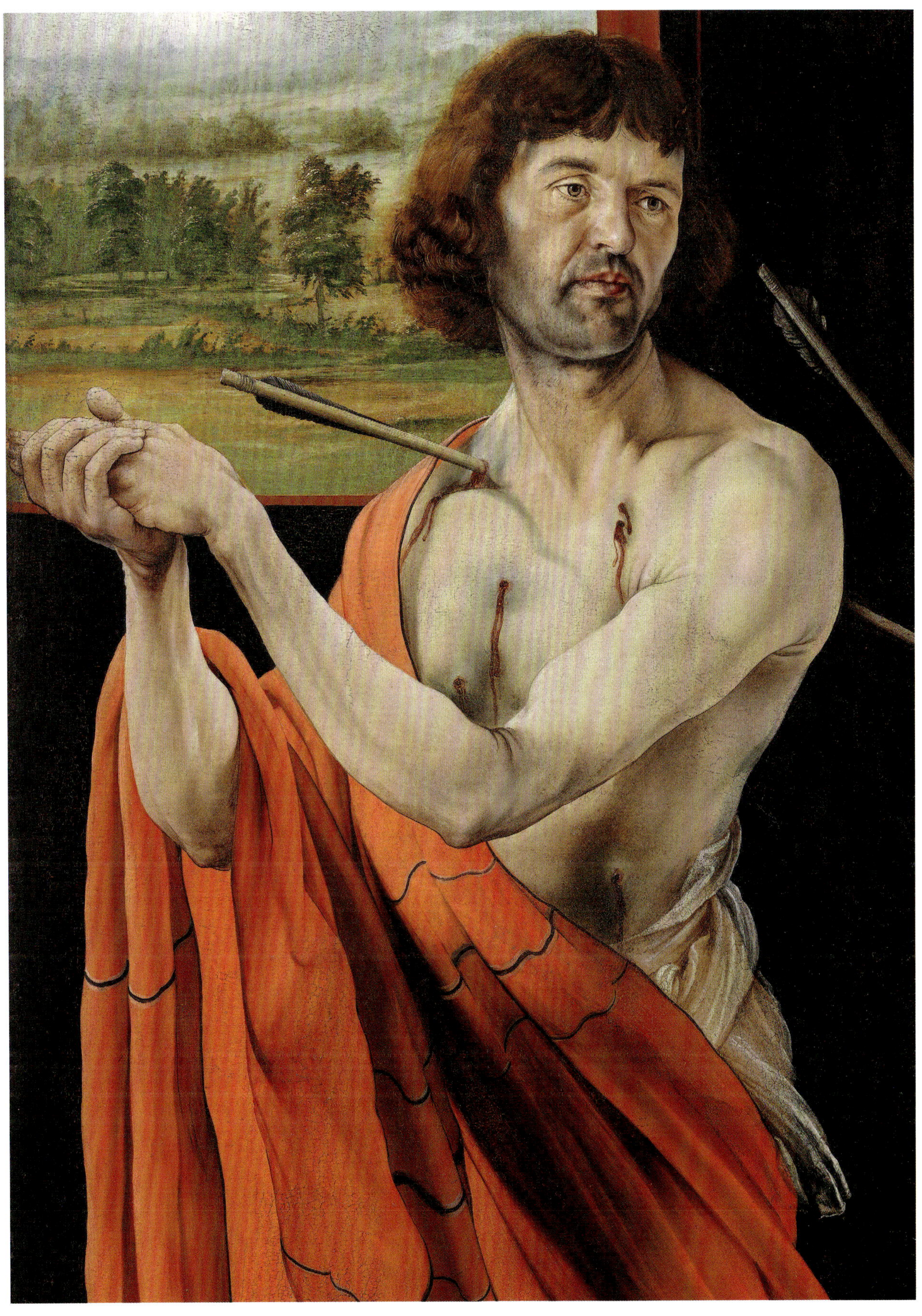

Meeting of Saints Anthony and Paul the Hermit (265 × 141 cm) [fig. 129]. This may not be proof, but it is at least a clue for the chronological order in which the paintings were done. Having completed the fixed panels and those on the initial side, Grünewald likely progressed to the next wings, beginning precisely with this scene, the most serene of the entire work. The depiction of the crystalline luminosity of the outdoor encounter, amidst a rugged, yet not foreboding or hostile, natural setting—marked by the ominous outlines of the dried, mossy trees and rocky spur in the background, leading to the solemn vista of the blue Vosges mountains in the distance—also explains the absence of Grünewald's characteristic red, as keenly noted by Bianconi.[89] The absence of blood, mystic light, heavy, costly fabrics, suggests a preference for the rough beauty of nature that is unspoiled and wild, to return to when possible to immerse oneself in, as an escape from the world.

According to the *Legenda Aurea* by Jacobus de Voragine, a very popular 13th-century collection of the lives of saints, which deserves to be read as a very likely iconographic source and perhaps even in preference to the *Vita Antonii* by Athanasius, written in the fourth century and well-known throughout Europe in its Latin version, also because of its courteous style:

> In this time S. Anthony was a hermit in another desert and was then ninety years of age. And on a time he thought in himself that in the world was none so good ne so great an hermit as he was himself. Hereupon came to him a revelation as he slept that, beneath all, low down in that desert was an hermit better than he.

127 | Mathis Grünewald, *Study for Saint Anthony the Abbott seating*, ca. 1514. Berlin, Staatliche Museen, Kupferstichkabinett, inv. KdZ 17659 verso.

128 | Mathis Grünewald, *Study for Saint Anthony the Abbott seating*, ca. 1514. Dresden, Staatliche Kunsthalle, Kupferstichkabinett, inv. C 1919-43 verso.

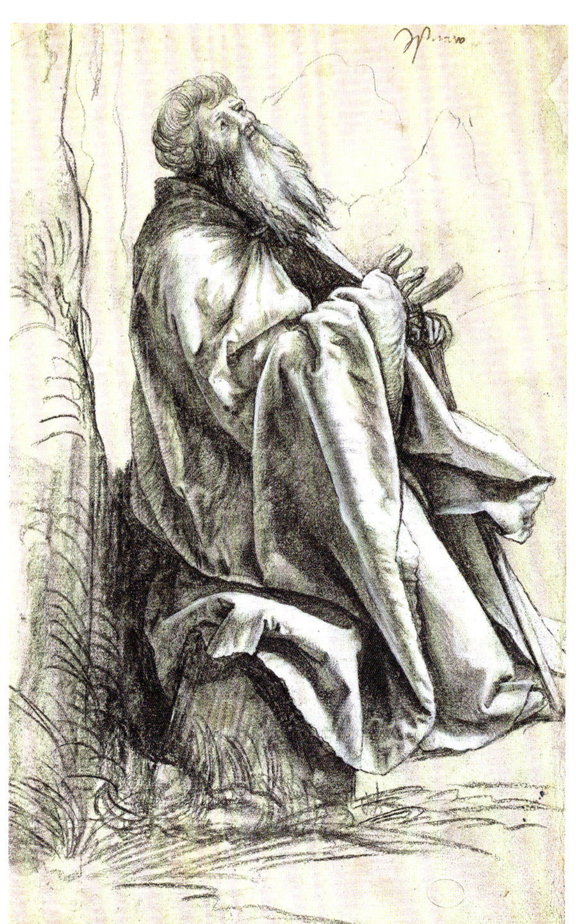

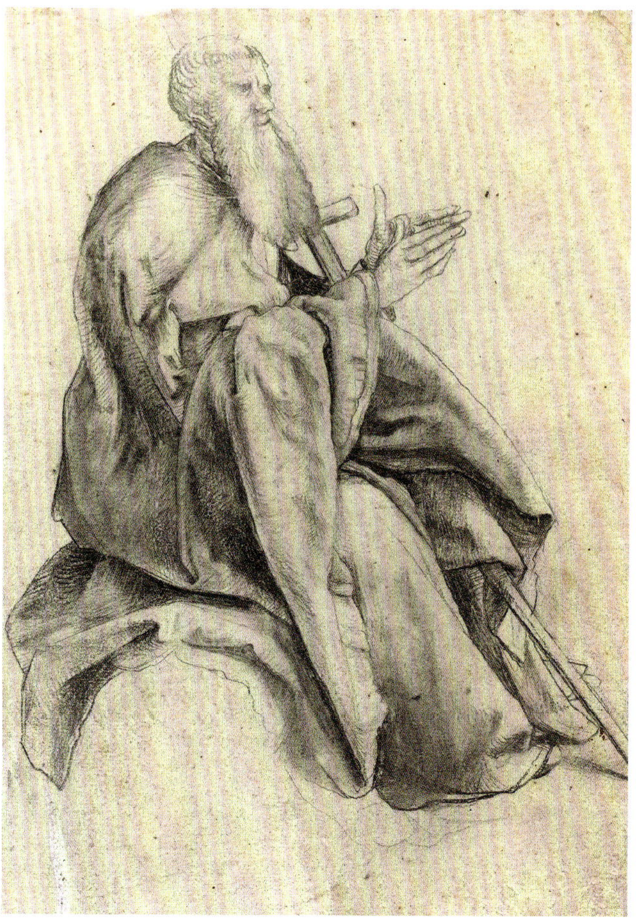

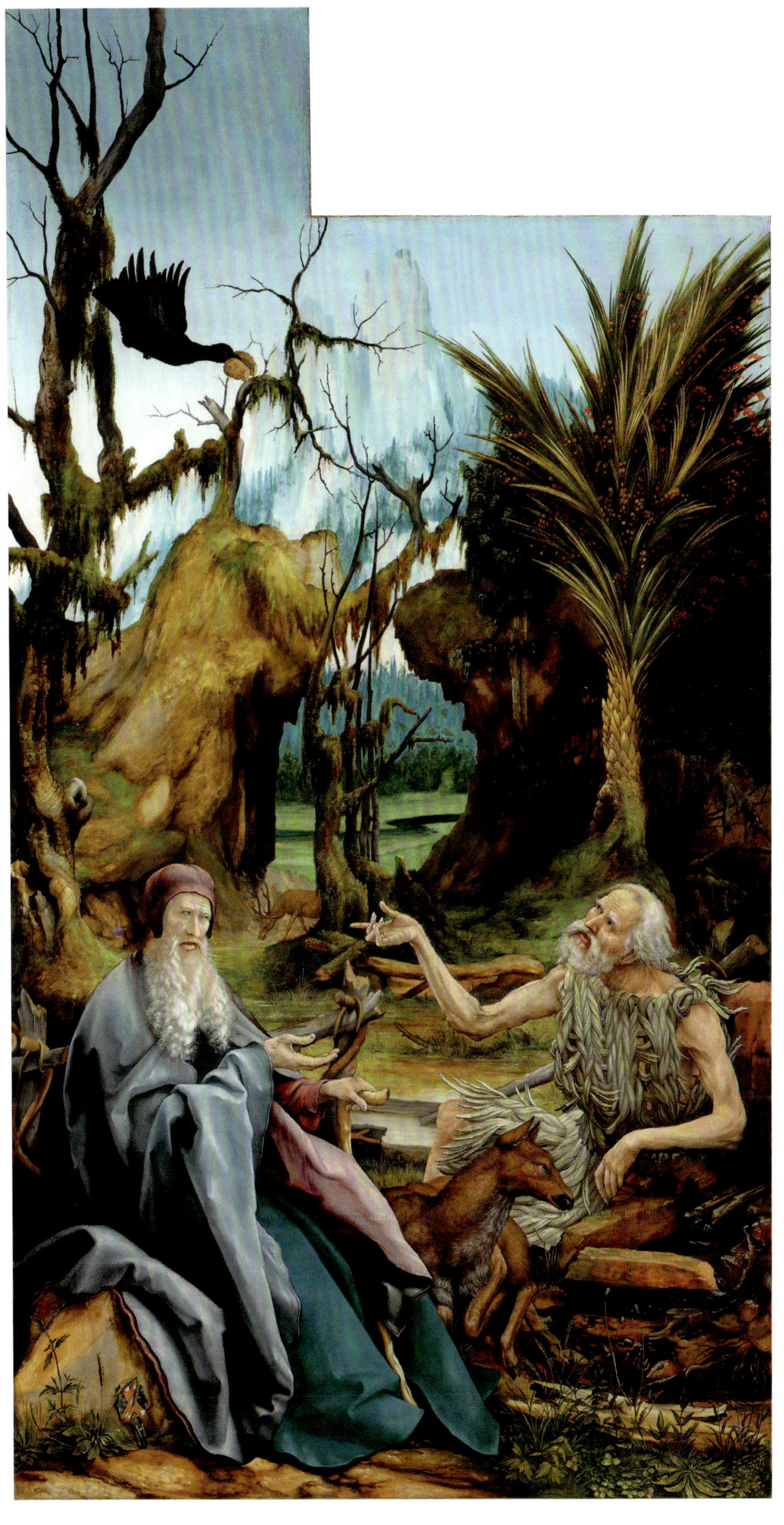

129 | Mathis Grünewald, *Meeting of the Saints Anthony the Abbott and Paul the Hermite* (from the Isenheim altarpiece), ca. 1514. Colmar, Muséè d'Unterlinden.

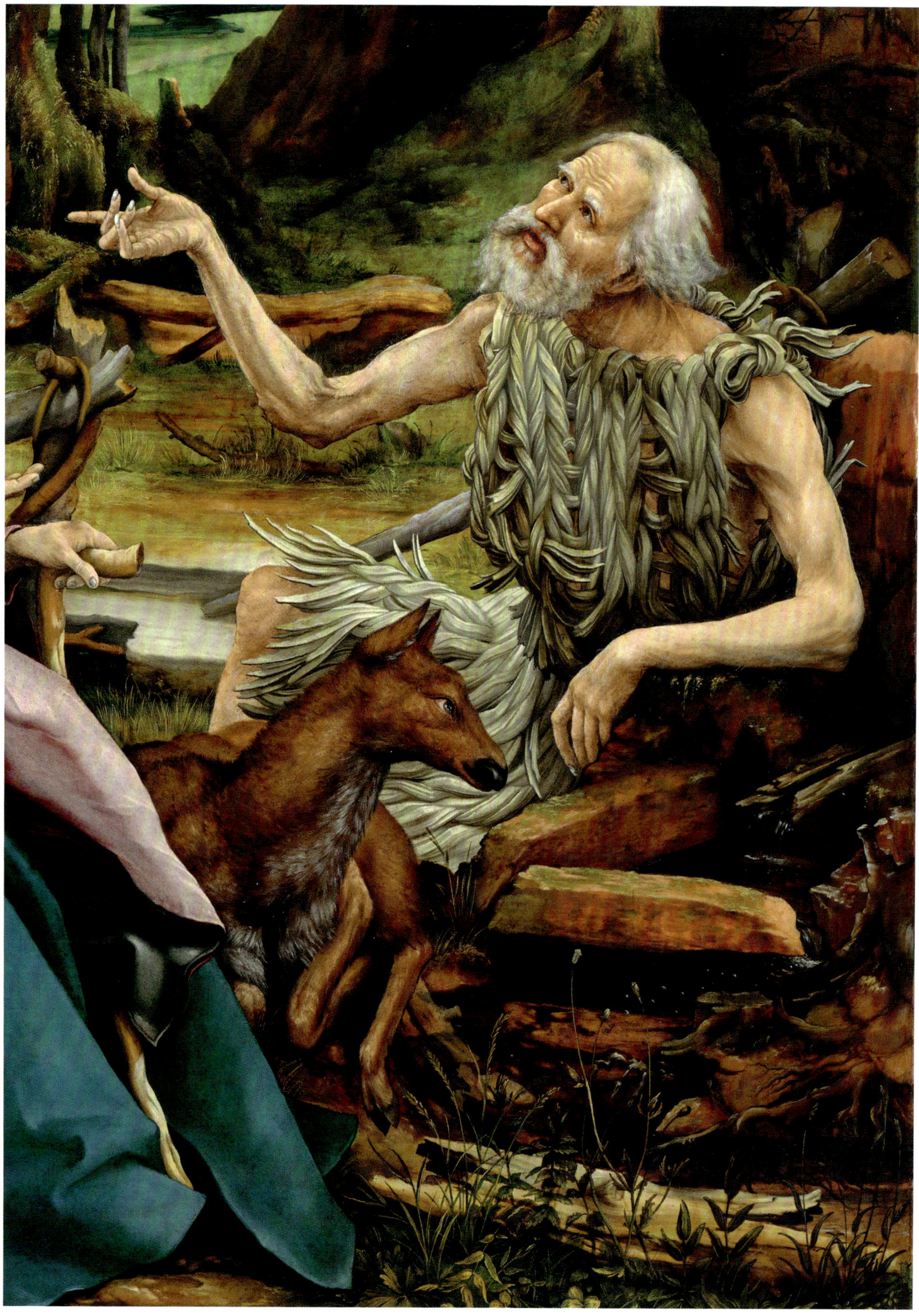

And whiles they were thus talking a crow came flying and brought to them two loaves of bread; and when the crow was gone S. Paul said: Be thou glad and joyful, for our Lord is debonair and merciful, he hath sent us bread for to eat. It is forty years passed that every day he hath sent me half a loaf, but now at thy coming he hath sent two whole loaves, and double provender. And they had question together until evensong time which of them both should entame or begin to take of the bread. At the last the bread departed even between their hands, and then they ate, and drank of the well or fountain. After graces said they had all that night collation together. On the morn said S. Paul: Brother, it is long sith that I knew that thou dwelledst in this region and in this country, and God had promised to me thy company, I shall now shortly die and shall go to Jesu Christ for to receive the crown to me promised, thou art come hither for to bury my body. When S. Anthony heard that, anon he began tenderly to weep, and wailed, praying that he might die with him and go in his company. S. Paul said: It is need yet that thou live for thy brethren, to the end that they by the ensample of thee be made firm and taught [. . .].

It happened in the second journey, where S. Anthony went through the desert the third hour of the day, he saw the soul of S. Paul, shining, ascend into heaven among a great company of angels, of prophets, and also of apostles, and anon he fell down to the earth weeping and wailing, and crying with a high voice: Alas, Paul! wherefore leavest thou me so soon, which have so little seen thee? Then he had so great desire to see the corpse or body that he passed all the remnant of his way as soon as a bird flying, like as he was wont to tell and rehearse, and when he came to the cell of S. Paul he found that the body was right up on his knees and the visage and hands addressed towards heaven and supposed he had been alive and had made his prayers, but when he had advised it, he knew well that he was passed out of this world. What weepings and what wailings he made upon the body it were a piteous thing to hear; among all other he said: O holy soul, thy body showeth in death this that thou didst in thy life. After this he was much abashed how he should bury the body, for he had no instrument to make his sepulchre; then came two lions which much debonairly made a pit after the quantity of his body, and S. Anthony buried his body therein. And he took with him the coat of S. Paul which was made and and afterward, for great reverence, S. Anthony ware this coat and clad him withal in great and solemn feasts.[90]

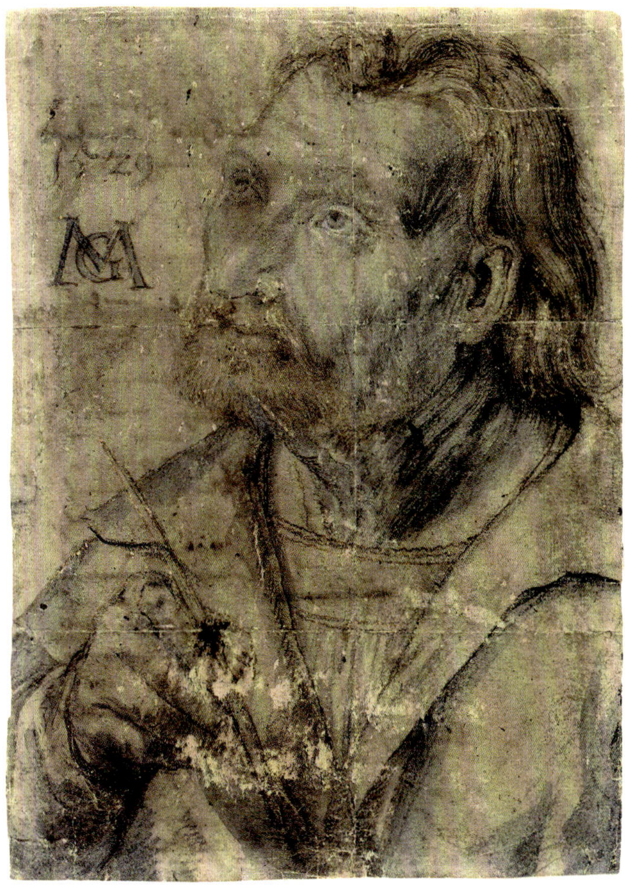

130 | Mathis Grünewald, *Meeting of the Saints Anthony the Abbott and Paul the Hermite* (detail, from the Isenheim altarpiece), ca. 1514. Colmar, Muséè d'Unterlinden.

131 | After (?) Mathis Grünewald, *Portrait of a Draftsman*, 1529 (?). Erlangen, Universty Libraru, inv. II F 18.

Perhaps without this painting, we would not imagine Grünewald as a "nature painter".[91] And yet, the beauty and accuracy of the plants in the foreground (according to the various commentators, allusions to the medicinal herbs used to treat the sick in Isenheim,[92] or for Christ's sacrifice), and the peaceful calm of the doe, which has

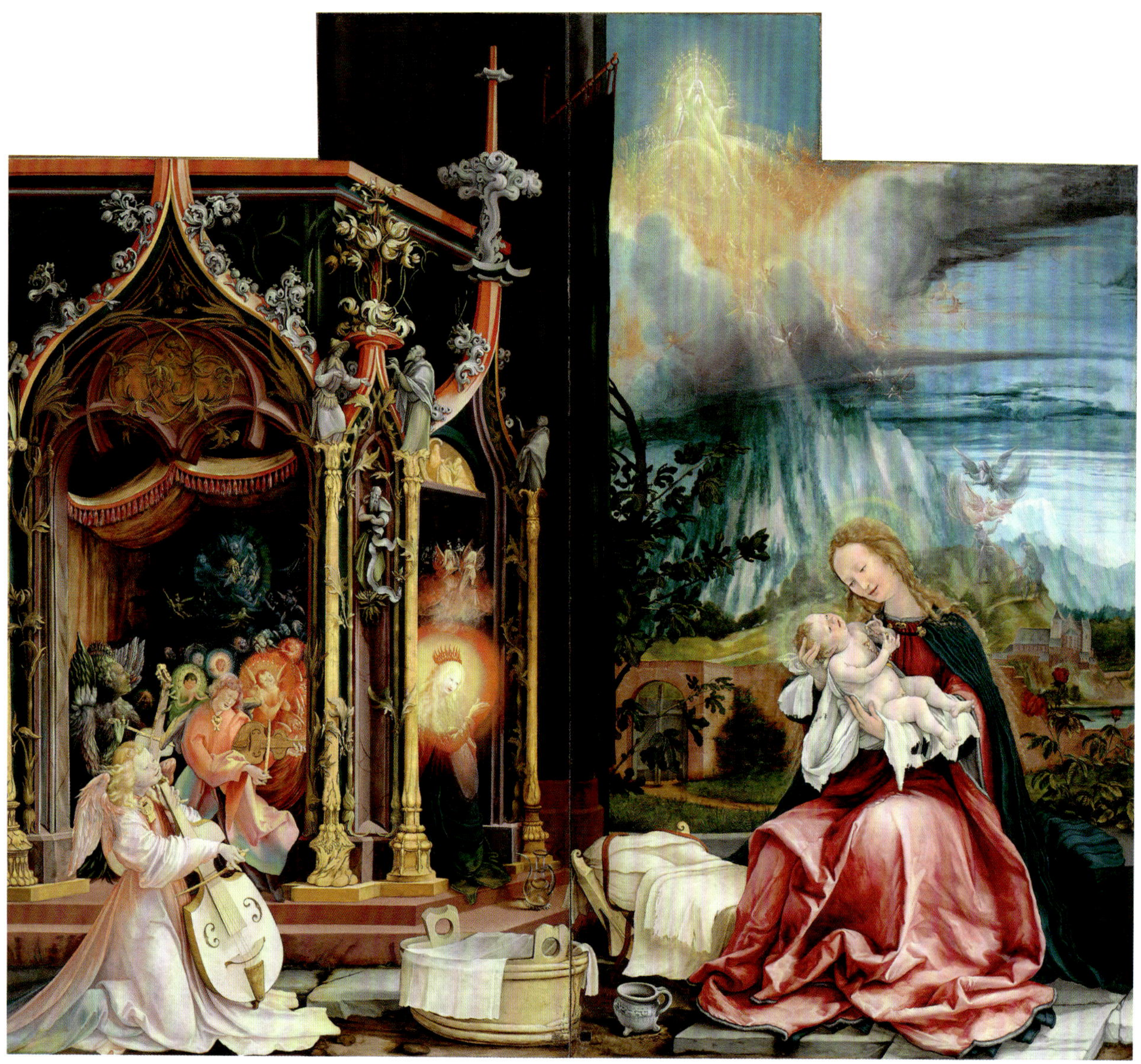

132 | Mathis Grünewald, *Allegory of the Incarnation* (from the Isenheim altarpiece), ca. 1514–1515. Colmar, Muséè d'Unterlinden.

left behind the buck seen in the clearing to sit at the feet of St. Paul, are all explicit indications of this inclination. The excruciating digging into the human figure is no longer enough for Mathis who, as he was painting the *Isenheim Altarpiece* began to experience a growth in his artistic ambitions and figurative emancipation.

Often, this face is held to be the portrait of Preceptor Guy Guers, given the advanced age and the fact that at the feet of the saint, his coat of arms is painted on the panel, on the back of a hand mirror leaning against the rock used as a seat [fig. 82]. But the opportune mention of Béguerie-De Paepe of the 1478 Antonite statutes that forbade monks from having beards[93] is enough to exclude this possibility.

The face of the elderly St. Paul, busy explaining to his fellow hermit his own, very personal food delivery service,[94] also seems more idealized than based on an actual model [fig. 130]. There are noted facial similarities with a drawing in the collection of the Erlangen University Library (black chalk and white lead, partially inked with brown ink, 208 × 150 mm, inv. II F 18), depicting a painter and "authenticated" with the monogram MG and dated 1529, both apocryphal [fig. 131].[95] The attribution of the drawing is still uncertain and it received some popularity, including visual, as a

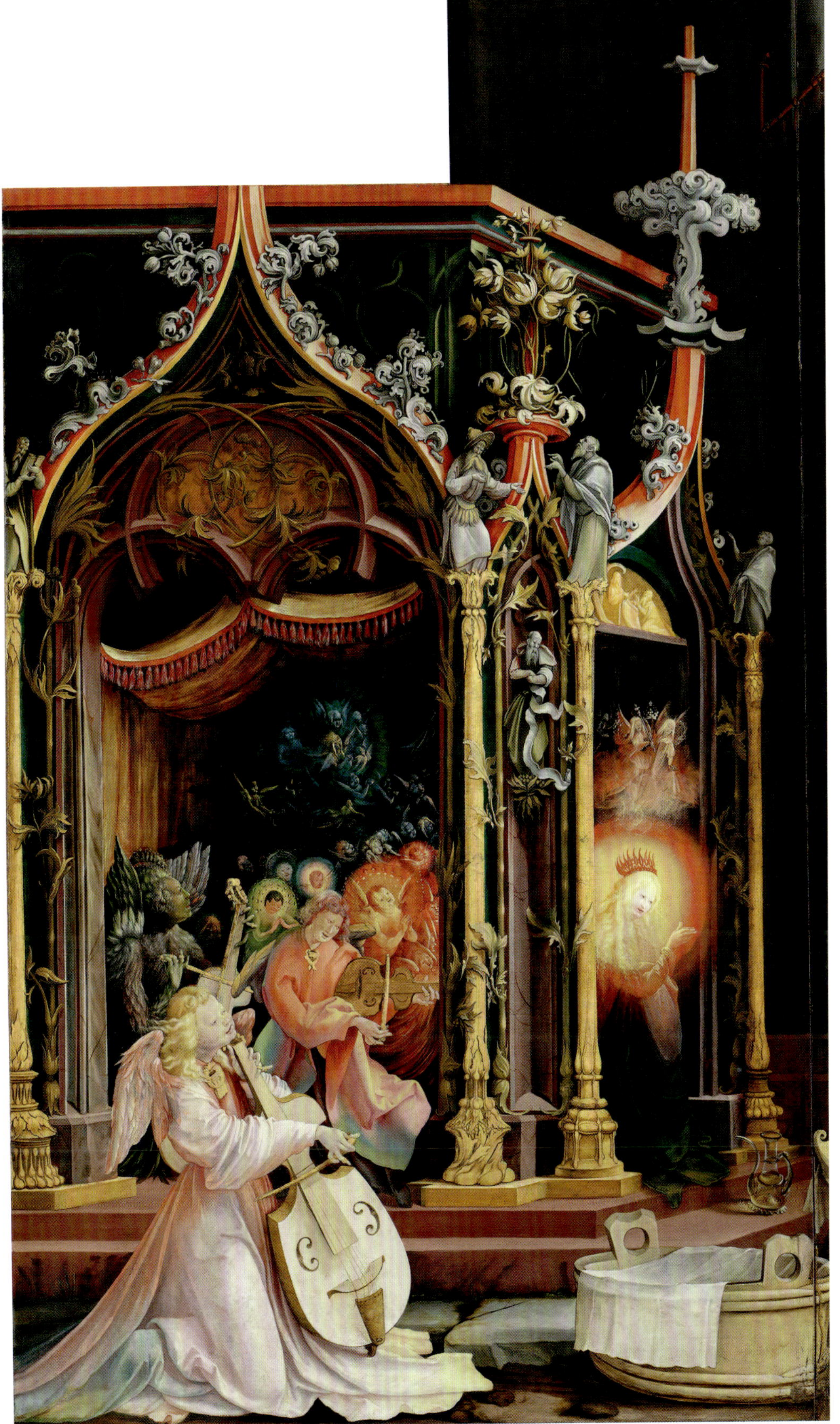

133 | Mathis Grünewald, *Allegory of the Incarnation* (detail. from the Isenheim altarpiece), ca. 1514–1515. Colmar, Musée d'Unterlinden.

134 | Mathis Grünewald, *Allegory of the Incarnation* (detail, from the Isenheim altarpiece), ca. 1514–1515. Colmar, Musée d'Unterlinden.

135 | Mathis Grünewald, *Allegory of the Incarnation* (detail, from the Isenheim altarpiece), ca. 1514–1515. Colmar, Musée d'Unterlinden.

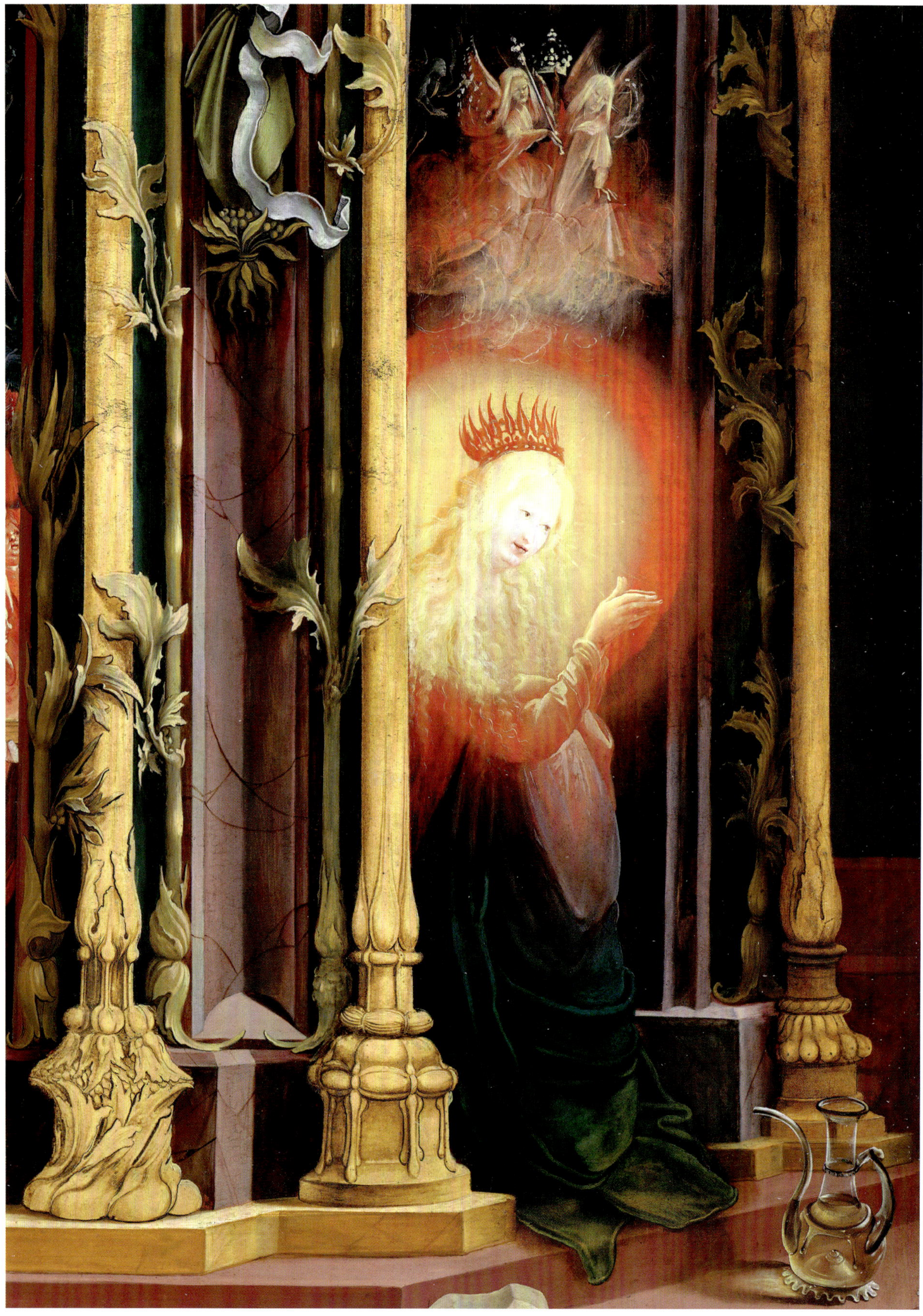

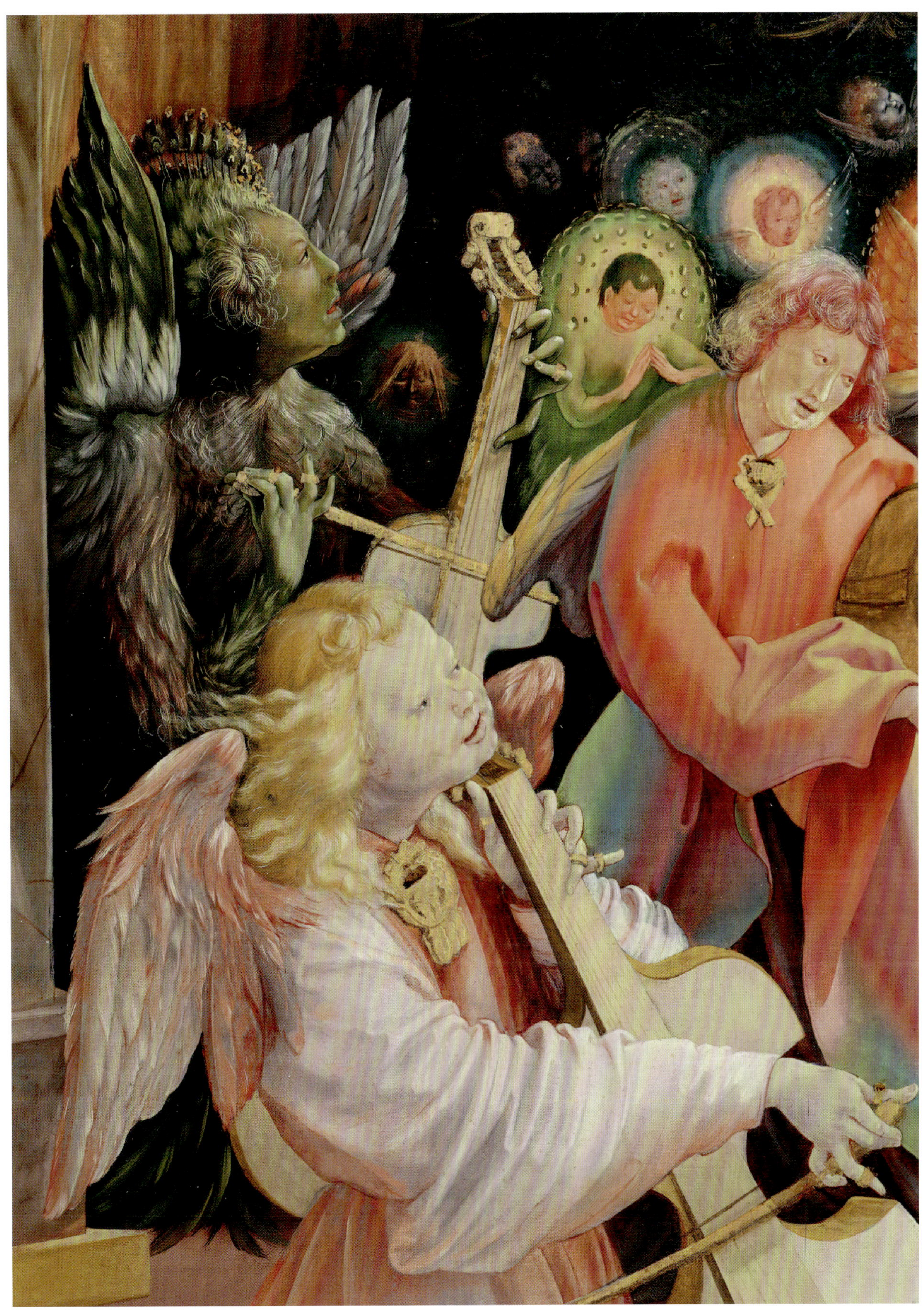

self-portrait of Grünewald but, although its state of conservation is not the best, the quality would not seem worthy of Mathis. I would not be against considering it an old copy of one of his drawings, and how nice it would be to think that this Klaus Kinski-like face was truly that of our artist.[96]

We can also see an iconographic subtlety that reveals the painter's strict fidelity to his literary source. St. Paul's hermitic "superiority", asserted by Jacobus de Voragine, is indicated by the contrast between the elegant and still-sumptuous clothing of St. Anthony and the tunic made of interwoven dried leaves worn by St. Paul. This distinction is also seen in the difference between the well-manicured nails of the former and the unkempt appearance of the latter with his long nails and bony arm covered in a disorderly white down.

As previously mentioned, the backs of the two Berlin and Dresden fragments with the *Arm of St. Sebastian* offer two different versions of the seated St. Anthony: the Dresden version is rendered in black chalk only, while the Berlin version includes evident additions of white lead. The latter version is particularly intriguing due to the new aspects it introduces. After having outlined the general mass of the figure in the drawing now in Dresden, Grünewald is no longer satisfied with using chalk to indicate the mobility of the light. Instead, again as in the Berlin drawings of *St. Catherine* and *St. Dorothy*, he utilizes whiting, but much more generously, in large and compact masses, all on full, loose drapery filled with indentations to create a series of mountainous ravines to give three-dimensionality to the form. Among the fully lit sections, identified by the white lead, and those in the shade, indicated by the build-up of black chalk, we see a dense network of intermediate areas in which the natural and "neutral" color of the paper becomes, itself, a color, suggesting a surface that is both more receptive to half tones and with a more convincing volumetry. These innovations have a parallel in the painted version where the garment of the saint has a virtually infinite chromatic richness. It is useless to search for anything similar in his German contemporaries. Mathis had embarked on a quest all his own, which, very soon and urged on by stimuli as yet beyond his horizon, would lead him to completely unforeseeable results.

Logically speaking, having completed this peaceful scene, Grünewald dedicated himself to painting the other side of the panel, the left half [fig. 132] of an image that is complex and difficult to understand in its integrity [fig. 133].[97]

We see here an elaborate Gothic tabernacle set against a dark curtain. Inside it, an orchestra of fanciful multi-colored angels plays for the Madonna who is kneeling on the very edge, her face as resplendent as the sun—a smaller-scale repetition of the identification between face and light we already admired in the *Resurrection*. Its radiant light scalds nearby objects, and even her blonde head carries an unusual crown with tongues of fire. Perhaps the reference proposed by Feuerstein to the familiar *Revelations* of St. Birgitta is correct: "thanks to her supreme joy she exceeded all creatures to come", Mary is "the vessel irradiated by the true sun, Christ" and she, herself, "the one that generates Christ, the true sun" (X, 14; IB, 11).[98] The Madonna, kneeling in prayer, her face in paradisiacal bliss, is visibly pregnant. At her feet is a glass ewer, perhaps a symbol of the purity of Mary penetrated by the Divine Word but remaining intact like glass permeated by the sun's rays. It is also a precise reminder of the mimetic skill of the Flemish artists he studied in his youth, but very few of them would have been able to equal the imprint of the colored reflection of the liquid contained in the ewer on the pink marble of the step [fig. 134].

136 | Mathis Grünewald, *Allegory of the Incarnation* (detail, from the Isenheim altarpiece), ca. 1514–1515. Colmar, Muséè d'Unterlinden.

137 | Mathis Grünewald, *Allegory of the Incarnation* (detail, from the Isenheim altarpiece), ca. 1514–1515. Colmar, Musée d'Unterlinden.

The crown on her head would seem a reference to the Holy Spirit, promised by the angel during the Annunciation: "Spiritus Sanctus superveniet in te, et virtus Altissimi obumbrabit tibi: ideoque et quod nascetur sanctum, vocabitur filius Dei" (Luke 1:35). Being pregnant and filled with the Holy Spirit is, for Mary, the same thing, and here Grünewald portrays the Spirit as tongues of fire, as in the manifestation of the Pentecost (Acts 2:2–4).[99] Scheja's interpretation of this scene as an allusion to Mary's coronation, though fairly unusual, is plausible.[100]

However, it seems quite obvious that the iconographic basis of this scene is the image of the *Virgo gravida*, a fairly codified iconography of which numerous elements here are part.[101] The curtain and niche itself in which the pregnant Virgin Mary is portrayed are rather clear references to the tabernacle of Moses, whose interpretation as the foreshadowing of Mary as the expectant mother became commonplace in the Christian exegesis.[102] Very apropos is a citation from the *Commentum in Psalmos Centum et quinquaginta Psalmi Davidici cum expositione* (Valencia, Imprenta Luis Arinyo y Alfonso Fernández de Córdoba, 1484) of the theologian Jaime Perez, a work so popular that it was reprinted a sixth and seventh time in 1509 and 1514, and especially likely to have been included in the Isenheim monastery library, given that Perez was an Augustinian:

> ita tabernaculum Moysi figurabat Virginem Mariam. Nam sicut arca testamenti fuit reposita in tabernaculo illo, ut patet *Exodo* 45, ita pariter totus Christus fuit repositus et requievit in utero virginali tamquam in tabernaculo materiali.[103]

In a similar context, the presence of the pomegranate leaves and fruit as part of the tabernacle decorations only support the interpretation here proposed.[104] I would also add, drawing above all from the studies by Lechner and Father Pozzi, that the three-quarter pose of the Madonna, in order to emphasize her physical status, is the norm in this type of representation,[105] and also that the serene expression of the mother-to-be can be explained within the context of a similar iconography, drawing on the fairly well-known text, *Sermones aurei de Maria Virgine Dei matre* by Jacobus de Voragine, the author of the *Legenda Aurea*:

> partus beatae Mariae fuit dissimilis a partu aliorum mulierum. Caterae mulieres habent timorem ante partum, quia in partu periclitantur, in partu dolorem et post partum languorem. Beata autem virgo nec ante partum timorem habuit, nec in partu dolorem sensit, nec post partum languorem incurrit[106]

Behind her back, the angels appear more dreamlike and unsettling. (Who inhabits the blue globe just below the tabernacle? Is the scaly, green-colored being on the right [fig. 135] really an angel? Or who knows, throwing open the mystic abysses, is it a converted demon?).[107] And the most unexpected displays of chromatic virtuosity, including—as was discovered during restoration—the reflection of the golden light, perhaps imprinted by the divine apparition among the clouds on the side panel, that dances across the smiling face of the viola da gamba-playing angel: everything is so beautiful that it is almost unbearable.[108] Sooner or later some learned scholar will provide us with the definitive iconological key for these parts of the painting, but what matters is that, as far as I know, there is no previous artist on which our painter could have based his work.

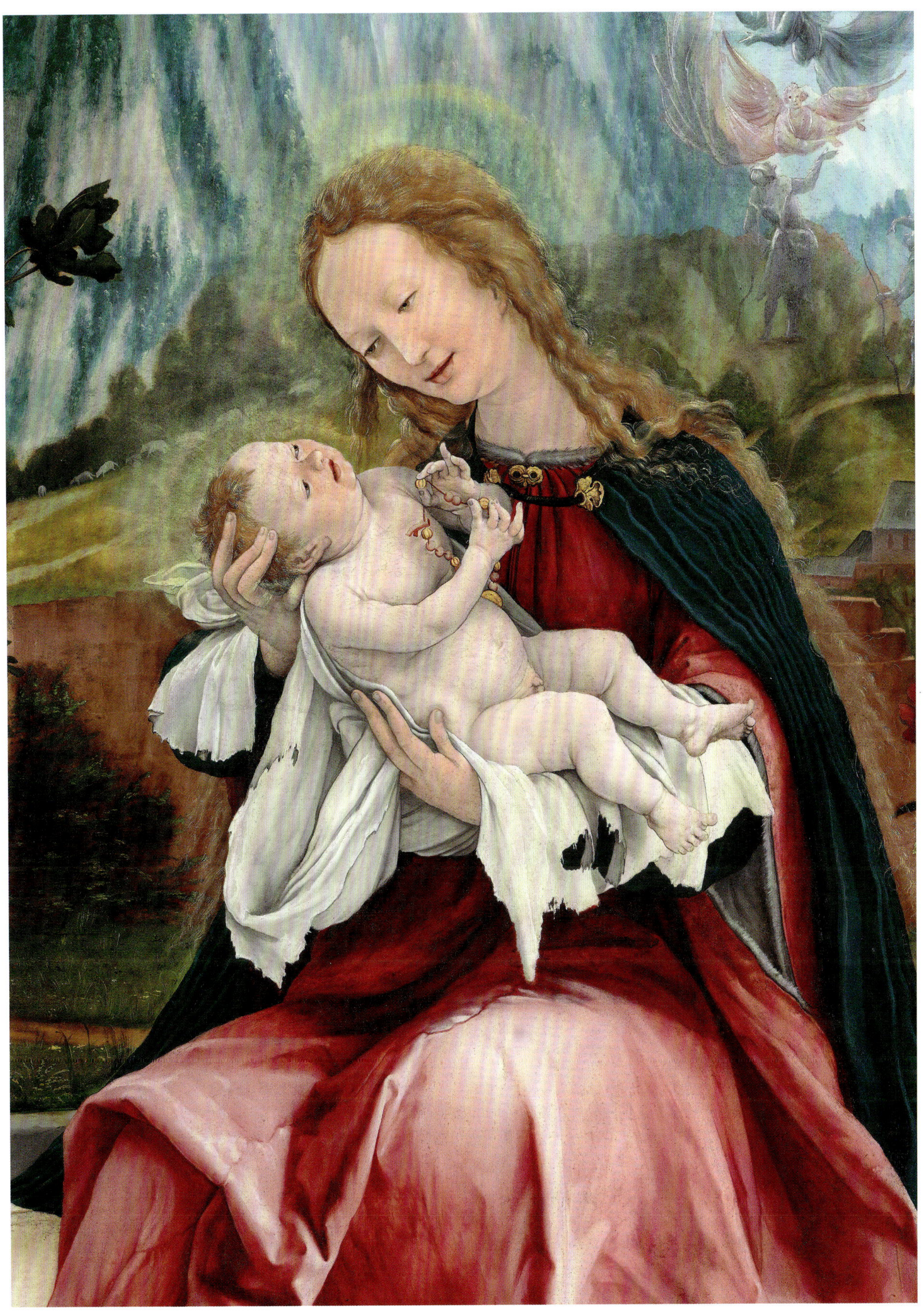

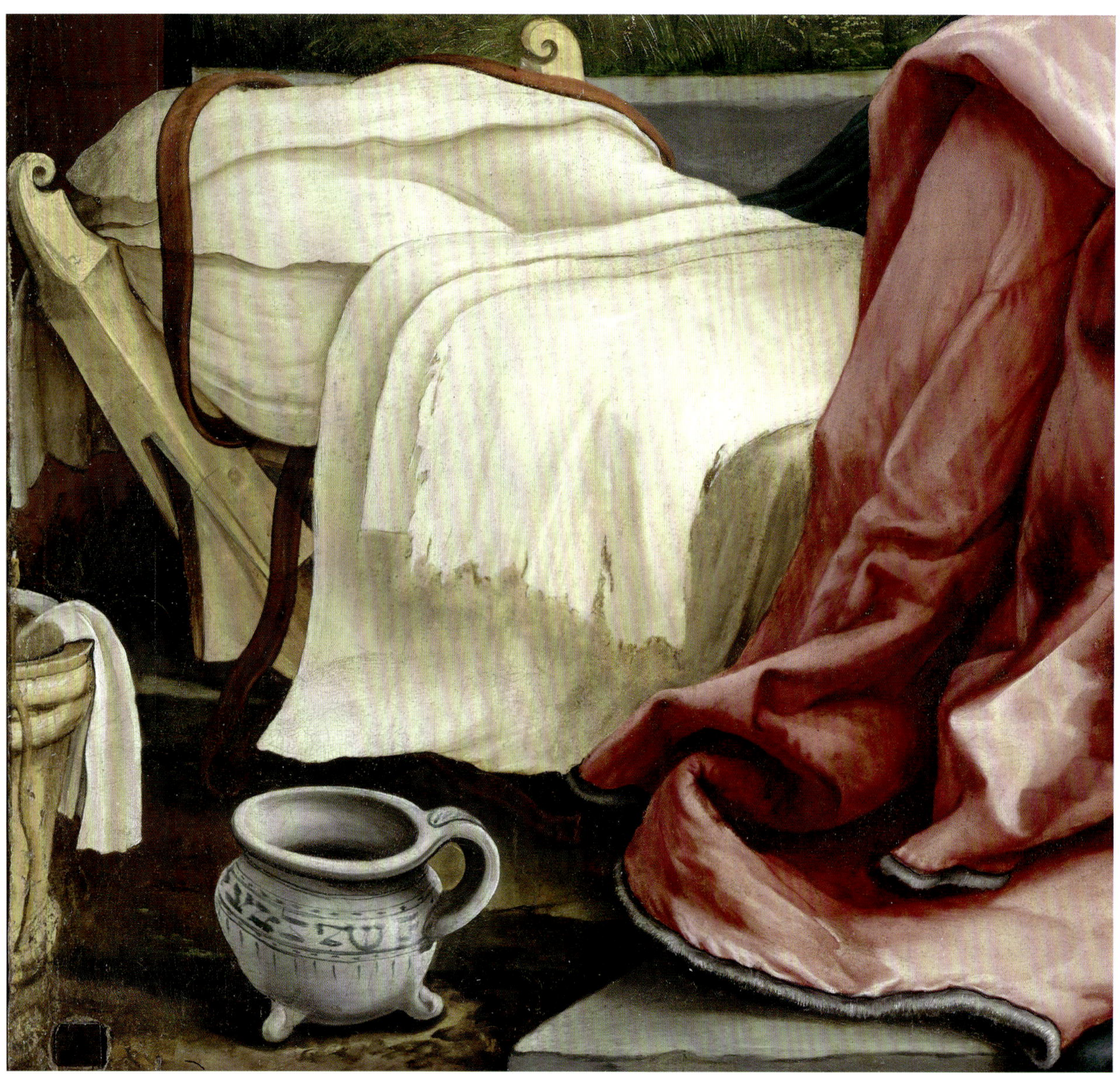

138 | Mathis Grünewald, *Allegory of the Incarnation* (detail, from the Isenheim altarpiece), ca. 1514–1515. Colmar, Musée d'Unterlinden.

The scene continues, without interruption, on the adjoining panel [fig. 136]. It should be recalled that these panels were visible on feast days, flanked by the *Annunciation* and the *Resurrection*: following the carnage shown in the *Crucifixion* during the regular church calendar, we are now presented with the glorious face of Christianity.

The Madonna is relaxing in a garden, smilingly cradling the Christ Child. They are totally absorbed in the interplay of their gazes and smiles, seemingly oblivious to everything else [fig. 137]. This depiction recalls an audacious passage by Staupitz (here, however, strongly influenced by Bernard of Clairvaux), taken from his *Libellus de executione aeterne praedestinationis:*

> In the fourth stage [of the love for God] the virgin Mary alone who is the Mother of God, is found. She alone tasted how sweet he is: Jesus is subjected to her, and he smiles when she wants him to, or he weeps, or he flatters her with his talk, or throws kisses at her, sleeps naked with her naked and he shows other signs of such love.[109]

It is perhaps no accident that in the background we see a bed whose interpretation remains ambiguous: it could be seen as a cot, according to contemporary interpretations, or rather a double bed, or even deliberately both simultaneously [fig. 138].[110] Within this resplendent and glorious context, the objects gathered within it are the everyday objects of recent motherhood: a washbasin (still on the table on the left), a potty for basic necessities to underscore Jesus's absolute humanity, even in the lowliest of physical activities. We even have a glimpse of its content: Christ's feces, no more no less, unique in the history of art. In fact, true mysticism, which is not the same as devotion, fears nothing.[111]

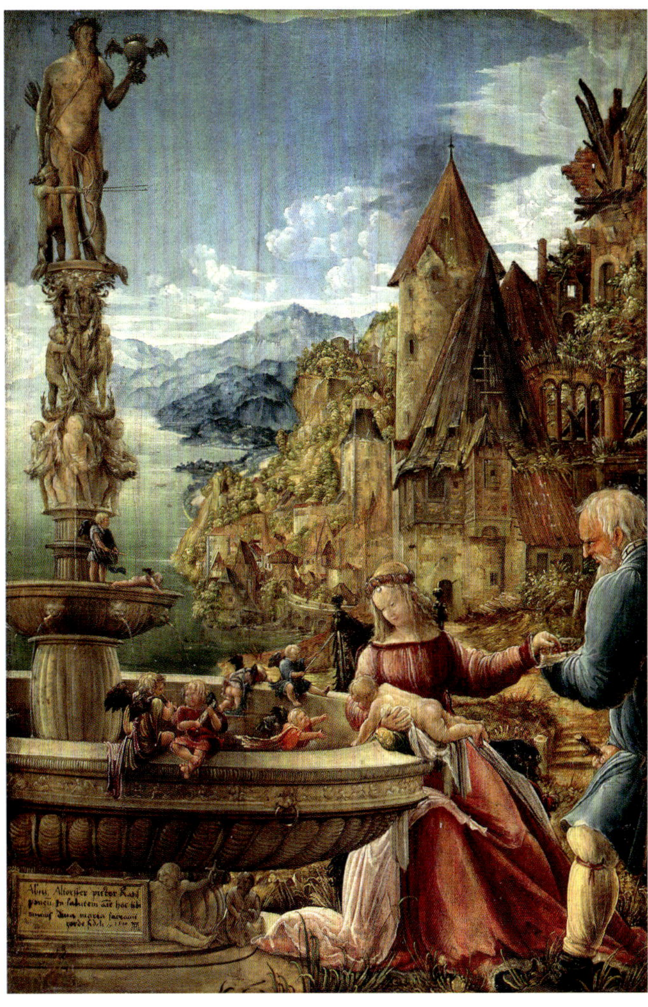

139 | Albrecht Altdorfer, *The Bath of the sleeping Jesus during the Flight into Egypt*, 1510. Berlin, Staatliche Museen, Gemäldegalerie, inv. 638B.

The garden, in which we see a rose bush (a symbol of Mary par excellence, but perhaps also inspired by Schongauer's masterpiece in the Dominican church in nearby Colmar), continues the naturalistic spell already seen in the *Meeting between Saints Peter and Paul.* Here, however, it is interrupted by the divine apparition, like the sudden appearance of the sun from behind clouds heavy with rain. From this golden epiphany descends something like a downpour that is quickly dispelled in the air.

There is nothing casual about the two rays emerging forcefully from the clouds. The first seems focused directly on the figure of the Madonna, as if to illustrate the passage from the antiphon *Ave Regina coelurum*: "Felix coeli porta Ex qua mundo lux est orta", which is usually a reference to the incarnation of Christ in Mary's womb (thus creating a solid connection with the image of the pregnant Virgin Mary on the left).[112] The divine light then passes and becomes incarnate through the "portal" of the Virgin Mary, perhaps also alluding to the non-metaphorical gate of the garden in the shape of a cross. Here it divides into a second ray towards the church in the background, in turn a *ianua coeli* of the contingent world. The Madonna is, thus, the tabernacle, the portal of light (a meaning also alluded to by the garden gate, *hortus conclusus*, with its beams forming a cross), and finally the image of the church. This way, in a highly condensed figurative synthesis, an entire Mariology that starts from the Exodus to arrive at the "historic" church is revealed before the eyes of the Ishenheim faithful.

It is difficult to find precedents for this image of God the Father as light whose flashes are angels. Scheja proposes a comparison with Bosch's triptych of *The Last Judgement*, perhaps commissioned for Lille in 1506 and now at the Akademie der bildenden Künste in Vienna. This work was also known in Germany (it was copied by Cranach in a painting at the Gemäldegalerie in Berlin) and it would confirm Mathis's solid interest in the Dutch painter.[113]

However, it would seem that all Grünewalds own the extraordinary mystic

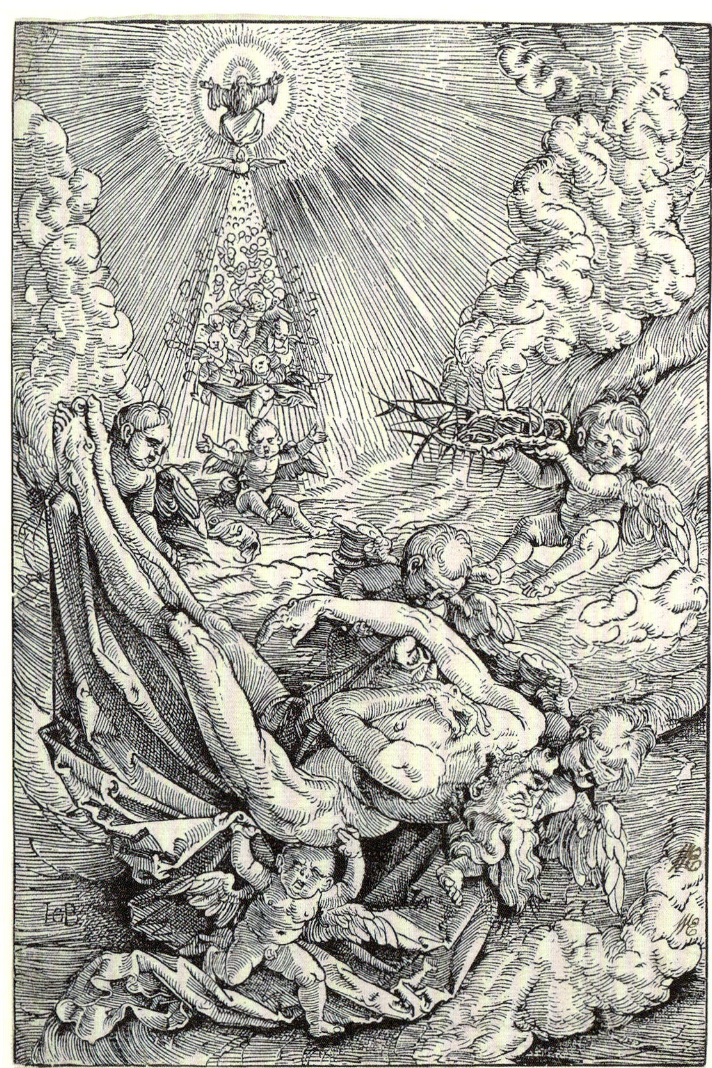

140 | Hans Baldung Grien, *The dead Christ mourned in heaven by the angels in the presence of God the Father*, woodcut, ca. 1515–1517.

tension already apparent in the *Resurrection*, the same desire to portray the indescribable. Who can say if playing a role in this flight of creativity there was not, once again, the *Liber Scivias* by Hildegard von Bingen:

> I am the supreme, fiery energy that ignited all living sparks and I did not issue with my breath anything that was mortal, but I distinguish these things judging them as they are; placing myself around the circle and flying around it with its superior wings, with knowledge, I ordered it with righteousness. [. . .]. I, the energy of fire [. . .].[114]

In the background, two angels bring the news to two shepherds, just as it occurred on the night of the Nativity. Below is a church seen from its apse, which has sometimes been perceived as a reference to the church of the Benedictine convent of Hildegard.[115]

It was here that the "public" affirmation of Mathis's works in Isenheim began. The already-mentioned Karlsruhe drawing copying one of the guards in the *Resurrection* and Jerg Ratgeb's consideration of this divine apparition highlight its significance. But it is no accident that the Grünewald of Isenheim is the piece important to Baldung Grien, who, as we know, was working at the very same time in nearby Freiburg. The opening of the sky in the strange woodcut depicting the *Dead Christ mourned in heaven by the angels in the presence of God the Father*, dated 1515–1517 [fig. 140], is unthinkable without the Grünewald work described above.[116] Naturally, these consecutive, unusual images of the pregnant Madonna and the Madonna as mother have prompted extensive iconological interpretations.[117] However, I have already amply discussed these aspects, and I prefer to take the discussion to a more historically and philologically solid ground.

Probably relevant to this moving image of Madonna with Child is a now-faded drawing on the verso of a sheet at the Kupferstichkabinett, Berlin (black chalk, 288 × 367 mm, inv. KdZ 2040)[118] [fig. 141]. The Christ Child is completely different, not concentrated on his mother's smile, but intently observing something to his right. Behind the Madonna's back is a clambering second child, probably St. John, while the Virgin Mary, with slightly inclined head, appears to be the same as the one in the *Isenheim Altarpiece*. On the recto of the sheet is a peculiar image, identical in terms of technique, style and paper to the Berlin study for St. Anthony, confirming the immediate chronological succession of these paintings. A figure with an

141 | Mathis Grünewald, *Madonna and Child with Saint John (?)*, ca. 1515. Berlin, Staatliche Museen, Kupferstichkabinett, inv. KdZ 2040 verso.

indistinct headpiece (?), holding an object (scepter?) in his left hand and pointing, or perhaps better, blessing with his right, flanked by an astrolabe, is wearing a sumptuous mantle whose train is being borne by two angels [fig. 142].

In the past, I had proposed an iconographic interpretation related to the diocese of Mainz. Seeing the main character as a bishop. I hypothesized he might be St. Boniface, the first archbishop of that city, "apostle to the Germans" and martyr. He was famous not only for his apostolate but also the controversy about the antipodes with Virgil of Salzburg who dared to admit that people also lived south of the equator.[119] However, although the dress of a cleric, it is not that of a bishop, and it is also difficult to identify what he is holding in his hand as a crozier. In terms of his headgear, which is certainly not a tiara, or even a crown absurdly worn askew

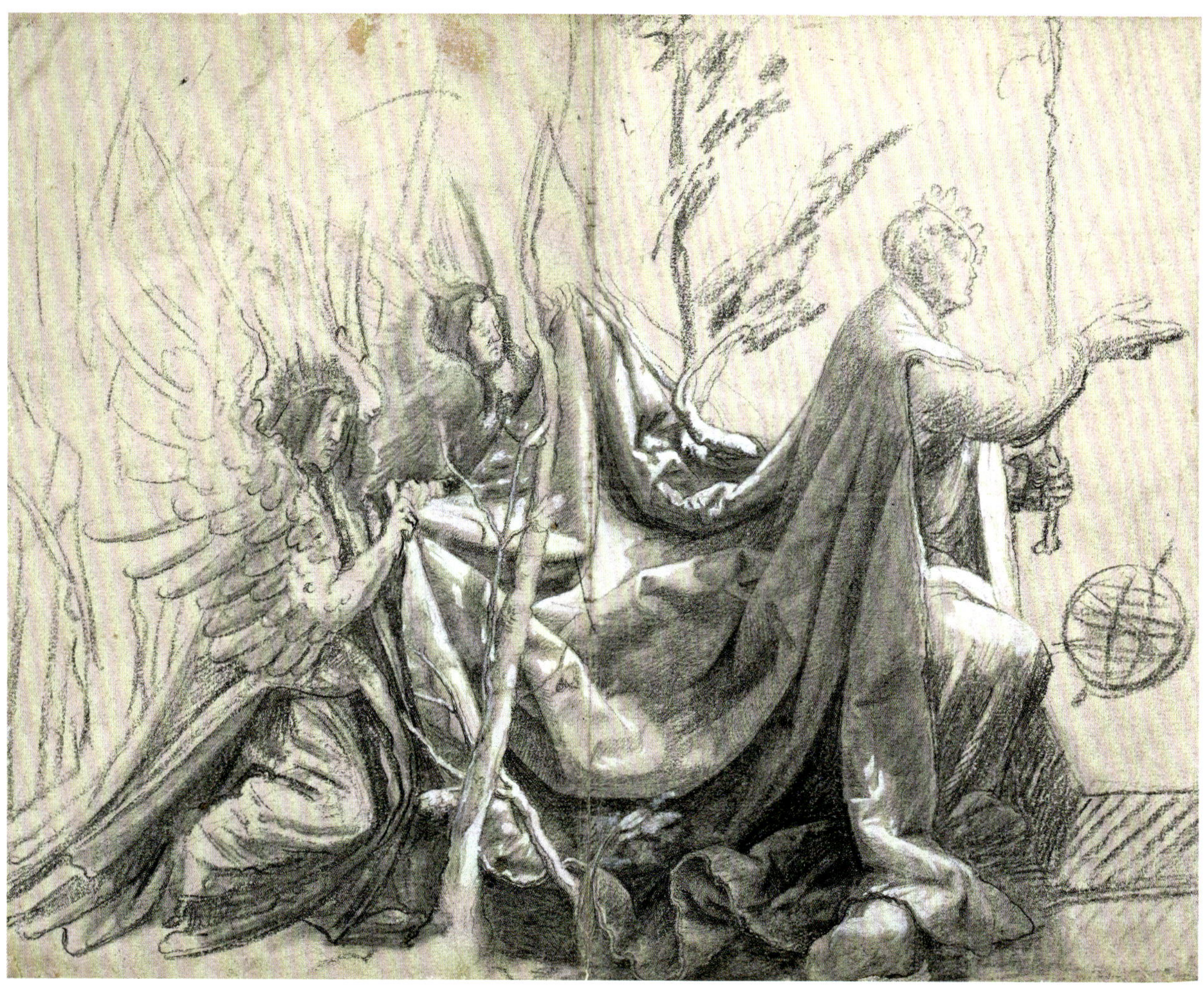

142 | Mathis Grünewald, *Angel of the Annunciation (?)*, ca. 1515. Berlin, Staatliche Museen, Kupferstichkabinett, inv. KdZ 2040 recto.

like a jaunty cap, I think it is a ray of light, or one of tongues of fire like those that adorn the head of the Virgin Mary in *the Allegory of the Incarnation*. Although his hypothesis has essentially come to nothing, I cannot exclude that Bernhard Saran was correct in suggesting that the initial setting of the *Allegory of the Incarnation* was completely different, with the image based on this drawing planned instead of the niche and orchestra of angels.[120] In that case, the figure in the flowing mantle could perhaps be a majestic God the Father with scepter (while the astrolabe would take the place of the more usual globe), or a beardless Christ involved in crowning his mother, a hypothesis that would support Scheja's iconographic interpretation, which, as we have seen, saw the Isenheim *Allegory* as the coronation of Mary. Nonetheless, I lean towards identifying the figure as an announcing angel, a scene that had been planned from the beginning, but in the context of an altarpiece conceived completely differently from what was actually painted. A comparison can be drawn with a painting quite close to it in time and location, the *Annunciation* dated 1527, by Strasbourg painter Wilhelm Stetter and today at the Augustinermuseum in Freiburg im Breisgau (inv. M 66/004) [fig. 143],[121] in which the angel makes the identical gesture of blessing with his right hand and holds a scepter in his left. A similar gesture had already been seen in the announcing angel painted by Schongauer in the altarpiece for the Antonites in Isenheim, which was mentioned earlier.

Furthermore, there is another anomaly in the painting, or at least something new. At first glance, the Madonna's red dress seems similar to the mantle of the standing St. Anthony. And yet it is difficult to confuse the compact and mineral rendering of that fabric, like an enormous cherry, with the much more material, rich and dense texture of the mantle, which includes a touch of pink (returned to its vibrant luminosity following restoration) that had not yet been explored by Grünewald [fig. 144]. Could something similar be found in Dürer, Baldung Grien or any other German painter? No. I admit that one example, just one, seems to me so apt and conclusive that nothing more need be said: the mantle of St. Martha and of the Madonna in the altar perhaps created for the Oratory of St. Martha in Brescia and now in the parish church of St. John the Evangelist, painted by Gerolamo Romanino around 1509 [fig. 145].[122] I think that even a spectrometric exam would produce similar results for the two mantles. How can such a destabilizing similarity be explained? Should we consider Mathis traveled to Brescia, right before he gave the final touches to the altarpiece? A hypothesis that is seemingly not just far-fetched, but absurd. However, before pronouncing a verdict, we should conclude the detailed analysis of the altarpiece.

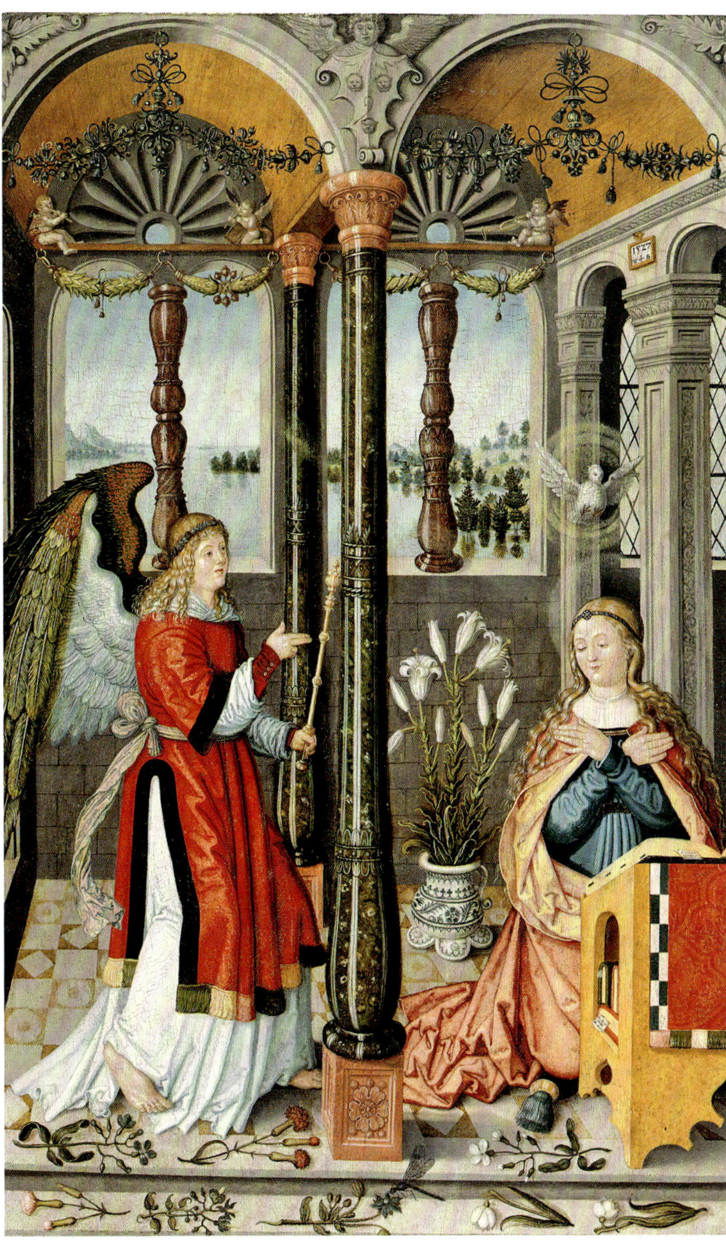

143 | Wilhelm Stetter, *Annunciation* 1527. Freiburg im Breisgau, Augustinermuseum, inv. M 66/004.

We have yet to examine the spectacular reverse side of the panel with the Madonna cradling Baby Jesus: the *Temptation of St. Anthony* (265 × 139 cm) [fig. 146]. The iconographic source is not hard to identify: once again, the *Vita Antonii* in the Latin translation by Evagrius of Antioch and the *Legenda Aurea*.

> After, he went into a hole or cave to hide him, and anon he found there a great multitude of devils, that so much beat him that his servant bare him upon his shoulders in to his house as he had been dead. When the other hermits were assembled and wept his death, and would have done his service, suddenly S. Anthony revived and made his servant to bear him into the pit again where the devils had so evil beaten him, and began to summon the devils again, which had beaten him, to battles. And anon they came in form of diverse beasts wild and savage, of whom that one howled, another siffled, and another cried, and another brayed and assailed S. Anthony, that one with the horns, the others with their teeth, and the others with their paws and

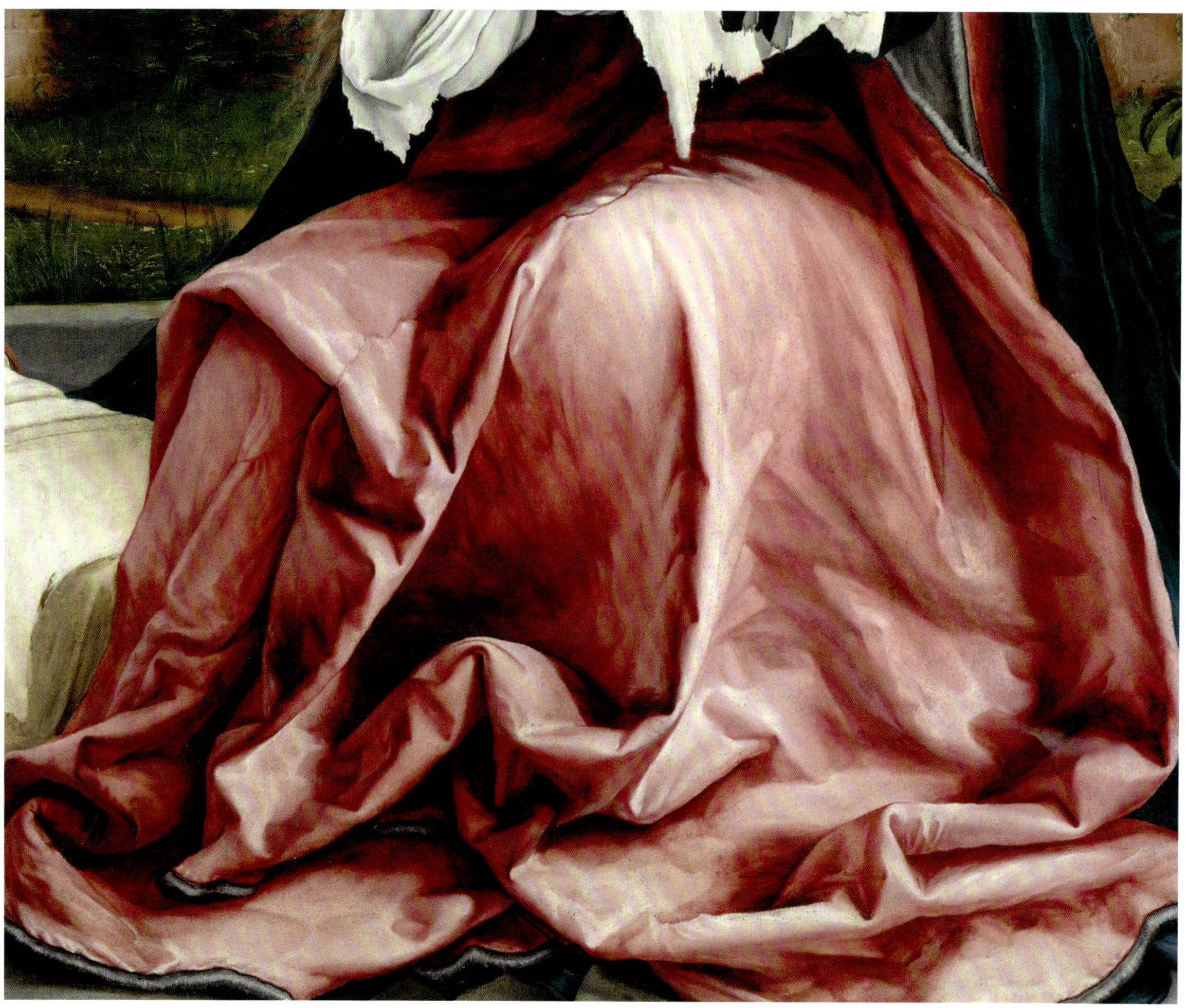

144 | Mathis Grünewald, *Allegory of the Incarnation* (detail, from the Isenheim altarpiece), ca. 1514–1515. Colmar, Muséè d'Unterlinden.

ongles, and disturned, and all to-rent his body that he supposed well to die. Then came a clear brightness, and all the beasts fled away, and S. Anthony understood that in this great light our Lord came, and he said twice: Who art thou? The good Jesu answered: I am here, Anthony. Then said S. Anthony: O good Jesu! where hast thou been so long? why wert thou not here with me at the beginning to help me and to heal my wounds? Then our Lord said: I was here but I would see and abide to see thy battle, and because thou hast manly fought and well maintained thy battle, I shall make thy name to be spread through all the world.[123] .

The scroll in the lower right bears the reprimand of St. Anthony: "ubi eras Ihesu bone ubi eras quare non affuisti ut sanares vulnera mea."[124] Even if I fear not very accurate, I very much like Schubert's idea of who reads, in the crevices of the dry, felled trunk to which the scroll is attached, the words "FIDE ME", interpreting them as the implicit response to the saint's desperate invocation.[125]

I also do not exclude the possibility that in addition to Athanasius/Evagrius and Jacobus de Voragine, Grünewald was also familiar with a third source, the epitome of the life of St. Anthony compiled by Johannes Marcellarii, *sacrista* of the mother house of the Antonite Order, the Monastery of St. Anthony at Viennois. In fact, it is only there we read that the saint "reperit se in quodam monte igneo ubi a daemonibus in

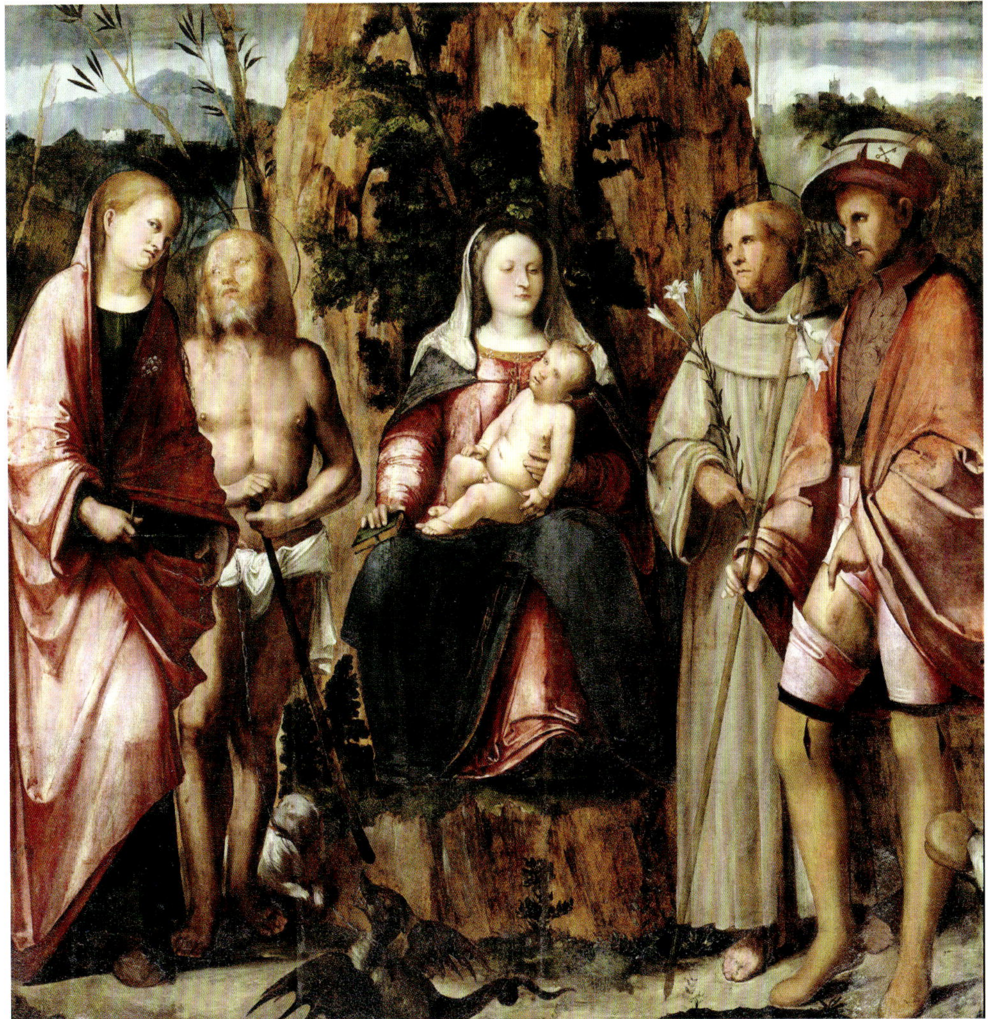

145 | Gerolamo de Romanis called Romanino, *Madonna and Child with the Saints Martha, Lazar, Anthony of Padua and Roch*, ca. 1509. Brescia, church of San Giovanni Evangelista.

sua figura apparentibus verberatus, traxinatus et mortaliter vulneratus fuit".[126]

Around the unfortunate hermit, all hell breaks loose—literally. Here, Mathis gives free rein to his macabre imagination: the setting teems with monsters and imaginary beasts that attack the saint, but also fight among themselves (in the background, two imaginary beings are savagely beating a frog) [fig. 147]. In the lower left, there is even a fetid monster about which much—perhaps too much—has been written (is he suffering from shingles or syphilis? [fig. 146]).[127] I would like to note, however, on the suggestion of Stefano Zuffi, that the demon with the head of a dragon (whose arms are also covered with pustules and sores [fig. 149]) seems to have been inspired by oriental, perhaps Chinese, iconography. For example, porcelain from the Ming dynasty, which was also well-known in Europe, includes a type of white and blue vases and plates decorated using a range of motifs, a quite common one being dragons. Examples spanning the entire 15th and early 16th centuries (Yongle, Xuande eras) include dragons with heads exhibiting comparable iconographic features: horns, elongated muzzles with open jaws and gaping white eyes [fig. 150].[128] There is nothing strange in thinking that Grünewald would have come in contact with an object of this type and that he would have examined it with his curious and unprejudiced eye, transforming the traditional motif of a far-off, unknown land into an habitué of his world of terrifying or (as in this case) comical monsters.

146 | Mathis Grünewald, *Temptations of Saint Anthony* (from the Isenheim altarpiece), ca. 1515. Colmar, Musée d'Unterlinden.

147 | Mathis Grünewald, *Temptations of Saint Anthony* (detail, from the Isenheim altarpiece), ca. 1515. Colmar, Musée d'Unterlinden.

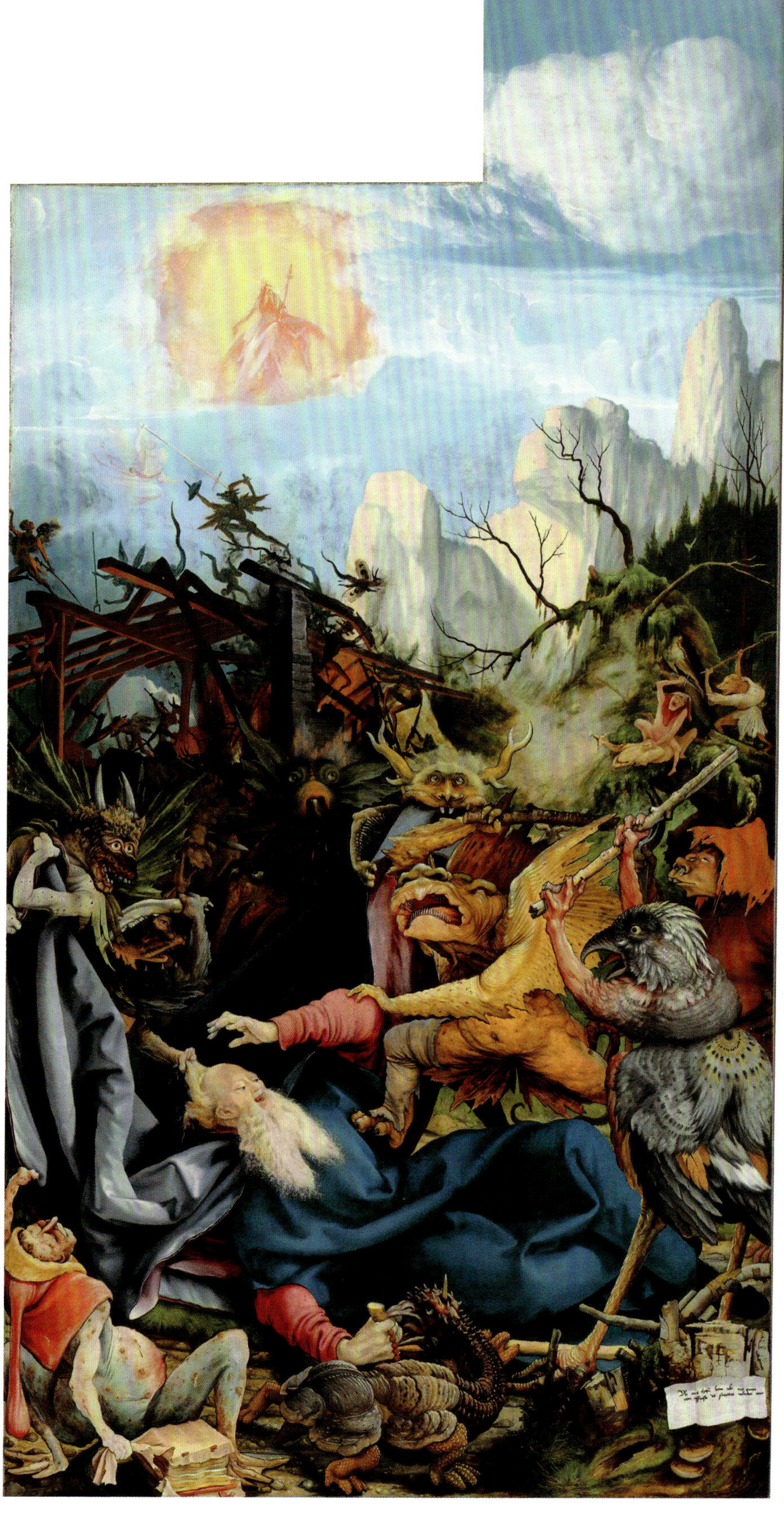

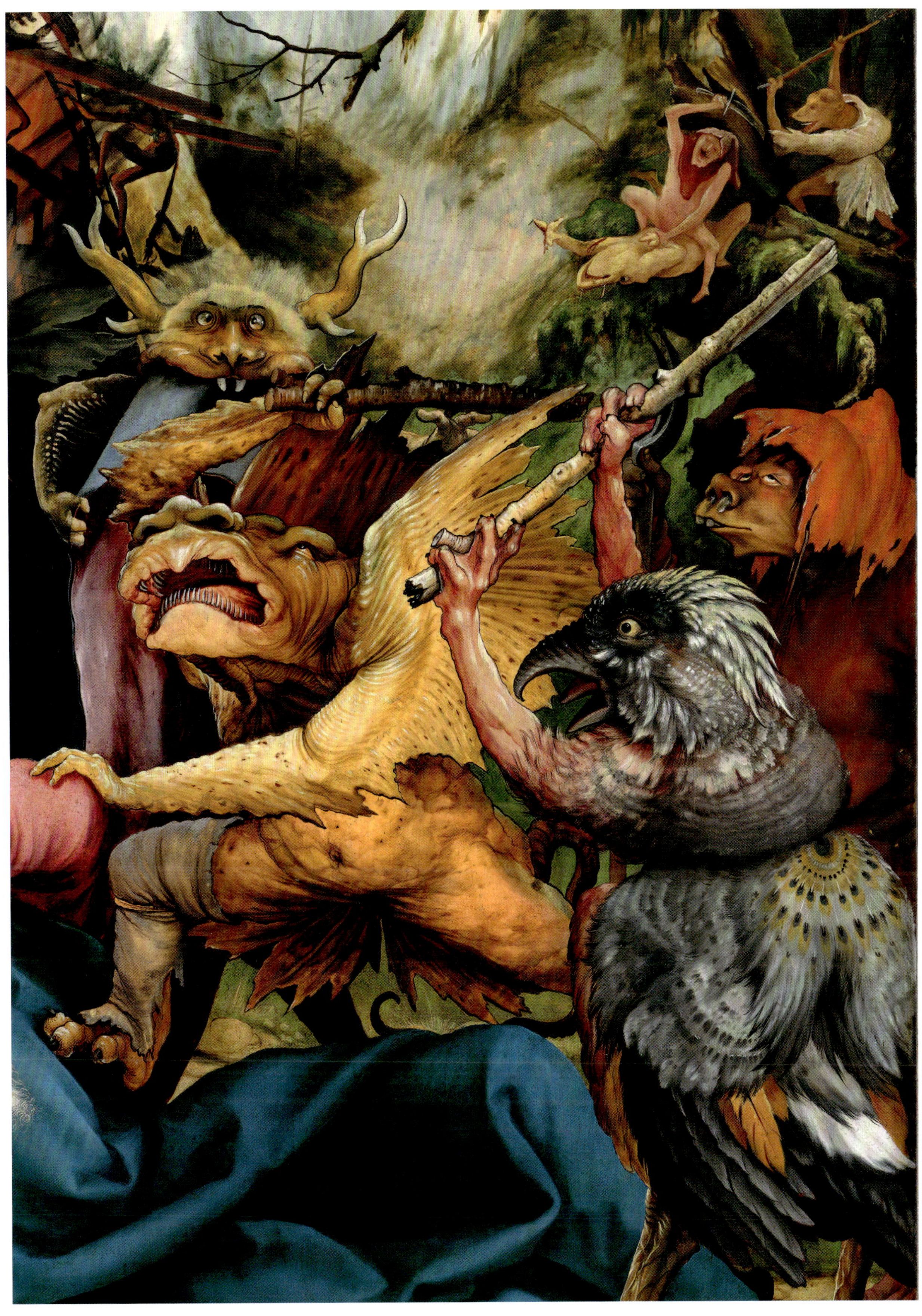

148 | Mathis Grünewald, *Temptations of Saint Anthony* (detail, from the Isenheim altarpiece), ca. 1515. Colmar, Musée d'Unterlinden.

It is clear that St. Anthony is not fighting back: his right hand, grabbing in resistance a stick in the form of a tau, is in the jaws of a demon, and he is lying on the ground, defenseless against all attacks.[129] I wonder again if this detail is connected with the thought of Johann von Staupitz. Starting in 1498, in the sermons he gave in Tübingen, Staupitz claimed, in a pre-Lutheran manner: "ideo autem [Deus] temptacionem admittit, ut miseros se agnoscant et misericordiam petant aut ad ipsam accipiendam consenciant. O vere nimis necessaria temptacio! Nam et in medio temptacionis nos ipsos negligimus."[130] This was central to Staupitz's theological

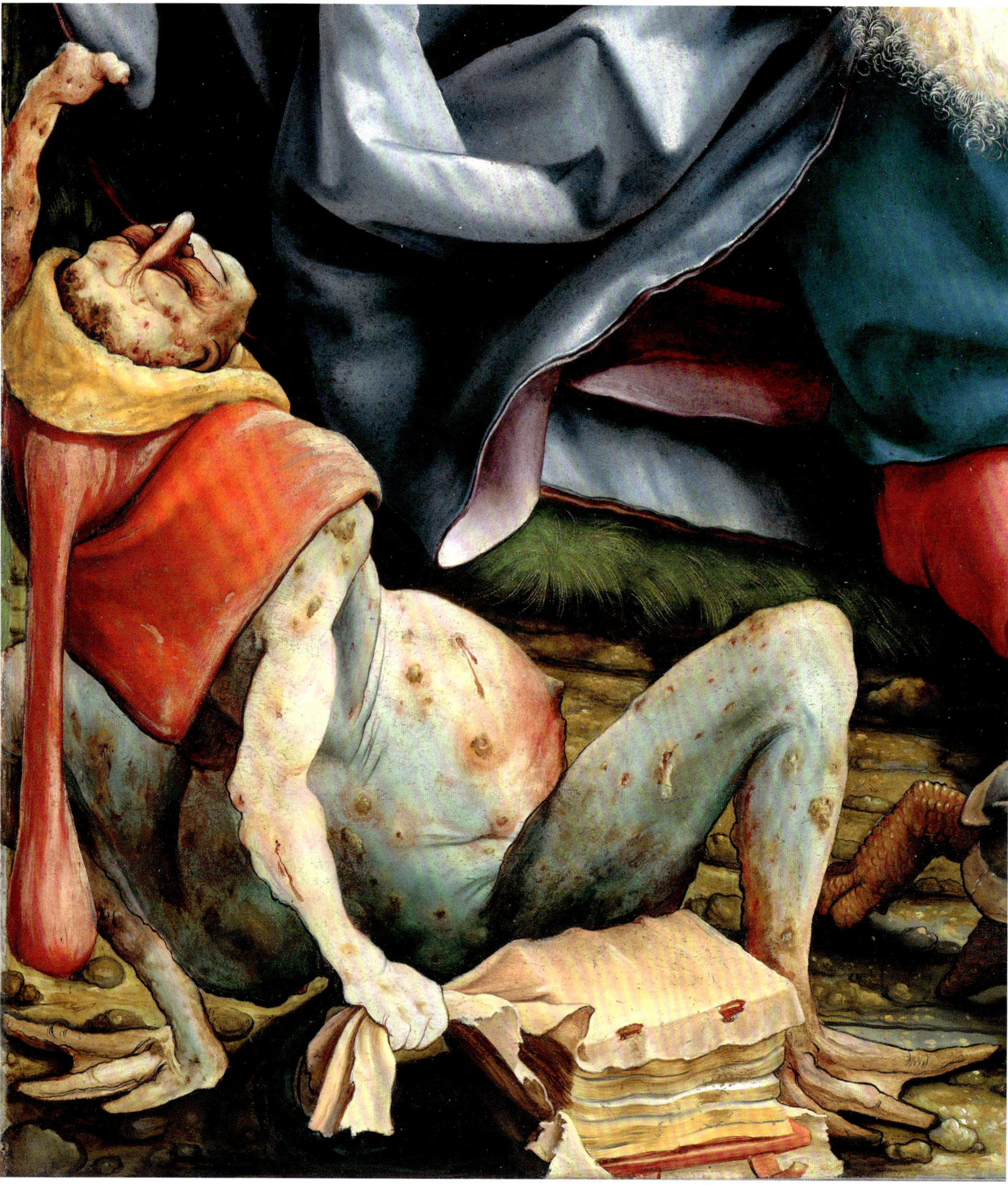

thinking, and he returned to it many years later in the now-familiar 1512 Salzburg sermons: "Ideo apertissime sequitur, quod non est fugienda temptacio, sed cum timore amplectanda in spe triumphi."[131]

Only a casual similarity? Staupitz's voice was certainly well-known and very authoritative throughout "Germany", and his Salzburg sermons were delivered just before Mathis began painting the altarpiece for the main altar. Therefore, it is not strange that the cultural and (also) spiritual climate that imbued the Antonite preceptory, in the end, would have led the painter to accept the Lutheran philosophy he so intimately and dramatically experienced, as we shall see. And there is even more regarding this. While Bosch is often mentioned as a precedent and perhaps as an inspiration for the images of the monstrous demons (a combination of grotesque, comical, frightening and repulsive) that attack the saint, the woodcut of the same subject done by Lucas Cranach the Elder in 1506 [fig. 151] provides a closer visual source.[132] Certainly, Grünewald did not need Cranach to unleash his ebullient imagination, but some key details seem to unquestionably point to the Cranach design. For example, the demon with the beaked head wielding a stick, the one pulling the hair of the hermit, or the one with an animal head (canine in Cranach, rodent in Grünewald) seen face-on [fig. 152]. Mathis's imagination, focused on transforming reality rather than creating something that does not exist in the physical world, needs an external impetus from sources like Chinese porcelain or German woodcuts to immerse himself in inventing a demon-infested hell. In other words, Grünewald is a mystic for whom reality, taken as a whole and in its materiality, is a reflection of something that transcends it, both in glory and horror. However, he is absolutely not a Bosch-style visionary or even, more morbidly, like Baldung Grien. Once again Huysmans accurately described him as "le plus forcené des realistes".[133]

Yet it is logical that Mathis would have that print in his files, and not just because of the subject. In the background is the no-longer extant monastery that has been identified as that of the Antonites in Lichtenburg, whose preceptor was Goswin von Orsoy, whom we have already encountered. In addition to being an important

149 | Mathis Grünewald, *Temptations of Saint Anthony* (detail, from the Isenheim altarpiece), ca. 1515. Colmar, Musée d'Unterlinden.

150 | Chinese Artist, Vase with Dragoon motif, Ming Dynasty, Xuande era, 1426–1435. New York, The Metropolitan Museum of Art, inv. 37.191.1.

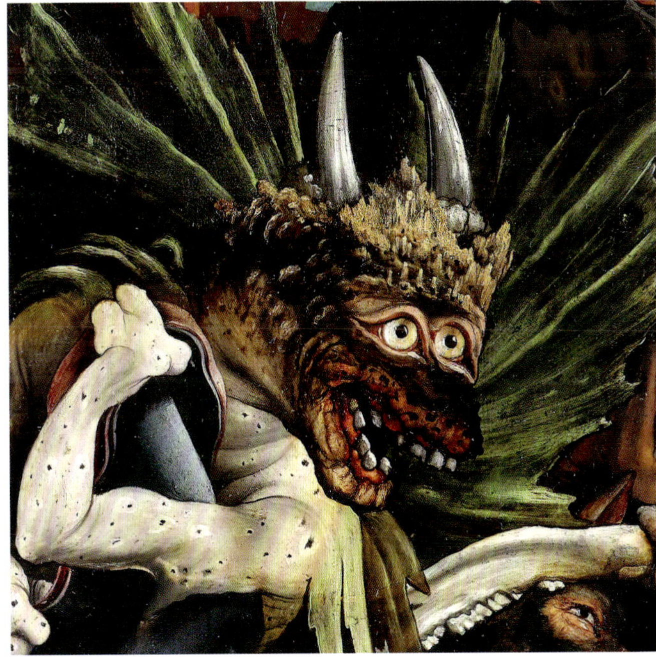

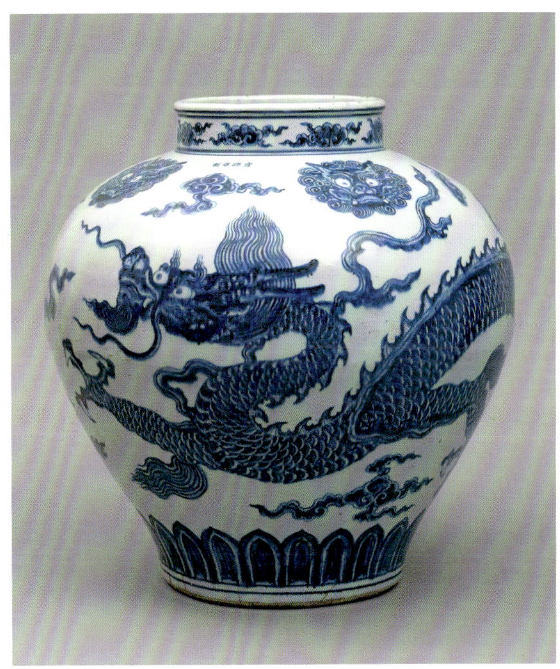

individual in the Order and one with ties to the Mainz court, Goswin (1450–1515) was also the chancellor of Wittenberg University (the city in which the Lichtenberg Antonite preceptory had its own chapel), precisely the university where a brilliant student of Staupitz, named Martin Luder (later Hellenized in Luther), delivered lectures on the Epistle to the Romans.[134]

This panel was one of the most admired and imitated from the early days.[135]

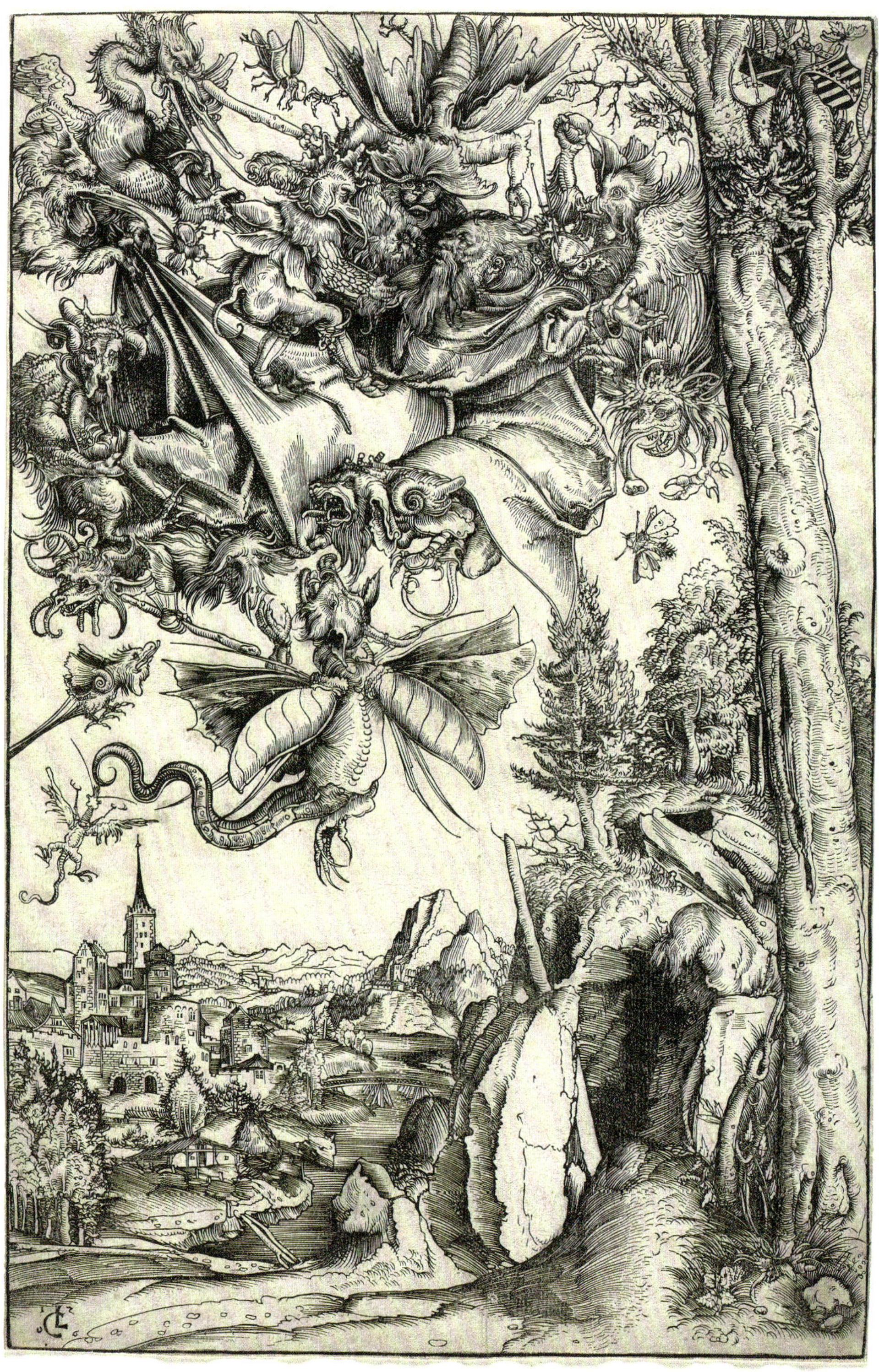

151 | Lucas Cranach the Elder, *Temptations of Saint Anthony*, 1506, woodcut.

Purged of all its expressive frenzy, the analogous scene painted by Martin Schaffner (1478/79–1546/49) is also derived, in one of the four panels now at the Staatliche Kunsthalle in Karlsruhe (inv. 2900), but previously in Salem on Lake Constance [fig. 153].[136] Similarly, Hans Baldung Grien, from nearby Strasbourg, must also have seen it. The figure of an unseated servant in the woodcut depicting the *Conversion of St. Paul* seems to have been taken, in turn, from Grünewald's *St. Anthony* [fig. 154].[137] In both cases, we are talking about pieces dated 1517, proof of the immediate authority of Grünewald's work. Additionally, there is also a watercolor copy that is quite similar (and seemingly by the same artist) to the one already seen of the soldier in the *Resurrection*, also now in Karlsruhe, inv. VIII 1498 [fig. 155].[138] This drawing, a historical document of primary importance, shows us the painting is still unfinished. The hut in the background demolished by the demons is missing and, above all, in addition to some detailing in the demons in the foreground, also the entire figure of the saint. The scientific examination recently performed on the Grünewald panels at the Musée d'Unterlinden confirmed this was not the copyist's choice. This showed that specifically the missing portion of the drawing, with the corresponding area left white, overflows into the already-painted edges, and that can also be seen in the paper copy—the only details not always in perfect correspondence given

152 | Mathis Grünewald, *Temptations of Saint Anthony* (detail, from the Isenheim altarpiece), ca. 1515. Colmar, Musée d'Unterlinden.

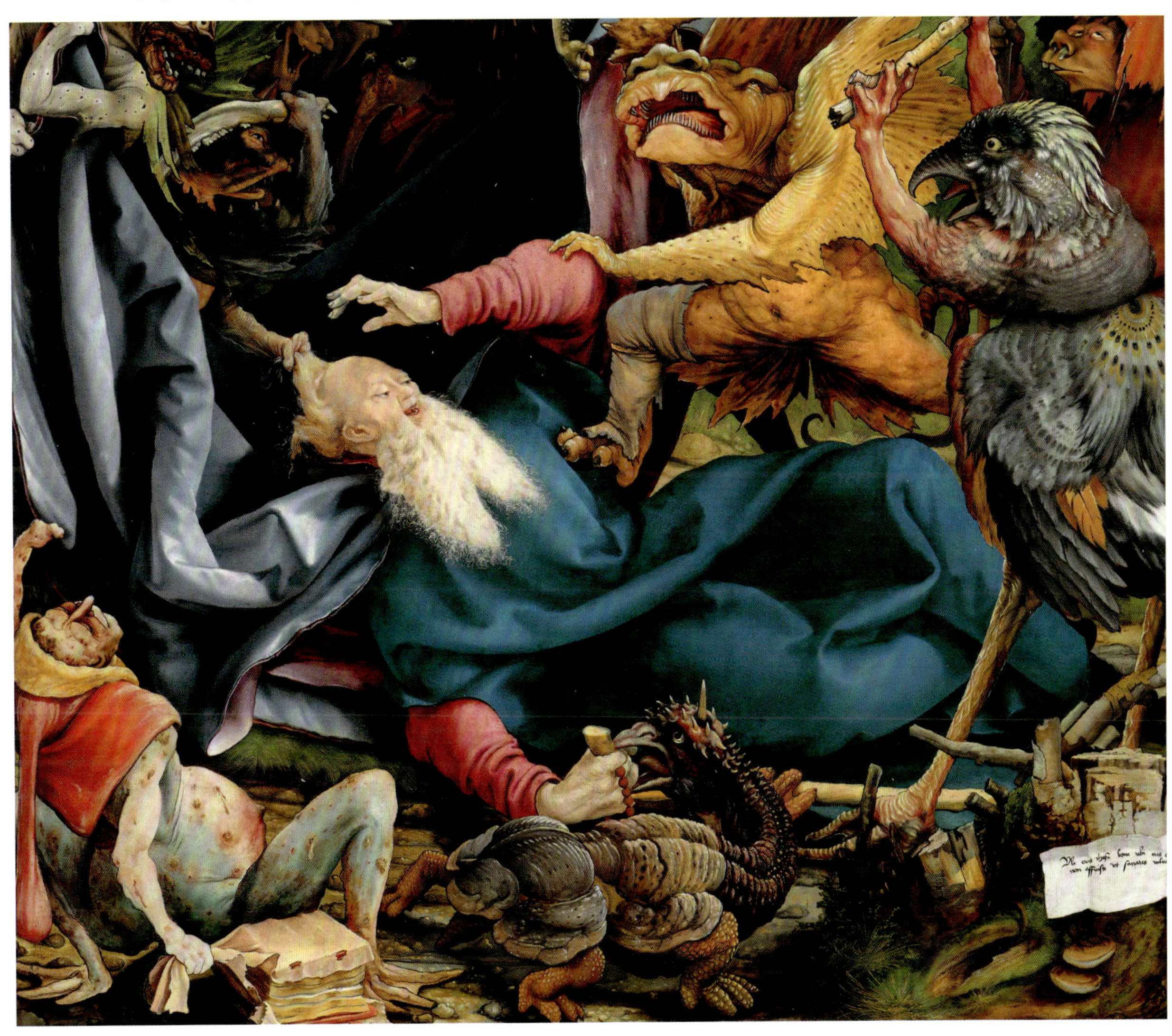

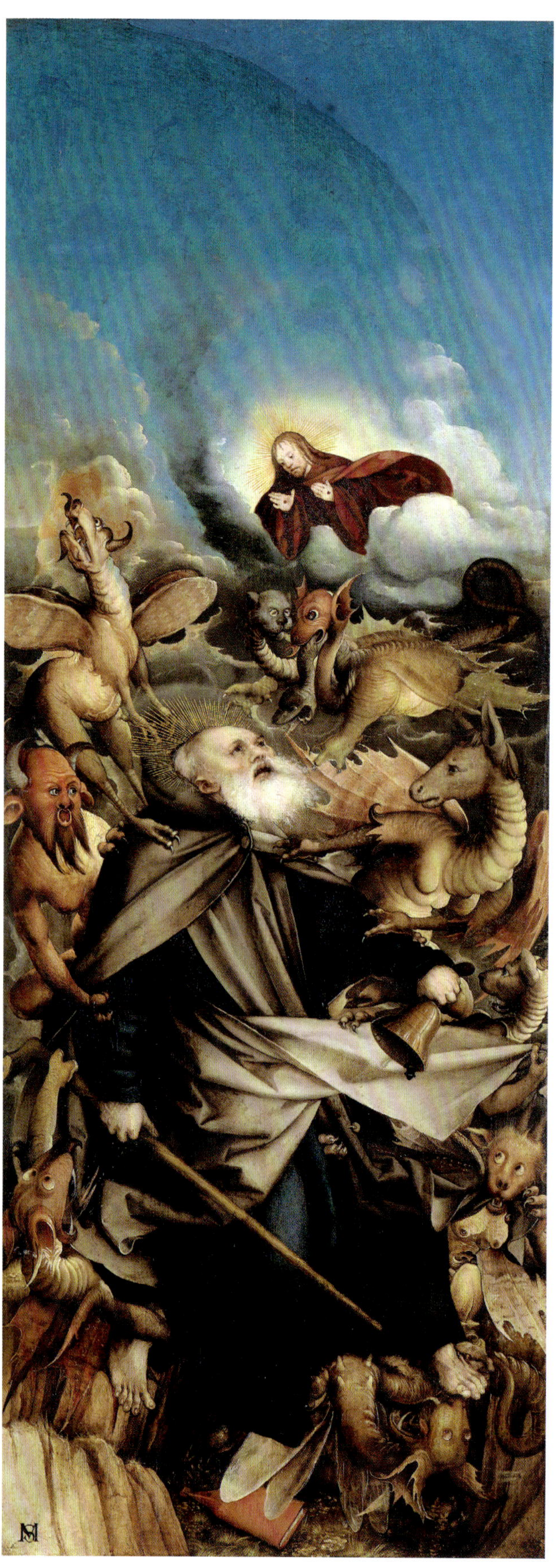

the actual state of the painting.[139] It necessarily follows that the figure of the saint and the assailants closest to him were added by Grünewald later, after the scene, still unfinished, had been copied by an anonymous artist who also turned his attention to other parts of the altarpiece (as is shown by the copy of the soldier in the *Resurrection*).[140] However, the entire work, including the still-unfinished panel, could already have been copied (in the workshop, or already present in the church?) by an artist unlikely to be an assistant to Mathis who seems to have painted the entire altarpiece himself, inch by inch,[141] means that there must have been an interruption in work, even if short-lived.

An added curiosity, starting at least from Rolfs,[142] is that the saint was considered a mirrored reworking of a Padua work, the *Temptation of St. Anthony* by Bernardo Parentino (Rome, Galleria Doria Pamphilj, inv. FC 419 [fig. 157]). It was painted in 1494 and thwarts the virtually impossible attempt to reconcile the concise and powerful language of Mantegna with a world of monsters and hellfires typical of a certain concept of Dutch painting antonomastically represented by Bosch. Of course, this apparent derivation is no proof of a trip to Italy by Mathis, also because the reference itself is not conclusive.[143] In fact, held in the Département de Arts Graphiques of the Louvre is a very interesting drawing (inv. 18643 recto, pen, brown ink and white lead on dark ochre-prepared paper, 15.7 × 28.3 mm), previously attributed to Baldung Grien by Franz Winzinger, according to museum records, which is a copy of the figure of the beaten St. Anthony [fig. 158]. However, it would seem a (very faithful) copy taken from a preparatory drawing rather than the painting, given that the saint's head is resting on a rectangular object, perhaps a book, that is not seen in the altarpiece panel. Also, the entire figure of St. Anthony is seen frontally and—it could be said—more relaxed compared with the more forceful view with much greater tension seen in the final version. The presentation of the saint in the Paris drawing has little in common with Parentino's painting. If my interpretation is correct, in the process of conceiving the hermit saint within the cornice of the already-painted riot of demons,

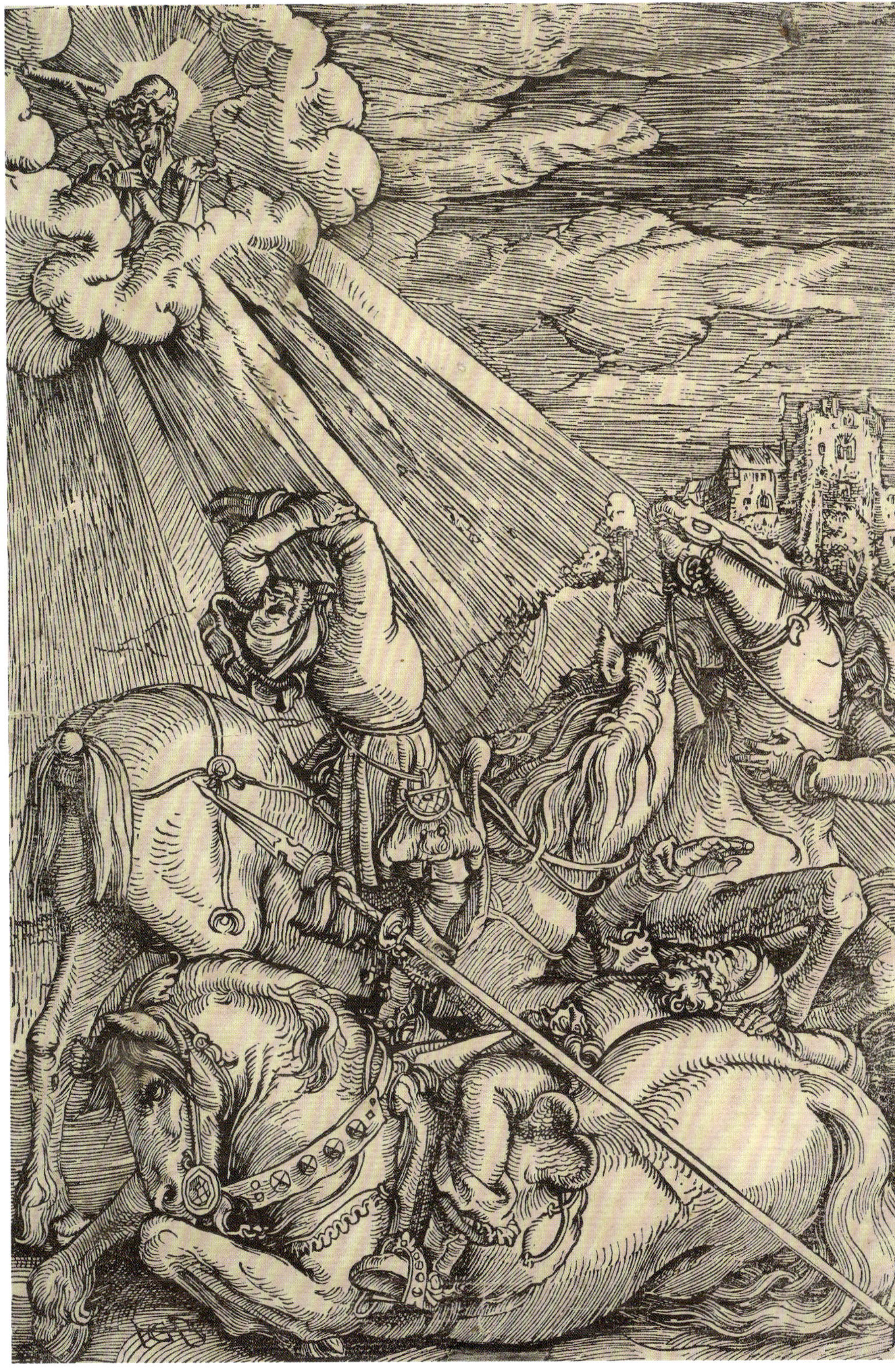

153 | Martin Schaffner, *Temptations of Saint Anthony*, 1517. Karlsruhe, Staatliche Kunsthalle, inv. 2900.

154 | Hans Baldung Grien, *The Conversion of Saint Paul*, 1517, woodcut.

Grünewald worked solely with his own ideas, putting a model in a sufficiently comfortable pose, but then forcing the pose in the transition from the preparatory study to the painting. In any case, the image of St. Anthony "traxinatus" by his hair, like a lifeless sack, was already well-established, from Agnolo Gaddi to Sassetta,[144] and therefore does not require any direct parentage.

However, the potential contact with Italy and, in that case, the specifics of "which"

Italy, remain a recurring theme with scholars of leading German Renaissance painters. Aside from the two well-documented and much-studied trips to Italy of Albrecht Dürer (or more precisely, the documented trip in 1505, while the one in 1494 has been challenged by a number of scholars, although erroneously, I think),[145] the question has been raised a number of times about Albrecht Altdorfer, Hans Holbein (we will be returning to him) and others. Even Mathis Grünewald, perhaps apparently the least "Italianate" of German painters, has been involved. Among the first to raise this question, in addition to the pioneering references by Franz Rieffel,[146] was Oskar Frank Hagen, who places an Italian visit of the painter before his known works (the occasion would have been the 1500 Jubilee), thus making it a cornerstone of his figurative approach.[147]

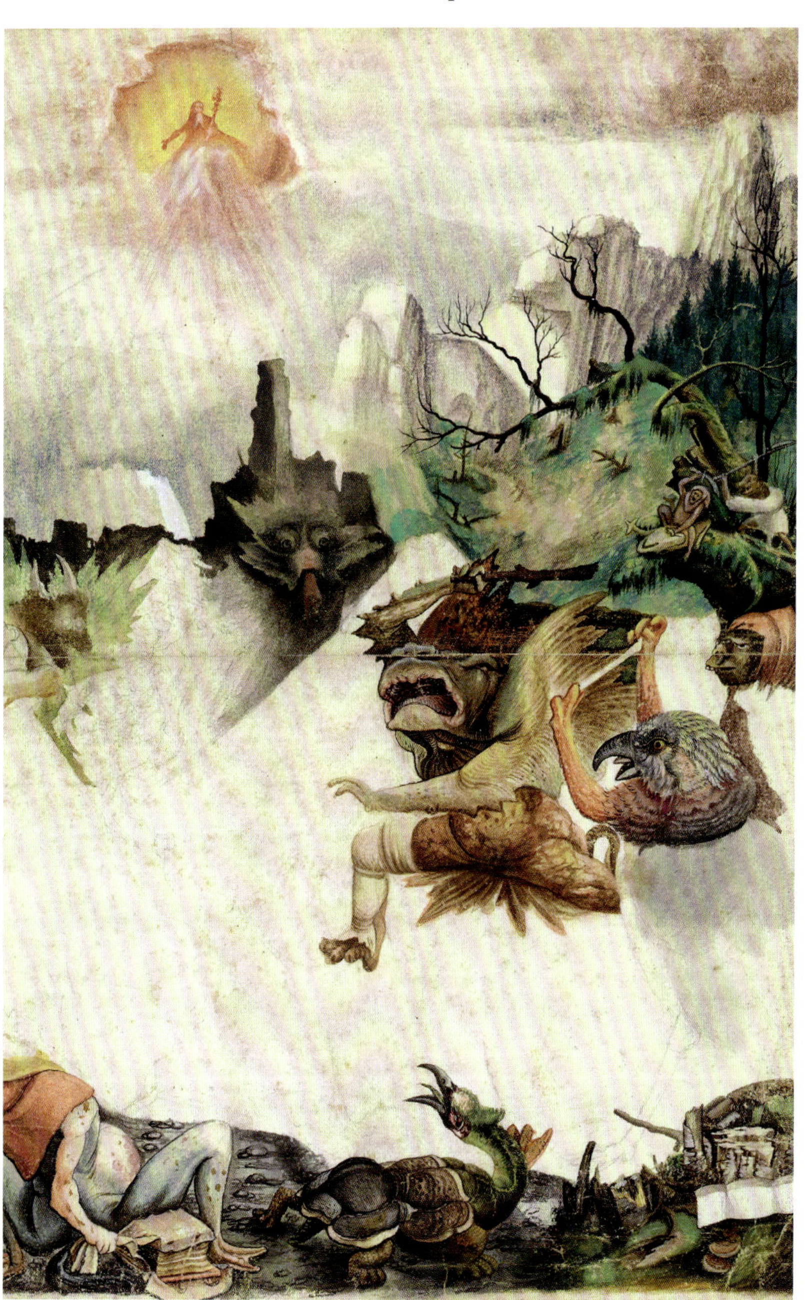

155 | After Mathis Grünewald, *The Temptations of Saint Anthony*, ca. 1515–1516. Karlsruhe, Staatliche Kunsthalle, inv. VIII 1498.

However, this question encountered moderate skepticism from Louis Réau, who offered some astute observations that will be examined later,[148] and from Eberhard Ruhmer,[149] yet it was taken up with exaggerated enthusiasm in one of the books dedicated to Mathis by Maria Lanckoronska.[150] She extended to the extreme the *modus operandi* of those previous scholars who supported the hypothesis of a Grünewald trip to Italy by inferring from actual (or more often presumed) similarities in individual details of the artist's works and details of this or that Italian artist (usually the best-known: Mantegna, Leonardo, Piero della Francesca) his direct acquaintance with the works in question. Lanckoronska's book abounds with comparisons, and with them, the wanderings of the German painter throughout almost all of central Italy, as well as Padua and Venice.[151]

Coming closer to the present day, the question of the relationship between Grünewald and Italy has perhaps somewhat lost its edge, despite some observations already discussed, such as that of Scheja and Ziermann who interpret the soldier on the ground in the front of the *Resurrection* as corresponding with the same scene sculpted by Luca Della

Robbia for Santa Maria del Fiore in Florence. Or the comparison by Philippe Lorentz of details of Grünewald's drapery taken from works of very different moments in his career, such as the triptych now in the parish church of Lindehardt and the major work in Isenheim, and the famous little monochrome canvases of drapery by the young Leonardo.[152]

In any case, they are all 15th-century Florentine works, which would imply reconsidering the view of Hagen and imagining a trip to Italy by Grünewald, or, more specifically, to Florence, no later than 1500. If this were the case, it would be reasonable to expect that other works from there, and in a significant manner, could have

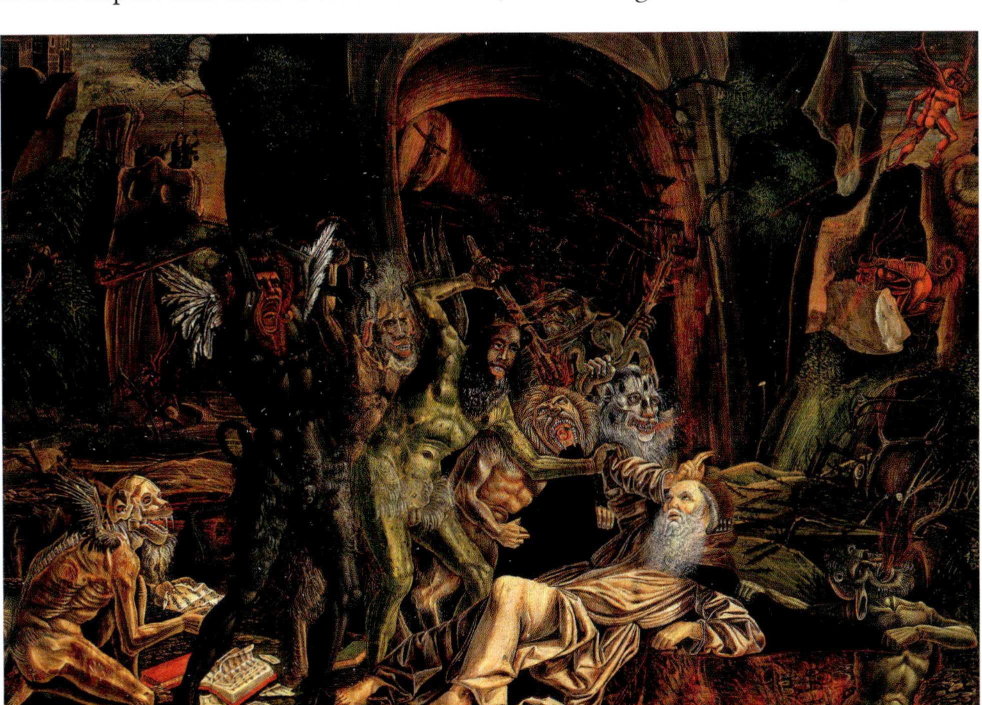

156 | Bernardo Parentino, *Temptations of Saint Anthony*. Rome, Galleria Doria-Pamphilj, inv. FC 419.

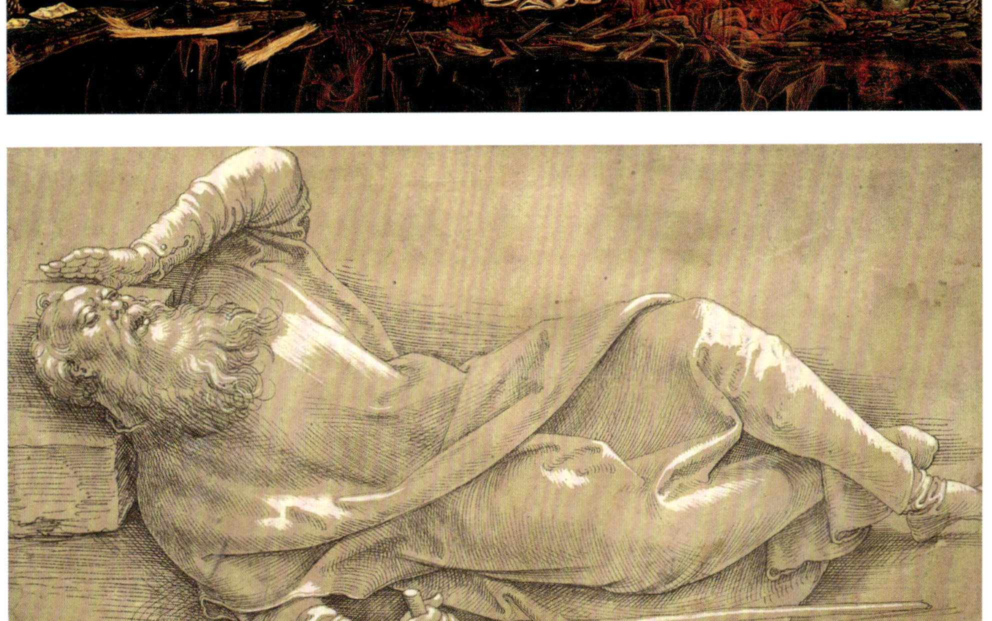

157 | After Mathis Grünewald, *Saint Anthony the Abbott*. Paris, Musée du Louvre, Département des Arts Graphiques, inv. 18643 recto.

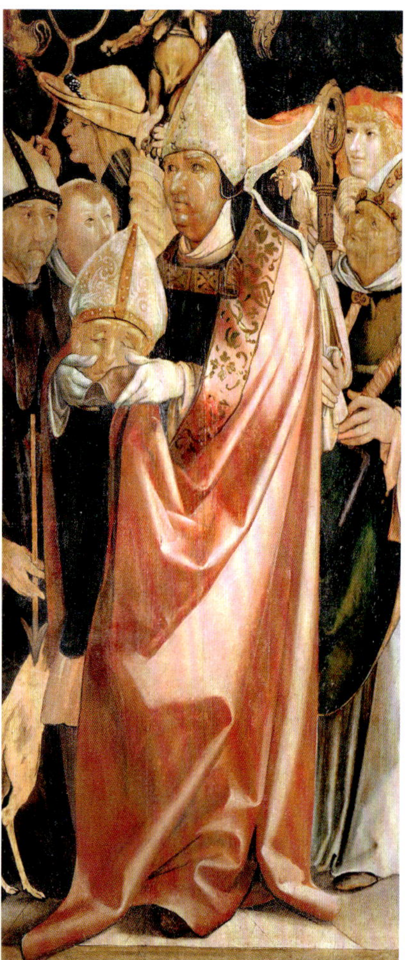
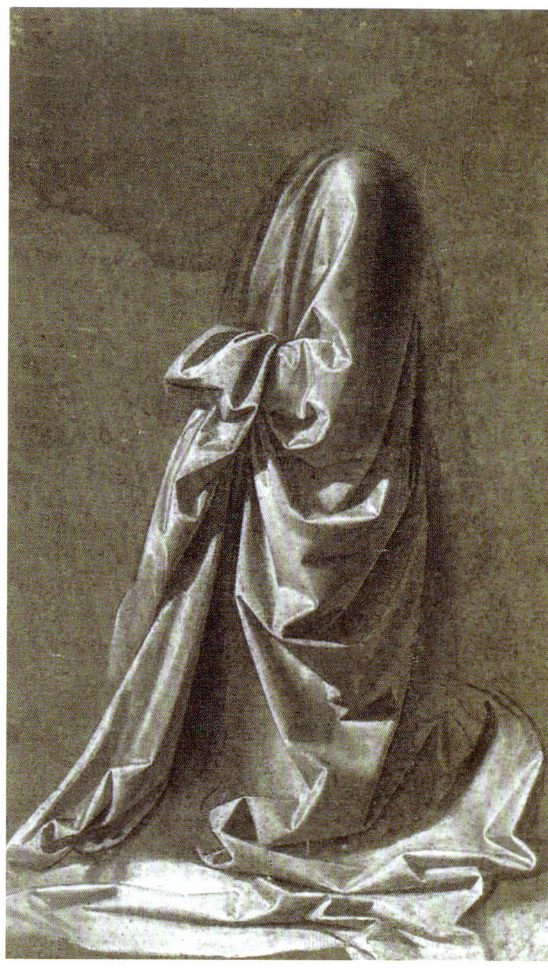

158 | Mathis Grünewald, *Saint Denys and six Holy Helpers* (detail), 1503 Lindenhardt, Parish church, in comparison with Leonardo da Vinci, *Study of drapery*, Paris, Musée du Louvre, Département des Arts Graphiques, inv. RF41904. From Philippe Lorentz, «Grünewald et Léonard de Vinci: les draperies dans le retable d'Issenheim», in Béguerie-De Paepe and Lorentz (eds.), *Grünewald et le retable d'Issenheim. Rehards sur un chef-d'œuvre*, Paris and Colmar 2007, p. 29.

become part of his collected experience. But none of this appears in his paintings and, in fact, the authors cited do not really mention this quandary.

The comparisons offered by Lorentz between the *St. Denys* in Lindenhardt and Leonardo's drapery study now in Princeton, or the viola da gamba-playing angel of the *Allegory of the Incarnation* in the *Isenheim Altarpiece* and the RF41904 study in the Louvre (not even a very good choice, given that it is a study in Verrocchiesque style parallel to the Leonardo 2256 at the same museum and 420E at the Uffizi, but not a Leonardo autograph) remain simply juxtapositions: it is only too clear that there is no interaction among the images [fig. 158]. Slightly more than a mere hint of dialogue, but not enough to be considered historically significant, is that between the beautiful drapery of the Madonna cradling the Christ Child in the *Isenheim Altarpiece* and the Leonardo drapery 2255 at the Louvre. Finally, and surprisingly so given what has been said to this point, there is, in fact, some correspondence between the details of the folds of the mantle of the tempted St. Anthony and yet another Leonardo drapery, RF 41905 at the Louvre [fig. 159]. Mathis's drapery is softer, less starchy, thc light hits it in small patches that are damp, cold and pearly. But it is hard not to see actual similarities between the two images, as if, above and beyond any direct relationship that would seem difficult to recognize, there were some minimum common denominators in the restless folds and mobility in the use of the white light against the gray background. It is very little, but we can notice one thing: the works of Leonardo that Lorentz has placed in comparison are close chronologically. They are from the later period of Leonardo's experience with Andrea del Verrocchio (approximately in the second half of the 1470s), while those of Grünewald are from different phases of his career. If there is a relationship, it is the German who, at a certain point, moves towards Leonardo (I mention him simply because this is the name Lorentz cites in his comparison).

The fact is, Leonardo is certainly pertinent, but we must be careful to identify the works that truly correspond, and it is not the young Leonardo of Florence, but the Leonardo of Milan or, perhaps even better, the art of some of his followers of the 1490s. In fact, we find something analogous in the flowing, amber light seen only in the painting of the Milan period, and not prior to the 1490s (subsequent to the London *Virgin of the Rocks*).[153] Perhaps nothing corresponds as well as the silvery mantle of Christ in the *Resurrection with Saints Leonard and Lucy*, painted by Giovanni Antonio Boltraffio and Marco D'Oggiono between 1491 and 1496 for the Grifi Chapel in San Giovanni Sul Muro in Milan (today at the Gemäldegalerie Berlin, inv. 90 B) [fig. 160].[154]

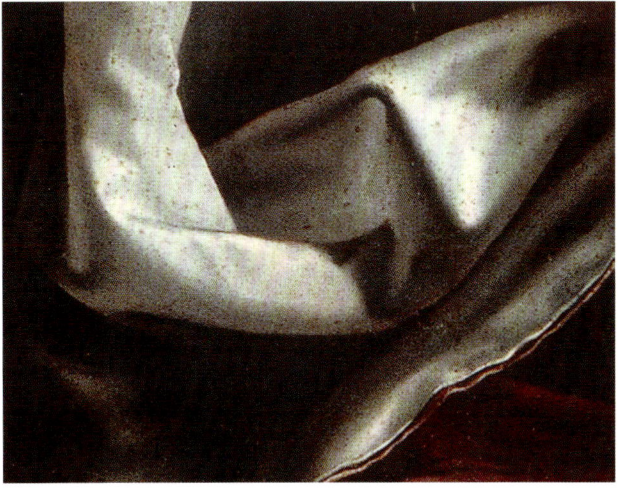

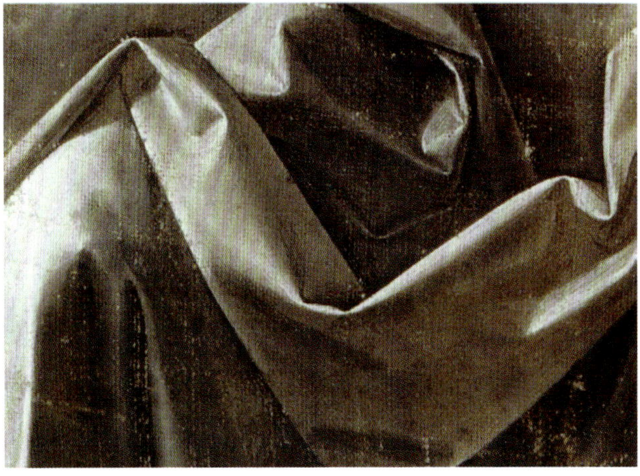

159 | Mathis Grünewald, *Temptations of Saint Anthony* (detail, from the Isenheim altarpiece), ca. 1515, Colmar, Musée d'Unterlinden, in comparison with Leonardo da Vinci, *Study of drapery*, Paris, Musée du Louvre, Département des Arts Graphiques, inv. 2255. From Philippe Lorentz, «Grünewald et Léonard de Vinci: les draperies dans le retable d'Issenheim», in Béguerie-De Paepe and Lorentz (eds.), *Grünewald et le retable d'Issenheim. Regards sur un chef-d'œuvre*, Paris and Colmar 2007, p. 28.

Is it possible to imagine Grünewald traveling to northern Italy, and more precisely current-day Lombardy (recalling the Brescia contact noted earlier in the Madonna's mantle, painted on the reverse side of the panel with the *Temptation of St. Anthony*), before having completed the *Isenheim Altarpiece*? Available dates would seem to exclude this possibility. The 1515 contract with Michael Wesser listed in the *post mortem* inventory would logically seem to refer to assembly work in the presbytery of the church of the *Isenheim Altarpiece*. The year 1515 also seems painted on the jar of Mary Magdalene at the foot of the Crucifixion, confirming the date of the work's completion.

In any case, this hypothesized Italian trip could not have taken place before 1515, precisely September 1515, when peace was made between France and the Holy League, which ceded the Duchy of Milan to the French King Francis I. Traveling before this date, amidst war, would have been highly reckless. Furthermore, the supposed Italian influences are only evident in what we identify as the last panel painted, while the rest of the altar remains totally extraneous to these influences or is merely lightly touched by them, probably as a result of Dürerian influences.

Should we consider that Mathis left the Isenheim (or Strasbourg) worksite for some reason, and then extended his absence going as far as Italy? Why then sign a contract with Wesser and probably have someone else assemble the altar? One might speculate that, having to leave Isenheim, the painter was urged by an impatient Guy Guers to install the altarpiece, even though it lacked only the mantle of the Madonna and the figure of St. Anthony, on the two sides of a panel that was visible for only a few days a year. Guy Guers in fact died the following year on

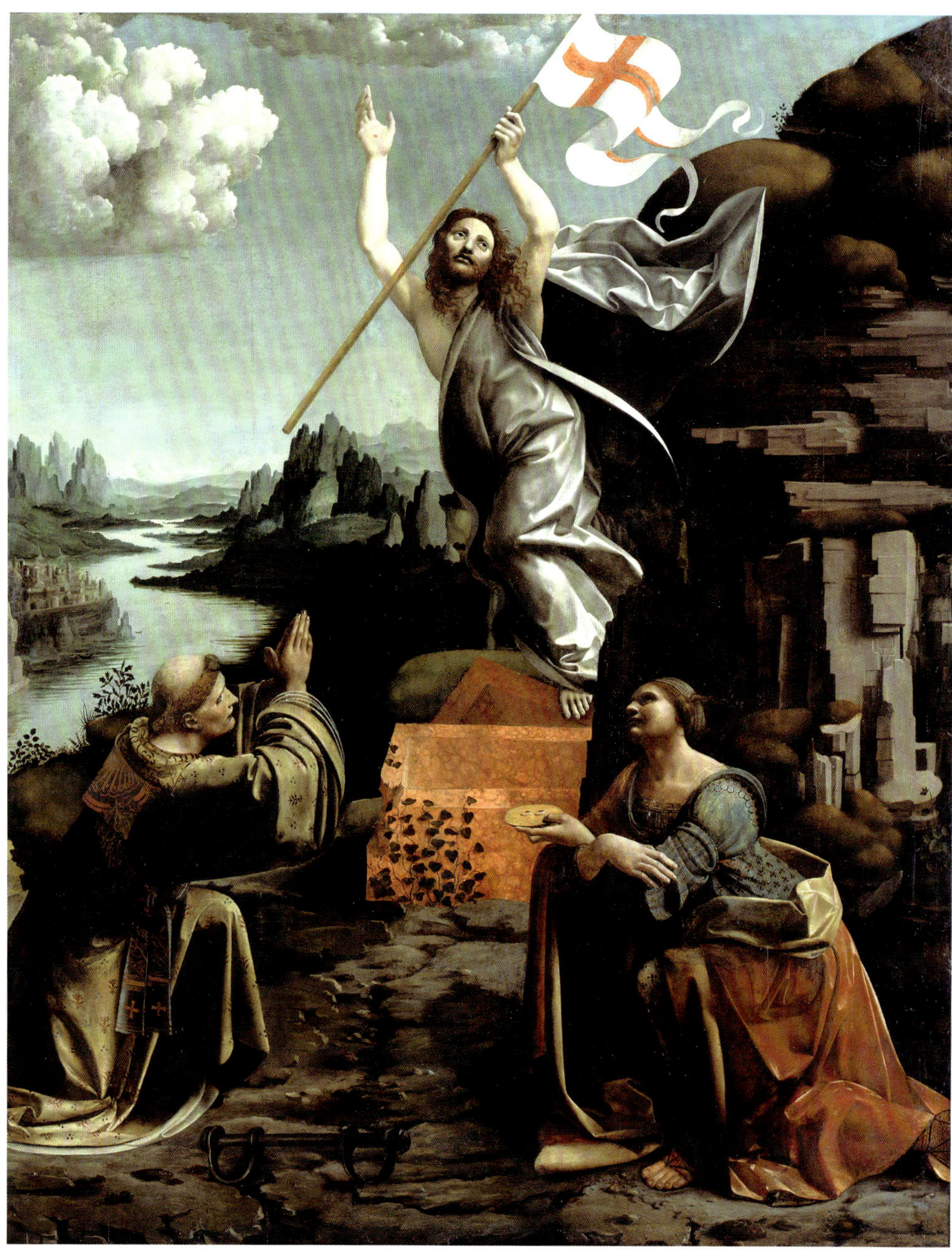

160 | Giovanni Antonio Boltraffio and Marco d'Oggiono, *Resurrection of Christ with the Saints Leonard and Lucy*, ca. 1491–1496. Berlin, Staatliche Museen, Gemäldegalerie, inv. 90B.

February 19, 1516.[155] This would explain why the anonymous Karlsruhe copyist took on a still-unfinished painting.

For this hypothesis to be plausible, this reconstruction requires a good explanation for why Grünewald would have had to leave his work in Isenheim. It is not difficult to find one. On February 9, 1514, Uriel von Gemmingen, the archbishop of Mainz, died, and Mathis, his employee if not member of his court, would have felt it necessary to return to his place to avoid running the risk of being removed from his position by whomever the new archbishop might be. After an absence of three years, it would not have been difficult for some competitor to usurp his place.

Grünewald was called as a witness in a trial related to his service for Uriel von Gemmingen at the Aschaffenburg castle in 1511. The citations were dated September 4, 1514, when Mathis was still probably in Isenheim or Strasbourg, and once again, without locating him, on February 23, 1516. At that point, the Antonite altarpiece should have been finished, or at least installed in place. It is evident that Grünewald was not in Mainz, where he would have been easy to locate, and where he reappeared on August 27, 1516, when "magister Mathis Gothart pictor" requested payment from the representative of the new archbishop, Albrecht von Brandenburg, obtaining the result that the canon Johann von Gutenberg be charged with requesting from the lord of Königstein (Eberhard IV von Eppstein) that the payment be granted. From this we learn that Mathis was not in Mainz on February 23, 1516, while six months later he was definitely in the city and was able to retain his position (or even improve it) under a new archbishop.

Therefore, the hypothesis I would like to propose is the following. At some unspecified date in 1515, Grünewald likely installed the *Isenheim Altarpiece*, although the *Madonna cuddling the Baby Jesus* and the *Temptation of St. Anthony* were still unfinished. He then traveled to Mainz and from there, for reasons unknown but certainly after September 1515, he went to northern Italy and returned to Germany no later than August of the following year. Upon his return, he completed the relatively little left to do in Isenheim and, finally, also the protective panels for the Heller altarpiece in Frankfurt. His reasons for returning to Mainz were unassailable, as we saw, and once again I suspect that Goswin von Orsoy de Wesalia played a role.

If we consider the historical context, we might even be able to imagine the reasons why Mathis, evidently reassured about his position at the Mainz court, did not return to Isenheim immediately. While in Lombardy the war was over, in the early months of 1516 the Vosges area of France was embroiled in hostilities between Count Gangolf von Geroldseck and Duke Anthony of Austria.[156] These were the same hostilities that convinced Erasmus of Rotterdam to return to the Netherlands via the longer but more tranquil route of the Rhein, and which perhaps also prompted Grünewald to not return to Alsace immediately.

In fact, I believe it is possible that it was precisely the learned Archbishop Albrecht who sent Mathis to Italy, precisely when he was working to bring from Bologna to Mainz the humanist Ulrich von Hutten, whom we will speak about again. If this journey occurred, it did not appear in the chapterhouse records of the Mainz cathedral: there is no trace of it in the diocese document register during Albrecht's episcopate.[157]

Before concluding our examination of the *Isenheim Altarpiece*, it is pertinent to review the main events involving it. The altarpiece maintained its prominence even when, strangely early, the fame of its artist waned. The Antonites resisted attempts by Emperor Rudolph II in 1597 and by Maximilian of Bavaria in the mid-17th century to acquire the work. Despite the loss of the monumental wooden structure, the altarpiece was preserved intact following the suppression of the Antonite monastery in 1796 thanks to former Goethe schoolmate Franz Christian Lerse who, still erroneously attributing the work to Dürer, was able to ensure its preservation and transfer to Colmar.[158]

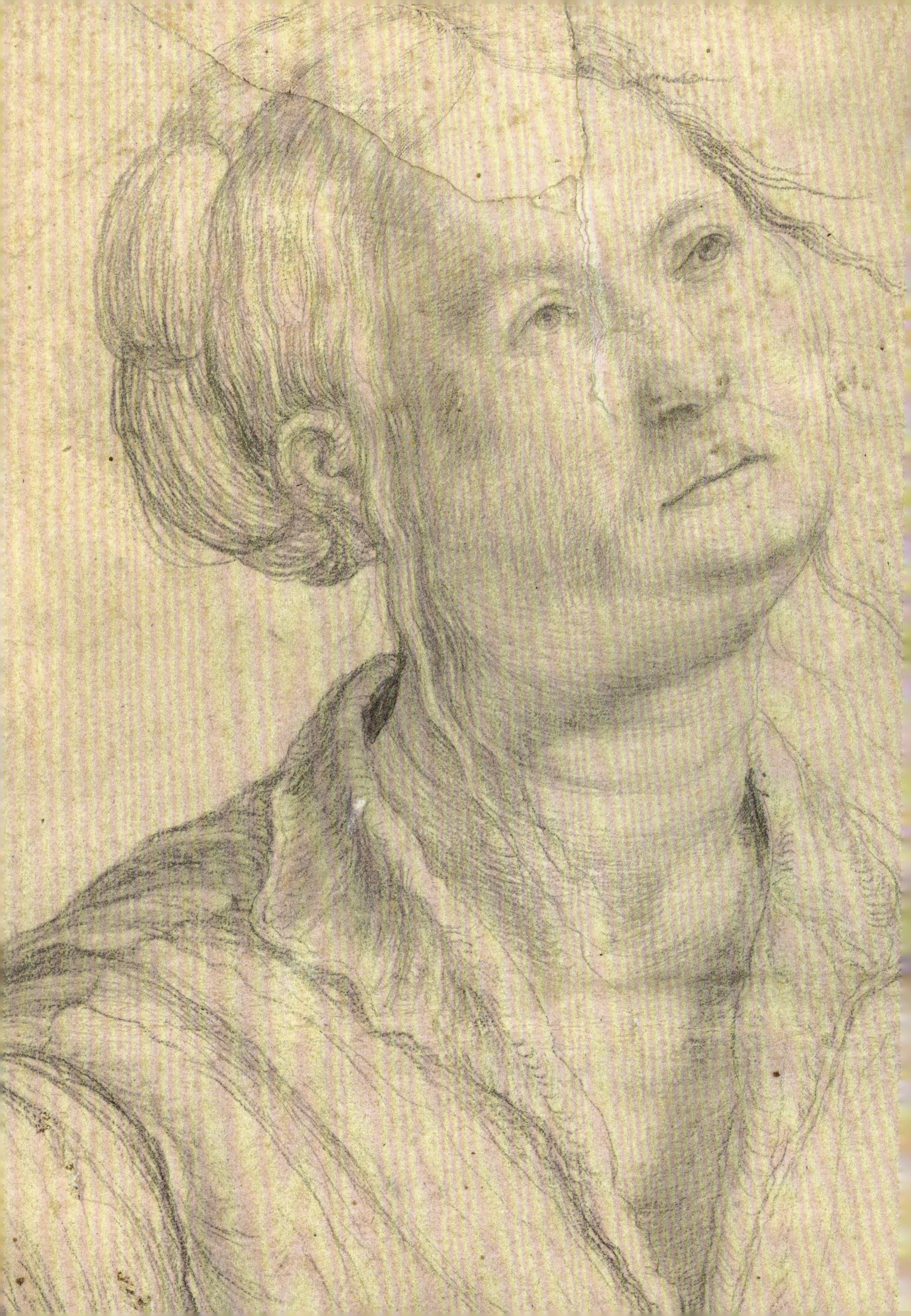

CHAPTER IV

Italy

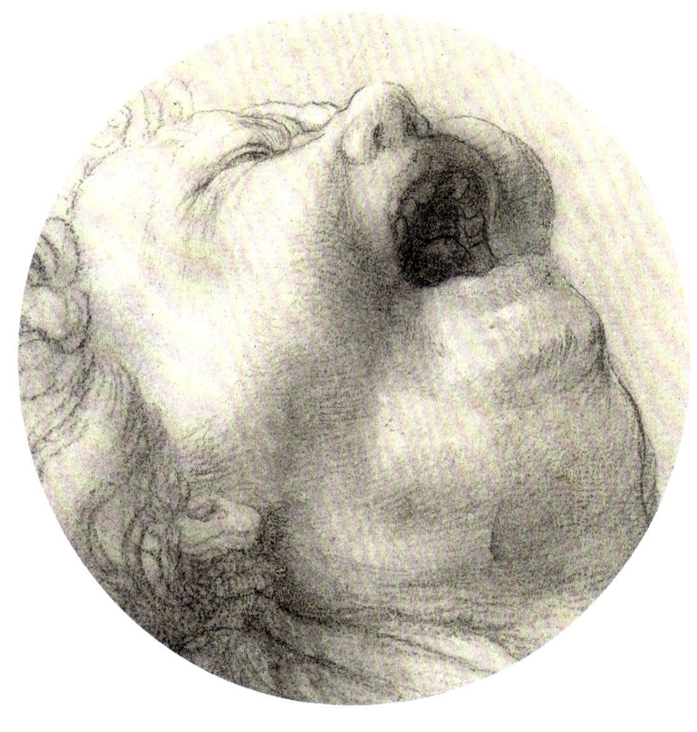

Finding German artists in northern Italy, particularly the Duchy of Milan and even besides the Milan Cathedral construction site, was certainly nothing new.[1] For example, Justus Amman von Ravensburg in Genoa in 1451,[2] or the extraordinary anonymous master who, a decade later, painted the *Ecce Homo* in the Oratory dedicated to St. Bernard in Chiaravalle Abbey, Milan.[3] Sisto Frei is also a significant example. Frei was a wood carver from Nuremberg, documented from 1500 to 1515,

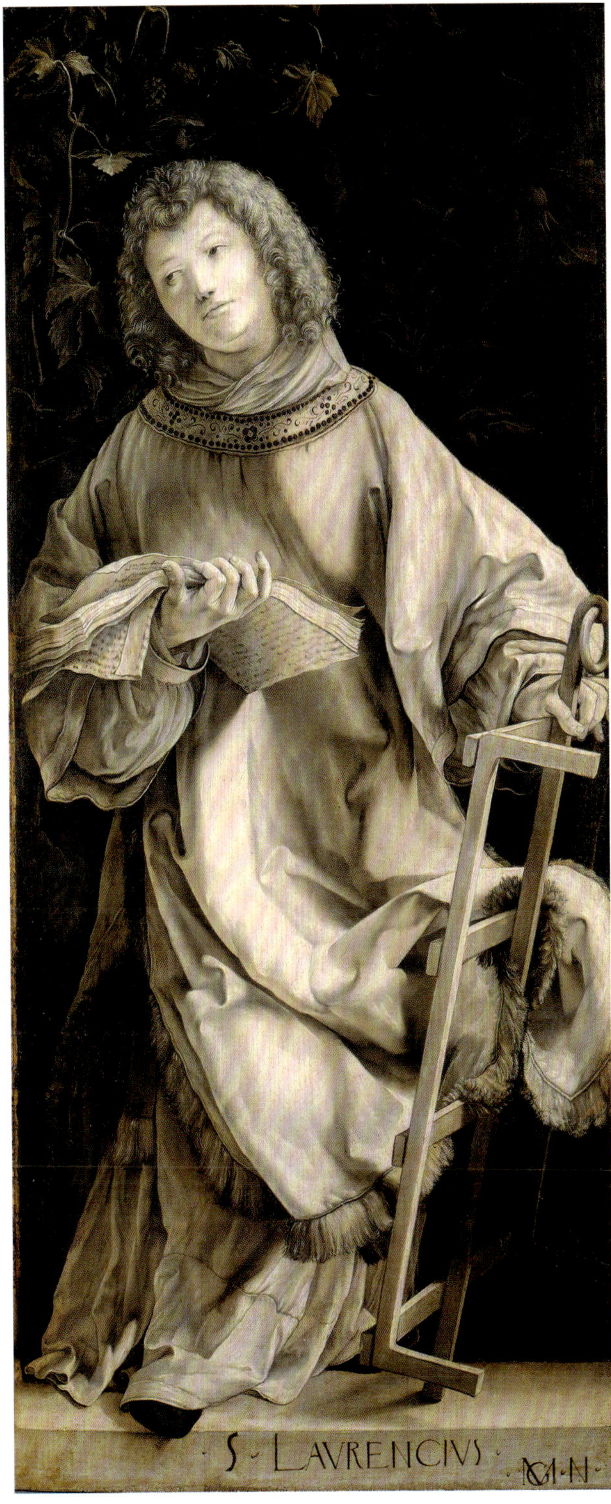

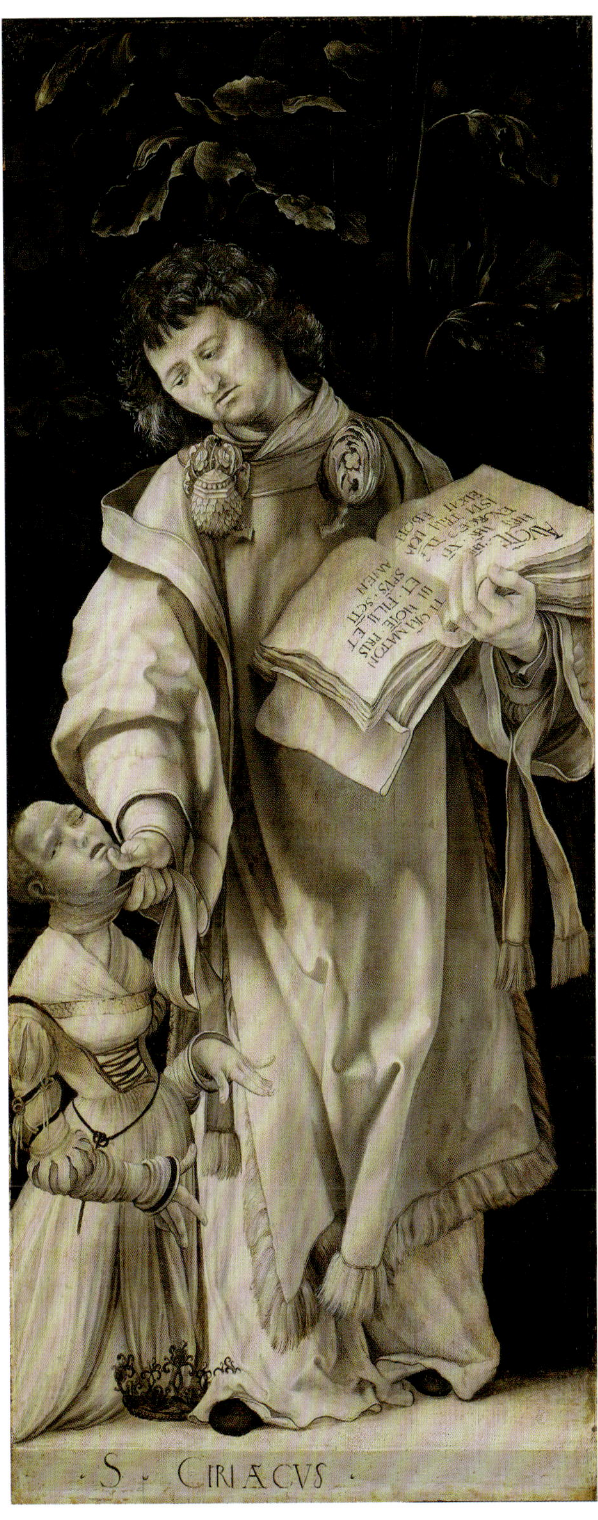

162 | Mathis Grünewald, *Saint Lawrence*, ca. 1516. Frankfurt am Main, Städel Museum, inv. 2604.

163 | Mathis Grünewald, *Saint Cyriacus*, ca. 1516. Frankfurt am Main, Städel Museum, inv. 2605.

but certainly established in northern Italy even before this. He was active in prestigious sites including the Colleoni Chapel in Bergamo and Trent Cathedral, and he is even likened to the young Grünewald for the formal and expressive tenacity of his *Crucifixion* in Trent.[4] Dürer also drew more than one idea from Leonardo's Milanese works,[5] and much is known about Hans Holbein the Younger's Lombard journey in 1518.[6] However, it is unlikely that this is what lured Mathis south.

Naturally, this question will only be relevant if we find actual, not just incidental, parallels with Lombard figurative output in Grünewald's works from this moment on.

Seen from this standpoint, the two panels with *Saints Lawrence and Cyriacus* at the Städel Museum become less problematic [figs. 162–163]. These panels, featuring much more incisive and monumental renderings of the corresponding female saints, are characterized by a vacillating, oleaginous light that we had never seen in Grünewald's development, and the geometrically simplified faces is also something new. I find striking the similarity between the view from below, resembling a geometric reduction, of Grünewald's St. Lawrence (the first to have on its base the

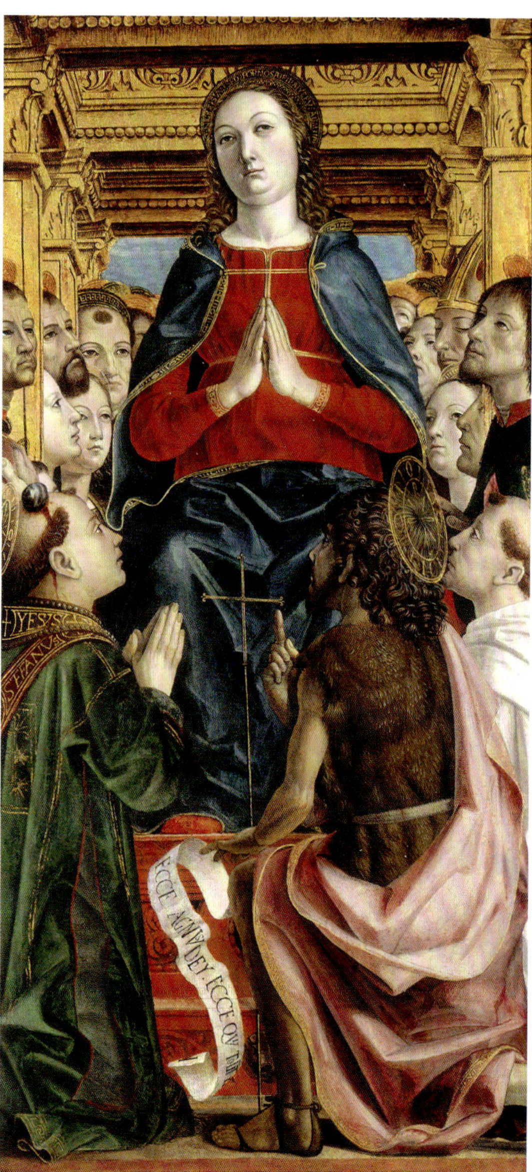

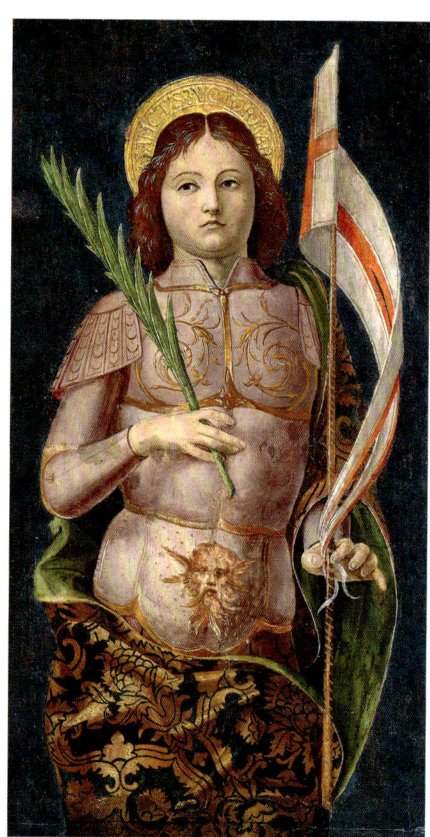

monogram used by Mathis Gothart Nithart in imitation of other German artists: MG N), and the works of the Milanese "perspective" artist Bernardo Zenale. Zenale's works from the 1490s, such as the *Madonna with Saints* at the Spencer Museum of Art in Lawrence, Kansas (inv. 1960.0049, gift from the Samuel H. Kress Foundation) [fig. 164], the *St. Martin* at the Musèe des Beaux-Arts in Grenoble (inv. MG 1295) [fig. 165], or the *Assumption of the Virgin* in the Church of San Carlo al Corso in Milan, but also later works like the altarpiece formerly in the Church of St. Francesco

164 | Bernardo Zenale, *Madonna with Saints*. Lawrence (Kansas), The Spencer Museum of Art, inv. 1960.0049.

165 | Bernardo Zenale, *St. Martin* (from a polyptych) Grenoble, Musée des Beaux-Arts, inv. MG 1295.

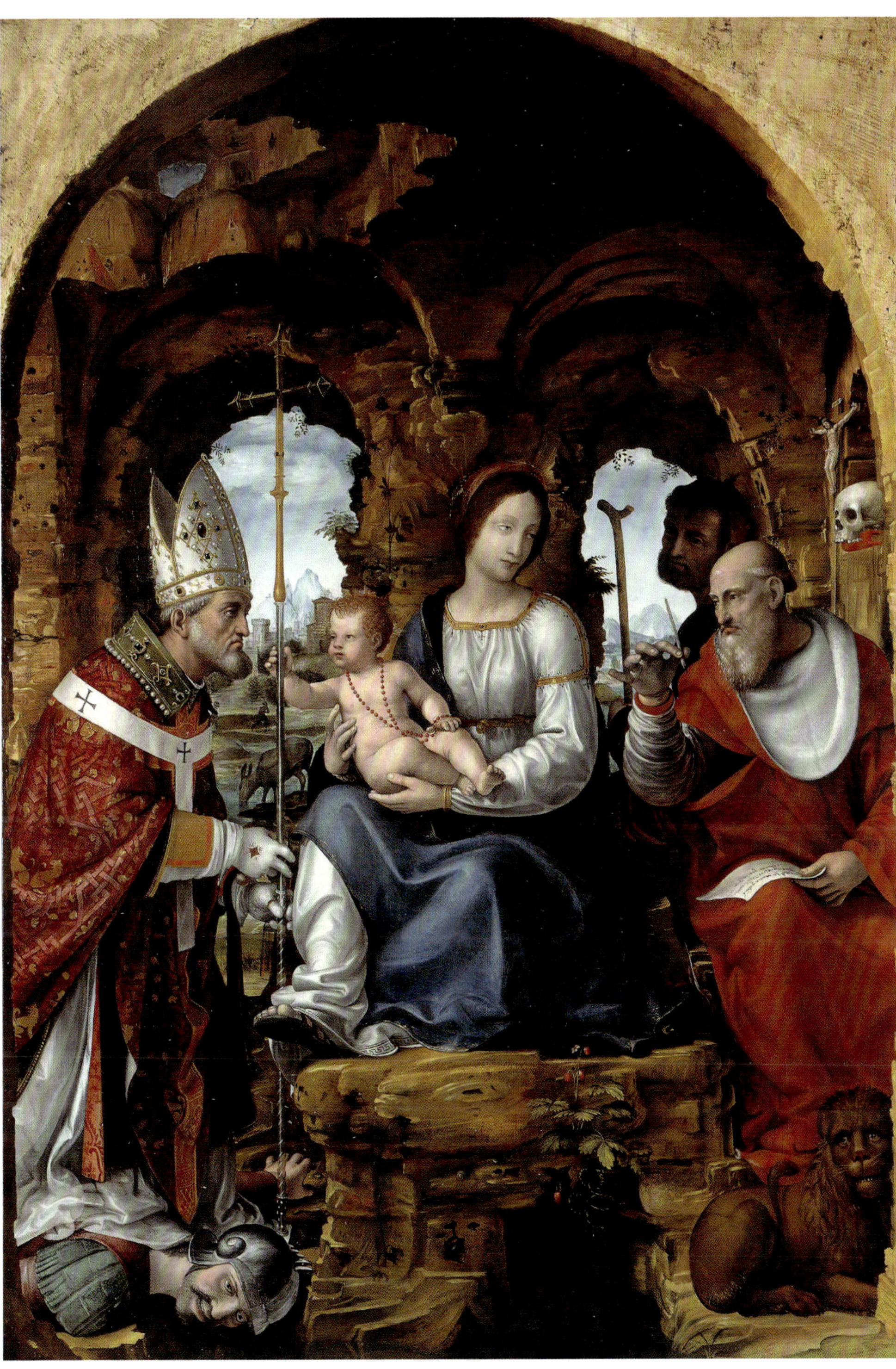

166 | Bernardo Zenale, *Madonna and Child with Saints Joseph, Ambrose and Jerome*, 1510. Denver, Denver Art Museum, inv. 1961.173.

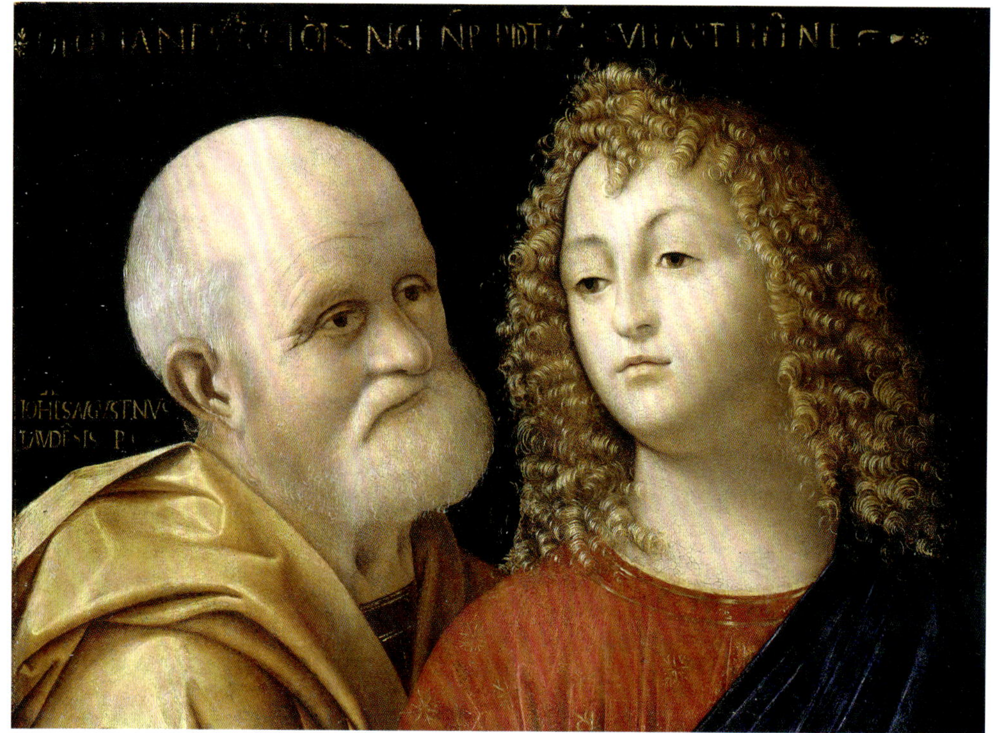

167 | Giovanni Agostino da Lodi, *The Apostles Peter and John*. Milan, Brera Gallery, inv. 2119.

168 | Bartolomeo Suardi called Bramantino, *Christ resurrected*. Madrid, Museo Nacional Thyssen Bornemisza, inv. 61 (1937.1).

169 | Mathis Grünewald, *Saint Lawrence* (detail), ca. 1516. Frankfurt am Main, Städel Museum, inv. 2604.

in Cantù (ca. 1502–1507) and now scattered among the Bagatti Valsecchi and Poldi Pezzoli Museums in Milan (respectively inv. 987–988 and 1621–1622) and the Getty Museum in Los Angeles (inv. 71.PB.60),[7] or the altarpiece representing the *Virgin Mary with Saints Joseph, Ambrose and Jerome* (Denver Art Museum, inv. 1961.173, gift from the Samuel H. Kress Foundation), painted in 1510 for the Raimondi Chapel in the Church of San Francesco Grande in Milan [fig. 166].[8] This dense, stagnant light gives the saints their shiny, marble-like surface allowing the shadows to settle on the extraordinarily rich folds of their clothing.

Chiara Cassinelli has suggested to me a comparison with the head of the apostle John in the small panel representing *Saints Peter and John*, certainly part of a predella, in the Pinacoteca di Brera (inv. 2119), a work by Giovanni Agostino of Lodi [fig. 167], a painter certainly not immune to the appeal of German painting, and a copy of the Brera painting is, in fact, German.[9] The similarity, in terms of physiognomy and perspective point, is clear and compelling (direct observation or reference to shared models?). However, Grünewald's lighting choice is not Venetian (the other attraction point of Giovanni Agostino's culture, together with Milan), but aligns completely and precisely with the style of Zenale.

It is precisely this last aspect that displays a profound engagement with the greatest of Lombard Renaissance painters, Bramantino. Evidence of this can be seen not only in the blue-gray molding of the drapery but also in the very unusual way of portraying shadow in the so-called *Man of Sorrows* (actually a *Resurrected Christ*: Madrid, Thyssen-Bornemisza Museum, inv. 61 (1937.1)) by Bramantino[10] [fig. 168]. I find it truly impossible to think that these numerous innovations are not the result of Mathis's interaction with these works (or other similar ones, difficult for us to identify, by these artists). Without Dürer's theoretical restraint, Grünewald seems to confidently identify in Zenale and Bramantino inspiration for a new softness in his lighting and, even more, a novel three-dimensional peremptoriness.

Also noteworthy is the utterly convinced rendering of the hand of St. Lawrence holding the book, seen in perspective as a multi-faceted polygon [fig. 169]. Is the similarity to the outstretched and equally perspectival hand of the grieving St. John in the *Crucifixion* today at the Brera (inv. 981), a masterpiece by Bramantino of the early 16th century, to be seen as merely coincidental [fig. 170]?[11]

Additionally, the idea of creating highlights with yellow paint—perfectly logical from the standpoint of rendering relief—represents a stunning evolution from Grünewald's earlier use of paper as a color during the Isenheim years, as seen in the Berlin studies for St. Anthony and the figure escorted by angels.

To confirm that Grünewald actually traveled to northern Italy, we must verify that aesthetic suggestions of Italian origin are actually found in his later works. Though, before exploring this, it is worth noting that if the theory holds, Grünewald's stay in Italy would have been quite brief, at most lasting from September 1515 to early-August 1516, including the outward and return journeys. Therefore, it is difficult to imagine that he could have produced something significant enough in Lombardy to have had an impact on Italian painters. However, if some indication of his passage were to be found, we would have further confirmation of the veracity of this hypothesis. In fact, such an indication does exist, specifically in a painter in the vicinity of the areas Mathis visited: Amico Aspertini. Longhi had already linked the German painter with the altarpiece by Aspertini in San Martino Maggiore in Bologna [fig. 171].[12] The bright colors and the feline expression of the bishop's profile are promising, but above all, the contorted hands, never before seen in Amico's repertoire, seem to Longhi to be those of Grünewald up to and not later than the *Isenheim Altarpiece*, which could

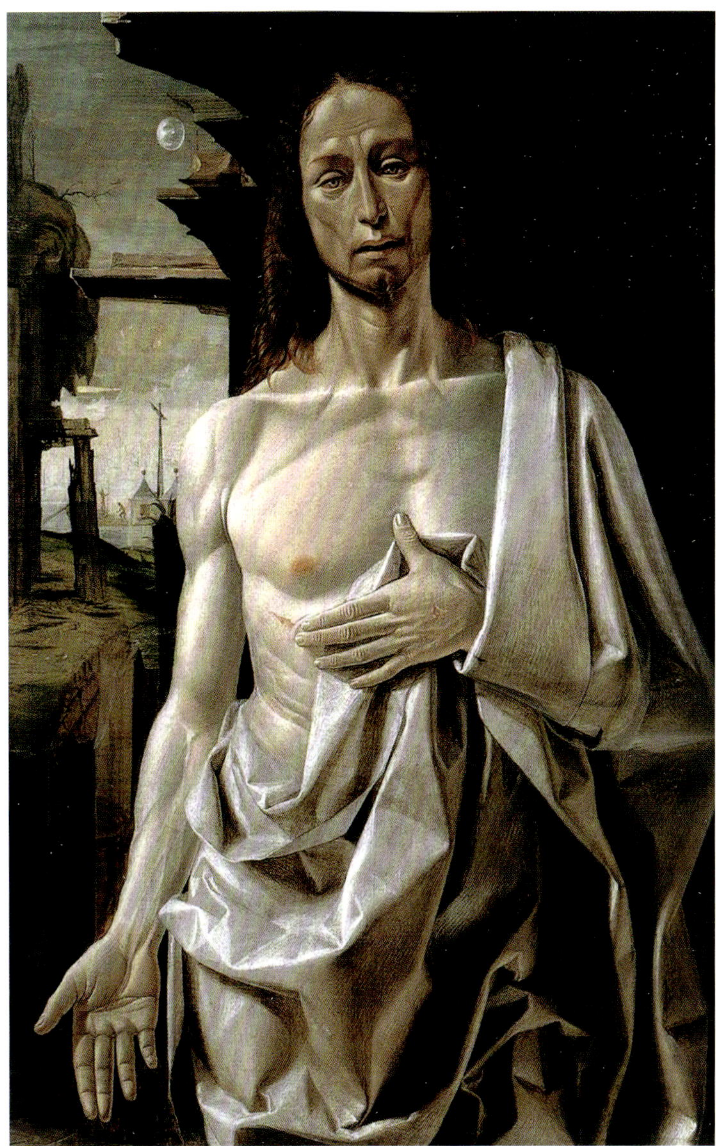

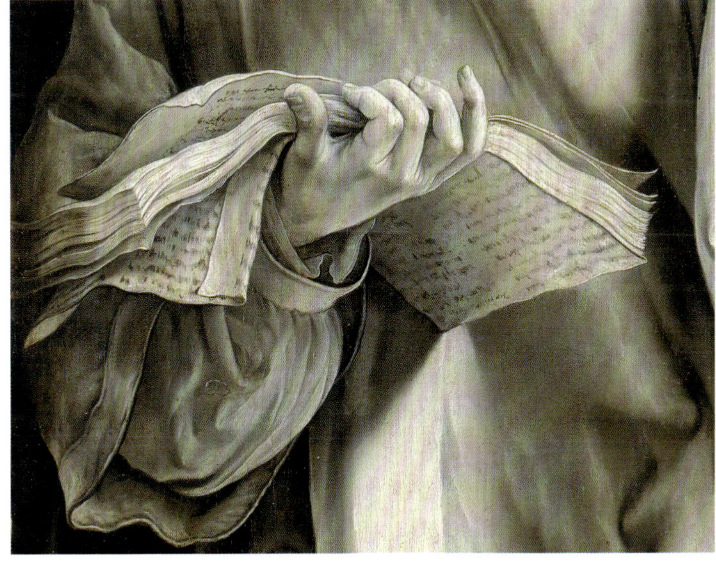

170 | Bartolomeo Suardi called Bramantino, *Crucifixion* (detail). Milan, Brera Gallery, inv. 981.

171 | Amico Aspertini, *Madonna and Child with Saints*, ca. 1515–1516. Bologna, Church of San Martino Maggiore.

172 | Amico Aspertini, *Albertus Magnus and Johannes Duns Scotus*. Como, Museo Civico, Pinacoteca di Palazzo Volpi, inv. 594.

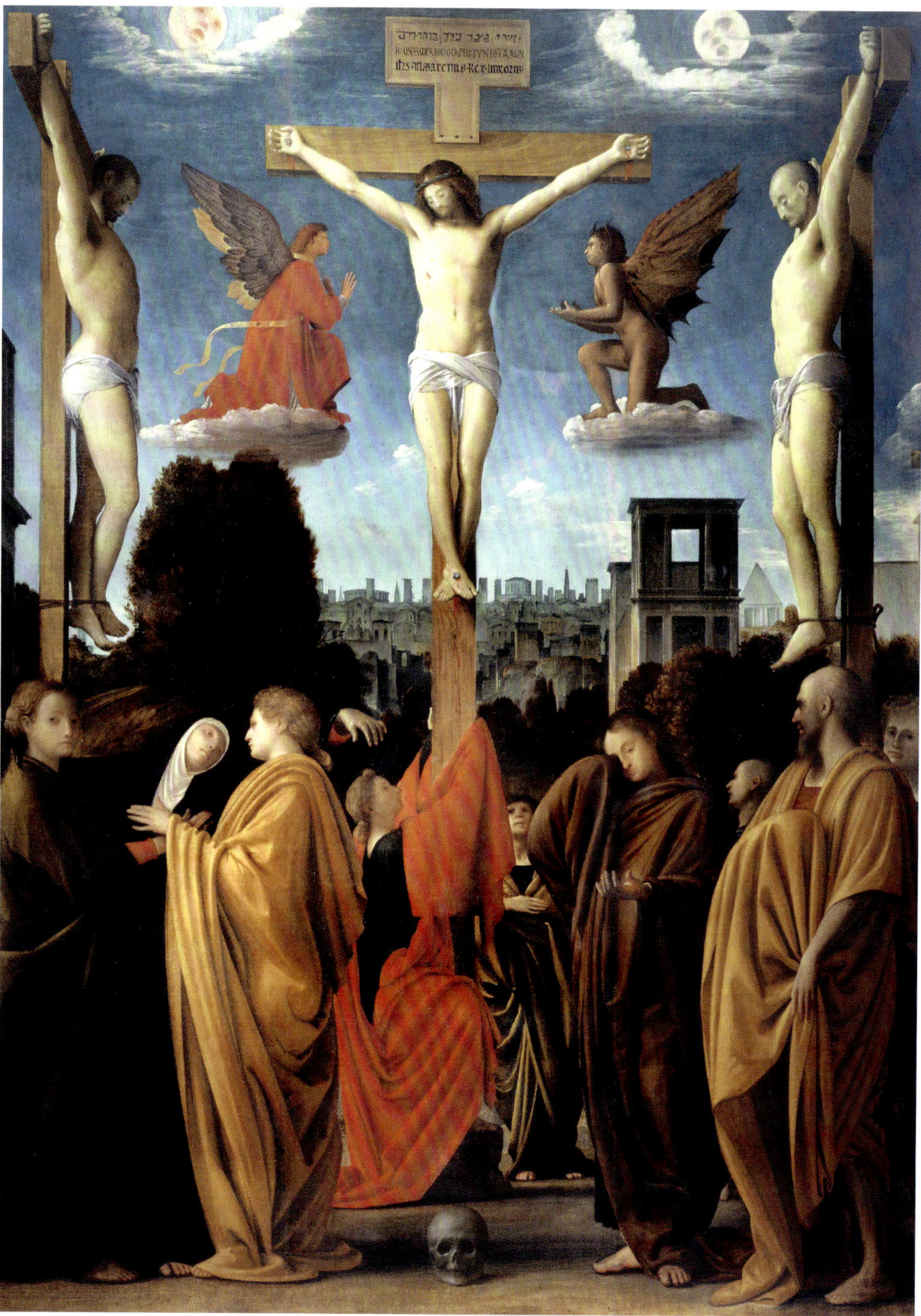

have been known as soon as he arrived in Italy. The same, if not more, could be said of the panel painting by Aspertini at the Museo Civico in Como (inv. 594) that depicts *Albertus Magnus and Johannes Duns Scotus* [fig. 172]. It dates from the same time, or just after, and in this panel the arthritic electrification of the hands is, if possible, even more extreme (and a comparison should be made of the monochrome heads of Grünewald's *St. Lawrence* today in Frankfurt and Aspertini's *Duns Scotus*). If we add to this that the chronology of Aspertini's altarpiece in Bologna is precisely 1515–1516, I would say the picture is complete.[13] In fact, it should be recalled that in the summer of 1517, the knight and humanist Ulrich von Hutten entered the service of the archbishop of Mainz following a long period of study that began in 1512 and included Pavia, Venice, Padua and, finally, Bologna. Ulrich and Mathis certainly knew each other in Mainz, but it is not at all impossible that their paths would have crossed earlier, further south.[14]

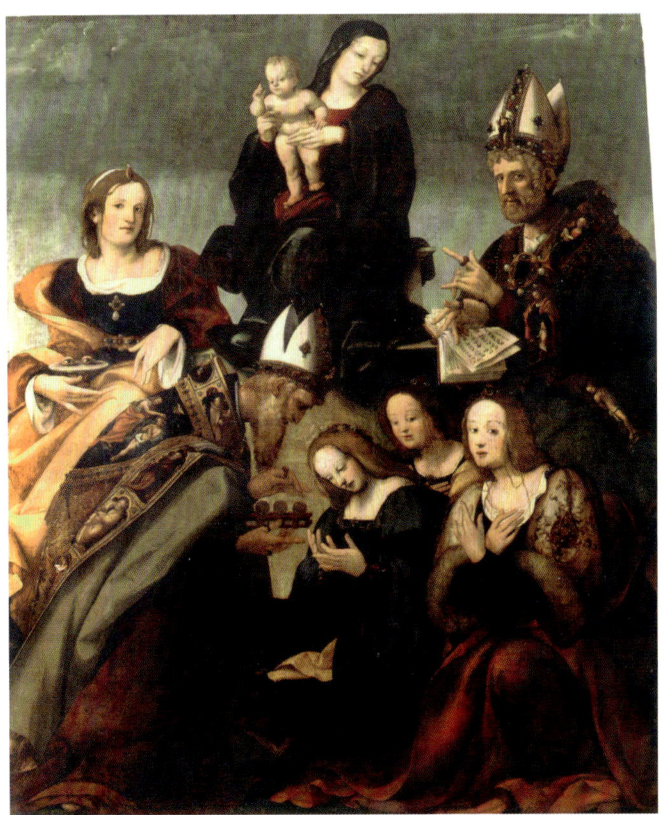

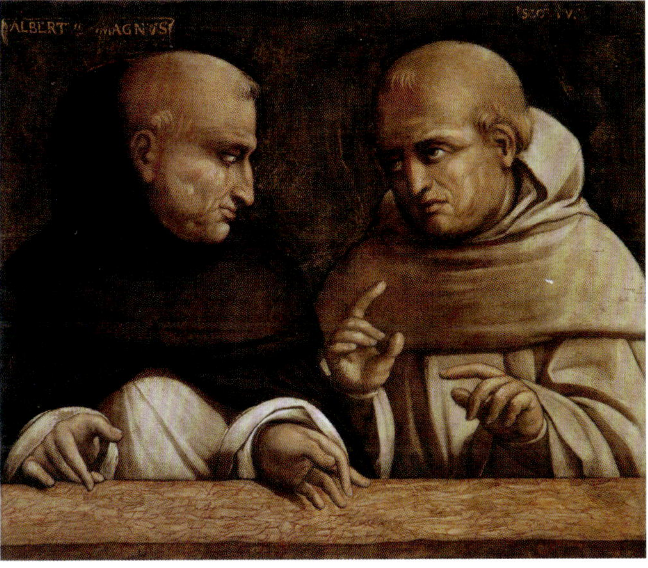

If I am correct, the fourth drawing, glued into his German Bible, by Hans Plock (Berlin, Kupferstichkabinett, inv. AM 22–1953 [fig. 173]) should be dated to this period.[15] The effect of the gleaming, metallic surfaces of the garments is like that of the Frankfurt panels, and it attests to the amazing richness of possibilities in Grünewald's graphic approach in this period (which, again, should be ca. 1516–1517).

The man, with upraised hands, exudes self-satisfaction, showcasing the exacting bravura of the head seen from below and the foreshortened arms, while his robe—marked by a long diagonal pleat reminiscent of Christ's garment in the *Agony in the Garden* from the *Small Passion* by Dürer (1508) [fig. 174],[16]—offers the same contorted metallic effects we have already seen. This figure has been variously, and implausibly, interpreted as Jesus transfigured (though the man appears too elderly), as a prophet in the *Transfiguration* scene (his elegantly middle-class clothes would belie this interpretation) or Moses with his arms raised during the battle with the Amalekites (but in that case, he should be brandishing the "staff of God", as cited in Exodus 17:8–14). Actually, a more plausible comparison with the panels by Wolf Huber, dated 1521 and today in Feldkirch Cathedral, shows a very convincing similarity with Joachim receiving from the angel the order to re-enter Jerusalem.[17] In fact, an earlier similar depiction of Joachim in the same pose can also be found in a small woodcut by Altdorfer, dated ca. 1513, that was part of an extensive series dedicated to the Fall and redemption of humanity [fig. 175].[18] For sure this was a model for Huber, which indicates a certain level of diffusion. It is conceivable that Grünewald was familiar with Altdorfer's work and that he had it in mind while creating his drawing. However, during this period Grünewald was an artist too original and inventive to merely rework external ideas and influences. Thus, the timid figure seen in Altdorfer and Huber's works transforms under Grünewald's hand into a majestic hero of the spirit, where the gesture of surprise and perhaps terror takes on the solemnity of a liturgical act, performed standing.

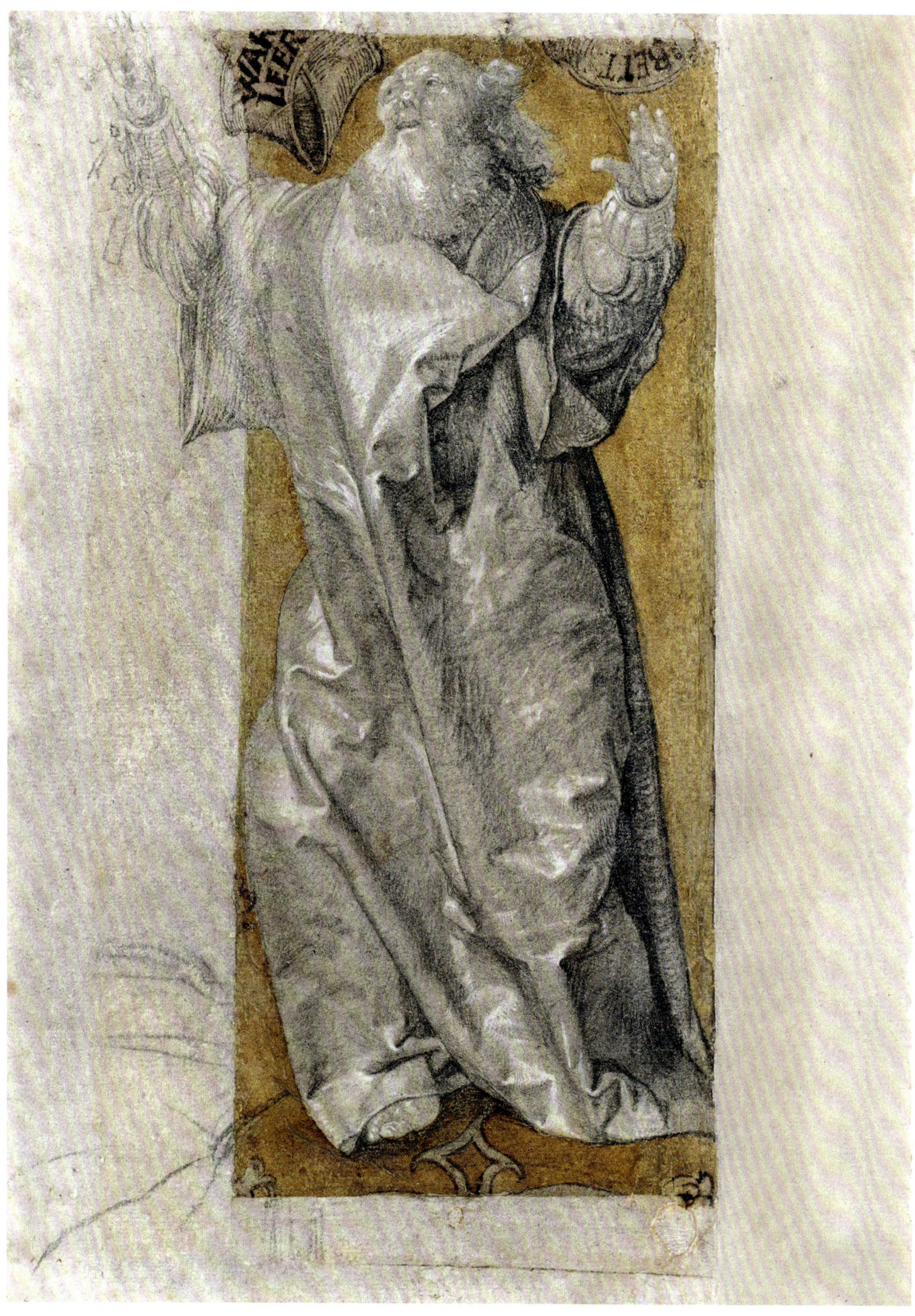

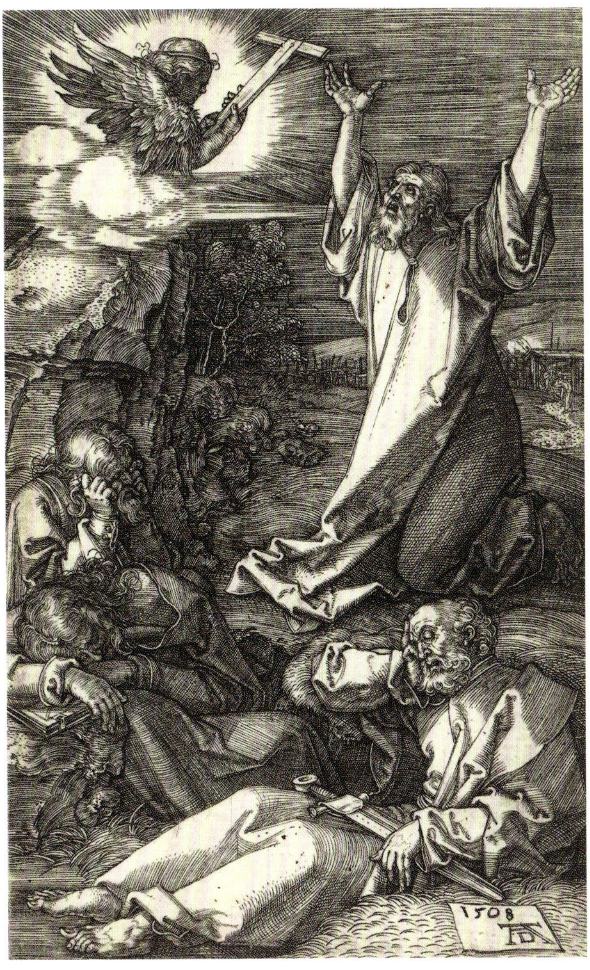

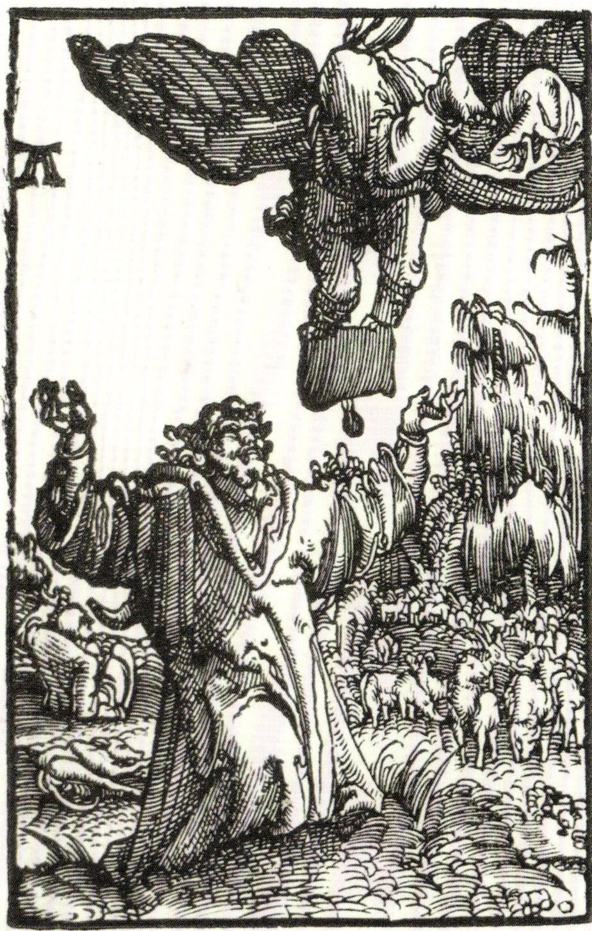

173 | Mathis Grünewald, *Saint Joachim (?)*, ca. 1516–1517. Berlin, Staatliche Museen, Kupferstichkabinett, inv. AM 22-1953.

174 | Albrecht Dürer, *Oration in the Garden*, woodcut, 1508.

175 | Albrecht Altdorfer, *Apparition of the Angel to Joachim*, 1510, woodcut.

However, it must be excluded, for chronological incompatibility, that the fourth "Plock drawing" could have some pertinence to the lost 1511 *Transfiguration*, a hypothesis posited by scholars more for inertia than real stylistic necessity. Instead, it might relate to one of the works documented in Mainz Cathedral, perhaps of a Marian subject, but given the information currently available, there is no evidence to confirm this beyond a vague hypothesis.

I wonder if the noteworthy drawing in Vienna (Graphische Sammlung Albertina, inv. 3047,[19] black chalk and white lead, 363 × 294 mm) [fig. 176] might belong to the same group. This drawing features a similar way of treating the drapery and the solemn, monumental figure that stands in majestic isolation, galvanized by a subtle rotary movement. The folds of the garments are primarily characterized by the light resting on the folds which is administered with superb skill using the white lead. The crisp, moist creases are very similar to those of the Frankfurt saints. Recently, Christof Metzger offered an interesting iconographic interpretation, identifying the figure as Moses and the burning bush, and hypothesizing that the drawing was for one of the hinged wings of the *Our Lady of the Snows* altarpiece in Aschaffenburg, which we will be discussing soon. This interpretation aligns with both the iconography and dating Metzger suggests, placing the Vienna drawing in the latter part of the second decade, and potentially associating it with an altarpiece dedicated to the Virgin Mary in Mainz Cathedral.[20] On the reverse side, just barely visible, there is a sketch of a bishop saint, and the key (?) held in his right hand would suggest

176 | Mathis Grünewald, *An aged man praying*, ca. 1516–1517. Vienna, Graphische Sammlung Albertina, inv. 3047 recto.

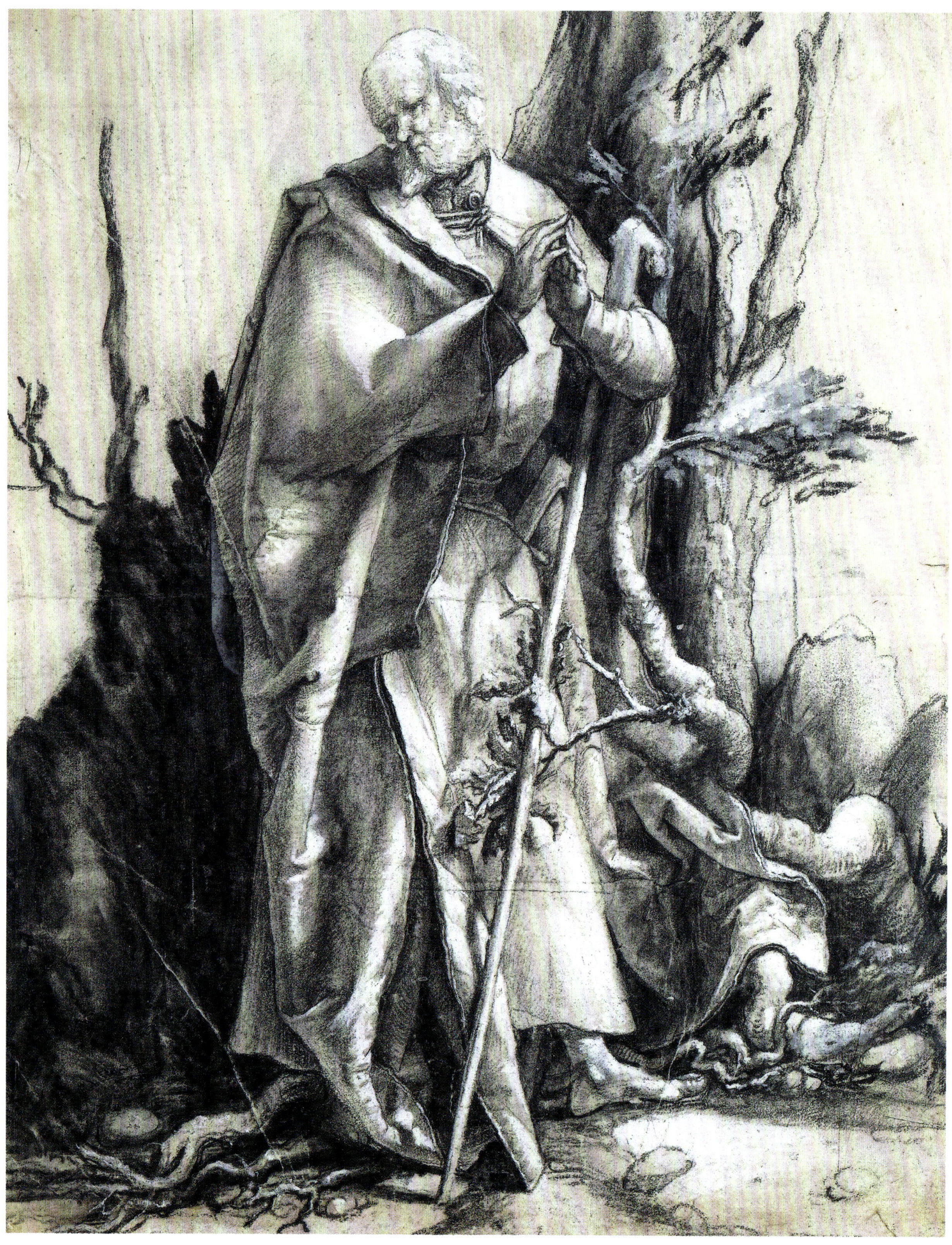

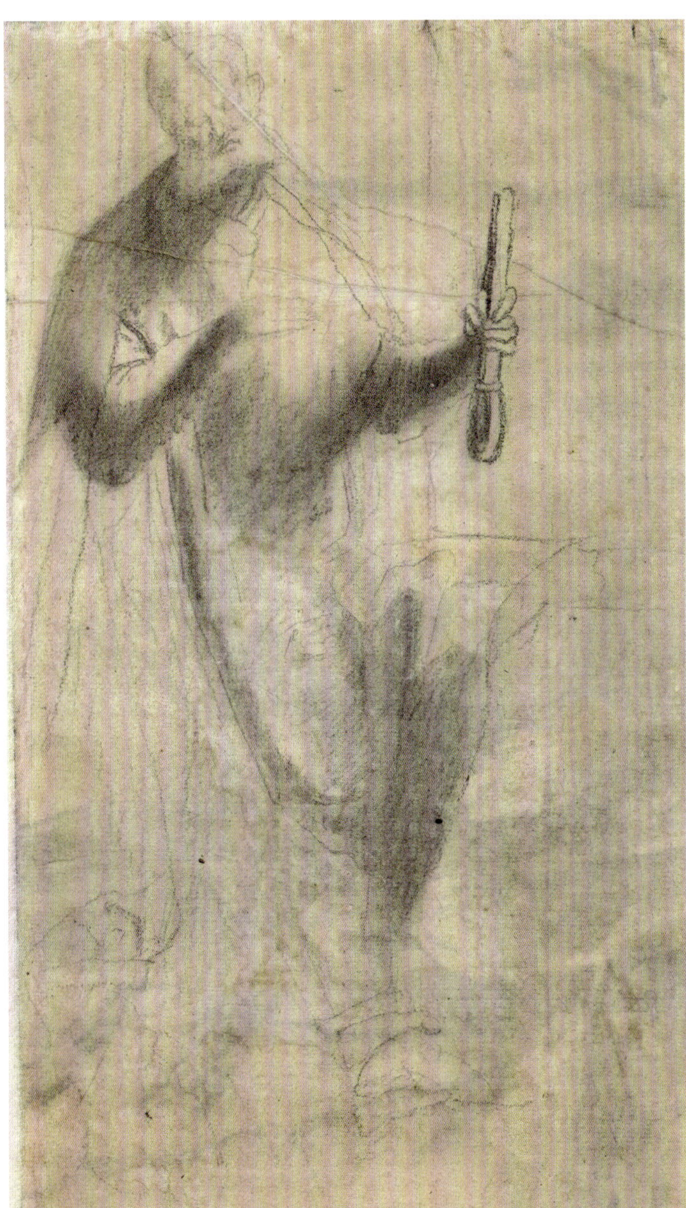

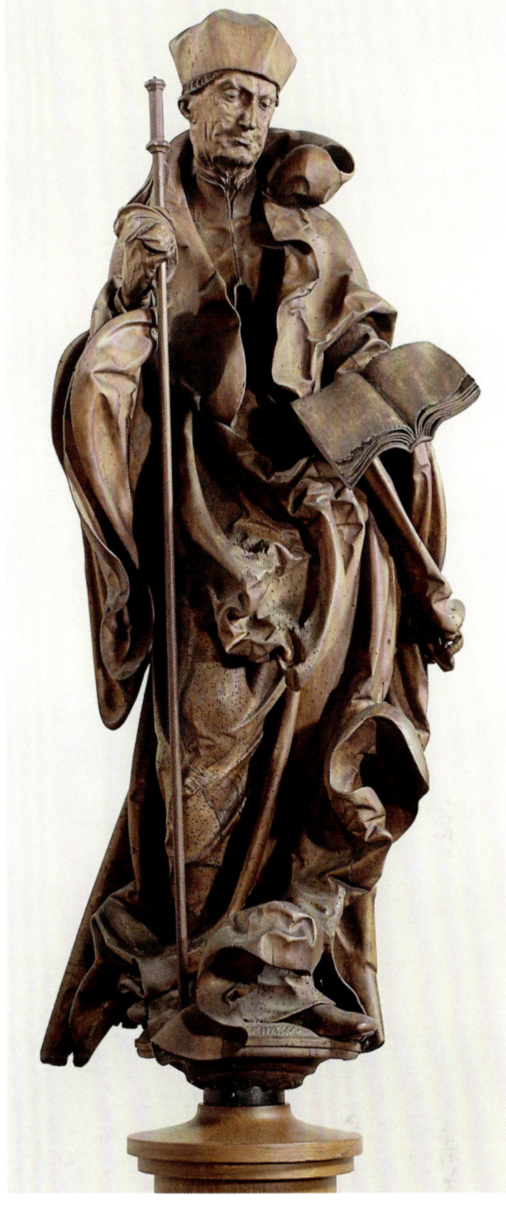

that it be interpreted as St. Peter [fig. 177]. A similar turning point must necessarily have impacted the sculptural world. For example, the beautiful *Abbot Saint* at the Liebighaus in Frankfurt (linden wood, 132 × 47 × 39 cm, inv. 958) [fig. 178]: a sculpture sometimes linked also to Master H.L., though stylistically less sophisticated, and in any case extraordinarily similar in terms of its volume, expressive power, and metallic and whirling drapery, to Mathis's panels also in Frankfurt.[21] However, despite the tremendous expressive impact and extreme virtuosity in the rendering of the drapery, it is not by him: too insistent is the physiognomic data in a somewhat self-serving way. Grünewald never digresses. What he inserts in his works is always strictly necessary, while these self-satisfied wrinkles and powerful jaw are not needed. We must limit ourselves to considering it a highly eloquent testimony of the authority given to Mathis by the artistic world of Mainz, Frankfurt, Franconia and Bavaria.

177 | Mathis Grünewald, *Study of Saint Peter (?)*, ca. 1516–1517. Vienna, Graphische Sammlung Albertina, inv. 3047 verso.

178 | Sculptor close to Grünewald, *Saint Abbot*. Frankfurt am Main, Liebighaus, inv. 958.

On August 5, 1517, our Canon Heinrich Reitzmann of Aschaffenburg dictated a

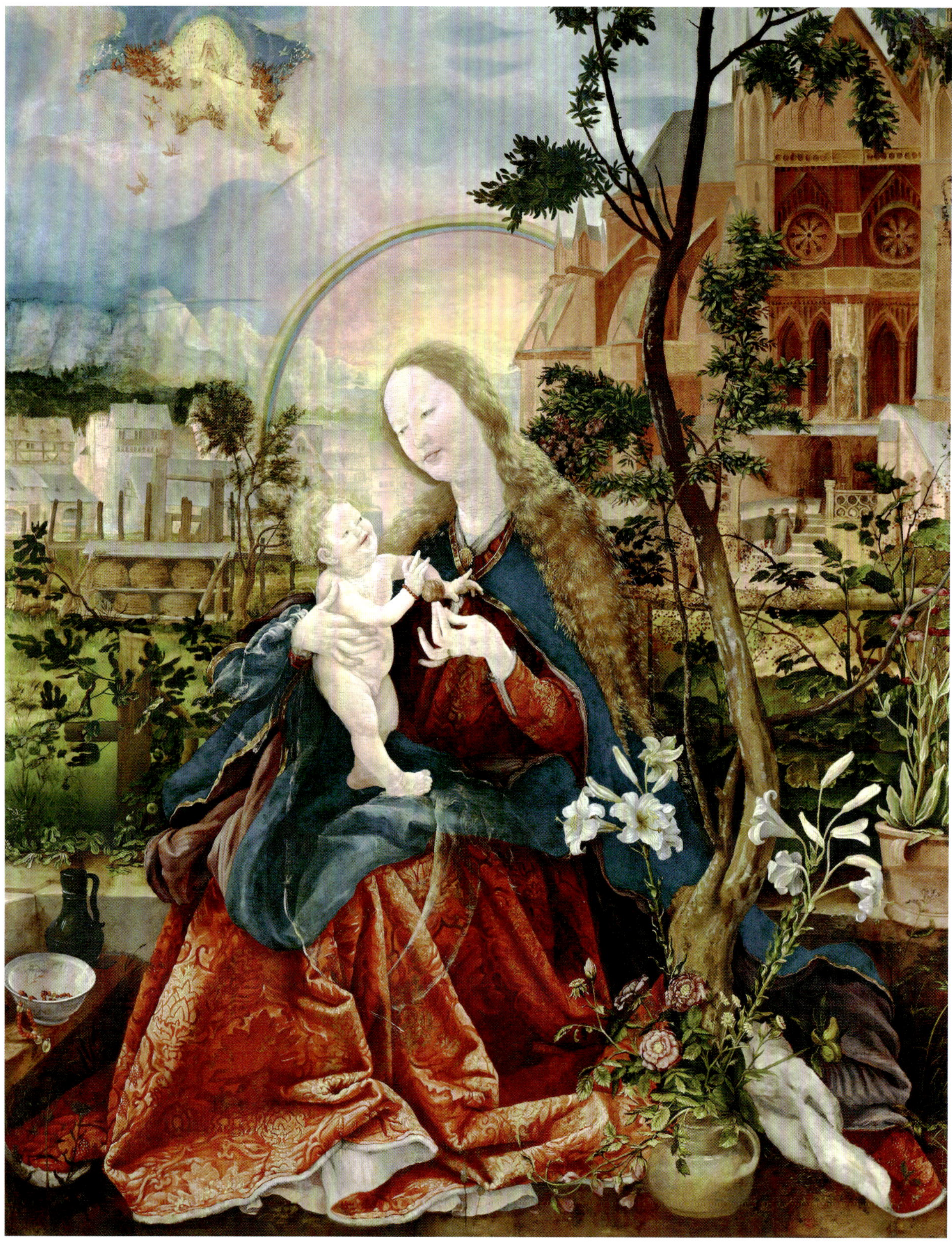

new version of his will, including twenty-five florins to be given to "magister Matheus pinctor" (it is not clear whether he was present or not) for him to paint an altarpiece of the Miracle of the Snows, the devotion of which Reitzmann had been promoting for some time. In 1515, a new edition of his treatise on Our Lady of the Snows was published, enhanced by a woodcut we will be discussing again, and a dedication to Albrecht von Brandenburg.[22]

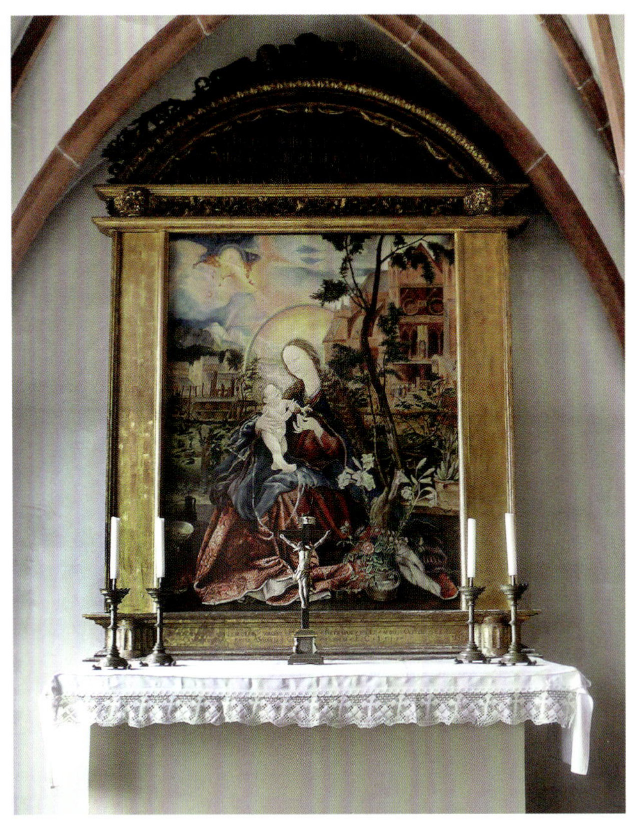

> Item lego 25 florenos ad facendum pingere festum Nivis per magistrum Matheum pinctorem in tabulam iam confectam, que locari debet in nova capella dominorum Casparis et Georgii Schantzen fratrum; materialia utpote colores reperiuntur in mensa serata in aula.[23]

Hanns Hubach produced a detailed reconstruction of the story of the chapel of Our Lady of the Snows (later of the Magi) at the collegiate church in Aschaffenburg and focused the attention on Reitzmann's earlier will, dictated, as usual, on August 5, in the year 1516.[24] In that will, the canon does not mention the altarpiece to be painted. According to Hubach, this means that Grünewald was already working on the painting today in Stuppach, or had perhaps even finished it. Such a deterministic interpretation of documents does not fit the process outlined to this point based on the results of the painter's figurative approach and the evolution of his style. However, I do not believe it is difficult to find a point of agreement in the hypothesis that on August 5, 1516, immediately upon his return to Germany, Mathis (who would appear once again in Mainz on the 27th) was immediately commissioned by Reitzmann to paint the altarpiece that had been planned.

179 | Mathis Grünewald, *Madonna and Child*, ca. 1516–1517. Stuppach (Bad Mergentheim), Parish church.

180 | Photo reconstruction of the Stuppach *Madonna* within its original frame in the Collegiate church of Aschaffenburg.

It was the *Madonna with Child* today in the Stuppach parish church near Bad Mergentheim (186 × 150 cm) [fig. 179], dated and signed by the painter on the bottom of the wooden frame, still surviving in the collegiate church in Aschaffenburg (the original painting was replaced with a copy by Christian Schad, dated 1947)[25] [fig. 180]:

> Ad honorem festi nivis deipaerae [sic] virginis, Henricus Retzmann huius aed is custos et canonicus ac Caspar Schantz, canonicus eiusdem ecclesiae. 1519. MGN.[26]

This is one of Grünewald's most impressive works, striking in its grandeur, chromatic intensity and naturalistic detail, with a tenderness that seems to fall back on itself, almost unbearable to the viewer to the point of becoming disquieting.

Standing out against the intense, fluid red of the Virgin's dress is the blue, again so similar to the blue seen in the youthful work of Romanino. In the background, we see the more finished landscape painted by Mathis, with a Gothic structure that has been identified as the transept of Strasbourg Cathedral.[27] The divine apparition in

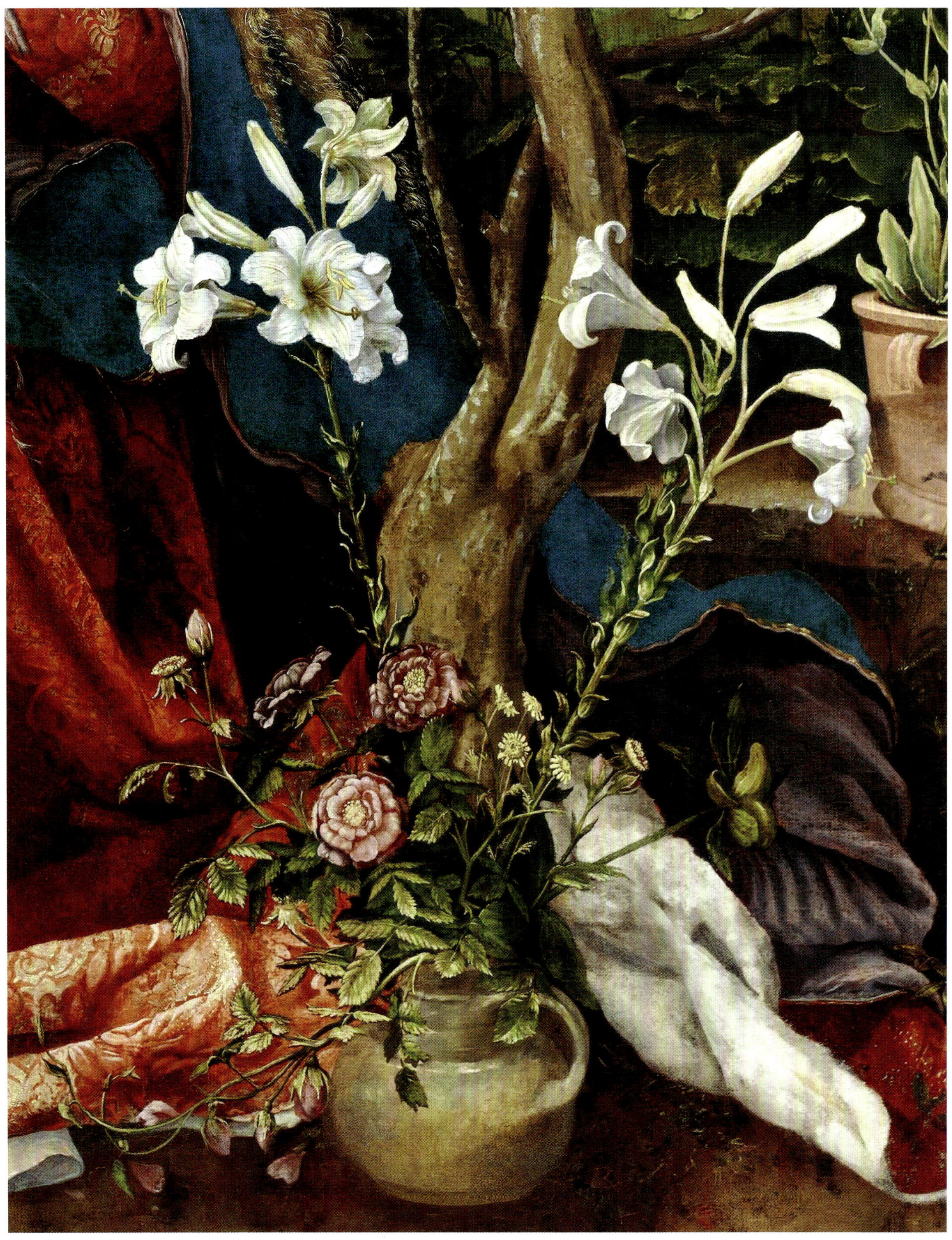

the upper left (incredibly altered in the 1936 restoration which transformed the Christ-like God of the original into a more obvious "Ancient of Days") looks towards the rainbow that acts as a bridge between the Gothic church and the nearby town. A garden grows all around, painted with amazing precision: from the vase with lilies and roses (Marian flowers par excellence) [fig. 181], to the tree oozing sap. Everything—the texture of the dress, the bowl with cherries and the jug—is painted with a Flemish-like meticulousness that Grünewald never lost. Yet what strikes us the most, in a figure reminiscent of Schongauer and Dürer, is the extremely elegant loop formed by the left arm and hand of the Virgin who gives a flower to Jesus. This is unquestionably based on the analogous, but reversed, detail of Leonardo's *Benois Madonna* (Saint Petersbourg, The State Hermitage, inv. 2773) [fig. 182], or perhaps a copy of it. The Butinonesque *Madonna* at the Pushkin Museum in Moscow (inv. 1545) shows that this theme, although developed in Florence, was known in Milan.[28] And not only. I am convinced—perhaps out of a sentimental and professional bias—that this mother with a healthy glow and long blonde hair (made of true gold, as the result of an alchemical transmutation),[29] intent on coddling her happily smiling child, is conversing with the world of Gaudenzio Ferrari. Although the similarity between this composition and Gaudenzio's terracotta *Madonna* in the small church of the Madonna of Loreto in Varallo, ca. 1513–1514[30] [fig. 183], might seem tangential, there appears to be an exchange of ideas. How much does this *Madonna* by Mathis presage the one painted by Gaudenzio around 1521 for the altarpiece of San Silano in Romagnano Sesia, and today part of the Borromeo collection in Isola Bella[31] [fig. 184]? It would not be surprising if Mathis, urged on by his religious ferment, actually visited the Saint Sepulchre sanctuary (later Holy Mountain) in Varallo, where, during the time in which he was likely visiting Lombardy, the French government of the Duchy of Milan, the diocese of Novara and the Franciscan Order were promoting its devotion.

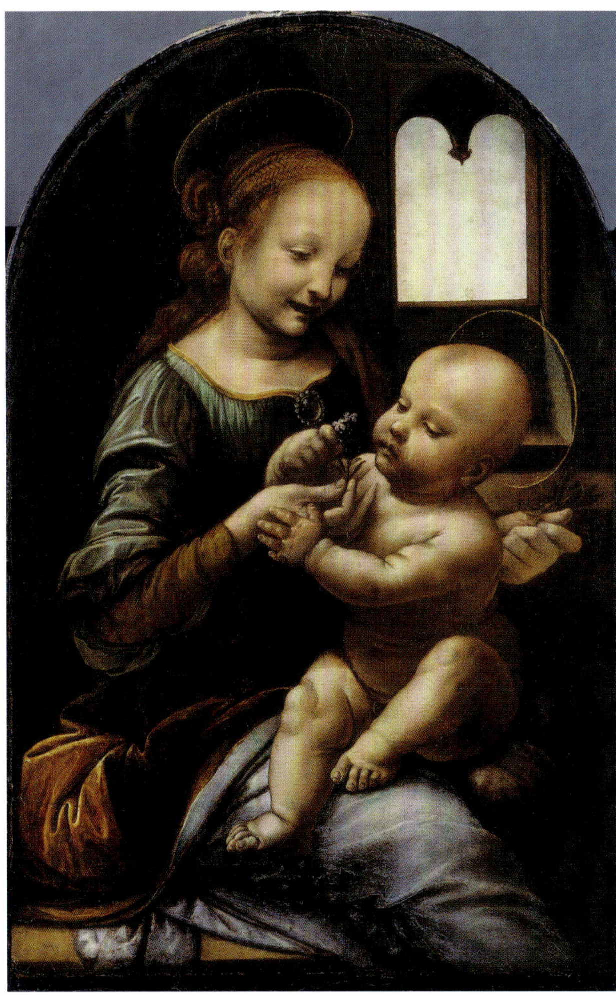

181 | Mathis Grünewald, *Madonna and Child* (detail), ca. 1516–1517. Stuppach, Parish church.

182 | Leonardo da Vinci, *Madonna and Child* (*Benois Madonna*), ca. 1478–1480. Saint Petersbourg, The State Hermitage, inv. 2773.

For those familiar with Grünewald's earlier works from Mainz and Aschaffenburg, such as the two Heller saints or the *Small Crucifixion* in Washington, this highly colored and uncommonly monumental painting would have come as a major surprise. It would have been clear that the still-immature painter called years earlier to Isenheim had evolved into a more inventive and irrepressible one, with perfect mastery of all painting technique, now returned after a long absence.

The Stuppach *Madonna* also stands out for its underlying sketch, typically very simple, drawn with a brush in red, instead of black.[32]

There is a preparatory drawing for the Stuppach *Madonna*, a sheet in black chalk, also in Berlin (inv. KdZ 12039, 315 × 279 mm)[33] [fig. 185]. The style, it must be noted, is

183 | Gaudenzio Ferrari, *Madonna suckling the Child*, ca. 1513.1514. Roccapietra (Varallo Sesia), Cappella di Loreto.

184 | Gaudenzio Ferrari, *Madonna and Child with the Saints Joseph and Anthony the Abbott* (from a polyptych). Isola Bella, Collezione Borromeo.

surprisingly that of the *Madonna in Glory* in Rotterdam and the studies of the apostles for the *Transfiguration* previously in Frankfurt. After having admired the magnificent freedom of light and movement in the drawings of the presumed *Moses* and *Joachim* in Vienna and Berlin, and the exhilarating result of the Stuppach painting, this drawing seems rigid and hesitant in comparison. The pose is only apparently the same, the "Leonardesque" arm is more banal, the Madonna's expression less tenderly regal, the draping of the folds more predictable, and mastery of the space not even comparable. In fact, it could even be said that the comparison is more explicit with the woodcut by Hans Baldung Grien depicting the *Madonna and Child on a Grassy Bench* [fig. 186], datable to ca. 1505–1507, reworked in reverse.[34] Nor can I exclude that Mathis might have had access to other etchings, even more recent ones, such as Dürer's burin, dated 1513[35] [fig. 187], or the one by Albrecht Altdorfer, usually dated ca. 1515–1520, but probably somewhat earlier[36] [fig. 188]. How can this apparent regression be explained? And more importantly, how to explain in 1516–1517 a drawing which, in terms of Grünewald's development, belongs to the early part of the second decade and, in any case, within and not subsequent to the early phase in Isenheim? If this is a sheet from 1516–1517, then all our reconstruction based on a close examination of his style is ephemeral, and the effort made to this point nothing more than an illusion. Fortunately, style never lies. This drawing, for reasons of style and technique, must necessarily date from the period 1510–1513, no earlier, no later. The clear relationship with the Stuppach *Madonna* can be explained easily thanks to Mathis's association with Canon Reitzmann. It should be remembered that Reitzmann had expressed his intent to create a painting dedicated to Our Lady of the Snows in his very first will on

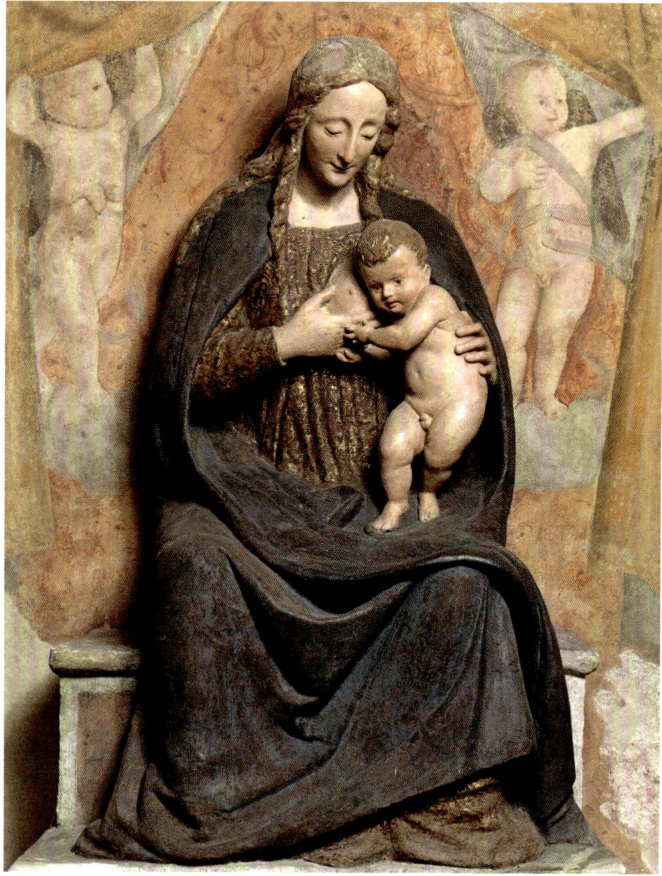

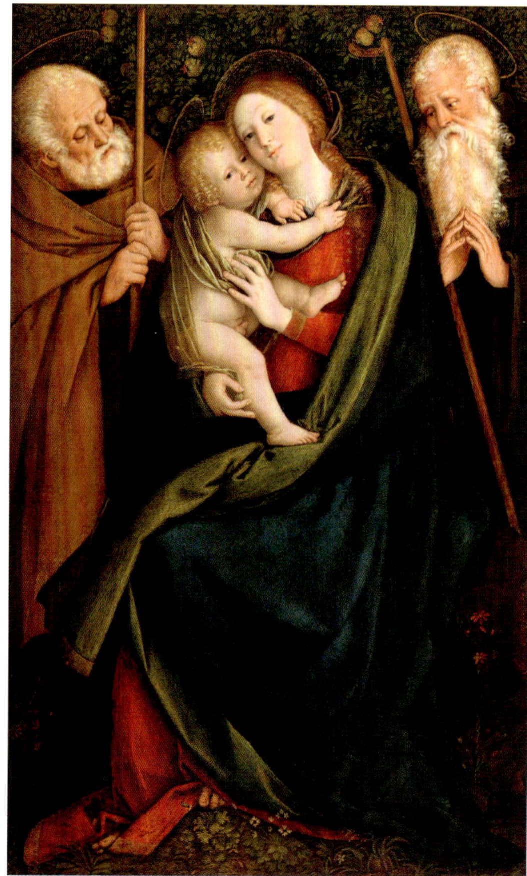

August 5, 1513. Clearly, from that date, Mathis reached an agreement with the canon of Aschaffenburg on the layout of the altarpiece. The will dated August 5, 1514, is very clear about this: "Item similiter volo et ordino quod festum Nivis gloriosissime Marie virginis in tabula depingatur *prout in proximo elapso anno* [i.e., 1513] *in testamento meo ordinavi*" (the italic emphasis is mine).[37] Thus, a project for the altarpiece already existed in 1513. Therefore, this sheet is not connected with the actual painting of the altarpiece, but with Reitzmann's initial request. It is a drawing from 1513, evidently made right before leaving for Isenheim and probably left with his friend, the canon,

185 | Mathis Grünewald, *Study for a Madonna and Child*, ca. 1513. Berlin, Staatliche Museen, Kupferstichkabinett, inv. KdZ 12039.

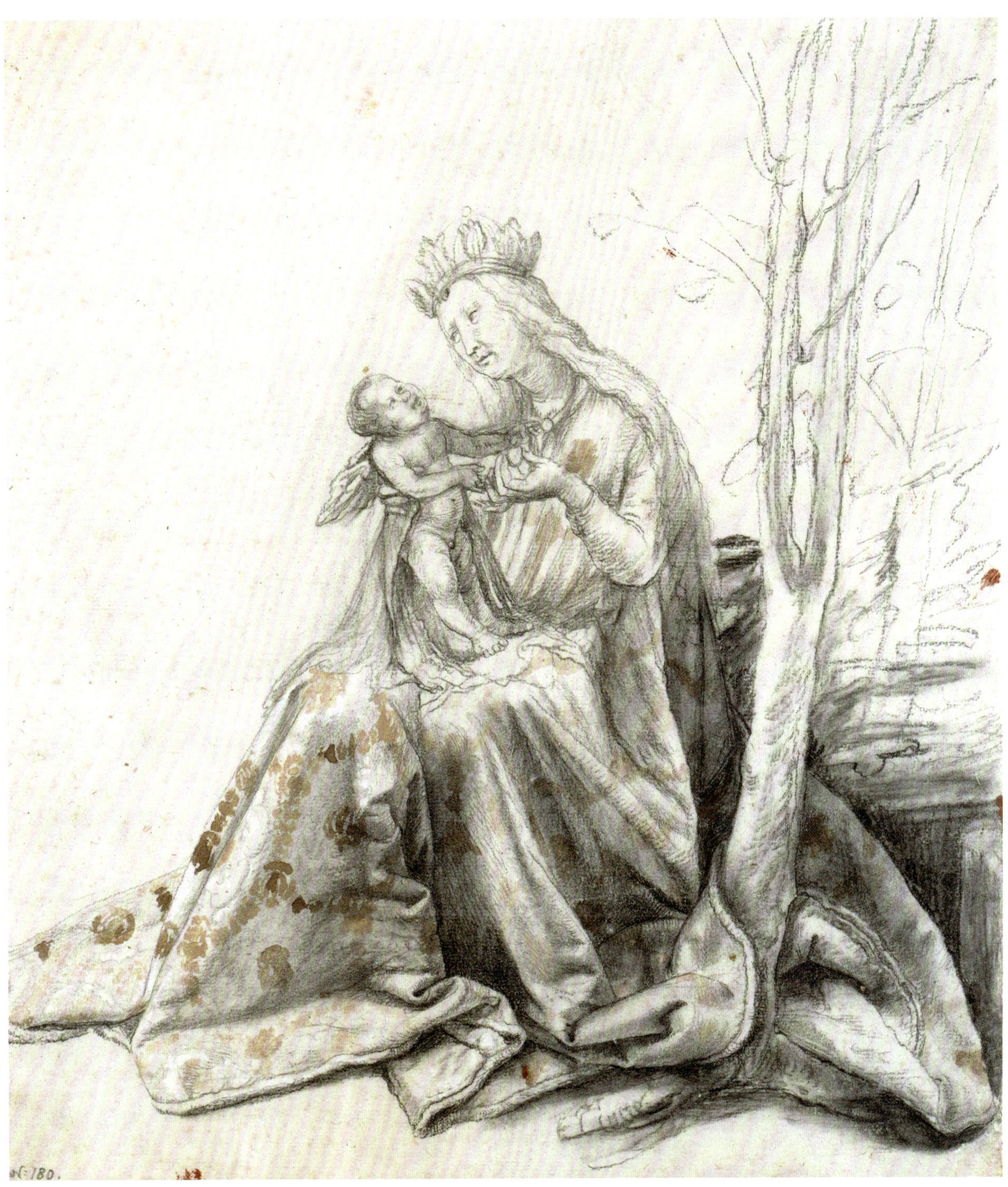

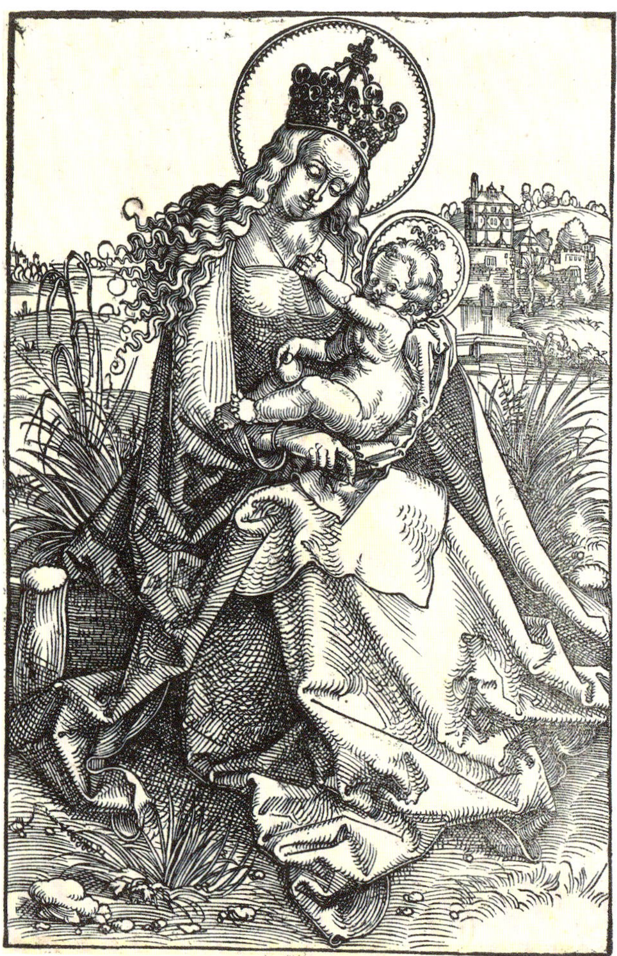

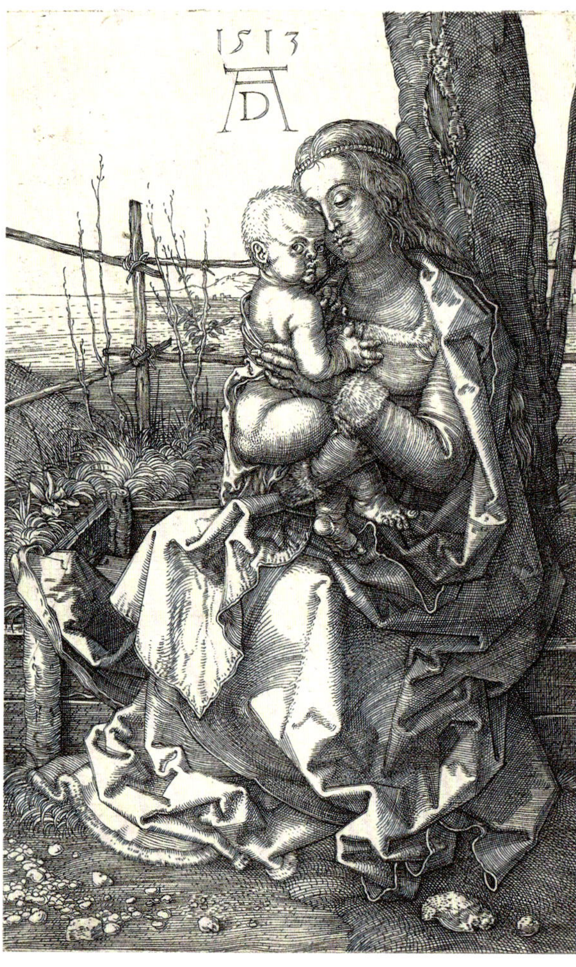

186 | Hans Baldung Grien, *Madonna and Child on a grassy bench*, woodcut.

187 | Albrecht Dürer, *Madonna and Child*, 1513, burin.

as a pledge for the future painting (which gives us a likely early dating limit for the Altdorfer burin). Rather than undermining our reconstruction, this fact highlights Grünewald's enormous growth within just five years. The experience in Isenheim was decisive in every way.

Regardless, the work would require some time, and it appears that Mathis returned in 1517. During this period, the chapterhouse of the collegiate church in Aschaffenburg sent a messenger to nearby Sailauf, where the painter (by now once again in service) was likely residing, to inspect the Pilgrim Fountain.[38] Reitzmann is once again the executor of the will of Canon Michael Kremmel, who died October 18, 1517. Mathis, who probably had just married and seeking a more stable life divided between Mainz and Aschaffenburg, bought some of Kremmel's furniture.[39] On the same occasion (we are near the end of 1517), Reitzmann donated two bed sheets from the inheritance of the deceased canon to the chapel of Our Lady of the Snows. These sheets were probably not used for the Stuppach *Madonna* (which at this point can be dated between the second half of 1516 and 1517), but for preparing other paintings for the same chapel.

According to Hubach's concise reconstruction, in which the documents and technical information flow effortlessly, the altarpiece, vaguely Italianate (though based on a model already common in Germany, so in this case Grünewald's Italian experience does not apply), designed as a unified modern piece, is transformed into a triptych on the basis of Heinrich Reitzmann's August 5, 1517 will.[40] Of the two new panels, only one remains, and after numerous vicissitudes, it is now at the Freiburg Augustinermuseum in Freiburg im Breisgau, and depicts the *Miracle of the Snow* (inv. 11480, 179 × 91.5 cm).[41] Its dating would thus be between late 1517 and the 1519 inscription on the frame [fig. 189].

In the background, we see the apparition of the Virgin Mary to Pope Liberius and John, a Roman patrician, on the night between August 4 and 5, 362. In the foreground, the pope traces the foundation of the church to be built (the basilica of Santa Maria Maggiore) over the snow that fell miraculously in Rome in August. On the back of the panel, a later painting shows the Magi in adoration (who, along with Saints Martin and George shared the dedication to Our Lady of the Snows, the chapel's namesake), created at a later date by another artist, today attributed to be Jörg Isenhart, around 1530 [fig. 190]. Therefore, it must be hypothesized that another panel existed, to the left of the *Madonna*, of an unknown subject (notable is Metzger's interesting hypothesis that mentions the Vienna drawing of *Moses and the burning bush*), or, according to Ziermann (but less probable), the two works might have been separated and belonged to different contexts.[42]

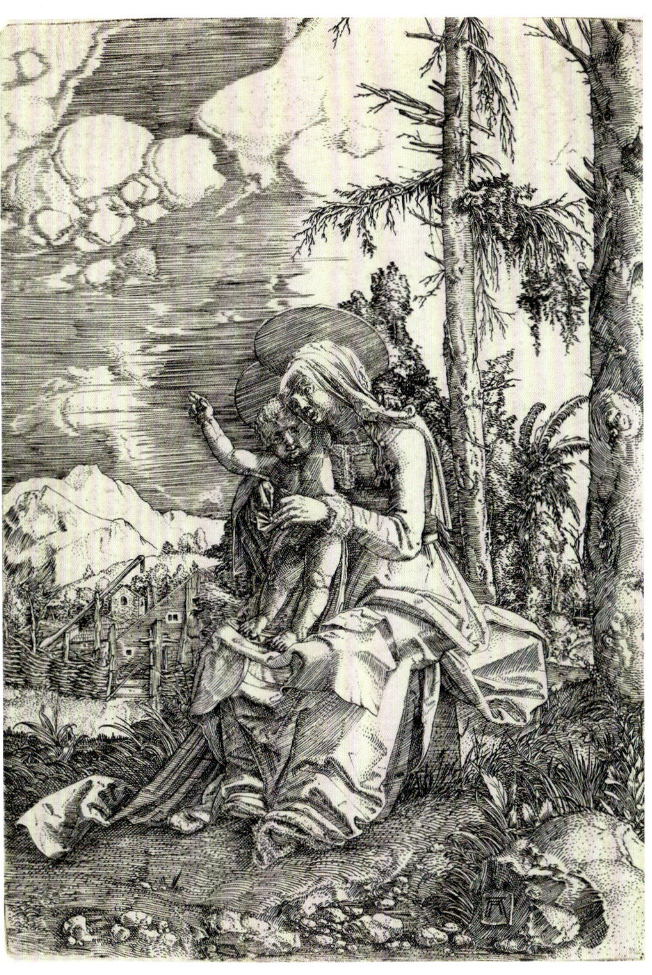

188 | Albrecht Altdorfer, *Madonna and Child*, woodcut.

Here Grünewald condenses (according to Leonardo's rule, consciously or not) all the scenes that in the frontispiece of Reitzmann's 1515 tract were portrayed in four vignettes [fig. 191]. From a narrative point of view, the only difference is that the depiction of the miraculous dream of the elderly couple (which would have annoyingly repeated the similar event with Pope Liberius) was replaced by the heavenly apparition towards which the elderly couple points (of course, the woodcut has very little to do with Mathis).

Unquestionably, this new painting by Grünewald, datable as has been said to 1517–1519, explicitly confirms the dialectical comparison initiated by him with the painting of Bramantino. First of all, the buildings of the imaginary Rome seen in the background are fully in his style: square towers and cylindrical mausoleums as in a De Chirico painting, or the architecture of Marcello Piacentini; and buildings decorated with roundels, monumental statues, and pilasters adorned with candelabra. A classical-style arsenal familiar to Lombard Renaissance scholars. But also, the solemn composure of the movements, the geometrical rendering of the figures and even the physiological accentuation of those in the papal entourage are all aspects that reference Bramantino. Could the subdued pace of the scene recall the Trivulzio Tapestries (or the *Disputation* by Gaudenzio in Varallo, 1507–1508, whose layout it is derived from [fig. 192])? And could the dominant red be the same used by Suardi? Doesn't John's elderly spouse, kneeling in a perfectly frontal pose behind the pope

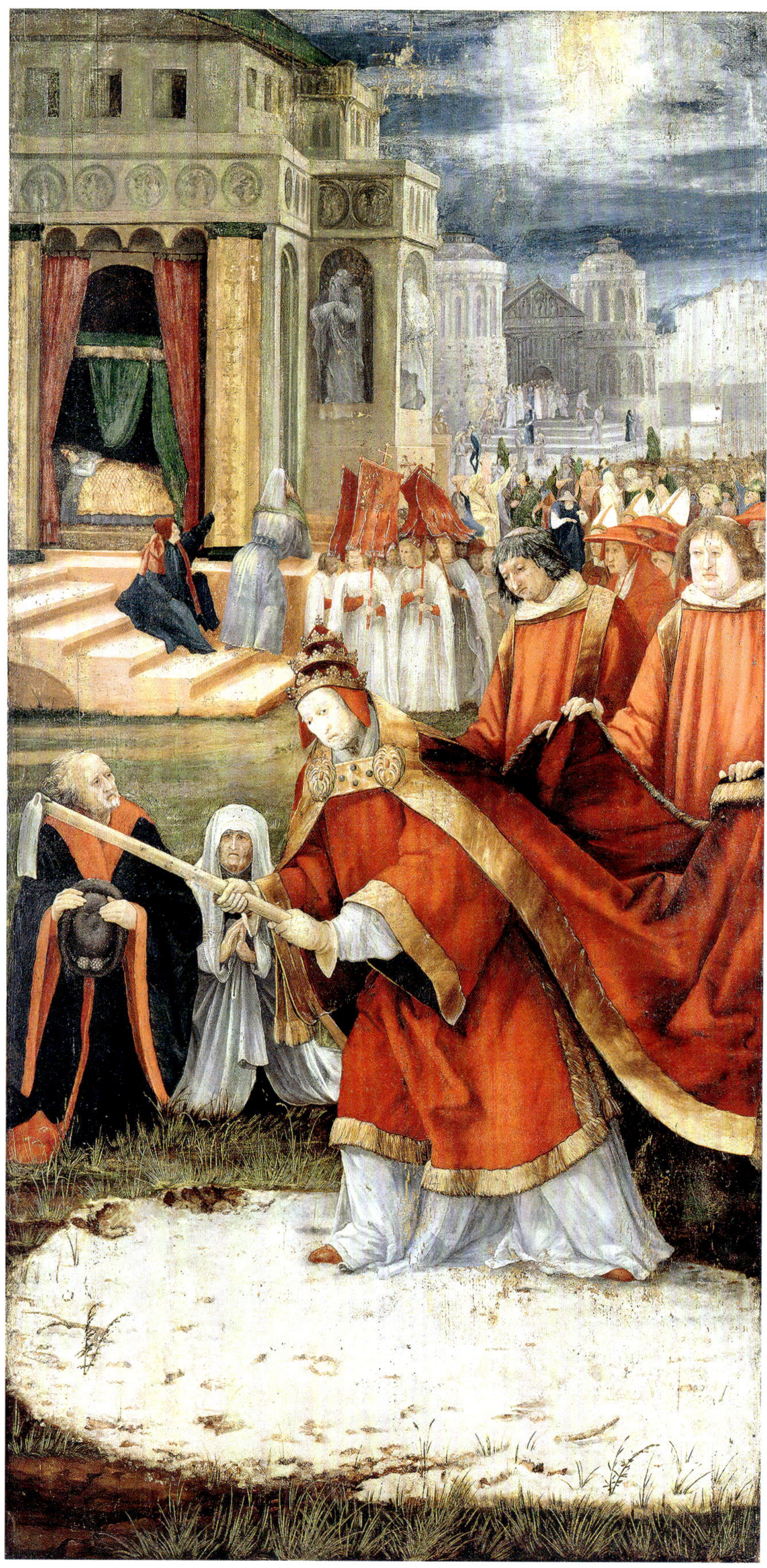

189 | Mathis Grünewald, *Miracle of the Snow*, ca. 1519. Freiburg am Breisgau, Augustinermuseum, inv. 11480.

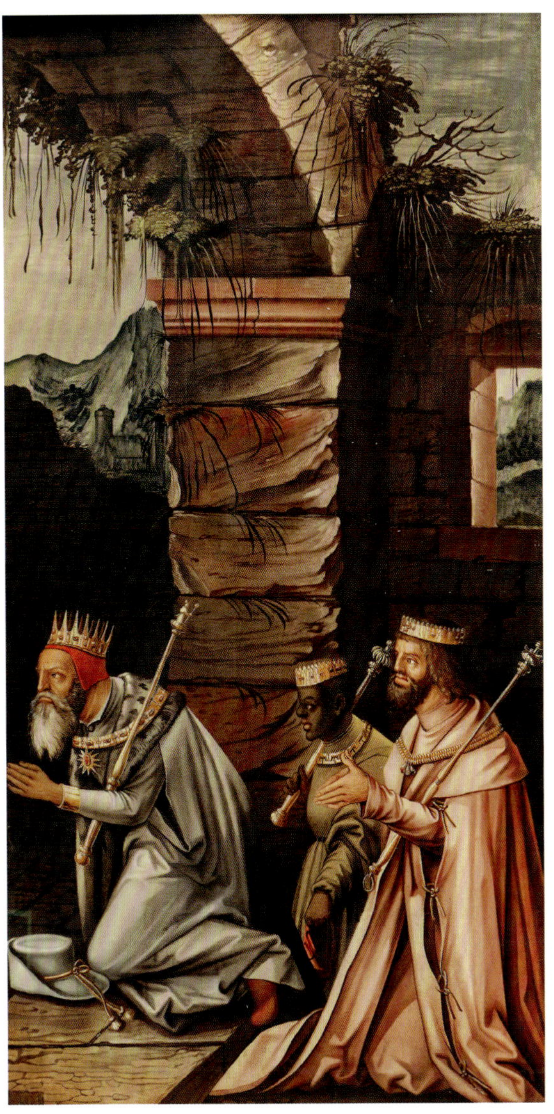

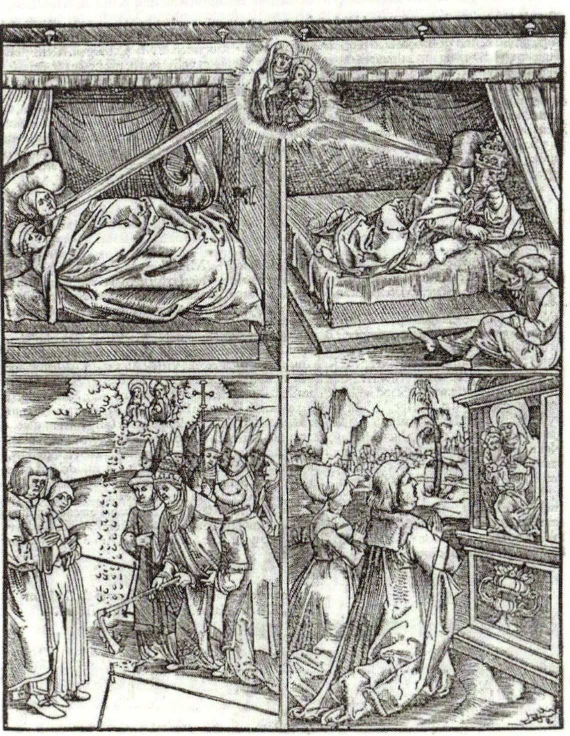

Hyſtoria de feſto niuis glorioſiſſime
dei genitricis ⁊ virginis Marie in ea forma qua Ro
me in Baſilica eiuſdem ad Mariam maiorem nuncu
pata: vbi mirabile ſumpſit exordium: obſeruatur:
Indulgētijs ſummoꝝ pontificū corroborata et nup
in notis ⁊ verbis adamuſſim correcta ⁊ emendata.

190 | Jörg Isenhart, *Adoration of the Magi*, ca. 1530. Freiburg am Breisgau, Augustinermuseum, inv. 11480.

191 | *Hystoria de festo nivis gloriosissime Dei genitricis et virginis Marie in ea forma qua Rome in Basilica eiusdem ad Mariam maiorem nuncupata*, Basel, Jakob von Pfortzheim, May 12, 1515, frontispiece.

[fig. 193], fit into the half-hidden depiction of the scene, like the pious woman with her arms crossed on her chest in Bramantino's *Crucifixion* at the Brera [fig. 194]? Here we are at the pinnacle of Mathis's infatuation with the cerebral and subtle painting style of the Lombard master, apparently diametrically opposed to his expressive world. In fact, if I knew nothing about Grünewald and I found myself in front of this work, ignoring completely its origins and history, I could find no better way to describe it than "Foreign (German?) follower of Bramantino".

I would like to think that the figure of John's elderly wife is a point of reference for the *Head of the woman with turban* at the Louvre (Département des Arts Graphiques, inv. 18588; black chalk with slight white lead highlights, 204 × 150 mm) [fig. 195].[43] The image continues in the most genteel direction of the full maturity of the painter which began with the Stuppach *Madonna*. Stunning smile, the most beautiful depiction ever done of maternity, not as an objective, biological fact, but as a sentiment. The same gentle, luminous smile, the same sweetness of the Stuppach *Madonna*, suggesting that Mathis might have intentionally captured that smile specifically, even if from a face no longer youthful, for the *Madonna* he painted for Heinrich Reitzmann. But it can be seen that the head and neck of the woman are above

192 | Gaudenzio Ferrari, *Christ disputing in the Temple*, ca. 1507–1508, Varallo Sesia, Church of Santa Maria delle Grazie.

193 | Mathis Grünewald, *Miracle of the Snow* (detail), ca. 1519. Freiburg am Breisgau, Augustinermuseum, inv. 11480.

194 | Bartolomeo Suardi called Bramantino, *Crucifixion* (detail). Milan, Brera Galleri, inv. 981.

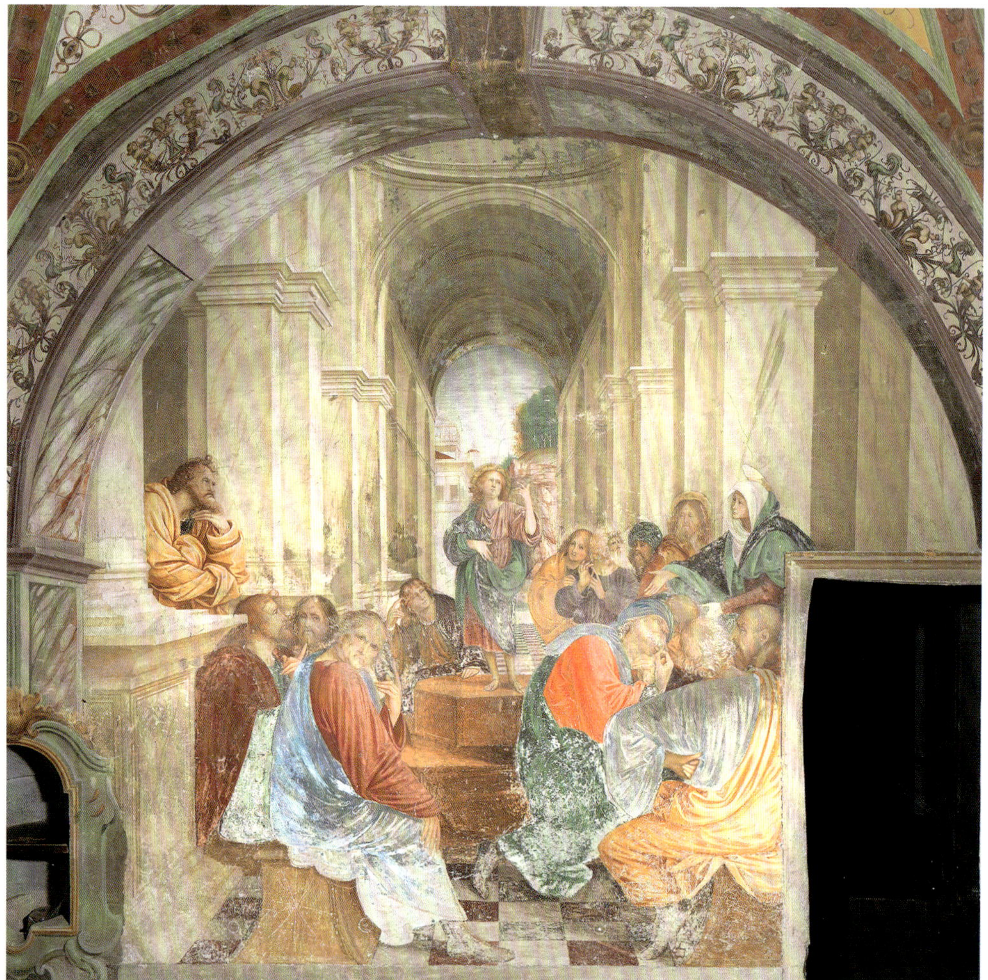

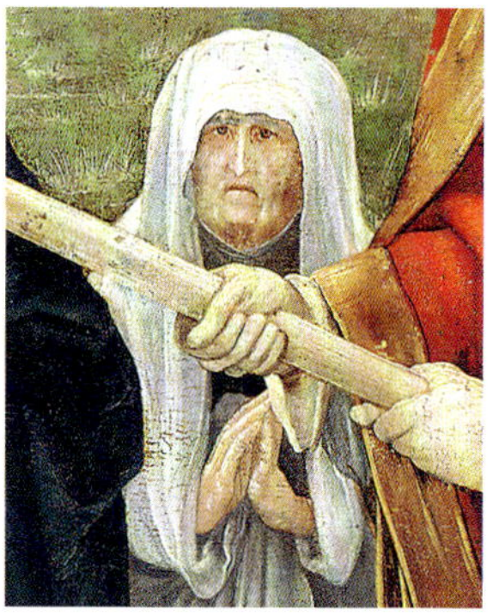

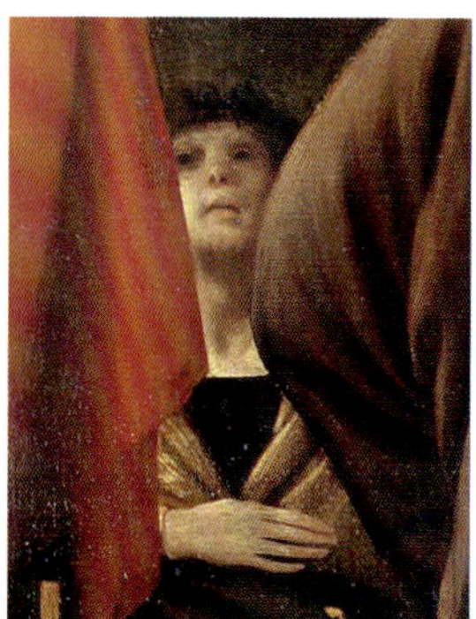

all rendered (of course with tremendous respect for reality) as shapes that have volume, whose shadows intersect. With consummate skill and economy of means, the curved line hugs the body to underscore its three-dimensionality, and the hint of a double chin is simply a blade of light that interrupts the shading of the neck. At the same time, through reflected light, there is a hint of the air circulating between the fabric of her headpiece and face. It seems clear to me that this drawing cannot be attributed to the period of the *Isenheim Altarpiece*.

The same means, and perhaps also the same model, were used in a drawing now at the Ashmolean Museum in Oxford [inv. WA 1863.421 (P. I. 297), black chalk, 377 × 236 mm][44] [fig. 196], in which the woman appears posed in prayer, or perhaps suffering, as for a Crucifixion. The curved line is even more insistent, as are the diagonal rays of light, with the intention to make tangible not only the variations in light but also the folds of her dress, the texture of her gathered hair, her strong hands and even her face muscles. It might seem we are not that distant from the drawing of

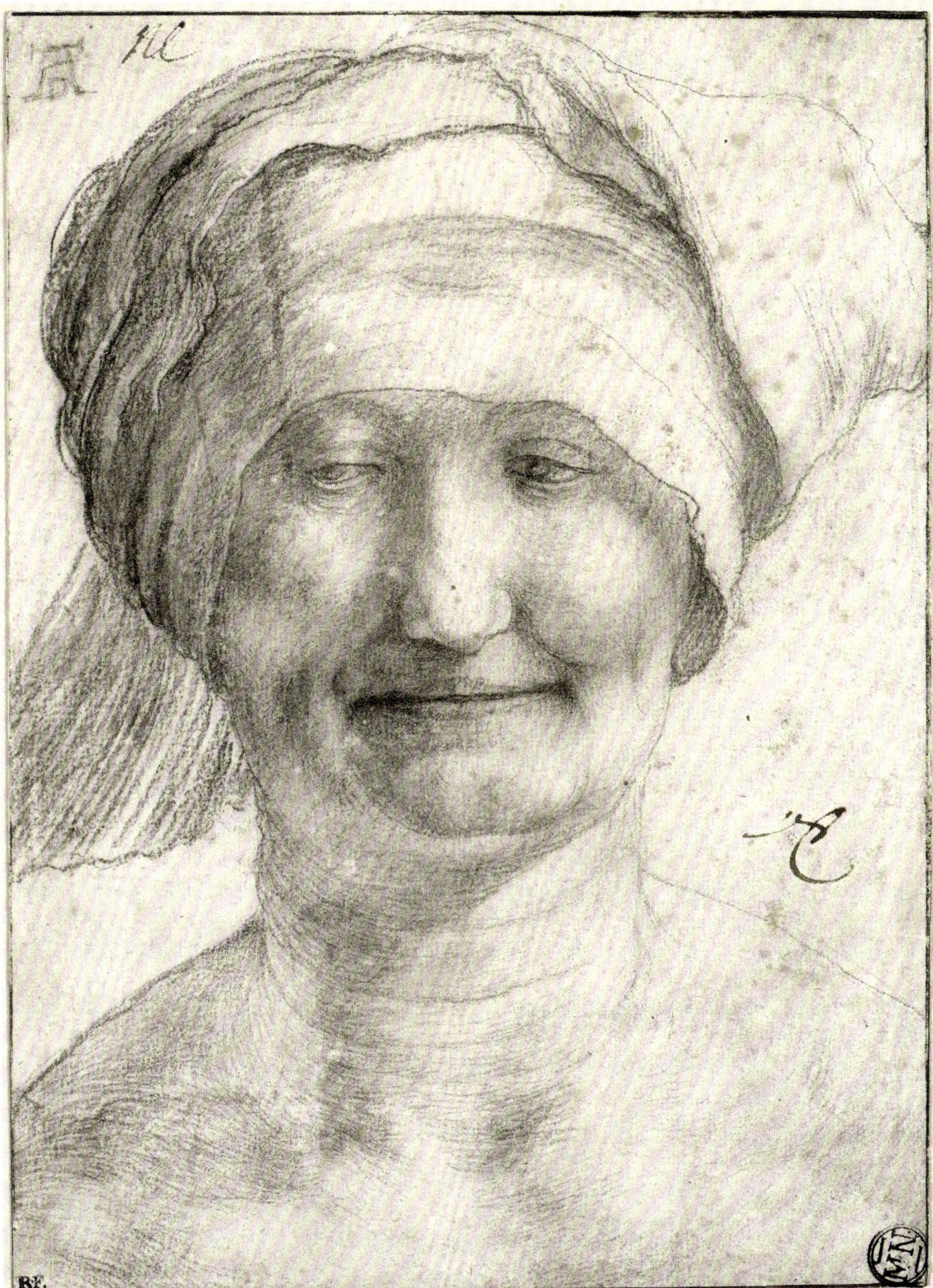

195 | Mathis Grünewald, *Head of a woman with turban, smiling*, ca. 1518–1519. Paris, Musée du Louvre, Département des Arts graphiques, inv. 18588.

Mary Magdalene at Winterthur which was analysed previously. But here, everything seems less violent: the light flows on the surface without undue pressure of the chalk on the paper to obtain dramatic effects. The overall impact is one of greater plasticity and, at the same time, a more meditative atmosphere. I suspect that in Milan, Mathis was exposed to some drawings by Leonardo from the early 1500s, almost certainly a face or half-length study from which he gleaned everything he could (we will be returning to this aspect). It should be noted that this sheet, clearly trimmed on the left side, includes a name [M]athis, almost certainly the painter's signature, while on the right a 17th-century hand has written: "This was done by Mathis d'Ossenburg [Aschaffenburg], painter to the Archbishop of Mainz, and when you see 'Mathis' written, it is his personal signature."[45] It goes without saying that this is the only drawing we are aware of that is signed by the artist, but the collector who added this note (perhaps Sandrart?) clearly knew of others.

It would not be surprising if the Oxford study were intended for a new *Crucifixion*. In fact, we know that Grünewald was once again involved in this subject, for an altarpiece perhaps destined for an altar dedicated to Mary Magdalene. In 1920, Heinrich Feurstein discovered a dramatic *Crucifixion* painted in 1648 by Christoph Krafft (156 × 72 cm, Künzelsau, Würth Collection, inv. 6576 [fig. 197]), which he believed was a copy of a lost work by Mathis, perhaps painted for Isenheim.[46] The hypothesis that it was a copy of an original by our artist was generally accepted by scholars, many of whom, however, rightly believe the lost prototype work to be from the 1520s.

Here Grünewald concentrates not so much on portraying Jesus's dreadful wounds, but rather, through an abstraction that renders everything even more horrific, on the foreshortening of the unnaturally stretched body, the nail protruding from the crossbeam of the crucifix, the wooden beams seen in perspective, the ladder, and the macabre dancing of the light on the crucified corpse which receives the dark shadow of the arm of the cross and the pitiful glow of the light of the moon. There is no doubt that this work, which can be imagined to be less violent than the previous versions of this theme, falls perfectly within this "broad" and perspectival phase of Grünewald's works, i.e., around 1520 or just after.

The dorsal viewpoint has often been interpreted in relation to the "lateral" presentation of many German Renaissance *Crucifixions*, starting from the one already mentioned by the young Cranach, now in Munich. However, I believe there is a more specific reference: the impenitent thief seen from behind in the *Crucifixion* that is part of the St. Sebastian altar (whose structure was not so different from the *Isenheim Altarpiece*) painted by Albrecht Altdorfer between 1509 and 1516 for the St. Florian Monastery in Linz, where it is still part of its collection [fig. 198].[47]

The compositional layout of *Christ Bearing the Cross* today in Karlsruhe, which will be discussed shortly, despite the presence of radically different figurative results, is compositionally related to the *Christ Going to Calvary* that is part of the same St. Florian altarpiece. Perhaps, even the last altarpiece painted for Mainz Cathedral, as we shall see, retains something from the St. Sebastian altarpiece. If this observation is correct, it gives us some indication of Grünewald's itinerary to and from Italy, which seems to have included stopovers in Linz and Brescia.

On more than one occasion, Dietmar Lüdke compared this lost work by Mathis to a drawing in the British Museum (inv. 1880.0214.345) attributed to the Monogrammist G Z, a follower of Baldung Grien (therefore an artist geographically appropriate to reflect a creation by Grünewald)[48] [fig. 199]. At least two other drawings reproducing the same image, one at the Kupferstichkabinett in Berlin (KdZ 291) and one in a private collection, act as confirmation of an authoritative prototype (not necessarily the work of Grünewald, but very likely dependent on him).[49] Lüdke himself, perhaps not completely consciously, adds a reference (for both the pose of Mary Magdalene and the viewpoint of the Crucifix) to the *Penitent St. Jerome* by Vincenzo Foppa today at the Pinacoteca dell'Accademia Carrara in Bergamo (inv. 81LC00225)[50] [fig. 200]: a reference which, in light of what has been presented so far, sounds extremely valuable.

An intriguing link exists between the presumed altar dedicated to Mary Magdalene (a saint who, in the painting by Krafft, is given special visibility) and an

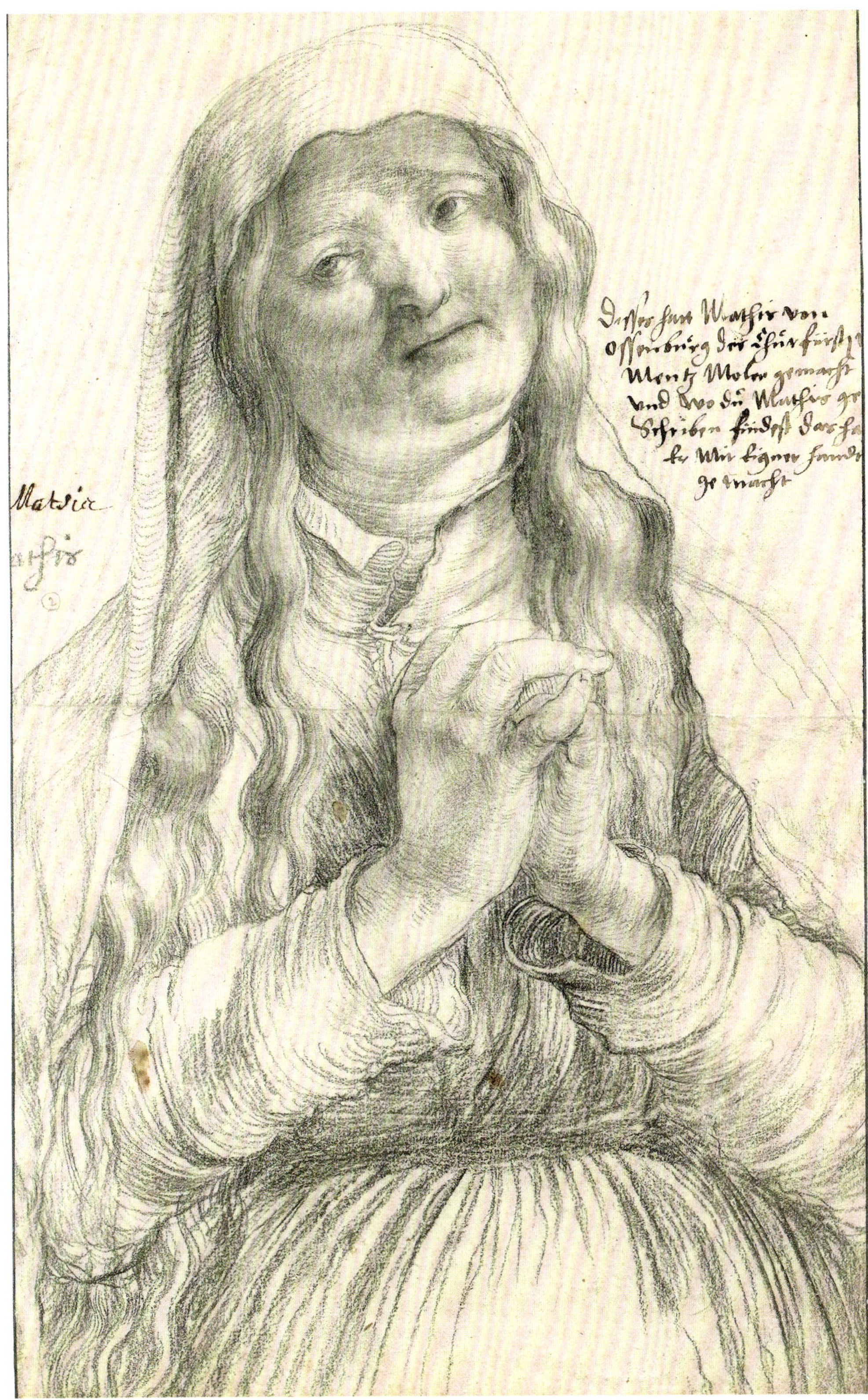

196 | Mathis Grünewald, *Study of a mourning woman*, ca. 1518–1519. Oxford, Ashmolean Museum, inv. WA 1863.421 (P. l. 297).

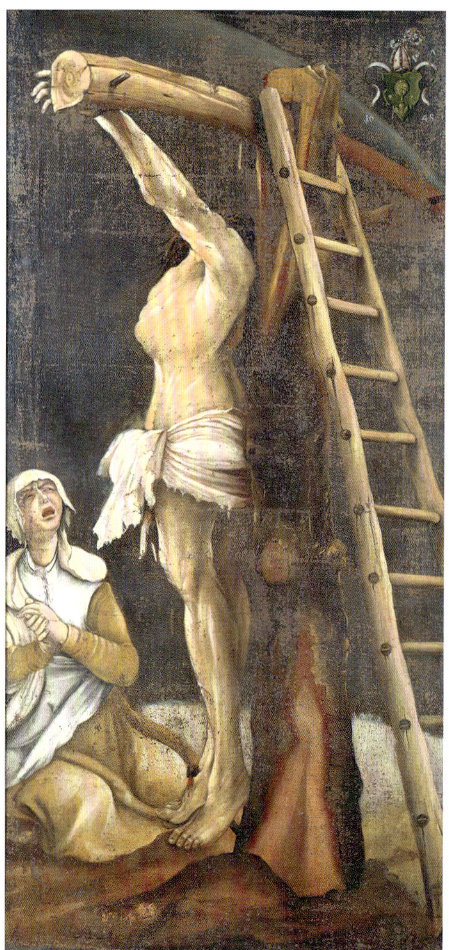

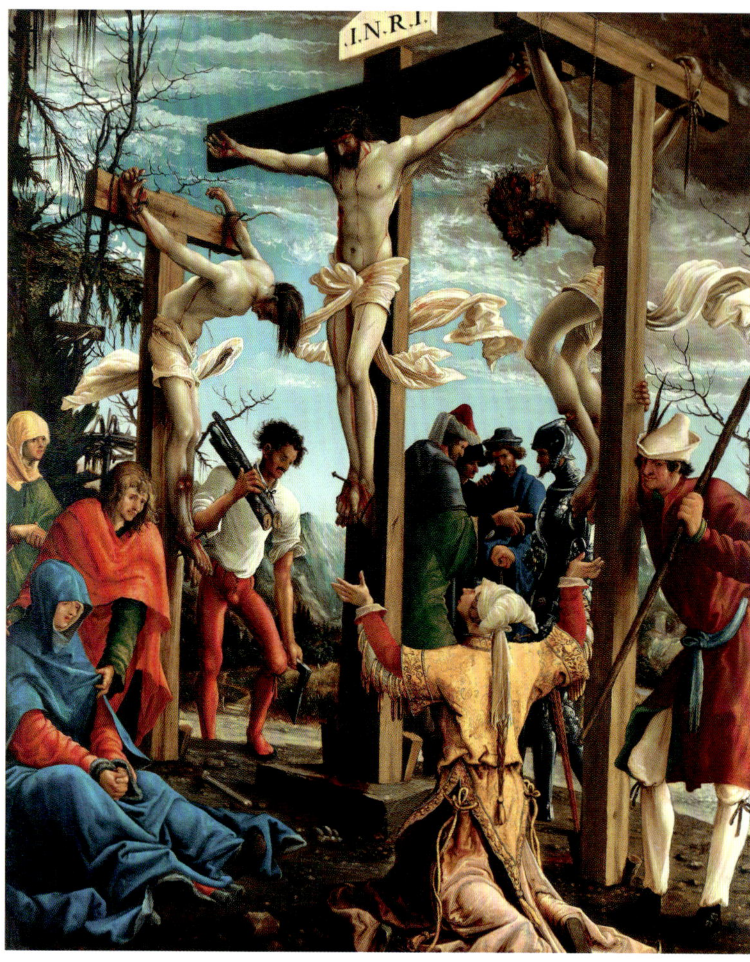

197 | Christoph Krafft (after Grünewald), *Crucifixion*, 1648. Künzelsau, Sammlung Würth, inv. 6576.

198 | Albrecht Altdorfer, *Crucifixion*, 1509–1516. Linz, Collection of Sankt Florian Abbey.

important sheet at the Staatliche Graphische Sammlung in Munich (inv. 1983: 85Z, black chalk, 390 × 299 mm).[51] On both the recto and verso we see the half-length figure of a woman [figs. 201–202], perhaps not the same one, in prayer. In fact, one has a meditative expression, while the other is in ecstasy, rather than pain. The recto technique and style are completely analogous to the Oxford drawing, and this tends to increase the probability that these are two studies intended for the same work, the *Crucifixion* partially copied by Krafft. However, the verso drawing, with its delicate and soft stroke, introduces a further variant, perhaps more technical than stylistic, in Grünewald's art. We will only look at the head, the most finished part. It is impossible not to admire the simplicity with which the artist was able to render the tossed hair which seems to gush out like water, the partially open mouth and the delicate shadows that provide volume to the well-shaped neck.

If I am correct, we are approximately in the same time period as two other Grünewald drawings, two studies in black chalk, both in Berlin and done very closely to each other, as attested by the fact that Mathis seems to use the same model, a youth or perhaps a man suffering from achondroplasia. It seems obvious to compare these sheets (inv. KdZ 1070 and KdZ 12319: respectively, 276 × 196 mm, the one sneering [fig. 203], and 247 × 202 mm, the one screaming [fig. 204])[52] with the lost altarpiece of Mainz Cathedral that portrays a hermit accompanied by a young boy, attacked and killed while crossing the frozen Rhine, perhaps a depiction of the martyrdom of St. Alban.

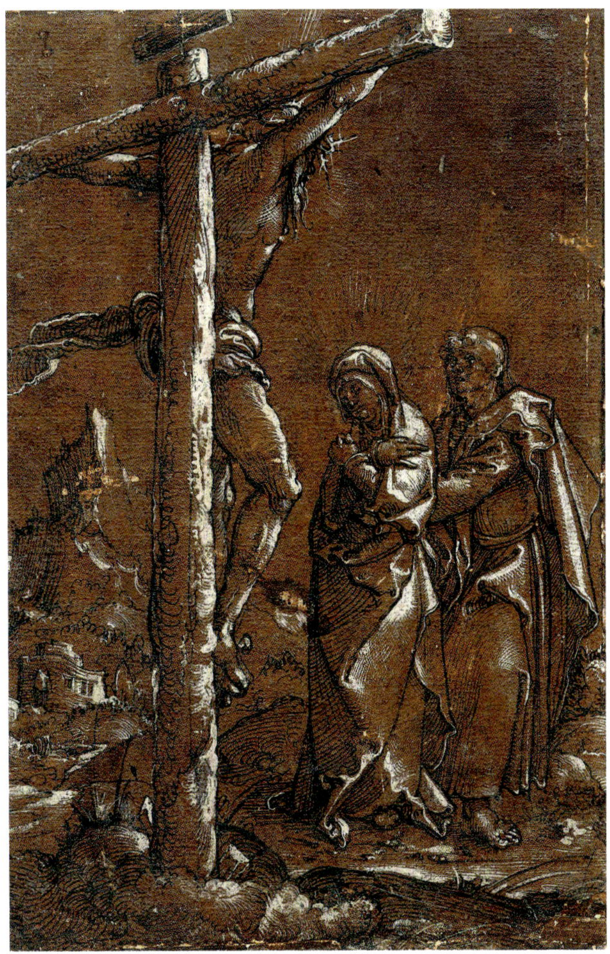

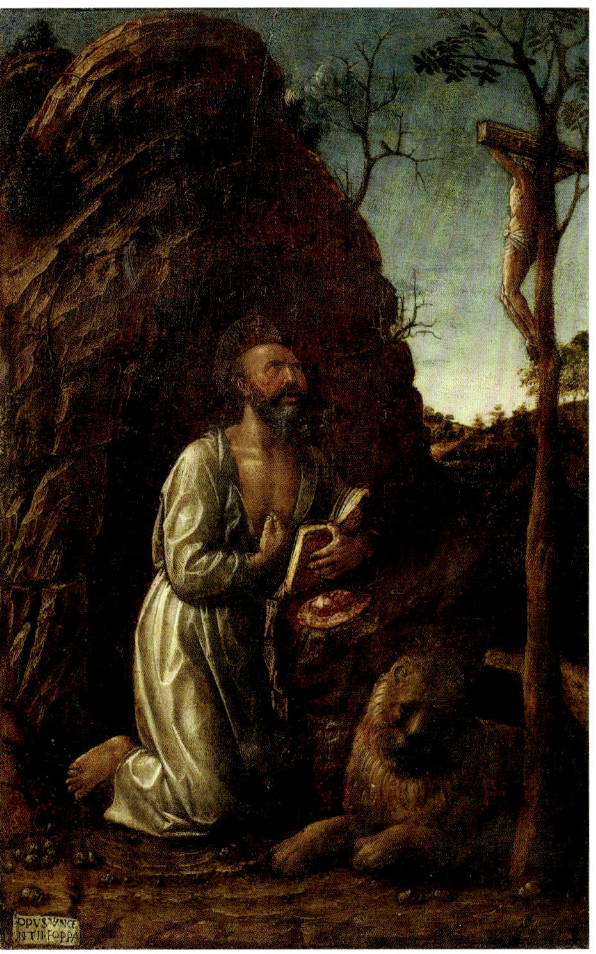

199 | Monogrammist G Z, *Study for a Crucifixion*. London, The British Museum, inv. 1880.0214.345.

200 | Vincenzo Foppa, *Saint Jerome*. Bergamo, Pinacoteca dell'Accademia Carrara, inv. 81LC00225.

Any work by Mathis for Mainz Cathedral must necessarily involve Albrecht von Brandenburg, and therefore it is useful to point out that the painter received two payments from the Mainz court: one, quite large, of 147 florins in 1524, and another, much smaller but still significant, of 20 florins in 1525.[53] It is not unlikely that included in this sum of 147 florins could potentially be the presumed Mary Magdalene altar, this altarpiece for the cathedral and two other paintings we will be discussing soon.

With the lost altarpiece, we turn to examine the surviving drawings. We see the same delicate stroke found in the verso of the Munich sheet and, above all, an exceptionally mature use of the line following the form. Grünewald explores effects that are extremely difficult to achieve, such as the semi-open mouth in a cruel grimace that exposes the tongue and teeth, and the foreshortened view of the head tipped back in a scream. The receding chin merges into the round mass of the neck whose soft, flabby consistency is ruthlessly drawn. I believe these two drawings betray an undeniable link to Leonardo's artistic style. As an example, we should examine the famous study at the Budapest Fine Arts Museum of Nicolò Orsini for the *Battle of Anghiari* (inv. D_1775) [fig. 205]. Aside from the different classical allure of Leonardo's drawing, it seems difficult not to see in the effects indicated above a precise connection between the two graphic works of these artists. And doesn't the throbbing, repulsive rotundity of Leonardo's studies of *Leda* have more than just a little to do with the results of these masterpieces by Grünewald as a drawing master?

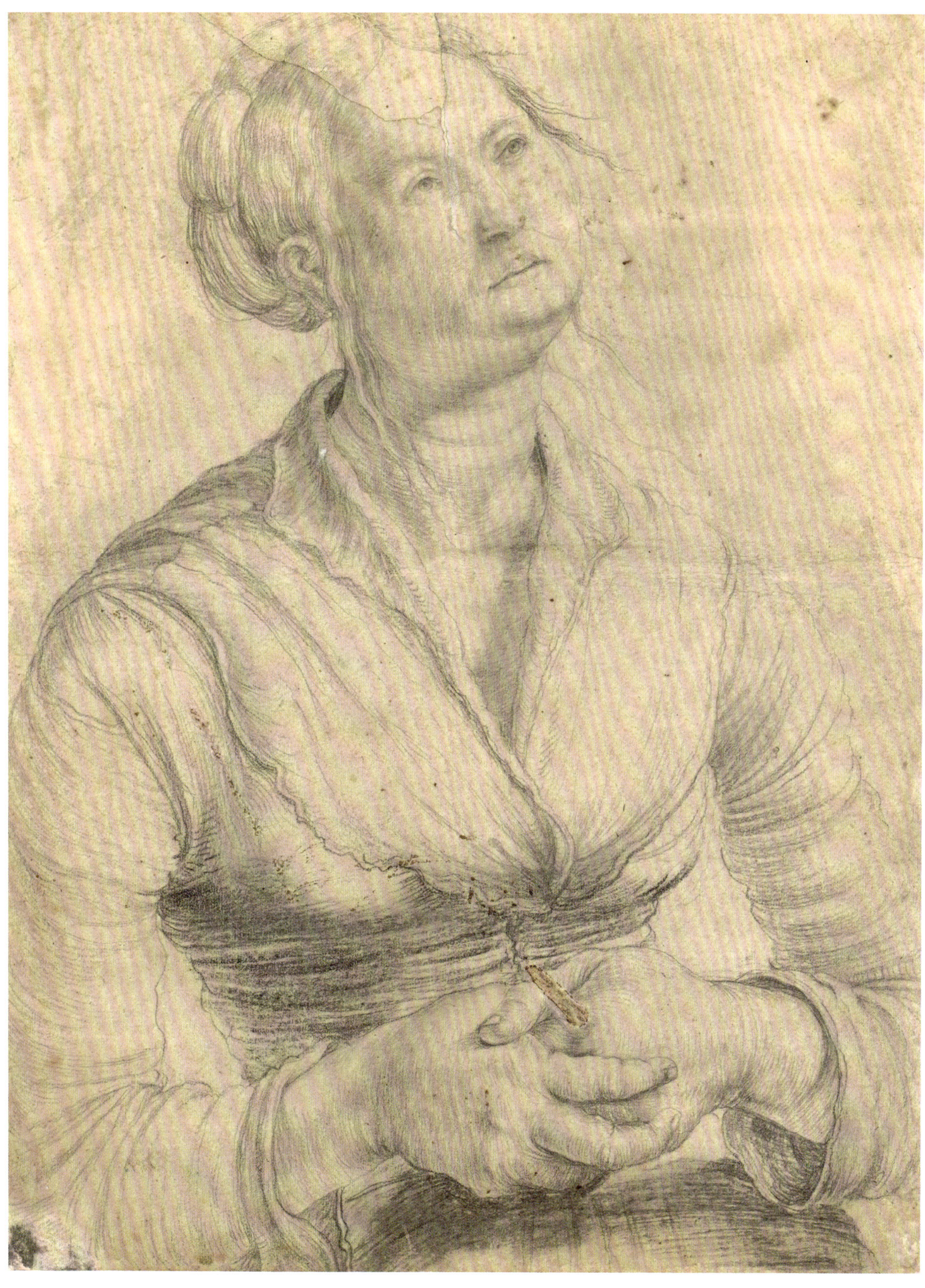

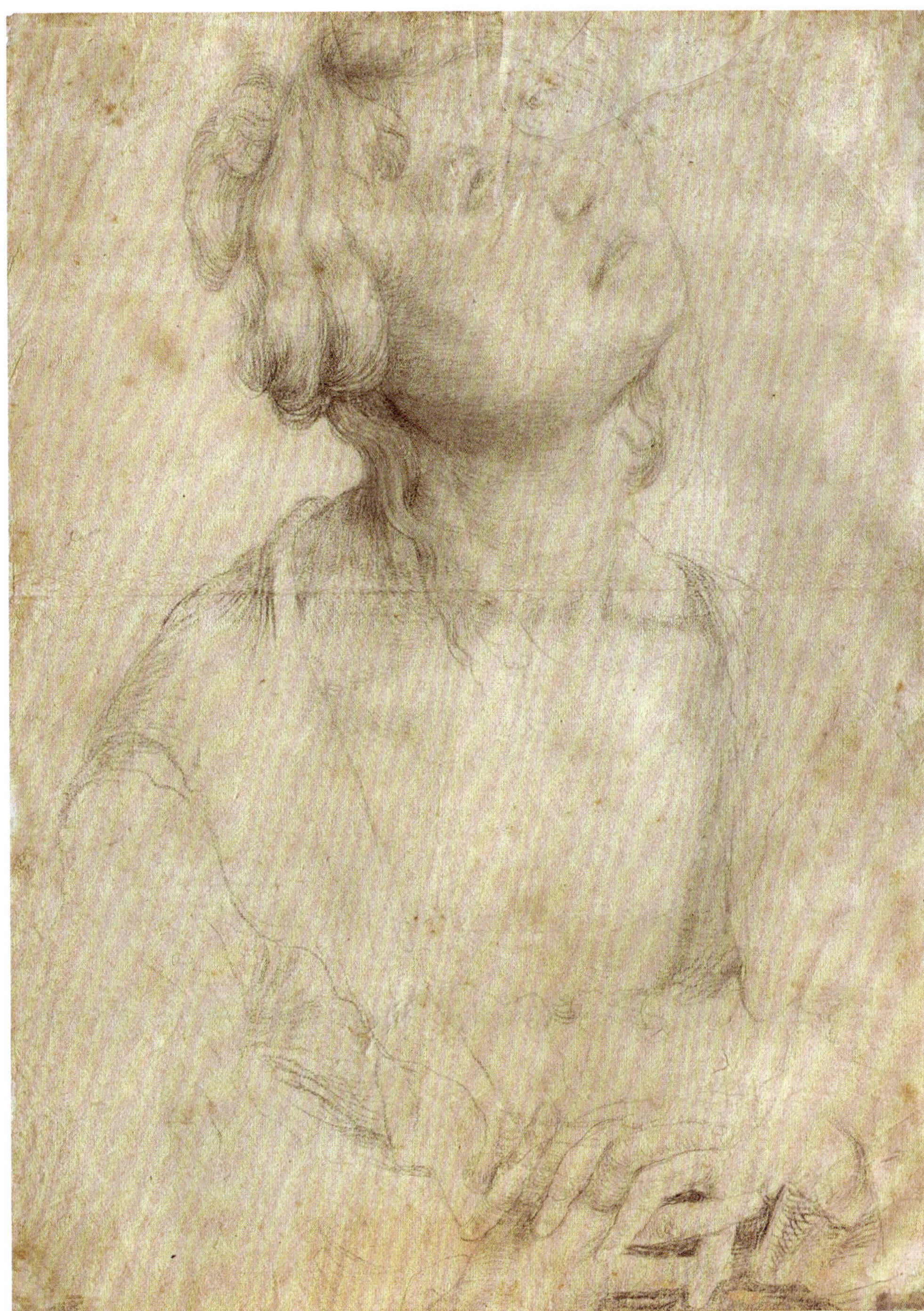

201 | Mathis Grünewald, *Woman praying*, ca. 1520. Munich, Staatliche Graphische Sammlung, inv. 1983: 85Z recto.

202 | Mathis Grünewald, *Woman praying*, ca. 1520. Munich, Staatliche Graphische Sammlung, inv. 1983: 85Z verso.

Nevertheless, we will never find in Mathis the reverent approach to Italian art and its "secrets" always kept by Dürer. Perhaps less intellectual, perhaps stronger, our painter uses Italian models with obvious admiration, but always in a very personal way, adapting everything to his own implacable expressive needs. The same is also true for what could be reminiscent of Altdorfer in the tipped-back head that might, perhaps, have some connection with the image of the corpse of St. Sebastian with its dangling head, painted for the St. Florian Monastery in Linz.

The verso of the sheet with the sneering face contains the *Head of a woman* [fig. 206], unquestionably from the same time, but with a completely different expressive feel.

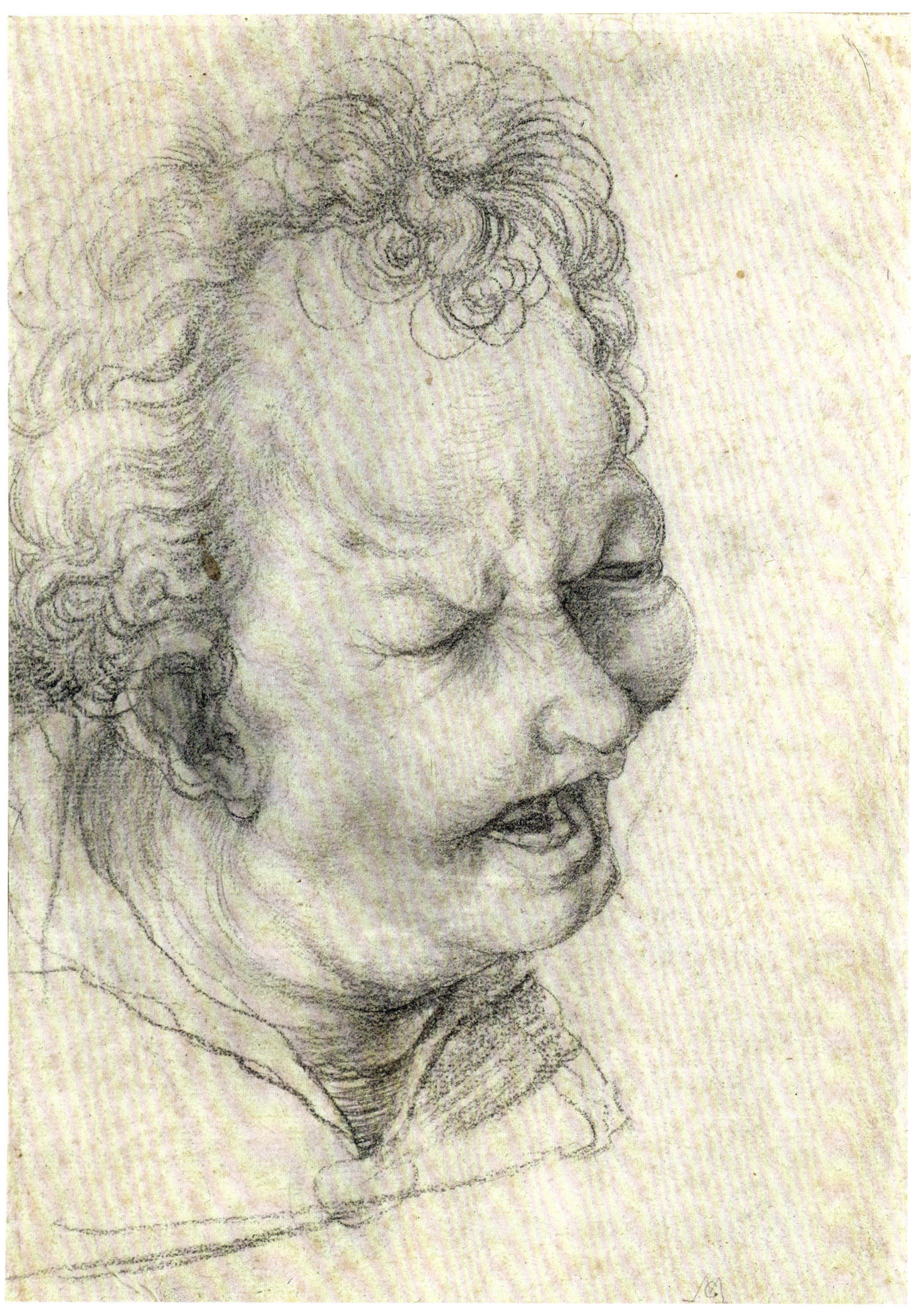

203 | Mathis Grünewald,
Head of a sneering man, ca. 1520.
Berlin, Staatliche Museen,
Kupferstichkabinett, KdZ 1070 recto.

204 | Mathis Grünewald,
Head of a crying man, ca. 1520.
Berlin, Staatliche Museen,
Kupferstichkabinett, inv. KdZ 12319.

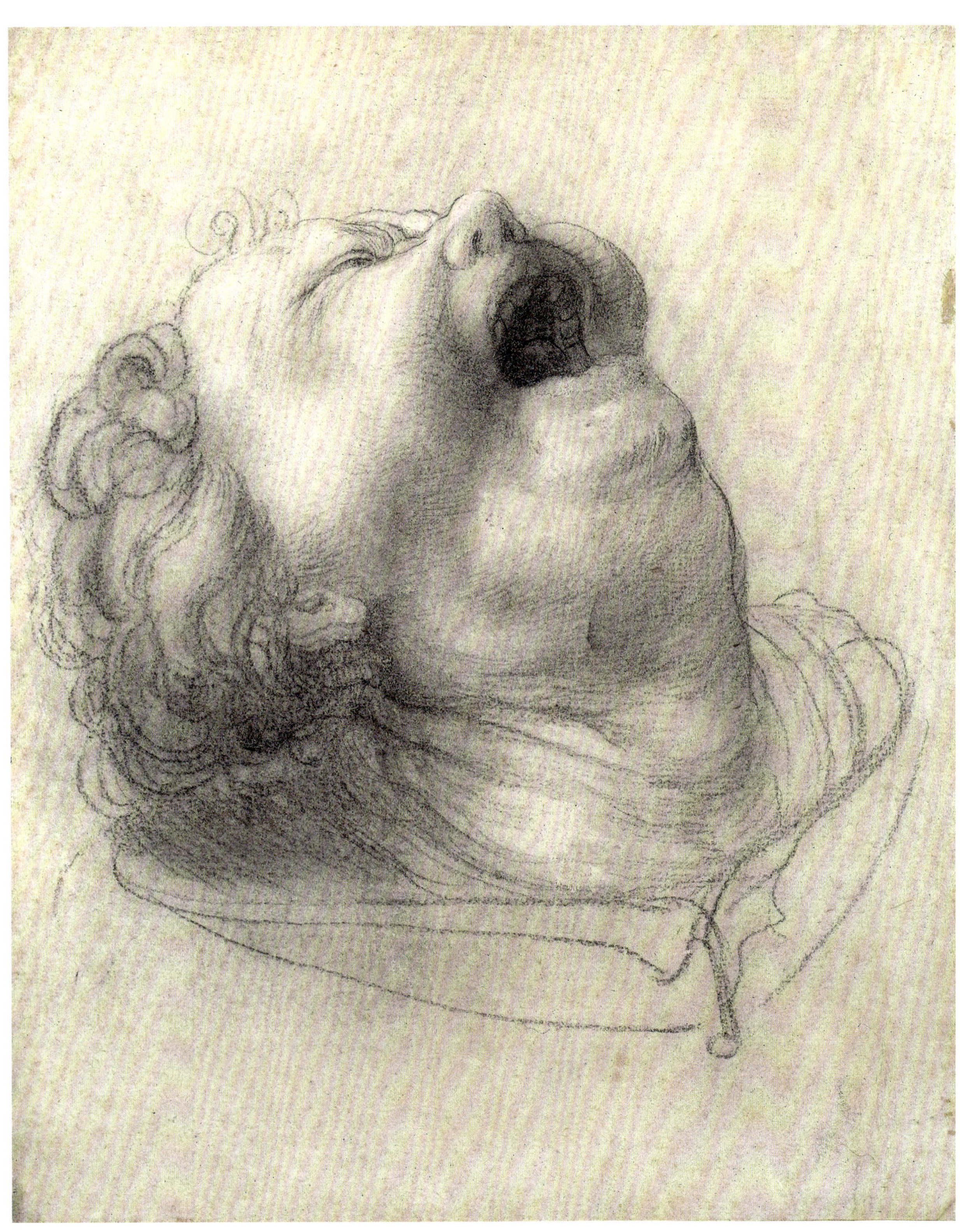

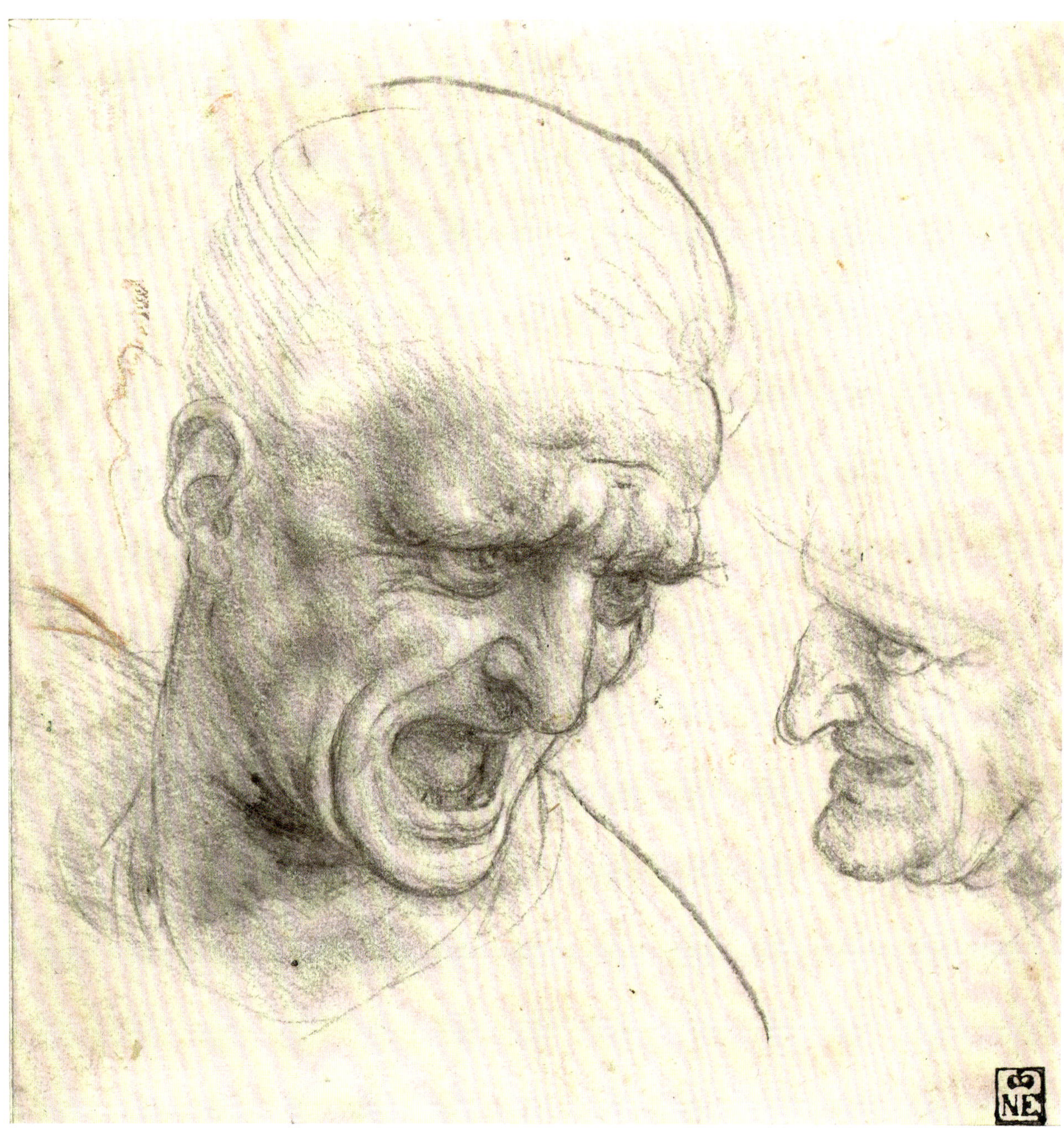

205 | Leonardo, *Study for the Battle of Anghiari*, ca. 1504–1505. Budapest, Szépművészeti Múzeum, inv. D_1775.

206 | Mathis Grünewald, *Female head*, ca. 1520. Berlin, Staatliche Museen, Kupferstichkabinett, inv. KdZ 1070 verso.

The nobly melancholic face could be that of the Madonna in adoration, even if it seems, above all, to be a beautiful, serene portrait. Mathis's portrayal of women appears more intimate, emotional and aware. Whether a calm middle-class matron, a sweet elderly woman, or an ardent young woman in prayer, his depictions no longer represent the elegant manikins of his youthful drawings, but instead pulsating, alive and worldly-wise individuals—not the idealized women of Dürer, or the erotic or necrotic obsessions of Baldung Grien.

The panel painted for the collegiate church in Halle an der Saale, dedicated to St. Maurice, the city's patron saint, and Mary Magdalene, was installed by 1525, the year which is already mentioned in the inventory. The panel depicts the *Meeting of Saints Erasmus and Maurice* (Munich, Alte Pinakothek, inv. 1044, 226 × 176 cm) [fig. 207], commissioned by Albrecht von Brandenburg who ordered the inclusion of the coats of

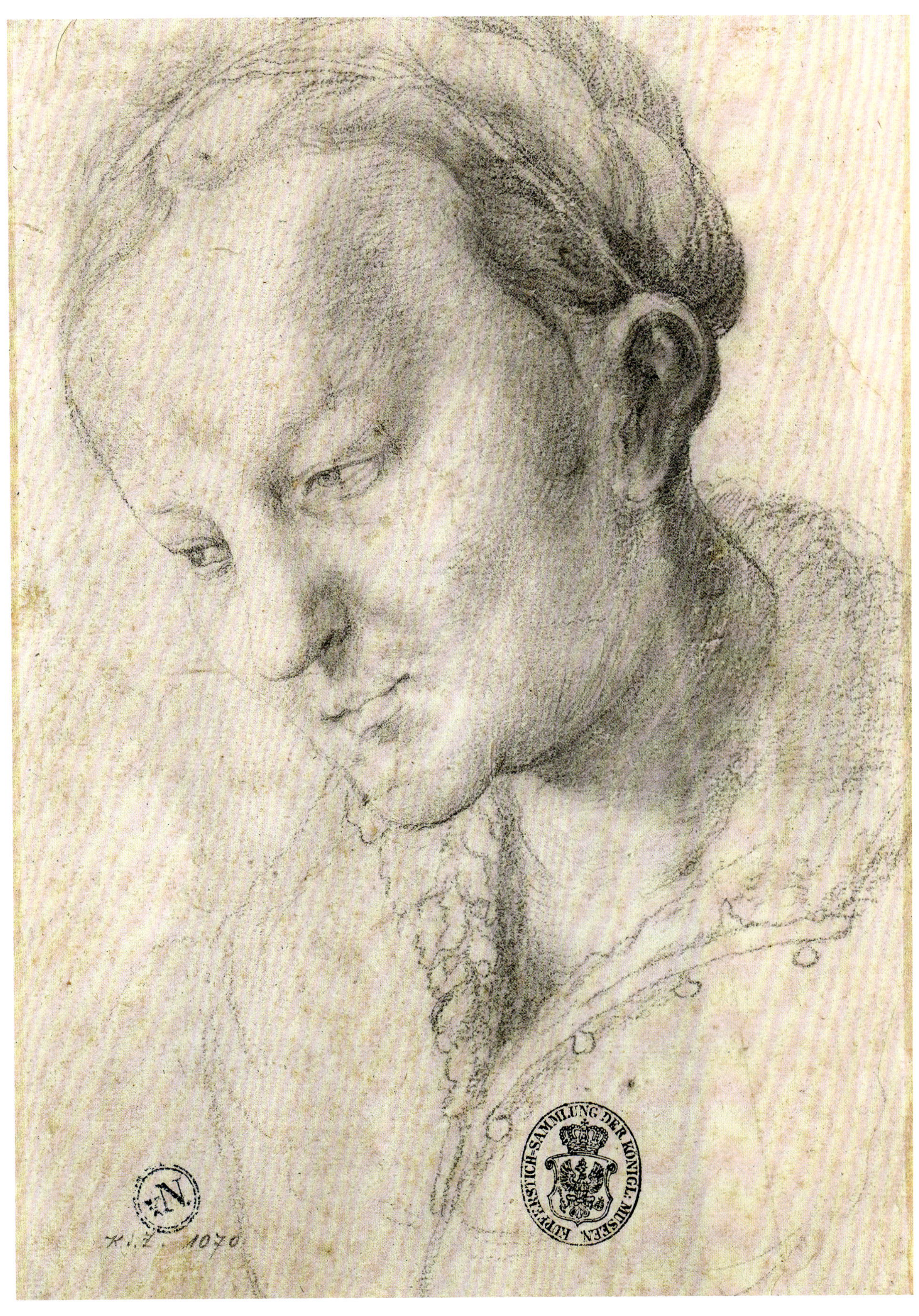
KUPFERSTICH-SAMMLUNG DER KÖNIGL. MUSEEN
N.

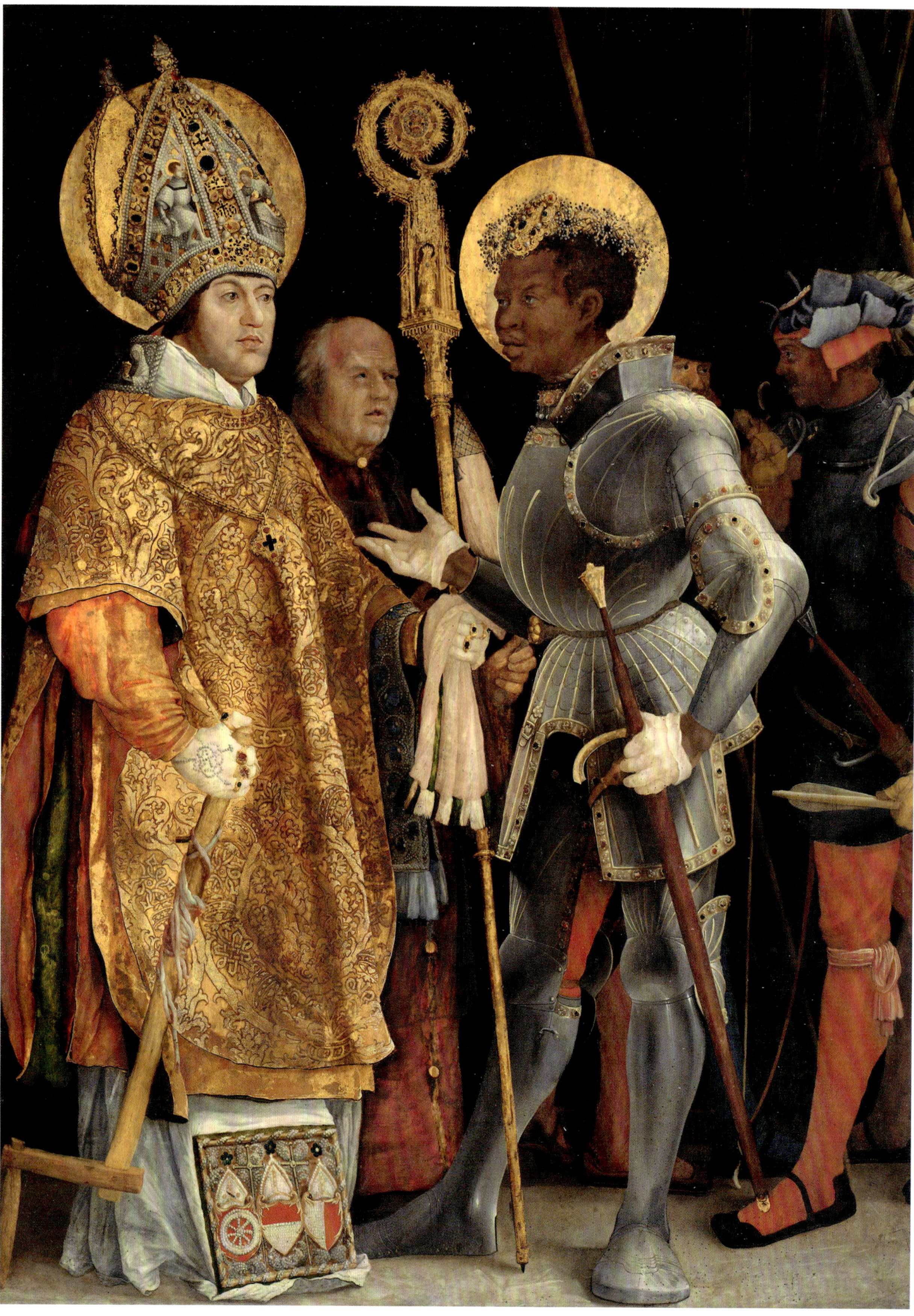

arms of the cities of Halle, Mainz and Halberstadt, of which he was also the bishop.[54]

While Maurice, head of the Theban Legion of Rome, is portrayed with armor similar to that of the silver statue containing his relics (owned by Albrecht at least since 1521 and taken to Halle, and of which a drawing still exists [fig. 208]),[55] Erasmus clearly resembles Albrecht himself, reflecting the numerous known portraits of the archbishop.

I must confess that this work poses some challenges for me: spatially undefined, it makes ample use of gold almost as if to saturate the coloring of the painting without requiring additional formal research; and the two protagonists are placed traditionally in the foreground, filling the space with secondary figures that do not provide measurement points, almost as if in a return, with the right proportions, to the solutions adopted years earlier in the *Mocking of Christ*. Even the two protagonists are borrowed without much creativity from pre-existing models. St. Erasmus's pose is almost banal and could derive from Pacher or even Holbein the Elder, and his features are taken, without even that much dissimulation, from a portrait of Albrecht etched by Dürer in 1519 [fig. 209].[56] Maurice, on the other hand, comes directly from an old etching by Lucas Cranach, his 1506 *St. George* [fig. 210] (dating from the peak of Mathis's interest in Cranach).[57] We seem to find in this dazzling panel (if on this one occasion we may resort to psychological analysis), something lacking conviction, almost forced.

And yet, even here, the artist reveals his greatness. The almost frightened, hesitant (certainly not relaxed) expression of St. Erasmus seems to capture, much more than the official portraits, including Dürer's, the vacillating character of Archbishop Albrecht. He was ambitious, yet irresolute, ambiguous but not malevolent, an admirer of Erasmus and the cause of what unleashed the revolt of Luther, his fiercest opponent in the initial phases of the Reformation, but protector of Luther's earliest humanist followers. He was a strong opponent of the Peasants' Revolt, but also capable of creating the secularization of his archbishopric, and he was ready to send a wedding gift of 20 florins when in 1525 Katharina von Bora married the reformer, even after he had banished all Lutherans from his court.[58]

It is perhaps works like this, relatively calm, yet charged with latent tension, that Melanchton had in mind in his *Elementorum rhetorices libri duo* (1531) when he described Mathis as a sort of "happy medium" between the sublime—the highly intellectual but impervious Dürer—and the amiable Cranach.

207 | Mathis Grünewald, *Meeting of the Saints Erasmus and Maurice*, ca. 1521–1523, Munich, Alte Pinakothek, inv. 1044.

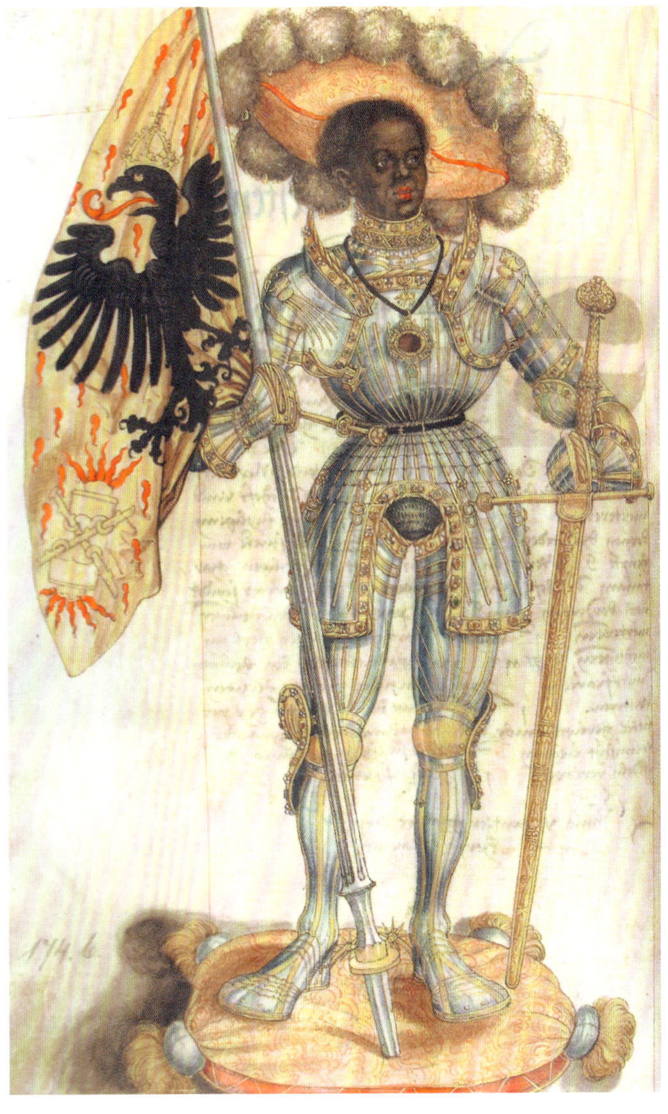

208 | Anonymous XVIth century Artist, *The Reliquary of Saint Maurice at Halle*. Aschaffenburg, Hofbibliothek, ms. 14, f. 227v.

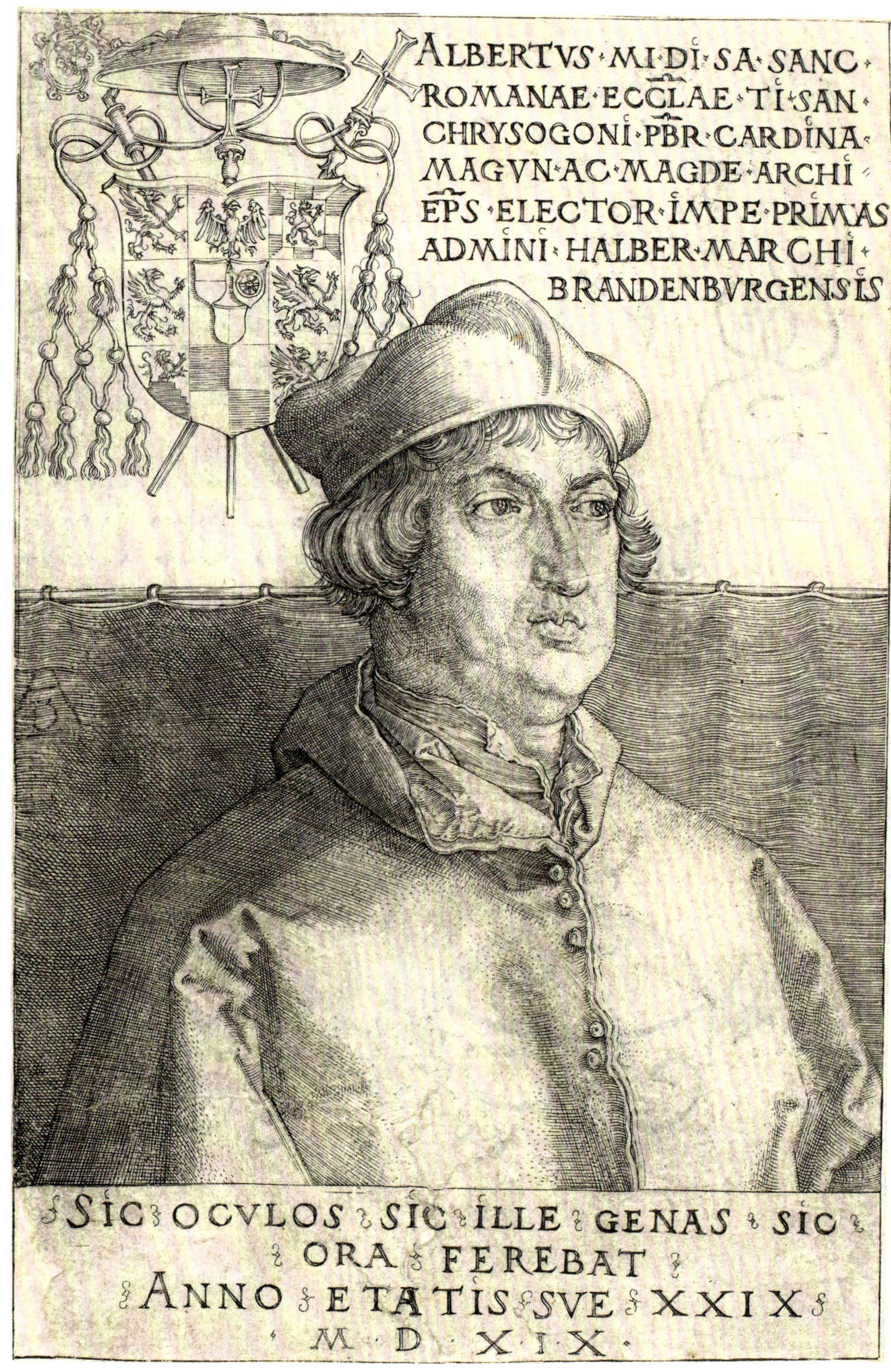

209 | Albrecht Dürer, *Portrait of Albrecht von Brandenburg*, 1519, woodcut.

This is what Melanchton wrote:

> Plurimum etiam conducit ad iudicandum agnoscere diversas formas, seu ut Graeci nominant χαρακτῆρας operum, non solum in hac arte. Sed in plerisque aliis peperit. Et tamen certi quasi gradus animadversi sunt, intra quos hae formae consistunt, videlicet humile genus, et illi oppositum grande. Tertium est mediocre, quis primo genere plenius est, et tamen aliquantulum a summo abest, in picturis facile deprehendi hae differentiae possunt. Durerus enim pingebat omnia grandiora, et frequentissimis lineis variata. Lucae picturae gracile sunt, quae etsi blandae sunt, tamen quantum distent a Dureri operibus, collatio ostendit. Matthias quasi mediocritatem servabat.[59]

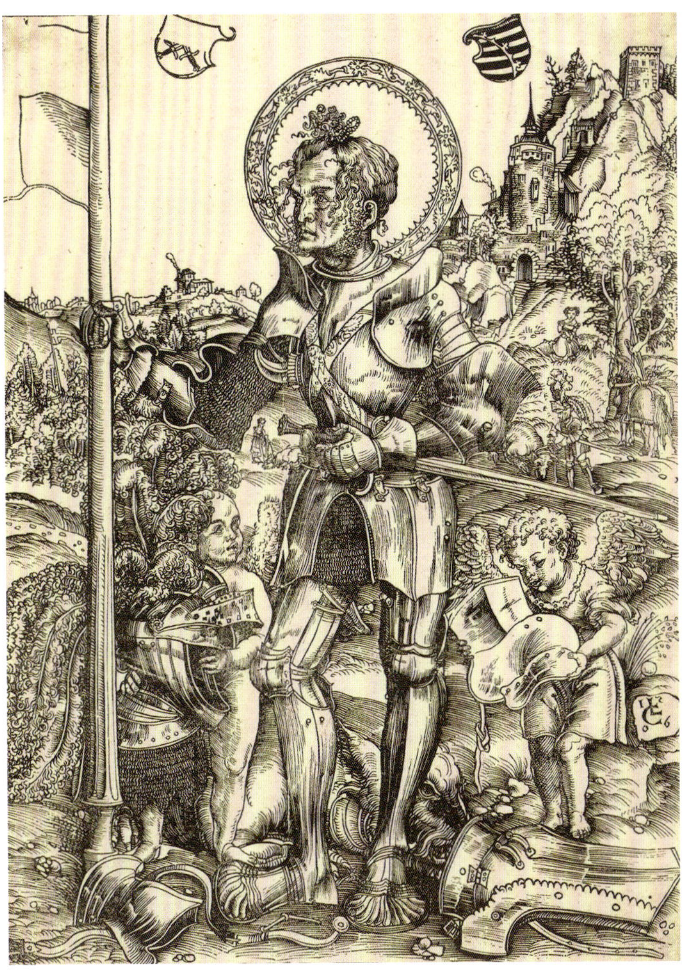

210 | Lucas Cranach the Elder, *Saint George*, 1506, woodcut.

Undoubtedly, he had something in mind that escapes us. We can consider Grünewald to be many things, but not the representative of a "middle style". Unless we consider this to mean that, in Melanchton's eyes, the painter is not driven by the same intellectual and scientific tension (especially regarding human proportions and perspective) as Dürer or, rather, that he does not share his geometric and mathematical rigor, and that he is just as removed from the occasionally shallow pleasantness of Cranach. From this standpoint,[60] the appreciation of the great German humanist is at least comprehensible, although his few and somewhat generic comments on Mathis would seem to reveal a fairly superficial knowledge of him.[61] Nonetheless, this actually only underscores his desire to mention him in any case. It is also possible that the *praeceptor Germanie* was addressing three painters whose formal or substantial involvement in Luther's Reformation was familiar to him.[62]

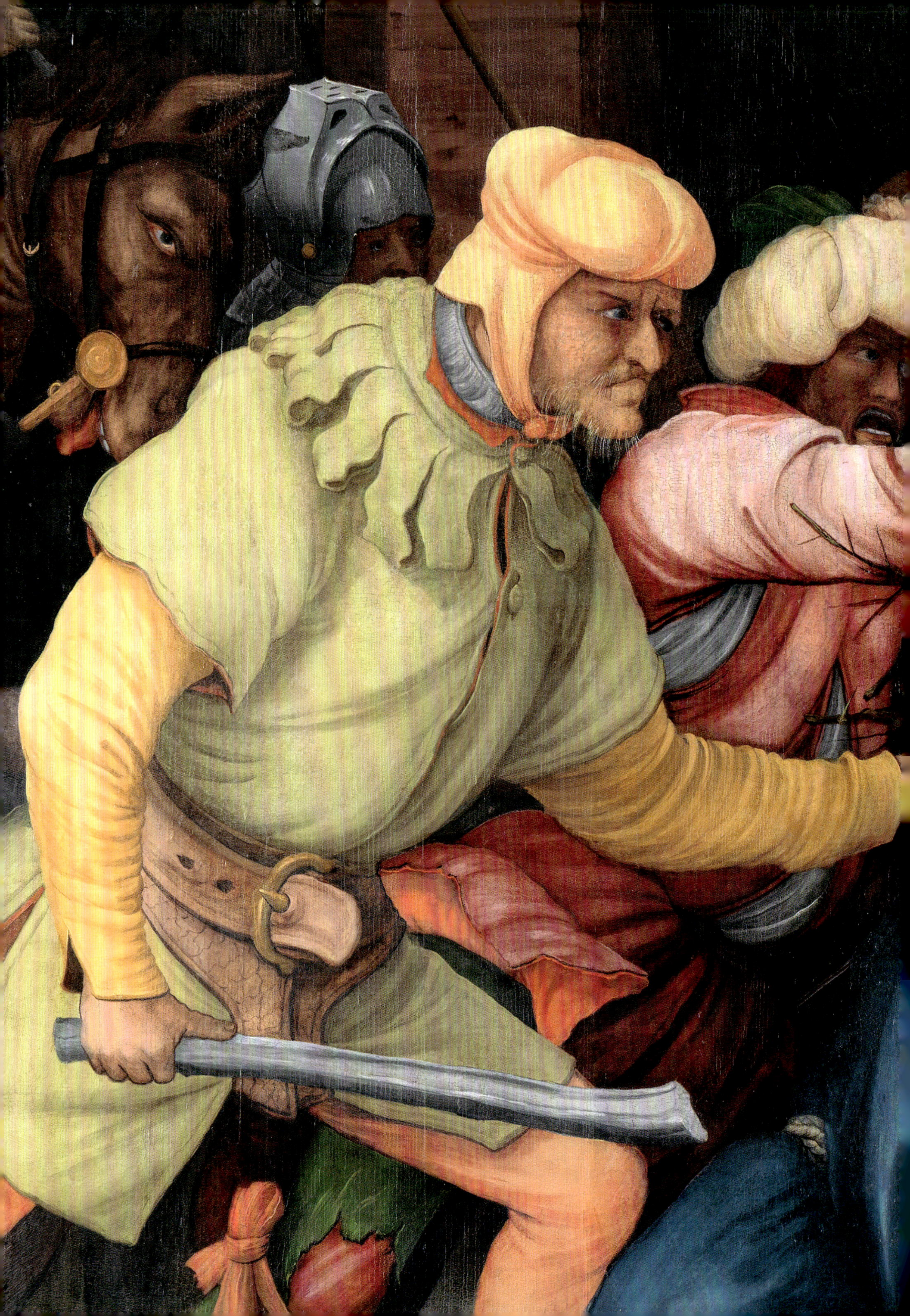

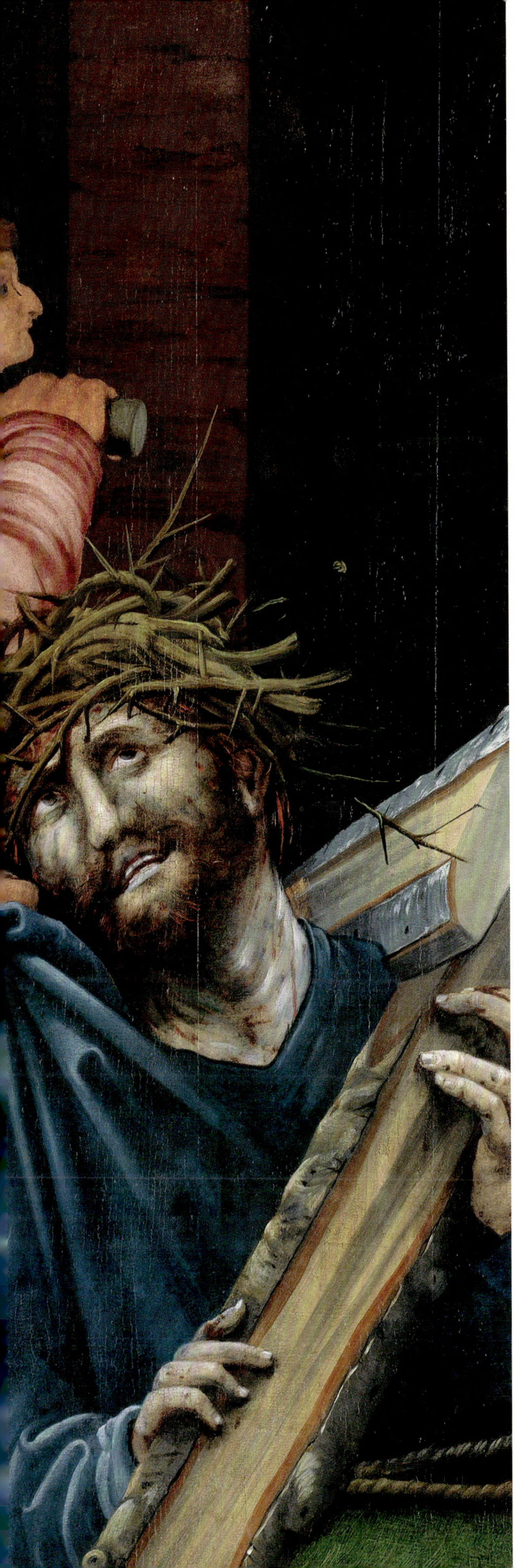

CHAPTER V

Luther, the Revolt, the Death

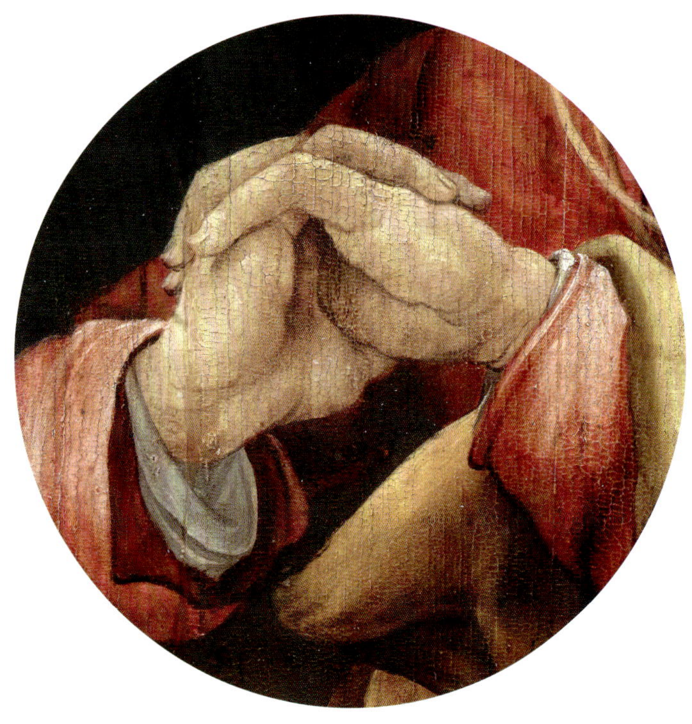

We have reached an essential final juncture. In theory, Albrecht, bishop of Halberstadt, would not have been able to concurrently claim the archbishopric of Mainz, a position that also conferred upon him the status of prince-elector.[1] To obtain permission, he was forced to pay Pope Leo X a large sum which was partially financed through a loan from the Fugger banking family who received, in return, control over the management of the sale of indulgences that were shamelessly pushed by the Dominican Johann Tetzel. As is well-known, the theological dilemma of indulgences and their impact on personal salvation was the key point of the Ninety-five Theses proposed by Luther at the academic debate in Wittenberg on October 31, 1517. Luther sent a copy of his Theses to Archbishop Albrecht who forwarded it to Rome, thus triggering a process, at the time unimaginable to all those involved in this story, that would launch the Reformation. This is not the place to delve into this issue, nor to provide a detailed examination of Lutheran theology, although some basic points will need to be addressed.[2] Nonetheless, it is certain that Luther's emergence created a very profound crisis in Grünewald. Albrecht von Brandenburg, noted for his vacillating tendency, was at the forefront of this revolution, and Mathis, serving as a key figure in this historical turning point—alongside individuals who played a leading role in the early days of the Reformation, such as Hutten, Capito and Hedio—inevitably absorbed the tension of the years between 1517 and 1525, which culminated in the tragic Peasants' War. In addition, his long-time association with the Antonites in Isenheim probably introduced him to Augustinian theology and, as we have seen, the preaching of Staupitz, from which Luther also came. All this is confirmed by the fact that in the *post mortem* inventory of his goods, compiled in Frankfurt between October 21 and 27, 1528 under the instructions of the Halle authorities (in order to compensate the creditors of the deceased painter),[3] a number of Lutheran writings were listed, which we will examine below. And as we will see, this evidence is already enough to suggest Mathis's significant, if not formal, adhesion to Lutheranism, in opposition to his generous patron.

Undoubtedly generous, Albrecht nevertheless maintained (nor could he have done otherwise) the lifestyle characteristic of a Renaissance prince, complete with its grandeur and ardent support for humanistic culture and arts, and mistresses who were anything but secret: nevertheless, he was not at all spiritually naive. We can ascertain this through the correspondence between him and Luther in late 1521. The *casus belli* was the cardinal's desire to exhibit his collection of relics alongside the indulgences connected to them in the new collegiate church in Halle for which, at that time, Grünewald was creating the altarpiece today in Munich.[4] Consequently, it is likely that the correspondence of the Wittenberg reformer provides the most plausible dating for Mathis's painting. Luther, the son of a miner as he liked to define himself, employed harsh, even arrogant language in his letters, threatening Albrecht with the publication of an inflammatory slander *Against the Idol of Halle*, if the latter did not abandon his project, imposing a strict deadline of eleven days within which a response was expected. The archbishop of Mainz replied with surprising patience and humility, expressing a declaration of faith that was very close to the foundations of Lutheran theology: "I confess that I have need of God's grace, given that I am a poor sinner [. . .] and without God's grace, I cannot bring about anything good."[5]

Unfortunately, this courageous opening arrived too late. Luther had already embarked irreversibly on the road to separation from Rome, and the polemical text

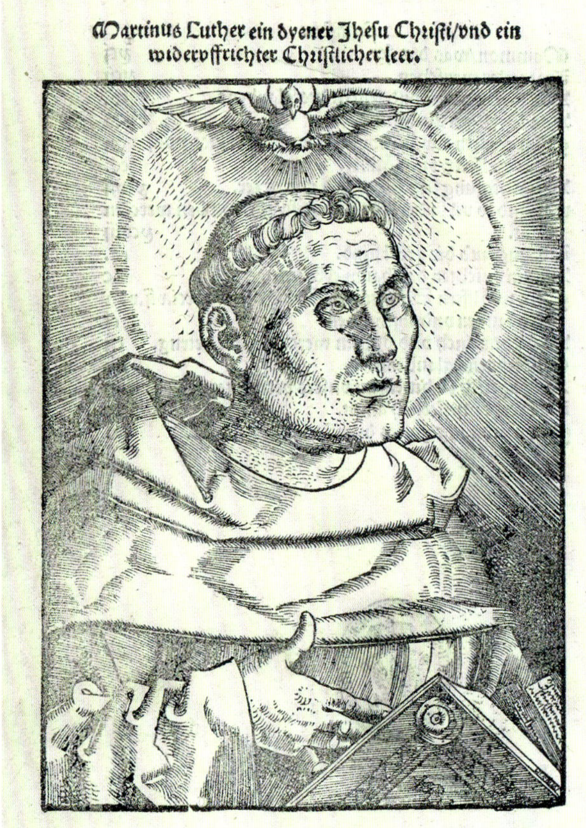

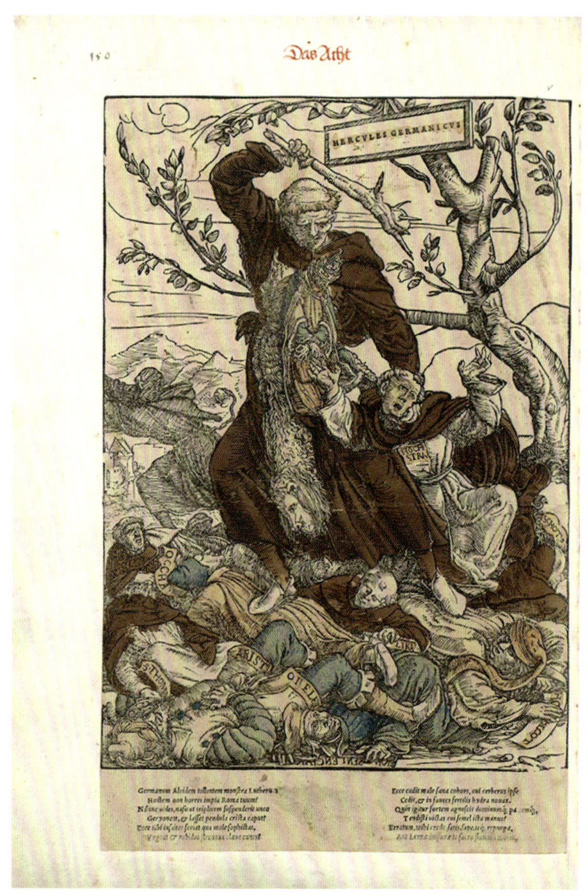

211 | Hans Baldung Grien, *Portrait of Martin Luther*, ca. 1520, woodcut.

212 | Hans Holbein the Younger, *Martin Luther as Hercules Germanicus*, 1517, woodcut.

213 | Mathis Grünewald, *Christ bearing the Cross*, ca. 1524. Karlsruhe, Staatliche Kunsthalle, inv. 993.

against Halle was published as promised. However, it is difficult to underestimate the impact this event (which, after all, involved him directly) could have had on Mathis. It should also be added that, as Schilling notes, Albrecht's response was likely suggested by Wolfgang Capito, in confirmation of how the cornerstones of Luther's thinking were already circulating in the Mainz archbishop's court.

It should be highlighted once again that Mathis was painting the altarpiece for Halle, a celebration of Archbishop Albrecht and the cult of relics, while other artists such as Cranach, Baldung Grien and Holbein the Younger were already celebrating the Augustinian Saxon as a living saint or the "Hercules Germanicus" [figs. 211–212].[6] Thus, Grünewald's adhesion or at least approach was neither immediate nor impulsive and above all, I think, his alignment was the result of a painful religious crisis and not of a political interpretation of events. For Mathis, at the end of a difficult intellectual and spiritual journey, which I will attempt to outline in the following pages, Luther must have appeared as the true rediscoverer of the Gospel, not a national hero. These observations may serve as an introduction to the examination of Grünewald's most difficult and tormented masterpiece: the double-sided panel formerly in Tauberbischofsheim.

This work, after experiencing a tumultuous history (it was relegated to the presbytery due to its perceived incompatibility to the aesthetics of a modern church; in 1893, its two sides were separated from each other causing significant damage to the painted surfaces), in 1899 finally arrived at the Kunsthalle in Karlsruhe.

Previously, the work belonged to the collegiate church in Tauberbischofsheim, which featured an altar dedicated to the True Cross. Though little is known about

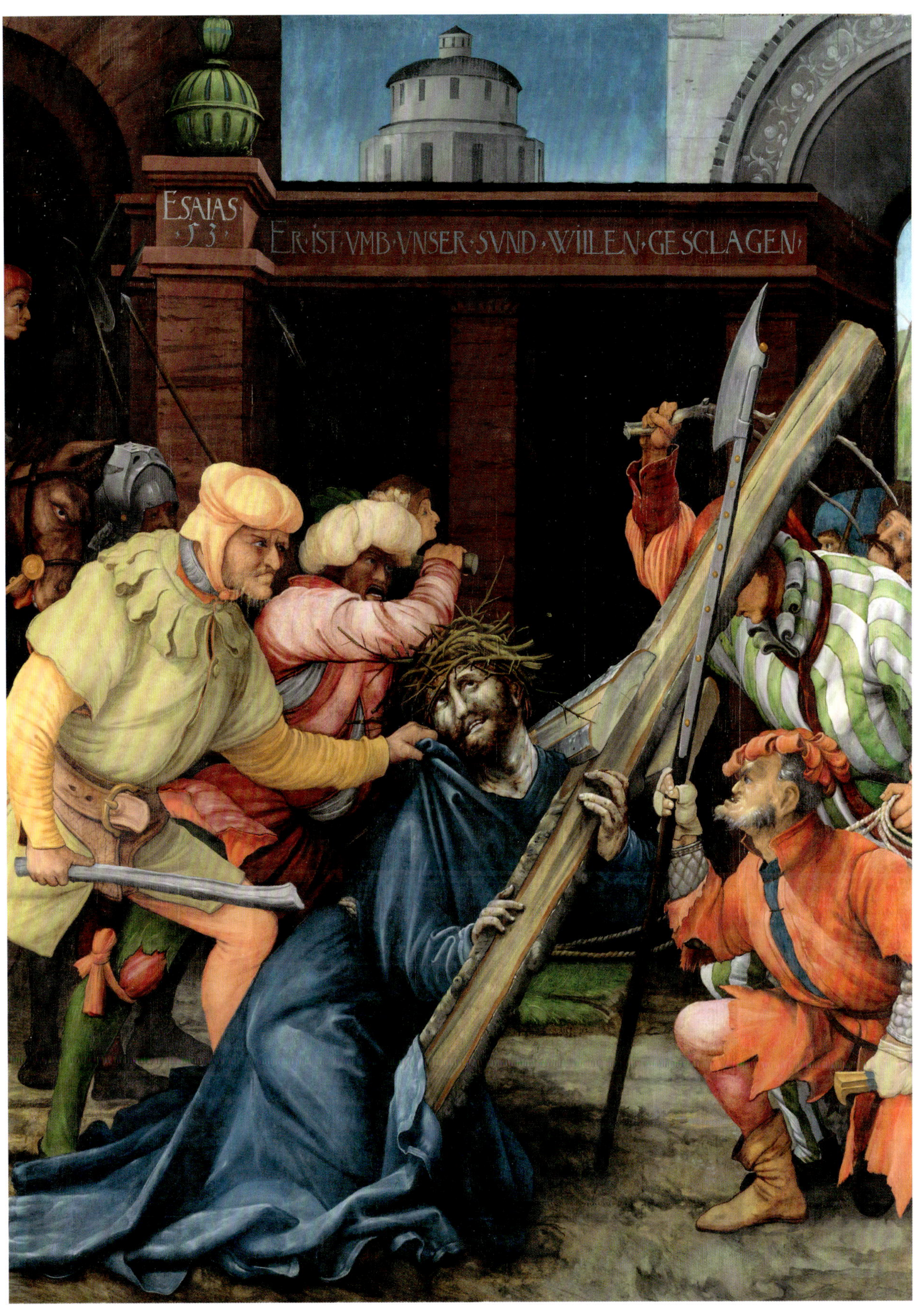
ESAIAS
53
ER·IST·VMB·VNSER·SVND·WILLEN·GESCLAGEN·

214 | Mathis Grünewald, *Christ bearing the Cross*, ca. 1524 (at the beginning of the cleaning work). Karlsruhe, Staatliche Kunsthalle, inv. 99.

215 | Bartolomeo Suardi called Bramantino, *Lamentation of Christ*, ca. 1510. Mezzana di Somma Lombardo, church of Santo Stefano.

216 | Gaudenzio Ferrari, *Male head with red hat* (fragment from a fresco). Varallo Sesia, Pinacoteca, inv. 680.

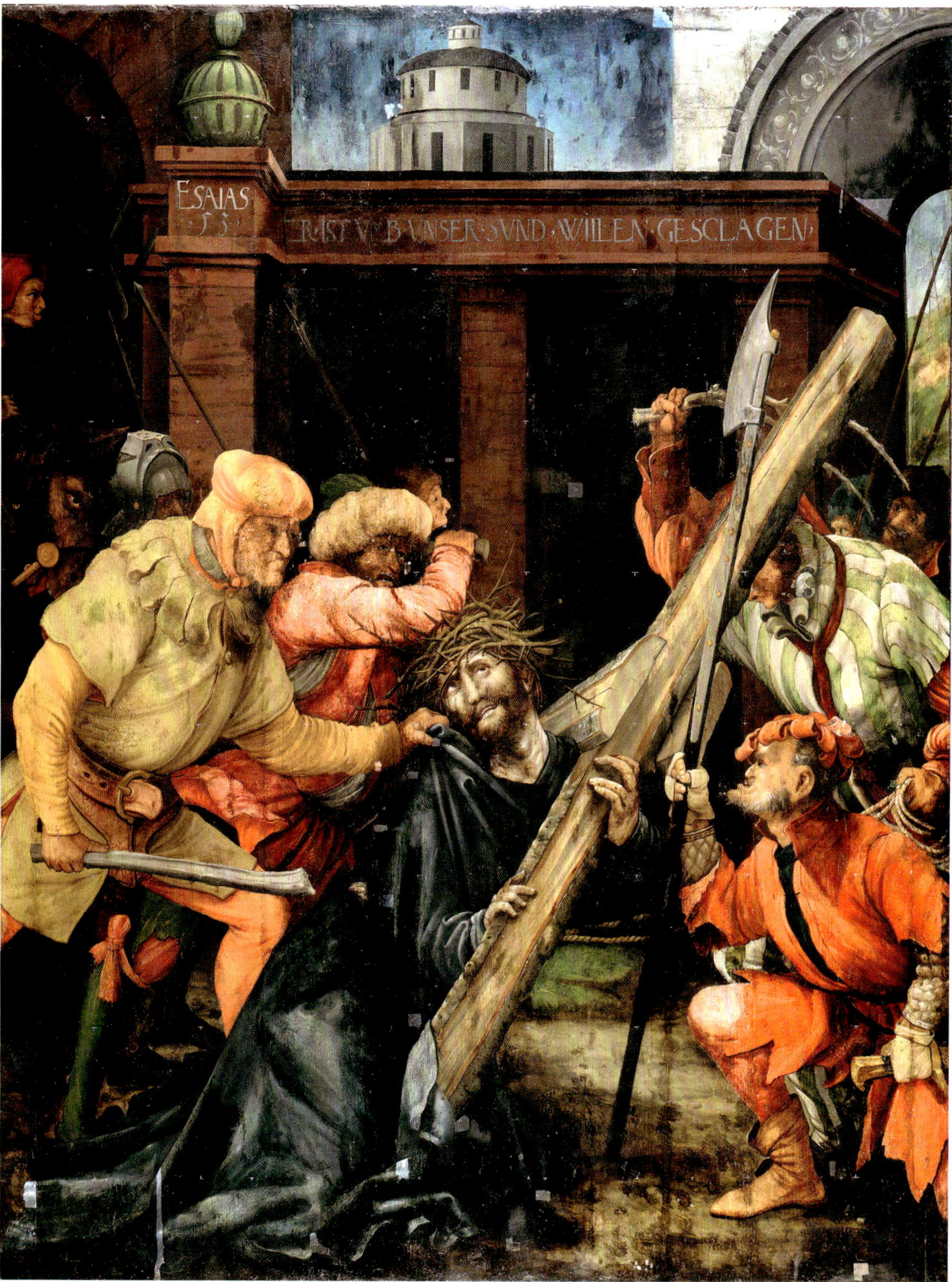

its early history, it is highly probable that the painting dates back to the later period of Grünewald's activity as a painter, 1524–1525.[7]

We begin with *Christ Carrying the Cross* (inv. 993, 193 × 151 cm) [fig. 213]. The painting is in a very poor state of preservation. The cleaning test windows, which I had the opportunity to examine closely in 2010 thanks to the courtesy of Hölger Jacob-Friesen, revealed comforting signs in terms of conservation status and offered aesthetically exacting insights: the sky is an intense turquoise blue that gradually fades into white towards the horizon; Christ's mantel is a very deep cobalt blue; and the freshly cut wood of the cross is unexpectedly still covered with a marvelous gray bark below the old overpainting.[8]

This explosion of bright colors is clearly detectable in the photo taken at the very beginning of the meticulous cleaning that lasted nearly a decade, the only one I am allowed to publish on this occasion [fig. 214]. However, following the completion of the restoration, which included pictorial reintegrations, the final result raised a number of questions. The coloring of the painting today is completely based on strong contrasts, not unlike that of a Florentine mannerist, even if some details (Christ's neck, the sleeve of the villain behind him and the cuff of the other one on the right brandishing the club) still preserve the extraordinary mobility we know so well from Grünewald's previous works. This new coloristic accordance sounds now a little harsh and forced, but probably and surprisingly it reveals the direction of Grünewald's late style. However, a number of faces seem tightened in a mask-like quality, and some background colors emerge even too homogeneously. To be clear, the problem does not pertain solely to this specific restoration but represents a broader concern. In cases such as this one, involving an extraordinary masterpiece with significant deterioration of its painted surfaces, should we prioritize the unity of the image as the primary criterion for restoration, or might a more archaeological restoration be preferable? In the latter approach the reintegrations function as mends, or better, tonal enhancements. This way, personal responsibility regarding the work is left to history and its qualities are free to emerge from what is conserved.

Bianconi[9] had already hypothesized the octagonal temple references to Bramantino, but without investigating further this possibility, not taken up by subsequent scholars. However, this suggestion warrants thorough consideration, and it could even be posited that the model could be the analogous temple in the background of the severely damaged *Lamentation of Christ* by Bramantino in the Church of Santo Stefano in Mezzana di Somma Lombardo, but formerly in the Franciscan Church of Sant'Angelo in Milan, a work datable to around 1510–1511[10] [fig. 215]. Furthermore, even the sky revealed by the restoration is analogous to that of the Brera *Crucifixion*, leaving me to conclude that Mathis's Lombard visit can now be regarded as historically substantiated.

And if this is not enough, there is also the

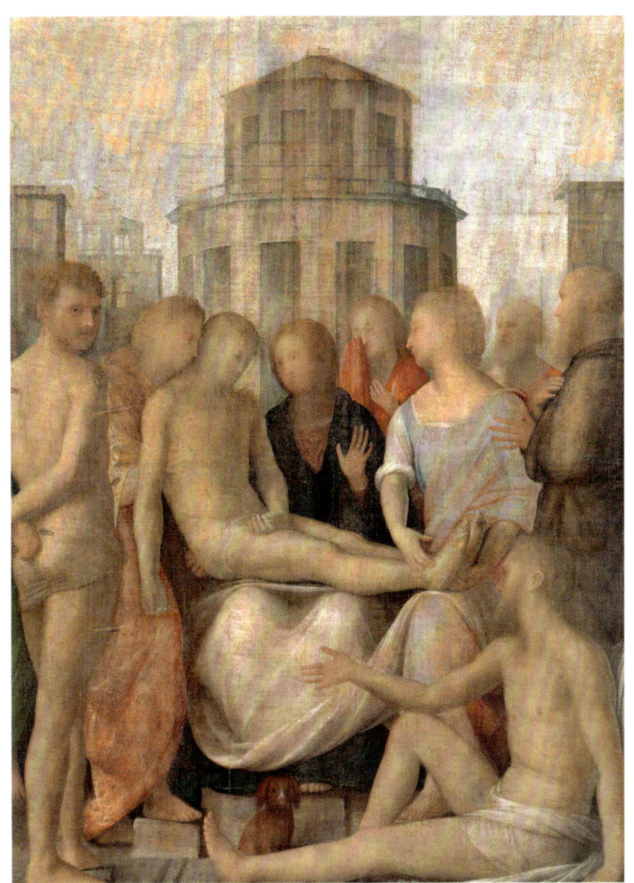

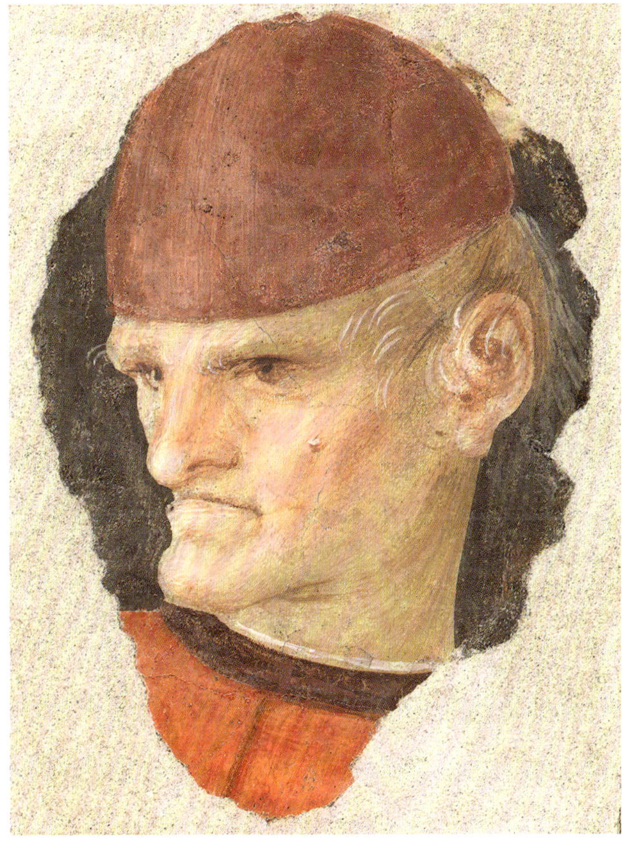

217 | Gaudenzio Ferrari, *Women crying on Jesus, a Thief and Soldiers*, ca. 1505. Varallo Sesia, Holy Mountain, Chapel 40, the *Pietà* (formerly Jesus Stripped of His Garments).

218 | Mathis Grünewald, *Christ bearing the Cross* (detail), ca. 1524. Karlsruhe, Staatliche Kunsthalle, inv. 993.

219 | Leonardo, *Groteseque Head*, ca. 1490. Chatsworth, The Devonshire Collection, inv. 823D.

220 | Mathis Grünewald, *Christ bearing the Cross* (detail), ca. 1524. Karlsruhe, Staatliche Kunsthalle, inv. 993.

221 | Giulio Campagnola after Andrea Mantegna, *Fight of Pagan Gods* (left side), burin. Pavia, Museo Civico.

resemblance between the thug with the yellow cap holding the club and, for example, the fragmentary fresco with the *Head of a man with a red cap* by Gaudenzio Ferrari (Varallo Sesia, Pinacoteca, inv. 680) [fig. 216], perhaps coming from a destroyed or reshaped Sacro Monte Chapel, and a work I think dates from around 1506.[11] It is also a type of face found in Bramantino and in Leonardo's circle, so it could simply be considered (and this is already something) a shared figurative background for both artists. The intense violence of the blows of the other hitmen could also bring to mind some drawings by Leonardo for the *Battle of Anghiari*, but, even more so, the intoxicated pathetism of the frescoes by Gaudenzio in Chapel no. 40, formerly dedicated to *Jesus Stripped of His Garments* (currently to the *Pietà*) at the Holy Mountain of Varallo, datable to 1505[12] [fig. 217]. And the profile of the elderly soldier kneeling

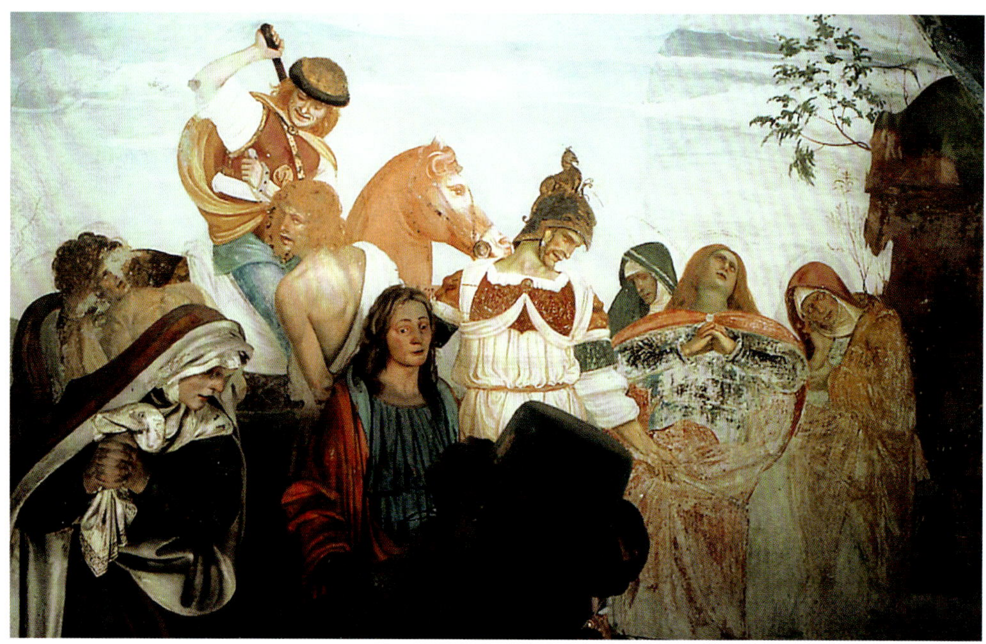

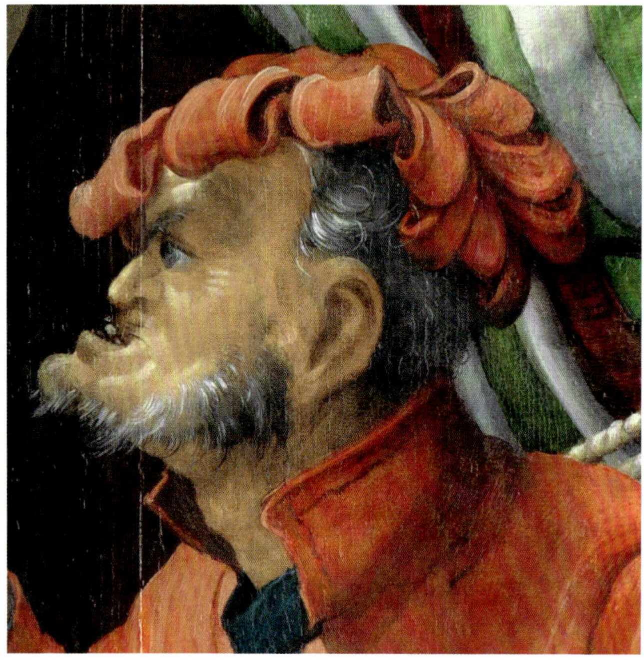

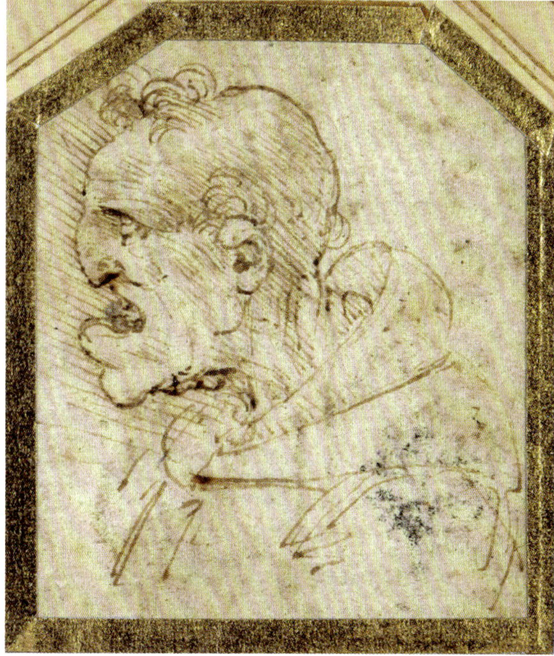

in derision [fig. 218] is a direct derivation of a "grotesque head" drawing by Leonardo, now in the Devonshire Collection (inv. 823 D), datable to the early years of the 16th century [fig. 219].[13] In this context, recognizing that the gesture of the hitman with the raised arm and face hidden by the beam on Christ's right [fig. 220] derives from the *Battle of the Sea Gods* by Mantegna [fig. 221] seems less incidental.[14] Yet despite these references, which reveal Grünewald's tremendous figurative background, few works appear as personal and innovative as this one. Below the looming pseudo-classical architecture that muddles the compositional layout—once again based on intersecting diagonals (one seen in the arm of the turbaned hitman behind Jesus and the chest and left arm of the kneeling soldier, the other from the profile of Christ's clothing) and the lines parallel to them—the middle pillar seems to weigh on the head of Jesus like a hyperbaric column.

A Jesus who is desperately alone, as Weixlgärtner notes, left to the mercy of the sadism of his tormentors: "His mother is not present, nor

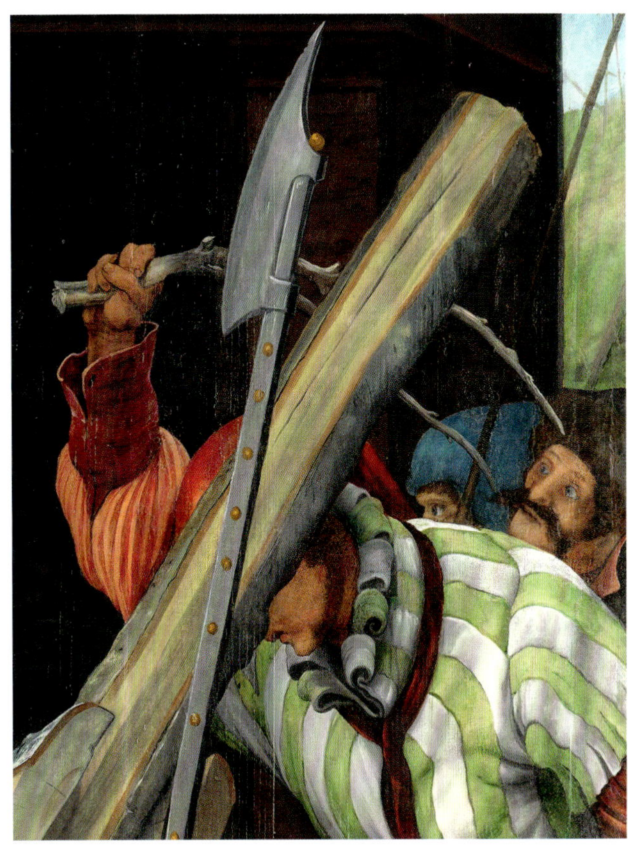

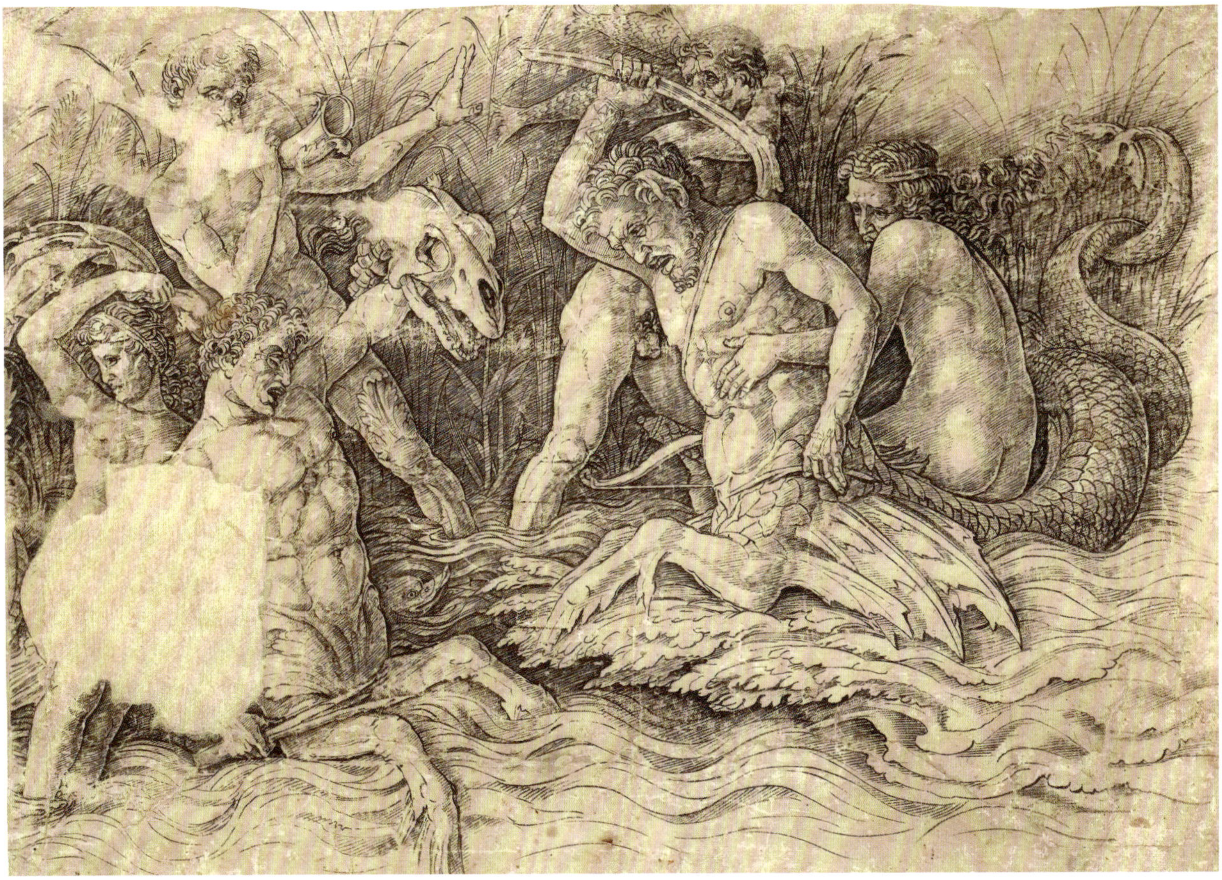

222 | Mathis Grünewald, *Crucifixion*, ca. 1524. Karlsruhe, Staatliche Kunsthalle, inv. 994.

is John or Mary Magdalene; no Veronica washes the blood and sweat from his face, no Simon of Cyrene carries his cross."[15] No Jesus is portrayed as abandoned as he is, not even in Isenheim. He is both crushed by pain and terrified, void of any resources, divinity or nobility, his hands clutching the wood of the cross with fingers like overgrown chicken feet.[16]

And yet Christ is monumental, as are the figures of the henchmen. Everything is in movement: the torsional poses of Jesus and the kneeling soldier are obvious even from the most cursory glance; as always, the use of light is extremely precise (for example, the straight shadow from the cross stamped on the elderly soldier on the right); and the intense hues seem to collide with each other, like the peach color of the pants of the thug with the club against the blue of Jesus's robes.

The German inscription on the façade of the building, from the Book of Isaiah: "But he was wounded for our transgressions" already seems to carry with it a quiver of Lutheran thought. The writing on the panel "ESAIS 53. ER IST VMB VNSER SVND WILLEN GESCLAGEN" is slightly different from Luther's, but the first Lutheran translation of Isaiah was not printed until the fall of 1528, which means it would not have been possible for the artist (who died at the same time) to use it.[17] In truth, Karl Arndt and Bernd Moeller compare the citation from Isaiah in the panel today in Karlsruhe with another Lutheran text, *Eyn Sermon von der Betrachtung des heiligen Leidens Christi* from 1519 (which by 1524 had already been reprinted more than twenty times[18]), which reads, however: "Isaia 53. Umb d'sund willen meyns volcks hab ich yhn geschlagen."[19] Grünewald certainly did not utilize the vernacular edition published by Johann Mentelin in 1466 and reprinted fourteen times up to the year 1518. Even consulting the other pre-Lutheran editions of the Bible in German (Nuremberg, Johann Sensenschmidt and Andreas Frisner, 1475; Cologne, Heinrich Quentell, ca. 1478; Nuremberg, Anton Koberger, 1483; Strasburg, Johann Grüninger, 1485; Augsburg, Johannes Schönsperger the Elder, 1487; Lübeck, Steffan Arndes, 1494; Augsburg, Johann Otner, 1507; Halberstadt, Lorenz Stuchs, 1522) I was not able to find a precise inference, and the same result has been confirmed to me by Mons. Franco Buzzi, who carried out a similar verification in parallel (also including the translation by Johannes Dietenberger, Cologne and Mainz, 1534). Therefore, it might be a translation that came to him on the spur of the moment (perhaps bearing in mind Luther's sermon in 1519 mentioned above, which will be discussed later) based on the Latin text, "ipse autem vulneratus est propter iniquitates nostras". In any case, it must be acknowledged that the inscription on the Karlsruhe painting that combines verses 53 and 5 from Isaiah, is very similar to the Lutheran translation: "Aber er ist umb unser missethat willen werwundet und umb unser sunde willen zuschlagen."[20] Subsequently, it would seem that this could be a citation from a flawed edition, or even recalled from memory. This, combined with the poor epigraphic quality, raises doubts regarding its authenticity, suggesting it might have been added at a later date. This suspicion is reinforced by the fact that the inscription is found on areas of the artwork that were unquestionably repainted over time, as early restoration analysis has shown. Therefore, it is not from the *Christ Carrying the Cross* that we can obtain information about Grünewald's proximity to the Reformation.

Nonetheless, a para-Lutheran, or perhaps even fully Lutheran, inspiration becomes evident in Mathis tragic portrayal of Christ, who is truly reduced to nothing, overtaken by sin, a wrongdoer, a condemned man. This is a theme that Luther had treated powerfully in his comment to the Letter to the Romans (1515–1516), much

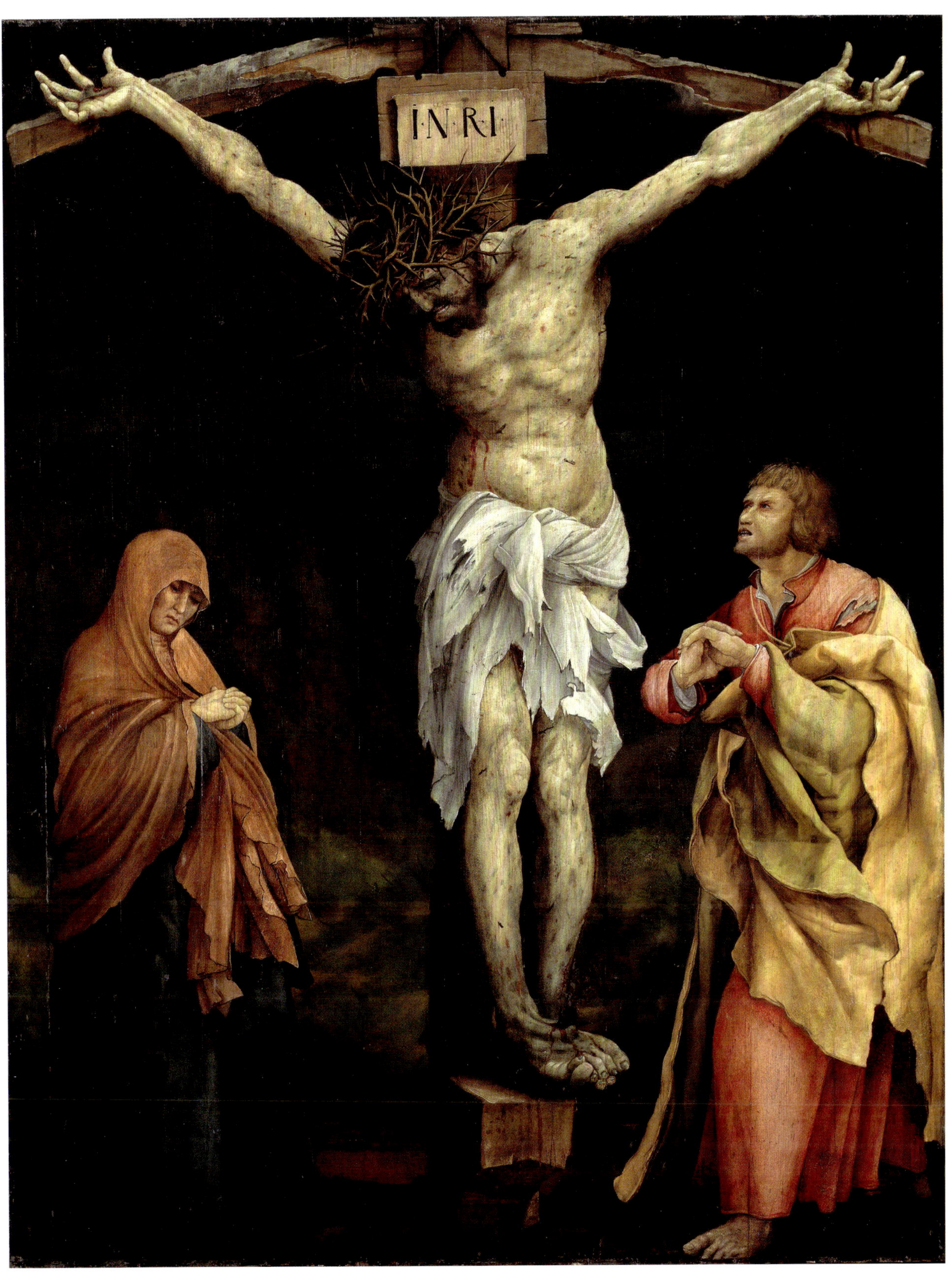

INRI

before entering into open conflict with Rome: "When he [God] wanted to glorify him and establish him in his Kingship, he made him die, he caused him to be confounded and to descend into hell."[21] The similarities found in the already-mentioned 1519 sermon are more generic, but at least this passage deserves quoting:

If pain or sickness afflicts you, just consider how paltry this is in comparison with

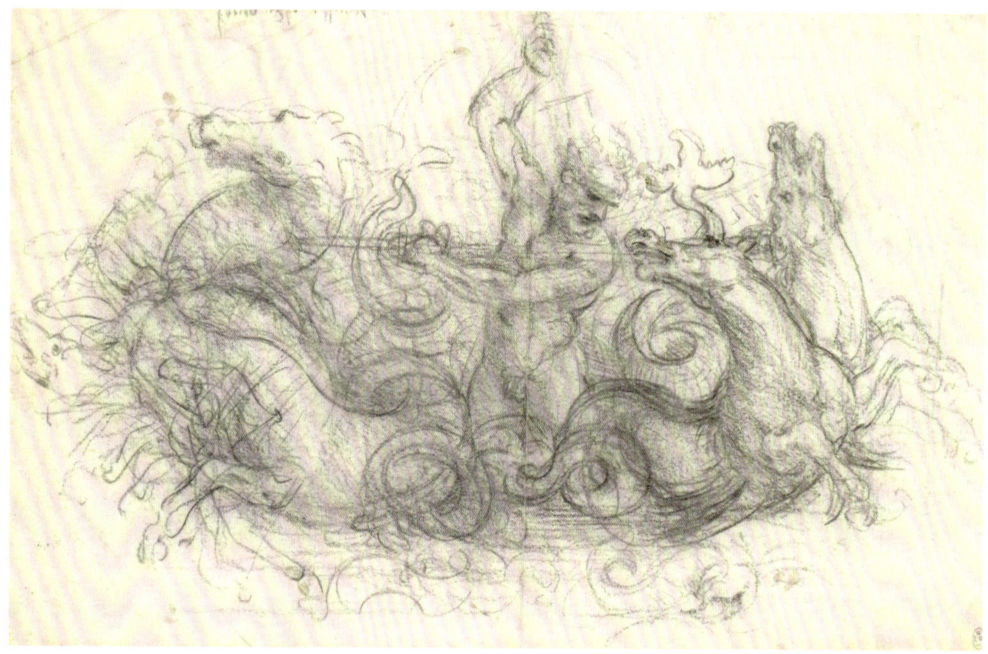

223 | Leonardo da Vinci, *Neptune*, ca. 1508. Windsor Castle, The Royal Library, inv. RCIN 12570.

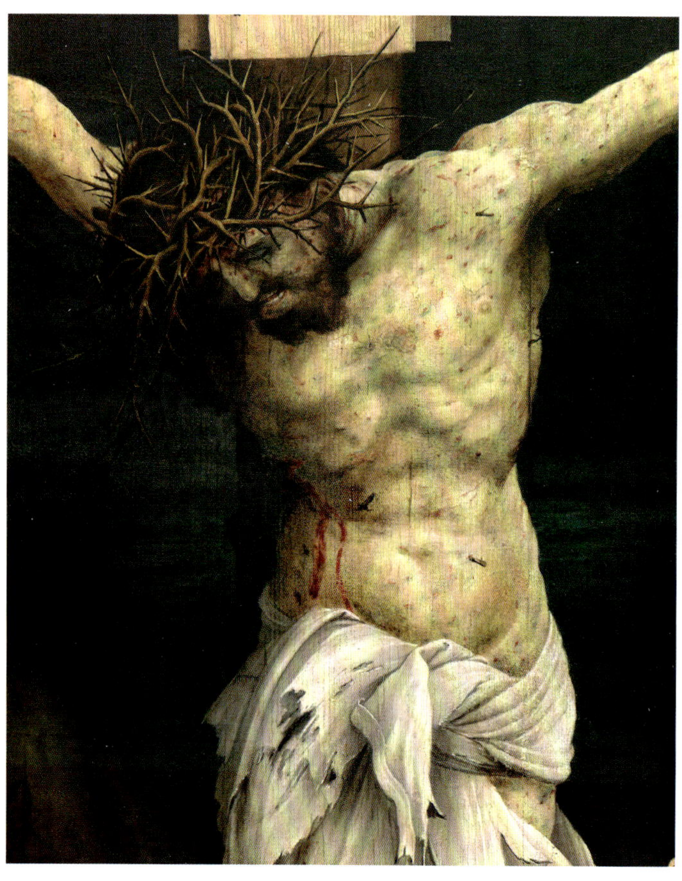

224 | Mathis Grünewald, *Crucifixion* (detail), ca. 1524. Karlsruhe, Staatliche Kunsthalle, inv. 994.

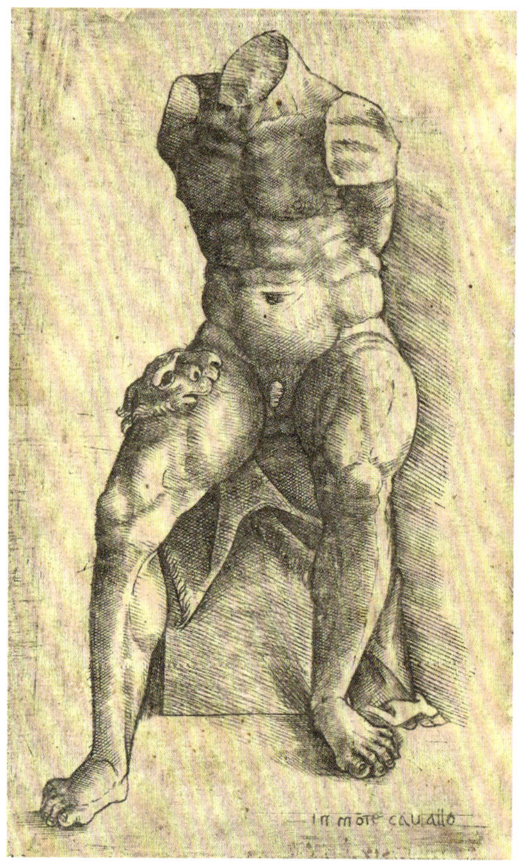

225 | Giovanni Antonio da Brescia, *The Belvedere Torso*, etching. London, The British Museum, inv. 1845.0825.258.

the thorny crown and the nails of Christ. If you are obliged to do or to refrain from doing things against your wishes, ponder how Christ was bound and captured and let hiter and yon. If you are beset by pride, see how your Lord was mocked and ridiculed along with criminals. If unchastity and lust assail you, remember how ruthlessly Christ's tender flesh was scourged, pierced, and beaten. If hatred, envy, and vindictiveness beset you, recall that Christ, who indeed had more reason to avenge himself, interceded with tears and cries for you and for all his enemies.[22]

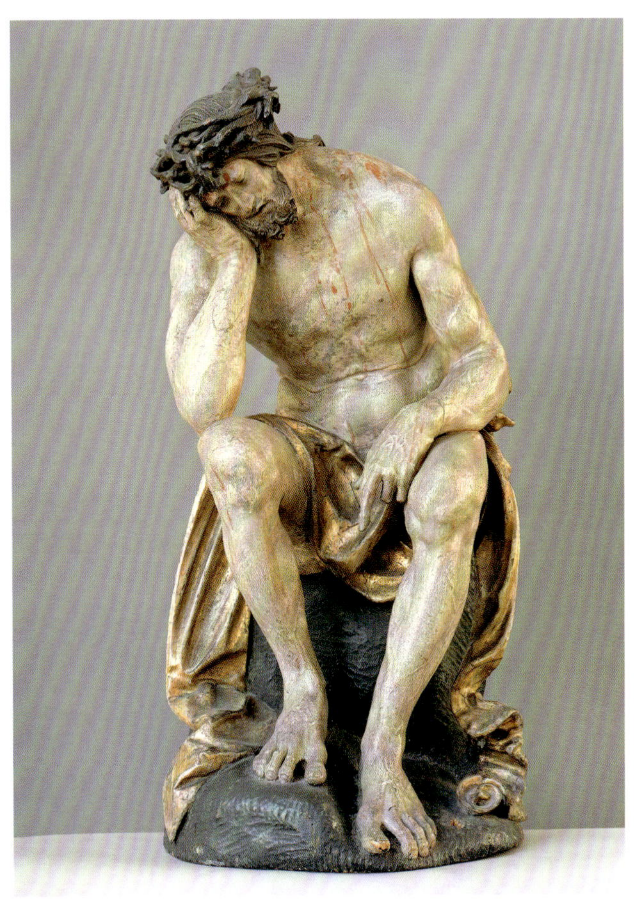

226 | Hans Leinberger, *Man of Sorrow*, ca. 1525. Berlin, Staatliche Museen, Skulpturensammlung und Museum für Byzantinische Kunst (Bode Museum). inv. 8347.

The same "poor wretch", is also seen on the other side of the panel (now separate, as noted previously: inv. no. 994, 195.5 × 142.5 cm) representing the *Crucifixion* [fig. 222]. At first glance, it would seem a less extreme depiction than the one in Isenheim. The composition is simplified and imposing, and the figures are majestic, comparable to large statues. Christ is depicted with an explosive physique, suggesting a strength capable of enduring torture and martyrdom.[23] The dramatic torsion of his chest, pushed forward by the weight of his head, creates an amazing plastic effect. Again here, we can observe an affinity with Lombard wooden sculptures (De Donati more than Del Maino) and perhaps the drawing style of Leonardo as in the *Neptune* at Windsor Castle (RCIN 12570)[24] [fig. 223]. Additionally, Mathis seems to be engaging with a prestigious model of the past: the chest of Christ pushed forward [fig. 224] is an almost derisive citation of the *Belvedere Torso*, one of the best-known Roman sculptures in the Renaissance, popularized through drawings and at least one etching by Giovanni Antonio da Brescia around 1515 [fig. 225].[25]

In turn, this explosively plastic and wild masterpiece would make its own impact. Once again, sculptors were the first ones ready to grasp the potential. For example, the *Man of Sorrows* at the Staatliche Museen, Skulpturensammlung und Museum für Byzantinische Kunst (Bode Museum) in Berlin (inv. 8347) by Hans Leinberger [fig. 226], the sculptor from the Landshut court, documented from 1510 to 1513.[26] This iconography was well-known in Germany, and at least one other version by Leinberger is known, probably datable to around 1520, in the Church of St. Nicholas in Landshut. But the Berlin piece stands out for the massive grandeur of its proportions, the protruding chest (perhaps a subtle reminder of the *Belvedere Torso*?), its immense feet and the more desperate than painful facial expression. I find it difficult to think of this remarkable linden wood sculpture (75 cm tall) without drawing connections to the Karlsruhe *Crucifixion*.

The support to which his feet are nailed has become a parallelepiped in perspective, flooded by a fixed patch of white light. The two onlookers, Mary and John, are also dignified with measured gestures. St. John [fig. 227] was studied from life, as revealed by the preparatory study at the Berlin Kupferstichkabinett (inv. KdZ

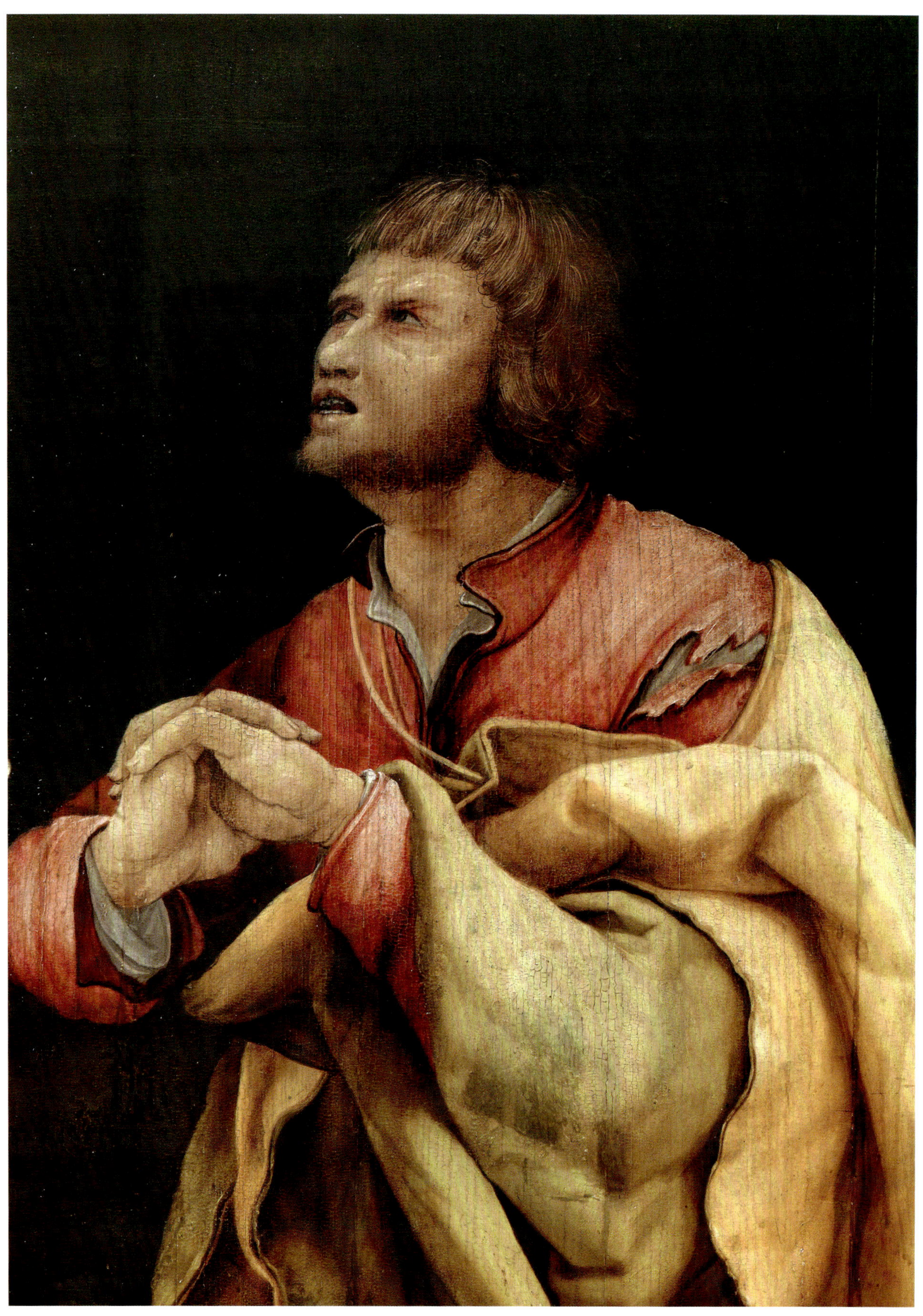

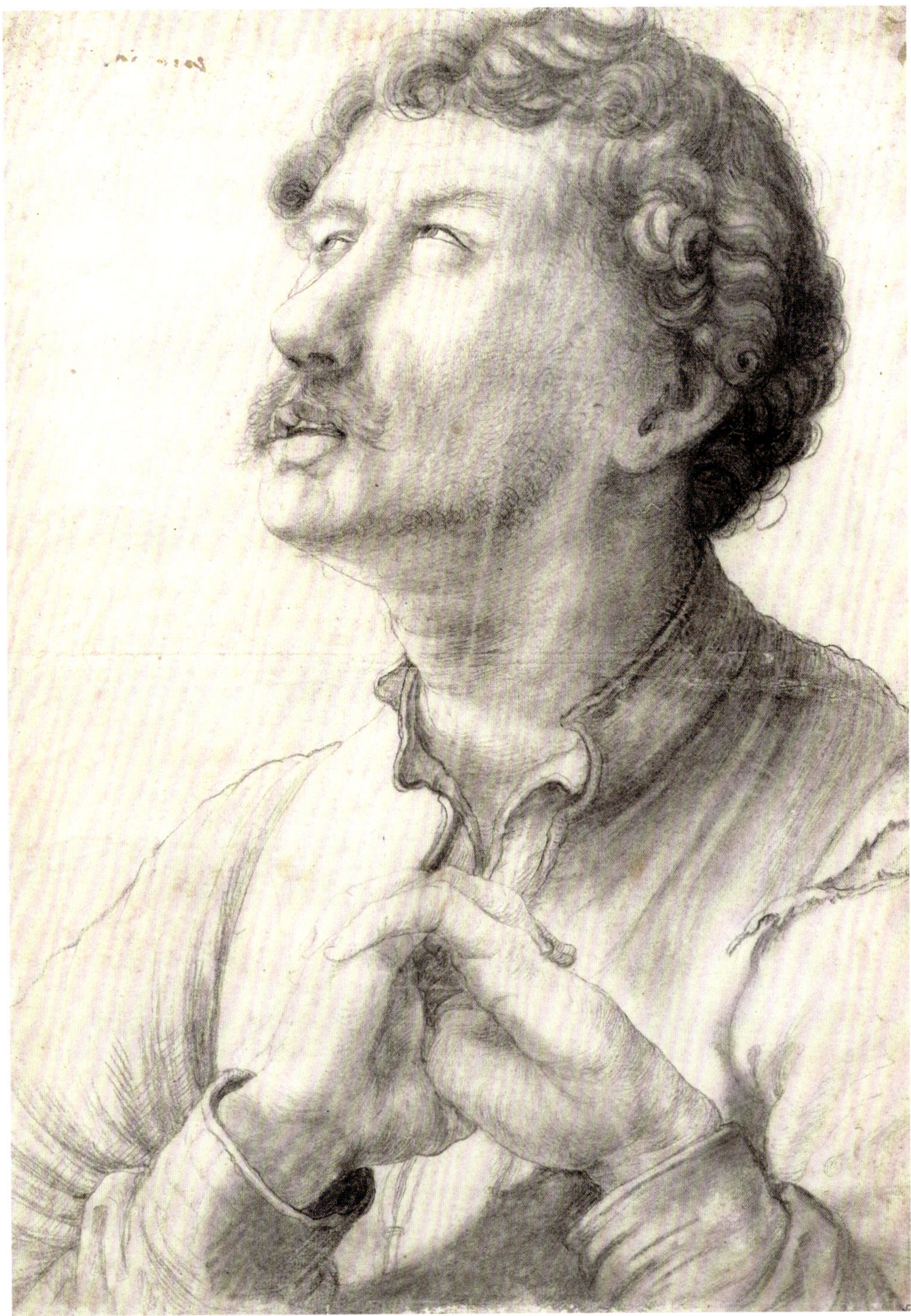

227 | Mathis Grünewald, *Crucifixion* (detail), ca. 1524. Karlsruhe, Staatliche Kunsthalle, inv. 994.

228 | Mathis Grünewald, *Study of a man praying*, ca. 1524. Berlin, Staatliche Museen, Kupferstichkabinett, inv. KdZ 12036.

12036, black chalk, 436 × 321 mm)[27] [fig. 228], in which all the characteristics of the last phase of Grünewald's drawing style can be seen, from the monumental presence to the wavy curls, like whorls of water in 16th-century drawings by Leonardo. However, despite the noteworthy tonal micro-interlacing, the granular stroke that creates volume and the rich wildness of the hair, one would not anticipate from this drawing the magnificent blend of the pink-ochre colors found in the painted clothing (exactly the same as the pants of St. Roch in the Romanino altarpiece in Brescia mentioned previously!), employed with a breadth and delicacy that can be

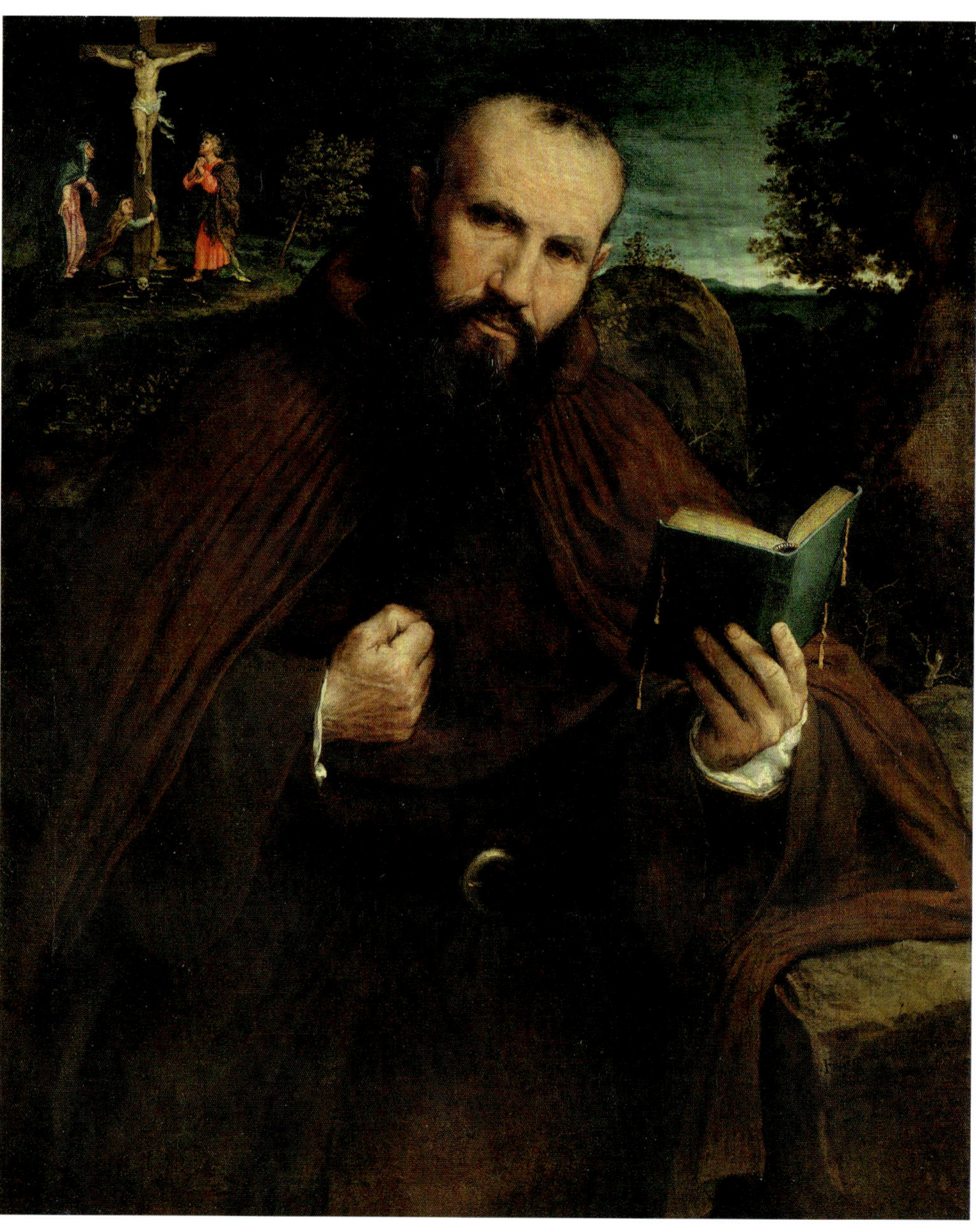

229 | Lorenzo Lotto, *Portrait of Fra Gregorio Belo*, 1547. New York, The Metropolitan Museum of Art, inv. 65.117.

described as proto-mannerist and which would have certainly garnered the approval of Pontormo.

It is somewhat surprising to find what would seem to be a fairly explicit reference to Grünewald's St. John in the Crucifixion scene inserted in a late work by Lorenzo Lotto, the *Portrait of Brother Gregorio Belo*, now at the Metropolitan Museum in New York (inv. 65.117), dated 1547 [fig. 229]. In the background of the Lotto painting, we see a scene of the Crucifixion in which John the Evangelist almost seems to be a small copy of the one in Karlsruhe. It is hard to say how Grünewald's inspiration could have reached the Venetian painter. But certainly, no one was better equipped than Lotto—a painter known for his connections with doctrinally borderline figures and for creating a now-lost portrait of Luther—to grasp the religious tension in the German painting, wracked by a painful and unresolved balance between "catholic" rigor and "discovery of the Gospel by Luther".[28] It would be the final seal on Lotto's attraction for the most extreme of German artists.

Compared to previous investigations into this question, in addition to the figurative aspects, here the expressive ambiance changes significantly. Once again, the correct interpretation was detected by Huysmans with amazing certitude in his famous 1891 novel *Là-bas*:

> This was the Christ of St. Justin, St. Basil, St. Cyrill and Tertullian, the Christ of the Early Church, a Christ who looked vulgar and ugly because he took upon himself all the sins of the world and assumed, in his humility, the most abject of appearances.
> This was the Christ of the Poors, a Christ who had become flesh in the likeness of the most wretched of those he had come to redeem, the ill-favoured and the indigent, all those in fact upon whose ugliness or poverty mankind wreaks its cowardly spite. This was also the most human of Christs, a Christ frail of flesh, forsaken by the Father until such time as no further torments were possible, a Christ succoured only by his Mother, to whom he must have cried out, as do all who suffer, like a child, though by then she was powerless to help him.
> By what was doubtless a supreme act of humility, he had willed that the Passion should not exceed the limits imposed by the human senses; and, in obedience to incomprehensible laws, he had consented that his Divinity should be suspended, as it were, from the first blows and insults, through the spitting and the scourging till the unspeakable torments of an interminable death-agony. [. . .]
> Never before had realism attempted such a subject; never before had a painter explored the divine charnel-house so thoroughly, or dipped his brush so brutally in running sores and bleeding wounds. It was outrageous and it was horrifying. Grünewald was the most daring of realists, without a doubt; but as one gazed upon this Redeemer of the doss-house, this God of the morgue, there was wrought a chance. Gleams of light filtered from the ulcerous head; a superhuman radiance illumined the gangrened flesh and the tortured features. This carrion spread-eagled on the cross was the tabernacle of a God; and here, his head [is] adorned with no aureole or nimbus but a tangled crown of thorns beaded with drops of blood.[29]

The restrained gestures, the absence of any type of secondary elements and the fact itself that the landscape is not enveloped in a dark, supernatural shadow, but a very common haze in which banks of fog are moving, strip this image of any excess of pathos or mysticism. What we see is only the anguish of a criminal: one who is well-built, as befits a working man driven by necessity to misdeeds or crime, who bears the clear signs of torment, but without exaggeration, yet sufficient to indicate, in any case, a sense of exceptionality, of Isenheim. The face, void of any idealization, dangles with the mouth open in a grimace of pain set in rigor mortis; not the mystic decay of the Isenheim corpse, but the realistic mechanical workings of muscles twisted by the effort of the unnatural pose. Nothing more than a cruel routine execution: one less criminal. And, if this man proclaimed himself to be the son of God and now is just a regular drudge who has been beaten and crucified, those who derided him were right ("if you are truly the son of God, come down off the cross and we will believe you"). In fact, it would be an act of true piety, of true devotion, to join in the derision. No resurrection is possible, no glory. When the dense fog has cleared, everyone will get back to work and it will all end there. What light is there from the outside? Even the nails, which always reflected light, are now, for the first time, opaque, soiled, almost emblematic.

Luther offers us the key to understanding this masterpiece of painting, and of mysticism itself in a text dated a few years later, 1530:

> Before he can be God he must first appear to be the Devil. We cannot reach heaven until we first descend into hell. We cannot be God's children unless first we are the Devil's children. Again before the world can be seen to be a lie it must first appear to be the truth.[30]

Even more clearly, in his comment to the Letter to the Romans, he had written:

> For even Christ suffered damnation and dereliction to a greater degree than all the saints. And his sufferings were not, as some imagine, easy for him. For he really and truly offered himself for us to eternal damnation to God the Father. And in his human nature, he behaved in no other way than as a man eternally damned to hell.[31]

In fact, in *On Christian Liberty*, published in 1520 in a double Latin and German edition (and, therefore, with broad dissemination also among the laity), Luther states that faith marries the soul to Christ and, following these marriages, Christ takes on the sins of man: "As a matter of fact, he makes them his own and acts as if they were his own and as if he himself had sinned."[32] Moreover, paraphrasing Paul, he says that Christ "nevertheless stripped himself of everything and became as a servant, doing and suffering everything [. . .]; and so, despite being free, because of his love for us, became a servant".[33] It might not seem that much, but as has already been said, we cannot help but notice how the character of the crucified Christ has changed from Isenheim to Tauberbischofsheim. He is superhuman even in his suffering, transfigured in a mystic sense thanks to the "timeless" presence of John the Baptist and the lamb—the first radically human, and the second hopelessly inanimate.

It will be objected that it is very unlikely that Mathis could have known Luther's commentary on St. Paul. But aside from the fact that his association with the Antonites could have provided him with some of the theological discussion promoted in Germany by the Augustinian Order during that period involving Staupitz and Luther, in 1520, Luther himself observed: "vulgus civium, artificum et quo qui sunt a Magistrorum istorum studiis remotiores rectius et certius de Christiana re iudicent quam Theologi doctrinales".[34] A fact, that of the theological involvement of laity and the "craftsmen", confirmed by the involvement in the Reformation, in varying degrees, of a number of artists, including Dürer, Cranach, Baldung Grien, Ratgeb and Riemenschneider, which we will discuss again.[35] In fact, we have observed that Luther actively promulgated his thinking through a prolific, grass-roots vernacular output that was reproduced in vast quantities by the printers who recognized him as a true "goose that lays the golden egg".

Secondly, it should be remembered that in 1517 Archbishop Albrecht enlisted Ulrich von Hutten into his service. Consequently, for some time Grünewald worked alongside one of the most inflammatory polemicists of the early years of the Reformation, and it is quite plausible that the famous—perhaps satirical—drawing now at the Kupferstichkabinett in Berlin (inv. KdZ 1071, black chalk, 272 × 199 mm [fig. 230]),[36] datable by its style to the early 1520s, was inspired by Hutten's ferocious anti-Rome satire, *Vadiscus*, published in 1520, although it is impossible to pinpoint a precise correspondence between the drawn image and the written text.[37] Although

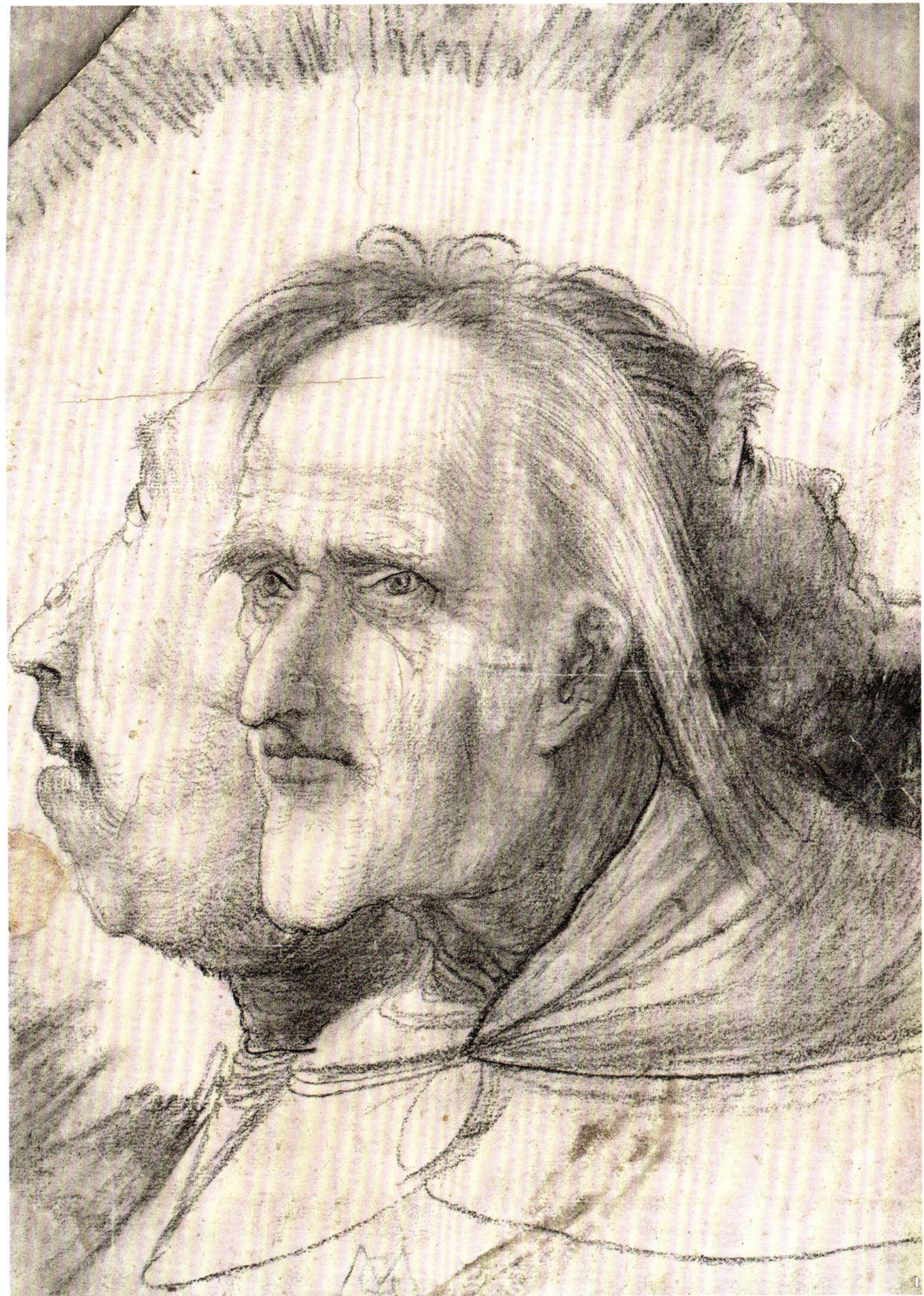

230 | Mathis Grünewald, *Study of Grotesques Heads ("Trias Romana")*, ca. 1524–1525. Berlin, Staatliche Museen, Kupferstichkabinett, inv. KdZ 1071.

the sense of this representation is elusive, the traditional interpretation as an anti-papist satire could essentially be on the mark. However, I do not want to get into dubious hermeneutic territory. For now, it is enough to acknowledge the debt to the Leonardesque "grotesque heads", rather than the much vaster output of German satirical etchings.

It might seem that this interpretation diverges from my established methodological approach based on the utmost primacy of philology. However, in this instance, I believe the Lutheran interpretation of the work is essential for its understanding and, above all, historically justified or even necessary.

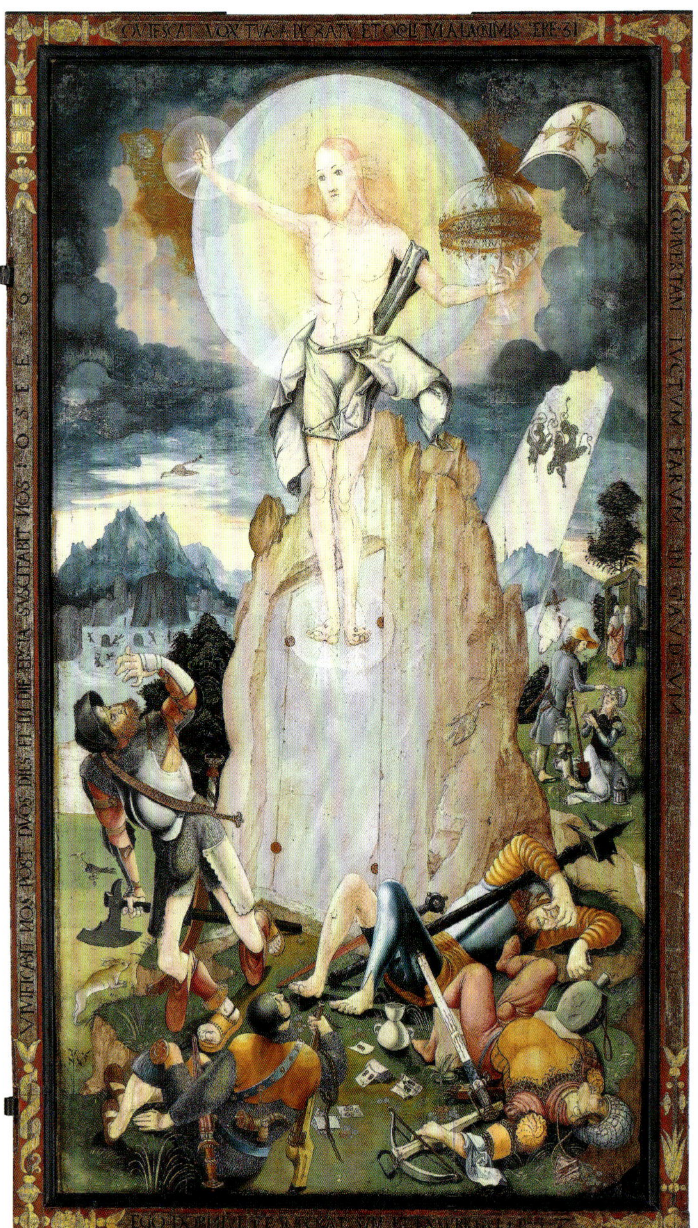

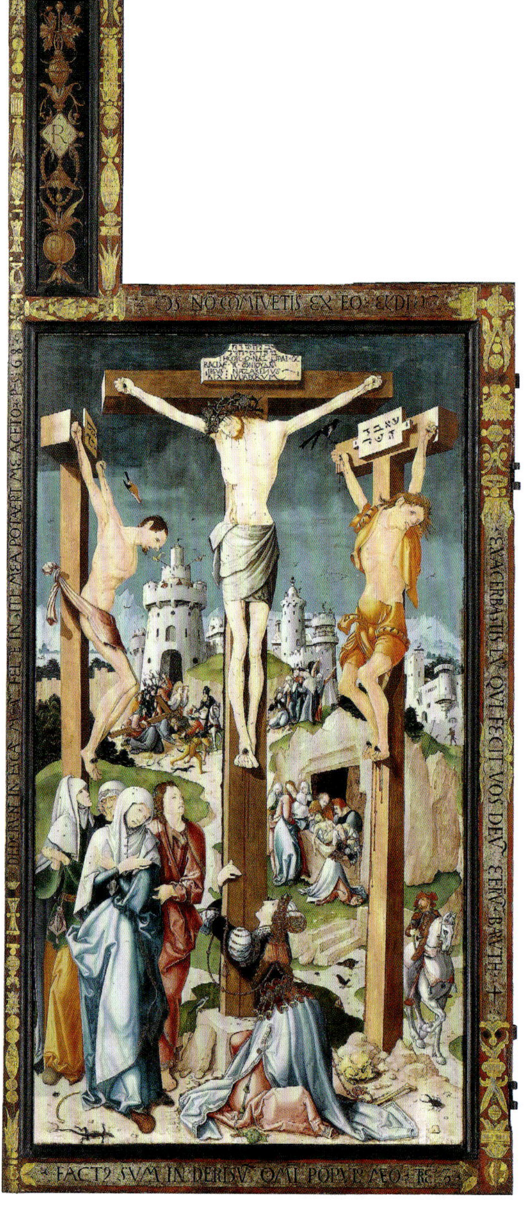

231 | Jerg Ratgeb, *Resurrection of Christ* (from a polyptich), ca. 1517–1519. Stuttgart, Staatliche Kunstgalerie, inv. 1523d.

232 | Jerg Ratgeb, *Crucifixion* (from a polyptych), ca. 1517–1519. Stuttgart, Staatliche Kunstgalerie, inv. 1523c.

It should be noted that after 1525, Grünewald unexpectedly left service at the Mainz court. It is often thought that this was the result of his proximity to the tragic Peasants' War, which had in Archbishop Albrecht (but also, we might add, Luther himself) an unyielding enemy. This is because of the coincidence of dates and circumstances, and also the fact that the 1528 inventory of the goods left by Mathis included a text with "the twelve articles of faith", generally interpreted as the twelve peasants' demands.[38] Certainly, other artists supported the revolt, and some had significant connections to Grünewald.[39]

The most glaring example is Jerg Ratgeb, "martyr of the Peasants' War", to borrow the expression of his most famous scholar, Wilhelm Fraenger.[40] We must resist the temptation to interpret his work, so difficult to evaluate critically, in light of the radical existential choices taken by the painter and his tragic end (which is an approach Fraenger adopted with tremendous empathetic involvement). It might be more

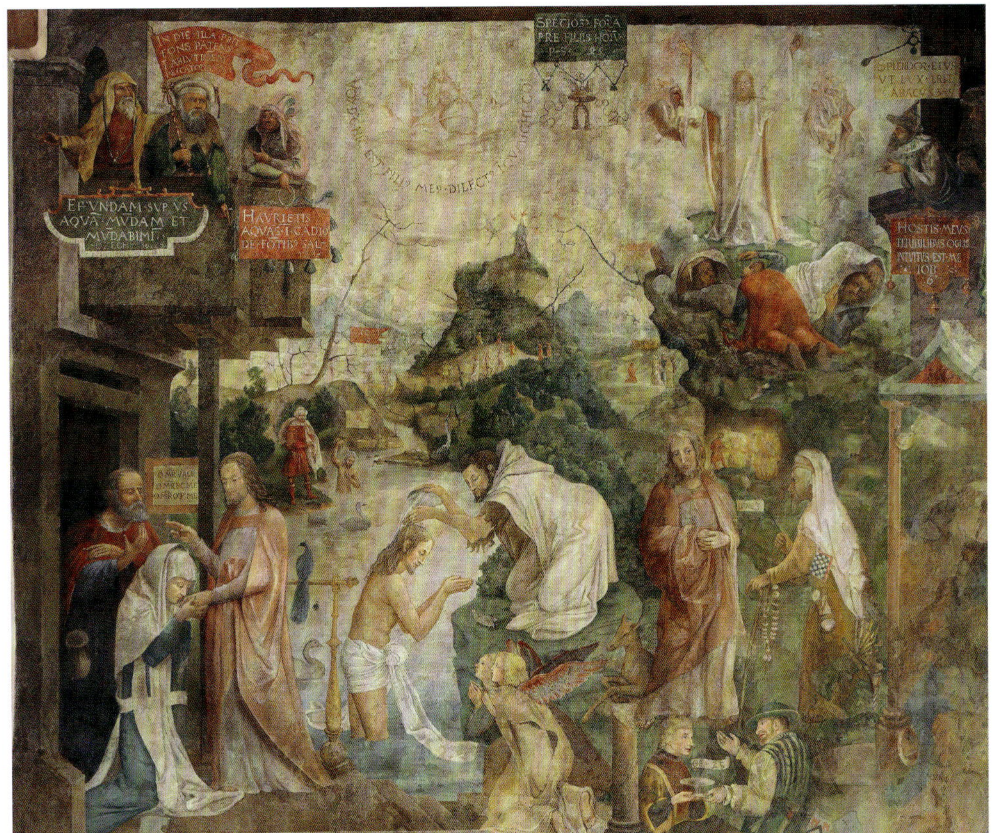

233 | Jerg Ratgeb, *Transfiguration*, ca. 1515. Frankfurt am Main, Carmelite Cloister.

useful to review, as far as they are known, the facts regarding his involvement in the Müntzerian venture. On April 17, 1525, Ratgeb was appointed Stuttgart City Councilman, when he was already on the side of the peasants, but ten days later he was appointed to the supreme military council and chancellor. In fact, Ratgeb, who lived in Stuttgart and worked for the Carmelites in Frankfurt and still in 1524 received the balance for the large *St. Mary* altarpiece in Herrenberg completed in 1519 (now at the Stuttgart Staatsgalerie, inv. 1523 a-e), became one of the key figures in the Peasants' movement precisely when it evolved into a military issue, and extremely violent on both sides. It should also be noted that those taking part in the riot had also cut their ties with Luther who, for his part, did not hesitate to call for military repression. Ratgeb was part of the delegation that attempted a final negotiation on May 9, before the fatal battle of Boblingen and Sindelfingen, where he was taken prisoner. Despite the trial documentation loss, we know he was executed on an unspecified day in 1526, though his death by quartering may only be apocryphal, perhaps suggested by a similar death he, himself, depicted in a detail of the Frankfurt frescoes.

It is not easy to understand what induced the painter to embrace the path of armed revolt, above and beyond the fevered emotions of the day. Though it would not explain the radical nature of his choice, an influence may have been the spirituality of the Brethren of the Common Life who, at least, he had time to know in Herrenberg, an Augustinian monastery entrusted to them (the prior died in 1517, and Prince Ulrich of Wittenberg replaced the Brethren with the Canons Regular of the Lateran, but Ratgeb had begun work on the large altarpiece in 1516). There was nothing inherently violent in the spirituality of the Brethren of the Common Life, but the emphasis on the inner life of the individual in direct contact with the Word of God, the scarce importance attributed to traditional devotional practices and the tension involved in conforming one's life to that of Christ (it is no coincidence that the manifesto text of the Brethren is the *Imitation of Christ*), just as they were aspects that influenced the Augustinian Luther,[41] could have at least created tension in the painter's religious energy. Unquestionably, in the Stuttgart altarpiece, Ratgeb shows that he was influenced by the knowledge of Grünewaldian innovations in Isenheim. More than once, in fact, the dependence of his Resurrection [fig. 231] on Mathis's unparalleled one has been emphasized. However, I would say that this panel also demonstrates knowledge of the Stuppach *Madonna*, particularly in that unforgettable rainbow-iris-crown-aureole, Mathis's inimitable invention. As an aside, it is worth noting that Ratgeb's altarpiece was finished in 1519 and this offers an upper limit for the Grünewald *Madonna* (the 1519 written, as we have seen, on the frame now in Aschaffenburg, provides evidence of the completion date of the work in the chapel dedicated to Our Lady of the Snows). Moreover, the connection does not end there, given that the type of Crucifix depicted by Ratgeb in this altarpiece [fig. 232] and even earlier in the fragmentary fresco in Frankfurt [fig. 233], appears to be based on those by Grünewald, especially the ones prior to the altarpiece now in Colmar, notably in the depiction of the divine apparition, similar to that behind the Virgin Mary in the *Isenheim Altarpiece*.[42]

The other, even greater artist who was certainly involved in the disastrous epic of the Peasants' War is the sculptor Tilman Riemenschneider. Although still significantly affected, he paid a lesser price than Ratgeb, even if he did not play a forefront role, as was the case with the Stuttgart painter.

Born in Heiligenstadt, Riemenschneider moved to Würzburg as early as 1483, enrolling in the local Guild of St. Luke, a professional association of artists. Two years later he married, obtained citizenship and opened his own workshop. The prolific output of his clearly large and well-organized workshop and the significance of his commissions indicate his professional and social stature, which culminated with his presence in the 1505 municipal delegation welcoming Emperor Maximilian I during his visit to Würzburg, and his election to the city council four years later. Riemenschneider was also re-elected in 1514 and 1518, and even held a two-year term as burgomaster in 1520–1521 and emeritus burgomaster in 1521–1522, after which he resumed his council duties. In this position, Tilman was part of the Würzburg faction against its prince-bishop Konrad von Thüngen and was on the side of the rebels.[43] Together with other members of the city council, Riemenschneider was arrested and held prisoner in the Marienberg Fortress until August 8, 1525. He was stripped of all official roles and had part of his significant assets confiscated.

It seems clear from Riemenschneider's example how dangerous it can be to indulge in comparisons based on stylistic overstatement, biographical restlessness and spiritual and political extremism, which seem to work so well for Jerg Ratgeb. Tilman was a member of the middle class who did well for himself, who enjoyed a major rise in his social standing, and whose art has long crystalized into a recognizable hallmark of high-level craftsmanship which, in a certain way, succeeded in touching all aspects of the expressive range from sophisticated elegance to intense pathos, but always within the limits of rational control of his stylistic choices. The trauma of the events of 1525 obviously affected him, but in the six years he had left to live (he died on July 7, 1531, and was buried without discussion in Würzburg Cathedral with a majestic memorial tombstone [fig. 234]) he continued to work for Catholic patrons.

The drastic way he was treated, including the legendary claim that his hands were broken to prevent him from continuing his activity as a sculptor, suggests a more profound reason than just spreading the news of the bishop's troops approaching the city, as reported in the chronicles of Lorenz Fries and Martin Cronthal.[44]

We have already examined the truly formative relationship between Grünewald and Riemenschneider, and there is no point in repeating it here, but we can note that Mathis's initial model was an artist later involved in the Revolt, and he, himself, was a figurative reference point for a colleague who became a prominent leader of the riots. Although there is no evidence of an active involvement in the war, it would seem legitimate to suspect that Mathis had at least open sympathy for the peasants, not enough to provoke violent consequences as with Riemenschneider and worse with Ratgeb, but at least enough to result in removal from his prestigious appointment at court. Perhaps anticipating this, Mathis placed his adopted son Endres (who later would be a schoolteacher in Frankfurt) in the workshop of sculptor Arnold Rücker in Seligenstadt (once again a special relationship with sculpture!) at the end of 1525, rather than in Mainz.[45] However, it should be said that Rücker was not only a sculptor but also an organ builder. Specifically, once again on the orders of Canon Reitzmann, in 1516 he created the instrument for the collegiate church in Aschaffenburg, and then restored it for Archbishop Albrecht following the Peasants' War.[46] Therefore, he was an artist with whom Grünewald had shared commitments and work experiences.

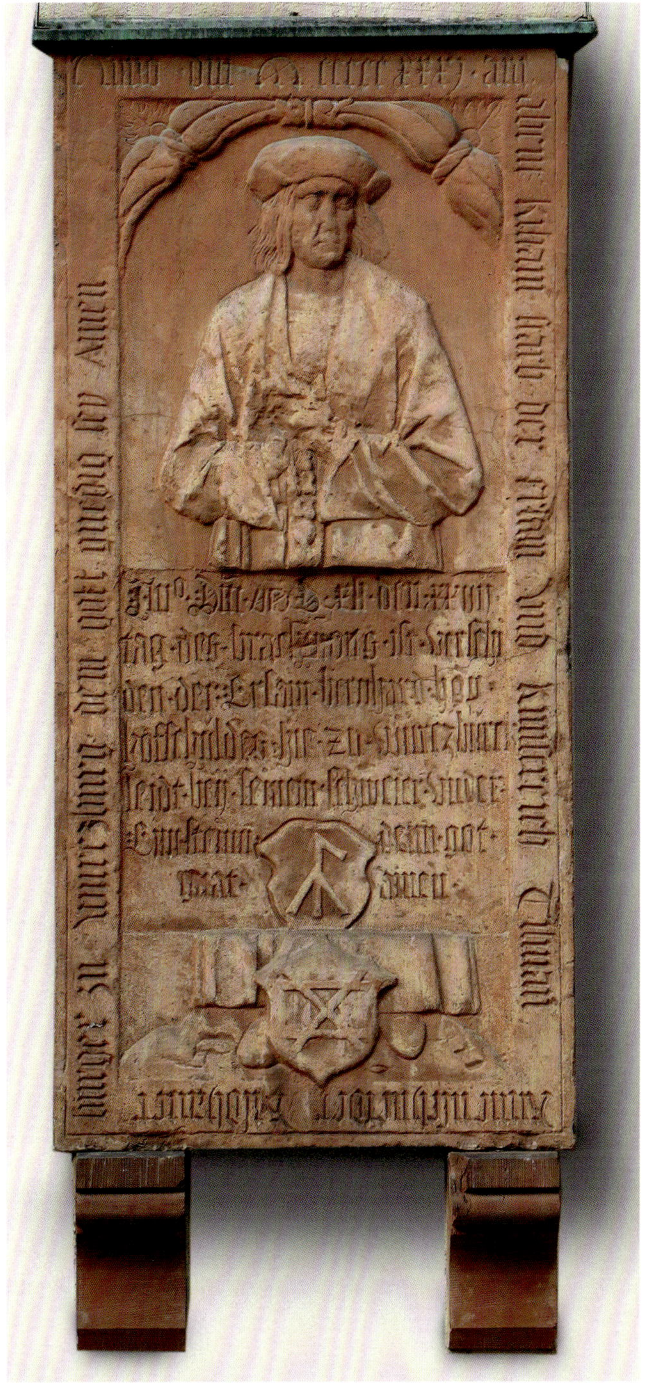

234 | *Tombstone of Tilman Riemenschneider*, 1532. Würzburg Cathedral.

It is also worth noting that on May 4, 1525, peasants in revolt sacked the Isenheim preceptory that had been abandoned by the monks who took refuge in Nancy. A number of contemporary sources report this fact, but there is no reason to think that the Grünewald altarpiece was touched, almost as if the rebels saw it as something that was truly part of their world, or saw its painter as one of their own.[47]

In June 1526, Archbishop Albrecht condemned his courtiers involved in the peasant revolt in Aschaffenburg. It may just be a coincidence, but Grünewald was replaced as court painter in the same year by the far less talented Simon Franck of Halle, and subsequently left Mainz for good.[48]

From the standpoint of affinity with the peasants, historical accounts provided by Hans Stolz and taken up in the next century by Dominican Seraphin Dietler, chroniclers of Gebwiller (today Guebwiller), in Alsace, suggest that an "evil person named Mathis Nithart" had instigated local residents to join the ranks of Müntzer followers.[49] The coincidence is striking, and yet it does not seem very likely that Mathis left the archbishop's service in 1525 to join the Alsatian rebels. Furthermore, as noted by Georges Bischoff,[50] the last name Nithart is also found in Alsace and, in fact, a Mathis with that last name, native of Eschentzwiller (other families with that name are found in Beblenheim, Turkheim, Soultzmatt and Strasburg), was banned in 1526 from Basel where he had taken refuge with other scattered rebels, thus becoming a candidate for the "evil person" reviled by Dietler. Therefore, we can essentially exclude that this Mathis Nithart was our painter.

Also, the "12 articles of faith" (specifically: "1 cleyn buchelge ingebunden erclerung der 12 artikolen des christlichen glaubens") referenced in Mathis's inventory need to be re-examined. The text of the rebels' demands was never given this name which, more generally, indicates the articles of the Creed.[51] Locating a possible German-language publisher of the edition owned by Mathis is not difficult. For example, it could be the *Erklärung der zwölf Artikel des christlichen Glaubens*, published in Ulma by Conrad Dinckmut on April 21, 1485, but the doubt arises if, in those tense times, Grünewald could really have been interested in such an old edition (it was reprinted in Nuremberg by Hans Guldenmundt in 1542, but as a "Catholic" text in opposition to "Protestant" theology), without considering that, being almost 30 cm tall and 538 pages long, it is difficult to consider it the "1 cleyn buchelge". Given the lack of similarity in the title, it is even more difficult that it could be identified with *Eyne verklerunge des eynigen waren Apostolischen Christlilchen gloubens* by Petrus Sylvius, published in Dresden by Emser on August 11, 1525. The most plausible candidate is unquestionably the text by Urbanus Rhegius, which was reprinted many times between 1521 and 1525, of which the most probable is that edited by Simprecht Küff in Augsburg on December 22, 1523, entitled *Erklärung der zwölff artickel Christliches gelaubens*, or even better, the re-edited edition published in Leipzig (publisher unknown) on March 9, 1525, entitled *Eyn erklarung der zwölff artickel Christlichs glawbens*. Smaller in size (9.62 × 13.52 cm) and with 75 sheets of paper, it would truly fit the criteria of a "cleyn buchelge" and, combined with the texts by Luther, could form the hardy nucleus of a proto-Reformation library in the vernacular.

There is an additional and decisive argument against Grünewald's active participation in the Peasants' War. Thanks to Hanns Hubach—who unquestionably has made the most important contribution regarding Grünewald in recent years—we have a clear idea of how the *Lamentation of Christ* in the collegiate church of Aschaffenburg (panel, 36 × 138 cm) was painted [fig. 235]. On the left of this painting is the coat of arms of Albrecht von Brandenburg and on the right is that of his predecessor, Dietrich von Erlach (1434–1459), who is buried in this very collegiate church, thus providing an important clue regarding the original location of the work.[52]

X-ray analysis[53] has revealed that the initial depiction, almost certainly by a 15th-century painter, showed Christ lying down according to traditional iconography, and not bent, an expedient that increases the sense of torment and also purely and simply the body's spatial command that the panel is unable to contain.[54] Mary Magdalene on the right appears tiny, and with extremely audacious creativity, the Madonna's presence is marked only by the clasped hands that just brush her son's head, as if in a caress, or as if to accompany with her hands a sad lullaby (the marvelous final chorale of the *Matthäus-Passion* by Johann Sebastian Bach comes to

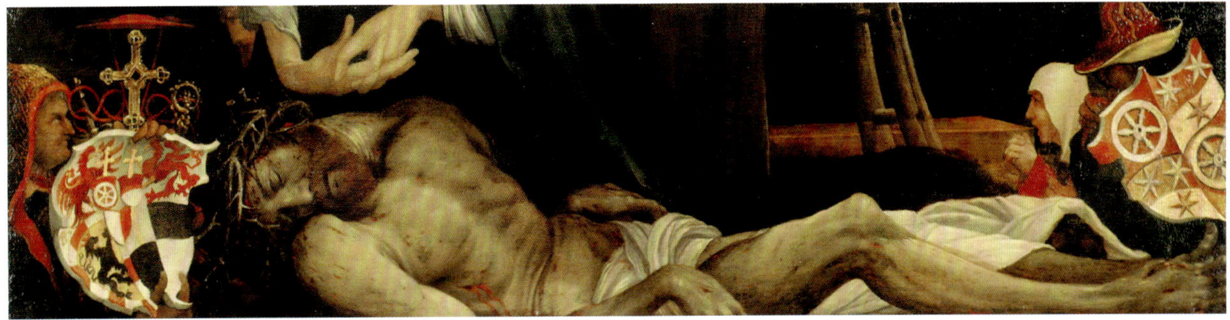

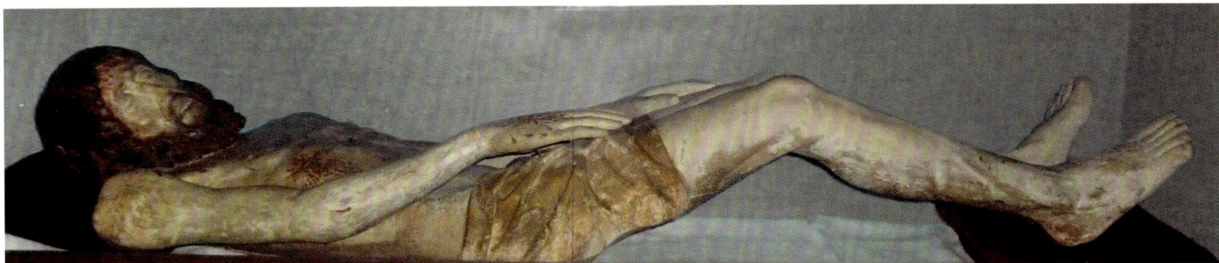

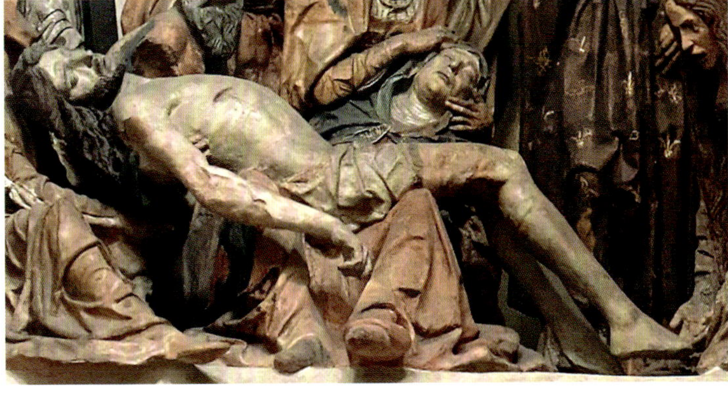

mind: "Mein Jesu, gute Nacht"![55]). Behind the dark frame of her robes, we barely glimpse the semi-hidden face of St. John. Compared with the analogous image of the *Isenheim Altarpiece*, we are struck by the proportional growth of Christ. He is no longer a heavy mass of dead flesh but, even in the agony of martyrdom, a powerful, robust body with an almost classical appearance in its anatomical perfection. Again, I must offer what I believe is an interesting comparison: a painted wooden sculpture of a *Dead Christ*, preserved in the Church of San Giuseppe in Arona, on Lake Maggiore [fig. 236]. This work, dating from the 1490s, was created in the prolific workshop of brothers Giovanni Pietro and Giovanni Ambrogio de Donati,[56] active throughout the Duchy of Milan. It has been suggested that this statue is what remains of a wooden Sepulchre, commissioned in 1501 to the sculptor Andrea da Riva San Vitale and painter Giovanni Antonio da Montonate for the Church of Santa Maria Nuova in Arona—a plausible hypothesis which, in any case, does not modify the work's critical standing.[57] Even if Grünewald did not specifically visit Arona, it is likely that during his 1516 stay in Lombardy he encountered similar works to this for sure (today, objects like this are quite rare, but in the early 1500s they were very common)[58] . An even more fitting comparison might be with the numbed Christ in the terracotta *Compianto* modeled by Agostino de Fondulis (or Fonduli) for the Church of Santa Maria presso San Satiro in Milan, about 1483 [fig. 237] (he created a further *Compianto* for the Church of San Sepolcro in Milan around 1514, though it only partially survives).[59] The way in which the figures are positioned in the limited space available is reminiscent of bas-relief techniques. It is unlikely that Grünewald, the long-standing admirer of Tilman Riemenschneider, would not have been influenced by the great sculptural tradition of the Duchy of Milan.

235 | Mathis Grünewald, Lamentation of Christ, 1525–1526. Aschaffenburg, Collegiate church.

236 | Circle of Giovan Pietro e Giovan Ambrogio De Donato (Andrea da Riva San Vitale?), *Dead Christ*. Arona, church of San Giuseppe.

237 | Agostino de Fondulis, *Lamentation of Christ*, ca. 1483. Milan, church of Santa Maria presso San Satiro.

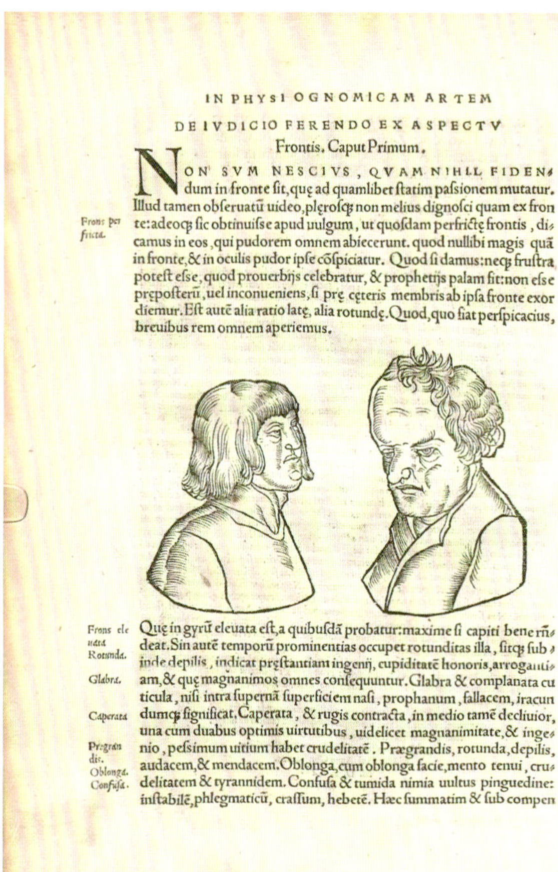

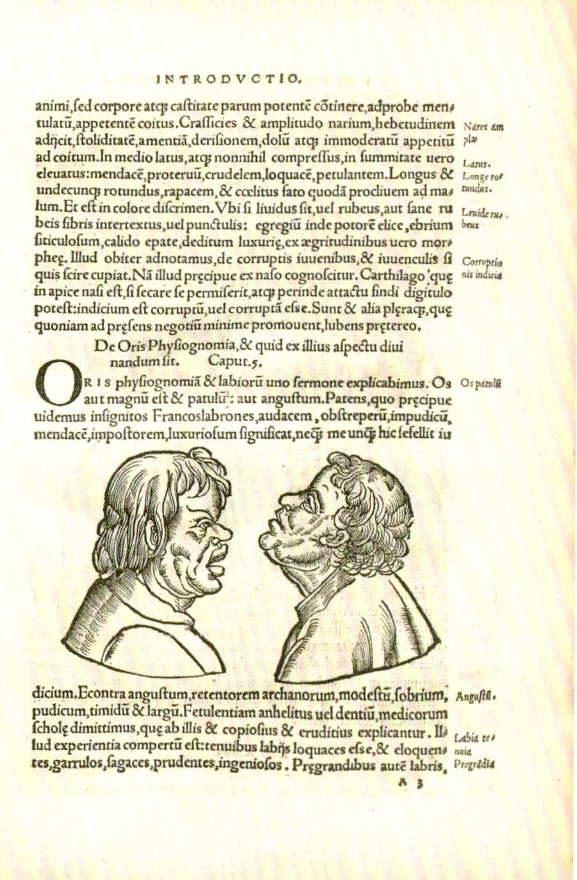

238 | Johannes de Indagine, *Introductiones Apotelesmaticae elegantes...*, Strasbourg, Johann Schott, 1522, c. 31 verso.

239 | Johannes de Indagine, *Introductiones Apotelesmaticae elegantes...*, Strasbourg, Johann Schott, 1522, c. A 3 recto.

According to Hubach, who succeeds brilliantly in keeping together technical data and information regarding style, heraldry and the archives, Mathis's contribution would in fact be "restoration" work. The painter would have intervened in the pre-existing painting that had been in the Chapel of the Holy Sepulchre in the Aschaffenburg collegiate church, following damage caused by the rebels, whose presence also involved the city.[60] This reconstruction provides an explanation for the presence of an older painting underneath and the von Erlach coat of arms (to which Albrecht, as a votive gesture, added his own), and offers a dating of 1525 for the panel which is totally convincing stylistically. It also explains the small payment (10 gulden) that Grünewald received from the Mainz court on February 27, 1526, "in abschlag seiner schuldt zu Aschaffenburg",[61] reasonable for a minor job. On the other hand, at this point we are forced to conclude that Mathis had no role in the Peasants' War.[62]

Grünewald reappears in Frankfurt on January 30, 1527, guest or tenant of the embroiderer Hans von Saarbrücken at his house "the Unicorn" (zum Einhorn). Despite being referred to as a "Maler" in the Frankfurt documents, it seems he no longer painted but rather sold paints and healing soaps in collaboration with someone named Lorenz Schneberger or Schnefeberger. On May 8 of the following year he was granted authorization to take over the plans of a mill on the Main, at the request of residents of Magdeburg, but this project almost certainly remained unfulfilled as it would once again be entrusted to Kaspar Weitz in 1528.[63] On November 5, 1535, Lorenz Schneberger was involved in a court case with Johannes Bremer von Hagen (also known as ab Indagine), a Steinheim curate and famed astrologer and "natural philosopher". The dispute over soap manufacturing tools left by Mathis to Indagine but claimed for himself by Schneberger is of particular interest, as the friendship between the painter and Steinheim clergyman opens interesting considerations about Grünewald's unusual cultural horizons. It is even more interesting that Indagine's best-known work, the *Introductiones apotelesmaticae elegantes in Chyromantiam, Physiognomiam, Astrologiam naturalem, Complexionem hominum, Naturas planetarum*, published in Strasburg in 1522 by Johann Schott (with a German edition published the following year, *Die Kunst der Chiromatzey Physiognomey, Natürlichen Astrologey, Complexion eins yegklichen mensches, Natürlichen ynflüss der planeten*), has as its frontispiece a portrait of the author based on a drawing by Hans Baldung Grien and not Mathis.[64] However, it should be noted that the second book of Indagine's treatise is dedicated to physiognomy and includes drawings of human "types" that border on caricatures, some of which are not that far (aside from a mediocre woodcut rendering) from the Berlin drawing of the three heads, to the point of suggesting a purpose behind the folio other than political-religious satire [figs. 238–239].

In the summer of 1528, Mathis journeyed to Halle, perhaps to escape the plague epidemic that had broken out in Frankfurt, or perhaps because the city so dear to Albrecht von Brandenburg had at least partially joined the Reformation. Or, more simply, because he had been called by the city council almost certainly because of his engineering skills. It seems probable that an important role in Mathis being called to Albrecht von Brandenburg's beloved city was played by the embroiderer Hans Plock, whom we have already met. Like Mathis, Plock was an artist in the service of the Mainz archbishop (it is not at all improbable that the two had worked together), and was also, in an apparently more direct and radical way, a follower of Lutheranism. He had also been elected a councilman of the city of Halle where he had been living since 1525.[65] On September 1, three city councilmen (the superintendent of the saltworks Heinrich Rumpe, the cabinet-maker Gabriel Tuntzell and the afore-mentioned Hans Plock) informed the city magistrates that "master Mathis Gothard painter and plumber, here in Halle at your service, is now with God", specifying that "his service to the city was little or nothing".[66]

The Halle authorities subsequently wrote to Frankfurt, requesting, as we have already seen, an inventory of the goods of the dead man who had left a number of creditors. The inventory was drafted between October 21 and 23. Among a number of things, paints, hydraulic equipment, elegant clothes, a title of nobility granted by the archbishop of Mainz (or perhaps a sort of proof of good behavior during the war, issued by Archbishop Albrecht on his departure: "1 rol uff eyn gebugen der uffror halben"), and ledgers of a mine. Among these belongings there were also, in a nailed case, a Bible, the twelve articles of the Creed and twenty-seven sermons by Luther. In another case there was a bound New Testament (almost certainly Luther's translation, published the first time in the famous edition of September 21, 1522, therefore the second edition revised in December of the same year, but already in 1523 at least fourteen unauthorized editions had already been printed)[67] and "many other Lutheran writings" ("das nu testament ingebunden und sunst viel scharteken luterich").[68] Also among his goods were a number of pieces of evidence of the "old" faith, indicating that Mathis had followed traditional devotional practices for some time, and perhaps had not even abandoned them completely after Luther's "discovery of the Gospel" (for example, "1 holzen paternostergen mit 6 bolger und 1 cleyn besam appell"). It would also be interesting to learn more details about the "klein bild" and, most importantly, about the two altar wings still in the priming stage (unfinished or interrupted?), one of which was once again an extreme *Crucifixion* flanked by the Madonna and St. John ("2 lid an eyn taffel sin wiss bereidt unnd uff dem einen 1 cruzifix maria und sant johannes").

If we exclude the possibility that he left the archbishop's court as a result of a disciplinary measure, his departure can be seen as a difficult personal decision, maybe driven by his inability to remain in the service of a man of power who, following the horrors of the war, he saw as being tyrannical and perhaps anti-Christian. While this interpretation might appear overly romantic, reports from those tension-filled years are replete with decisions even more dramatic than this one.

In reality, Grünewald appears to have abandoned not only his service at the archbishop's court but also painting itself. In fact, there are no reports of other works by him in his last years, which seem to have been troubled. An existential shift which, above and beyond any specific area of specialization, was amazingly sensed by Paul Hindemith in the moving finale of his *Mathis der Maler* (1938), an undisputed masterpiece of 20th-century opera, for which he also wrote the libretto:[69]

> [Part 7, Scene 2]
> ALBRECHT
> You dare to deliver
> such a message to me? Where have I failed you?
> To offer suitable remuneration
> for your truly heavenly work
> my wealth is not sufficient.
> Spare my love this torment.
> MATHIS
> Who more than you can understand my actions,
> You, who understood
> my wrongs? As you see, the work
> is finished. I have not wasted a single hour.
> I have given the world and God that which
> I did with my limited powers.
> It is time to tie up my little boat,
> and I, an old man, with nostalgia
> but without pain, can look out to sea.
> ALBRECHT
> Accept my house: a serene
> observatory towards the horizon.
> No one will distract you, only
> a friend will visit you sometimes.
> MATHIS
> Please do what is best for me. Do not waste
> anything. Little time remains me, before
> the final call. My soul
> is too weak to serve art.
> My body is worn down by the effort.
> Both calmly await
> the end, far away from those places

that saw my old ambitions.
Allow me to find a niche
in which to die, like
an animal in its forest.
ALBRECHT
As painful as the wound
you have inflicted is,
I must silently obey. Separating us is a power
we do not control. Bearing testimony
of you will always be your work:
when your body is no more,
when your name has been forgotten. Farewell.
[Last scene]
MATHIS, *alone*
The journey along this final stretch
of road I want to tread lightly.
All my fruit has fallen,
these last autumn leaves
I want to restore to the earth.
(He opens a chest and begins to place his possessions in it, tenderly taking his time over each one)
Coffer as deep as the tomb,
these small bits of death my hand
delivers to sleep: so that they preserve,
when I am buried, a final breath
(he places a roll of paper in the chest)
of the good I have done,
(he places a ruler and a compass)
of my aspirations,
(he places paints and brushes, after having caressed them)
of what I have created,
(he places a gold necklace)
of the honors,
(he places some books)
of what has disturbed me,
(he kisses the colored ribbon) [given to him by Regina, daughter of the head of the peasants, Hans Schwalb, a character invented by Hindemith]
of what I loved.[70]

I suspect that such a radical life choice, not that unlike the one intuited by Hindemith, must have arisen in this great German painter from a searing existential crisis,[71] perhaps triggered by the debate around the use and role of images which came to the forefront starting in the years immediately prior to the Peasants' War. Banned, not without iconoclastic episodes, by Andreas Karlstadt during Luther's absence from Wittenberg, hidden at the Wartburg in 1521, they were partially rehabilitated by the latter, but in a somewhat ambiguous way. As it has been seen, among the possessions listed in the 1528 inventory were twenty-seven sermons by Luther, bound in a single volume. This proves, without a shadow of doubt, that Mathis had at least read works in German of the leader of the Reformation. There is no uncertainty, as persuasively hypothesized by Reiner Marquard, that these were the *XXVII Predig D. Martin Luthers newlich vszgang en Anno XXIII* published in 1523 in Strasburg by Johann Schott and then again in Haguenau by Amandus Farckall in 1524.[72] Included in this collection are the eight famous *Invokavitpredigten*, of which there was a virtually contemporaneous edition in Mainz in 1524. Among the sermons, the theme of the one for Tuesday following *Invocabit* Sunday was *On images*, in which Luther embarks on the difficult task of blunting the weapons of intransigent iconoclasts like Andreas Karlstadt without contradicting the undoubted scriptural premises. As this important text reads:

But we must come to the images, and concerning them also it is true that they are unnecessary, and we are free to have them or not, although it would be much better if we did not have them. I am not partial to them. A great controversy arose on the subject of images between the Roman emperor and the pope; the emperor held that he had the authority to banish the images, but the pope insisted that they should remain, and both were wrong. Much blood was shed, but the pope emerged as victor and the emperor lost. [. . .] Here we must admit, that we may make images and have images, but we must not worship them, and when they are worshiped, they should be put away and destroyed, just as King Hezekiah brake in pieces the serpent erected by Moses. [. . .] Therefore it should have been preached that images were nothing and that God is not served by their erection, and they would have fallen of themselves. That is what I did; that is what Paul did in Athens, when he went into their churches and saw all their idols. He did not strike at any of them, but stood in the market-place and said, "Ye men of Athens, ye are all idolatrous." [. . .] outward things could do no harm to faith, if only the heart does not cleave to them nor put its trust in them.[73]

In the best of cases, the images, even those Grünewald painted, did not cause any damage. However, the man who must have appeared to him and many of his contemporaries as "the man of God", explicitly declared his reservations against images.[74]

And when, to a certain extent, Luther took a more favorable position towards images, in the violent tract, *Against the Heavenly Prophets*, written in 1525 against Thomas Müntzer and his followers,[75] the final step was perhaps taken. It made Luther seem—and not wrongly—a conservative: Müntzer was radically, and even violently, against images, and new blood would have to be shed.

Above all, it would seem that "the" Luther of Grünewald, that truly impacted him, was that of the twenty-seven sermons. It was that version of him, if I am right, that so shook his conscience, while it is probable that Mathis was not even aware of Luther's later 1525 tract.[76]

If my understanding of him is correct, Grünewald was not one to engage in actions he perceived as meaningless or essentially useless, nor was he one to dedicate himself to profane issues or accept commissions from both the Catholic and Reformed sides at the same time, like some Cranach. Certainly not him, who with the nails of his *Crucifixions* had crucified himself, his piercing and boundless faith, his own great figurative culture. To Mathis it was either all or nothing: thus, nothing, as always, in the Lutheran way, befits a Christian. Better to disappear as a painter, to leave the final *Crucifixion* unfinished. Better to dedicate himself to the mines, the trade, and the healing soaps. Better, finally, to die as a guest in a city which would deplore the mere fact that he had done "little or nothing".

NOTES

Preface

1. Exhibition catalogues edited respectively by: Pantxika De Paepe, Philippe Lorentz, *Grünewald et le retable d'Issenheim. Regards sur un chef-d'œuvre*, Colmar, Musée Unterlinden, 2007; Dietmar Lüdcke, *Grünewald und seine Zeit*, Karlsruhe, Staatliche Kunsthalle, 2007; Michael Roth, *Matthias Grünewald. Zeichnungen und Gemälde*, Berlin, Kupferstichkabinett, Staatliche Museen zu Berlin, 2008.

Chapter I | The Beginning

1. Joachim von Sandrart, *L'Academia Todesca della Architectura, Scultura et Pittura: Oder Teutsche Akademie der Edlen Bau-Bild-und-Malerey-Künste* (Nuremberg: Froberger, 1675, 236–237). In 1683, a Latin edition was published: *Academia nobilissimae artis pictoriae* (Nuremberg: Froberger, 1683), in which the biography of Grünewald is found on pp. 225–226. As a general reference for Sandrart, see: *Joachim von Sandrart. Ein europaeischer Künstler und Theoretiker zwischen Italien und Deutschland*, ed. by Sybille Ebert-Schifferer (Hirmer: München, 2009), and more specifically, Reiner Marquard, «Mathias Grünewald-"übel verheuratet». Eine Überprüfung von Joachim Sandrarts Grünewald-Notiz », *Aschaffenburger Jahrbuch für Geschichte, Landeskunde und Kunst den Untermaingebietes*, 21, 2001, 259–274. More generally, a detailed examination of early criticism of Grünewald is provided in Margarete Hausenberg, *Matthias Grünewald im Wandel der deutschen Kunstanschauung* (Lepzig: J. J. Weber, 1927).

2. Bernhart Jobin and Johann Fischart, *Accuratae Effigies Pontificorum Maximorum numero XXVIII ab anno Christi MCCCXXXVIII ad aetatem usque nostram praesidentium* (Strassburg: Bernhart Jobin, 1573).

3. Vincenz Steinmeyer, *Newe Künstliche, Wohlgerissene, vnnd in Holtz geschnittene Figuren dergleichen niemahlen gesehen worden. Von den fürtrefflichsten künstlichsten vnnd Berühmtesten Mahlern Reissern vnnd Formschneydern als nemlich Albrecht Dürer, Hanß Holbeyn, Hanß Sebaldt Böhem, Hanß Scheuflin und andern* (Frankfurt: Vincenz Steinmeyer, 1620).

4. A good overview of Grünewald's early fortunes is offered by François-René Martin, "Les formes de l'attribution. Réflexions sur l'historiographie de Grünewald (XVIe-XIXe siècle)", in *La technique picturale de Grünewald et de ses contemporaines*, conference proceedings (Colmar January 24–26, 2006), ed. by Pantxika Béguerie-De Paepe, Michel Menu (Colmar: Musée d'Unterlinden, 2007), 5–16. Even more accurate is that by Maristella Cervi, *Prospettive d'ékphrasis: il polittico d'Isenheim nella letteratura tedesca del Novecento*, PhD dissertation, Textual Theory and Analysis, XXI cycle, Università degli Studi di Bergamo, academic year 2008/2009, dissertation advisor Amelia Valtolina, 11–29, and Anna Schreurs-Morét, "Matthias Grünewald und der Isenheimer Altar. Vom Leuchten der Farbe zur Fama eines Künstlers", in *Der Isenheimer Altar. Werk und Wirkung*, ed. by Werner Frick, Günther Schnitzler (Freiburg im Breisgau: Rombach Verlag, 2019), 40–64. For the first modern instance, see: Thomas Noll, "Rilke und die Rezeption des sog. Matthias Grünewald im späten 19. und früher 20. Jahrundert", in *Im Schwarzwald. Uncollected Poems 1906–1911* (Blätter der Rilke-Gesellschaft, 31), ed. by Erich Unglaub, Jörg Paulus (Göttingen: Wallstein, 2012), 133–156.
A synthesis of the sources, which generally remain reliable, is provided by Piero Bianconi, *L'opera completa di Grünewald*, (Milan: Rizzoli, 1972), 82–84. The main monographs that will be referred to repeatedly in this study and which provide the documentary sources are: Heinrich Alfred Schmid, *Die Gemälde und Zeichnungen von Matthias Grünewald* (Strassburg: W. Heinrich, 1911); Louis Réau, *Matthias Grünewald et le retable de Colmar* (Nancy, Paris and Strasbourg: Berger-Levrault, 1920); Walter Karl Zülch, *Der historische Grünewald. Mathis Gothart-Neithardt* (München: Bruckmann, 1938). Of special importance are: August. L. Mayer, *Matthias Grünewald* (München: Delphin-Verlag, 1919); Hanns Heinz Josten, *Matthias Grünewald* (Bielefeld and Leipzig: Velhagen & Klasing, 1921); Willy Pastor, *Matthias Grünewald* (Berlin: Amsler & Ruthardt, 1921); Oskar F. L. Hagen, *Matthias Grünewald* (1919, definitive edition München: Piper & Co., 1922); Heinrich Feurstein, *Matthias Grünewald* (Bonn am Rhein: Verlag der Buchgemeinde, 1930); Fritz Knapp, *Grünewald* (Bielefeld and Lepizig: Velhagen & Klasing, 1935); Arthur Burkhard, *Matthias Grünewald. Personality and Accomplishment* (Cambridge (Mass.): Cambridge University Press, 1936); Marcel Brion, *Grünewald* (Paris: Librairie Plon, 1939); Adolf Max Vogt, *Grünewald. Mathis Gothart Nithart Meister gegenklassicher Malerei* (Zürich and Stuttgart: Artemis-Verlag, 1957); Nikolaus Pevsner and Michael Meier, *Grünewald* (London: Thames and Hudson, 1958); Eberhard Ruhmer, *Grünewald. The Paintings* (London: Phaidon, 1958); Arpad Weixlgärtner, *Grünewald* (Vienna and Munich: Anton Schroll & Co., 1962); Maria Lanckoronska, *Matthias Gothart-Neithart. Singgehalt und historischer Untergrund der Gemälde* (Darmstadt: Eduard Rether Verlag, 1963); Anton Kehl, *"Grünewald"-Forschungen* (Neustadt an der Aisch: Schmidt, 1964); Wilhelm Fraenger, *Matthias Grünewald*, ed. Gustel Fraenger e Ingeborg Baier-Fraenger (Dresden: Veb Verlag der Kunst, 1983: this is the reissue of two publications that already appeared in 1929 and 1936); Fedja Anzelewskj, *Matthias Grünewald. Das Gesamtwerk* (Berlin: Ullstein Taschenbuch, 1980, Italian edition *Grünewald. Tutti i dipinti*, Milano: Rizzoli, 1981); Lottlise Behling, *Matthias Grünewald* (Strasbourg: Editions des dernières nouvelles d'Alsace, 1981); Berta Reichenau, *Grünewald* (Thaur, Vienna and Munich: Kulturverlag, 1992); Pantxika Béguerie and Georges Bischoff, *Grünewald le maître d'Issenheim* (Paris: Casterman, 1996); Horst Ziermann, *Matthias Grünewald* (Munich, London and New York: Prestel, 2001); Hanns Hubach, under "Grünewald, Matthias", in *Saur. Allgemeine Künstlerlexikon*, vol. 63 (Munich: De Gruyter, 2009), 386–396, available online at https://www.degruyter.com/database/AKL/entry/_00069638T/html. These texts should be seen as underlying this entire book and they will only be referenced in specific instances. The bibliographies for individual works by Grünewald also assume the support of these texts, and solely in exceptional cases will I cite explicitly only works dedicated specifically to each painting not included in this general compendium. Notwithstanding its clear intent, I have chosen not to include in the list of primary monographs the monumental book by François-René Martin, Michel Menu

and Sylvie Ramond, *Grünewald* (Paris: Hazan, 2012, consulted in its Italian co-edition, Milan: Jaca Book, 2013). Notwithstanding Menu's essay, offering significant results from the scientific and technological analysis performed on Grünewald's paintings, and the noteworthy iconographic apparatus, the book falls short in the historical-artistic aspects, lacking philological depth and containing major gaps in the bibliography. It reflects a typically "French" approach, influenced by authors such as Daniel Arasse, Hubert Damisch, Georges Didi-Huberman, Philippe Morel, and Victor Stoichita. This approach, to varying extents, leans more towards elegant entertainment and (more or less) dazzling conversational rhetoric rather than what I can call true "art history".

5. Balthazar de Monconys, *Journal des voyages*, seconde partie (Lyon: Horace Boissat et Georges Remeus, 1666), 280.

6. According to Nicholas Meier, "Commentary on the Drawings", in Pevsner-Meier, *Grünewald*, 26–28, in particular 26, the six drawings (which will be examined in more detail later) belong to the Grimmer-Uffenbach-Schelkens album and were rediscovered by Max Friedlaender in the Savigny collection in Frankfurt, currently owned by the Berlin Staatliche Museen where they arrived in 1925 (nos. KdZ 12035–12040).

For Uffenbach, see the monograph by Ursula Opitz, *Philipp Uffenbach. Ein Frankfurter Maler um 1600* (Berlin: Deutscher Kunstverlag, 2014). For Balthasar de Monconys, one of the few contemporaries to take an interest in Vermeer, as a source on art history: Arthur comte de Marsy, *Balthasar de Monconys: analyse de ses voyages au point de vue artistique* (Caen: Le Blanc-Hardel, 1880). See also: Schmid, *Die Gemälde und Zeichnungen*, 14, and Réau, *Mathias Grünewald*, XXIX.

7. "ain schöne gemalte tafel, so mit sonderer kunst von ainem fürnemen maister". The following September 8th, the emperor wrote to Albrecht H. Zimmermann again, and for the last time on this topic, on October 27th: Heinrich Zimerman, "Urkunden, Akten und Regesten aus dem Archiv des K. K. Ministeriums des Innern" [2], *Kunsthistorische Sammlungen des Allerhöchsten Kaiserhauses*, VII, 1888, XV-LXXXIV, in particular XLIV-XLVI.

8. Elisabeth Clementz, *Les Antonins d'Issenheim. Essor et derive d'une vocation hospitalière à la lumière du temporal* (Strasbourg: Société Savante d'Alsace, 1998), 290. However, it is possible that mid-century, perhaps starting in 1632, the altarpiece, together with many other pieces of sacred art and furnishings from the Isenheim preceptory were transferred to the monastic house in Thann. In 1628, the precious objects had already been transferred from Isenheim to Thann (Clementz, *Les Antonins d'Issenheim*, 1998, 263 note 132), and two years earlier, on August 25, the Grünewald altarpiece is still mentioned in its original location (*ibidem*, 290). However, on September 25, 1650, a visitor to the monastery, although describing the Church of St. Anthony in Isenheim in glowing terms, does not seem to mention the altarpiece. Given its size, it could not have been part of "les dix autels garnis de leurs petits retables antiques" (*ibidem*, 249). In any case, the altarpiece was once again (or still?) in place on December 18, 1658, for the visit of Prince Ferdinand Maria of Bavaria, who thought it to be the work of Dürer (*ibidem*, 290).

9. Burckhardt mentions Grünewald a number of times in the second edition of the *Handbuch des Geschichte der Malerei seit Constantin dem Grossen* by Franz Theodor Kugler (Berlin: Duncker und Humblot, 1847), II, 248–251, and also in his later works (for Burckhardt's interest in Grünewald, see: Wolfgang Minaty, *Grünewald im Dialog. 500 Jahre Isenheimer Altar in Kunst, Literatur und Musik* (Regensburg: Schnell & Schneider, 2016), 16–17, 92, 145. But the entire book is useful as a summary of the critical and visual fortunes of the *Isenheim Altarpiece* and its creator. For Burkhardt as Kugler's editor and proofreader, see: Heinrich Dilly, "'Riveduta e ampliata da Jacob Burckhardt in collaborazione con l'autore'. La seconda edizione dei manuali sulla pittura e la storia dell'arte di Franz Kugler", in *La formazione del vedere. A partire da Burckhardt*, Milan conference proceedings, February 19–20, 2009, Andrea Pinotti and Maria Luisa Roli, eds., Macerata: Quodlibet, 2011, 51–71). Burckhardt's attribution of the *Isenheim Altarpiece* to Matthias can be found in "Mitteilungen aus Basel", *Kunstblatt*, 36, 1844, 151–152.

10. The report by Lerse, written in 1781, can now be found in the critical edition with commentary in: Reiner Marquard, *Matthias Grünewald und die Reformation* (Berlin: Frank & Timme, 2009), 230–253.

11. Johann Wolfgang Goethe, *Au seiner Reise am Rhein, Main und Neckar 1814 und 1815*, in *Sämtliche Werke*, hsg. von Ernst Beutler, vol. 12 (Zürich: Artemis, 1949, reprint Zürich and München: Artemis-Deutscher Taschenbuch Verlag, 1977), 565.

12. To document the research activity that led to this result, a very readable synthesis can be found in Ziermann, *Matthias Grünewald*, 9–33.

13. Hans J. Rieckenberg, "Zum Namen und zur Biographie des Malers Matthias Grünewald", in *Festschrift Hermann Heimpel* (Göttingen: Vandenkoeck & Ruprecht, 1971), I, 741–758; Idem, "Matthias Grünewald. Name und Leben neu betrachtet", *Jahrbuch der Staatlichen Kunstsammlungen in Baden-Württemberg*, II, 1974, 47–20; see also the actual monograph: *Matthias Grünewald* (Herrsching-Ammersee: Pawlak Verlag, 1976). "Rieckenberg is an historian who [. . .] has no idea of art history" (Ziermann, *Matthias Grünewald*, 29).

14. Giovanni Reale, *I misteri dell'altare di Isenheim di Grünewald. Una interpretazione storico-ermeneutica* (Milano: Bompiani, 2005), XVII–XXV, often refers to Rieckenberg, calling him "Rieckenberger".

15. In particular by Schmid, *Die Gemälde und Zeichnungen*, I, 50–56; this hypothesis found some favor, also thanks to the authoritativeness of the early-to-mid-19th-century Swiss scholar: Josten, *Matthias Grünewald*, 16–22; Hagen, *Matthias Grünewald*, 35–44 and related footnotes, although in a problematic way; Feurstein, *Matthias Grünewald*, 45–46; open skepticism of Burkhard, *Matthias Grünewald*, 6–7. Possible influence from Holbein the Elder is still acknowledged by Weixlgärtner, *Grünewald*, 17–19.

16. Regarding the works cited and the painter in general, see the edited collection: *Hans Holbein d. Ä. Die Graue Passion in ihrer Zeit*, exhibition catalogue, Stuttgart, ed. by Elsbeth Wiemann (Ostfildern: Hatje Cantz, 2010); Christoph Trepesch, Andreas Tacke, *Der ältere Holbein. Augsburg an der Schwelle zur europäische Kunstmetropole*, exhibition catalogue, Augsburg (Munich; Michel Imhof Verlag, 2024).

17. For Schongauer, see, in general: *Der hübsche Martin. Kupferstiche und Zeichnungen von Martin Schongauer (ca 1450–1491)*, ed. by Pantxika Béguerie (Colmar: Unterlinden Museum, 1991); *Le beau Martin. Études et mises au point*, conference

proceedings (Colmar, September 30–October 2, 1991), ed. by Albert Châtelet (Colmar: Musée d'Unterlinden, 1994); Pantxika Béguerie-De Paepe and Magali Haas, *Schongauer á Colmar*, exhibition catalogue, Colmar (Antwerp: Ludion, 2011).

18. Franz Bock, *Die Werke des Matthias Grünewald* (Strassburg: Heitz & Mündel, 1904), 52, who saw Mathis coming from Schongauer's workshop.

19. Feurstein, *Matthias Grünewald*, 40–43. The scholar most explicit in underscoring the contrast between Dürer and Grünewald, perhaps even going to extremes, is Eberhard Ruhmer, *Grünewald. Drawings. Complete edition* (London: Phaidon, 1970). But see also: Fedja Anzelewsky, "Albrecht Dürer und Mathis Gothart Nithardt", in *Erwin Redslob zum 70 Geburstag. Eine Festgabe* (Berlin: Blaschker, 1955), 292–300.

20. In truth, there have even been those who have seen in Grünewald's early works significant influence from Michael and also Friedrich Pacher: Hans Friedrich Schmidt, "Voraussetzungen der Kunst Grünewalds", *Zeitschrift des deutschen Vereins für Kunstwissenschaft*, VII, 1940, 89–103.

21. Daniel Hess, *Das Gothaer Liebespaar: ein ungleiches Paar im Gewand höfischer Minne* (Frankfurt am Main: Fischer, 1996); *Jahreszeiten der Gefühle. Das Gothaer Liebespaar und die Minne im Spätmittelalter*, ed. by Allmuth Schuttwolf (Ostfildern-Ruit: Verlag Gerd Hatje,1998): see also the review by Ulf Häder, in "Journal für Kunstgeschichte", II, 1998, 4, 348–352.

22. A close examination of the relationship between the Master of the Housebook and Grünewald is pointed out by Réau, *Mathias Grünewald*, 53-57 and Josten, *Matthias Grünewald*, 13–14. The comparison and substantial unification of the two works was proposed earlier by Henry Thode, "Die Malerei am Mittelrhein im XV. Jahrhundert und der Meister der Damstadter Passionscene", *Jahrbuch der preusseuschen Kunstsammlungen*, XXI, 1900, 59–74, 113–135; Bock, *Die Werke des Mathis*, 53; Friedrich Back, *Mittelrheinische Kunst. Beiträge zur Geschichte der Malerei und Plastik in vierzehnten und fünfzehnten Jahrundert* (Frankfurt am Main: Baer, 1910), 76–77. However, this meant having to set Mathis's birth date significantly earlier, leading to unresolvable contradictions. Greater kinship in the edgy graphism and pathos-filled anatomic accentuation—but not so far as to become a shared style—can be found in the panels of the Dominikusaltar, the work of a Middle Rhine painter housed in the Darmstadt Landesmuseum, as already noted by Josten, *Matthias Grünewald*, 14.

23. Robert Suckale, "Grünewald und die ältere fränkische Malerei", in Béguerie-De Paepe, Menu (eds.), *La technique picturale*, 161–166.

24. Noted when it was part of a private collection, by Kurt Bauch, "Aus Grünewalds Frühzeit", *Pantheon*, XXVII, 1969, March-April, 83–98. See also: Howard Creel Collinson, "Sacerdotal Themes in a Predella Panel of the Last Supper by Mathis Gothart-Neithart, called Grünewald", *Zeitschrift für Kunstgeschichte*, 49, 1986, 301–322; Eike Oellermann, "Der Choralaltar in der St. Michaelskirche in Lindenhardt", *Zeitschrift des deutschen Vereins für Kunstwissenschaft*, 45, 1991, 131–157 (she believes it to be the predella of the Lindenhardt altar, which we will speak about shortly); Reichenauer, *Grünewald*, 21–28.

25. Antje-Fee Köllermann, entry no. 1, in *Matthias Grünewald. Zeichnungen und Gemälde*, exhibition catalogue, Berlin, ed. by Michael Roth (Berlin: Hatje Cantz-Staatliche Museen, 2008), 79–85. On the Dürer drawing, see: Wolfgang Hütt, *Albrecht Dürer 1471 bis 1528. Das gesamte graphische Werk*, 1, *Handzeichnungen* (Herrsching: Manfred Pawlak, 1978), 1, *Handzeichnungen*, 53.

26. Stephan Fridolin, *Schatzbehalter oder Schrein der wahren Reichtümer des Heils und ewigen Seligkeit* (Nuremberg: Anton Koberger, 1491), f. q iii. The comparison is proposed in Collinson, "Sacerdotal Themes", 305.

27. For Riemenschneider, in general: Georg Anton Weber, *Til Riemenschneider. Sein Leben und Wirken* (Regensburg: J. Habbel, 1911); Justus Bier, *Tilmann Riemenschneider*, I, *Die frühen Weke* (Würzburg: Verlagsdruckerei Würzburg, 1925); II, *Die reifen Werke* (Augsburg: Dr. Benno Filser Verlag, 1930); III, *Die späten Werke in Stein* (Wien: Anton Schroll, 1973); IV, *Die Späten Werke in Holz* (Wien: Anton Schroll, 1978); Kurt Pfister, *Riemenschneider* (Dresden: Carl Reissner Verlag, 1927); Kurt Gerstenberg, *Tilman Riemenschneider* (1941, 5° ed. München: Bruckmann, 1955); *Tilman Riemenschneider. Frühe Werke*, exhibition catalogue, Würzburg, ed. by Hartmut Krohm (Berlin: Staatliche Museen Preussischer Kulturbesitz,1981); Justus Bier, *Tilmann Riemenschneider. His Life and Work* (Lexington: The University Press of Kentucky, 1982); *Tilman Riemenschneider Master Sculptor of the Late Middle Ages*, exhibition catalogue, Washington, ed. by Julien Chapuis (Washington: National Gallery of Art, 1999); Iris Kalden-Rosenfeld, *Tilman Riemenschneider. The Sculptor and his workshop* (Königstein im Taunus: Karl Robert Langewiesche Nachfolger Hans Köster Verlagsbuchandlung, 2004); *Tilman Riemenschneider c. 1460–1513*, conference proceedings (Washington, December 3–4, 1999), ed. by Julien Chapuis, Washington-New Haven-London: National Gallery of Art-Yale University Press, 2004); *Tilman Riemenschneider. Werke seiner Blütezeit*, exhibition catalogue, Würzburg, ed. by Claudia Lichte (Regensburg: Schnell Steiner, 2004); *Tilman Riemenschneider. Werke seiner Glaubenswelt*, exhibition catalogue, Würzburg, ed. by Wolfgang Schneider (Regensburg: Schnell Steiner, 2004); Matthias Weniger, *Tilman Riemenschneider. Die Werke in Bayerischen Nationalmuseum* (Petersberg: Michael Imhoff, 2017); *Riemenschneider in Situ*, ed. by Katherine M. Boivin, Gregory C. Bryda (Turnhout: Harvey Miller, 2022). For the Holy Blood Altar see also Katherine M. Boivin, *Riemenschneider in Rothenburg. Sacred Space and Civic Identity in the Late Medieval City* (University Park, PA: Pennsylvania State University Press, 2021), and first of all and especially, Michael Baxandall, *The Limewood Sculptors of Renaissance Germany* (New Haven and London: Yale University Press, 1980), 172–190, 262.

28. Collinson, "Sacerdotal Themes", 306–307, had the brilliant insight to consider "The dependence of Grünewald's panel on sculptural syntax", but it was wasted in a sterile comparison with the later predella depicting the *Last Supper* in the Church of Sts. John and Martin in Schwabach, a work dated 1506–1508 from the workshop of Michael Wolgemut, and, above all, for not being able to bring the comparison from an iconographic to a stylistic plane.

29. Grete Tiemann, "Zur Grünewaldfrage", *Cicerone*, 16 (22), 1924, 1079–1081, at 1079.

30. Wolf Lücking, *Mathis. Nachforschungen über Grünewald* (Berlin: Fröhlich & Kaufmann, 1983), 39.

31. Regarding the decision not to use color in general and in Riemenschneider's works in particular, see especially the

contributions of Jőrg Rosenfeld, "Die nichtpolychromierte Retableskulptur als bildreformerisches Phänomen im ausgehenden Mittelalter und in der beginnenden Neuzeit", in Krohm, Oellermann (eds.) *Flügel-Altäre des Späten*, 64–82; Eike Oellermann, "Polychrome or Not? That is the Question", and Michele Marincola, "Riemenschneider's Use of the Decorative Punch in Unpolychromed Sculpture", in Chapuis (ed.), *Tilman Riemenschneider c. 1460*, respectively 112–123 and 130–147; Manfred Schümann, "Gefass oder holzsichtig? Zur Problem der Fassung im Werk Tilman Riemenschneiders", in Lichte (ed.), *Tilman Riemenschneider*, 166–173.

32. This comparison is already suggested by Köllerman in the entry quoted above, but see also: Anna Morat-Fromm, "Eine Begegnung mit Folgen? Grünewald und Baldung", in *Grünewald und seine Zeit*, Karlsruhe exhibition catalogue, Karlsruhe, ed. by Dietmar Lüdke (München-Berlin: Deutsche Kunstverlag, 2007), 39–47. See also Daniel Hess and Johanna Scherer, entry no. 7–8, in *Hans Baldung Grien sacré/profane*, exhibition catalogue, Karlsruhe, ed. by Hölger Jakob-Friesen (Berlin-Munich: Deutscher Kunstverlag, 2019). 88–89.

33. For these works, see, respectively: Timothy H. Husband, entries nos. 1, 4, 21 in Chapuis (ed.), *Tilman Riemenschneider Master*, 160–162, 172–175, 246–249; and finally, for *Our Lady of the Annunciation* in the Louvre: Gerhard Lutz, entry nos. 1,2, in *Riemenschneider and Late Medieval Alabaster*, exhibition catalogue (Cleveland), ed. by Gerhard Lutz (Cleveland: The Cleveland Museum of Art in association with D Giles Limited, 2023), 90–101.

34. The 1502 dating of the panel in Saint-Germain-en-Laye proposed by Bernard Vermet, "Hieronymus Bosch: pittore, tecnica o stile?", in Jan Koldeweij, Paul Vandenbroeck and Bernard Vermet, *Hieronymus Bosch. Catalogo completo* (Milano: Rizzoli, 2001), 84–99, based on dendrochronological results from the wood base. Although this date fits within the proposed reconstruction, it should be evaluated with extreme caution, I believe. Currently, the leading view is that the painting in Saint-Germain-en-Laye is only a copy, even if the best one known, from a prototype by Bosch. See, for example: Stefan Fischer, *Hieronymus Bosch. The Complete Works* (Köln: Taschen, 2016), 265–266; Alexandra Zvereva, entry no. 14, in *Between Hell and Paradise. The Enigmatic World of Hieronymus Bosch*, exhibition catalogue, Budapest, ed. by Bernadett Tóth, Ágota Varga (Budapest: Fine Arts Museum, 2022), 116–119; and Frédéric Elsig, "L'Escamoteur de Saint-Germain-en-Laye, une oeuvre de Gielis Panhedel?" in Frédéric Elsig, Patrick Le Chanu, Agnès Virole, *Jérôme Bosch et l'Escamoteur* (Paris: Somogy, 2002), 27–31, suggests the paternity of Gielis Panhedel (ca. 1490–post 1546). Given the existence of other versions and a drawing signed by Bosch with a similar scene at the Louvre and dated around the year 1500 (Département des Arts Graphiques, inv. 19197: Erwin Pokorny, entry no. 15, in Tóth, Varga (eds.), *Between Hell and Paradise*, 120–123, with partial bibliography), the most likely hypothesis remains the earlier presence of a popular, authoritative Bosch prototype dating from the very late 15th century or the beginning of the 16th.

35. The reasons for identifying Judas in the apostle with the yellow mantle are explained by Collinson, "Sacerdotal Themes", whose liturgical interpretation of the scene, although perhaps a bit too over-elaborate, is useful in confirming the original function as a predella as the most likely one for the Grünewald painting in Coburg.

36. For example, in Krakow, this period must have been at least two years: Fritz Hellwag, *Die Geschichte des deutschen Tischlerhandwerks* (Berlin: Verlagsanstalt des deutschen Holzarbeiter-Verbandes, 1924, reprint Hannover: Schäfer, 1995), 157.

37. Roger H. Marijnissen, *Hieronymus Bosch. The Complete Works* (Oxshott: Tabard Press, 1987), 260–264; Fischer, *Hieronymus Bosch*, 251–252 (with the theory that it was created in two different time periods, starting in 1505, for reasons anything but conclusive). Dendrochronological testing would suggest a fairly acceptable 1491–1497 dating (toward the later date) on a stylistic level, bearing in mind, as already noted, all the reservations regarding a methodology that is certainly useful, but always to be taken with a grain of salt (Vermet, "Hieronymus Bosch: pittore", 88).

38. The triptych was published, already attributed to Grünewald, by Karl Sitzmann, *Der Lindenhardter Tafelbilder* (Bayreuth: Carl Giekel, 1926); also see the important essay by Oellermann, "Der Choralaltar", 131–157.

39. Maria Lanckoronska, *Matthäus Neithart sculptor. Der Meister des Blaubeurer Altars und seine Werke* (München: A. Fruhmorgen, 1965). Despite the unlikely identification, the intuition regarding the importance of sculpture in Grünewald's career is very astute, and in particular the relationship with Riemenschneider (see 143–160).

40. Ziermann, *Matthias Grünewald*, 40–44. In light of the observations made to this point and those that will follow, the sententiousness of the following affirmation is rather disturbing: "One can be fairly safe to assuming that the panels of the *Lindenhardt Altarpiece* had no connection with Master Mathis." Others contrary to attributing it to Grünewald are Wilhelm Pinder, *Die deutsche Kunst der Dürerzeit* (Leipzig: E. A. Seeman, 1940), 253–275; Lorenz Dittmann, *Die Farbe bei Grünewald* (München: Ludwig-Maximilians-Universität, Diss., 1955), 112, 172–173. The altar as the work of a "studio" is held by Vogt, *Grünewald. Meister gegenklassicher*, 33; copy of the Grünewald original for Zülch, *Der historische Grünewald*, 81, 323, also responsible for the suggestion in favor of Arnold Rücker for the sculptures (while Karl Sitzmann and Heinrich Meyer, "Hans Nussbaum. Ein Bamberger Bildschnitzer der Dürerzeit. Mit Notizen und Zuschreibungen", *Bericht des Historischen Vereins für die Pflege der Geschichte des ehemaligen Fürstbistums Bamberg*, 90, 1951, 279–320, thought of Hans Nussbaum, while more recently reference to the Michael Wolgemut studio is found in Hubach, "Grünewald, Matthias"). Also speaking about a work of uncertain attribution, due to the incompatibility with the *Mocking of Christ* in Munich (which will be discussed shortly), also dated 1503, is Ruhmer, *Grünewald. Paintings*, 127–128.

41. Italo Bacigalupo, *Der Lindenhardter Altar. Grünewald oder Hans von Kulmbach? Die Entsehungs-und Gebrauchtsgeschichte der Tafelbilder* (Petersberg: Michael Imhof Verlag, 2011). The idea to attribute the painted parts of the altarpiece to Hans von Kulmbach, collaborator of Dürer, is objectively inadmissible, and none of the numerous comparisons offered truly enter into the area of style, the only one valid in philology. But the book is noteworthy for the quality of its illustrations and wealth of bibliographical material, an indicator of very serious research,

albeit misguided, unfortunately. However this was sufficient to suspend judgement on the panels by other scholars. This approach stems from implicit distrust in attribution as a cognitive method (Michael Roth, "Dürer-Baldung-Grünewald?", in *Hans Baldung Grien. Neue Perspektiven auf sein Werk*, ed. by Hölger Jacob-Friesen, Oliver Jehle (Berlin-München: Deutscher Kunstverlag, 2019), 68–79, particularly 73). The hypothesis, recently pointed out, of a probable intervention of Grünewald in the Bindlach/ Lindenhardt altarpiece as a collaborator of the workshop of Michael Wolgemut, sounds definitely unconvincing (Isabella Sturm and Manuel Teget-Welz. "Kollegen oder Konkurrenten? Die Kooperationen des Hans von Kulmbach", in *Renaissance in Franken. Hans von Kulmbach und die Kunst um Dürer*, exhibition catalogue, Kronach, ed. by Manuel Teget-Welz and Hans Dickel (Petersberg: Michael Imhof Verlag, 2022), 87-103, at 88). The style and quality of the painted panels are homogeneous and too close to Mathis, and the several references to Tilman Riemenschneider declare the work as done by an artist trained in Würzburg.

42. Bier, *Tilmann Riemenschneider*, I, 78–86; Bodo Buczynski and Artur Kratz, "Untersuchungen an Steinbildwerken Tilman Riemenschneiders", in Bloch (ed.), *Tilman Riemenschneider. Frühe*, 335–375, particularly 343–346; Kalden-Rosenfeld, *Tilman Riemenschneider. The sculptor*, 56–59; Hartmuth Krohm, "Rudolphus de Scherenberg, Episcopus herbipolensis, Franciaeque orientalis Dux: Effigy and Rhetoric", in Chapuis (ed.), *Tilman Riemenschneider c. 1460*, 28–35.

43. Hartmuth Krohm, entry in Bloch (ed.), *Tilman Riemenschneider. Frühe*, 210–211; Kalden-Rosenfeld, *Tilman Riemenschneider. The sculptor*, 129; Jean Chapuis, entry no. 17 in Chapuis (ed.), *Tilman Riemenschneider. Master*, 233–235.

44. Bier, *Tilmann Riemenschneider*, I, 87–90; Buczynski and Kratz, in Bloch (ed.), *Tilman Riemenschneider. Frühe*, 349–351; Kalden-Rosenfeld, *Tilman Riemenschneider. The sculptor*, 50–52.

45. Lanckoronska, *Matthias Gotthart-Neithart*, 40–41; Lücking, *Mathis-Nachforschungen*, 22–23 (the Grünewald St. George is defined "Ein Kompliment für Tilman Riemenschneider"). Curiously, in the first three little poems in the collection *Nach der Natur. Ein Elementargedichte* (1988), Winifred G. Sebald identifies in the visage of St. Denys of Lindenhardt a crypto-portrait of Riemenschneider (English translation by Michael Hamburger, *After Nature*, London: Hamish Hamilton, 2003), 6–7.

46. Kalden-Rosenfeld, *Tilman Riemenschneider. The sculptor*, 127–128.

47. Hartmut Krohm, Eike Oellerman and Andrea Kleberger, "Malereien von Martinus Schwarz", in Bloch (ed.), *Tilman Riemenschneider. Frühe*, 106–114.

48. Leo Andergassen, *Bartlmä Dill Riemenschneider. Ein Würzburger Maler in Südtirol*, in Schneider (ed.), *Tilman Riemenschneider. Werke*, 150–167; Linda A. Huebert Hecht and Hanns-Paul Ties, "The Tirolian Anabaptist Artist. Bartlme Dill Riemenschneider and the Anabaptist Women in His Household, 1526–1549", *The Mennonite Quarterly Review*, 92, July 2018, 439–460; and finally, Wolfgang Strobl, "<<Ianus Bifrons>>. Ein Künstlerleben in Widerspruch und Einheit. Zu einem subversiven täuferischen Freskenzyklus Bartlme Dill Riemenschneiders in Tramin, Ansitz Lagenmantel (1547)", *Zeitschrift für bayerische Landesgeschichte*, 82, 2, 2019, 381–445, with extensive bibliography.

49. Fritz Koreny, "Riemenschneider and the Graphic Arts", in Chapuis (ed.), *Tilman Riemenschneider. Master*, 98–112 interprets the figure as a foolish Virgin. A relief depicting *Christ in the Garden*, now in the Berchetsgaden Schlossmuseum, includes on the back a black chalk drawing of a sword.

50. Paulus Weissenberger, "Die Künstlergilde St. Lukas in Würzburg", in *Archiv des historischen Vereins von Unterfranken und Aschaffenburg*, 70, 1935–1936, 175–242, at 208 no. 8.

51. Weissenberger, "Die Künstlergilde ", 209 no. 24.

52. Weissenberger, "Die Künstlergilde", 214 no. 64.

53. *Der Rats-Chronik der stadt Würzburg (XV. Und XVI. Jahrundert)*, ed. by Wilhelm Engel (Würzburg: Kommissionsverlag Ferdinand Schöning, 1950), 74–75, 93.

54. *Galerie Aschaffenburg Katalog* (München: Bayerische Staatsgemäldesammlungen, 1975), 88. The work was purchased at an auction of Hugo Helbing, Frankfurt am Main (June 12, 1928, lot 63), where it was presented as being by an "Oberdeutscher Meister". A handwritten note in the auction catalogue attributes the work to Grünewald, explaining the reasons for the purchase. The 1975 catalogue is more prudent, lamenting the lesser quality compared with the Lindenhardt altar, but its similarity and influence are noted. It is surprising that this work, which is even on public display, has not really entered into the most recent literature on Grünewald.

55. Zdzisław Kępiński, *Veit Stoss* (Warszawa and Dresden: Verlag der Kunst-Auriga, 1981), 102–107.

56. Weniger, *Tilman Riemenschneider. Die Werke*, 164–183.

57. Attributed to Grünewald by Heinz Braune, "Ein Bild von Matthias Grünewald", *Repertorium für Kunstwissenschaft*, 12, 1909, 504–507. In addition to the monographs on this painter, see also the following specific bibliography: Margrit Lurz, *Die Verspottung Christi des Mathis Gothard Nithart gen Grünewald. Ikonographie der Verspottung Christi unter besonderer Berücksichtigung des Werkes Grünewalds und seiner Beziehung zu den vorhandenen Kopien* (Köln-Wien: Böhlau Verlag, 1979), especially useful for the ample repertory of copies (80–95); Howard Creel Collinson, *Three Paintings by Mathis Gothart-Neithart, called Grünewald: the Trascendent Narrative as Devotional Image*, PhD dissertation (New Haven: Yale University, May 1986, consulted in a microfilm copy at the Bibliothèque Nationale Universitaire in Strasbourg), 77–107, with further review of the copies; Reichenau, *Grünewald*, 29–48; Jessica Mack-Andrick, entry no. 159 in Lüdke (ed.), *Grünewald und seine Zeit*, 158–159.

58. Collinson, *Three Paintings*, 85. Following a different line of reasoning, Collinson also believes "the painting would have been executed sometime during 1504".

59. It seems obvious to me that the construction of Grünewald's paintings is in no way naive, but that does not mean we have to identify them as being the extremely complicated "schlüsselcompositionen" identified by Joachim Kromer, *Matthoas Grünewald. Die Schlüsselkompositionen seiner Tafeln* (Baden-Baden: Verlag Valentin Koerner, 1978), 93–100 for the Munich *Mocking of Christ*. Similar analyses have been made of later paintings (and we will discuss these further on), such as the *Isenheim Altarpiece*, the Stuppach *Madonna*, the *Meeting of Saints Erasmus and Maurice*, also in Munich, and the double panel in Karlsruhe.

60. Zülch *Der historische Grünewald*, 104. Also see: Wolfgang Hütt, *Albrecht Dürer 1471 bis 1528. Das gesamte graphische Werk*,

2, *Das gesamte graphische Werk. Druckgrahik* (Herrsching: Manfred Pawlak, 1978), 1926; Ulrich Schulz, *Albrecht Dürer. Das druckgraphische Werk. Kupferstiche, Holzschnitte und Bücher*, I, *Die frühen Jahre bis zur zweiten italienischen Reise*, exhibition catalogue, Bad Schussenried, Erfurt and Augsburg (Bad Schussenried: Staatlichen Schlösser und Gärten Baden-Württemberg, 2011), 54–55. The bearded figure who seems to be trying to calm the fat guard could be Nicodemus, according to Gertrud Schiller, *Iconography of Christian Art*, 2 vols. (London: Lund Humphries, 1971), II, 58.

61. Baxandall, *The Limewood Sculptors*, 123–127.

62. Daantje Meuwissen, "A Painter in Black and White? The Symbiotic Relationship between the Paintings and the Woodcuts of Jacob Cornelisz. van Oostanen", in *Making and Marketing. Studies of the Painting Process in Fifteenth- and Sixteenth-Century Netherlandish Workshops*, ed. by Molly Faries (Turnhout: Brepols, 2006), 55–81.

63. Kępiński, *Veit Stoss*, 64–66; Rainer Kahsnitz, "Volckamersche Gedächtnisstiftung", in *Veit Stoss in Nürnberg. Werke des Meisters und seiner Schule in Nürnberg und Umgebung*, exhibition catalogue, Nuremberg, ed. by Rainer Kashnitz (Munich: Deutscher Kunstverlag, 1983), 218–258. As stressed by Collinson, *Three Paintings*, 105–106, the Volckamer monument was also a memorial, even if sculpted.

64. The presence in Nuremberg of the young Mathis, even if seen from the perspective of Dürer and within the context of a reconstruction of our painter's youth that is quite different from the one here traced, was already asserted by Charles Sterling, "Grünewald vers 1500–1505", *Cahiers Alsaciens d'archéologie d'art et d'histoire*, XIX, 1975–76, 127–144. See also: Anzelewsky, "Albrecht Dürer und Mathis", 292–300.

65. Gert von der Osten, "Job and Christ. The Development of a Devotional Image", *Journal of the Warburg and Courtauld Institute*, XVI, 1953, 153–158.

66. James H. Marrow, *Passion Iconography in Northern European Art of the Late Middle Ages and Early Renaissance. A Study of the Transformation of Sacred Metaphor into Descriptive Narrative* (Kortrijk: Van Ghemmert Publishing Co.), 1979, 319.

67. Erwin Panofsky, *The Life and Art of Albrecht Dürer* (Princeton: Princeton University Press, 1955, ed. 1971), 92–94.

68. Stephan Kemperdick, "Die *Kreuzigung* im Kunstmuseum Basel", in Béguerie-De Paepe, Menu (eds.), *La technique picturale*, 65–72. But also see for more on this question.

69. Ruhmer, *Grünewald Paintings*, 117.

70. Bier, *Tilmann* Riemenschneider, IV, 72–80. Also see the entries by Hartmut Krohm, Andrea Kleberger and Erwin Meyer in Bloch [ed.], *Tilman Riemenschneider. Frühe*, 56–72; Manfred Schürmann and Claudia Lichte, entry nos. 30–31 in Lichte (ed.), *Tilman Riemenschneider. Werke*, 280–281; Michael Koller, entries nos. 24–25 in Schneider (ed.), *Tilman Riemenschneider. Werke*, 230–233.

71. These observations are again thanks to Kemperdick, "Die *Kreuzigung*", in Béguerie-De Paepe, Menu (eds.), *La technique picturale*, 65–72. On the etching by the Master of the Calvary see also Tobias Pfeifer-Helke, entry, in *Mit den Gezeiten. Frühe Druckgraphik der Niederlande: Katalog der niederländischen Druckgraphik von den Anfängen bis um 1560 in der Sammlung des Dresdener Kupferstich-Kabinetts*, exhibition catalogue, Dresden (Petersberg: Imhof, 2013), 82.

72. Szilvia Bodnár, *German Drawings of the Fifteenth and Sixteenth Century in the Museum of Fine Arts, Budapest* (Budapest: Museum of Fine Arts, 2020), 23–24.

73. About Hans Geiler, see: Stephan Gasser, Katharina Simon-Muscheid, Alain Fretz, *Die Freiburger Skulptur des 16. Jahrhunderts. Herstellung, Funktion und Auftraggeberschaft* (Petersberg: Michael Imhoff Verlag, 2011), II, 182–369.

74. It is perhaps no accident that a piece very similar and certainly also attributable to the circle of Hans Geiler, found in the Szépművészéti Múzeum in Budapest, has been connected to the studio of Tilman Riemenschneider: Jolán Balogh and Éva Szmodis-Eszlàry, *Katalog der Ausländischen Bildwerke des Museums der Bildenden Kunste in Budapest. IV.-XVIII. Jahrhundert*, III, *Neuerwerbungen* (Budapest: Akademiai Kiadó, 1994), 55.

Chapter II | Early Maturity

1. Élisabeth Ravaud, Elsa Lambert and Patrick Le Chanu, « Le *Retable d'Issenheim*. Résultats de l'imagerie scientifique», in Béguerie-De Paepe, Menu (eds.), *La technique picturale*, 40–48.

2. On the function and technique of the drawings in Grünewald's work, see Michael Roth, *Mit Licht gemalt und zeichnet- Grünewalds Zeichnungen und Grisaillen*, and Georg Josef Dietz, Irene Brücle, Gerhard Banik, *Grünewalds Zeichentechnik*, in Roth (ed.), *Matthias Grünewald. Zeichnungen*, respectively 54–61 and 62–69.

3. See the good entry by Michael Roth, *Matthias Grünewald. Die Zeichnungen* (Berlin and Ostfildern: Hatje Cantz, 2008), 36–37, with bibliography and proposed dating to ca. 1509–1511; less cogent the parallel one by Jessica Mack-Andrick, in Lüdke (ed.) *Grünewald und seine Zeit*, 164–166. Here is the fundamental bibliography for the drawings. This includes the standard monographs and the catalogues cited above, which will serve as a constant point of reference, unless otherwise stated. It includes: Max I. Friedländer, *Die Zeichnungen des Matthias Grünewald* (Berlin: Grote'sche Verlagsbuchhandlungen, 1927); Guido Schoenberger, *The drawings of Mathis Gothart Nithart, called Grünewald* (New York: Bittner, 1948); Lottlise Behling, *Die Handzeichnungen des Mathis Gothart Nithart genannt Grünewald* (Weimar: Hermann Böhlaus Nachfolger, 1955); Günther Jacobi, *Kritische Studien zu den Handzeichnungen von Matthias Grünewald. Versuch einer Chronologie*, Inaugural-Dissertation zur Erlagungen des Docktorgradee der Philosophischer Fakultät der Universität Köln, July 14, 1956; Ruhmer, 1970; Fritz Baumgart, *Grünewald. I disegni* (Florence: La Nuova Italia, 1974).

4. Albert Châtelet, entry no. 80 in *Der hübsche Martin*, 358–359.

5. Dieter Koepplin, in Dieter Koepplin and Tilman Falk, *Lukas Cranach. Gemälde Zeichnungen Druckgraphik*, Basel exhibition catalogue, (Basel and Stuttgart: Birkhäuser, 1974), I, 252–253; Joachim Jacoby, entry no. 51 in *Cranach l'altro Rinascimento*, exhibition catalogue, Rome, ed. by Anna Coliva, Bernard Aikema (Milan: 24 Ore Cultura, 2011), 288–289.

6. Susanne Kern, *Deutsche Malerei des 15. Und 16. Jahrunderts im Landesmuseum Mainz. Ausgewälte Werke* (Mainz: Landesmuseun Mainz, 1999), 52–61, with previous bibliography; Stephan Kemperdick, entry no. 77 in *Geschichte der bildenden*

Kunst in Deutschland, 4, *Spätgotik und Renaissance* (Munich: Prestel-Deutscher Taschenbuch Verlag, 2007), 333.

7. *Gemäldegalerie Berlin. Gesamtverzeichnis* (Berlin: Staatliche Museen zu Berlin-Preussische Kulturbesitz, 1996), 14.

8. Regarding the Aschaffenburg fireplace, see especially Bernhard Saran, *Matthias Grünewald. Mensch und Weltbild*, (Munich: Wilhelm Goldmann, 1982), 75–121; Ziermann, *Matthias Grünewald*, 19–22. Precisely Saran, *Matthias Grünewald. Mensch*, 21, notes that the profession of hydraulic engineer required expertise in the use of carpentry and sculpting materials, a fact that would fit well into the hypothesis of Grünewald training alongside, or at least in close contact with, Tilman Riemenschneider.

9. Bodo Brinkmann, entry in Bodo Brinkmann, Stephan Kemperdick, *Deutsche Gemälde im Städel 1500–1550* (Mainz am Rhein: Verlag Philipp von Zabern, 2005), 352–373; Astrid Reuter, "Zur Geschicthe des Heller-Altars" and entry nos. 6–7 in Lüdke (ed.), *Grünewald und seine Zeit*, 127–130, 136–139. On the "Heller monochromes" see, especially, Saran, *Matthias Grünewald. Mensch*, 122–188; Franziska Sarwey, *Grünewald-Studien. Zur Realsymbolik des Isenheimer Altars* (Stuttgart: Urachhaus, 1983), 30–39; Bernhard Decker, "Notizen zum *Heller-Altar*", *Städel-Jahrbuch*, N. F., 10, 1985,179–192; Bernhard Decker, *Dürer und Grünewald. Der Frankfurter Heller-Altar. Rahmnenbedingungen der Altarmalerei* (Frankfurt am Main: Fischer, 1996; Ewald M. Vetter, *Grünewald. Die Altäre in Frankfurt, Isenheim und Aschaffenburg und ihre Ikonographie* (Weissenhorn: Anton H. Konrad, 2009), 9–18; Elsbeth Wiemann, entry nos. 36–39 in Eadem (ed.), *Hans Holbein d. Ä* , 228–239.

10. Dietmar Lüdke, entry nos. 4–5 in Idem (ed.), *Grünewald und seine Zeit*, 131–135.

11. On Heller, see the lovely profile in Wolfgang Schmid, "Jakob Heller—ein Frankfurter Stifter und Auftraggeber", in Lüdke (ed.), *Grünewald und seine Zeit*, 48–57.

12. So reads the original text (I cite the excellent transcription in the appendix to Marquard, *Grünewald und die Reformation*, 220–229): "Dieser fürtrefliche Künstler hat zur Zeit Albrecht Dürers ungefehr Anno 1505. gelebet/ welches an dem Altar von der Himmelfahrt Mariae/ in der Prediger Closter zu Frankfurt von Albrecht Dürer gefärtiget/ abzunehmen/ als andessen vier Flügel von aussenher/ wann der Altar zugeschlossen wird/ dieser Matthaeus vom Aschaffenburg mit liecht in grau und schwarz diese Bilder gemahlt/ auf einem ist S. Lorenz mit dem Rost/ auf dem andern eine S. Elisabeth/ auf dem dritten ein S. Stephan/ und auf dem vierdten ein ander Bild/ so mir entfallen/ sehr zierlich gestellet/ wie es noch allda zu Frankfurt zu sehen." There is some ambiguity, but which seems to be clarified in the 1683 Latin edition, which I quote from Réau, *Mathias Grünewald*, 344–345: "Vixit autem artifex hic noster temporibus Alberti Dureri, circa annum Christi 1505, quod apparet ex altari quodam historia Assuntionis Mariae in coenobio Praedicatorum Francofurtensi ab Alberto Durero exornato, cujus valvae quatuor Matthaeus hic Aschaffenburgensis monochromate griseo pinxit, in una S. Laurentium cum crate; altera S. Elisabetham; in tertia S. Stephanum et in quarta imaginem quandam similem repraesentans, quae omnia Francofurti adhuc spectari queunt." Strangely, Sandrart states that the monocromatic columns painted on the back of the four saints are the work of a "Johannes Grunewald", a different artist: "valvas illas tabulae Dürerianae supra commemoratas, quas Matthaeus Aschaffenburgensis extrorsum pinxerat, hic noster interius magna industria atque elegantia pinxerit. Deinde et diagraphica quaedam ab illo facta supersunt; nec non xylographica quaedam, ubi mulieres quaedam pingues igni assidentes ollam penes se habent unguentariam cum furcis et hircis, quasi jamjam ad choreas nocturnas advolaturae" (Sandrart, *Academia nobilissimae artis*, 226). I cannot explain why Sandrart introduces this fictitious Johannes Grunewald, evidently confused with Hans Baldung Grien (author of a lot of drawings depicting witches in frightful, ridiculous or even pornographic situations), attributing to him a role in the "Heller panels". But his description informs us that at Sandrart's time the saints were placed in the external, and the columns in the internal part of the polyptych. We can think at least that the panels painted by Grünewald had been dismembered from the original position and replaced, because it is logical that the side with the columns was the most exterior of the whole altarpiece.

13. The story behind the purchase by the Karlsruhe museum is told in Jens Lauts, *Staatliche Kunsthalle Karlsruhe. Neuerwerbungen alter Meister 1966–1972* (Karlsruhe: Staatliche Kunsthalle, 1973), 10–23.

14. For this story, see Panofsky, *The Life and Work* (ed. 1971), 161–165). Briefly, also see again Christof Metzger, *The Heller Altarpiece*, in *Dürer*, Vienna exhibition catalogue, ed. by Christof Metzger (Munich-London: Prestel, 2020), 302–318. Full documentation on the Heller altar is published with commentary in *Albrecht Dürer. Documentary Biography*, Edition Translation Commentary by Jeoffrey Ashcroft (New Haven-London: Yale University Press, 2016), I, 208–231.

15. *Albrecht Dürer. Documentary Biography*, I, 224.

16. Ruhmer, *Grünewald drawings*, 83; Ewald M. Vetter, "Die 'Hellerflügel' Grünewalds und das Verklärungs-Retabel der Dominikanerkirche in Frankfurt", *Jahrbuch der Staalichen Kunstsammlungen in Baden-Württemberg*, 13, 1976, 23–54; Idem, *Grünewald. Die Altäre*, 9–25.

17. *Galerie Aschaffenburg Katalog*, 87, with bibliography; Johann Georg von Hohenzollern, *Staatsgalerie Aschaffenburg* (München-Zürich: Schnell & Steiner, 1984), 43.

18. Ernst Buchner, *Die Alte Pinakothek München. Meisterwerke der europäische Malerei* (Munich: Hirmer, 1957), 12; Weixlgärtner, *Grünewald*, 129 (who admits, however, that he only knows the painting from photographs); Bianconi, *L'opera completa*, 101. The 1975 museum catalogue's observation that the *Portrait of a Priest* is stylistically similar to the predella with the *Fourteen Holy Helpers* mentioned earlier is, in my opinion, no less significant. Through a tortuous path, the Portrait was purchased by the London antiques dealer Agnew's in 1938, which received in exchange, with the approval of Adolf Hitler himself, the *Portrait of Bindo Altoviti* by Raphael (which Buchner erroneously believed to be a workshop piece, and described it as such in the last catalogue in which it appeared in Munich: *Illustrated Catalogue Alte Pinakothek Munich*, Munich: Carl Gerber, 1938, 207–208), *The Quack Doctor* by Gerrit Dou, today at the Boijmans van Beuningen Museum in Rotterdam and a Madonna by Rubens which ended up at the Snijders and Rockoxhuis, Antwerp: Jane van Nimmen, "Italy, Germany, America: the Migration of a Raphael Portrait", in *Raphael, Cellini and a Renaissance Banker: the Patronage of Bindo Altoviti*, Boston and Florence

exhibition catalogue, ed. by Alan Chong, Daniele Pegazzano and Demetrios Zikos (Boston: Isabella Stewart Gardner Museum, 2003), 214–236, especially 225–226 and accompanying notes. Quite astonishing is the disdain expressed by François-René Martin, 2013, 39, who dismisses the work as being of "very poor quality". But it becomes somewhat less surprising if we consider that soon after (48) the same author defines as "very beautiful" the *Portrait of a Young Artist* at the Art Institute di Chicago, inv. 1947.77 [fig. 51], which attained a certain fame in the 1930s as a self-portrait of Mathis (identified again as such by Walter Karl Zülch, *Grünewald. Mathis Neithart genannt Gothart*, Leipzig: E. A. Seeman, not dated but 1949, tav. I) but which could reasonably be considered a forgery (this also seems the veiled opinion of A. Weixlgärtner, *Grünewald*, 25). For an updated bibliography on this painting, optimistically dated ca. 1500, see: Martha Wöllfl (ed.), *Northern European and Spanish Painting before 1600 in the Art Institute of Chicago*, Chicago: Art Institute of Chicago, 2008, 424–430). The face of the young artist is a faithful, but somewhat younger, version of that of the *St. Sebastian* in the *Isenheim Altarpiece* (often considered to be a crypto-self-portrait of Grünewald), starting with the dissymmetry of the eyes and the uneven bangs on his forehead. The hands are generically Grünewaldian, while the half-filled glass decanter on the shelf on the back wall imitates the one in the *Allegory of the Incarnation* in Isenheim. There is also a sly *pentimento*, and the monogram MN. After all, in Martin's analysis, superficiality abounds. If the work really was "certainly painted prior to 1500—perhaps even before 1480", it would take its place alongside, or even pre-date, the very early self-portraits of the young Dürer, and therefore would have to be considered a very important work for Rhenish painting. At that point, analogies with Grünewald's mature works would demand much greater attention, but this is not forthcoming from the French scholar who, after offering his hasty opinion, completely ignores it.

19. On this, see the entry by Bodo Brinkmann, in Brinkmann, Kemperdick (eds.), *Deutsche Gemälde im Städel*, 142–152.

20. Stephan Kemperdick, entry in Brinkmann, Kemperdick (eds.), *Deutsche Gemälde im Städel*, 124–141.

21. It should be noted that already Lücking, *Mathis-Nachforschungen*, 46–59, and then as a monograph in Idem, *Grünewald. Der Stalburg-Altar* (Berlin: Fröhlich & Kaufmann, 1986), compared the Stalburg panels with works by Grünewald, even going so far as to identify Mathis as the artist of the Stalburg panels. This hypothesis may go too far, but his intuition deserved greater interest in later historiography.

22. Fritz Herrmann, *Die Protokolle des Mainzer Domkapitels*, III, *Die Protokolle aus der Zeit des Erzbischofs Albrecht v. Brandenburg 1514–1545*, vol. I (Paderborn 1932: Verlag Ferdinand Schöning anastatic reprint Darmstadt: Hessische Historische Kommission, 1974), 165, 348, 587.

23. Kehl, *"Grünewald"-Forschungen*, 77–83.

24. Wolfgang Brückner, *Kult und Kunst um 1500. Riemenschneider und die Glaubenswelt seiner Zeit*, in Schneider (ed. by), *Tilman Riemenschneider. Werke*, 31–49, especially 43.

25. The largest collection of information about Reitzmann is provided by Hanns Hubach, *Matthias Grünewald. Der Aschaffenburger Maria-Schnee-Altar. Geschichte-Rekonstruktion-Ikonographie* (Speyer; Verlag der Gesellschaft für mittelrheinische Kirchengeschichte, 1996), 14–28.

26. Schmid, *Die Gemälde und Zeichnungen*, 287: Zülch, *Der historiche Grünewald*, 409, footnote 17.

27. Very correctly, Roth, *Matthias Grünewald die Zeichnungen*, 38, already suggests a dating of about 1509–1511, although the same author, in *Grünewald et le retable d'Issenheim. Regards sur un chef-d'oeuvre*, exhibition catalogue, Comar, ed. by Pantxika Béguerie-De Paepe, Philippe Lorentz (Paris-Comar: Somogy Editions d'Art-Musée d'Unterlinden-Societé Schongauer, 2007), 121, had just given a later chronology.

28. Ruhmer, *Grünewald drawings*, 21.

29. This is the original German text: "Ferner waren von dieser edlen Hand zu Maynz in dem Domm auf der linken Seiten des Chors/ in drey unterschiedlichen Capellen/ drey Altar-Blätter/ jedes mit zweyen Flügeln in- und auswendig gemahlt/ gewesen// deren erstes war unsere liebe Frau mit dem Christkindlein in der Wolke/ unten zur Erden warten viele Heiligen in sonderbarer Zierlichkeit auf/ als S. Catharina/ S. Barbara/ Caecilia/ Elisabetha/ Apollonia und Ursula/ alle dermassen adelich/ natürlich/ holdselig und *correct* gezeichnet/ auch so wohl *colorirt* dass sie mehr im Himmel/ als auf Erden zu seyn scheinen. Auf ein anderes Blat war gebildet ein blinder Einsidler/ der mit seinen Leitbuben/ über den zugefrornen Rheinstrom gehend/ auf dem Eiss von zween Mördern überfallen/ und zu todt geschlagen wird/ und auf seinem schreyenden Knaben ligt/ an Affecten und Ausbildung mit verwunderlich natürlichen wahren Gedanken gleichsam überhäuft anzusehen; das dritte Blat war etwas *imperfecter*/ als vorige zwey/ und sind sie zusammen Anno 1631. oder 32. in damaligem wilden Krieg wggenommen/ und n einem Schiff nach Schweden versandt worden/ aber nemen vielen andern dergleichen Kunststücken durch Schiffbruch in dem Meer zu Grund gegangen" (Marquard, *Grünewald und die Reformation*, 224–225). This is the original 1683 Latin text: "Deinde et Moguntiae in aede Dominica ad sinistram chori in tribus sacellis trium ab ipso pictae erant altarium tabulae, duabus valvis singulae utrinque expictis instructae quarum una D. referebat Virginem cum filiolo in nube quadam, sub qua in terra multae Sanctae elegantissime appositae, quales S. Catharina, S. Barbara, Caecilia, Elisabetha, Apollonia et Ursula, tam nobili omnes invento, naturam tam proximae imitantes, tantaque gratia delineatae, coloribus ram conspicuae, ut in coelo potius quam in terra apparere viderentur. In tabula altera exhibitus erat eremitas quidam caecus, quem cum puero duce per Rheni glaciem transeuntem duo latrones obrutum occidebant, clamanti puero suo incumbentem, tanto affectu tantaque natura ut admiratione obrueretur spectator. Tertia autem tabula paulo quidem erat imperfectior. Sed et haec cum coeteris anno 1631 vel 32 inter alias belli praedes navi quadam in Sueciam transmittendas, exorta in mari tempestate, naufragio cum pluribus artificiis similibus absorpta periit" (Réau, *Mathias Grünewald*, 345). Bianconi, *L'opera completa*, 95–96, hypothesizes that at least one of these works actually did not end up at the bottom of sea, but instead among the works of collector Pieter Spieringh. This line of investigation has recently been studied by Wolfgang Minaty, *Grünewalds verschollenes Bild Untergegangen? Der Fall Alban wird wieder aufgerollt* (Mainz: Nünnerich-Asmus, 2018), who points out that the Grünewald works could not have been taken from the Mainz Cathedral in 1631 or 1632 (though it must be said

that Sandrart indicates that date with a certain margin of doubt). About Spieringh, also see Badeloch Noldus, "An "unvergleichbarer Liebhaber". Pieter Spierinck, the art-dealer diplomat", *Scandinavian Journal of History*, 31, 2006, 173–185; Susanne Meurer," <<Yearning for Biography>>. The Elusive Life of Mathis Grünewald", in *The Challenge of the Object*, conference proceedings (Nuremberg, July 15–20, 2012), ed. by Georg Ulrich Grossmann, Petra Krutisch (Nuremberg: Verlag des Germanischen Nationalmuseums, 2013), 1050–1054, especially 1052. Regarding the Swedish domination of Mainz, see Hermann-Dieter Müller, *Der schwedischer Staat in Mainz, 1631–1636. Einnahme, Verwaltung, Absichten, Restitution* (Mainz: Stadtbibliothek, 1979). The Aschaffenburg paintings didn't meet the same fate: Christian Leo, *Würzburg unter schwedischer Herrschaft, 1631–1633. Die "Summarische Beschreibung" des Joachim Ganzhorn* (Würzburg: Echter Verlag, 2017).

30. Renate Kolle, entry no. 11.3, in *Dürer Holbein Grünewald. Meisterzeichungen der deutscher Renaissance aus Berlin und Basel* exhibition catalogue, Berlin and Basel (Ostfildern-Ruit: Verlag Gerd Hatje, 1997), 179–181 dated "um 1511/12"; Roth, Matthias *Grünewald die Zeichnungens*, entry, 39–40, dated "um 1509–11 (?)".

31. Weniger, *Tilman Riemenschneider. Die Werke*, 72–104.

32. Roth, entry in Béguerie-De Paepe, Lorentz (eds.), *Grünewald et le retable*, 116–117, and Idem, *Matthias Grünewald die Zeichnungen*, 41.

33. "Absonderlich aber ist sehr preiswürdig die von ihme mit Wasserfarben gebildete Verklärung Christi auf dem Berg Thabor/ als worinnen zuvordest eine verwunderlich-schöne Wolke/ darinnen Moyses und Elias erscheinen/ samt denen auf der Erden knienden Aposteln/ con *Invention, Colorit* und alle Zierlichkeiten so fürtrefflich gebildet/ dass es Selzsamkeit halber von nichts übertroffen wird/ ja es ist in Manner und Eigenschaft unvergleichlich/ und eine Mutter aller *Gratien*" (Marquard, *Grünewald und die Reformation*, 223–224). This is the 1683 text in Latin: "Prae ceteris autem magnam meretur laudem ejusdem Transfiguratio Christi colore aquario picta, in qua imprimis nubes illa pulcherrima, in qua Moyses et Elias apparent, cum Apostolis genibus in terra nixis tam elegantem prae se fert inventionem, colores tam vividos et venustatem tam admirabilem ut carius nihil dici queat, opusque vere sit incomparabile" (Réau, *Mathias Grünewald*, 345).

34. Kehl, *"Grünewald"-Forschungen*, 120–121.

35. Roth, *Matthias Grünewald die Zeichnungen*, 24–27, dated "Um 1510/11". It should not be excluded that both the Rotterdam and Dresden drawings belonged in the past to the same collector, such a connoisseur of Grünewald's work as to indicate on the drawings the city to which the work is connected.

36. Roth, *Matthias Grünewald die Zeichnungen*, 28–33, 63–64, dated "Um 1510–11", except for no. AM 21–1953 with a more convincing dating of "Um 1516–19". Regarding the "Hans Plock Bible" (edition published by Hans Lufft in Wittenberg in 1541 with the Luther translation) see Werner Timm, "Die Einklebungen der Lutherbibel mit den Grünewaldzeichnungen", *Forschungen und Berichte der Staatlichen Museen zu Berlin*, 3, 1957, 105–121; Maria Deiters, "Bible, Image, Artist–The Bible of Hans Plock", in *"Wading Lambs and Swimming Elephants". The Bible for the Laity and Theologians in the Late Medieval and Early Modern Era*, ed. by Wim François and August den Hollander (Leuven-Paris-Walpole, MA: Peeters Publishers, 2012), 153–180; *Die Hausbibel des Seidenstickerts Hans Plock (ca. 1490–1570). Wege der Erschliessung*, ed. by Albrecht Henkys, Claudine Moulin (Heidelberg: Universität Winter, 2022), and below in this book.

37. Behling, *Die Handzeichnungen des Mathis*, 24–29; Vetter, *Grünewald Die Altäre*, 14–25 and accompanying notes. The relationship between Grünewald and Ratgeb, and with the Halle *Heiltumsbuch*, printed in Nuremberg in December 1520, will be discussed later in Chapter 5. See the anastatic reprint, with foreword by Heinrich L. Nickel (Halle: Verlag Janos Stekovics, 2001).

38. Colin Eisler, *Paintings from the Samuel H. Kress Collection. European Schools Excluding Italians*, (Oxford: Oxford University Press, 1977), 19–23; John Oliver Hand, *German Paintings of the Fifteenth through Seventeenth Centuries* (Washington and Cambridge: National Gallery of Art–Cambridge University Press, 1995), 70–81, extremely detailed technical, historical and bibliographical information, but fairly elusive regarding chronology which remains broad (and therefore definitely inconclusive) to between 1511–1520.

39. For the entire documentation Zülch, *Der historische Grünewald*, 324–326.

40. Reference to the eclipse is offered by Zülch, *Der historische Grünewald*, 1938, 123–131, who, however, in his discussion, inserts the "Small Crucifixion" immediately prior to Isenheim; the astronomical event becomes a dating criterion for Weixlgärtner, *Grünewald*, 28–34. The same eclipse was depicted by Bosch in this triptych of the *Temptation of St. Anthony*, today at the Museu Nacional de Arte Antiga in Lisbon, datable no later than 1505: Gloria Vallese and Giangiacomo Gandolfi, "1 Ottobre 1502: Jheronimus Bosch, un'eclissi anulare e la passione di Cristo", in *"Ad una ad una annoverar le stelle"*, XIX Congresso della Società Italiana di Archeoastronomia Università di Bari, ed. by Elio Antonello (Padua: Padova University Press, 2022, 195–214.

41. Ruhmer, *Grünewald paintings*, 120–121; Ziermann. *Matthias Grünewald*, 164–166.

42. Antje-Fee Köllermann, entry no. 36 in Roth (ed.), *Matthias Grünewald Zeichnungen*, 219–223 (important for the survey of the copies). It is important to note that, although without explaining the reasons, Hubach, "Grünewald, Matthias", dates the work to around 1511–1512. However, based on the discussion that follows, I also believe this is the correct chronology.

43. See the precise and cogent analysis of E. Melanie Gifford, Susanna P. Griswold, Norma Uemura, "Matthias Grünewald's *Small Crucifixion*. Painting Practice and Personal Style", in Béguerie-De Paepe, Menu (eds.), *La technique picturale*, 73–80.

44. Hütt, *Albrecht Dürer*, 1, 515.

45. The reference to Birgitta of Sweden is thanks to Feurstein, *Matthias Grünewald*, 86. The text is from *The Revelations of St. Birgitta of Sweden*, translated by Denis Searby, introductions and notes by Bridget Morris, vol. 2 (Oxford: Oxford University Press, 2006), 126. For the reception, including popular, of the texts of St. Brigitta, see Marjorie Reeves, *The Influence of Prophecy in the Later Middle Ages (*Oxford: Clarendon Press, 1969), 553.

46. Anne-Sophie Pellé, *Aemulatio Italorum. La réception culturelle des gravures du Mantegna dans l'art germanique au temps d'Albrecht Dürer* (Turnhout: Brepols, 2023), 216–218. The similarity between the two images of the grieving St. John

is limited to the fully traditional and codified gesture of the clasped hands, and does not presume at all a direct relationship between the two works.

47. A survey of the painted copies is provided in Feurstein, *Matthias Grünewald*, 114–118.

48. Katharina Heinemann, entry no. 186 in *Das Rätsel Grünewald*, exhibition catalogue, Aschaffenburg, ed. by Rainhard Riepertinger et al. (Augsburg: Haus der Bayerischen Geschichte, 2002), 303.

49. Ingrid Jenderko-Sichelschmidt, entry no. 187 in *Das Rätsel Grünewald*, 303.

50. Weixlgärtner, *Grünewald*, 28.

51. Roth, *Matthias Grünewald die Zeichnungen*, 73–74, "Um 1515–25". The chronology of the drawing has undergone significant variations, with a prevalence for very early dates (for example Guido Schoenberger, *The drawings of Mathis Gothart Nithart, called Grünewald* (New York: H. Bittner & Co., 1948), 25, suggests 1504–1505, while Baumgart, *Grünewald. I disegni*, n. 1, suggests 1506–1507).

52. An old copy exists at the Basel Museum (Zülch, *Der historische Grünewald*, 281).

53. Recently also Roth, *Matthias Grünewald die Zeichnungen*, 47–49, with dating to the years of the Isenheim altar or after, ca. 1512–1519.

54. Suggested by Zülch, *Der historische Grünewald*, 122 and 333, taken up by Ziermann, *Matthias Grünewald*, 63.

55. Willi Kurth, *The Complete Woodcuts of Albecht Dürer* (London: W. and G. Foyle, 1927, reprint New York: Dover Publications 1963), 27 and tav. 193; Hütt, *Albrecht Dürer*, 2, *Druckgraphik*, 1712; Schulz, *Albrecht Dürer. Das druckgraphische*, I, 178–179.

56. Edoardo Villata, "Grünewald in Lombardia?", in *Cultura oltremontana in Lombardia al tempo degli Sforza (1450–1535)*, Geneva conference proceedings, April 12–13, 2013, ed. by Frédéric Elsig, Claudia Gaggetta (Rome: Viella, 2014), 281–314, particularly 290.

57. Roth, *Matthias Grünewald die Zeichnungen*, 57–58, "Uhm 1512–16".

58. Ruhmer, *Grünewald drawings*, 86.

59. Behling, *Die Handzeichnungen des Mathis*, 102.

60. As already suggested by Schmid, *Die Gemälde und Zeichnungen*, 287, who published the important document we will examine later, and by Zülch, *Der historische Grünewald*, 409.

61. No mention is made of this by Pellé, *Aemulatio Italorum. La rèception*, who nonetheless discerns quite imaginative references to Mantegna in Grünewald's works, even if, as we shall now see, they are not necessarily etchings based on drawings by Mantegna.

62. Jean-Michel Massing, "Jaconus Argentoratensis. Etude preliminaire", and "The Triumph of Caesar by Benedetto Bordon and Jacobus Argentoratensis. Its iconography and influence", in *Studies in Imagery*, vol. I, *Text and Images* (London: The Pindar Press, 2004), 69–97, 108–140. See also Pellé, *Aemulatio Italorum. La rèception*,75–76.

63. Suzanne Boorsch, entry no. 118 in *Andrea Mantegna*, exhibition catalogue, London, ed. by Jane Martineau (Milan: Electa, 1992), 376–377: Vera Segre, entry nos. 7–8 in *Andrea Mantegna e l'incisione italiana del Rinascimento nelle collezioni dei Musei Civici di Pavia*, exhibition catalogue, Pavia, ed. by Saverio Lomartire (Milan: Electa, 2004), 90–91.

64. Roth, *Matthias Grünewald die Zeichnungen*, 71–72.

Chapter III | Isenheim

1. For all technical and historical information summarized here, see the general description in Bianconi, *L'opera completa*, 1972, 89–93, and the fine detailed explanations in Pantxika Béguerie, *Unterlinden. Le Retable d'Issenheim* (Strasbourg: La Nuèe Bleue, 1991); "Le Retable d'Issenheim", in Béguerie and Bischoff, *Grünewald le maître d'Issenheim*, 12–39; Béguerie-de Paepe and Haas, *Le Retable d'Issenheim.* Other specific bibliographical references: Linda Nochlin, *Mathis at Colmar. A Visual Confrontation* (New York: Red Dust, 1963); Georg Scheja, *Der Isenheimer Altar des Matthias Grünewald (Mathis Gothart Nithart)* (Cologne: DuMont Schauberg, 1969); Wilhelm Nyssen, *Choral des Glaubens. Meditationen zum Isenheimer Altar* (Freiburg im Breisgau: Christophorus Verlag, 1984); Max Seidel, *Grünewald Der Isenheimer Altar* (Stuttgart: Belser, 1986, new ed. 1990); Ruth Mellinkoff, *The Devil at Isenheim. Refliections of Popular Belief in Grünewald's Altarpiece* (Berkeley, Los Angeles and London: University of California Press. 1988); Andrée Hayum, *The Isenheim Altarpiece. God's Medicine and the Painter's Vision* (Princeton: Princeton University Press, 1989); Christian Heck, "De Nicolas de Haguenau à Grünewald: origine et structure du retable d'Issenheim", in Krohm, Oellermann (eds.) *Flügel-Altäre des Späten*, 223–237; Reichenauer, *Grünewald*, 81–182; Eugene Monick, *Evil, Sexuality and Disease in Grünewald's Body of Christ* (Dallas: Spring Publications, 1993); Marie Anne Hartmann, *Mathias Grunewald le retable d'Issenheim. Peinture et spiritualité* (Obernai : J. Do. Bentzinger, 1994); Reiner Marquard, *Mathias Grünewald und der Isenheimer Altar. Erläuterungen Erwägungen Deutungen* (Stuttgart: Calwer, 1996); Gottfried Richter, *Der Isenheimer Altar* (Stuttgart, Urachhaus, 1997, English edition *The Isenheim Altar. Suffering and Salvation in the Art of Grünewald*, Edinburgh: Floris Books, 1998; Hubert Comte, *Grünewald, le retable d'Issenheim* (Sarreguemines: Pierron, 1999); Marquard, *Grünewald und die Reformation*, 96–156; Adriano. Mariuz, *L'altare di Isenheim. Mathis Grünewald pittore della Morte e della Resurrezione* (Verona: Scripta, 2011); Béguerie-De Paepe and Haas, *Le retable d'Issenheim*; Michael Schubert, *The Isenheim Altarpiece. History-Interpretation-Background* (Stuttgart: Steiner Books, 2017, first edition 2007): it is a curious jumble of exaggerated interpretations taken to the absurd and keen and detailed observations; Frick, Schnitzler (eds.), *Der Isenheimer Altar*; Giorgio Gualdrini, *Trittico delle cose ultime. Grünewald, Holbein, Raffaello* (Villa Verucchio: Pazzini Editore, 2023), 33–156, 249–324 (this last section is particularly relevant and detailed regarding museological events and the altarpiece's literary and visual success). Also fundamental Béguerie-De Paepe, Lorentz (eds.) *Grünewald et le retable d'Issenheim.* On the contrary, little of use is found in Reale, *I misteri dell'altare*, and in Mario Dal Bello, *Matthias Grünewald. Orrore e visione* (Rome: Dei Merangoli, 2023).

2. The main historical source for the Antonites is Aymar Falco, *Antonianae Historiae Compendium ex variis iisdemque gravissimis ecclesiasticis scriptoribus, necnon rerum gestarum*

monumentis collectum, una cum externis rebus quam plurimis scitu memoratuque dignissimi (Lugdunum: Theobaldus Payen, 1534); more generally, see Adalbert Mischlewski, *Gründzuge der Geschichte des Antoniterordens bis zum Ausgang des 15. Jahrhunderts* (Cologne: Böhlau-Verlag, 1976); Laura Fenelli, *Il tau, il fuoco, il maiale. I canonici regolari di sant'Antonio Abate tra assistenza e devozione* (Spoleto: Fondazione CISAM, 2006); for a more detailed treatment, see Paul Stintzi, *Les Antonites d'Issenheim* (Mulhouse: no indication of publisher, 1972), and, especially, Clementz, *Les Antonins d'Issenheim.*

3. For Johann von Staupitz (ca. 1460–1524), of whom we will speak again, see in particular David Curtis Steinmetz, *Misericordia Dei. The Theology of Johannes von Staupitz in Its Late Medieval Setting* (Leiden: Brill, 1968); Franz Posset, *The Front-Runner of the Catholic Reformation. The Life and Work of Johann von Staupitz* (Aldershot: Routledge, 2003). For his role in the Augustinian Order, see Theodor Kolde, *Die deutsche Augustiner-Congregation und Johann von Staupitz. Ein Beitrag zur Ordens- und Reformationsgeschichte nach meistens ungedruckten Quellen* (Gotha: Friedrich Andreas Berthes, 1879).

4. Posset, *The Front-Runner*, 183–184. It is open to debate whether there existed at this time a specifically "Augustinian" theology, or simply the study and the commentaries of Augustine's works. For this, see the detailed survey in David Curtis Steinmetz, *Luther and Staupitz. An Essay in the Intellectual Origins of the Protestant Reformation* (Durham, North Carolina: Duke University Press, 1980), 13–34. The term *sodalitas staupiciana* is used by Christoph Scheurl in a letter to Staupitz himself dated January 15, 1518, to indicate a group of Nuremberg intellectuals who admired this Augustinian preacher, one of the group members being Dürer, "our German Apelles" (*Albrecht Dürer. Documentary*, I, 480).

5. Clementz, *Les Antonins d'Issenheim*, 68–107.

6. Until just a few years ago he was believed to have been Italian, but for more on this see the learned and specific details in Adalbert Mischlewski, "Die Antoniter und Isenheim", in Seidel, *Grünewald Der Isenheimer*, ed. 1990, 102–121, and Elisabeth Clementz, "Les précepteurs d'Issenheim, Bâle et Strasbourg, et leur rédeaux e relations", in Béguerie-De Paepe, Lorentz (eds.), *Grünewald et le retable*, 46–53, at 52, and also Eadem, *Les Antonins d'Issenheim*, 271–273.

7. About him, in addition to the pioneering work of Wilhelm Vöge, *Niclas Hagnower der Meister des Isenheimer Hochaltars und seine Frühwerke* (Freiburg: Urban-Verlag, 1931), see Christian Heck and Roland Recht, *Le Retable d'Issenheim avant Grünewald. Les sculptures de Nicolas de Haguenau* (Colmar: Musée d'Unterlinden, 1987); Berenike Berentzen, *Niclaus Hagnower. Studien zum Bildhauerischen Werk* (Petershof: Imhof, 2014). It should be noted that Roland Recht, "Les sculptures du retable d'Issenheim", *Cahiers Alsaciens d'archéologie d'art et d'histoire*, XIX, 1975–76, 27–48, offered doubts about identifying Niclaus as the creator of the sculpted parts of the Isenheim altarpiece, and was followed by Schubert, *The Isenheim Altarpiece*, 148–149.

8. Hubach, "Grünewald, Matthias"; Gregory C. Bryda, "The Exuding Wood of the Cross of Isenheim", *The Art Bulletin*, 100, 2018, 2, 6–36, at 6.

9. On the Orlier altarpiece see Stephan Kemperdick, entry no. 6.3, in *Peintures germaniques des collections françaises (1370–1580)*, exhibition catalogue, Besançon, Colmar, Dijon, ed. by Isabelle Dubois-Brinkmann, Aude Briau (Dijon-Paris: Éditions Faton-Institut National d'Histoire de l'Art, 2024), 212–213, with bibliography.

10. Pantxika Béguerie-De Paepe, "La réalisation du retable d'Issenheim: Nicolas de Haguenau à Strasbourg", in Béguerie-De Paepe, Lorentz (eds.), *Grünewald et le retable*, 54–65.

11. Susanne Meurer, "Wer ist schuld an Grünewald?", in Anna Schreurs-Morêt. Lucia Simonato, Susanne Meurer (ed.), *Die Künstler der "Teutesche Academie" Joachim von Sandrarts. "Aus aller Herren Länder"* (Turnhout: Brepols, 2015), 181–194.

12. Jean Fuchs, *Inventaire des Archives de la Ville de Strasbourg antérieurs à 1790*, Sèrie V (Strasbourg: Ville de Strasbourg, undated), 179 no. 136/6. Hochfeld could be a place in the Rhineland or, more likely, current-day Hochfelden in Alsace.

13. Villata, "Grünewald in Lombardia?", in Elsig, Gaggetta (eds.), *Cultura oltremontana in Lombardia*, 284. According to the reconstruction by Meurer, "Wer ist schuld", in Schreurs-Morêt, Simonato, Meurer S. Meurer (ed.), 2015; Eadem, "Yearning for Biography", 1050–1054, the name Grünewald originated in the sphere of the Frankfurt intelligentsia involved in deciphering the MGN monogram found on one of the monochromes currently at the Städel Museum. However, it should be noted that in the known documents regarding Hagnower (reviewed by B. Berentzen, *Niclaus Hagenower*, 27–33 and accompanying notes) there is no association of the name Grunwalt or Grünewalt with the sculptor.

14. A. Kehl, *"Grünewald"-Forschungen*, 211–212. The surnames Grünwalt, Grünewald or Grünenwald recur a number of times in Strasbourg between the 16th and 17th centuries. A Louis Grünewald is documented in 1562 (J. Fuchs, *Inventaire des Achives*, V, 18 no. 8/45), the same year in which Arbogast Grünewald, engineer and machine builder, offers his skills to the city, after having designed a bridge two years earlier (*ibidem*, respectively, 20 no. 9/34, and 125 no. 66/8, and in the latter instance, the surname is written Grienwald). In 1574, a Wolf Grienwald is documented in relation to the mines of the Lapoutroie Valley and Sante-Marie-aux-mines (*ibidem*, 56 no. 18/112), and in the same year a Luc Grienwald, hatter, also appears (*ibidem*, 66 no. 19/181). In the 17th century we find Johann Caspar and Johann Adolf Grünewald, in 1625 and 1629, respectively (*ibidem*, 159 no. 107/25 and 150 no. 93/ 3).

15. Pantxika Béguerie-De Paepe, *Nouvelles hypothèses sur la genèse du retable d'Issenheim: Grünewald et Strasbourg?*, in Béguerie-De Paepe, Lorentz (eds.), *Grünewald et le retable*, 12–15. The fact that the altarpiece was painted directly in Alsace had already been hypothesized by Behling, *Matthias Grünewald*, 4–5.

16. For the moment, reference is to the lovely online conference of Juliette Levy-Hinstin held on April 12, 2021, available here: https://www.youtube.com/watch?v=qOguPl4Oq7E, and to Pantxika Béguerie-De Paepe, *Colmar. Musèe Unterlinden.Un nouveau regard sur le retable d'Issenheim. Quelques apports de la restauration sur l'étude de l'œuvre*, in « Revue des musées de France », 4, 2023, 9–14.

17. Alan Shestack, "An Introduction to Hans Baldung Grien", in *Hans Baldung Grien Prints and Drawings*, exhibition catalogue, Washington, ed. by James H. Marrow, Alan Shestack (New Haven: Yale University Press, 1981), 2–18, at 9–15; Frank

Muller, *Hans Baldung Grien. Entre christianisme et paganisme* (Strasbourg: Editions du Signe, 2019), 40–46; Johanna Scherer, entry in *Hans Baldung Grien sacré/profane*, Karlsruhe exhibition catalogue, ed. by Hölger Jacob-Friesen (Berlin and Munich: Deutscher Kunstverlag, 2019), 174–177. Specifically concerning the large altarpiece in the Freiburg cathedral, see Carmen Zils, Constanze Albecker, Annette Rauscher, Yumiko Yuguchi, Barbara Eicholz, Juliane Bett, Susanne Becker and Ruth Gresser, *Der Freiburg Hochaltar. Tradition und Signatur des Neuen*, in *Hans Baldung Grien in Freiburg*, exhibition catalogue, Freiburg im Breisgau, ed. by Saskia Durian-Ress (Freiburg im Breisgau: Rombach Verlag, 2001), 261–300.

18. Weixlgärtner, *Grünewald*, 45–46.

19. Clementz, *Les Antonins d'Issenheim*, 167–168.

20. Interesting observations and hypotheses on this individual based on archival research, in Georges Bischoff, "Grünewald? Un mystère", in Béguerie and Bischoff, *Grünewald le maître d'Issenheim*, 63–111, at 96–97. On the inventory of the goods left by Mathis, see the last chapter.

21. This had already been intuited by Behling, *Matthias Grünewald*, 4.

22. Clementz, *Les Antonins d'Issenheim*, 249–251.

23. Some observations about the Isenheim liturgical calendar are available in Hayum, *The Isenheim Altarpiece*, 58–80 and accompanying notes. Also see Comte, *Grünewald, le retable*, 10–12. Interesting, but inevitably generic, the interpretation of the initial face of the altarpiece as a liturgical object provided by Reichenauer, *Grünewald*, 89–100.

24. However, it is not underrated by one of Grünewald's very first exegetes, Émile Verhaeren ("Le peintre Mathias Grünewald, d'Aschaffenburg", *La Société nouvelle*, December 1894, 661–679, republished in Émile Verhaeren, *Écrits sur l'art*, ed. by Paul Aron, vol. II, *1893–1916*, Brussels: Labor, 1997, 626–643, at 639, English translation in Émile Verhaeren, *Essays on the Northern Renaissance. Rembrandt, Rubens, Grünewald and Others*, ed. by Albert Alhadeff, New York: Peter Lang Publishing, 2012, 129–147, at 142), which dwells in particular on the figure of Mary Magdalene: "The long ordeal of her master has enfeebled her, has reduced her to a thing that wends its way from one painful rise to another [. . .] one hears more than one sees her sobs and her shrieks before the open sepulcher [. . .] the Magdalene excruciatingly proclaims her agony, abandoning herself to her grief as she once abandoned herself to her love, forever the victim of her heart." The Belgian critic was already interested in Mathis starting in 1886 ("En voyage. Les Gothiques allemands", *L'Art moderne*, August 15, 1886, 257–258, republished in Verhaeren, *Écrits sur l'art*, II, 250–252).

25. Hölger Jacob-Friesen, entry nos. 74–75 in Jacob-Friesen, Jehle (eds.), *Hans Baldung Grien*, 182–183.

26. Pantxika Béguerie-De Paepe, entry no. 2 in Béguerie-De Paepe, Lorentz (eds.), *Grünewald et le retable*, 82–83.

27. Laure Fagnart, *Léonard de Vinci en France. Collections et collectionneurs (Xvéme-XVIIéme siècles)* (Rome: L'Erma di Bretschneider, 2009), 311–312.

28. John Berger, *Between Two Colmar*, in *About Looking* (London: Pantheon Books, 1980), 134–140, republished in Idem, *Portraits: John Berger on Artists*, ed. by Tom Overton (London and New York: Verso, 2017), 49–55, at 51.

29. Margherita Guidacci, *L'altare di Isenheim* (Milan: Rusconi, 1980; then in Eadem, *Le poesie*, ed. by Maura Del Serra, Florence: Le Lettere, 1999), 295: "Piomba il falco dal cielo, non colomba—la colomba è lei, spaventata,/ che distoglie lo sguardo e vorrebbe nascondersi/ e congiunge tremante, quasi a difesa, le mani".

30. Roth, *Matthias Grünewald die Zeichnungen*, 45–46.

31. Reported by Ravaud, Lambert and Le Chanu, "Le *Retable d'Issenheim*. Résultats", in De Paepe, Menu (eds.), *La technique picturale*, 40–48, which should be consulted from here on for the results of the investigations of the Isenheim altarpiece; but see also Élisabeth Ravaud, Elsa Lambert, "Les étapes d'élaboration du retable à travers l'imagerie scientifique", in Béguerie-De Paepe, Lorentz (eds.), *Grünewald et le retable*, 232–243, and Michel Menu, "Materia e tecnica", in Martin, Menu, Ramond, *Grünewald*, 256–275.

32. Schiller, *Iconography of Christian Art*, I, 52.

33. Also see the anastatic reprint of the 1505 and 1509 editions (though the plate in question does not appear in the latter) in William M. Ivins Jr., *On the Rationalization of Sight. With an Examination of Three Renaissance Texts on Perspective* (New York: Da Capo Press, 1975); in general, see Pelerin Viator Liliane Brion-Guerry, *Jean Pélerin Viator. Sa place dans l'histoire de la perspective* (Paris: Les Belles Lettres, 1962), and specifically 248–249 for the illustration in question. See also Raphäel Tassin, entry, in *La Renaissance à Toul. Morceaux choisi*, exhibition catalogue, Toul, ed. by Alde Harmand, Philippe Masson (Toul : Musée d'Art ed d'Histoire de Toul, 2013), 66–67.

34. Truly curious the interpretation of Schubert, *The Isenheim Altarpiece*, 72–73, who sees the repetition as simply a calligraphy exercise by Mary and, even worse, as an esoteric reference to the alleged presence of two different Jesuses, one the protagonist of the Gospel of Matthew and the other that of Luke. Putting aside such pseudo-iconological meandering, it could be that Grünewald was given only a portion of the text "Ecce virgo concipiet et pariet filiu(m) et vocabitur nomen eius emanuel butiru(m) et mel comedet ut sciat reprobare malu(m) et eligere bonu(m)", and not knowing Latin, as is highly likely for a painter, the best solution he could find to fill the remaining space was to repeat the citation.

35. A shocking sampling, including visual, of the therapeutic practices is given in *Feldtbuch der Wundtartzney* (Strasbourg: Johannes Schott, 1517, consulted in the anastatic reprint of Baiersbronn: Medicina rara editions, undated), the work of Hans von Gersdorff, who was a surgeon at the Antonite hospital in nearby Strasbourg, and enhanced by the wood-engravings based on the drawings of Hans Wechtlin: Melanie Panse, *Hans von Gersdorff's "Feldtbuch der Wundtartzney". Produktion, Präsentation und Rezeption von Wissen* (Wiesbaden: Reicher Verlag, 2012); Chiara Benati, "Surgeon or Lexicographer? The Latin-German Glossaries in Addendum to Hans von Gersdorff's *Feldtbuch der Wunderarzney*", *Linguistica e Filologia*, 33, 2013, 35–57; Eadem, "The Field Surgery Manual Which Became a Medical Commonplace Book: Hans von Gersdorff's *Feldtbuch der Wundarzney* (1517) Translated into Low German", in *Bodily and Spiritual Hygiene in Medieval and Early Modern Literature. Explorations of Textual Presentations of Filth and Water*, ed. by Albrecht Classen (Berlin and Boston: De Gruyter, 2017), 501–528.

36. "Nondum considerastine quanti ponderis sit peccatum?" (*Cur Deus homo*, in Sancti Anselmi ex Beccensi abbate

Cantuariensi archiepiscopi *Opera Omnia*, ed. by Gabriele Gerberon, Venice: Giuseppe Corona 1744, vol. I, 124, caput XXI). The only scholar to offer Anselm's text as a possible iconographic source for Grünewald was, I believe, Siegfrid Kettling, *Das Evangelium des Malers Mathis. Betrachtungen zum Isenheimer Altar* (Wuppertal: Brockhaus, 1985), 29. On this theological point, see Notger Slenczka, "'Nondum considerasti quanti ponderis sit peccatum—Du hast noch nicht ermessen, welches Gewicht die Sünde hat'. Die Bedeutung des Kreuzes für das Selbstverständnis des Menschen", *Kerygma und Dogma*, 62, 2016, 2, 160–182.

37. "un véritable buisson de ronce disposé en 'nid de pie' renversé (Louis Charbonneau-Lassay, *Le Vulnéraire du Christ. Le mystérieuse emblématiqume des plaies du corps et du coeur de Jésus Christ*, ed. by Gauthier Pierozak (Paris : Gutenberg Reprint, 2018), 125. As stressed with great sensitivity by Karen van den Berg, *Die Passion zu malen. Zur Bildauffassung bei Matthias Grünewald* (Duisburg and Berlin: Pict Im, 1997), 28–30, Grünewald creates the figures of this scene in a differentiated manner, also within the same individual, as a way of amplifying the three-dimensionality and make them, themselves, the only markers in the space which, otherwise, is essentially negated by the almost totally black background. In particular, notes van den Berg, this procedure is evident in the crucified Christ, whose parts are depicted starting from different points of observation: for the head, the hands and even two different points for the torso, and for the feet. Ensuring coherence in an image created in this way is the rendering of the surfaces which are extraordinarily, cruelly real and based on real-life study (*ibidem*, 43–44).

38. Interesting technical observations of Bryda, "The Exuding Wood" 2018, 18: "In addition to the two tones of color, Grünewald differentiated the coagulated blood with an impasto application of the darker pigment, which appear as bas-relief globules on the otherwise smooth panel. To build up such a thick glaze, he increased the ratio of medium to pigment—likely with unusually high proportions of tree resin in his paint mixture —which would have rendered the original texture and appearance of the congealed blood as more vitreous and translucent than is visible today."

39. Nochlin, *Mathis at Colmar*, 15, underscores "the enhancement of expressive potential created by opening and enlarging the semi-circular webs of skin between thumb and fore-finger, so that, especially in Christ's hands, seen against the black sky, these become open mouths". Perhaps the most powerful description of the light in the Grünewald Crucifixion is by Thomas Wolfe, *On Time and the River. A Legend of Man's Hunger in his Youth* (1935), ed. with an introduction of Elisabeth Kostava (London: Penguin Books, 2016), 761: "A supernatural light falls upon the immense twisted length of the body [of Christ] (a grey-white green) and yet *completely solid light*—you can count the ribs, the muscles (the head falling to the right), full of brutal agony—it is crowned with long thorns and rusty blood—it droops over, it is too big." Immediately after, Wolfe wrote, "There is nothing like it in the world", adding a bit later: "This is the greatest and also the most 'modern' picture I have ever seen" (*ibidem*, 762).

40. On Staupitz's Salzburg sermons see Steinmetz, *Misericordia Dei*, 126–129; F. Posset, *The Front-Runner*, 134–156.

41. "Si haben darnach strick angelegt an hendt und füess und also erpärmlich zogen, das alles das kracht hat und zertent ist, das kain saiten nimer also ausgespant wirt als di süess lautent saiten, daraus erklingt di süess stim gots": Johann von Staupitz, *Salzburger Predigten 1512*, critical edition ed. by Wolfram Schneider-Lastin (Tübingen: Universität Tübingen, 1990), 107.

42. "Da fleust aus allen adern und painen das götlich pluet heraus, das smeckt nach der götlichen parmherzikait. Es ist nindert ain so lains wündlein noch löchlein, du mügst wol dadurch eintringen zu der sel und durch die sel zu der gothait, Da soltu smecken und kosten aller süessisten parmherzikait. Das verleich mir und euch got. Amen" (Staupitz, *Salzburger Predigten 1512*, 94–95). The English translation is taken from Posset, *The Front-Runner*, 149. It was not until 1523 that a comparison was made of the disfigured skin of the crucified Christ and the coarse, wrinkled parchment of the Book of Life, a simile already found, however, in Heinrich Suso, one of the great Rheinland mystics of the 14th century (Posset, *The Front-Runner*, 154).

43. *Two Essays by J. K. Huysmans*, in Ruhmer, *Grünewald Paintings*, 25 (English translation by R. Baldick). This is the original text: "Ce Christ affreux qui se mourait sur l'autel de l'hospice d'Issenheim semble fait à l'image des affigés du mal des ardents qui le priaient; ils se consolaient en songeant que ce Dieuqu'ils imploraient avait éprouvé leurs tortures et qu'il s'était incarné dans une forme aussi repoussante que la leur, et ils se sentaient moins désherités et moins vils. [. . .] Son Christ des pèstiferés eût choqé le goût des Cours; il ne pouvait être compris que par les infirmes, les désespérés et les moines, par les membres souffrants du Christ" (Joris-Karl Huysmans, *Trois Primitifs. Les Grünewald du Musée de Colmar. Le maître de Flemalle et la Florentine du Musée de Francfort-sur-le-Mein*, Paris: Albert Meissen, 1905, 50–51); firstly published, as "Les Grünewald du Musée de Colmar", in *Le mois littéraire et pittoresque*, 62, mars 1904, 282-300; see also Joris-Karl Huysmas, *Les Grünewald du Musée de Colmar*, critical edition by Pierre Brunel, ndré guyaux and Christian Heck, Paris: Hermann, 1988. On Huysmans as interpreter of Grünewald see Gustave Vanvelkenhuyzen, "Le manuscrit de *Trois Primitifs*", *Bulletin de la societé J.K. Huysmans*, 15, décembre 1986, 12-23; Christian Heck, "Grünewald et le culte des primitifs septentrionaux chez Huysmans", in *Huysmans: une esthéthique de la decadence*, conference proceedings (Basel, Mulhouse and Colmar, November 5–7, 1984), ed. by Robert Kopp. Christian Heck, André Guyaux (Paris: Slatkine, 1987), 271–284; Anthony Zielonka, "Huysmans and Grünewald: the Discovery of Spiritual Naturalism", *Nineteenth-Century French Studies*, 18, 1989–1990, 1–2, 212–230; Pierre Brunel, "Des carnets de Huysmans au *Trois Primitifs*", *Genesis (Manuscrits-Recherche-Invention*, 7, 1995, 115-121; Nancy Davenport, "The Revival of Fra Angelico and Matthias Grünewald in Nineteenth-Century French Religious Art", *French Studies*, 27, 1–2, 1998–1999, 1–2, 157–199; Cervi, *Prospettive d'ékphrasis* 2008/2009, 30–32; Nicolas Valazza, "Du 'charnier divin au 'triomphe de la Chair'. Huysmans face à Grünewald", in *Les Religions du xixè siècle*, conference proceedings (Paris, November 26–28, 2009), ed. by Sophie Guermès, Bertrand Marchal, published online (2011): https://serd.hypotheses.org/files/2018/08/NicolasValazza.pdf; Pierre Vaisse, "L'art religieux en République", and André Guyaux, "'Le seul art véridique et grand': Huysmans et les Primitifs", in *Joris-*

Karl Huysmans. De Degas à Grünewald, Paris and Strasbourg exhibition catalogue, Paris, Strasbourg, ed, by Stéphane Guégan and André Guyaux (Paris-Strasbourg: Musée d'Orsay, Musée de la ville de Strasbourg-Gallimard, 2020), respectively, 141–157, at 142–143, and 158–167, at 164–166; Simone Ferrari, "Huysmans critico d'arte. La fortuna dei primitivi fiamminghi", *Il Capitale Culturale*, 27, 2023, 3–16.

44. *The Rivers North of the Future. The Testament of Ivan Illich as told to David Cayley* (Toronto: Anansi, 2005), 211–212.

45. Rudolph Arbesmann O. S. A., "The Concept of 'Christus Medicus' in St. Augustine", *Traditio*, X, 1954, 1–28; A. Hayum, *The Isenheim Altarpiece*, 37.

46. Caroline Walker Bynum, *Wonderful Blood. Theology and Practice in Late Medieval Germany and Beyond* (Philadelphia: University of Pennsylvania Press, 2007), 256. Also see Danielle Buschinger, *Sang versé, sang guérisseur, sang aliment et sang du Christ dans la littérature médiévale allemande*, in *Le sang au moyen âge*, international conference proceedings (Montpellier, November 27–29, 1997), ed. by Marcel Fauré (Montpellier: Université Montpellier III Paul Valéry, 1999), 257–266.

47. Petrus Dorlandus, *Viola animae per modum dyalogi*, Köln, Heinrich Quentell, May 29, 1499 (cited from the 1501, July 16, reprinting, c. D i recto: "[Christus] voluit. . .plagis vulnerari ut bene saucium reformeret, et sanguinem fundere ut semianimem ad vitam gratie animaret." The English translation is taken from Walker Bynum, *Wonderful Blood*, 163.

48. Albert Châtelet, "Unité ou diversité du theme du retable d'Issenheim", *Cahiers Alsaciens d'archeologie d'art et d'histoire*, XIX, 1975–76, 60–68, at 63–64. The import of his conclusions is reassessed, however, in Hayum, *The Isenheim Altarpiece*, 157 note 34.

49. "aber alspald du anzünt wirst in der betrachtung, so tue die augen zue, stee nit darauf. Das ausser gesicht oder pild des leibs, das zaigt dir an das leiden Christi, die betrachtung der sel macht dirs fruchtper, in der gothait ligt der keren des süessikait verporgen" (Staupitz, *Salzburger Predigten 1512*, 28). The English translation is taken from Posset, *The Front-Runner*, 140. See also Franz Posset, "Preaching the Passion of Christ on the Eve of the Reformation", *Concordia Theological Quarterly*, 59, 4, 1995, 279–300, at 287, cited by Marco Fratini in the major review of the Italian edition of this volume, *Riforma e movimenti religiosi*, 5, 2019, 233–237, at 235.

50. Staupitz, *Salzburger Predigten 1512*, 123.

51. *Ibidem*, 27 (from the first sermon).

52. Elias Canetti, *Die Fackel im Ohr. Lebensgeschichte 1921–1931* (Vienna: Fischer, 1980; English translation *The Torch in my Ear*, New York: Farrar, Straus and Giroux, 1983, 217). I would like to thank Marco Fratini for informing me about this important passage.

53. Marrow, *Passion Iconography*, 52–54, including the reference to Ludolph of Saxony. The Latin text of the Vulgate is taken from the *Biblia Sacra iuxta vulgatam versionem*, ed. by Robert Weber, revised by Roger Gryson (Stuttgart: Deutsche Bibelgesellschaft, 2007), 1151–1152. The classic English version from the *King James Bible* is not as effective: "Surely he hath borne our griefes, and caried our sorrows: yet we did esteeme him striken, smitten of God, and afflicted.

But he was wounded for our transgressions, He was bruised for our iniquities: the chastisement of our peace was upon him, and with his stripes we are healed." (*The Holy Bible 1611 Edition King James Version*, Peabody: Hendrikson Publishers, 2008.

54. *Biblia Sacra*, 2007, 1249. From the King James translation: "From above hath he sent fire into my bones, and it prevaileth against them: he hath spread a net for my feete, he hath turned me backe; he hath made me desolate, and faint all the day."

55. Michael Roth, "Les dessins de Matthias Grünewald pour le retable d'Issenheim", in Béguerie-De Paepe, Lorentz (eds.), *Grünewald et le retable*, 92–104, at 98–99; Roth, *Matthias Grünewald die Zeichnungen*, 49–50.

56. See, in brief, Kristina Herrmann Fiore, entry no. VI.1 in *Dürer e l'Italia*, exhibition catalogue, Rome, ed. by Kristina Herrmann Fiore (Milan: Electa, 2007), 270–271; Andrew J. Martin, entry no. 1/18 in *Dürer e il Rinascimento tra Germania e Italia*, exhibition catalogue, Milan, ed. by Bernard Aikema (Milan: 24 Ore Cultura, 2018), 329–330.

57. Schmid, *Die Gemälde und Zeichnungen*, I, 138.

58. The interpretation of Schubert, *The Isenheim Altarpiece*, 58—according to whom the veil over her eyes would allude to the fact that Mary Magdalene had not yet experienced the revelation of the final sense of the Crucifixion, seen only with the earthly eyes of love—is very poetic, but not convincing given that in the predella with the Lamentation of Mary Magdalene, her eyes are open and not veiled, while it is the Madonna whose eyes are covered.

59. Van den Berg, *Die Passion zu Malen*, 29, stresses that John the Baptist is present as a unitary figure thanks to the intensity of his color rendering, but that only the pointed figure, as if a sudden movement, actually achieves physical reality, "while all else recedes in the face of this gesture".

60. Fratini, review, 2019, 235–236. Also see the catalogue of Heimo Reinitzer, *Gesetz und Evangelium. Über ein reformatorisches Bildthema, seine Tradition, Funktion und Wirkungsgeschichte* (Hamburg: Christians Verlag, 2006), 2 vols. An earlier indication in this direction was made by Hayum, *The Isenheim Altarpiece*, 83–84.

61. For the connection between late-14th-century Augustinian mysticism and homiletics and Lutheran spirituality, with Staupitz as a fundamental intermediary, see Steinmetz, *Misericordia Dei*, 25–30. An explicitly pre-Lutheran interpretation is offered by Reiner Marquard. "Die Versuchungtafel als Schlüsselbild des Isenheimer Altars. Anmerkungen zum reformatiomsgeschichtlichen Hintergrund der Kunst Mathias Grünewalds", Frick, Schnitzler (eds.), *Der Isenheimer Altar*, 65–93, at 75–79, who considers it, quite irrefutably, an autonomous conclusion of the artist.

62. Schiller, *Iconography of Christian Art*, II, 158.

63. Wilhelm Rugamer, "Der Isenheimer Altar Matthias Grünewalds im Lichte der Liturgie und der kirchlichen Reformbewegung", *Theologische Quartalschrift*, CXX, 1939, 145–163; W. Stephen Kayser, "Grünewald's Christianity", *Review of Religion*, V, 1, 1940, 3–35; Hayum, *The Isenheim Altarpiece*, 89–98. According to a 1628 inventory, there was a baptismal font in the Church of St. Anthony in Isenheim whose copper basin was kept right behind the main altar (Jean Jacques Dietrich, "La Depouille du convent des Antonites d'Issenheim", *Revue d'Alsace*, n. s., II, 2, 1873, 70–78). My warmest thanks to Pantxika Béguerie-De Paepe, who demonstrated to me that, however, no river is painted behind St. John.

64. It is striking that already in a note for the play *Die Schwärmer*, written on February 27, 1912, Robert Musil (in a way, one of the great mystics of the 20th century) had compared Suso and Grünewald: "suddenly finding oneself having to live in God, as Suso and the painter Grünewald did" (unfortunately, this passage was left out of the English translation of the anthology of Musil's diaries: Robert Musil, *Diaries 1899–1941*, ed. by Philip Payne, Mark Mirsky, New York: Basic Books, 1998). Also see Gualdrini, *Trittico delle cose*, 289–290.

65. Huysmans, "Two Essays", in Ruhmer, *Grünewald, The paintings*, 14. The original: "Grünewald s'y révèle, tel quel le peintre le plus audacieux qui ait jamais existé, le premier qui ait tenté d'exprimer avec la pauvreté des couleurs terrestres la vision de la divinité mise en suspens sur la croix et revenant, visible à l'oeil nu, au sortir de la tombe. Nous sommes avec lui en plein hallali mystique, devant une art sommé dans ses retranchements, oblige de s'aventurer ans l'au-delá plus loin qu'aucun théologien n'aurait pu, cette fois, lui enjoindre d'aller" (Huysmans, *Trois promitifs*, 23–24). Also particularly insightful the interpretation of Scheja, *Der Isenheimer Altar*, 34–40.

66. Konrad Oberhuber, Sylvia Ferino-Pagden and Ernst Wolfgang Huber, "Catalogo dei disegni", in *Raffaello. I disegni*, ed. by Eckhart Knab, Eewin Mitsche, Konrad Oberhuber, Italian ed. italiana by Paolo Dal Poggetto (Florence: Nardini, 1983), 625.

67. Roberto Longhi, "Arte italiana e arte tedesca" (1941), in *"Arte italiana e arte tedesca" con altre congiunture tra Italia ed Europa (1939–1969)* (Complete works of Roberto Longhi, vol. IX, Florence: Sansoni, 1979), 3–21, at 16. Also see François-René Martin, "Estrema Tule. Sur une métaphore géographique chez Roberto Longhi", *Predella*, 10, 2014, 151–159.

68. Martin Buber, "The Altar" (1917), in Martin Buber, "The Altar"—Jean-Luc Nancy, "Chromatic Atheology", *Journal of Visual Culture*, 4, 1, 2005, 116–128, at 122 (English translation by Marion Picker).

69. It should be noted that the starry sky seems painted with true cosmological expertise, not surprising if we consider the precision with which Grünewald painted the eclipse in the Crucifixion today in Washington (see the fine observations by Schubert, *The Isenheimer Altarpiece*, 108–109).

70. This had already been noted by Fraenger, *Grünewald*, 76. See also Kettling, *Das Evangelium des Malers*, 54. For the concept of "second creation" in Augustine, see *De Civitate Dei*, XXII, 17, and even more the Augustinian theologian Hugh of Saint Victor, "Noah's Ark (De archa Noe)", IV, 11, in *Selected Spiritual Writings*, Foreword by Aelred Squire O. P. (London: Faber & Faber, 1962), 137–138: "For the elect reckon the works of restoration as superior to those of the first creation." See also Leo Steinberg, *The Sexuality of Christ in Renaissance Art and in Modern Oblivion* (New York: Pantheon, 1983), 127.

71. It should be noted that the unnamed Antonite visitor in 1650, mentioned several times, stated that "Je n'ay veu aucune maison de l'Ordre en laquelle il y eust tant et de si bons livres qu'icy, exceptué Saint-Antoine et Paris", thus informing us of the excellence of the Isenheim Preceptory library, a fact to be remembered, including in the pages that follow.

72. Hildegard von Bingen, *Scivias*, ed. by Adelgundis Fuhrkötter OSB, vol. II, tome 2 (Turnhout: Brepols, 1978), 124. Also see Reichenauer, *Grünewald*, 158–168.

73. Jakob Boehme, *The signature of all things* [1622], Foreword by Clifford Bax, chapters XI, nos. 84–85, XII, 22 (London and New York: J. Dent & Sons, 1912), 84–85, 157. This is the original text: "wie die Kertze im Fewer erstirbet, vnd gehet auss demselben sterben das Liecht vnd die krafft, als das grosse vnfuehlende Leben auss, also solte vnd muste auss Christi sterben, auss seinem tode die ewige Goettliche Sonne in Menschlicher eigenschafft auffgehen [. . .]. Vnd wie Adam das Ebenbild Gottes in finster todes gestalt vervandelte, also verwandelte Gott das Ebenbilde auss dem Tode, durch seinen Fewergrim wieder ins Liecht er zog das Ebenbilde wieder auss dem Tode gleich wie eine Blume auss der wilden Erden waechset.[. . .] Der Todt stehet in einem newen Leibe auss der Finsternuss dess todes auff, in weisser schoener Farbe: aber gleich wie ein verborgener glantz, da man die Farbe nicht recht erkennen kan, also lange biss sichs *resolviret*, vnd die *materia* wieder begehrent wird, so gehet im *Centro Saturnus* in *Iovis* vnd *Veneris* eigenschafft, die Sonne in allen sieben Gestalten auff, das ist im *verbo fiat*, gleich als eine newe Schoepfung, vnd lauffen aller sieben Gestalte begierde in *Solis* glantz, als in die weisse vnd rohte Farbe, vom Fewer vnd Liecht, das ist Majestaetische" (Jakob Böhme, *Werke. Morgenroete im Aufgangk, De Signatura Rerum*, hrsg. von Ferdinand van Ingen (Frankfurt am Main: Deutscher Klassiker Verlag, 2009), 697–698, 708).

74. Alessandro Ballarin, "Giovanni Gerolamo Savoldo" (1966), in Idem, *La Salomè del Romanino ed altri studi sulla pittura bresciana del Cinquecento*, vol. I (Cittadella: Bertoncello Arti Grafiche, 2005), 11–22, at 19. See also Luigi Dania, "Una inedita pala d'altare di Lorenzo Lotto", *Antichità viva*, 19, 1980, 4, 7–11 (my thanks go to Maria Grazia Albertini Ottolenghi for this suggestion); for the Lotto altarpiece, see Enrico Maria Dal Pozzolo, *Lorenzo Lotto. Catalogo generale dei dipinti*, with the participation of Raffaella Poltronieri, Valentina Castegnaro and Marta Paravanti, (Milan: Skira, 2022), 178–179; Simone Facchinetti, entry no. II.3, in *Moroni 1521–1580 il ritratto del suo tempo*, exhibition catalogue, Milan, ed. by Simone Facchinetti, Arturo Galansino, (Milan: Gallerie d'Italia-Skira, 2023), 114. A further parallelism (though earlier and almost impossible to verify historically) between the Lotto altarpiece for the Church of San Domenico in Recanati, completed in 1508, and Grünewald's two female saints in the Heller altarpiece. It is notable that *Saints Stephen and Cyriacus*, often associated with Grünewald, are not referenced in this context, suggesting that they may pertain to a different phase in the German artist's oeuvre. Alessandro Ballarin discusses this potential connection in *Giorgione e l'umanesimo veneziano* (Verona: Aurora, 2016 but 2018), vol. II, *Giorgione e la Compagnia degli Amici*, 990, but without offering solutions regarding its historical feasibility, except: "these are real problems [sono bei problemi]". A potential explanation could be seen in possible common denominators between the two painters. The easiest and most intuitive is unquestionably Dürer, the Dürer of the *Feast of the Rosary* for Lotto and the Heller altarpiece for Grünewald. Another possible, yet objectively less probable, common acquaintance could be Veit Stoss. As already mentioned, he was well-known to Mathis, but Lotto could also have run into some work of his, given that the sculptor was known in Italy (for example, the *St. Roch* in the basilica of the Santissima

Annunziata in Florence, whose dating still vacillates: see the detailed explanation of Hartmut Krohm, "Due sculture di Veit Stoss. L'arte dell'intaglio nel suo massimo compimento intorno al 1500", in *"Fece di scoltura di legname e colori". Scultura del Quattrocento in legno dipinto a Firenze*, exhibition catalogue by Alfredo Bellandi (Florence: Giunti, 2016), 139–159, at 139–148.

75. This relationship was suggested by Scheja, *Der Isenheimer Altar*, 23, and taken up by Ziermann, *Matthias Grünewald*, 116, but already rejected by Charles D. Cuttler, "Further Grünewald sources", *Zeitschrift für Kunstgeschichte*, 50, 1987, 539–549, at 548.

76. We will be discussing this artist again. As it could be expected, the fame of the altarpiece would seem to center on the *Crucifixion*, the most easily observable image. At least a drawing at the Kunstmuseum in Basel should be mentioned, published by Zülch, *Der historische Grünewald*, ill. 169 and a late 16th-century painting in a private collection (previously belonging to Remy Faesch of Basel), that offers a simplified version of the Crucifixion and the Lamentation, cited by Hans Reinhardt, "Les notices du collectionneur balois Henry Faesch mentionnant une copie de l'autel d'Issenheim exécutée au XVIe siècle", *Cahiers Alsaciens d'archeologie d'art et d'histoire*, XIX, 1975–76, 195–198.

77. It goes without saying that I do not agree with the opinion of Heike Wetzig, "Die Standflügel des Isenheimer Altars", in Krohm, Oellermann (eds.) *Flügel-Altäre des Späten*, 238–259, at 253, according to whom the two panels were painted last.

78. Sarwey, *Grünewald-Studien*, 50–52. The Lerse's text is now available in Marquard, *Grünewald und die Reformation*, 230–253.

79. Pierre Vaisse, in Piero Bianconi and Pierre Vaisse, *Toute l'oeuvre peint de Grünewald* (Paris: Flammarion, 1974), 108; Idem, "Faut-il modifier la presentation du Retable d'Issenheim?", *La Tribune de l'art*, April 29, 2012; Reinhardt, "Les notices", 194; Behling, *Matthias Grünewald*, 13; Cuttler, "Further Grünewald sources", at 540; Marquard, *Grünewald und die Reformation*, 45–48; Gualdrini, *Trittico delle cose*, 265–266.

80. I do not find convincing, in support of the current arrangement of the two panels, the aesthetic-chromatic considerations offered by Wetzig, "Die Standflügel des Isenheimer", in Krohm, Oellermann (eds.) *Flügel-Altäre des Späten*, 251–253, according to whom the image of St. Sebastian is too similar, in its pose and dominant red tones, to that of St. John the Baptist in the *Crucifixion*, to be able to imagine one next to the other. In terms of the first point, it is not difficult to imagine the faithful led by the praying gesture of St. Sebastian towards the scene of the Cross, in which it is St. John the Baptist, with his pointing finger, who indicates the dead Christ. In terms of color, I find enchanting the idea of the red darting like a tongue of fire from the cloak of St. Sebastian to that of St. John the Baptist, then re-emerging, almost spent, on Mary Magdalene's cloak. Analogously, the same logic applies in the movement of the red on St. Sebastian's cloak to that of the Madonna in the second opening, then disappearing and reappearing in the curtain of the *Annunciation*.

81. Aubert Gérard, "Rapport d'étude du support et des encadrements du Retable d'Issenheim", in Béguerie-De Paepe, Menu (eds.), *La technique picturale*, 171–176.

82. Schmid, *Die Gemälde und Zeichnungen*, I, 140.

83. I am not completely convinced by it, but unquestionably ingenious is the interpretation of Henri Blum, "Grünewald, les deux volets fixes du Retable d'Issenheim", *L'information d'histoire de l'art*, XVII, 5, 1972, 199–207, who sees St. Anthony as a "doctor" and St. Sebastian as being a "sick person", drawing on the iconography of the illustrations in illuminated medical manuscripts which show the former as being larger than the latter.

84. That the diabolic figure is female—therefore referencing lust (the only type of "temptation" not present in the panel, which we will discuss soon, that portrays St. Anthony assailed by devils) and also ignored by the elderly St. Anthony—is properly clarified by Schubert, *The Isenheimer Altarpiece*, 38.

85. Roth, *Matthias Grünewald die Zeichnungen*, 43–46. Also see Ulrike Heinrichs-Schreiber, "*Natura contra idolon*. Zur Frage des Antikebezugs in Mathis Gothart-Nithart Gemälde des hl. Senbastian am Isenheimer Altar", in *Die Präsenz der Antike im Übergang vom Mittelalter zur Frühen Neuzeit*, ed. by Ludger Grenzmann, Klaus Grubmüller, Fidel Rädl, Martin Stahelin (Göttingen: Vandenhoeck & Ruprecht, 2004), 351–388, at 362–383.

86. The assertion by Kurt Bauch and Charles Sterling, who sees the landscape behind St. Sebastian as a 17th-century addition, appears to be a case of hypercorrection ("Discussion sur la communication de Henri Blum", *Cahiers Alsaciens d'archéologie d'art et d'histoire*, XIX, 1975–76, 74).

87. Ziermann, *Matthias Grünewald*, 100.

88. Adolf Max Vogt, "Grünewalds Sebastianstafel und die Sebastianthema in der Renaissance", *Zeitschrift für schweizerische Archäologie und Kunstgeschichte*, 18, 1958, 1–2, 172–176; Ziermann, *Matthias Grünewald*, 100. Less far-fetched is the reference to a drawing by Antonio del Pollaiolo today in Bayonne proposed by Van den Berg, *Die Passion zu Malen*, 45–46. The similarity of the pose is, in fact, noteworthy, but there is no similarity of style, leading one to think either of second-hand knowledge (but how?) or, perhaps more simply, a regular pose of the models of both the Italian and German painters. In that case, the similarity would simply be a random coincidence.

89. Bianconi, *L'opera completa*, 93.

90. Jacopo da Voragine, *The Golden Legend or Lives of the Saints, Englished by William Caxton (1483)*, ed. by Frederick Startridge Ellis (London: J. M. Dent & Co., 1900), II, 91.

91. "The background of nature here portrayed by Grünewald is the most remarkable German landscape of the entire sixteenth century" (Burkhard, *Matthias Grünewald*, 40).

92. In this scene and in that of the Madonna with Child which will be discussed later, there is a significant number of carefully depicted botanical species, probably based on the pharmacopoeia used in the monastery, as suggested by Wolfgang Kühn, "Grünewalds Isenheimer Altar als Darstellung mittelalterlicher Heilkräuter", *Kosmos*, XLIV, 1948, 327–333, and Lottlise Behling, *Die Pflanze in der mittelalterlichen Tapfelmalerei* (Cologne: Hermann Böhlaus Nachfolger, 1967), 141–147. Also see Comte, *Grünewald, le retable*, 14, and the detailed catalogueing in Schubert, *The Isenheimer Altarpiece*, 159–164.

93. Pantxika Béguerie-De Paepe, entry no. 1, in Béguerie-De Paepe, Lorentz (eds.), *Grünewald et le retable*. 68–70, at 70.

94. The crow, actually a Northern bald Ibis (*geronticus*

eremita), called "Rappvogel" in Alsatian dialect, is also a superb example of painting from life. This bird, today virtually extinct but quite common in 16th-century Germany, was identified by Schubert, *The Isenheimer Altarpiece*, 128–130.

95. Antje-Fee Köllermann, entry no. 31, in Roth (ed.), *Matthias Grünewald Zeichnungen*, 201–205, backs the idea of the autograph; as does, it would seem, Hanns Hubach, entry *Grünewald, Matthias*, 386–396, consulted online at https://www.degruyter.com/database/AKL/entry/_00069638T/html, which also summarizes the hypothesis of seeing in the face of St. Paul a crypto-portrait of the artist.

96. How felicitous it would have been if Kinski had actually met Grünewald's character in his work, considering that the Polish-German actor was the protagonist of some the most memorable movies directed by Werner Herzog, who declared "if I had to name names of painters, those who influenced me, I would call Grünewald": *Herzog on Herzog*, ed. by Paul Cronin, (London: Faber & Faber, 2002), 136.

97. In addition to the standard monographs and the bibliography cited in the footnotes below, see Joseph Bernhart, *Die Symbolik im Menschwerdungsbild des Isenheimer Altares* (Munich: Patmos Verlag, 1921); Egid Beitz, *Grünewalds Isenheimer Menschwerdungsbild und seine Quellen* (Cologne: F. J. Marcan Verlag, 1924); Erwin Poeschel, "Zur Deutung von Grünewalds Weihnachtsbild", *Zeitschrift für Kunstgeschichte*, XIII, 1950, 92–104; Herbert von Einem, "Die 'Menschwerdung Christi' des Isenheimer Altares", in *Kunstgeschichtlichen Studien für Hans Kauffmann*, ed. by Wolfgang Braunfels (Berlin: Mann, 1956), 152–171; Van den Berg, *Die Passion zu Malen*, 69–86; Søren Kaspersen, "'Die drei Marien'. Menschwerdung als Andachtsbild neue Erwägungen über Grünewalds Isenheimer Altar", *Acta ad archaelogiam et artium pertinentia*, 21, 7, 2017, 197–242.

98. Feurstein, *Matthias Grünewald*, 90–98.

99. Mellinkoff, *The Devil at Isenheim*, 77–87, on the other hand interprets the figure as the image of the *Ecclesia*. I do not exclude that this meaning (which is often superimposed on the image of Mary) could be suggested, but I believe that the *Annunciation/Incarnation* sequence depicted on the second side face of the *Isenheim Altarpiece* can only refer to the Virgin Mary in person.

100. Scheja, *Der Isenheimer Altar*, 40–55. This scholar takes up an intriguing idea from Lerse (see Marquard, *Grünewald und die Reformation*, 247–249), according to which the image on the left is nothing other than a vision of the Madonna, ecstatically intent on the right in contemplating the Child.

101. Regarding this iconography, see in particular Caroline Feudale, "The Iconography of the Madonna del Parto", *Marsyas. Studies in the History of Art*, 7, 1954–1957, 8–24; Martin Gregor Lechner, *Maria Gravida. Zum Schwangerschaftsmotiv in der Bildenden Kunst* (Munich: Schnell, 1981); Giovanni Pozzi, "Maria tabernacolo", *Italia medioevale e umanistica*, 32, 1989, 263–326 [focused on the *Madonna del Parto* (Our Lady of Parturition) by Piero della Francesca but with a wealth of more general references]; Massimo Cesareo, "Arte e teologia nel Medioevo: l'iconografia della "Madonna del Parto"", *Arte Cristiana*, LXXXVIII, 796, 2000, 43–63; Jack Dewhurst and Franco Crainz, *The Pregnant Madonna in Christian Art* (Rome: Peliti Associati, 2001).

102. Pozzi, "Maria tabernacolo", 282–283, 313.

103. Jacob Perez, *Commentum in Psalmos Centum et quinquaginta Psalmi Davidici cum expositione*, (Valencia: Imprenta Luis Arinyo y Alfonso Fernández de Córdoba, 1484), cited by Pozzi, "Maria tabernacolo", 290, in the Lyons edition, Antonio Du Ry, 1521.

104. On the pomegranate as a nuptial attribute taken from the *Song of Songs* and in reference to Mary, see Mirella Levi D'Ancona, *The Garden of the Renaissance. Botanical Symbolism in Italian Painting* (Florence: Leo S. Olschki, 1974), 316; Pozzi, "Maria tabernacolo", 305.

105. Lechner, *Maria Gravida*, 223, 231.

106. Jacopo Da Varagine, *Sermones aurei de Maria Virgine Dei matre*, (Venetiis: ad Signum Concordiae, 1590), 138. Also see Pozzi, "Maria tabernacolo", 314.

107. Mellinkoff, *The Devil at Isenheim*, 19–43, has no doubt believing it is a demon, in fact, Lucifer himself, the fallen angel, as also does Schubert, *The Isenheimer Altarpiece*, 79–80. However, the fact that he is also kneeling and playing with an inspired air in a not very "demonic" way cannot be ignored. Diametrically opposed the interpretation of Reichenauer, *Grünewald*, 148–153, who even considers it to be the image of the Archangel Gabriel, before becoming entangled in fruitless esoteric details that even call into question Giovanni Pico della Mirandola. Finally, it should be noted that angels with a comparable semblance are sometimes represented in German art, for example the woodcut portraying *Mary Magdalene in Ecstasy* by Meister E S, translated into a sculpture around 1490 by the workshop of János Weiss in the Berki altarpiece, today at the Szépművészeti Múzeum in Budapest (Mária Aggházy, *Early Wood Carvings in Hungary*, Budapest: Publishing House of the Hungarian Academy of Sciences, 1965, 20. However, I must report that I did not find the etching by Master E S mentioned by this Hungarian scholar), nor even in the Münnerstadt altarpiece by Tilman Riemenschneider [fig. 58], which was mentioned previously.

108. Particularly intense comments regarding the angelic concert are found in Nochlin, *Mathis at Colmar*, 17–21, and Hayum, *The Isenheim Altarpiece*, 46–47. The latter, a bit later on (49), provides an unusual and fascinating interpretation of the reverse side of the altarpiece: "through light and color, [it] provokes the kind of visual fixation precedent to a trancelike state. This effect is a perceptual equivalent to the content, where occult beliefs and magical means are marshaled to combat the evil spirits associated with disease."

109. "Im virdten grad ist die einig iunkcfraw, die gots gepererin Maria, die allein geschmeckt hat, wie sues er sei, dero ist unterwurffig Iesus, zu irem wolgeuallen lachet er ytso, schier weint er, nun redt er susiglich, nun felt er sie an vand kust sie, nun schlest er nackent bey der nackenden, und beweisst yr der gleichen allerley worzeichen seiner lieb" (Johann von Staupitz, *Opera quae reperiri potuerunt omnia*, ed. by Joachim Karl. Friedrich Knaake, I, Potsdam: Krausnick, 1867, 161). This sermon, delivered in Nuremberg in 1516 during Advent, was published in January 1517 and, therefore, falls just outside the chronological limits for the creation of the Isenheim altarpiece. However, as noted in the introduction, the text was "tantopere efflagitatus", in essence, something difficult to obtain in such a short time, and it could be thought that Staupitz assembled in the Nuremberg sermon, probably delivered in German,

material he had already used in his homiletic activity (for the entire question, see Posset, *The Front-Runner*, 162–190, from which the English translation of the passage is taken).

110. Supporting the thesis of the bed is the passage by Staupitz quoted above. In support of the cot is the spread of "sacred cradles" of Baby Jesus as very popular devotional objects in German, Flemish and Dutch areas: see the detailed disucssion in Caroline Walker Bynum, *Dissimilar Similitudes. Devotional Objects in Late Medieval Europe* (New York: Zone Books, 2020), 58–96, even if the gender-oriented interpretation seems quite forced. Schubert, *The Isenheimer Altarpiece*, 96, also puts forward the idea of interpreting the cradle also as a bed, even linking it to the hospital beds in Isenheim. Similarly, although within the context of a complicated and ingenious interpretation of the entire altarpiece linked to vegetal symbology (with many overlapping interpretations, as always occurs in authentically iconological essays), it is again interpreted as a hospital bed by Bryda, "The Exuding Wood", 22, who, perceptively, also admits the interpretation of this Madonna as the *Sponsa Christi* and so attributes to the "bed" the meaning of "flowering nuptial bed", in accordance with the *Song of Songs*, 1:15.

111. Mellinkoff, *The Devil at Isenheim*, 61–67, interprets the Hebrew lettering that decorates the potty in a negative sense, associating the Hebrew alphabet with the content of the potty. I suspect, rather, that the connection should be interpreted from the standpoint of the flesh (and also, therefore, in terms of physiology!). Jesus was Jewish, therefore rendering more inseparable physicalness and Jewishness. As Stefano Zuffi has suggested to me, a euphemistic version of this theme could perhaps be suggested in the make-shift bath in a fountain by the *Madonna with Sleeping Child during the flight into Egypt* at the Berlin Gemäldegalerie (inv. 638B), by Albrecht Altdorfer, dated 1510 [fig. 140]. A different interpretation in which the first letter (from the right) *Shin* would have apotropaic significance, is suggested by Hayum, *The Isenheim Altarpiece*, 42. On the other hand, and in my view totally convincingly, Van den Berg, *Die Passion zu Malen*, 85, writes that "the concept of the incarnation of Christ is depicted here in both its fullest and most fundamentally earthly sense", although not referring explicitly to this specific detail. However, I find overly far-fetched the Kabbalistic interpretation proposed by Reichenauer, *Grünewald*, 153–158; as is the although creative one by Schubert, *The Isenheimer Altarpiece*, 89–97, which interprets the entire scene as alluding to the rite of circumcision. Schubert notes that the Baby Jesus, although theoretically portrayed at the age of eight or nine months, is still uncircumcised and, implausibly, interprets this fact from an esoteric standpoint. I wonder if, in the polysemic organization of this image, the non-circumcision of Jesus does not characterize this image, *as well as* that of the Nativity, which, alone, would justify the presence, on the mountain in the background, of shepherds being announced by angels of the Savior's birth.

112. Karl Harmuth, *Die verschlossene Pforte. Eine Untersuchung zu Ez. 41, 1–3* (Breslau: Universität, Dissertation, 1933), and Pozzi, "Maria tabernacolo", 306.

113. Scheja, *Der Isenheimer Altar*, 23; for the Bosch triptych Fischer, *Hieronymus Bosch*, 154–175, 250–251.

114. "Ego summa et ignea vis, quae omnes viventes scintillas accendi et nulla mortalia efflavi, sed illa diiudico ut sunt [. . .]. Ego itaque vis ignea [. . .]." (Ildegarda di Bingen, *Il libro delle opere divine*, ed. by Marta Cristiani, Michela Pereira, Milan: Mondadori, 2003, 138–139). The English translation of Hildegard's text, *Book of Divine Works with Letters and Songs*, ed. by Matthew Fox, (Rochester (VT), Bear & Company, 1987), could not have had the benefit of the critical edition published in 1996, and this is the reason why it was not utilized here. For the circulation of Hildegard's texts, see M. Reeves, *The Influence of Prophecy*, 560.

115. Reichenauer, *Grünewald*, 126–128.

116. Lynn Jacobs, entry no. 50 in Marrow, Shestack (eds.), *Hans Baldung Grien*, 204–206; Sybille Bock and Saskia Durian-Ress, entry no. 15, in Durian-Ress (ed.), *Hans Baldung Grien*, 130–131. More generally on the relationship between the two painters, see François-Georges Pariset, "Grünewald et Baldung", *Cahiers Alsaciens d'archéologie d'art et d'histoire*, XIX, 1975–76, 147–172; Morat-Fromm, "Eine Begegnung mit Folgen?". On a literary level (which is nonetheless plausible), a meeting between the two painters during work on the monumental altarpieces in Isenheim and Freiburg is imagined by Christoph Meckel, *H. B. G.* (Freiburg im Breisgau: Modo Verlag, 2005, ed, 2012), 17–37; thanks to Philippe Sénéchal for suggesting this source.

117. For example, Rudolf Günther, *Die Bilder des Genten und Isenheimer Altars* (Studien über christliche Denkmäler, 16, Leipzig: Dieterich'sche Verlagsbuchhandlung), 1925; Erwin Poeschel, "Zur Deutung von Grünewalds Weihnachtsbild", 92–104; Gustav Münzel, "Eine neue Erklärung zu dem Menschwerdungsbild im Isenheimer Altar", *Zeitschrift für Kunstgeschichte*, XV, 1952, 75–77; Herbert von Einem, "Grünewalds Auferstehung Christi aus Isenheim", in *Festschrift der Arbeitsgemeinschaft für Forschung des Landes Nordrhein-Westphalen* (Cologne and Opladen: Westdeutscher Verlag, 1955), 23–24; Lanckoronska, *Matthias Gothart-Neithart*, 123–144; Scheja, *Der Isenheimer Altar* 1969; E. M. Vetter (1971), 2009, 69–101; Mellinkoff, *The Devil at Isenheim*; Reale, *I misteri dell'altare*.

118. Renate Kolle, entry no. 11.4, in *Dürer Holbein Grünewald*, 183–187; Roth, *Matthias Grünewald die Zeichnungen*, 59–60.

119. *Vita e lettere di san Bonifacio*, ed. by Enrica Mascherpa (Bari: Le noci, 1991).

120. Bernard Saran, "Von der Macht des Wortes im Bild", in Seidel, *Grünewald Der Isenheimer*, ed. 1990, 80–97. However, I cannot agree with the next step in this scholar's reconstruction which imagined the male figure in the Vienna drawing, discussed later, as St. Joseph, next to the Madonna with Child.

121. Detlef Zinke, *Masterpieces from Middle Age to Baroque at the Augustinermuseum of Freiburg i. Br.* (Berlin-München: Deutscher Kunstverlag, 2010), 152–153.

122. Alessandro Ballarin, "La Salomè del Romanino" (1971), in Idem, *La Salomè del Romanino* 2005, I, 43–121, at 78–81; Alessandro Nova, *Romanino* (Turin: Allemandi, 1994), 211–212. Coming very close to the truth, Scheja, *Der Isenheimer Altar*, 24, suggested a color comparison with Titian. It is a pity that neither he nor subsequent studies developed this promising line of investigation.

123. Jacobus of Voragine, *The Golden Legend*, 1900, II, 225. For a useful, detailed iconographic interpretation of the scene, see Jean-Michel Massing, "Étude iconographique de l'Agression de Saint Antoine de Grünewald", *Cahiers Alsaciens d'archéologie d'art et d'histoire*, XIX, 1975–76, 105–126. See also Jerry Marino,

"Touch of Evil: Disease and the Diabolical in Grünewald's *Temptation of St. Anthony*", *Athanor*, XXVI, 2008, 23–33. For the *Legenda Aurea* as the main iconographic source, see also Massing, "Étude conographique de l'Agression de Saint Antoine de Grünewald", in *Studies in Imagery*, I, 363–391.

124. Very interesting the observation of Hayum, *The Isenheim Altarpiece* 79, according to whom there is a graphic hierarchy in the altarpiece's inscriptions: Upper case Roman for the phrase of John the Baptist in the Crucifixion; elegant Gothic for the citation from Isaiah in the Annunciation, and lower-case Italic for the scroll in the Temptation of St. Anthony.

125. Schubert, *The Isenheimer Altarpiece*, 122.

126. Enrico Castelli, *Il demoniaco nell'arte* (Milan and Florence: Electa, 1952, new edition edited by Enrico Castelli Gattinara, Turin: Bollati Boringhieri, 2007), 114–119.

127. See, for example, Jean-Martin Charcot and Paul Richier, *Les difformes et les malades dans l'art* (Paris: Lecrosnier et Babé, 1889), 79–80; a rich and perceptive survey is offered by Gualdrini, *Trittico delle cose*, 147–154. See also Marquard, "Die Versuchunstafel als Schlüsselbild", 79–88. In addition, there are also the intense verses of Margherita Guidacci, *L'altare di Isenheim*, subsequently in *Le Poesie*, 298–299, who interprets the scene as a sort of terrifying obsession that is also relevant today, except that she replaces Grünewald's demons with the military and technocracy in general. As commented by Graziella Magherini, "Perturbante estetica e creazione artistica: Margherita Guidacci e l'altare di Isenheim", in *Per Margherita Guidacci*, conference proceedings (Florence, October 15–16, 1999), ed. by Margherita Ghilardi (Florence: Le Lettere, 2001), 119–133, at 131: "The terrors from the psychotic point of view are always the same [. . .], what changes over time is the iconography of terror." See also Diletta Gamberini, "Margherita Guidacci e la riflessione sulla modernità attraverso il prisma di un'ecfrasi da Grünewald", *IPR Italian Poetry Revew*, XVIII, 2023, 249–280, with extensive bibliography.

128. Suzanne G. Valenstein, *A Handbook of Chinese Ceramics* (New York: Metropolitan Museum of Art, 1989), plate 21; Alexandre Hougron, *La céramique chinoise ancienne* (Paris: Editions de l'Amateur, 2015), 96. Thanks to the special affinity (*secundum quid*, obviously) with the Grünewald demon, I am including the vase from the Xuande era (1426–1435) at the Metropolitan Museum of Art, Washington (inv. 37.191.1) [fig. 151].

129. I find very astute the observation of Gamberini, "Margherita Guidacci e la riflessione", 261: "His upward glance—but in the opposite direction to that where a ray of light from the sky reveals a God the Father already focused on aiding the ascetic by supervising the armed angel he has sent to rout the demons—suggests that his faith is equally irresolute."

130. Ernst Wolf, *Staupitz und Luther. Ein Beitrag zur Theologie des Johannes von Staupitz und deren Bedeutung für Luthers theologischen Werdegang* (Quellen und Forschungen zur Reformationsgeschichte, 9, Leipzig: Heinsius, 1927), 16–27. It should be noted that the Brethren of the Common Life was a brotherhood founded in the second half of the 14th century by Gert Groote, who was a disciple of Jan van Ruysbroeck (in turn influenced by the great Rheinland mystics, Meister Eckhart and, above all, Heinrich Suso and Johannes Tauler). The Order Brotherhood became culturally prestigious at the end of the 15th century (Staupitz himself was not immune to its influence, nor was Bosch, and the young Luther would attend their schools), and it believed that *massima temptatio est non temptari* (Castelli, *Il demoniaco nell'arte*, ed, 2007, 47–49; for a more detailed discussion, see John van Engen, *Sisters and Brothers of the Common Life: The Devotio Moderna and the World of the Later Middle Ages*, Philadelphia: University of Pennsylvania Press, 2008).

131. See also the observations of Steinmetz, *Luther and Staupitz*, 74–75, in reference to Staupitz's youthful commentary to the Book of Job: "Temptation is important in the Christian life. While every temptation can be overcome by resignation to the will of God, the process of temptation is essential as a means of sanctification and as a ground for certitude."

132. Koepplin and Falk, *Lucas Cranach. Gemälde-Zeichnungen-Grafik*, exhibition catalogue (Basel: Birkhaus, 1974), II, no. 398; Giulia Bartrum, *German Renaissance Prints 1490–1550*, exhibition catalogue (London: British Museum, 1995), no. 168.

133. Defining what he called the "devotion of the decline" of late Gothic sculpture, Henri Focillon unintentionally stated perfectly the spiritual character of the *Isenheim Altarpiece*: "Finally, the devotion of the decline, more demanding and perhaps more sensitive in its emotions, replaced this serenity with its own unease, passionately devoted itself to the terrible scenes of the Calvary, fixed them, contemplated them, made them live again, suffered them anew, with a dramatic pageantry and mystic power of re-creation which conferred holiness even on the accessory and the indifferent object" (Henri Focillon, *The Art of the West in the Middle Ages*, II, *Gothic Art*, edited and introduced by Jean Bony, translated by Donald King, London and New York: Phaidon, 1963, 2° ed. 1969, 72). The original French text, more precise and powerful, sounds as follows: Enfin la devotion du déclin, plus exigeante et peut-être plus sensible, substitue son inquiétude à cette sérénité, s'attache passionnément aux scénes terribles du Calvaire, les fixe, les voit, les fait revivre, les souffre à nouveau, avec un faste dramatique et un pouvoir mystique de résurrection, qui conferent à l'accessoire et à l'objet une valeur sacrée. » (Henri Focillon, *Art d'Occident*, II, *Le Moyen Age gothique* (1938), Paris : Librairie Armand Colin, 1965, 164.

134. A broader examination of the cultural level of the Antoniteswould probably still need to be carried out, but some aspects of it can be found in Peter Macardle, "Matthias Wegener and Traces of Antonite Humanism in Cologne", *Journal of the Warburg and Courtauld Institutes*, 57, 1994, 254–263.

135. In this case, I am in disagreement with Massing, "Schongauer, Bosch, Grünewald et les autres. De quelques *Tribulations de saint Antoine* et leurs influences", in *Studies in Imagery*, I, 392–420, which essentially denies any early visual popularity for the Grünewald panel.

136. Dietmar Lüdke, *Martin Schaffner. Die vier Antonius-Tafeln von 1517* (Karlsruhe: Staatliche Kunsthalle Karlsruhe, 1999); Manuel Teget-Welz, *Martin Schaffner. Leben und Werk eines Ulmer Malers zwischen Spätmittelalter und Renaissance* (Forschungen zur Geschichte der Stadt Ulm, 32, Ulm: Kohlhammer, 2008), 88–90, 405–417.

137. Sybille Bock and Saskia Durian-Res, entry no. 28, in Durian-Ress (ed.), *Hans Baldung Grien*, 156–157.

138. Dorit Schäfer, entry no. 16 in Béguerie-De Paepe, Lorentz (eds.), *Grünewald et le retable*, 136–139.

139. Therefore, I am not convinced by the interpretation of Marquard, "Die Versuchunstafel als Schlüsselbild", 86–88.

140. Élisabeth Ravaud and Elsa Lambert, "Les étapes d'elaboration", in Béguerie-De Paepe, Lorentz (eds.), *Grünewald et le retable*, 232–243, and above all Carole Juillet, "Quelques hypothèses sur le panneau de la Tentation de Saint Antoine", *La technique picturale*, in Béguerie-De Paepe, Menu (eds.), *La technique picturale*, 61–64. It seems to me that this very important observation is not at all shared by François-René Martin, "Grünewald e la sua arte", in Martin, Menu and Ramond, *Grünewald*, 10–233, at 110–120.

141. Berger, *Portraits*, 51, writes that the Isenheim Crucifix "is painted inch by inch. No contour, no cavity, no rise within the contours, reveals a moment's flickering of the intensity of depiction", but this comment could certainly be applied to the entire painted surface of the altarpiece.

142. Wilhelm Rolfs, "Eine Italienische Vorlage Grünewalds für die Versuchung des hl. Anton vom Isenheimer Altar", *Repertorium für Kunstwissenschaft*, XLII, 1920, 227–238; see also Zülch, *Der historische Grünewald*, 202.

143. In addition, Massing, "Étude iconographique", 107–110, also cites unlikely alternative figurative texts, such as Starnina or the Master of the Osservanza, but also a 15th-century Florentine etching which is more interesting and could likely be taken into consideration.

144. For the moment, I limit myself to the overview offered by Castelli, *Il demoniaco nell'arte*, ed. 2007, 98.

145. For this, see, in general, Hermann Fiore (ed.), *Dürer e l'Italia*.

146. Franz Rieffel, "Grünewald-Studien (II)", *Zeitschrift für Christliche Kunst*, 10, 1897, 65–78.

147. Oskar Hagen, "Zur Frage der Italienreise Matthias Grünewalds", *Kunstchronik*, XXVII, 1917, 73; Idem, "Grünewald und das Montagna-Tryptychon in den Uffizien", *ibidem*, 411. The theme of a trip to Italy also runs through the monograph by Hagen, *Matthias Grünewald*. Hagen's short articles triggered opposition from Emmy Voigtländer, "Ist Matthias Grünewald in Italien gewesen?", *Tägliche Rundschau*, February 19, 1918, and Eadem, "Zur Italienreise Grünewalds", *Kunstchronik*, XXIX, 1918, 187, with the reply by Hagen, "Einheit der künstlerischen Persönlichkeit: Grünewald", *ibidem*, 225. The idea also circulated in the book by Josten, *Matthias Grünewald*, 27.

148. Réau, *Mathias Grünewald*, 64–68.

149. Ruhmer, *Grünewald, The paintings*, 119.

150. Maria Lanckoronska, *Neithart in Italien. Ein Versuch* (München: Frühmorgen, 1967).

151. However, it must be said that Lanckoronska—excessive and sometimes disarmingly naive in the answers she offers, all from a bookish perspective—is quite perceptive in the questions she poses. As we will see, Grünewald's Italian trip is a real theme for critique, as is, in a fundamental way, his relationship with sculpture as she discussed in another book which has already been spoken of.

152. Philippe Lorentz, "Grünewald et Léonard de Vinci: les draperies dans le retable d'Issenheim", in Béguerie-De Paepe, Lorentz (eds.), *Grünewald et le retable*, 16–31. Significantly, Lorentz writes that the German painter's familiarity with Leonardo's drapery studies "ne relève pas de la simple observation des dessins du maître italien, qui *d'une manière ou d'une autre*, seraient parvenu dans le stock de modèles de l'artiste allemand" (26, italic emphasis is mine).

153. The dating around 1490 of the second *Virgin of the Rocks*, both given the internal aspects of Leonardo's development and his measurable influence on Milanese painting in the last decade of the 15th century, is thanks to Alessandro Ballarin, *Leonardo a Milano. Problemi di leonardismo milanese tra Quattrocento e Cinquecento. Giovanni Antonio Boltraffio prima della Pala Casio* (Verona: Aurora, 2010), I, 3–262 (texts written between 1985 and 2000). Specifically, 1489 is the chronology argued, on the basis of style and new documentation, by Edoardo Villata, *Leonardo* (Rome: Istituto della Enciclopedia Italiana, 2015), 97–107.

154. Maria Teresa Fiorio, *Giovanni Antonio Boltraffio. Un pittore milanese nel lume di Leonardo* (Rome-Milan: Jandi Sapi, 2000), 78–80; Ballarin, *Leonardo a Milano*, I, 41–45, 622–628, 676; Antonio Mazzotta, entry no. 65, in *Leonardo da Vinci Painter at the Court of Milan*, exhibition catalogue, London, ed. by Luke Syson, Larry Keith (London: National Gallery Company, 2011), 240–241.

155. This information is provided by the contemporary report of Hans Stolz: Wolfram Stolz, *Die Hans Stolz'sche Gebweiler Chronik. Zeugenbericht über den Bauernkrieg am Oberrhein* (Freiburg am Breisgau: Stolz, 1979), 128: "Am Dienstag vor St. Mathäus 1516 [appunto il 19 febbraio 1516] starb der Präzeptor der Issenheimer Antoniter, ein frommer Mann, der den Glockenturm sowie u. a. auch das Gewölbe der Issenheimer Kirche errichten und die Tafel auf dem Hochaltar aufstellen liess. Er hatte den Antonitern grosse Ehre erwiesen". This is, and is not to be underestimated, the absolutely first mention of the Grünewald altarpiece. In the next century, the Stolz chronicle is essentially copied by the Dominican Seraphin Dietler (1650–1724), who, regarding the altarpiece, feels it necessary to add: "die tafflen so iberaus thünstlich gearbeitet, von dem weltberiembten künstler Albrecht Dyrrer mahler undt bildhauer zugleich, liess er [Guers] auch machen auff den Fronaltar" (*Die Gebweiler Chronik des dominikaners Fr. Seraphin Dietler*, a cura di Johann von Schlumberger, Gebweiler: Verlag der J. Bolsse'schen Buchhandlung, 1898, 88).

156. Bischoff, "Grünewald? Un mystère", in Béguerie and Bischoff, *Grünewald le maître d'Issenheim*, 63–111, at 92–93.

157. Herrmann, *Die Protokolle des Mainzer Domkapitels*, III/ I.

158. For these and other historical events involving the altarpiece, see Béguerie-De Paepe and Haas, *Le retable d'Issenheim*; François Desseilles, *Les temps juridiques du retable d'Issenheim, Dépasser l'étude de cas ?*, in *Nouveaux regards sur les saisies patrimoniales en Europe à l'époque de la Révolution française*, conference proceedings (Bruxelles, May 30-31, 2018), ed. by Pierre-Yves Kairis (Turnhout: Brepols, 2023), 343–362.

Chapter IV | Italy

1. See, in particular, Hermann Kellenbenz, "Augsburg, Nürnberg und Mailand in der Zeit von Ludovico il Moro", in *Milano nell'età di Ludovico il Moro*, conference proceedings (Milan: Comune di Milano, 1983), 65–78; Patrizia Mainoni, "La nazione che non c'è: i tedeschi a Milano e a Como fra Tre e Quattocento", in *Comunità forestiere e nationes nell'Europa dei secoli XIII-XVI*, ed. by Giovanna Petti Balbi (Naples: Liguori,

2001), 200–228; Patrizia Mainoni, "Attraverso i valichi svizzeri. Merci oltremontane e mercati lombardi", in *Le Alpi medievali nello sviluppo delle regioni contermini*, ed. by Gian Maria Varanini (Naples: Liguori, 2004), 99–122. Starting at the end of the 1400s, the German community in Milan, although not organized in a formal "fondaco", tended to meet around the school of St. Catherine in the Basilica of San Nazaro Maggiore: Carlo Cairati and Edoardo Rossetti, "Luoghi di diffusione della cultura oltremontana nella Milano sforzesca: suggestioni "todesche" a Santa Caterina di San Nazaro", in Elsig, Gaggetta (eds.), *Cultura oltremontana in Lombardia*, 81–128, at 95–109.

2. Giuliana Algeri, "Ai confini del Medioevo", in Giuliana Algeri and Anna De Floriani, *La pittura in Liguria. Il Quattrocento* (Genuaa: Tormena, 1992), 15–224, especially 170–181; A. De Marchi, "Genua Amman von Ravensburg, Zanetto Bugatto e la parte fiamminga nella pittura lombarda di età sforzesca", *Nuovi Studi*, 27, 2022–2023, 61–86, especially 75–85 and accompanying notes.

3. Federico Cavalieri, "Una nuova presenza oltremontana nella pittura milanese dell'età sforzesca", *Nuovi Studi*, 5, 1998, 29–37; Frédéric Elsig, entry no. IV.5, in *Arte lombarda dai Visconti agli Sforza. Milano al centro dell'Europa*, exhibition catalogue, Milan, ed. by Mauro Natale, Serena Romano (Milan: Skira, 2015), 287–288.

4. Gianfranco Bortolotto, "Sisto Frei scultore (notizie 1500–1515)", *Arte Veneta*, 41, 1987, 176–184; Laura dal Pra, entry in *Rinascimento e passione per l'antico. Andrea Riccio e il suo tempo*, exhibition catalogue, Trento, ed. by Andrea Bacchi, Laura Giacomelli (Trento: Provincia Autonoma di Trento, 2008), 598–605; Marco Rossati, "Sculture oltremontane nella Lombardia del Quattro e Cinquecento: presenza, scambi, importazioni", Elsig and Gaggetta (eds.), *Cultura oltremontana in Lombardia*, 129–165, at 151–152. At an earlier time we can also mention the cases of the sculptors Johannes Teutonicus and Paul Moerich von Rott: see Sara Cavatorti, *Giovanni Teutonico. Scultura lignea tedesca nell'Italia del Quattrocento* (Perugia: Aguaplano, 2016); Mauro Grazioli, "Il caso di Giovanni Tedesco: documenti d'archivio", in *Rinascimento sul Garda*, exhibition catalogue, Riva del Garda, ed. by Luca Gabrielli, Giuseppe Sava, Luca Siracusano, Marco Tanzi (Florence: Edifir. 2024), 243-245; Aldo Galli, Matteo Mazzalupi, "Sulle tracce di don Paolo Moerich, chierico e scultore", *Analecta Pomposiana. Studi di storia religiosa delle diocesi di Ferrara e Comacchio*, 39, 2015, *Quattrocento bondense. Religiosità, stampa, arte, cultura*, ed. by Silvia Superbi, 13-60.

5. This is a difficult matter that still requires further inquiries. Following the preliminary essay by Pietro C. Marani, "Dürer, Leonardo e i pittori lombardi del Quattrocento", in Herrmann Fiore (ed.), *Dürer e l'Italia*, 51–61, there is now the more in-depth Simone Ferrari, *Dürer e Leonardo. Il Paragone delle Arti e nord e a sud delle Alpi* (Genoa: Genova University Press, 2020).

6. Heinrich Alfred Schmid, *Hans Holbein der Jüngere. Sein Aufstieg zur Meisterschaft und sein Englischer Stil*, I (Basel: Holbein Verlag, 1948), 73–127; Roberto Salvini, *La pittura tedesca* (Milan: Garzanti, 1959), 180; Alessandro Ballarin, "Holbein e la Lombardia" (2000), in Idem, *Leonardo a Milano*, III, 901–945. Ballarin (*ibidem*, 907) establishes a parallel between Holbein's famous *Dead Christ* and Grünewald's *Lamentation* in the *Isenheim Altarpiece*, noting in the former "a Lombard cultural background that Grünewald does not have", which, if the comparison is limited to these two works, is unquestionably true. If anything, the problem lies in the fact that, as we have already seen and will be expanded on in the pages that follow, after the altarpiece now in Colmar, Mathis also created other works in which, if I am seeing correctly, Lombard references clearly emerge. References in Holbein to Leonardo and Andrea Solario are also noted in Jochen Sander, "The Artistic Development of Hans Holbein the Younger as Panel Painter during his Basel Years", in *Hans Holbein the Younger. The Basel Years 1515–1532*, Basel, Munich and Berlin exhibition catalogue (Munich: Prestel, 2006), 14–18, but hypothesizing that Hans could have seen works by Italian painters during his 1524 stay in France.

7. Mauro Natale, "L'ancona dell'Immacolata Concezione a Cantù" and entry no. 27–29, Paola Astrua and Giovanni Romano, entry no. 30, in *Zenale e Leonardo. Tradizione e rinnovamento della pittura lombarda*, exhibition catalogue (Milan: Electa, 1982), 24–33, 96–99, 99–101; Stefania Buganza, entry in *Santa Maria dei Servi tra Medioevo e Rinascimento. Arte superstite di una chiesa scomparsa nel cuore di Milano*, exhibition catalogue Milan, ed. by Ermes Maria Ronchi (Milan: Mondadori, 1997), 48–51; Stefania Buganza, "Bernardo Zenale alla certosa di Pavia", *Nuovi Studi*, 4, 1997, 109–130.

8. Stefania Buganza, entry, in *Bramantino. L'arte nuova del Rinascimanto lombardo*, exhibition catalogue, Lugano, ed. by Mauro Natale (Milan: Skira, 2014), 250–253, with bibliography; Alessandra Galizzi Kroegel, "The Altarpieces by Bernardo Zenale at the Getty and Denver Art Museums: Two Case Studies for the Iconography of the Immaculate Conception", *Ikon. Journal of Iconographic Studies*, 4, 2017, 201–216; Gianluca Poldi, "Una diversa Vergine delle Rocce. *Underdrawing* e osservazioni visive intorno alla pala di Denver di Bernardo Zenale", *Artibus et Historiae*, 2025 (forthcoming).

9. For the small Brera panel, likely part of a predella depicting *Christ among the apostles*, see *La riscoperta di un dipinto della Pinacoteca di Brera. Giovanni Agostino da Lodi. Il maestro e il giovane allievo*, ed. by Sandrina Bandera (Milan: Le Nuove Grafiche, 2007), even if the hypothesis according to which St. Peter would be a crypto-portrait of Leonardo is, to put it kindly, bizarre.

10. Mauro Natale, entry no. 7 in *Bramantino. L'arte nuova del Rinascimento lombardo*, exhibition catalogue Luganom ed. by Mauro Natale (Milan: Skira, 2014), 106–111 for the historical information. In terms of critique and philology, I see no reason to revise what I wrote in Edoardo Villata, *Tristezza della resurrezione. Bramantino negli anni di Ludovico il Moro* (Milan: Ennerre, 2012), 41–45.

11. Giovanni Agosti and Jacopo Stoppa, entry no. 8 in *Bramantino a Milano*, exhibition catalogue, Milan, ed. by Giovanni Agosti, Jacopo Stoppa, Marco Tanzi (Milan: Officina Libraria, 2012), 136–151 (but I really do not think that the hand in perspective is an "invention" of the restoration work, as suggested in this text). I continue to believe—and sooner or later I will discuss this in detail—that the hypothesis of a provenance from the St. Jerome monastery in Milan and a commission from Bernardino de Carvajal around 1510, apparently confirmed by documentation, are philologically untenable and essentially the result of a misunderstanding (Edoardo Rossetti, "Uno spagnolo

tra i francesi e la devozione gesuata: il cardinale Bernardino Carvajal e il monastero di San Girolamo di porta Vercellina a Milano", in *Le Duché de Milan et les commanditaires français (1499–1521)*, conference proceedings, Geneva, March 30–31, 2012, ed. by Frédéric Elsig, Mauro Natale (Rome: Viella, 2013), 181–235, especially 199–212).

12. Roberto Longhi, "Ampliamenti" (1940), in *Officina ferrarese* (def. ed. 1956, Florence: Sansoni, 1974), 188; Daniela Scaglietti Kelescian, in Marzia Faietti, Daniela Scaglietti Kelescian, *Amico Aspertini* (Modena: Artioli, 1995), 164; Gianni Nigrelli, entry no. 40 in *Amico Aspertini 1474–1552, artista bizzarro nell'età di Dürer e Raffaello*, exhibition catalogue Bologna, ed. by Andrea Emiliani, Daniela Scaglietti Kelescian (Cinisello Balsamo: Silvana Editoriale, 2008),164–165.

13. For the Como panel attributed to Aspertini by Giovanni Romano, "Verso la "maniera moderna": da Mantegna a Raffaello", in *Storia dell'arte italiana*, 6, *Cinquecento e Seicento* (Turin: Einaudi, 1981), 5–83, especially 52 footnote 5 (English translation by Claire Dorey, "Towards the Modern Manner: From Mantegna to Raphael", in *History of Italian Art*, vol. 2, Cambridge: Polity Books, 1994, 373–488, especially 479–480 footnote 82), see at least Alessandro Ballarin, *Dosso Dossi. La pittura a Ferrara negli anni del Ducato di Alfonso I*, 2 vols. (Cittadella: Bertoncello, 1994–1995, I, 1995), 36, II, 1994, fig. 57 (ca. 1515–1520), D. Scaglietti Kelescian, in Faietti, Scaglietti Kelescian, *Amico Aspertini*, 91 (ca. 1519, contemporaneous with the altarpiece of St. Petronius); Andrea Luigi Casero, entry no. 56 in Emiliani, Scaglietti Kelescian (eds.), *Amico Aspertini*, 200–201. I must say that the Como panel seems closer to me to the Bologna altarpiece in San Martino Maggiore, rather than that of St. Petronius, already marked by the encounter with Dosso and, above all, Pordenone. On the other hand, I find it difficult to recognize specific Grünewaldian elements in the *Crucifixion* by Vincenzo Pagani at the Fermo Pinacoteca Civica (Wolfgang Minaty, "Ein Grünewald in Italien? Wie plötzlich der Maler Vincenzo Pagani ins Visier kommt", *Mainfrankisches Jahrbuch für Geschichte und Kunst*, 67, 2015, 49–64; also see footnote 367). I also note the similarity with Lotto already noted previously, especially in terms of the *Trinity* in Sant'Alessandro in Colonna, a work datable, I repeat, to 1519–1520, according to Dal Pozzolo. I believe it is significant that critics have noted similarities between Grünewald and Lotto, specifically in the latter's works created in Bergamo and datable to the early 1520s, such as the altarpiece in Santo Spirito, 1521 (Mario Dal Bello, *Lorenzo Lotto. Un incontro*, Città del Vaticano: Libreria Editrice Vaticana, 2011, 60–61; Dal Pozzolo, *Lorenzo Lotto. Catalogo*, 188–189), the announcing angel in the Ponteranica altarpiece, 1522 (Rodolfo Pallucchini, "Un solitario confessore del suo tempo", in Giordana Mariani Canova, *L'opera completa del Lotto*, Milan: Rizzoli, 1975, 5–10, especially 8; Dal Pozzolo, *Lorenzo Lotto. Catalogo*, 200–201), or the *Lamentation* in Sant'Alessandro, ca. 1522–1523 (Mariani Canova, *L'opera completa del Lotto*, 96; Giovanni Carlo Federico Villa, entry in *Maitres vénitiens, Chefs d'Oeuvre de l'Accademia Carrara de Bergamo et du Musée Royale d'Anvers*, Brussels exhibition catalogue ed. by Giovanni Carlo Federico Villa, Cinisello Balsamo: Silvana Editoriale, 2011, 144–145; Dal Pozzolo, *Lorenzo Lotto. Catalogo*, 270–271).

14. Regarding Hutten's years in Italy, see Hajo Holborn, *Ulrich von Hutten and the German Reformation* (1937), ed. by Roland Herbert Bainton (New York: Harper, 1967), 39–86.

15. Roth, *Matthias Grünewald die Zeichnungen*, 28–29, with dating "Um 1510–11".

16. Hütt, *Albrecht Dürer*, 2, 1850.

17. Jochen Sander, entry no. 26–27 in *Fantastische Welten. Albrecht Altdorfer und das Expressive in der Kunst um 1500*, exhibition catalogue, Frankfurt and Vienna ed. by Stefan Roller, Jochen Sander (Munich: Hirmer, 2010), 76–79, with previous bibliography.

18. Olivia Savatier Sjöholm, entry no. 27b, in *Albrecht Altdorfer maître de la Renaissance allemande*, exhibition catalogue ed. by Hélène Grollemund, Séverine Lepape, Olivia Savatier Sjöholm (Paris: Louvre éditions-Lienart 2020),110–115.

19. Roth, *Matthias Grünewald die Zeichnungen*, 63–64, with shareable dating "Um 1516–19".

20. Christof Metzger, "Feuer und Eis. Matthias Grünewalds 'Moses unter dem brennenden Dornbusch' und der Aschaffenburger 'Maria-schnee Altar'", in *Linien-Musik des Sichtbaren. Festschrift für Michael Semff*, ed. by Kurt Zeitler (Berlin and Munich: De Gruyter, 2015), 178–187.

21. *Der heilige Abt. Ein spätgotische Holzskulptur im Liebighaus*, Frankfurt conference proceedings (March 6–8, 1998), ed. by Valentina Torri (Berlin: Dietrich Reimer, 2001), particularly, about Grünewald, the essay by Hanns Hubach, "Der heilige Abt und Grünewald. Chronologie eines Missverständisses", 127–144; Stefan Roller, entry no. 122 in Roller, Sander (eds.), *Fantastische Welte. Albrecht*, 218–219. It should be remembered that Lanckoronska, *Matthias Neithart*, 203–207, had already compared the Frankfurt sculpture and Grünewald.

22. *Hystoria de festo nivis gloriosissime Dei genitricis et virginis Marie in ea forma qua Rome in Basilica eiusdem ad Mariam maiorem nuncupata*, Basel, Jakob von Pfortzheim, May 12, 1515.

23. Zülch, *Der historische Grünewald*, 368; Kehl, *"Grünewald"-Forschungen*, 137–138. Reitzmann dictated eight versions of his will, of which seven have survived, and all dated August 5, the feast day of Our Lady of the Snows (Paul Fraundorfer, "Altes und Neues zur Grünewaldforschung", *Würzburger Diözesangeschichtsblätter*, 14–15, 1952–1953, 373–431, especially 412–414).

24. Hubach, *Matthias Grünewald. Der Aschaffenburger*, to be consulted in full for its wealth of information, sources and iconographic analysis; see, in particular, 73 for the 1516 dating of the Stuppach Madonna, and 245–256 for the sequence of Heinrich Reitzmann's wills up to 1517.

25. Elwine Rothfuss-Stein, "Christian Schads Kopie der 'Stuppacher Madonna' von Matthias Grünewald", in *Christian Schad. Die Späten Jahre, 1942–1982*, exhibition catalogue, Aschaffenburg and Passau, ed. by Brigitte Schad (Aschaffenburg: Galerie der Stadt), 1994, 70–83.

26. Lottlise Behling, "Neue Forschungen zu Grünewalds Stuppacher Maria", *Pantheon*, 36, 1968, 11–20; Bruno Hilsenbeck, *Die Stuppacher Madonna des Mathis Gothart Nithart-Matthias Grünewald und ihre Botschaft* (Bad Mergentheim: Kapellenpflege Stuppacher Madonna, 1974); Sarwey, *Grünewald-Studien*, 20–29; Reichenauer, *Grünewald*, 61–80; Hubach, *Matthias Grünewald. Der Aschaffenburger, passim*; Brigitte Barz, *Die Stuppacher Madonna von Matthias Grünewald* (Stuttgart: Urachhaus, 1998); Hanns Hubach, "Die Stuppacher Madonna des Mathis Grünewald", *Zeitschrift des Deutschen Vereins für Kunstwissenschaft*,

54–55, 2000–2001, 141–175; Ludwig A. Mayer, "Neue Erkenntnisse zur Entstehung des Maria-Schnee-Altares und gegenteilige Ansichten zu einigen MGN-Dokumenten", *Aschaffenburger Jahrbuch für Geschichte, Landeskunde und Kunst des Untermaingebietes*, 22, 2002, 11–38; Hanns Hubach, "Der Aschaffenburger Maria-Schnee Altar", and Tilman Daiber, "Der Aschaffenburger Maria-Schnee Altar. Betrachtungen zu Maltechnik und Zustand", in Béguerie-De Paepe, Menu (eds.) *La technique picturale*, respectively, 81–88 and 89–96; Vetter, *Grünewald. Die Altäre*, 102–142; Julia Ricker, *Grünewalds Stuppacher Madonna ist restauriert. Schönheit hinter Glas*, in "Monumente. Magazin für Denkmalkultur in Deutschland", 2013, 6 (www.monumente-online.de); Andreas Menrad, "Grünewalds Ikone im Landesamt für Denkmalpflege. Die Restaurierung der 'Stuppacher Madonna'", *Denkmalpflege in Baden-Württemberg*, 2013, 2, 62–68; Ursula Fuhrer and Annette Kollmann, "Die 'Stuppacher Madonna' im Licht der restauratorischen Untersuchungen. Zu Bestand, Schadensbildern, Konservierungs- und Restaurierungsmassnahmen", *Denkmalpflege in Baden-Württemberg*, 2013, 2, 69–74; Wolfgang Minaty, "Führt Höttinger zu Grünewald? Der Aschaffenburger Maria-Schnee-Altar auf Spurensuche", *Aschaffenburger Jahrbuch für Geschichte, Landeskunde und Kunst des Untermaingebietes*, 34, 2020, 56–108; Judith Breuer, "Die Kapelle für Grünewalds Madonnenbild in Stuppach", *Denkmalpflege in Baden-Württemberg*, 2022, 4, 270–277; Ludwig Schönbein, *'Sei mein Heute, sei mein Morgen!' Frieden finden in einer 'verkehrten Welt'—aufgezeigt am Projekt der Stuppacher Madonna* (Lindenberg: Kunstverlag Josef Fink), 2023.

27. Schmid, *Die Gemälde und Zeichnungen*, I, 212–213; Lanckoronska, *Matthias Gothart-Neithart*, 189–195; L. Behling, "Neue Forschungen", 14; Hubach, *Matthias Grünewald. Der Aschaffenburger*, 102–103 ; B, Barz, 1998, 33; Béguerie-De Paepe, "Nouvelles hypothèses", in Béguerie-De Paepe, Lorentz (eds.), *Grünewald et le retable*, 14.

28. Jack Wasserman, *Leonardo da Vinci* (New York: Harry N. Abrams, 1975), 42; a proposal for the stylistic and cultural classification of the Moscow painting, offered by Giovanni Romano, is pointed out by Giovanni Agosti, Jacopo Stoppa and Marco Tanzi, "Il Rinascimento lombardo (visto da Rancate)", in *Il Rinascimento nelle terre ticinesi. Da Bramantino a Bernardino Luini*, exhibition catalogue Rancate, ed. by Giovanni Agosti, Jacopo Stoppa, Marco Tanzi (Milan: Officina Libraria, 2010), 21–69, at 35–36. It should be noted that Leonardo also drew on this formal idea of the Madonna with Child and Angels by Hans Memling, today at the Berline Gemäldegalerie but painted for Florence (Edoardo Villata, *1478, A Year in Leonardo da Vinci's Career*, Newcastle upon Tyne: Cambridge Scholars Publishing, 2021), 154. But it would seem that Mathis had no knowledge of Memling. It is also noteworthy that A. Ballarin, "Problemi di leonardismo milanese tra Quattro e Cinquecento: Giovanni Antonio Boltraffio prima della Pala Casio" (1985), in Idem, *Leonardo a Milano* , I, 5–45, at 9, states that the *Benois Madonna* was surely brought with him to Milan by Leonardo. I am not so sure of it, because it is true that its composition was known in Lombardy, but it was known as well in Florence. But I couldn't hope for a stronger confirmation of the link between the two *Madonnas* by Leonardo and Mathis than the assurance that the former's was actually in Milan at the beginning of16th century.

29. I wonder if some alchemical element could be actually detected in this painting. "Gold" is a symbol of Sun (Sol), which is at its turn "the most exacte image of God himself", as stated by the most important treatise on magic of the 16th century, Cornelius Agrippa von Nettesheim's 1531 *De Occulta Philosophia* (Book II, chapter XXXII). Agrippa wrote: "For it [Sun] is amongst the other stars the image and statue of the great Prince of both worlds, viz. terrestrial, and celestial; the true light, and the most exacte image of God himself; whose essence resembles the Father, light the Son, heat the Holy Ghost" (Henry Cornelius Agrippa, *Three Books of Occult Philosophy*, translated by James Freake, 1651, ed. by Donald Tyson, Woodbury, MN: Llewellyn Worldwide, 1992, 365). The original Latin text sounds as follows: "Ipse [Sol] inter reliqua sydera est imago et statua summi principis, utriusque mundi terrestris et coelestis vera lux atque ipsius Dei exactissimum simulachrumm cuius essentia Patrem, splendor Filium, calor Spiritum Sanctum resignat" (Cornelius Agrippa, *De Occulta Philosophia Libri Tres*, ed. by Vittoria Perrone Compagni, Leiden: Brill, 1992, 345). It is tempting to read also the very skin of Virgin Mary (for sure emphasized by some ancient and strong cleaning) as a reference to Moon (which metal is silver). Just after the passage quoted above, in the same chapter, Agrippa wrote: "But the Moon, the nighest to the Earth, the receptacle of all the heavenly influences [...] is the most fruitful of the stars, and receiving the beams and influences of all the other planets and stars as a conception, bringing them forth to the inferior world as being next to itself" (Agrippa, *Three Books of Occult*, 366). The original text is more precise: "Luna autem terris finitima, receptaculum omnium coelestium influxuum [...], stellarum foecundissima, Solis coeterorumque planetarum atque stellarum radios et influxus quasi foetum suscipiens, inferiori mundo sibi vicino velut parturiens edit" (Agrippa, *De Occulta Philosophia*, 346). It is noteworthy that the first draft of Agrippa's book was written in Würzburg in 1509–10 and dedicated to the philosopher and alchemist Johannes Trithemius, who was abbot at the benedictine convent of St. Jakob in the same city; the letter to Trithemius was published also in the printed version of Agrippa's treatise. The correspondence Sun/Gold and Moon/Silver is a commonplace of alchemical literature.

30. A work for which this remains unsurpassed Giovanni Testori, *Gaudenzio alle porte di Varallo* (Milan: Arti Grafiche Amilcare Pizzi, 1960); for an updated bibliography, see Paolo Angeleri, entry no. 29 in *Il Rinascimento di Gaudenzio Ferrari*, exhibition catalogue, Varallo, Vercelli and Novara, ed. by Giovanni Agosti, Jacopo Stoppa (Milan: Officina Libraria, 2018), 228–236.

31. Edoardo Villata, entry no. 23 in *Capolavori da scoprire. La collezione Borromeo*, exhibition catalogue, Milan, ed. by Mauro Natale, Andrea Di Lorenzo (Milan: Skira, 2006), 208–213; Massimo Romeri, entry no. 48–52 in Agosti, Stoppa (eds.), *Il Rinascimento di Gaudenzio Ferrari*, 357–365, with a dating of 1520–1525 that is too broad; but is important to notice that the relationship between the two images had already been pointed out by Polish writer and art critic Théodore de Wizewa (pseudonym of Teodor Wyżewski), "Le mouvement artistique à l'étranger", *La Revue de l'art ancien et moderne*, XX, 1904, 30–38, who interpreted it as a result of time Gaudenzio supposedly spent in Germany.

32. Daiber, "Der Aschaffenburger Maria-Schnee".

33. Roth, *Matthias Grünewald die Zeichnungen*, 65–66.

34. Lorraine Karafel, entry no. 4, in Marrow, Shestack (eds.) *Hans Baldung Grien*, 72–73.

35. Hütt, *Albrecht Dürer*, 2, 1889: Schulz, *Albrecht Dürer. Das druckgraphische Werk*, II, *Kupferstiche, Kaltmadelarbeiten, Radierungen, Holzschnitte und Bücher*, exhibition catalogue, Bad Schussenried, Erfurt and Augsburg (Bad Schussenried: Staatliche Schlösser und Gärten Baden Württemberg, 2011), 80–81; Roberta d'Adda, entry no. 29, in *Albrecht Dürer. Incisioni della Pinacoteca Tosio Marinengo*, exhibition catalogue, Brescia, ed. by Elena Lucchesi Ragni, Maurizio Mondini (Cinisello Balsamo: Silvana Editoriale, 2006), 130–131.

36. Olivia Savatier Sjőholm, entry no. 39, in Grollemund, Lepape, Savatier Sjöholm (eds.), *Albrecht Altdorfer maître*, 150–153. The primary reason for the proposed dating lies in the rendering of the landscape, cirrus clouds and hatched sky, analogous to the etchings dated just prior to 1520. However, it seems to me that, here, these elements do not attain the full plasticity of the landscape etchings and, also, the hatched sky is also seen in the woodcut of the Resurrection dated 1512, just as the "ungracious" facial style and multi-directional hatching connect the Madonna with other graphic works by Altdorfer, such as the *Beheading of John the Baptist*, another woodcut from 1512, or the pen drawing at the Munich Staatliche Graphische Sammlung (inv. 1919–269), datable to ca. 1513 (Hans Mielke, *Albrecht Altdorfer. Zeichnungen Deckfarbenmalerei Druckgraphik*, Berlin and Regensburg exhibition catalogue, Berlin: Reimer Verlag, 1988, 148–151).

37. Schmid, *Die Gemälde und Zeichnungen*, I, 286–287; Zülch, *Der historische Grünewald*, 358; Kehl, *"Grünewald"-Forschungen*, 134.

38. Kehl, *"Grünewald"-Forschungen*, 141.

39. *Ibidem*, 138–139.

40. Hubach, *Matthias Grünewald. Der Aschaffenburger*, 57–73.

41. See the bibliography cited in footnotes 290–292, to which could be added Zinke, *Masterpieces from Middle Age*, 156–157.

42. Ziermann, *Matthias Grünewald*, 162.

43. Roth, *Matthias Grünewald die Zeichnungen*, 53–54, with dating "Um 1512–16". Also see Van den Berg, *Die Passion zu Malen*, 91–98.

44. Roth, *Matthias Grünewald die Zeichnungen*, 51–52. Again here, the proposed chronology is "Um 1512–16".

45. "Disses hatt Mathis von// Ossenburg des Churfürsten v[on] Mentz/ Moler gemacht/ und wo du Mathis ge/ schriben findest, das ha[t]/ Er mit Eigner handt/ gemacht".

46. S. Kemperdick. entry no. 83, in Krause (ed.), *Geschichte der bildenden Kunst*, IV, 336–337; Dietmar Lüdke, *Die "Donaueschinger Magdalenenklage" der Sammlung Würth in Schwäbisch Hall*, and entry no. 114, in Idem (ed.), *Grünewald und seine Zeit*, 331–335, 336, with previous bibliography.

47. Friedbert Ficker, *Altdorfer* (Milan: Mondadori, 1977), 52–66; Anne-Marie Bonnet and Gabriele Kopp-Schmidt, *Die Malerei der Deutschen Renaissance 1484–1555* (Munich: Schirmer Mosel, 2014), 244–245.

48. Dietmar Lüdke, entry no. 120, in *Grünewald und seine Zeit*, 345–346; Idem, "Grünewalds Kreuzigungsbilder aus Tauberbischofsheim und den ehemaligen Fürstenberg-Sammlungen Donaueschingen", in Frick-Schnitzler (eds.), *Der Isenheimer Altar*, 95–130, at 120–127.

49. See the detailed note on the British Museum website: https://www.britishmuseum.org/collection/object/P_1880-0214-345.

50. Lüdke, Grünewalds Kreuzigungsbilder", in Frick, Schnitzler (eds.), *Der Isenheimer Altar*, 124–125. For the Foppa panel, see the detailed entry by Marco Albertario, in *Accademia Carrara Bergamo. Dipinti italiani del Trecento e del Quattrocento. Catalogo completo*, ed. by Giovanni Valagussa (Milan: Officina Libraria, 2018, 164–167, even if the dating of the 1480s proposed by Giovanni Romano and shared here, seems impossible to me for precise stylistic and philological reasons.

51. Roth, *Matthias Grünewald die Zeichnungen*, 49–50, with dating "Um 1512–16".

52. Renate Kolle, entry no. 11.5, in *Dürer Holbein Grünewald*, 187–190; Roth, *Matthias Grünewald die Zeichnungen*, 67–70.

53. Schmid, *Die Gemälde und Zeichnungen*, I, 288; Zülch, *Der historische Grünewald*, 369; Kehl, *"Grünewald"-Forschungen*, 142.

54. In addition to the standard monographs, for this work see Edgar Wind, "Albrecht von Brandenburg as St. Erasmus", *Journal of the Warburg Institute*, 1, 1937, 142–162; Ludwig Grote, *Die Erasmus-Mauritius-Tafel von Matthias Grünewald* (Berlin: Mann, 1947). I have not been able to look at Karin Stober, *Die Erasmus-Mauritius tafel von Matthias Grünewald als programmatischer Ausdruck der machtpolitischen Ansprüche eines Kirchenfürsten im Zeitalter der Glaubenserneuerung*, Mag.-Arbeit (Freiburg im Breisgau: Freiburger Universität, 1984).

55. Dagmar Eichberger, "Rencontres. Matthias Grünewald à travers ses contemporaine" in Béguerie-De Paepe, Lorentz (eds.), *Grünewald et le retable*, 32–44.

56. Hütt, *Albrecht Dürer*, 2, 1915; Anna Bartl, entry no. 113 in *Das Rätsel Grünewald*, 231–234; Schulz, *Albrecht Dürer. Das druckgraphische*, 2, 140–141.

57. Koepplin and Falk, *Lucas Cranach*, I, 60–62.

58. Roland H. Bainton, *Here I Stand. A Life of Martin Luther* (Cambridge: Cambridge University Press, 1960, n. ed. Tring: Lion Books, 1983), 291–292.

59. Philipp Schwartzherdt (Melanchton), *Elementorum rhetorices libri duo*, Wittemberg: Georg Rhau, 1531, h v recto-verso. See also Marquard, *Grünewald und die Reformation*, 185–193. Previously, the same author (in *Mathias Grünewald und der Isenheimer*, 30), had interpreted a reference to the pointing finger of John the Baptist, contained in a hymn by Melanchton, *Aeterno gratias patri*, from 1539, as a reference to the same detail in the Isenheim altarpiece. In this case, however, I believe it is a more generic reference to an iconographic attribute typical of St. John, significantly pre-dating Grünewald.

60. I generally follow the interpretation of Marquard. *Grünewald und die Reformation*, 185–193. See also the sensitive essay by Donald B. Kuspit, "Melanchton and Dürer: the search for the simple style", *The Journal of Medieval and Renaissance Studies*, 3, 1973, 177–202, in which an English translation of Melanchton's text, provided by George Houston, is also published at page 187: "It is also very useful, in forming a judgment, to distinguish the various styles of speaking, for the variation in personal talents has given rise, in speaking as in many other arts to various types of works, or, as the Greeks say, to different 'characters' of works. And yet certain gradations, so to speak, have been distinguished, within which these types

are contained: there is the Simple style, and its opposite the Grand. The third is the Middle, which is fuller than the first, but yet lacks something of the Grand style. These differences may be readily discerned in paintings. For example, Dürer painted everything in the Grand manner, variegated with innumerable lines. The paintings of Lucas are Simple; although they are charming, a comparison will show how far removed they are from the works of Dürer. Matthias remained more or less in the Middle style. These styles, moreover, intermingle with. one another, just as musicians mix their notes: even those which are rather thin occasionally give rise to something which is quite full. Then too, at the same time, some *loci* (topics) are full, others thin, according to the variety of matter which one is discussing."

61. Direct contact between the two, which could have occurred in Halle or Frankfurt, has been hypothesized by various authors, including Zülch, *Grünewald. Mathis Neithart*, 11, and Reiner Marquard, "Philipp Melanchton und Mathis Grünewald", *Zeitschrift für Kirchengeschichte*, 3, 1997, 295–308.

62. The comparison with painting is absent in his previous *De rhetorica libri tres*, Parisiis, Robert Etienne, February 14, 1528. Very likely, it was inspired to Melanchton by Dürer's evaluation pointed out by Erasmus in his 1528 *Dialogus de recte Latini Grecisque sermonis pronuntiae*: see Erwin Panofsky, "'Nebulae in pariete'. Notes on Erasmus' Eulogy on Dürer", *Journal of the Warburg and Courtauld Institutes*, 14, 1951, 34–41.

Chapter V | Luther, the Revolt, the Death

1. On Albrecht von Brandenburg see at least *Erzbischof Albrecht von Brandenburg 1490–1545. Ein Kirchen- und und Reichsfürst der Frühen Neuzeit*, ed. by Friedhelm Jürgensmeier (Frankfurt am Main: Knecht, 1991); *Der Kardinal Albrecht von Brandenburg. Renaissancefürst und Mäzen*, exhibition catalogue, Halle, ed. by Thomas Schauerte, Katje Schneider, Andreas Tacke, 2 vols. (Regensburg: Schnell & Steiner, 2006); Armin Stein, *Kardinal Albrecht* (Halle: Projekte Verlag-Cornelius, 2013).

2. In any case, in addition to the bibliography cited above, see at least the following easily obtainable texts: Giovanni Miegge, *Lutero*, I (Torre Pellice: Claudiana, 1949), 190–234 (but the entire book is a pivotal historic and theological introduction to Luther, especially in the years of interest to us); Roland H. Bainton, *The Reformation of the Sixteenth Century* (Boston: Beacon Press, 1952), 36–71; Martin Brecht, *Martin Luther: sein Weg zu Reformation 1483–1521* (Stuttgart: Calwert, 1981), English edition *Martin Luther: his Road to Reformation 1483–1521* (Minneapolis: Fortress Press 1993) 175–221; Adriano Prosperi, *Lutero. Gli anni della fede e della libertà* (Milan: Mondadori, 2017).

3. This extremely important document, destroyed during World War II but available in microfilm, has been republished a number of times with even significant variations among the following editions: Ludwig Seibert, *Sippenbuch der Stadt und Zent Seligenstadt*, I, Seligenstadt: Sprey, 1934, 41–54; Zülch, *Der historische Grünewald*, 373–375; Kehl, *"Grünewald". Forschungen*, 151–160; Saran, *Matthias Grünewald. Mensch*, 210–213; Bernhard Müller Wirthmann, *Von Fellen, Farben und Vermischtem. Das Nachlassinventar des Mathis Gothart-Nithart*, in *Das Rätsel Grünewald*, 71–80; Marquard, *Grünewald und die Reformation*, 203–219 which provides an especially precise transcription that will be used each time the 1528 inventory is mentioned.

4. Also in this context, the writing of the *Hallesches Heiltumsbuch*, published in Nuremberg in 1520 with woodcuts by the city's artists, including Wolf Traut and Dürer himself, author of the portrait of Albrecht (dated 1519) in the frontispiece, which Grünewald probably had in mind when painting his *St. Erasmus*. Cranach was also involved, confirmation of just how fluid the boundaries between "papists" and "Lutherans" were in the hot, early days of Reformation (*Hallisches Heilightums Buch vom 1520*, ed. by Richard Muther (Munich-Leipzig: Bard, Marquardt & Cle, 1889); Gábor von Térey, *Cardinal Albrecht von Brandenburg und das Halle'sches Heiligthumsbuch von 1520* (Strasbourg: Heitz, 1892); *Das Hallesches Heiltum*, ed. by Philipp Maria Halm, Rudolf Berliner (Berlin: Deutscher Verein für Kunstwissenschaft, 1931); Kerstin Merkel, "Die Reliquien von Halle und Wittemberg. Ihre Heiltumsbücher und Inszenierung", in *Cranach Meisterwerke auf Vorrate. Die Erlanger Handzeichnungen der Universitätbibliothek*, exhibition catalogue, Erlangen, Halle and Augsburg, ed. by Andreas Tacke (Munich: Form-Druck, 1994), 37–50; Dagmar Eichberger, "A Renaissance Reliquary Collection in Halle and its Illustrated Catalogue", *Art Journal of the National Gallery of Victoria*, 37, 1996, 19–36); Rushena Abduramanova, *Kardinal Albrecht von Brandenburg und das Hallesche Heiltumsbuch* (Potsdam: GRIN Verlag, 2013).

5. This important phase in the relations between Luther and Albrecht von Brandenburg is detailed well in Heinz Schilling, *Martin Luther. Rebell in einer Zeit des Umbruchs* (Munich: Beck, 2012), which I read in the Italian edition, *Martin Lutero. Ribelle in un'epoca di cambiamenti radicali* (Turin: Claudiana, 2016), 219–222.

6. Peter-Klaud Schuster, "Abstraktion, Agitation und Einfühlung. Formen protestantischer Kunst im 16. Jahrhundert", and entry nos. 27–32 in *Luther und die Folgen für die Kunst*, exhibition catalogue, Hamburg, ed. by Werner Hoffmann (Munich-Hamburg: Prestel, 1983), 115–125, 152–159. See also Robert. W. Scribner, *For the Sake of Simple Folk. Popular Propaganda for the German Reformation* (Oxford: Oxford University Press. 1994), 14–36.

7. Our scant information is summarized well in Bianconi, *L'opera completa*, 96. See also Reichenauer, *Grünewald*, 49–60. There is also the hypothesis of Jessica Mack-Andrick, "Von beiden Seiten betrachtet. Überlegungen zum Tauberbischofsheim Altar", in Lüdke (ed.), *Grünewald und seine Zeit*, 2007, 68–77, especially 74–77, picked up again by Marquard, *Grünewald und die Reformation*, 173, according to whom the work could have been part of a legacy of Friedrich Virnkorn, parish priest of Distelhausen, but also chaplain in Tauberbischofsheim and the Church of St. Agatha in Aschaffenburg, who died in 1518.

8. An initial report in Karin Achenbach-Stolz, *Die "Kreuztragung" von Matthias Grünewald aus restauratorischer Sicht*, in Lüdke (ed.), *Grünewald und seine Zeit*, 2007, 104–115; Karin Achenbach-Stolz and Hölger Jacob-Friesen, *Grünewalds Kreuztragung. Die Restaurierung eines Hauptwerkes deutscher Kunst* (Karlsruhe: Staatliche Kunsthalle, 2014); Hölger Jacob-Friesen, "Matthias Grünewald, Kreuztragung Christi", in *Förderprojekte der Rudolf-August Oetker-Stiftung 2016 bis*

2020, ed. by Monika Bachtler, Susanne Lindhorst (Bielefeld: Sieveking Verlag, 2020), 212–217.

9. Bianconi, *L'opera completa*, 97.

10. Mauro Natale, Edoardo Rossetti, entry no. 39–40 in Natale (ed.) *Bramantino. L'arte nuova*, 238–248. However, I have difficulty seeing the resemblance between the architectural elements in Grünewald's panel and those in the etching by Dirck Jacobsz Vellert depicting *St. Bernard in adoration of the Madonna with Child*, dated September 1524, emphasized by Jessica Mack-Andrick, entry no. 66, in Lüdke (ed.), *Grünewald und seine Zeit*, 244–246, and Dietmar Lüdke, "Grünewalds Kreuzigungsbilder aus Tauberbischofsheim", in Frick, Schnitzler (eds.), *Der Isenheimer Altar*, 102–103.

11. Simone Amerigo and Carla Falcone, entry in *Dossier gaudenziani. Restauri alla Pinacoteca di Varallo*, ed. by Simone Amerigo, Carla Falcone (Varallo: Società per l'Incoraggiamento allo Studio del Disegno, 2014), 96–110.

12. Edoardo Villata, "Gaudenzio Ferrari e la *Spogliazione delle vesti* al Sacro Monte di Varallo", *Arte Lombarda*, 145, 2005, 76–92. I consider the attribution to Gaudenzio and the 1505 date to be one of the fundamental differentiations between understanding and not understanding the development of that master. I realize that this statement is a blanket judgement of Agosti, Stoppa (eds.), *Il Rinascimento di Gaudenzio*, considered as a historiographic enterprise.

13. Carmen C. Bambach, entry no. 73 in *Leonardo da Vinci master Draftsman*, exhibition catalogue, New York ed. by Carmen C. Bambach (New Haven-London: Yale University Press, 2003), 459–461.

14. Christian Müller, *Grünewalds Werke in Karlsruhe* (Karlsruhe: Staatliche Kunsthalle, 1984), 17–18.

15. Weixlgärtner, *Grünewald*, 104.

16. The ultra- (or pseudo-) iconology of Pellé, *Aemulatio Italorum. La réception*, 282–285, who even provides a phallic interpretation of the club held by the thug dressed in yellow, and the beam of the cross itself, in a sort of grotesque game of "mine is bigger than yours", might mean something to a psychiatrist, but most likely not to an art historian.

17. Martin Brecht, *Martin Luther*, III. *Die Erhaltung der Kirche 1532–1546* (Stuttgart: Calwert, 1987), Eng. trad. *Martin Luther. The Preservation of the Church 1532–1546* (Minneapolis: Fortress Press, 1999), 96. Se also the summary by Franco Buzzi, *La Bibbia di Lutero* (Turin: Claudiana, 2016), 24–27. It seems likely that Mathis owned an edition of the New Testament translated by Luther starting in 1522. In fact, in the 1528 inventory we find: "item das nu testament ingebunden und sunst viel scharteken luterich" (Marquard, *Grünewald und die Reformation*, 213).

18. Bridget Heal, *A Magnificent Faith. Art and Identity in Lutheran Germany* (Oxford: Oxford University Press, 2017), 130.

19. Karl Arndt and Bernd Moeller, "Die Bücher und letzten Bilder Mathis Gothart-Nitharts, des so genannten Grünewald", in *Das Rätsel Grünewald*, 45–60, especially 52. Also see Reiner Marquard, "Mathias Grünewalds Tauberbischofsheimer Andachtsbilder in der Kunsthalle Karlsruhe und Martin *Luthers teologia crucis*", *Zeitschrift für die Geschichte des Oberrheins*, 156, 2008, 179–194; Idem, *Matthias Grünewald*, 171–172, 179–185; Angelika Michael, *Luther und die Bilder. Von Bildern, die man sicht, und solchen, die man nicht sicht*, in h"Lutherjahrbuch", 79, 2011, 101–137, especially 112–115. The text of the sermon can be found in *Luthers Werke in Auswahl*, I, ed. by Otto Clemen (Berlin: De Gruyter, 1933), 154–160, at 156.

20. Citation from the first complete edition of 1534, consulted in the recent anastatic reprint: *Das Buch der Bücher. Die Luther-Bibel von 1534*, ed. by Stephan Füssel (Cologne: Taschen, 2017), I, c. XXVIIv.

21. "Quem tunc, quando voluit glorificare et in regnum statuere [. . .] maxime contrarie fecit mori, confundi et ad inferos descendere" (*Luthers Werke in Auswahl*, vol. V, *Der junge Luther*, ed. by Erich Vogelsang (Berlin: De Gruyter, 1933), 263; the English translation is from Martin Luther, *Lectures on Romans*, ed. by Wilhelm Pauck (Louisville: Westminster Press, 1961), 242).

22. "Szo dich eynn weetag odder krancheit beschweret dencke wie geringe das sey gegen der dornenn kronen und negell Christi.
Szo du must thun adder lassenn was dir widdert dencke wie Christus gepunden und gefangen hyn unnd her gefurt wirt.
Ficht dich die hoffert an sich wie deyn herr vorspottet und mit den schechern voracht wirt.
Stost dich unkeuscheit und lust an gedenck wie bitterlich Christus zartes fleysch zur geysselt durch stochen und durch schlagen wirt.
Ficht dich hasz und neyt an ader rachesuchst denck wie Christus mit vielen threnen und ruffen fur dich und alle seyne feynd gepeten hatt der wol billicher gerochen hette" (*Luthers Werke in Auswahl*, I, 160; the English translation, by Martin H. Bertram, is from *Martin Luthers's Works*, vol. 55, *Devotional Writings*, I, ed. by Martin O. Dietrich (Philadelphia: Fortress Press, 1969), 13–14). Already, Van den Berg, *Die Passion zu Malen*, 138–142, interpreted *Christ Bearing the Cross* from a Lutheran perspective, even if her references to the Heidelberg Disputation in 1518, although plausible chronologically, would not seem the most relevant. Strong emphasis regarding the relationship between the double altarpiece in Tauberbischofsheim and the 1519 Luther sermon is found in Marquard, *Grünewald und die Reformation*, 179–185.

23. Van den Berg, *Die Passion zu Malen*, 45, already noted, in comparison with the Isenheim Crucifixion, the enhanced three-dimensionality of the Tauberbishofsheim Christ (he "works more with foreshortening and *chiaroscuro*" than in Isenheim).

24. Kenneth Clark, *The Drawings of Leonardo da Vinci in the Collection of His Majesty the King at Windsor Castle* (New York and Cambridge: Cambridge University Press, 1935), I, 94.

25. Phyllis P. Bober and Ruth O. Rubinstein, *Renaissance Artists and Antique Sculpture. A Handbook of Sources* (Oxford: Oxford University Press, 1986), 166–168. It is unlikely that this theme could have reached him by way of the Dürer woodcut known only as the "Study for five figures", ca. 1515 (Sandra Kaden, entry no. 6/6 in Aikema (ed.), *Dürer e il Rinascimento tra Germania*, 375–376). The *Belvedere Torso* has also been suggested as the figurative source for the *Flagellation of Christ* painted in 1525 by Wolf Huber as part of the Augustinian altarpiece of St. Florian (Katrin Dyballa, entry no. 28, in Roller, Sander (eds.), *Fantastische Welten*, 80–81. Potential contact between Huber and Grünewald was noted previously, and the coincidence in the dates here is also emblematic. The suspicion arises that either one depends on the other (Wolf on Mathis, probably), or, perhaps more likely, that both painters were

reacting independently and in parallel to the same stimulus, possibly the appearance of copies or derivations of the Roman sculpture.

26. Regarding the sculpture now in Berlin see Mikhail Jakovlevich Liebmann, *Die deutsche Plastik 1350–1550*, Leipzig: Seeman, 1982, 383–386; Baxandall, *The Limewood Sculptors of Renaissance*, 202–216; in general about Leinberger: Georg Lill, *Hans Leinberger. Der Bildschnitzer von Landshut. Welt und Umwelt des Künstlers*, Munich: Bruckmann, 1942; Hans Thoma, *Hans Leinberger. Seine Stadt, seine Zeit, sein Werk*, Regensburg: Friedrich Pustet, 1979; Claudia Behle, *Hans Leinberger. Leben und Eigenart des Künstlers. Stilistische Entwicklung. Rekonstruktion der Gruppen und Altäre*, Munich: UNI-Druck, 1984.

27. Renate Kolle, entry no. 11, 6, in *Dürer Holbein Grünewald*, 190–192; Roth, *Matthias Grünewald die Zeichnungen*, 75–76.

28. The derivation is pointed out by Edoardo Villata, "Lotto e Pordenone a Venezia: vite parallele (asimmetriche)", in *Lorenzo Lotto. Contesti, significati, conservazione*, Loreto conference proceedings (February 1–3, 2018), ed. by Francesca Coltrinari, Enrico Maria Dal Pozzolo (Treviso: Zel, 2019), 262–275, at 272, but Mariani Canova, *L'opera completa di Lorenzo*, 121, had already seen in the small Crucifixion in the Lotto painting "a dramatic revival of grunewaldian taste". The portrait of Gregorio Belo was painted in Venice between 1546 and 1548 (Lorenzo Lotto, *Il libro di spese diverse*, ed. by Francesco De Carolis, Trieste: Trieste University Press, 2017, 172–173; Dal Pozzolo, *Lorenzo Lotto. Catalogo*, 416–417). Immediately after, in 1549, Lotto traveled to Ancona and his presence in the Marche could be the vehicle for the presumed awareness of formal Grünewaldian themes by Vincenzo Pagani. The Madonna in the *Crucifixion* at the Pinacoteca Civica in Fermo, dated 1553, and its painted wooden twin in the Church of Santa Maria delle Grazie in Monteprandone were interpreted from a Grünewaldian (or Altdorferian) standpoint by Wolfgang Minaty, "Ein Grünewald in Italien?", 49–64. Admitting that this connection exists [I have many doubts, but Paola Pierangelini and Walter Scotucci, entry no. 24, in *Vincenzo Pagani un pittore devoto tra Crivelli e Raffaello*, exhibition catalogue, Fermo, ed. by Vittorio Sgarbi (Cinisello Balsamo: Silvana Editoriale, 2008), 160–161, had already discovered "Nordic origins"], Lotto as a go-between would be a more likely explanation than imagining Pagani (and only him?) influenced by the *St. John the Evangelist with hands clasped and head raised* that Sandrart saw in Rome and attributed to Grünewald, adding the apocryphal inscription "Mattahaeus Grünwald Alemann fecit" (*Teutsche Akademie*, II, 83). It should be noted that in the 1863 Latin edition of the *Academia nobilissimae artis pictoriae*, Sandrart omitted the passage regarding the Roman *St. John*, which perhaps could be seen as a distancing from his own "discovery", in the face of a broader audience than that of German art lovers. On the heterodox friendships of Lorenzo Lotto see Massimo Firpo, *Artisti, gioiellieri, eretici. Il mondo di Lorenzo Lotto tra Riforma e Controriforma* (Rome and Bari: Laterza, 2001). However, the two small panels by Lotto depicting the *Madonna and St. John at the foot of the cross*, today at the Fondazione Longhi in Florence, were the models that inspired Pagani. What should be noted, if anything, is that in the two paintings owned by Roberto Longhi references to Grünewald have sometimes been seen (once again by Mariani Canova, *L'opera completa di Lorenzo Lotto*, 121; see also Dal Pozzolo, *Lorenzo Lotto. Catalogo*, 414).

29. Joris-Karl Huysmans, in Ruhmer, *Grünewald, The paintings*, 8–9. The original text—even longer than the quote cited here—is as follows: "Celui-là, c'était le Christ de saint Justin, de saint Basile, de saint Cyrille, de Tertullien, le Christ des premieres siècles de l'Église, le Christ vulgaire, laid, parce qu'il assuma toute la somme des péchés et qu'il revêrit, par humilité, les frmes les plus abjectes.

C'était le Christ des Pauvres, Celui qui s'était assimilé aux plus miserables de ceux qu'il venait racheter, aux disgraciés et aux mendiants, à tous ceux sur la laideur ou l'indigence desquels s'acharne la lâcheté de l'homme; et c'était aussi le plus human des Christ, un Christ à la chair triste et faible, abandonné par le Père qui n'était intervenu que lorsque aucune douleur nouvelle n'était possible; le Christ assisté seulement de sa Mère qu'il avait dû, ainsi que tous ceux que l'on torture, appeler dans des cris d'enfant, de sa Mère, impuissante alors et inutile.

Par une derniére humilité sans doute, il avait supporté que la Passion ne dépassait point l'envergure permise aux sens; et, obéissant à d'incompréhensibles ordres, il avait accepté que sa Divinité fût comme interrompue depuis les soufflets et les coups de verges, les insultes et les crachats, depuis toutes ces maraudes de la souffrance, jusqu'aux effroyables douleurs d'une agonie sans fin. [. . .]

Certes, jamais le naturalisme ne s'était encore évadé dans des sujets pareils; jamais peintre n'avait brassé de la sorte le charnier divin et si brutalement trempé son pinceau dans les plaques des humeurs et dans les godets sanguinolentes des trous. C'était excessif et c'était terrible. Grünewald était le plus forcené des realistes; mais à regarder ce Rédempteur de vadrouille, ce Dieu de morgue, cela changeait. De cette tête exulcèrée filtraient des lueurs; une expression surhumaine illuminait l'effervescence des chairs, l'éclampsie des traits. Cette charogne éployée était celle d'un Dieu, et, sans aureole, sans nimbe, dans le simple accoutrement de cette couronne ébourriffée, semée de grains rouges par des points de sang. Jésus apparissait, dans sa celeste Superéssence, entre la Vierge, foudroyée, ivre de pleurs, et le saint Jean don't les yeux calcines ne parvenaient plus à fonder des larmes" (Joris-Karl Huysmans, *Là-bas* [1891]. ed. by Pierre Cogny (Paris: Flammarion. 1978), 37–43.

30. *Der 117 Psalm ausgelegt 1530*, hrsg. von Ernst Thiele, in D. Martin Luthers *Werke*, kritische Gesamtausgabe, vol. 31/1, ed. by Karl Drescher (Weimar: Hermann Bolhaus Nachfolger, 1913), 219–258, especially 249. The English translation is from Bainton, *Here I Stand*, ed. 1983, 218.

31. "Nam et Christus plus quam omnes sancti damnatus est et derelictus. Et non, ut aliqui imaginantur, facile fuit passus. Quid realiter et vere se in eternam daamnationem obtulit Deo patri pro nobis. Et humana eius natura non aliter se habuit quam homo eternaliter damnandus ad infernum" (*Luthers Werke in Auswahl*, V, 273). For the English translation, see Luther, *Lectures on Romans*, 263.

32. "ym selbs eygen macht und nit anders thut denn als hett er sie gethan": *On Christian Liberty*, translated by W. A. Lambert, revised by Harold J. Grimm, in *The Works of Martin Luther*, vol. 31 (Philadelphia: Fortress Press, 1957), 343–377, especially 352.

33. The German text reads: "Dennoch hatt er sich des alles geeussert und geperdet wie ein knecht allerley gethan und

gelidenn [. . .] und alsso ob er wol frey ware doch umb unser willen ein knecht wordenn." The current English translation is from the Latin text which is more faithful to the Pauline version; here I have preferred to translate the German text.

34. *Responsio Lutheriana ad condemnationem doctrinalem per Magistros nostros Lovanienses et Colonienses factam*, in *D. M. Luthers Werke*, kritische Ausgabe, vol. 6, ed. by Joachim Friedrich Karl Knaake, Weimar: Hermann Böhlaus Nachfolger, 1888, 181–195, especially 185.

35. For Dürer, see recently Thomas Schauerte, *Dürer e la Riforma: una conclusione aperta*, in Aikema (ed.), *Dürer e il Rinascimento tra Germania*, 107–113.

36. Renate Kolle, entry no. 11.7, in *Dürer Grünewald Holbein*, 192–194; Roth, *Matthias Grünewald die Zeichnungen*, 34–35, with dating "Um 1510–1515", perhaps excessively late.

37. Ulrich von Hutten, *Vadiscus oder Die römische Dreifaltigkeit*, in Hulrich von Hutten, Thomas Müntzer, Martin Luther, *Werke*, ed. by Siegrfid Streller, vol. I (Berlin and Weimar: Aufbau-Verlag, 1982), 54–144, also see the English edition: *The Triades or Trinities of Rome translated in to Englyshe*, London, Tho. Godfray, s. d. (1535?)

38. However, reticent on this question is Marquard, *Grünewald und die Reformation*. On the Peasants' Revolt in general, see at least these classics Friedrich Engels, *Der deutsche Bauernkrieg* (1850), Leipzig: Reklam Verlag, 1975); Ernest Belfort Bax, *The Peasants War in Germany, 1525–1526* (London: Sonnenschein, 1899); Peter Blickle, *Die Revolution von 1525* (Munich and Vienna: Oldenbourg, 1975).

39. Although to be taken with some caution, also useful is the interpretation of Maurice Pianzola, *Peintres et vilains. Les artistes de la Renaissance et la grande guerre des paysans de 1525* (1962, new ed. Clermont-Ferrand : L'Insomniaque, 2015).

40. Wilhelm Fraenger, *Jörg Ratgeb. Ein Maler und Märtyrer aus dem Bauernkrieg* (Dresden: Verlag der Kunst, 1971, 2nd ed. Munich: Beck, 1981), for the information that follows, together with Ute-Nortrup Kaiser, *Jerg Ratgeb. Spurensicherung*, exhibition catalogue, Frankfurt and Pforzheim (Frankfurt am Main: Starke, 1985).

41. On young Luther's contact with the school of the Brethren of the Common Life in Magdeburg: Brecht, *Martin Luther: his Road*, 15–17.

42. It is also worth mentioning the allegorical fresco in very poor condition in the chapterhouse of Mainz Cathedral, attributed to Ratgeb by recent scholars, but referred to Mathis around 1520 by Feurstein, *Matthias Grünewald*, 118–120.

43. For the document summary regarding Riemenschneider, see in synthesis *Chronology of Tilman Riemenschneider*, in Chapuis (ed.), *Tilman Riemenschneider. Master*, 16–17; for his career in Würzburg see Stephan Kemperdick, *A Sculptor in Würzburg*, in *Ibidem*, 69–82. For Riemenschneider and his civil activities, service to the bishop and support for the Peasants' Revolt, see the excellent documented summary by Thomas A. Brady Jr., "One Soul, Two Bodies: Lordship and Faith in the Prince-Bishopric of Würzburg", in Chapuis (ed.), *Tilman Riemenschneider c. 1460*, 15–27. Always worth reading, the posthumous historical novel published in Switzerland by Karl Heinrich Stein (pseudonym of the Austrian lawyer, educator and writer Heinrich Steinitz), *Tilman Rienenschneider in deutschen Bauernkrieg* (Zürich: Büchergilde, 1942). On Steinitz, who died at Auschwitz in 1942, see Christina Pol, *Heinrich Steinitz, Anwalt und Poet* (Vienna: Mandelbaum Verlag), 2006.

44. Lorenz Fries, *Die Geschichte des Bauern-Krieges in Ostfranken*, ed. by August Schäffer, Theodor Henner, 2 vols. (Würzburg: Druck der Tein'schen Druckerei, 1883), especially vol. I, 238–240; Martin Cronthal, *Die Stadt Würzburg im Bauernkriege*, ed.by Michael Wieland (Würzburg: Stürtz, 1887), 90–91 (but the entire text is relevant). See also Ulrich Wagner, *Der Bauernkrieg bei Lorenz Fries und Martin Cronthal*, in *Lorenz Fries und sein Werk. Bilanz und Einordnung*, ed. by Franz Fuchs, Stefan Petersen, Ulrich Wagner, Walter Ziegler (Würzburg: Verlag Ferdinand Schöningh, 2014), 150–178.

45. Kehl, *"Grünewald"-Forschungen*, 160–163.

46. Saran, *Matthias Grünewald. Mensch*, 29.

47. "Une autre bende avoit tout ravy en la commanderie sainct Anthoine de Isenam pres de tanne et faisoit semblant de tourner le chief droit de Remiremont et Espinal, tesmoingz les religieux et serviteurs dudit Isenam qui sen estoient venuz fuyans en habitz dissimulez droit à Nancy vers le susdit commissaire du pape, leur abbé" (Nicolas Volcyr, *L'Histoire et Recueil de la Triomphante et glorieuse victoire obtenue contre les seduyetz et abusez Lutheriens mescreans du pays d'Aulsays par Antoine duc de Calabre Lorrain et de Bar*, Paris: Gaillot Du Pré, 1526, c. Biii verso; see also Pierre Marot, "Notes sur Nicolas Volcyr de Serrouville, historiographe du duc de Lorraine Antoine", *Revue historique de la Lorraine*, 1931, 1, 5–13, and Denis Crouzet, "Un texte fondateur? Note sur l'*Histoire et recueil de la triumphante et glorieuse victoire. . .*", in *Foi, fidelité, amitié en Europe à la période modern. Mélanges offerts à Robert Sauzet*, ed. by Brigitte Maillard, Tours: Presses Universitaires François Rabelais, 1995, 313–331). Another source also dating from 1537 certifies that the rebels gathered at Isenheim "ont cause un dommage considerable a ladit Maison de Saint-Antoine, en se ses ornements, livres, papiers et autres choses" (Clementz, *Les Antonins d'Issenheim*, 196–197). Respect for the Grünewald altarpiece is even more surprising since the sacking and (probable) iconoclasm did not spare the "ornements" of the Antonite mother house in Isenheim.

48. About Albrecht von Brandenburg and Aschaffenburg see Heinrich Fussbahn, "Die Kirche des Kardinals Albrecht von Brandenburg", *Aschaffenburger Jahrbuch für Geschichte, Landeskunde und Kunst des Untermaingebietes*, 26, 2008, 9–55.

49. *Die Gebweiler* Chronik, 99–100; Stolz, *Die Hans Stolz'sche Gebweiler*, 137, and 398 footnote 301, in which the identification of this Mathis Nithart as Grünewald is accepted.

50. Bischoff, "Grünewald? Un mystère", in Béguerie and Bischoff, *Grünewald le maître d'Issenheim*, 106–107. See also Michel Krempper, *Mathis Nithard dans la guerre des Paysans 1525* (Mulhouse: Mulhousienne d'Edition / Milhüser Verlag, 2019), 42–50.

51. This was understood by Behling, *Matthias Grünewald*, 6, but without being further developed, and her suggestion was not taken up in subsequent research. In fact, Marquard, *Mathias Grünewald und der Isenheimer*, 27–31, beginning with the irrefutable identification of the "12 artikolen des christlichen glaubens" with those of the rebel peasants, argues—in a way that is no longer sustainable—that Mathis supported the Reformation, even—as a consequence—in its most radical forms.

52. Jessica Mack-Andrick, "Grünewalds 'Beweinung Christi'

und die ikonographische Tradition" and entry no. 105 in Lüdke (ed.), *Grünewald un seine Zeit*, 311–317. It should be noted that in Aschaffenburg there was also a church dedicated to the Holy Sepulchre that belonged to a Beguine community and was aided by Cardinal Albrecht, whose altarpiece found its way to the collegiate church on his death. This was the source of the hypothesis offered by Andreas Tacke, "Die Aschaffenburger Heiliggrabkirche der Beginen. Überlegungen zu einer Memorialkirche Kardinal Albrechts von Brandenburg mit Mutmaßungen zum Werk Grünewald", *Anzeiger des Germanischen Nationalmuseums*, 1992, 195–239, that the *Lamentation* painted by Grünewald comes from that Beguine church.

53. See, for example, Vetter, *Grünewald. Die Altäre*, 200.

54. Again here, the enhanced monumentality of Grünewald's Christ compared with the similar image in Isenheim (specifically, "the increasing weight of the figures") was stressed by Van den Berg, *Die Passion zu Malen*, 142, but without drawing any conclusions about the figurative approach.

55. A comparison of Bach's masterpiece and Grünewald, but focused on the Isenheim altarpiece, specifically the light, was offered by Albrecht Goes, *Stunden mit Bach* (Hamburg: Furche-Verlag, 1960; I consulted the Italian edition, *Incontri con Bach*, Turin: Claudiana, 1961, 13–23).

56. For this see Raffaele Casciaro, *La scultura lignea lombarda del Rinascimento* (Milan: Skira, 2000), 110–131, 290–320, with the previous bibliography; and for subsequent updates, the studies gathered in *Rassegna di studi e notizie*, XXXVI, 2009, vol. XXXII, especially the "Regesto dei documenti" by Carlo Cairati and Daniele Cassinelli, 133–158.

57. Davide Mirabile, "Un 'Presepe' ad Arona. Rinascimento nel Verbano tra pittura, scultura e arte vetraria", *Prospettiva*, 119–120, 2005, 98–104; Orso Maria Piavento, entry no. 37, in *Teatri del sacro e del dolore. I Compianti in legno e in terracotta in Lombardia e in Piemonte tra Quattrocento e Cinquecento*, ed. by Renzo Dionigi, Filippo Maria Ferro (Soncino: Edizioni dei Soncino, 2020). 199–201.

58. On the fashion for "Compianti" (sculptural scenes of the Mourning on dead Christ) see the comprehensive (even if sometimes redundant) Dionigi, Ferro (eds.), *Teatri del sacro.*

59. Sandrina Bandera, *Agostino de Fondulis e la riscoperta della terracotta nel Rinascimento lombardo* (Bergamo: Bolis, 1997); see also Paolo Bensi, "Impasti argillosi e policromie delle sculture in terracotta a Padova e in Lombardia intorno a Giovanni e Agostino de Fondulis", *Insula Fulcheria*, XLVI, 2016, 75–83; Francesca Tasso, entry no. 17, in Dionigi, Ferro (eds.), *Teatri del sacro*, 160–161; see also the important book by Marco Scansani, *Il fuoco sacro della terracotta. Giovanni de Fondulis tra Lombardia e Veneto* (Mantua: Tre Lune, 2024),

60. Hanns Hubach, "'. . .scrinium super sepulchrum aperiuntur'. Die Heilig-Grab-Kapelle der Aschaffenburger Stiftskirche und Matthias Grünewalds 'Beweinung Christi'", in *"Ich armer sundiger mensch". Heiligen-und-Reliquienkult am Übergang zumkonfessionnellen Zeitalter*, conference proceedings (Halle-Saale, October 8–10, 2004), ed. by Andreas Tacke (Göttingen: Kunstmuseum des Landes Sachsen-Anhalt), 2006, vol. 2, 415–498; Idem, "Mein hend, die mus ich winden. Grünewalds Aschaffenburger 'Beweinung Christi'", in *Cranach im Exil. Aschaffenburg um 1540: Zuflucht–Schatkammer–Residenz*, exhibition catalogue, Aschaffenburg, ed. by Gerhard Ermischer, Andreas Tacke (Regensburg: Schnell & Steiner, 2007), 136–155.

61. Kehl, *"Grünewald"-Forschungen*, 143.

62. With all due respect to Pellé, *Aemulatio Italorum. La réception*, 281–282, who assumes Mathis backed the Reformation and the cause of the peasants, ignoring, if nothing else, research by Marquard, Hubach and also, *si parva licet*, this author.

63. For all these documents, see Kehl, *"Grünewald"-Forschungen* 143–148, with reference to the previous bibliography.

64. Linda C. Hults, "Baldung and the Reformation", in Marrow, Shestack (eds.), *Hans Baldung Grien*, 38–55, at 40.

65. *Vom Kardinalsornat zur Luther-Bibel: Kunst und Leben des Seidenstickers Hans Plock im Spannungsfeld der Reformation*, exhibition catalogue Berlin, ed. by Tanja Baensch (Berlin: Stadtmuseum Berlin, 2005).

66. Kehl, *"Grünewald"-Forschungen*, 148–151. Bischoff, "Grünewald? Un mystère", in Béguerie and Bischoff, *Grünewald le maître d'Issenheim*, 1996, 95, a different interpretation is offered, in which it was a document relating to a mineral deposit, probably in the Vosges.

67. Buzzi, *La Bibbia di Lutero*, 20–21.

68. Marquard, *Grünewald und die Reformation*, 165–169.

69. Harold C. Schonberg, "Hindemith and Matthias the Painter", *The American Music Lover*, 8, 1941–1942, 163–168; Elaine Padmore, "Hindemith and Grünewald", *The Music Review*, XXXIII, 3, 1972, 190–193; Gudrun Breimann, *"Mathis der Maler" und der "Fall Hindemith"* (Frankfurt: Peter Lang), 1997; Michael Fuller, "Paul Hindemith's 'Mathis der Maler': Parable for our Times", *New Blackfriars*, 78, 916, 1997, 260–267; Siglind Bruhn, *The Temptation of Paul Hindemith. "Mathis der Maler" as a Spiritual Testimony* (Stuyvesant, NY: Pendragon Books), 1998 (see the review of it by John Williamson, *Notes*, second series, 56, 4, 2000, 951–954); Susanne Schaal-Gotthardt, "'Ist, dass du schaffst und bildest, genug?' Grünewald-Rezeption in Paul Hindemiths Sinfonie und Oper *Mathis der Maler*", in Frick, Schnitzler (eds.), *Der Isenheimer Altar*, 229–249. The anti-Nazi tension in Hindemith's work has been somewhat put into perspective, if not openly questioned, in some recent studies: for example, the latest by Lesley Hughes, "'A German Artwork for the German People'. An Altarpiece and an Accommodation in Paul Hindemith's *Mathis der Maler* (1935)", *The Journal of Musicology*, 40, 2, Spring 2023, 131–158 (essay referred to me by Federico Terzi),

70. ZWEITER AUFTRITT
ALBRECHT
Du bringst es über dich, mein Freund, mir solche Botschaft/ Zu senden! Woran hab' ich es fehlen lassen?/ Ich bin zu mindren Werts, um deinem wahrhaft/ Heiligen Tun Preise zu bieten. Lass meine/ Liebe nicht die Pein erdulden.
MATHIS
Wer kann so erfassen/ Wie ihr mein Handeln, da ihr selbst mein Unrecht verstandet./ Seht, alle Arbeit ist getan. Keine Stunde meines Wandels vergeudete ich. Der Welt/ Und Gott gab ich, was ich mit schwachen Kräften schuf./ Nun, da mein Schifflein landet,/ Kann ich, ein alter Mann, das weite Meer/ Mit Wehmut schauen, nicht mit Trauer.
ALBRECHT
Nimm mein/ Haus als eine Warte, die mit der Ruhe dir den

Blick/Ins Weite bietet. Nichts wird dich stören, nur ein/ Treuer Freund wird manchmal zu dir wallen.
MATHIS
Mein Glück/ Wollt ihr. Verschwendet nichts. Nur kurze Zeit/ Verbleibt mir, dann ergeht der letzte Ruf./ Mein Geist, zu matt, der Kunst zu dienen; mein Leib, der/ Schweren Mühen satt, sie beide sollen weit/ Von allen Stätten früheren Strebens geduldig/ Das Ende erharren. Lasst mich mein Sterbeplätzlein/ Suchen, wie ein Tier im Wald.
ALBRECHT
Wie sehr mich schmerzt, was/ Du mir zufügst, ich bin dir stumm Gehorsam schuldig./Uns trennt die Macht, die wir nicht meistern. Das/ Werk wird ewig von dir zeugen, wenn dein/ Leib vergeht, dein Name erlischt. Leb wohl.
umarmt ihn und geht ab

LETZTER AUFTRITT
MATHIS
allein
Auf denn zum letzten Stück des Weges. Leicht/ Will ich die Schwelle übertreten. Wie/ Sich alle Frucht von mir löste, sei auch das letzte Blatt/ Aus reifem Herbst dem Boden übergeben.
Er öffnet eine Truhe und beginnt, seine Habe hineinzulegen, bei jedem Gegenstand liebevoll verweilend.
Hohl/ Wie das Grab die Truhe. Dem Schlaf reicht/ Die Hand die kleinen Leichname. Sie/ Mögen noch bewahren, wenn man mich begraben hat/ Einen Hauch dessen,
legt eine Papierrolle in die Truhe
Was ich an Gutem übte,
versenkt Massstab und Zirkel
Was ich erstrebte,
legt Farben und Pinsel hinein, nachdem er sie gestreichelt hat
Was ich erschuf,
eine goldene Kette
Was mir an Ehren ward,
einige Bücher
Was mich bedrängte,
küsst das bunte Band
Was ich liebte.

The text is taken from the libretto in the program of the production staged in November 2010 at the Paris Opéra (Christoph Eschenbach, conductor; Oliver Py, stage director). Hindemith began work on this opera in the early 1930s, using the main themes for a symphony that has become a classic, whose world premiere was conducted by Wilhelm Furtwängler in Berlin in 1934.

71. I think Castelli, *Il demoniaco nell'arte*, ed. 2007, 81 is right: "The theological drama that split religious unity in Germany is summarized more in Grünewald than in Dürer."

72. Reiner Marquard, "Matthias Grünewald und die '27 predig Lutters ingebunden', Neue Aufschlüsse über Grünewalds Verhältnis zur Reformation", *Zeitschrift für die Geschichte des Oberrheins*, 146, 1998, 529–537; K. Arndt and B. Moeller, 2002, 45–60; Marquard, *Grünewald und die Reformation*, 159–165.

73. *The Works of Martin Luther with introductions and notes*, vol. 2 (Philadelphia: A. J. Holman Company, 1915), 401–406 (translation by August Steimle).

74. In a completely unintentional but very significant way, Luther took part in the 16th-century "Paragone of the arts", assuming a position in favor of hearing over seeing as the most important sense, referencing what was fundamental for him, the *fides ex auditu*, but also the importance he attributed to music—including performed—over the figurative arts: "Quia in humanitate [Deus] absconditus latet, que est tenebre eius, in quibus videri non potuit sed tantum audiri" (*Luthers Werke in Auswahl*, V, 94). See the comment by Steinmetz, *Luther and Staupitz*, 57: "God cannot be discerned by sight in Jesus of Nazareth but only by the hearing of faith. The ear is equipped by grace to discern what the eye cannot."

75. *The Works of Martin Luther*, vol. 40, *Church and Ministry*, tome II, ed. by Conrad Bergendoff (Philadelphia: Fortress Press, 1978), 73–223. See also Martin Brecht, *Martin Luther. Shaping and Defining the Reformation 1521–1532* (Minneapolis: Fortress Press 1990, ed. 1994), 164–172; Heal, *A Magnificent Faith*, 16–23.

76. Curiously Jonathan Jones considers the *Isenheim Altarpiece* an example of "art as therapy, and a tour de force of the kind of magical thinking Luther wanted to abolish" (*Earthly Delights. A History of the Renaissance*, London: Thames & Hudson, 2024, 207).

BIBLIOGRAPHY

1466

Biblia Übers. aus dem Lat. Mit dt. Tituli psalmorum, Strassburg: Johann Mentelin (before June 27).

1475

Biblia Germanica, Nuremberg: Johann Sensenschmidt and Andreas Frisner, December 9.

1478

Biblia Germanica, Cologne: Bartholomaeus de Unkel and Heinrich Quentell, ca. 1478.

1483

Biblia Germanica, Nuremberg: Anton Koberger, February 17, 1483.

1484

Jacob Perez, *Commentum in Psalmos. Centum et quinquaginta Psalmi Davidici cum expositione*, Valencia: Imprenta Luis Arinyo y Alfonso Fernández de Córdoba, September 6 (later Lugduni: Antonio Du Ry, 1521).

1485

Biblia, Strassburg: Johann Grüninger, May 2.

Erklärung der zwölf Artikel des christlichen Glaubens, Ulm: Conrad Dinckmut, April 21.

1487

Deutsche Bibel, Augsburg, Johannes Schönsperger der Älte, May 25.

1491

Stephan Fridolin, *Schatzbehalter oder Schrein der wahren Reichtümer des Heils und ewigen Seligkeit*, Nuremberg: Anton Koberger, November 8.

1494

Biblia Sacra Germanica, Lubeck: Steffan Arndes, November 14.

1499

Petrus Dorlandus, *Viola animae per modum dyalogi*, Cologne: Heinrich Quentell, May 29; reprint, July 16, 1501.

1505

Jean Pelerin Viator, *De Artificiali Perspectiva*, Toul: Pierre Jacobi, July 9.

1507

Biblia Germanica, Augsburg: Johann Otmar für Johann Rynmann, February 12.

1515

Heinrich Reitzmann, *Hystoria de festo nivis gloriosissime Dei genitricis et virginis Marie in ea forma qua Rome in Basilica eiusdem ad Mariam maiorem nuncupata*, Basilea: Jakob von Pfortzheim, May 12.

1517

Hans von Gersdorff, *Feldtbuch der Wundtartzney*, Strassburg: Johannes Schott; facsimile edition, Baiersbronn: Medicina Rara editions, no date (circa 1970).

1522

Biblia germanica inferiori–Biblia dudesch, Halberstadt: Lorenz Stuchs, July 8, 2 vols.

Johannes Bremer von Hagen (de Indagine), *Introductiones apotelesmaticae elegantes in Chyromantiam, Physiognomiam, Astrologiam naturalem, Complexiones hominum, Naturas planetarum*, Strassburg: Johann Schott, July.

1523

Johannes Bremer von Hagen (de Indagine), *Die Kunst der Chiromatzey Physiognomey, Natürlichen Astrologey, Complexion eins yegklichen mensches, Natürlichen ynflüss der planeten*, Strassburg: Johann Schott.

Urbanus Rhegius, *Erklärung der zwölff artickel Christliches gelaubens*, Augsburg: Simprecht Küff, December 22.

1525

Urbanus Rhegius, *Eyn erklarung der zwölff artickel Christlichs glawbens*, Leipzig, March 9.

Petrus Sylvius, *Eyne verklerunge des eynigen waren Apostolischen Christlilchen glaubens*, Dresden: Emser, August 11.

1526 (?)

Nicolas Volcyr, *L'Histoire et Recueil de la Triomphante et glorieuse victoire obtenue contre les seduyetz et abusez Lutheriens mescreans du pays d'Aulsays par Antoine duc de Calabre Lorrain et de Bar*; Paris: Gaillot Du Pré.

1528

Philipp Schwartzherdt (Melanchton), *De rhetorica libri tres*, Paris: Robert Etienne, February 14.

1531

Philipp Schwartzherdt (Melanchton), *Elementorum rhetorices libri duo*, Wittenberg: Georg Rhau.

1534

Johannes Dieterberger, *Biblia beider Allt vnnd Newen Testamenten*, Mainz and Cologne: Peter Jordan for Peter Quentel.

Aymar Falco, *Antonianae Historiae Compendium ex variis iisdemque gravissimis ecclesiasticis scriptoribus, necnon rerum gestarum monumentis collectum, una cum externis rebus quam plurimis scitumemoratuque dignissimi*, Lugduni: Theobaldus Payen.

1535 (?)

Ulrich von Hutten, *The Triades or Trinities of Rome translated in to Englyshe*, London, Tho. Godfray, s. d. (1535?).

1573

Bernhart Jobin and Johann Fischart, *Accuratae Effigies Pontificorum Maximorum numero XXVIII ab anno Christi MCCCXXXVIII ad aetatem usque nostram praesidentium*, Strassburg: Bernhart Jobin.

1590

Jacopo Da Varagine, *Sermones aurei de Maria Virgine Dei matre*, Venetiis: ad Signum Concordiae.

1620

Vincenz Steinmeyer, *Newe Künstliche, Wohlgerissene, vnnd in Holtz geschnittene Figuren dergleichen niemahlen gesehen worden. Von den fürtrefflichsten künstlichsten vnnd Berühmtesten Mahlern Reissern vnnd Formschneydern als nemlich Albrecht Dürer, Hanß Holbeyn, Hanß Sebaldt Böhem, Hanß Scheuflin und andern,* Frankfurt: Vincenz Steinmeyer.

1666

Balthazar de Monconys, *Iournal des voyages*, seconde partie, Lyon: Horace Boissat et Georges Remeus.

1675

Joachim von Sandrart, *L'Academia Todesca della Architectura, Scultura et Pittura: Oder Teutsche Akademie der Edlen Bau-Bild-und-Malerey-Künste*, Nuremberg: Froberger.

1683

Joachim von Sandrart, *Academia nobilissimae artis pictoriae*, Nuremberg: Froberger.

1744

Sancti Anselmi ex Beccensi abbate Cantuariensi archiepiscopi *Opera Omnia*, ed. by Gabriele Gerberon, Venice: Giuseppe Corona, 2 vols.

1844

Jakob Burckhardt, "Mitteilungen aus Basel", *Kunstblatt*, 36, 151–152.

1847

Franz Theodor Kugler, *Handbuch des Geschichte der Malerei seit Constantin dem Grossen*, Berlin: Duncker und Humblot; 2nd edition ed. by Jacob Burckhardt, tome II.

1867

Johann von Staupitz, *Opera quae reperiri potuerunt omnia*, ed. by Joachim Karl. Friedrich Knaake, vol. I, Potsdam: Krausnick.

1873

Jean Jacques Dietrich, "La Depouille du convent des Antonites d'Issenheim", *Revue d'Alsace*, n. s., II, 2, 70–78.

1879

Theodor Kolde, *Die deutsche Augustiner-Congregation und Johann von Staupitz. Ein Beitrag zur Ordens- und Reformationsgeschichte nach meistens ungedruckten Quellen*, Gotha: Friedrich Andreas Berthes.

1880

Arthur comte de Marsy, *Balthasar de Monconys: analyse de ses voyages au point de vue artistique*, Caen: Le Blanc-Hardel.

1883

Lorenz Fries, *Die Geschichte des Bauern-Krieges in Ostfranken*, ed. by August Schäffer and Theodor Henner, Würzburg: Druck der Tein'schen Druckerei, 2 vols.

1886

Émile Verhaeren, "En voyage. Les Gothiques allemands", *L'Art moderne*, August 15, 257–258.

1887

Martin Cronthal, *Die Stadt Würzburg im Bauernkriege*, ed. by Michael Wieland, Würzburg: Stürtz.

1888

Responsio Lutheriana ad condemnationem doctrinalem per Magistros nostros Lovanienses et Colonienses factam, in *D. Martin Luthers Werke*, kritische Ausgabe, vol. 6, ed. by Joachim Friedrich Karl Knaake, Weimar: Hermann Bohlaus Nachfolger,181–195.

Heinrich Zimerman, "Urkunden, Akten und Regesten aus dem Archiv des K. K. Ministeriums des Innern" [2], *Kunsthistorische Sammlungen des Allerhöchsten Kaiserhauses*, VII, XV–LXXXIV.

1889

Jean-Martin Charcot and Paul Richier, *Les difformes et les malades dans l'art,* Paris: Lecrosnier et Babé.

Hallisches Heilightums Buch vom 1520, ed. by Richard Muther, Munich-Leipzig: Bard, Marquardt & Cle.

1892

Gábor von Térey, *Cardinal Albrecht von Brandenburg und das Halle'sches Heiligthumsbuch von 1520*, Strassburg: Heitz.

1894

Émile Verhaeren, "Le peintre Mathias Grünewald, d'Aschaffenburg", *La Societé nouvelle*, December, 661–679.

1897

Franz Rieffel, "Grünewald-Studien (II)", *Zeitschrift für Christliche Kunst*, 10, 65–78.

1898

Die Gebweiler Chronik des dominikaners Fr. Seraphin Dietler, ed. by Johann von Schlumberger, Gebweiler: Verlag der J. Bolsse'schen Buchhandlung.

1899

Ernest Belfort Bax, *The Peasants War in Germany, 1525–1526*, London: Sonnenschein.

1900

Jacopo da Voragine, *The Golden Legend or Lives of the Saints, Englished by William Caxton (1483)*, ed. by Frederick Startridge Ellis (London: J. M. Dent & Co., 2 vols.

Henry Thode, "Die Malerei am Mittelrhein im XV. Jahrhundert und der Meister der Damstadter Passionscene", *Jahrbuch der preusseuschen Kunstsammlungen*, XXI, 59–74, 113–135.

1904

Franz Bock, *Die Werke des Matthias Grünewald*, Strassburg: Heitz & Mündel.

Joris-Karl Huysmans, "Les Grünewald du Musée de Colmar", *Le mois littéraire et pittoresque*, 62, mars 1904, 282-300.

Théodore de Wizewa (Teodor Wyżewski), "Le mouvement artistique à l'étranger", *La Revue de l'art ancien et moderne*, XX, 30–38.

1905

Joris-Karl Huysmans, *Trois Primitifs. Les Grünewald du Musée de Colmar. Le maître de Flemalle et la Florentine du Musée de Francfort-sur-le-Mein*, Paris: Albert Meissen.

1909

Heinz Braune, "Ein Bild von Matthias Grünewald", *Repertorium für Kunstwissenschaft*, 12, 504–507.

1910

Friedrich Back, *Mittelrheinische Kunst. Beiträge zur Geschichte der Malerei und Plastik in vierzehnten und fünfzehnten Jahrundert*, Frankfurt am Main: Baer.

1911

Heirich Alfred Schmid, *Die Gemälde und Zeichnungen von Matthias Grünewald*, Strassburg: W. Heinrich, 2 vols.

Georg Anton Weber, *Til Riemenschneider. Sein Leben und Wirken*, Regensburg: J. Habbel.

1912

Jakob Boehme, *The signature of all things* [1622], Foreword by Clifford Bax, London and New York: J. Dent & Sons.

1913

Martin Luther, *Der 117 Psalm ausgelegt 1530*, hrsg. von Ernst Thiele, in D. Martin Luthers *Werke*, kritische Gesamtausgabe, vol. 31, tome I, ed. by Karl Drescher, Weimar: Hermann Bolhaus Nachfolger, 219–258.

1915

The Works of Martin Luther with introductions and notes, vol. 2, Philadelphia: A. J. Holman Company.

1917

Oskar Hagen, Grünewald und das Montagna-Tryptychon in den Uffizien", *Kunstchronik*, XXVII, 411.

Oskar Hagen, "Zur Frage der Italienreise Matthias Grünewalds", *Kunstchronik*, XXVII, 73.

1918

Oskar Hagen, Hagen, "Einheit der künstlerischen Persönlichkeit: Grünewald", *Kunstchronik*, XXIX, 225.

Emmy Voigtländer, "Ist Matthias Grünewald in Italien gewesen?", *Tägliche Rundschau*, February 19.

Emmy Voigtländer, "Zur Italienreise Grünewalds", *Kunstchronik*, XXIX, 87.

1919

August. L. Mayer, *Matthias Grünewald*, Munich: Delphin-Verlag.

1920

Louis Réau, *Matthias Grünewald et le retable de Colmar*, Nancy, Paris and Strasbourg: Berger-Levrault.

Wilhelm Rolfs, "Eine Italienische Vorlage Grünewalds für die Versuchung des hl. Anton vom Isenheimer Altar", *Repertorium für Kunstwissenschaft*, XLII, 227–238.

1921

Joseph Bernhart, *Die Symbolik im Menschwerdungsbild des Isenheimer Altares*, Munich: Patmos Verlag.

Hanns Heinz Josten, *Matthias Grünewald*, Bielefeld and Leipzig: Velhagen & Klasing.

Willy Pastor, *Matthias Grünewald*, Berlin: Amsler & Ruthardt.

1922

Oskar F. L. Hagen, *Matthias Grünewald*, München: Piper & Co., (first edition 1919).

Egid Beitz, *Grünewalds Isenheimer Menschwerdungsbild und seine Quellen*, Cologne: F. J. Marcan Verlag.

1924

Fritz Hellwag, *Die Geschichte des deutschen Tischlerhandwerks*, Berlin: Verlagsanstalt des deutschen Holzarbeiter-Verbandes; reprint Hannover: Schäfer, 1995.

Grete Tiemann, "Zur Grünewaldfrage", *Cicerone*, 16 (22), 1079–1081.

1925

Justus Bier, *Tilmann Riemenschneider*, I, *Die frühen Werke*, Würzburg: Verlagsdruckerei Würzburg.

Rudolf Günther, *Die Bilder des Genten und Isenheimer Altars* (Studien über christliche Denkmäler, 16), Leipzig: Dieterich'sche Verlagsbuchhandlung.

1926

Karl Sitzmann, *Der Lindenhardter Tafelbilder*, Bayreuth: Carl Giekel.

1927

Max I. Friedländer, *Die Zeichnungen des Matthias Grünewald*, Berlin: Grote'sche Verlagsbuchhandlungen.

Margarete Hausenberg, *Matthias Grünewald im Wandel der deutschen Kunstanschauung*, Lepzig: J. J. Weber.

Willi Kurth, *The Complete Woodcuts of Albecht Dürer*, London: W. and G. Foyle; reprint New York: Dover Publications 1963.

Kurt Pfister, *Riemenschneider*, Dresden: Carl Reissner Verlag.

Ernst Wolf, *Staupitz und Luther. Ein Beitrag zur Theologie des Johannes von Staupitz und deren Bedeutung für Luthers theologischen Werdegang* (Quellen und Forschungen zur Reformationsgeschichte, 9), Leipzig: Heinsius.

1930

Justus Bier, *Tilmann Riemenschneider*, II, *Die reifen Werke*, Augsburg: Dr. Benno Filser Verlag.

Heinrich Feurstein, *Matthias Grünewald*, Bonn am Rhein: Verlag der Buchgemeinde.

1931

Das Hallesches Heiltum, ed. by Philipp Maria Halm, Rudolf Berliner, Berlin: Deutscher Verein für Kunstwissenschaft, 1931.

Pierre Marot, "Notes sur Nicolas Volcyr de Serrouville, historiographe du duc de Lorraine Antoine", *Revue historique de la Lorraine*, 1, 5–13.

Wilhelm Vöge, *Niclas Hagnower der Meister des Isenheimer Hochaltars und seine Frühwerke*, Freiburg: Urban-Verlag.

1932

Fritz Herrmann, *Die Protokolle des Mainzer Domkapitels*, III, *Die Protokolle aus der Zeit des Erzbischofs Albrecht v. Brandenburg 1514–1545*, tome I, Paderborn: Verlag Ferdinand Schöning ; reprint Darmstadt: Hessische Historische Kommission 1974.

1933

Karl Harmuth, *Die verschlossene Pforte. Eine Untersuchung zu Ez. 41, 1–3*, Breslau: Universität, Dissertation.

Luthers Werke in Auswahl, I, ed. by Otto Clemen, Berlin: De Gruyter.

Luthers Werke in Auswahl, vol. V, *Der junge Luther*, ed. by Erich Vogelsang, Berlin: De Gruyter.

1934

Ludwig Seibert, *Sippenbuch der Stadt und Zent Seligenstadt*, Seligenstadt: Sprey.

1935

Kenneth Clark, *The Drawings of Leonardo da Vinci in the Collection of His Majesty the King at Windsor Castle*, New York-Cambridge: Cambridge University Press, 2 vols.

Fritz Knapp, *Grünewald*, Bielefeld and Lepizig: Velhagen & Klasing.

1935–1935

Paulus Weissenberger, "Die Künstlergilde St. Lukas in Würzburg", in *Archiv des historischen Vereins von Unterfranken und Aschaffenburg*, 70, 175–24.

1936

Arthur Burkhard, *Matthias Grünewald. Personality and Accomplishment*, Cambridge (Mass.): Cambridge University Press.

1937

Edgar Wind, "Albrecht von Brandenburg as St. Erasmus", *Journal of the Warburg Institute*, 1, 142–162.

1938

Ernst Buchner, *Illustrated Catalogue Alte Pinakothek Munich*, Munich: Carl Gerber.

Walter Karl Zülch, *Der historische Grünewald. Mathis Gothart-Neithardt*, München: Bruckmann.

1939

Marcel Brion, *Grünewald*, Paris: Librairie Plon.

Wilhelm Rugamer, "Der Isenheimer Altar Matthias Grünewalds im Lichte der Liturgie und der kirchlichen Reformbewegung", *Theologische Quartalschrift*, CXX, 371–28.

1940

Wilhelm Pinder, *Die deutsche Kunst der Dürerzeit*, Leipzig: E. A. Seeman.

W. Stephen Kayser, "Grünewald's Christianity", *Review of Religion*, V, 1, 3–35.

Hans Friedrich Schmidt, "Voraussetzungen der Kunst Grünewalds", *Zeitschrift des deutschen Vereins für Kunstwissenschaft*, VII, 89–103.

1941–1942

Harold C. Schonberg, "Hindemith and Matthias the Painter", *The American Music Lover*, 8, 163–168.

1942

Georg Lill, *Hans Leinberger. Der Bildschnitzer von Landshut. Welt und Umwelt des Künstlers*, Munich: Bruckmann.

Karl Heinrich Stein (Heinrich Steinitz), *Tilman Rienenschneider in deutschen Bauernkrieg*, Zürich: Büchergilde.

1947

Ludwig Grote, *Die Erasmus-Mauritius-Tafel von Matthias Grünewald*, Berlin: Mann.

1948

Wolfgang Kühn, "Grünewalds Isenheimer Altar als Darstellung mittelalterlicher Heilkräuter", *Kosmos*, XLIV, 27–333.

Heinrich Alfred Schmid, *Hans Holbein der Jüngere. Sein Aufstieg zur Meisterschaft und sein Englischer Stil*, tome I, Basel: Holbein Verlag.

Guido Schoenberger, *The Drawings of Mathis Gothart Nithart, called Grünewald*, New York: Bittner.

1949

Giovanni Miegge, *Lutero*, I, Torre Pellice: Claudiana.

Johann Wolfgang Goethe, *Sämtliche Werke*, hsg. von Ernst Beutler, vol. 12, Zürich: Artemis; reprint Zürich and Munich: Artemis-Deutscher Taschenbuch Verlag 1977.

Walter Karl Zülch, *Grünewald. Mathis Neithart genannt Gothart*, Leipzig: E. A. Seeman, without date (but 1949).

1950

Erwin Poeschel, "Zur Deutung von Grünewalds Weihnachtsbild", *Zeitschrift für Kunstgeschichte*, XIII, 92–104.

Der Rats-Chronik der stadt Würzburg (XV. Und XVI. Jahrundert), ed. by Wilhelm Engel, Würzburg: Kommissionsverlag Ferdinand Schöning.

1951

Heinrich Meyer, "Hans Nussbaum. Ein Bamberger Bildschnitzer der Dürerzeit. Mit Notizen und Zuschreibungen", *Bericht des Historischen Vereins für die Pflege der Geschichte des ehemaligen Fürstbistums Bamberg*, 90, 279–320.

Erwin Panofsky, "'Nebulae in pariete'. Notes on Erasmus' Eulogy on Dürer", *Journal of the Warburg and Courtauld Institutes*, 14, 34–41.

1952

Roland H. Bainton, *The Reformation of the Sixteenth Century*, Boston: Beacon Press.

Gustav Münzel, "Eine neue Erklärung zu dem Menschwerdungsbild im Isenheimer Altar", *Zeitschrift für Kunstgeschichte*, XV, 75–77.

1952–1953

Paul Fraundorfer, "Altes und Neues zur Grünewaldforschung", *Würzburger Diözesangeschichtsblätter*, 14–15, 373–431.

1953

Gert von der Osten, "Job and Christ. The Development of a Devotional Image", *Journal of the Warburg and Courtauld Institute*, XVI, 153–158.

1954

Rudolph Arbesmann O. S. A., "The Concept of 'Christus Medicus' in St. Augustine", *Traditio*, X, 1–28.

1954–1957

Caroline Feudale, "The Iconography of the Madonna del Parto", *Marsyas. Studies in the History of Art*, 7, 8–24.

1955

Fedja Anzelewsky, "Albrecht Dürer und Mathis Gothart Nithardt", in *Erwin Redslob zum 70 Geburstag. Eine Festgabe*, Berlin: Blaschker, 292–300.

Lorenz Dittmann, *Die Farbe bei Grünewald*, Munich: Ludwig-Maximilians-Universität, Diss.

Herbert von Einem, "Grünewalds Auferstehung Christi aus Isenheim", in *Festschrift der Arbeitsgemeinschaft für Forschung des Landes Nordrhein-Westphalen*, Cologne-Opladen: Westdeutscher Verlag, 23–24.

Kurt Gerstenberg, *Tilman Riemenschneider*, Munich Bruckmann, (1° edition 1941).

Lottlise Behling, *Die Handzeichnungen des Mathis Gothart Nithart genannt Grünewald*, Weimar: Hermann Böhlaus Nachfolger.

Erwin Panofsky, *The Life and Art of Albrecht Dürer*, Princeton: Princeton University Press, cons. ed. 1971.

1956

Herbert von Einem, "Die 'Menschwerdung Christi' des Isenheimer Altares", in *Kunstgeschichtlichen Studien für Hans Kauffmann*, ed. by Wolfgang Braunfels Berlin: Mann.

Günther Jacobi, *Kritische Studien zu den Mandzeichnungen von Matthias Grünewald. Versuch einer Chronologie*, Inaugural-Dissertation zur Erlagungen des Docktorgradee der Philosophischer Fakultät der Universität Köln, July 14.

1957

Ernst Buchner, *Die Alte Pinakothek München. Meisterwerke der europäische Malerei*, München: Hirmer.

Martin Luther, *On Christian Liberty*, translated by W. A. Lambert, revised by Harold J. Grimm, in *The Works of Martin Luther*, vol. 31, Philadelphia: Fortress Press, 343–377.

Werner Timm, "Die Einklebungen der Lutherbibel mit den Grünewaldzeichnungen", *Forschungen und Berichte der Staatlichen Museen zu Berlin*, 3, 105–121.

Adolf Max Vogt, *Grünewald. Mathis Gothart Nithart Meister gegenklassicher Maleerei*, Zürich and Stuttgart: Artemis-Verlag.

1958

Nikolaus Pevsner and Michael Meier, *Grünewald*, London: Thames and Hudson.

Eberhard Ruhmer, *Grünewald. The Paintings*, London: Phaidon.

Adolf Max Vogt, "Grünewalds Sebastianstafel und die Sebastianthema in der Renaissance", *Zeitschrift für schweizerische Archáologie und Kunstgeschichte*, 18, 1–2, 172–176.

1959

Roberto Salvini, *La pittura tedesca*, Milan: Garzanti.

1960

Roland H. Bainton, *Here I Stand. A Life of Martin Luther*, Cambridge: Cambridge University Press, new ed. Tring: Lion Books, 1983.

Albrecht Goes, *Stunden mit Bach*, Hamburg: Furche-Verlag.

Giovanni Testori, *Gaudenzio alle porte di Varallo*, Milan: Arti Grafiche Amilcare Pizzi.

1961

Martin Luther, *Lectures on Romans*, ed. by Wilhelm Pauck, Louisville: Westminster Press.

Albrecht Goes, *Incontri con Bach*, Torino: Claudiana.

1962

Liliane Brion-Guerry, *Jean Pélerin Viator. Sa place dans l'histoire de la perspective*, Paris: Les Belles Lettres.

Hugh of Saint Victor, *Selected Spiritual Writings*, Foreword by Aelred Squire O. P., London: Faber & Faber.

Arpad Weixlgärtner, *Grünewald*, Vienna and Munich: Anton Schroll & Co.

1963

Henri Focillon, *The Art of the West in the Middle Ages*, II, *Gothic Art*, edited and introduced by Jean Bony, London and New York: Phaidon; 2nd ed. 1969.

Maria Lanckoronska, *Matthias Gothart-Neithart. Sinngehalt und historischer Untergrund der Gemälde*, Darmstadt: Eduard Rether Verlag.

Linda Nochlin, *Mathis at Colmar. A Visual Confrontation*, New York: Red Dust.

1964

Anton Kehl, *"Grünewald"-Forschungen*, Neustadt an der Aisch: Schmidt.

1965

Mária Aggházy, *Early Wood Carvings in Hungary*, Budapest: Publishing House of the Hungarian Academy of Sciences.

Henri Focillon, *Art d'Occident*, II, *Le Moyen Age gothique* (1938), Paris: Librairie Armand Colin.

Maria Lanckoronska, *Matthäus Neithart sculptor. Der Meister des Blaubeurer Altars und seine Werke*, Munich: A. Frühmorgen.

1967

Lottlise Behling, *Die Pflanze in der mittelalterlichen Tapfelmalerei*, Köln: Hermann Böhlaus Nachfolger.

Hajo Holborn, *Ulrich von Hutten and the German Reformation* (1937), English edition ed. by Roland Herbert Bainton, New York: Harper.

Maria Lanckoronska, *Neithart in Italien. Ein Versuch*, Munich: Frühmorgen.

1968

Lottlise Behling, "Neue Forschungen zu Grünewalds Stuppacher Maria", *Pantheon*, 36, 11–20.

David Curtis Steinmetz, *Misericordia Dei. The Theology of Johannes von Staupitz in Its Late Medieval Setting*, Leiden: Brill.

1969

Kurt Bauch, "Aus Grünewalds Frühzeit", *Pantheon*, XXVII, March–April, 83–98.

Martin Luthers's Works, vol. 55, *Devotional Writings*, I, ed. by Martin O. Dietrich, Philadelphia: Fortress Press.

Marjorie Reeves, *The Influence of Prophecy in the Later Middle Ages*, Oxford: Clarendon Press.

Georg Scheja, *Der Isenheimer Altar des Matthias Grünewald (Mathis Gothart Nithart)*, Cologne: DuMont Schauberg.

1970

Eberhard Ruhmer, *Grünewald. Drawings. Complete edition*, London: Phaidon.

1971

Wilhelm Fraenger, *Jörg Ratgeb. Ein Maler und Märtyrer aus dem Bauernkrieg*, Dresden: Verlag der Kunst; 2nd ed. Munich: Beck, 1981.

Hans J. Rieckenberg, "Zum Namen und zur Biographie des Malers Matthias Grünewald", in *Festschrift Hermann Heimpel*, Göttingen: Vandenkoeck & Ruprecht, I, 741–758.

Gertrud Schiller, *Iconography of Christian Art*, 2 vols., London: Lund Humphries.

1972

Piero Bianconi, *L'opera completa di Grünewald*, Milan: Rizzoli.

Henri Blum, "Grünewald, les deux volets fixes du Retable d'Issenheim", *L'information d'histoire de l'art*, XVII, 5, 199–207.

Elaine Padmore, "Hindemith and Grünewald", *The Music Review*, XXXIII, 3, 190–193.

Paul Stintzi, *Les Antonites d'Issenheim*, (without indication of publisher), Mulhouse.

1973

Justus Bier, *Tilmann Riemenschneider*, III, *Die späten Werke in Stein*, Vienna: Anton Schroll.

Donald B. Kuspit, "Melanchton and Dürer: the search for

the simple style", *The Journal of Medieval and Renaissance Studies*, 3, 177–202.

Jens Lauts, *Staatliche Kunsthalle Karlsruhe. Neuerwerbungen alter Meister 1966–1972* (Karlsruhe: Staatliche Kunsthalle.

1974

Fritz Baumgart, *Grünewald. I disegni*, Florence: La Nuova Italia.

Bruno Hilsenbeck, *Die Stuppacher Madonna des Mathis Gothart Nithart-Matthias Grünewald und ihre Botschaft*, Bad Mergentheim: Kapellenpflege Stuppacher Madonna.

Dieter Koepplin and Tilman Falk, *Lukas Cranach. Gemälde Zeichnungen Druckgraphik*, exhibition catalogue (Basel), Basel and Stuttgart: Birkhäuser, 2 vols.

Mirella Levi D'Ancona, *The Garden of the Renaissance. Botanical Symbolism in Italian Painting*, Florence: Leo S. Olschki.

Roberto Longhi, *Officina Ferrarese* [1940–1956] (Opere complete di Roberto Longhi, vol. 5), Florence: Sansoni.

Hans J. Rieckenberg, "Matthias Grünewald. Name und Leben neu betrachtet", *Jahrbuch der Staatlichen Kunstsammlungen in Baden-Württemberg*, II, 47–120.

Pierre Vaisse, in Piero Bianconi and Pierre Vaisse, *Toute l'oeuvre peint de Grünewald*, Paris: Flammarion, 108.

1975

Peter Blickle, *Die Revolution von 1525*, Munich-Vienna: Oldenbourg.

Friedrich Engels, *Der deutsche Bauernkrieg* (1850), Leipzig: Reklam Verlag.

Galerie Aschaffenburg Katalog (München: Bayerische Staatsgemäldesammlungen.

William M. Ivins Jr., *On the Rationalization of Sight. With an Examination of Three Renaissance Texts on Perspective*, New York: Da Capo Press.

Giordana Mariani Canova, *L'opera completa del Lotto*, Milan: Rizzoli.

Rodolfo Pallucchini, "Un solitario confessore del suo tempo", in Mariani Canova, *L'opera completa del Lotto*, 5–10.

Jack Wasserman, *Leonardo da Vinci*, New York: Harry N. Abrams.

1975–1976

Albert Chatelet, "Unité ou diversité du thème du retable d'Issenheim", *Cahiers Alsaciens d'archeologie d'art et d'histoire*, XIX, 1975–76, 60–68.

"Discussion sur la communication de Henri Blum", *Cahiers Alsaciens d'archéologie d'art et d'histoire*, XIX, 74.

Jean-Michel Massing, "*Étude iconographique de l'Agression de Saint Antoine de Grünewald*", *Cahiers Alsaciens d'archéologie d'art et d'histoire*, XIX, 105–126.

François-Georges Pariset, "Grünewald et Baldung", *Cahiers Alsaciens d'archéologie d'art et d'histoire*, XIX, 147–172.

Roland Recht, "Les sculptures du retable d'Issenheim", *Cahiers Alsaciens d'archéologie d'art et d'histoire*, XIX, 1975–76, 27–48.

Hans Reinhardt, "Les notices du collectionneur balois Henry Faesch mentionnant une copie de l'autel d'Issenheim exécutée au XVIe siècle", *Cahiers Alsaciens d'archeologie d'art et d'histoire*, XIX, 195–198.

Charles Sterling, "Grünewald verso 1500–1505", *Cahiers Alsaciens d'archéologie d'art et d'histoire*, XIX, 127–144.

1976

Adalbert Mischlewski, *Gründzuge der Geschichte des Antoniterordens bis zum Ausgang des 15. Jahrhunderts*, Cologne: Böhlau-Verlag.

Hans J. Rieckenberg, *Matthias Grünewald*, Herrsching-Ammersee: Pawlak Verlag.

Ewald M. Vetter, "Die 'Hellerflügel' Grünewalds und das Verklärungs-Retabel der Dominikanerkirche in Frankfurt", *Jahrbuch der Staalichen Kunstsammlungen in Baden-Württemberg*, 13, 23–54.

1977

Friedbert Ficker, *Altdorfer*, Milan: Mondadori.

Colin Eisler, *Paintings from the Samuel H. Kress Collection. European Schools Excluding Italians*, Oxford: Oxford University Press.

1978

Justus Bier, *Tilmann Riemenschneider*, IV, *Die Späten Werke in Holz*, Vienna: Anton Schroll.

Wolfgang Hütt, *Albrecht Dürer 1471 bis 1528. Das gesamte graphische Werk*, 1, *Handzeichnungen*, Herrsching: Manfred Pawlak.

Wolfgang Hütt, *Albrecht Dürer 1471 bis 1528. Das gesamte graphische Werk*, 2, *Das gesamte graphische Werk. Druckgrahik*, Herrsching: Manfred Pawlak.

Joris-Karl Huysmans, *Là-bas* [1891]. ed. by Pierre Cogny, Paris: Flammarion.

Joachim Kromer, *Matthoas Grünewald. Die Schlüsselkompositionen seiner Tafeln*, Baden-Baden: Verlag Valentin Koerner.

Hildegard von Bingen, *Scivias*, ed. by Adelgundis Fuhrkötter OSB, vol. II, tome 2, Turnhout: Brepols.

The Works of Martin Luther, vol. 40, *Church and Ministry*, tome II, ed. by Conrad Bergendoff, Philadelphia: Fortress Press.

1979

Margrit Lurz, *Die Verspottung Christi des Mathis Gothard Nithart gen Grünewald. Ikonographie der Verspottung Christi unter besonderer Berücksichtigung des Werkes Grünewalds und seiner Beziehung zu den vorhandenen Kopien*, Cologne and Vienna: Böhlau Verlag.

James H. Marrow, *Passion Iconography in Northern European Art of the Late Middle Ages and Early Renaissance. A Study of the Transformation of Sacred Metaphor into Descriptive Narrative*, Kortrijk: Van Ghemmert Publishing Co.).

Hermann-Dieter Müller, *Der schwedischer Staat in Mainz, 1631–1636. Einnahme, Verwaltung, Absichten, Restitution*, Mainz: Stadtbibliothek.

Roberto Longhi, "Arte italiana e arte tedesca" (1941), in *"Arte italiana e arte tedesca" con altre congiunture tra Italia ed Europa (1939–1969)* (*Opere complete di Roberto Longhi*, vol. IX), Florence: Sansoni, 3–21.

Wolfram Stolz, *Die Hans Stolz'sche Gebweiler Chronik. Zeugenbericht über den Bauernkrieg am Oberrhein*, Freiburg am Breisgau: Stolz.

Hans Thoma, *Hans Leinberger. Seine Stadt, seine Zeit, sein Werk*, Regensburg: Friedrich Pustet.

1980

Fedja Anzelewskj, *Matthias Grünewald. Das Gesamtwerk*, Berlin: Ullstein Taschenbuch.

Michael Baxandall, *The Limewood Sculptors of Renaissance*

Germany, New Haven and London: Yale University Press.

John Berger, *Between Two Colmar*, in *About Looking*, London: Pantheon Books, 134–140.

Elias Canetti, *Die Fackel im Ohr. Lebensgeschichte 1921–1931*, Wien: Fischer.

Luigi Dania, "Una inedita pala d'altare di Lorenzo Lotto", *Antichità viva*, 19, 4, 7–11.

Margherita Guidacci, *L'altare di Isenheim*, Milan: Rusconi.

David Curtis Steinmetz, *Luther and Staupitz. An Essay in the Intellectual Origins of the Protestant Reformation*, Durham, North Carolina: Duke University Press.

1981

Lottlise Behling, *Matthias Grünewald*, Strasbourg: Editions des dernières nouvelles d'Alsace.

Martin Brecht, *Martin Luther: sein Weg zu Reformation 1483–1521*, Stuttgart: Calwert.

Bodo Buczynski and Artur Kratz, "Untersuchungen an Steinbildwerken Tilman Riemenschneiders", in *Tilman Riemenschneider. Frühe*, 335–375.

Hans Baldung Grien Prints and Drawings, exhibition catalogue (Washington), ed. by James H. Marrow, Alan Shestack, New Haven: Yale University Press.

Linda C. Hults, "Baldung and the Reformation", in Marrow, Sestack (eds.), *Hans Baldung Grien*, 38–55.

Zdzisław Kępiński, *Veit Stoss*, Warszawa and Dresden: Verlag der Kunst-Auriga.

Hartmut Krohm, Eike Oellerman and Andrea Kleberger, "Malereien von Martinus Schwarz", in Bloch (ed.). *Tilman Riemenschneider. Frühe*, 106–114.

Martin Gregor Lechner, *Maria Gravida. Zum Schwangerschaftsmotiv in der Bildenden Kunst*, Munich: Schnell.

Giovanni Romano, "Verso la 'maniera moderna': da Mantegna a Raffaello", in *Storia dell'arte italiana*, 6, *Cinquecento e Seicento*, Turin: Einaudi, 5–83.

Alan Shestack, "An Introduction to Hans Baldung Grien", in Marrow, Sestack (eds.), in *Hans Baldung Grien*, 2–18.

Tilman Riemenschneider. Frühe Werke, exhibition catalogue (Würzburg), ed. by Peter Bloch, Berlin: Staatliche Museen Preussischer Kulturbesitz.

1982

Justus Bier, *Tilmann Riemenschneider. His Life and Work*, Lexington: The University Press of Kentucky.

Hulrich von Hutten, Thomas Müntzer, Martin Luther, *Werke*, ed. by Siegrfid Streller, vol. I (Berlin-Weimar: Aufbau-Verlag, 2 vols.

Mikhail Jakovlevich Liebmann, *Die deutsche Plastik 1350–1550*, Leipzig: Seeman.

Mauro Natale, "L'ancona dell'Immacolata Concezione a Cantù", in *Zenale e Leonardo. Tradizione*, 24–33.

Bernhard Saran, *Matthias Grünewald. Mensch und Weltbild*, München: Wilhelm Goldmann.

Zenale e Leonardo. Tradizione e rinnovamento della pittura lombarda, exhibition catalogue (Milan), Milan: Electa.

1983

Elias Canetti, *The Torch in my Ear*, New York: Farrar, Straus and Giroux.

Wilhelm Fraenger, *Matthias Grünewald*, ed. by Gustel Fraenger, Ingeborg Baier-Fraenger, Dresden: Veb Verlag der Kunst.

Rainer Kahsnitz, "Volckamersche Gedächtnisstiftung", in *Veit Stoss in Nürnberg. Werke des Meisters und seiner Schule in Nürnberg und Umgebung*, exhibition catalogue, Nurenberg, ed. by Rainer Kashnitz, München: Deutscher Kunstverlag, 218–258.

Hermann Kellenbenz, "Augsburg, Nürnberg und Mailand in der Zeit von Ludovico il Moro", in *Milano nell'età di Ludovico il Moro*, congress proceedings (Milan), Milan: Comune di Milano, 65–78.

Wolf Lücking, *Mathis. Nachforschungen über Grünewald*, Berlin: Fröhlich & Kaufmann.

Luther und die Folgen für die Kunst, exhibition catalogue (Hamburg), ed. by Werner Hoffmann, Munich-Hamburg: Prestel.

Konrad Oberhuber, Sylvia Ferino-Pagden and Ernst Wolfgang Huber, "Catalogo dei disegni", in *Raffaello. I disegni*, ed. by Eckhart Knab, Erwin Mitsche, K. Oberhuber, italian ediyion ed. iby Paolo Dal Poggetto, Florence: Nardini.

Franziska Sarwey, *Grünewald-Studien. Zur Realsymbolik des Isenheimer Altars*, Stuttgart: Urachhaus.

Peter-Klaud Schuster, "Abstraktion, Agitation und Einfühlung. Formen protestantischer Kunst im 16. Jahrhundert", in Hoffmann (ed.), *Luther und die Folgen*, 115–125.

Leo Steinberg, *The Sexuality of Christ in Renaissance Art and in Modern Oblivion*, New York: Pantheon.

1984

Claudia Behle, *Hans Leinberger. Leben und Eigenart des Künstlers. Stilistische Entwicklung. Rekonstruktion der Gruppen und Altäre*, Munich: UNI-Druck.

Johann Georg von Hohenzollern, *Staatsgalerie Aschaffenburg*, Munich and Zürich: Schnell & Steiner.

Christian Müller, *Grünewalds Werke in Karlsruhe*, Karlsruhe: Staatliche Kunsthalle.

Wilhelm Nyssen, *Choral des Glaubens. Meditationen zum Isenheimer Altar*, Freiburg im Breisgau: Christophorus Verlag.

1985

Bernhard Decker, "Notizen zum *Heller-Altar*", *Städel-Jahrbuch*, N. F., 10, 179–192.

Ute-Nortrup Kaiser, *Jerg Ratgeb. Spurensicherung*, exhibition catalogue (Frankfurt and Pforzheim), Frankfurt am Main: Starke.

Siegrfid Kettling, *Das Evangelium des Malers Mathis. Betrachtungen zum Isenheimer Altar*, Wuppertal: Brockhaus.

1986

Phyllis P. Bober and Ruth O. Rubinstein, *Renaissance Artists and Antique Sculpture. A Handbook of Sources*, Oxford: Oxford University Press.

Howard Creel Collinson, "Sacerdotal Themes in a Predella Panel of the Last Supper by Mathis Gothart-Neithart, called Grünewald", *Zeitschrift für Kunstgeschichte*, 49, 301–322.

Howard Creel Collinson, *Three Paintings by Mathis Gothart-Neithart, called Grünewald: the Transcendent Narrative as Devotional Image*, PhD dissertation, New Haven: Yale University, May.

Wolfgang Lücking, *Grünewald. Der Stalburg-Altar*, Berlin: Fröhlich & Kaufmann.

Max Seidel, *Grünewald Der Isenheimer Altar.* Stuttgart: Belser (new edition 1990).

Gustave Vanvelkenhuyzen, "Le manuscrit de *Trois Primitifs*", *Bulletin de la societé J.K. Huysmans*, 15, décembre, 12-23.

1987

Martin Brecht, *Martin Luther*, III. *Die Erhaltung der Kirche 1532–1546*, Stuttgart: Calwert.

Ildegarde von Bingen, *Book of Divine Works with Letters and Songs*, ed. by Matthew Fox, Rochester (VT), Bear & Company.

Robert Musil, *Diaries 1899–1941*, ed. by Philip Payne, Mark Mirsky, New York: Basic Books.

Gianfranco Bortolotto, "Sisto Frei scultore (notizie 1500–1515)", *Arte Veneta*, 41, 176–184.

Charles D. Cuttler, "Further Grünewald sources", *Zeitschrift für Kunstgeschichte*, 50, 539–549.

Christian Heck, "Grünewald et le culte des primitifs septentrionaux chez Huysmans", in *Huysmans: une esthéthique de la decadence*, conference proceedings (Basel, Mulhouse and Colmar, November 5–7, 1984), ed. by Robert Kopp. Christian Heck, André Guyaux, Paris: Slatkine, 271–284.

Christian Heck and Roland Recht, *Le Retable d'Issenheim avant Grünewald. Les sculptures de Nicolas de Haguenau*, Colmar: Musée d'Unterlinden.

Roger H. Marijnissen, *Hieronynus Bosch. The Complete Works*, Oxshott: Tabard Press.

1988

Joris-Karl Huysmas, *Les Grünewald du Musée de Colmar*, critical edition by Pierre Brunel, André Guyaux and Christian Heck, Paris: Hermann, 1988.

Ruth Mellinkoff, *The Devil at Isenheim. Refliections of Popular Belief in Grünewald's Altarpiece*, Berkeley, Los Angeles and London: University of California Press.

Hans Mielke, *Albrecht Altdorfer. Zeichnungen Deckfarbenmalerei Druckgraphik*, exhibition catalogue (Berlin and Regensburg), Berlin: Reimer Verlag.

1989

Andrée Hayum, *The Isenheim Altarpiece. God's Medicine and the Painter's Vision*, Princeton: Princeton University Press.

Giovanni Pozzi, "Maria tabernacolo", *Italia medioevale e umanistica*, 32, 263–326.

Suzanne G. Valenstein, *A Handbook of Chinese Ceramics*, New York: Metropolitan Museum of Art.

1989–1990

Anthony Zielonka, "Huysmans and Grünewald: the Discovery of Spiritual Naturalism", *Nineteenth-Century French Studies*, 18, 1–2, 212–230.

1990

Adalbert Mischlewski, "Die Antoniter und Isenheim", in Seidel (ed.), *Grünewald Der Isenheimer*, ed. 1990, 102–121.

Bernard Saran, "Von der Macht des Wortes im Bild", in Seidel (ed.), *Grünewald Der Isenheimer*, ed. 1990, 80–97.

Johann von Staupitz, *Salzburger Predigten 1512*, critical edition by Wolfram Schneider-Lastin, Tübingen: Universität Tü bingen.

1991

Pantxika Béguerie, *Unterlinden. Le Retable d'Issenheim*, Strasbourg: La Nuèe Bleue.

Erzbischof Albrecht von Brandenburg 1490–1545. Ein Kirchenund und Reichsfürst der Frühen Neuzeit, ed. by Friedhelm Jürgensmeier, Frankfurt am Main: Knecht.

Der hübsche Martin. Kupferstiche und Zeichnungen von Martin Schongauer (ca 1450–1491), ed. Pantxika Béguerie, Colmar: Unterlinden Museum.

Eike Oellermann, "Der Choralaltar in der St. Michaelskirche in Lindenhardt", *Zeitschrift des deutschen Vereins für Kunstwissenschaft*, 45, 131–157.

Vita e lettere di san Bonifacio, ed. by Enrica Mascherpa, Bari: Le noci.

1992

Cornelius Agrippa, *De Occulta Philosophia Libri Tres*, ed. by Vittoria Perrone Compagni, Leiden: Brill, 1992.

Henry Cornelius Agrippa, *Three Books of Occult Philosophy*, translated by James Freake, ed. by Donald Tyson, Woodbury, MN: Llewellyn Worldwide.

Andrea Mantegna, exhibition catalogue, London. ed. by Jane Martineau, Milan: Electa.

Giuliana Algeri, "Ai confini del Medioevo", in Giuliana Algeri and Anna De Floriani, *La pittura in Liguria. Il Quattrocento*, Genoa: Tormena, 15–224.

Flügel-Altäre des Späten Mittelalters, conference proceedings (Münnerstadtnin Unterfranken, October 1–3, 1990), ed. Hartmuth Krohm, Eike Oellermann, Berlin: Staatliche Museen zu Berlin-Preussischer Kulturbesitz.

Christian Heck, "De Nicolas de Haguenau à Grünewald: origine et structure du retable d'Issenheim", in Krohm, Oellermann (eds.), *Flügel-Altäre des Späten*, 223–237.

Berta Reichenau, *Grünewald*, Thaur, Vienna and Munich: Kulturverlag.

Jőrg Rosenfeld, "Die nichtpolychromierte Retableskulptur als bildreformerisches Phänomen im ausgehenden Mittelalter und in der beginnenden Neuzeit", in *Flügel-Altäre des Späten*, 64–82.

Andreas Tacke, "Die Aschaffenburger Heiliggrabkirche der Beginen. Überlegungen zu einer Memorialkirche Kardinal Albrechts von Brandenburg mit Mutmaßungen zum Werk Grünewald", *Anzeiger des Germanischen Nationalmuseums*, 195–239.

Barbara Welzel, "Tilman Riemenschneider und das Bildprogramm des Heiligblut-Altares in Rothenburg o. T.", *Flügel-Altäre des Späten*, 198–209.

Heike Wetzig, "Die Standflügel des Isenheimer Altars", in Krohm, Oellermann (eds.) *Flügel-Altäre des Späten*, 238–259.

1993

Martin Brecht, *Martin Luther: his Road to Reformation 1483–1521*, Minneapolis: Fortress Press.

Eugene Monick, *Evil, Sexuality and Disease in Grünewald's Body of Christ*, Dallas: Spring Publications.

1994

Jolán Balogh and Éva Szmodis-Eszlàry, *Katalog der Ausländischen Bildwerke des Museums der Bildenden Kunste in Budapest. IV.-XVIII. Jahrhundert*, III, *Neuerwerbungen*, Budapest: Akademiai Kiadó.

Le beau Martin. Études et mises au point, conference proceedings (Colmar, September 30–October 2, 1991), ed. by Albert Châtelet, Colmar: Musée d'Unterlinden.

Martin Brecht, *Martin Luther. Shaping and Defining the Reformation 1521–1532*, Minneapolis: Fortress Press.

Marie Anne Hartmann, *Mathias Grunewald le retable d'Issenheim. Peinture et spiritualité*, Obernai: J. Do. Bentzinger.

Peter Macardle, "Matthias Wegener and Traces of Antonite Humanism in Cologne", *Journal of the Warburg and Courtauld Institutes*, 57, 254–263.

Kerstin Merkel, "Die Reliquien von Halle und Wittemberg. Ihre Heiltumsbücher und Inszenierung", in *Cranach Meisterwerke auf Vorrate. Die Erlanger Handzeichnungen der Universitätbibliothek*, exhibition catalogue (Erlangen, Halle and Augsburg), ed. by Andreas Tacke, Munich: Form-Druck, 37–50.

Alessandro Nova, *Romanino*, Turin: Allemandi.

Giovanni Romano, "Towards the Modern Manner: From Mantegna to Raphael", in *History of Italian Art*, vol. 2, Cambridge: Polity Books, 373–488.

Elwine Rothfuss-Stein, "Christian Schads Kopie der 'Stuppacher Madonna' von Matthias Grünewald", in *Christian Schad. Die Späten Jahre, 1942–1982*, exhibition catalogue (Aschaffenburg and Passau), ed. by Brigitte Schad, Aschaffenburg: Galerie der Stadt, 70–83.

Robert. W. Scribner, *For the Sake of Simple Folk. Popular Propaganda for the German Reformation*, Oxford: Oxford University Press.

1994–1995

Alessandro Ballarin, *Dosso Dossi. La pittura a Ferrara negli anni del Ducato di Alfonso I*, 2 voll., Cittadella: Bertoncello.

1995

Giulia Bartrum, *German Renaissance Prints 1490–1550*, exhibition catalogue (London), London: British Museum.

Pierre Brunel, "Des carnets de Huysmans au *Trois Primitifs*", *Genesis Manuscrits-Recherche-Invention*, 7, 115-121.

Denis Crouzet, "Un texte fondateur? Note sur l'*Histoire et recueil de la triumphante et glorieuse victoire. . .*", in *Foi, fidelité, amitié en Europe à la période modern. Mélanges offerts à Robert Sauzet*, ed. by Brigitte Maillard, Tours: Presses Universitaires François Rabelais, 313–331.

Marzia Faietti and Daniela Scaglietti Kelescian, *Amico Aspertini*, Modena: Artioli.

John Oliver Hand, *German Paintings of the Fifteenth through Seventeenth Centuries*, Washington and Cambridge: National Gallery of Art-Cambridge University Press.

Franz Posset, "Preaching the Passion of Christ on the Eve of the Reformation", *Concordia Theological Quarterly*, 59, 4, 279–300.

1996

Pantxika Béguerie and Georges Bischoff, *Grünewald le maître d'Issenheim*, Paris: Casterman.

Pantxika Béguerie, "Le Retable d'Issenheim", in Béguerie and Bischoff, *Grünewald le maître d'Issenheim*, 12–13.

Georges Bischoff, "Grünewald? Un mystère", in Béguerie and Bischoff, *Grünewald le maître d'Issenheim*, 63–111.

Bernhard Decker, *Dürer und Grünewald. Der Frankfurter Heller-Altar. Rahmnenbedingungen der Altarmalerei*, Frankfurt am Main: Fischer.

Dagmar Eichberger, "A Renaissance Reliquary Collection in Halle and its Illustrated Catalogue", *Art Journal of the National Gallery of Victoria*, 37, 19–36.

Gemäldegalerie Berlin. Gesamtverzeichnis, Berlin:Staatliche Museen zu Berlin-Preussische Kulturbesitz.

Daniel Hess, *Das Gothaer Liebespaar: ein ungleiches Paar im Gewand höfischer Minne*, Frankfurt am Main: Fischer.

Hanns Hubach, *Matthias Grünewald. Der Aschaffenburger Maria-Schnee-Altar. Geschichte-Rekonstruktion-Ikonographie*, Speyer; Verlag der Gesellschaft für mittelrheinische Kirchengeschichte.

Reiner Marquard, *Mathias Grünewald und der Isenheimer Altar. Erläuterungen Erwägungen Deutungen*, Stuttgart: Calwer.

1997

Sandrina Bandera, *Agostino de Fondulis e la riscoperta della terracotta nel Rinascimento lombardo*, Bergamo: Bolis.

Karen van den Berg, *Die Passion zu malen. Zur Bildauffassung bei Matthias Grünewald*, Duisburg-Berlin: Pict Im.

Gudrun Breimann, *"Mathis der Maler" und der "Fall Hindemith"*, Frankfurt: Peter Lang.

Stefania Buganza, *Bernardo Zenale alla certosa di Pavia, Nuovi Studi*, 4, 109–130.

Dürer Holbein Grünewald. Meisterzeichnungen der deutschen Renaissance aus Berlin und Basel, exhibition catalogue (Basel and Berlin), Ostfildern: Verlag Gerd Hatje.

Michael Fuller, "Paul Hindemith's 'Mathis der Maler': Parable for our Times", *New Blackfriars*, 78, no. 916, 260–267.

Reiner Marquard, "Philipp Melanchton und Mathis Grünewald", *Zeitschrift für Kirchengeschichte*, 3, 295–308.

Santa Maria dei Servi tra Medioevo e Rinascimento. Arte superstite di una chiesa scomparsa nel cuore di Milano, exhibition catalogue (Milan), ed. by Ermes Maria Ronchi, Milan: Mondadori.

Émile Verhaeren, *Écrits sur l'art*, ed. by Paul Aron, vol. II, *1893–1916*, Bruxelles: Labor.

1998

Brigitte Barz, *Die Stuppacher Madonna von Matthias Grünewald*, Stuttgart: Urachhaus.

Siglind Bruhn, *The Temptation of Paul Hindenith. "Mathis der Maler" as a Spiritual Testimony*, Stuyvesant, NY: Pendragon Books.

Federico Cavalieri, "Una nuova presenza oltremontana nella pittura milanese dell'età sforzesca", *Nuovi Studi*, 5, 29–37.

Elisabeth Clementz, *Les Antonins d'Issenheim. Essor et derive d'une vocation hospitalière à la lumière du temporal*, Strasbourg: Société Savante d'Alsace.

Ulf Häder, review of *Jahreszeiten der Gefühle. Das Gothaer Liebespaar und die Minne im Spätmittelalter*, in "Journal für Kunstgeschichte", II, 4, 348–352.

Jahreszeiten der Gefühle. Das Gothaer Liebespaar und die Minne im Spätmittelalter, ed. by Allmuth Schuttwolf, Ostfildern-Ruit: Verlag Gerd Hatje.

Reiner Marquard, "Matthias Grünewald und die "27 predig Lutters ingebunden", Neue Aufschlüsse *über* Grünewalds Verhältnis zur Reformation", *Zeitschrift für die Geschichte des Oberrheins*, 146, 529–537.

Gottfried Richter, *Der Isenheimer Altar*, Stuttgart, Urachhaus, 1997, English edition *The Isenheim Altar. Suffering and Salvation in the Art of Grünewald*, Edinburgh: Floris Books.

1999

Martin Brecht, *Martin Luther. The Preservation of the Church 1532–1546*, Minneapolis: Fortress Press.

Nancy Davenport, "The Revival of Fra Angelico and Matthias Grünewald in Nineteenth-Century French Religious Art", *French Studies*, 27, 1–2, 157–199.

Danielle Buschinger, *Sang versé, sang guérisseur, sang aliment et sang du Christ dans la littérature médièvale allemande*, in *Le sang au moyen âge*, conference proceedings (Montpellier, November 27–29, 1997), ed. by Marcel Fauré, Montpellier: Université Montpellier III Paul Valéry, 257–266.

Chronology of Tilman Riemenschneider, in Chapuis (ed.), *Tilman Riemenschneider. Master*, 16–17.

Hubert Comte, *Grünewald, le retable d'Issenheim*, Sarreguemines: Pierron.

Margherita Guidacci, *Le Poesie*, ed. by Maura del Serra, Florence: Le Lettere.

Stephan Kemperdick, *A Sculptor in Würzburg*, in Chapuis (ed.), *Tilman Riemenschneider Master*, 69–82.

Susanne Kern, *Deutsche Malerei des 15. Und 16. Jahrunderts im Landesmuseum Mainz. Ausgewälte Werke*, Mainz: Landesmuseum Mainz.

Fritz Koreny, "Riemenschneider and the Graphic Arts", in Chapuis (ed.), *Tilman Riemenschneider. Master*, 98–112.

Dietmar Lüdke, *Martin Schaffner. Die vier Antonius-Tafeln von 1517*, Karlsruhe: Staatliche Kunsthalle Karlsruhe.

Tilman Riemenschneider Master Sculptor of the Late Middle Ages, exhibition catalogue, ed. by Julien Chapuis, Washington: National Gallery of Art.

2000

Raffaele Casciaro, *La scultura lignea lombarda del Rinascimento*, Milan: Skira.

Massimo Cesareo, "Arte e teologia nel Medioevo: l'iconografia della 'Madonna del Parto'", *Arte Cristiana*, LXXXVIII, 796, 43–63.

Maria Teresa Fiorio, *Giovanni Antonio Boltraffio. Un pittore milanese nel lume di Leonardo*, Rome-Milan: Jandi Sapi.

John Williamson, review of S. Bruhn, 1998, *Notes*, second series, 56, 4, 951–954.

2000–2001

Hanns Hubach, "Die Stuppacher Madonna des Mathis Grünewald", *Zeitschrift des Deutschen Vereins für Kunstwissenschaft*, 54–55, 141–175.

2001

Jack Dewhurst and Franco Crainz, *The Pregnant Madonna in Christian Art*, Rome: Peliti Associati.

Massimo Firpo, *Artisti, gioiellieri, eretici. Il mondo di Lorenzo Lotto tra Riforma e Controriforma*, Rome-Bari: Laterza.

Hans Baldung Grien in Freiburg, exhibition catalogue (Freiburg im Breisgau), ed. by Saskia Durian-Ress, Freiburg im Breisgau: Rombach Verlag.

Der heilige Abt. Ein spätgotische Holzskulptur im Liebighaus, conference proceedings (Frankfurt, March 6–8, 1998), ed. by Valentina Torri, Berlin: Dietrich Reimer.

Hanns Hubach, "Der heilige Abt und Grünewald. Chronologie eines Missverständisses", in Torri (ed.), *Der heilige Abt*, 127–144.

Graziella Magherini, "Perturbante estetica e creazione artistica: Margherita Guidacci e l'altare di Isenheim", in *Per Margherita Guidacci*, conference proceedings (Florence, Octobrer 15–16, 1999), ed. by Margherita Ghilardi, Florence: Le Lettere, 119–133.

Patrizia Mainoni, "La nazione che non c'è: i tedeschi a Milano e a Como fra Tre e Quattocento", in *Comunità forestiere e nationes nell'Europa dei secoli XIII-XVI*, ed. by Giovanna Petti Balbi, Napoli: Liguori, 200–228.

Reiner Marquard, "Mathias Grünewald-'*übel* verheuratet'. Eine *Überprüfung* von Joachim Sandrarts Grünewald-Notiz", *Aschaffenburger Jahrbuch für Geschichte, Landeskunde und Kunst den Untermaingebietes*, 21, 259–274.

Bernard Vermet, "Hieronymus Bosch: pittore, tecnica o stile?", in Jan Koldeweij, Paul Vandenbroeck and Bernard Vermet, *Hieronymus Bosch. Catalogo completo*, Milan: Rizzoli, 84–99.

Horst Ziermann, *Matthias Grünewald*, Munich, London and New York: Prestel.

Carmen Zils, Constanze Albecker, Annette Rauscher, Yumiko Yuguchi, Barbara Eicholz, Juliane Bett, Susanne Becker and Ruth Gresser, *Der Freiburg Hochaltar. Tradition und Signatur des Neuen*, in Durian-Ress (ed.). *Hans Baldung Grien*, 261–300.

2002

Karl Arndt and Bernd Moeller, "Die Bücher und letzten Bilder Mathis Gothart-Nitharts, des so genannten Grünewald", in Riepertinger et al. (eds.), *Das Rätsel Grünewald*, 45–60.

Frédéric Elsig, "L'Escamoteur de Saint-Germain-en-Laye, une oeuvre de Gielis Panhedel?" in Frédéric Elsig, Patrick Le Chanu and Agnès Virole, *Jérôme Bosch et l'Escamoteur*, Paris: Somogy, 27–31.

Herzog on Herzog, ed. by Paul Cronin, London: Faber & Faber.

Ludwig A. Mayer, "Neue Erkenntnisse zur Entstehung des Maria-Schnee-Altares und gegenteilige Ansichten zu einigen MGN-Dokumenten", *Aschaffenburger Jahrbuch für Geschichte, Landeskunde und Kunst des Untermaingebietes*, 22, 11–38.

Bernhard Müller Wirthmann, *Von Fellen, Farben und Vermischtem. Das Nachlassinventar des Mathis Gothart-Nithart*, in *Das Rätsel Grünewald*, 71–80.

Das Rätsel Grünewald, exhibition catalogue (Aschaffenburg), ed. by Riepertinger et al., Augsburg: Haus der Bayerischen Geschichte.

2003

Ildegarda di Bingen, *Il libro delle opere divine*, ed. by Marta Cristiani and Michela Pereira, Milan: Mondadori.

Leonardo da Vinci master Draftsman, exhibition catalogue (New York), ed. by Carmen C. Bambach, New Haven-London: Yale University Press.

Jane van Nimmen, "Italy, Germany, America: the Migration of a Raphael Portrait", in *Raphael, Cellini and a Renaissance Banker: the Patronage of Bindo Altoviti*, exhibition catalogue (Boston and Florence), ed. by Alan Chong, Daniele Pegazzano, Demetrios Zikos, Boston: Isabella Stewart Gardner Museum, 214–236.

Franz Posset, *The Front-Runner of the Catholic Reformation. The Life and Work of Johann von Staupitz*, Aldershot: Routledge.

Winifred G. Sebald, *Nach der Natur. Ein Elementargedichte* (1988), English translation by Michael Hamburger, *After Nature*, London: Hamish Hamilton.

2004

Andrea Mantegna e l'incisione italiana del Rinascimento nelle collezioni dei Musei Civici di Pavia, exhibition catalogue (Pavia), ed. by Saverio Lomartire, Milan: Electa.

Leo Andergassen, *Bartlmä Dill Riemenschneider. Ein Würzburger Maler in Südtirol*, in Schneider (ed.), *Tilman Riemenschneider. Werke seiner Glaubenswelt*, 150–167.

Thomas A. Brady Jr., "One Soul, Two Bodies: Lordship and Faith in the Prince-Bishopric of Würzburg", in Chapuis (ed.), *Tilman Riemenschneider c. 1460*, 15–27.

Wolfgang Brückner, *Kult und Kunst um 1500. Riemenschneider und die Glaubenswelt seiner Zeit*, in Schneider (ed.), *Tilman Riemenschneider. Werke*, 31–49.

Ulrike Heinrichs-Schreiber, "*Natura contra idolon*. Zur Frage des Antikebezugs in Mathis Gothart-Nithart Gemálde des hl. Senbastian am Isenheimer Altar", in *Die Prásenz der Antike im Übergang vom Mittelalter zur Frühen Neuzeit*, ed. by Ludger Grenzmann, Klaus Grubmüller, Fidel Rádle, Martin Stahelin, Göttingen: Vandenhoeck & Ruprecht, 351–388.

Iris Kalden-Rosenfeld, *Tilman Riemenschneider. The Sculptor and his workshop*, Königstein im Taunus: Karl Robert Langewiesche Nachfolger Hans Köster Verlagsbuchandlung.

Hartmuth Krohm, "Rudolphus de Scherenberg, Episcopus herbipolensis, Franciaeque orientalis Dux: Effigy and Rhetoric", in Chapuis (ed.), *Tilman Riemenschneider c. 1460*, 28–35.

Patrizia Mainoni, "Attraverso i valichi svizzeri. Merci oltremontane e mercati lombardi", in *Le Alpi medievali nello sviluppo delle regioni contermini*, ed. by Gian Maria Varanini, Napoli: Liguori, 99–122.

Michele Marincola, "Riemenschneider's Use of the Decorative Punch in Unpolychromed Sculpture", in Chapuis (ed.), *Tilman Riemenschneider c. 1460*, 2004, 130–147.

Jean-Michel Massing, *Studies in Imagery*, vol. I, *Text and Images*, London: The Pindar Press, 108–140.

Eike Oellermann, "Polychrome or Not? That is the Question", in Chapuis (ed.), *Tilman Riemenschneider c. 1460*, 112–123.

Manfred Schümann, "Gefass oder holzsichtig? Zur Problem der Fassung im Werk Tilman Riemenschneiders", *Tilman Riemenschneider. Werke seiner Blützeit*, 166–173.

Tilman Riemenschneider c. 1460–1513, conference proceedings (Washington, December 3–4, 1999), ed. by Julien Chapuis, Washington-New Haven and London: National Gallery of Art-Yale University Press.

Tilman Riemenschneider. Werke seiner Blützeit, exhibition catalogue, Würzburg, ed. by Claudia Lichte, Regensburg: Schnell & Steiner.

Tilman Riemenschneider. Werke seiner Glaubenswelt, exhibition catalogue, Würzburg, ed. by Wolfgang Schneider, Regensburg: Schnell & Steiner.

2005

Alessandro Ballarin, *La Salomè del Romanino ed altri studi sulla pittura bresciana del Cinquecento*, Cittadella: Bertoncello Arti Grafiche, 2 vols.

Martin Buber, "The Altar" (1917), in Martin Buber, "The Altar"—Jean-Luc Nancy, "Chromatic Atheology", *Journal of Visual Culture*, 4, 1, 116–128.

Bodo Brinkmann and Stephan Kemperdick, *Deutsche Gemälde im Städel 1500–1550*, Mainz am Rhein: Verlag Philipp von Zabern.

Vom Kardinalsornat zur Luther-Bibel: Kunst und Leben des Seidenstickers Hans Plock im Spannungsfeld der Reformation, exhibition catalogue (Berlin), ed. by Tanja Baensch, Berlin: Stadtmuseum Berlin.

Christoph Meckel, *H. B. G.*, Freiburg im Breisgau: Modo Verlag; reprint 2012.

Davide Mirabile, "Un 'Presepe' ad Arona. Rinascimento nel Verbano tra pittura, scultura e arte vetraria", *Prospettiva*, 119–120, 98–104.

Giovanni Reale, *I misteri dell'altare di Isenheim di Grünewald. Una interpretazione storico-ermeneutica*, Milan: Bompiani.

The Rivers North of the Future. The Testament of Ivan Illich as told to David Cayley, Toronto: Anansi.

Edoardo Villata, "Gaudenzio Ferrari e la *Spogliazione delle vesti* al Sacro Monte di Varallo", *Arte Lombarda*, 145, 76–92.

2006

Albrecht Dürer. Incisioni della Pinacoteca Tosio Marinengo, exhibition catalogue (Brescia), ed. by Elena Lucchesi Ragni, Maurizio Mondini, Cinisello Balsamo: Silvana Editoriale.

Capolavori da scoprire. La collezione Borromeo, exhibition catalogue (Milan), ed. by Mauro Natale, Andrea Di Lorenzo, Milan: Skira.

Laura Fenelli, *Il tau, il fuoco, il maiale. I canonici regolari di sant'Antonio Abate tra assistenza e devozione*, Spoleto: Fondazione CISAM.

Hanns Hubach, "'. . .scrinium super sepulchrum aperiuntur'. Die Heilig-Grab-Kapelle der Aschaffenburger Stiftskirche und Matthias Grünewalds 'Beweinung Christi'", in *"Ich armer sundiger mensch". Heiligen-und-Reliquienkult am Übergang zumkonfessionnellen Zeitalter*, conference proceedings (Halle-Saale, October 8–10, 2004), ed. by Andreas Tacke, Göttingen: Kunstmuseum des Landes Sachsen-Anhalt, vol. 2, 415–498.

Der Kardinal Albrecht von Brandenburg. Renaissancefürst und Mäzen, exhibition catalogue (Halle), ed. by Thomas Schauerte, Katje Schneider, Andreas Tacke, Regensburg: Schnell & Steiner, 2 vols.

Daantje Meuwissen, "A Painter in Black and White? The Symbiotic Relationship between the Paintings and the Woodcuts of Jacob Cornelisz. van Oostanen", in *Making and Marketing. Studies of the Painting Process in Fifteenth- and Sizteenth- Century Netherlandish Workshops*, ed. by Molly Faries, Turnhout: Brepols, 55–81.

Badeloch Noldus, "An 'unvergleichbarer Liebhaber'. Pieter Spierinck, the art-dealer diplomat", *Scandinavian Journal of History*, 31, 173–185.

Christina Pol, *Heinrich Steinitz, Anwalt und Poet*, Vienna: Mandelbaum.

Heimo Reinitzer, *Gesetz und Evangelium. Über ein reformatorisches Bildthema, seine Tradition, Funktion und Wirkungsgeschichte*, Hamburg: Christians Verlag, 2 vols.

The Revelations of St. Birgitta of Sweden, translated by Denis Searby, introductions and notes by Bridget Morris, vol. 2, Oxford: Oxford University Press.

Jochen Sander, "The Artistic Development of Hans Holbein the Younger as Panel Painter during his Basel Years", in *Hans Holbein the Younger. The Basel Years 1515–1532*, exhibition catalogue (Basel, Munich and Berlin), Munich: Prestel, 14–18.

2007

Karin Achenbach-Stolz, *Die "Kreuztragung" von Matthias Grünewald aus restauratorischer Sicht*, in Lüdke (ed.), *Grünewald und seine Zeit*, 104–115.

Pantxika Béguerie-De Paepe, "Nouvelles hypothèses sur la genèse du retable d'Issenheim: Grünewald et Strasbourg?", in Béguerie-De Paepe, Lorentz (eds.), *Grünewald et le retable*, 12–15, 82–83.

Pantxika Béguerie-De Paepe, "La réalisation du retable d'Issenheim: Nicolas de Haguenau à Strasbourg", in Béguerie-De Paepe, Lorentz (eds.), *Grünewald et le retable*, 54–65, 68–70.

Biblia Sacra iuxta vulgatam versionem, ed. by Robert Weber, revised by Roger Gryson, Stuttgart: Deutsche Bibelgesellschaft.

Enrico Castelli, *Il demoniaco nell'arte* (1952), new edition ed. by Enrico Castelli Gattinara, Turin: Bollati Boringhieri.

Elisabeth Clementz, "Les précepteurs d'Issenheim, Bâle et Strasbourg, et leur rédeaux e relations", in Béguerie-De Paepe, Lorentz (eds), *Grünewald et le retable*, 46–53.

Tilman Daiber, "Der Aschaffenburger Maria-Schnee Altar. Betrachtungen zu Maltechnik und Zustand", in Béguerie-De Paepe, Menu (eds.), *La technique picturale*, 89–96.

Dürer e l'Italia, ed. by Kristina Hermann Fiore, exhibition catalogue (Rome), Milan: Electa.

Dagmar Eichberger, "Rencontres. Matthias Grünewald à travers ses contemporaine" in Béguerie, Lorentz (eds.), *Grünewald et le retable*, 32–44.

Aubert Gérard, "Rapport d'étude du support et des encadrements du Retable d'Issenheim", *La technique picturale*, in Béguerie-De Paepe, Menu (eds.), *La technique picturale*, 171–176.

Geschichte der bildenden Kunst in Deutschland, 4, *Spätgotik und Renaissance*, ed. by Katharina Krause, Munich, Berlin, London and New York: Prestel-Deutscher Taschenbuch Verlag.

E. Melanie Gifford, Susanna P. Griswold, Norma Uemura, "Matthias Grünewald's *Small Crucifixion*. Painting Practice and Personal Style", in Béguerie-De Paepe, Menu (eds.), *La technique picturale*, 73–80.

Grünewald et le retable d'Issenheim. Regards sur un chef-d'oeuvre, exhibition catalogue (Colmar), ed. by Pantxika Béguerie-De Paepe and Philippe Lorentz, Paris and Colmar: Somogy Editions d'Art-Musée d'Unterlinden-Societé Schongauer.

Grünewald und seine Zeit, exhibition catalogue (Karlsruhe), ed. by Dietmar Lüdke, Munich and Berlin: Deutsche Kunstverlag.

Hanns Hubach, "Der Aschaffenburger Maria-Schnee Altar", in Béguerie-De Paepe, Menu (eds.) *La technique picturale*, 81–88.

Hanns Hubach, "Mein hend, die mus ich winden. Grünewalds Aschaffenburger 'Beweinung Christi'", in *Cranach im Exil. Aschaffenburg um 1540: Zuflucht—Schatkammer—Residenz*, exhibition catalogue (Aschaffenburg), ed. by Gerhard Ermischer and Andreas Tacke, Regensburg: Schnell & Steiner, 136–155.

Stephan Kemperdick, "Die *Kreuzigung* im Kunstmuseum Basel", in Béguerie-De Paepe, Menu (eds.), *La technique picturale*, 65–72.

Carole Juillet, "Quelques hypothèses sur le panneau de la Tentation de Saint Antoine", *in* Béguerie-De Paepe, Menu (eds.), *La technique picturale*, 61–64.

Philippe Lorentz, "Grünewald et Léonard de Vinci: les draperies dans le retable d'Issenheim", in Béguerie-de Paepe, Lorentz (eds.), *Grünewald et le retable*, 16–31.

Dietmar Lüdke, *Die "Donaueschinger Magdalenenklage" der Sammlung Würth in Schwäbisch Hall*, in Idem (ed.), *Grünewald und seine Zeit*, 345–346.

Jessica Mack-Andrick, "Von beiden Seiten betrachtet. Überlegungen zum Tauberbischofsheim Altar", "Grünewalds "Beweinung Christi" und die ikonographische Tradition", in Lüdke (ed.), *Grünewald und seine Zeit*, 68–77.

Pietro C. Marani, "Dürer, Leonardo e i pittori lombardi del Quattrocento", in Herrmann Fiore (ed.), *Dürer e l'Italia*, 51–61.

François-René Martin, "Les formes de l'attribution. Réflexions sur l'historiographie de Grünewald (XVIe-XIXe siècle)", in Béguerie-De Paepe, Menu (eds.), *La technique picturale*, 2007, 5–16.

Anna Morat-Fromm, "Eine Begegnung mit Folgen? Grünewald und Baldung", in *Grünewald und seine Zeit*, 39–47.

Elisabeth Ravaud and Elsa Lambert, "Les étapes d'élaboration du retable à travers l'imagerie scientifique", in Béguerie-De Paepe, Lorentz (eds.), *Grünewald et le retable*, 232–243.

Élisabeth Ravaud, Elsa Lambert and Patrick Le Chanu, "Le *Retable d'Issenheim*. Résultats de l'imagerie scientifique", in Béguerie-De Paepe, Menu (eds.) *La technique picturale*, ed., 40–48.

Astrid Reuter, "Zur Geschicthe des Heller-Altars", in Lüdke (ed.), *Grünewald und seine Zeit*, 127–130.

La riscoperta di un dipinto della Pinacoteca di Brera. Giovanni Agostino da Lodi. Il maestro e il giovane allievo, ed. by Sandrina Bandera, Milan: Le Nuove Grafiche.

Michael Roth, "Les dessins de Matthias Grünewald pour le retable d'Issenheim", in Béguerie-De Paepe, Lorentz (eds.), *Grünewald et le retable*, 92–104, 121.

Wolfgang Schmid, "Jakob Heller- ein Frankfurter Stifter und Auftraggeber", in Lüdke (ed.), *Grünewald und seine Zeit*, 48–57.

La technique picturale de Grünewald et de ses contemporaines, conference proceedings (Colmar, January 24–26, 2006), ed. by Pantxika Béguerie-De Paepe, Michel Menu, Colmar: Musée d'Unterlinden.

Robert Suckale, "Grünewald und die *ältere* fränkische Malerei", in Béguerie-De Paepe, Menu (eds.), *La technique picturale*, 161–166.

Caroline Walker Bynum, *Wonderful Blood. Theology and Practice in Late Medieval Germany and Beyond*, Philadelphia: University of Pennsylvania Press.

2008

Amico Aspertini 1474–1552, artista bizzarro nell'età di Dürer e Raffaello, exhibition catalogue (Bologna), ed. by Andrea Emiliani, Daniela Scaglietti Kelescian, Cinisello Balsamo: Silvana Editoriale.

John van Engen, *Sisters and Brothers of the Common Life: The Devotio Moderna and the World of the Later Middle Ages*, Philadelphia: University of Pennsylvania Press.

The Holy Bible 1611 Edition King James Version, Peabody: Hendrikson Publishers.

Georg Josef Dietz, Irene Brücle and Gerhard Banik, *Grünewalds Zeichentechnik*, in Roth (ed.), *Matthias Grünewald. Zeichnungen*, 62–69.

Heinrich Fussbahn, "Die Kirche des Kardinals Albrecht von Brandenburg", *Aschaffenburger Jahrbuch für Geschichte, Landeskunde und Kunst des Untermaingebietes*, 26, 9–55.

Jerry Marino, "Touch of Evil. Desease and the Diabolical in Grünewald's *Temptation of St. Anthony*", *Athanor*, XXVI, 23–33.

Reiner Marquard, "Mathias Grünewalds Tauberbischofsheimer Andachtsbilder in der Kunsthalle Karlsruhe und Martin *Luthers teologia crucis*", *Zeitschrift für die Geschichte des Oberrheins*, 156, 179–194.

Matthias Grünewald. Zeichnungen und Gemälde, exhibition catalogue (Berlin), ed. by Michael Roth. Berlin: Hatje Cantz-Staatliche Museen.

Northern European and Spanish Painting before 1600 in the Art Institute of Chicago, ed. by Martha Wöllfl Chicago: Art Institute of Chicago.

Rinascimento e passione per l'antico. Andrea Riccio e il suo tempo, exhibition catalogue (Trento, Castello del Buonconsiglio), ed. by Andrea Bacchi, Laura Giacomelli, Trento: Provincia Autonoma di Trento.

Michael Roth, *Matthias Grünewald. Die Zeichnungen*, Berlin and Ostfildern: Hatje Cantz.

Michael Roth, *Mit Licht gemalt und zeichnet- Grünewalds Zeichnungen und Grisaillen*, in Idem (ed.). *Matthias Grünewald. Zeichnungen*, 54–61.

Manuel Teget-Welz, *Martin Schaffner. Leben und Werk eines Ulmer Malers zwischen Spätmittelalter und Renaissance* (Forschungen zur Geschichte der Stadt Ulm, 32), Ulm: Kohlhammer.

Vincenzo Pagani un pittore devoto tra Crivelli e Raffaello, exhibition catalogue (Fermo), ed. by Vittorio Sgarbi, Cinisello Balsamo: Silvana Editoriale.

2008–2009

Maristella Cervi, *Prospettive d'ékphrasis: il polittico d'Isenheim nella letteratura tedesca del Novecento*, tesi di dottorato in Teoria e analisi del testo, XXI ciclo, Università degli Studi di Bergamo, relatore Amelia Valtolina.

2009

Jakob Böhme, *Werke. Morgenroete im Aufgangk*, *De Signatura Rerum*, ed. by Ferdinand van Ingen, Frankfurt am Main: Deutscher Klassiker Verlag.

Carlo Cairati and Daniele Cassinelli, "Regesto dei documenti", *Rassegna di studi e notizie*, XXXVI, vol. XXXII, 2009, 133–158.

Laure Fagnart, *Léonard de Vinci en France. Collections et collectionneurs (XVéme-XVIIéme siècles)*, Rome: L'Erma di Bretschneider.

Hanns Hubach, entry "Grünewald, Matthias", in *Saur. Allgemeine Künstlerlexikon*, vol. 63, Munich: De Gruyter, 386–396, https://www.degruyter.com/database/AKL/entry/_00069638T/html

Joachim von Sandrart. Ein europaeischer Künstler und Theoretiker zwischen Italien und Deutschland, ed. by Sybille Ebert-Schifferer, Hirmer: München.

Reiner Marquard, *Matthias Grünewald und die Reformation*, Berlin: Frank & Timme.

Ewald M. Vetter, *Grünewald. Die Altäre in Frankfurt, Isenheim und Aschaffenburg und ihre Ikonographie*, Weissenhorn: Anton H. Konrad.

2010

Giovanni Agosti, Jacopo Stoppa and Marco Tanzi, "Il Rinascimento lombardo (visto da Rancate)", in *Il Rinascimento nelle terre ticinesi. Da Bramantino a Bernardino Luini*, exhibition catalogue (Rancate), ed. by Giovanni Agosti, Jacopo Stoppa, Marco Tanzi, Milan: Officina Libraria, 21–69.

Alessandro Ballarin, *Leonardo a Milano. Problemi di leonardismo milanese tra Quattrocento e Cinquecento. Giovanni Antonio Boltraffio prima della Pala Casio*, Verona: Aurora, 4 vols.

Fantastische Welten. Albrecht Altdorfer und das Expressive in der Kunst um 1500, exhibition catalogue (Frankfurt and Vienna), ed. by Stefan Roller, Jochen Sander, Munich: Hirmer.

Hans Holbein d. Ä. Die Graue Passion in ihrer Zeit, exhibition catalogue (Stuttgart), ed. by Elsbeth Wiemann, Ostfildern: Hatje Cantz.

Detlef Zinke, *Masterpieces from Middle Age to Baroque at the Augustinermuseum of Freiburg i. Br.*, Berlin-Munich: Deutscher Kunstverlag.

2011

Italo Bacigalupo, *Der Lindenhardter Altar. Grünewald oder Hans von Kulmbach? Die Entsehungs- und Gebrauchtsgeschichte der Tafelbilder*, Petersberg: Michael Imhof Verlag.

Pantxika Béguerie-De Paepe and Magali Haas, *Schongauer á Colmar*, exhibition catalogue, Colmar, Antwerp: Ludion.

Cranach l'altro Rinascimento, exhibition catalogue (Rome), ed. by Anna Coliva, Bernard Aikema, Milano: 24 Ore Cultura.

Mario Dal Bello, *Lorenzo Lotto. Un incontro*, Città del Vaticano: Libreria Editrice Vaticana.

Heinrich Dilly, "'Riveduta e ampliata da Jacob Burckhardt in collaborazione con l'autore'. La seconda edizione dei manuali sulla pittura e la storia dell'arte di Franz Kugler", in *La formazione del vedere. A partire da Burckhardt*, conference proceedings (Milan, February 19–20, 2009), ed. by Andrea Pinotti, Maria Luisa Roli, Macerata: Quidlibet, 51–71.

Stephan Gasser, Katharina Simon-Muscheid, Alain Fretz, *Die Freiburger Skulptur des 16. Jahrhunderts. Herstellung, Funktion und Auftraggeberschaft*, Petersberg: Michael Imhoff Verlag, 2 vols.

Leonardo da Vinci Painter at the Court of Milan, exhibition catalogue (London), ed. by Luke Syson, Larry Keith, London: National Gallery Company.

Maitres vénitiens, Chefs d'Oeuvre de l'Accademia Carrara de Bergamo et du Musée Royale d'Anvers, exhibition catalogue (Bruxelles), ed. by Giovanni Carlo Federico Villa, Cinisello Balsamo: Silvana Editoriale.

Adriano Mariuz, *L'altare di Isenheim. Mathis Grünewald pittore della Morte e della Resurrezione*, Verona: Scripta.

Angelika Michael, "Luther und die Bilder. Von Bildern, die man sicht, und solchen, die man nicht sicht", *Lutherjahrbuch*, 79, 101–137.

Ulrich Schulz, *Albrecht Dűrer. Das druckgraphische Werk. Kupferstiche, Holzschnitte und Bűcher*, I, *Die frűhen Jahre bis zur zweiten italienischen Reise*, II, *Kupferstiche, Kaltmadelarbeiten, Radierungen, Holzschnitte und Bücher*, exhibition catalogue (Bad Schussenried, Erfurt and Augsburg), Bad Schussenried: Staatlichen Schlösser und Gärten Baden-Wűrttemberg.

Nicolas Valazza, "Du 'charnier divin au triomphe de la Chair'. Huysmans face à Grünewald", in *Les Religions du xixè siècle*, conference proceedings (Paris, November 26–28, 2009), ed. by Sophie Guermès, Bertrand Marchal, online publication: https://serd.hypotheses.org/files/2018/08/NicolasValazza.pdf

2012

Bramantino a Milano, exhibition catalogue (Milan), ed. by Giovanni Agosti, Jacopo Stoppa and Marco Tanzi, Milan: Officina Libraria, 2012.

Maria Deiters, "Bible, Image, Artist-The Bible of Hans Plock", in *"Wading Lambs and Swimming Elephants". The Bible for the Laity and Theologians in the Late Medieval and Early Modern Era*, ed. by Wim François, August den Hollander, Leuven, Paris and Walpole, MA: Peeters Publishers, 153–180.

Ursula Fuhrer and Annette Kollmann, "Die 'Stuppacher Madonna' im Licht der restauratorischen Untersuchungen. Zu Bestand, Schadensbildern, Konservierungs- und Restaurierungsmassnahmen", *Denkmalpflege in Baden-Württemberg*, 69–74.

François-René Martin, Michel Menu and Sylvie Ramond, *Grünewald*, Paris: Hazan, (Italian edition Milan: Jaca Book, 2013).

Michel Menu, "Matière et technicque", in Martin, Menu and Ramond, *Grünewald*, 256–275.

Thomas Noll, "Rilke und die Rezeption des sog. Matthias Grünewald im späten 19. und früher 20. Jahrundert", in *Im Schwarzwald. Uncollected Poems 1906–1911* (Blätter der Rilke-Gesellschaft, 31), ed. by Erich Unglaub, Jörg Paulus, Göttingen: Wallstein, 133–156.

Melanie Panse, *Hans von Gerdorff's "Feldtbuch der Wundtartzney". Produktion, Präsentation und Rezeption von Wissen*, Wiesbaden: Reicher Verlag.

Heinz Schilling, *Martin Luther. Rebell in einer Zeit des Umbruchs*, Munich: Beck.

Pierre Vaisse, "Faut-il modifier la presentation du Retable d'Issenheim?", *La Tribune de l'art*, April 29.

Émile Verhaeren, *Essays on the Northern Renaissance. Rembrandt, Rubens, Grünewald and Others*, ed. by Albert Alhadeff, New York: Peter Lang Publishing.

Edoardo Villata, *Tristezza della resurrezione. Bramantino negli anni di Ludovico il Moro*, Milan: Ennerre.

2013

Rushena Abduramanova, *Kardinal Albrecht von Brandenburg und das Hallesche Heiltumsbuch*, Potsdam: GRIN Verlag.

Chiara Benati, "Surgeon or Lexicographer? The Latin-German Glossaries in Addendum to Hans von Gersdorff's Feldtbuch der Wunderarzney", *Linguistica e Filologia*, 33, 35–57.

Andreas Menrad, "Grünewalds Ikone im Landesamt für Denkmalpflege. Die Restaurierung der 'Stuppacher Madonna'", *Denkmalpflege in Baden-Württemberg*, 2, 62–68.

Susanne Meurer, "'Yearning for Biography'. The Elusive Life of Mathis Grünewald", in *The Challenge of the Object*, conference proceedings (Nuremberg, July 15–20, 2012), ed. by Georg Ulrich Grossmann, Petra Krutisch, Nurenberg: Verlag des Germanischen Nationalmuseums, 1050–1054.

Mit den Gezeiten. Frühe Druckgraphik der Niederlande: Katalog der niederländischen Druckgraphik von den Anfängen bis um 1560 in der Sammlung des Dresdener Kupferstich-Kabinetts, exhibition catalogue (Dresden), Petersberg: Imhof.

La Renaissance à Toul. Morceaux choisi, exhibition catalogue, ed. by Alde Harmand, Philippe Masson, Toul : Musée d'Art et d'Histoire de Toul.

Julia Ricker, *Grünewalds Stuppacher Madonna ist restauriert. Schönheit hinter Glas*, in "Monumente. Magazin für Denkmalkultur in Deutschland", 6 (www.monumente-online.de).

Edoardo Rossetti, "Uno spagnolo tra i francesi e la devozione gesuata: il cardinale Bernardino Carvajal e il monastero di San Girolamo di porta Vercellina a Milano", in *Le Duché de Milan et les commanditaires français (1499–1521)*, conference proceedings (Geneva, March 30–31, 2012), ed. by Fréderic Elsig, Mauro Natale, Rome: Viella, 81–235.

Armin Stein, *Kardinal Albrecht*, Halle: Projekte Verlag-Cornelius.

2014

Karin Achenbach-Stolz and Holger Jacob-Friesen, *Grünewalds Kreuztragung. Die Retaurierung eines Hauptwerkes deutscher Kunst*, Karlsruhe: Staatliche Kunsthalle.

Berenike Berentzen, *Niclaus Hagnower. Studien zum Bildhauerischen Werk*, Petershof: Imhof.

Bramantino. L'arte nuova del Rinascimento lombardo, exhibition catalogue (Lugano), ed. by Mauro Natale, Milan: Skira.

Anne-Marie Bonnet and Gabriele Kopp-Schmidt, *Die Malerei der Deutschen Renaissance 1484–1555*, Munich: Schirmer Mosel.

Carlo Cairati and Edoardo Rossetti, "Luoghi di diffusione della cultura oltremontana nella Milano sforzesca: suggestioni 'todesche' a Santa Caterina di San Nazaro", in Elsig, Gaggetta (eds.), *Cultura oltremontana in Lombardia.*

Cultura oltremontana in Lombardia al tempo degli Sforza (1450–1535), conference proceedings (Geneva, April 12–13, 2013), ed. by Frédéric Elsig, Claudia Gaggetta, Rome: Viella.

Dossier gaudenziani. Restauri alla Pinacoteca di Varallo,ed. by Simone Amerigo, Carla Falcone, Varallo: Società per l'Incoraggiamento allo Studio del Disegno.

François-René Martin, "Estrema Tule. Sur une métaphore géographique chez Roberto Longhi", *Predella*, 10, 151–159.

Ursula Opitz, *Philipp Uffenbach. Ein Frankfurter Maler um 1600*, Berlin: Deutscher Kunstverlag.

Marco Rossati, "Sculture oltremontane nella Lombardia del Quattro e Cinquecento: presenza, scambi, importazioni", Elsig, Gaggetta (eds.), *Cultura oltremontana in Lombardia*, 129–165.

Edoardo Villata, "Grünewald in Lombardia?", in Elsig, Gaggetta (eds.), *Cultura oltremontana in Lombardia*, 281–314.

Ulrich Wagner, *Der Bauernkrieg bei Lorenz Fries und Martin Cronthal*, in *Lorenz Fries und sein Werk. Bilanz und Einordnung*, ed. by Franz Fuchs, Stefan Petersen, Ulrich Wagner, Walter Ziegler, Würzburg: Verlag Ferdinand Schöningh, 150–178.

2015

Arte lombarda dai Visconti agli Sforza. Milano al centro dell'Europa, exhibition catalogue (Milan) ed. by Mauro Natale, Serena Romano, Milan: Skira, 287–288.

Aldo Galli and Matteo Mazzalupi, "Sulle tracce di don Paolo Moerich, chierico e scultore", *Analecta Pomposiana. Studi di storia religiosa delle diocesi di Ferrara e Comacchio*, 39, 2015, *Quattrocento bondense. Religiosità, stampa, arte, cultura*, ed. by Silvia Superbi, 13-60

Alexandre Hougron, *La céramique chinoise ancienne*, Paris: Editions de l'Amateur.

Christof Metzger, "Feuer und Eis. Matthias Grünewalds 'Moses unter dem brennenden Dornbusch' und der Aschaffenburger 'Maria-schnee Altar'", in *Linien-Musik des Sichtbaren. Festschrift für Michael Semff*, ed. by Kurt Zeitler, Berlin-Munich: De Gruyter, 178–187.

Susanne Meurer, "Wer ist schuld an Grünewald?", in *Die Künstler der "Teutesche Academie" Joachim von Sandrarts. "Aus aller Herren Länder"*, ed. by Anna Schreurs-Morêt. Lucia Simonato, Susanne Meurer Turnhout: Brepols, 181–194.

Wolfgang Minaty, "Ein Grünewald in Italien? Wie plötzlich der Maler Vincenzo Pagani ins Visier kommt", *Mainfrankisches Jahrbuch für Geschichte und Kunst*, 67, 49–64.

Maurice Pianzola, *Peintres et vilains. Les artistes de la Renaissance et la grande guerre des paysans de 1525* (1962), new ed. Clermont-Ferrand: L'Insomniaque.

Edoardo Villata, *Leonardo*, Rome: Istituto della Enciclopedia Italiana.

2016

Alessandro Ballarin, *Giorgione e l'umanesimo veneziano*, Verona: Aurora (but 2018), tome II, *Giorgione e la Compagnia degli Amici.*

Paolo Bensi, "Impasti argillosi e policromie delle sculture in terracotta a Padova e in Lombardia intorno a Giovanni e Agostino de Fondulis", *Insula Fulcheria*, XLVI, 75–83.

Franco Buzzi, *La Bibbia di Lutero*, Turino: Claudiana.

Sara Cavatorti, *Giovanni Teutonico. Scultura lignea tedesca nell'Italia del Quattrocento*, Perugia: Aguaplano, 2016

Albrecht Dürer. Documentary Biography, Edition Translation Commentary by Jeoffrey Ashcroft, New Haven and London: Yale University Press, 2 vols.

Stefan Fischer, *Hieronymus Bosch. The Complete Works*, Cologne: Taschen.

Hartmut Krohm, "Due sculture di Veit Stoss. L'arte dell'intaglio nel suo massimo compimento intorno al 1500", in *"Fece di scoltura di legname e colori". Scultura del Quattrocento in legno dipinto a Firenze*, exhibition catalogue (Florence), ed. by Alfredo Bellandi, Florence: Giunti, 139–159.

Wolfgang Minaty, *Grünewald im Dialog. 500 Jahre Isenheimer Altar in Kunst, Literatur und Musik*, Regensburg: Schnell & Schneider.

Heinz Schilling, *Martin Lutero. Ribelle in un'epoca di cambiamenti radicali*, Turin: Claudiana.

Notger Slenczka, "'Nondum considerasti quanti ponderis sit peccatum—Du hast noch nicht ermessen, welches Gewicht die Sünde hat'. Die Bedeutung des Kreuzes für das Selbstverständnis des Menschen", *Kerygma und Dogma*, 62, 2, 160–182.

Thomas Wolfe, *On Time and the River. A Legend of Man's Hunger in his Youth* (1935), ed. with and introduction of Elisabeth Kostava, London: Penguin Books.

2017

Chiara Benati, "The Field Surgery Manual Which Became a Medical Commonplace Book: Hans von Gersdorff's Feldtbuch der Wundarzney (1517) Translated into Low German", in *Bodily and Spiritual Hygiene in Medieval and Early Modern Literature. Explorations of Textual Presentations of Filth and Water*, ed. by Albrecht Classen, Berlin and Boston: De Gruyter, 501–528.

John Berger, *Portraits: John Berger on Artists*, ed. by Tom Overton, London-New York: Verso.

Das Buch der Bücher. Die Luther-Bibel von 1534, ed. by Stephan Füssel, Cologne: Taschen, 23 vols.

Alessandra Galizzi Kroegel, "The Altarpieces by Bernardo Zenale at the Getty and Denver Art Museums: Two Case Studies for the Iconography of the Immaculate Conception", *Ikon. Journal of Iconographic Studies*, 4, 2017, 201–221.

Bridget Heal, *A Magnificent Faith. Art and Identity in Lutheran Germany*, Oxford: Oxford University Press.

Søren Kaspersen, "'Die drei Marien'. Menschwerdung als Andachtsbild neue Erwägungen über Grünewalds Isenheimer Altar", *Acta ad archaelogiam et artium pertinentia*, 21, 7, 197–242.

Christian Leo, *Würzburg unter schwedischer Herrschaft, 1631–1633. Die "Summarische Beschreibung" des Joachim Ganzhorn*, Würzburg: Echter Verlag7.

Lorenzo Lotto, *Il libro di spese diverse*, ed. by Francesco De Carolis, Trieste: Trieste University Press.

Adriano Prosperi, *Lutero. Gli anni della fede e della libertà*, Milan: Mondadori.

Michael Schubert, *The Isenheim Altarpiece. History-Interpretation-Background*, Stuttgart: Steiner Books (first edition 2007).

Matthias Weniger, *Tilman Riemenschneider. Die Werke in Bayerischen Nationalmuseum.* Petersberg: Michael Imhoff.

2018

Accademia Carrara Bergamo. Dipinti italiani del Trecento e del Quattrocento. Catalogo completo, ed. by Giovanni Valagussa, Milan: Officina Libraria, 2018.

Gregory C. Bryda, "The Exuding Wood of the Cross of Isenheim", *The Art Bulletin*, 100, 2, 6–36.

Louis Charbonneau-Lassay, *Le Vulnéraire du Christ. Le mystérieuse emblématiquue des plaies du corps et du coeur de Jésus Christ*, ed. by Gauthier Pierozak, Paris: Gutenberg Reprint.

Dürer e il Rinascimento tra Germania e Italia, exhibition catalogue (Milan), ed. by Bernard Aikema, Milan: 24 Ore Cultura.

Linda A. Huebert Hecht and Hanns-Paul Ties, "The Tirolian Anabaptist Artist. Bartlme Dill Riemenschneider and the Anabaptist Women in His Household, 1526–1549", *The Mennonite Quarterly Review*, 92, July, 439–460.

Wolfgang Minaty, *Grünewalds verschollenes Bild Untergegangen? Der Fall Alban wird wieder aufgerollt*, Mainz: Nünnerich-Asmus.

Il Rinascimento di Gaudenzio Ferrari, exhibition catalogue (Varallo, Vercelli, and Novara), ed. by Giovanni Agosti and Jacopo Stoppa, Milan: Officina Libraria.

2019

Der Isenheimer Altar. Werk und Wirkung, ed. by Werner Frick, Günther Schnitzler, Freiburg im Breisgau: Rombach.

Dietmar Lüdke, "Grünewalds Kreuzigungsbilder aus Tauberbischofsheim und den ehemaligen Fürstenberg-Sammlungen Donaueschingen", in Frick, Schnitzler (eds.), *Der Isenheimer Altar*, 95–130.

Reiner Marquard. "Die Versuchungtafel als Schlüsselbild des Isenheimer Altars. Anmerkungen zum reformatiomsgeschichtlichen Hintergrund der Kunst Mathias Grünewalds", in Frick, Schnitzler (eds.), *Der Isenheimer Altar*, 65–93.

Susanne Schaal-Gotthardt, "'Ist, dass du schaffst und bildest, genug?' Grünewald-Rezeption in Paul Hindemiths Sinfonie und Oper *Mathis der Maler*, in Frick, Schnitzler (eds.), *Der Isenheimer Altar*, 229–249.

Thomas Schauerte, *Dürer e la Riforma: una conclusione aperta*, in Aikema (ed.), *Dürer e il Rinascimento tra Germania*, 107–113.

Marco Fratini, review of E. Villata, *Grünewald pittore e mistico tra Lutero e Hindemith*, in *Riforma e movimenti religiosi*, 5, 2019, 233–237.

Hans Baldung Grien. Neue Perspektiven auf sein Werk, ed. by Hölger Jacob-Friesen, Oliver Jehle, Berlin and Munich: Deutscher Kunstverlag.

Hans Baldung Grien sacré/profane, exhibition catalogue (Karlsruhe), ed. by Hölger Jakob-Friesen, Berlin and Munich: Deutscher Kunstverlag: 2019.

Michel Krempper, *Mathis Nithard dans la guerre des Paysans 1525*, Mulhouse: Mulhousienne d'Edition / Milhüser Verlag.

Frank Muller, *Hans Baldung Grien. Entre christianisme et paganisme*, Strasbourg: Editions du Signe.

Michael Roth, "Dürer-Baldung-Grünewald?", in Jacob-Friesen, Jehle (eds.), *Hans Baldung Grien*, 68–79.

Anna Schreurs-Morét, "Matthias Grünewald und der Isenheimer Altar. Vom Leuchten der Farbe zur Fama eines Künstlers", in Frick, Schnitzler (eds.), *Der Isenheimer Altar*, 40–64.

Wolfgang Strobl, "'Ianus Bifrons'. Ein Künstlerleben in Widerspruch und Einheit. Zu einem subversiven täuferischen Freskenzyklus Bartlme Dill Riemenschneiders in Tramin, Ansitz Lagenmantel (1547)", *Zeitschrift für bayerische Landesgeschichte*, 82, 2, 381–445.

Edoardo Villata, "Lotto e Pordenone a Venezia: vite parallele (asimmetriche)", in *Lorenzo Lotto. Contesti, significati, conservazione*, conference proceedings (Loreto, February 1–3, 2018), ed. by Francesca Coltrinari, Enrico Maria Dal Pozzolo, Treviso: Zel, 262–275.

2020

Szilvia Bodnár, *German Drawings of the Fifteenth and Sixteenth Century in the Museum of Fine Arts, Budapest*, Budapest: Museum of Fine Arts.

Simone Ferrari, *Dürer e Leonardo. Il Paragone delle Arti e nord e a sud delle Alpi*, Genua: Genova University Press.

André Guyaux, "'Le seul art véridique et grand': Huysmans et les Primitifs", in Guégan, Guyaux (eds.), *Joris-Karl Huysmans*, 158–167.

Holger Jacob-Friesen, "Matthias Grünewald, Kreuztragung Christi", in *Förderprojekte der Rudolf-August Oetker-Stiftung 2016 bis 2020*, ed. by Monika Bachtler, Susanne Lindhorst, Bielefeld: Sieveking, 212–217.

Joris-Karl Huysmans. De Degas à Grünewald, exhibition catalogue (Paris and Strasbourg), ed, by Stéphane Guégan, André Guyaux, Paris-Strasbourg: Musée d'Orsay, Musée de la ville de Strasbourg-Gallimard.

Christof Metzger, *The Heller Altarpiece*, in *Dürer*, exhibition catalogue (Vienna), ed. by Christof Metzger, Munich and London: Prestel, 302–318.

Wolfgang Minaty, "Führt Höttinger zu Grünewald? Der Aschaffenburger Maria-Schnee-Altar auf Spurensuche", *Aschaffenburger Jahrbuch für Geschichte, Landeskunde und Kunst des Untermaingebietes*, 34, 56–108.

Teatri del sacro e del dolore. I Compianti in legno e in terracotta in Lombardia e in Piemonte tra Quattrocento e Cinquecento, ed. by Renzo Dionigi, Filippo Maria Ferro, Soncino: Edizioni dei Soncino.

Pierre Vaisse, "L'art religieux en République", in Guégan, Guyaux (eds.), *Joris-Karl Huysmans*, 141–157.

Caroline Walker Bynum, *Dissmilar Similitudes. Devotional Objects in Late Medieval Europe*, New York: Zone Books.

2021

Katherine M. Boivin, *Riemenschneider in Rothenburg. Sacred Space and Civic Identity in the Late Medieval City*, University Park, PA: Pennsylvania State University Press.

Edoardo Villata, *1478, A Year in Leonardo da Vinci's Career*, Newcastle upon Tyne: Cambridge Scholars Publishing.

2022

Between Hell and Paradise. The Enigmatic World of Hieronymus Bosch, exhibition catalogue (Budapest), ed. by Bernadett Tóth, Ágota Varga, Budapest: Fine Arts Museum.

Judith Breuer, "Die Kapelle für Grünewalds Madonnenbild in Stuppach", *Denkmalpflege in Baden-Württemberg*, 4, 270–277.

Enrico Maria Dal Pozzolo, *Lorenzo Lotto. Catalogo generale dei dipinti*, con la partecipazione di Raffaella Poltronieri e di Valentina Castegnaro e Marta Paravanti, Milan: Skira.

Die Hausbibel des Seidenstickerts Hans Plock (ca. 1490–1570). Wege der Erschliessung, ed. by Albrecht Henkys, Claudine Moulin Heidelberg: Universität Winter.

Riemenschneider in Situ, ed. by Katherine M. Boivin, Gregory C. Bryda, Turnhout: Harvey Miller.

Isabella Sturm and Manuel Teget-Welz. "Kollegen oder Konkurrenten? Die Kooperationen des Hans von Kulmbach", in *Renaissance in Franken. Hans von Kulmbach und die Kunst um Dürer*, exhibition catalogue, Kronach, ed. by Manuel Tehet-Welz and Hans Dickel, Petersberg: Michael Imhof Verlag, 87-103

Gloria Vallese and Giangiacomo Gandolfi, "1° Ottobre 1502: Jheronimus Bosch, un'eclissi anulare e la passione di Cristo", in *"Ad una ad una annoverar le stelle"*, XIX Congresso della Società Italiana di Archeoastronomia Università di Bari, ed. by Elio Antonello, Padova: Padova University Press, 195–214.

2022–2023

A. De Marchi, "Jos Amman von Ravensburg, Zanetto Bugatto e la parte fiamminga nella pittura lombarda di età sforzesca", *Nuovi Studi*, 27, 61–96.

2023

Pantxika Béguerie-De Paepe, "*Colmar. Musée Unterlinden.Un nouveau regard sur le retable d'Issenheim. Quelques apports de la restauration sur l'étude de l'œuvre*", in *Revue des musées de France*, 4, 9–14.

Mario Dal Bello, *Matthias Grünewald. Orrore e visione*, Rome: Dei Merangoli.

François Desseilles, *Les temps juridiques du retable d'Issenheim, Dépasser l'étude de cas?*, in *Nouveaux regards sur les saisies patrimoniales en Europe à l'époque de la Révolution française*, conference proceedings (Bruxelles, May 30th-31th, 2018), ed. by Pierre-Yves Kairis, Turnhout: Brepols, 343–362.

Simone Ferrari, "Huysmans critico d'arte. La fortuna dei primitivi fiamminghi", *Il Capitale Culturale*, 27, 3–16.

Diletta Gamberini, "Margherita Guidacci e la riflessione sulla modernità attraverso il prisma di un'ecfrasi da Grünewald", *IPR Italian Poetry Review*, XVIII, 249–280.

Giorgio Gualdrini, *Trittico delle cose ultime. Grünewald, Holbein, Raffaello*, Villa Verucchio: Pazzini Editore.

Lesley Hughes, "'A German Artwork for the German People'.

An Altarpiece and an Accommodation in Paul Hindemith's *Mathis der Maler* (1935)", *The Journal of Musicology*, 40, 2, Spring, 131–158.

Moroni 1521–1580 il ritratto del suo tempo, exhibition catalogue, ed. by Simone Facchinetti, Arturo Galansino, Milan: Gallerie d'Italia-Skira.

Anne-Sophie Pellé, *Aemulatio Italorum. La réception culturelle des gravures du Mantegna dans l'art germanique au temps d'Albrecht Dürer*, Turnhout: Brepols.

Riemenschneider and Late Medieval Alabaster, exhibition catalogue (Cleveland), ed. by Gerhard Lutz, Cleveland: The Cleveland Museum of Art in association with D Giles Limited.

Ludwig Schönbein, *'Sei mein Heute, sei mein Morgen!' Frieden finden in einer 'verkehrten Welt'—aufgezeigt am Projekt der Stuppacher Madonna*, Lindenberg: Kunstverlag Josef Fink.

2024

Jonathan Jones, *Earthly Delights. A History of the Renaissance*, London: Thames & Hudson.

Peintures germaniques des collections françaises (1370–1580), exhibition catalogue (Besançon, Colmar, Dijon), ed. by Isabelle Dubois-Brinkmann, Aude Briau, Dijon-Paris: Éditions Faton-Institut National d'Histoire de l'Art.

Marco Scansani, *Il fuoco sacro della terracotta. Giovanni de Fondulis tra Lombardia e Veneto,* Mantua: Tre Lune.

Christoph Trepesch, Andreas Tacke, *Der ältere Holbein. Augsburg an der Schwelle zur europäische Kunstmetropole*, exhibition catalogue, Augsburg, Munich; Michel Imhof.

2025

Gianluca Poldi, "Una diversa Vergine delle Rocce. *Underdrawing* e osservazioni visive intorno alla pala di Denver di Bernardo Zenale", *Artibus et Historiae* (forthcoming).

No date.

Jean Fuchs, *Inventaire des Archives de la Ville de Strasbourg antérieurs à 1790*, Sèrie V, Strasbourg: Ville de Strasbourg, no date.

INDEX OF NAMES

PHOTO CREDITS

1, 2: Augsburg, Hoher Dom/Diözese Augsburg: Hascher fotografie Augsburg
3: Musée Unterlinden Colmar, RMN-Grand Palais
4, 9, 17, 23, 25, 27, 38, 46, 55, 59, 67, 68, 75, 77, 87, 99, 116, 122, 159, 160, 181, 191, 208, 217 (photo Giorgio Olivero), 234, 235, 238, 239, 240: Edoardo Villata (private archive)
5, 6, 14: Kunstsammlungen der Veste Coburg/ Germany
7: Staatliche Museen zu Berlin, Kupferstichkabinett / Dietmar Katz, public domain Mark 1.0
8, 155, 175: The Cleveland Museum of Art, Public Domain
10, 11 : Evangelisch-luterische Pfarrkirche St. Martin, Schwabach
12 : RMN-Grand Palais (musée du Louvre) / Jean-Gilles Berizzi / Thierry Le Mage
13 : Saint Germain en Laye, Musée Municipal Ducastel-Vera
15: Gallerie dell'Accademia, Venice
16a, 16b, 18, 19, 22: Pfarrkirche St. Michael, Lindenhardt
20: CSvBibra, Public Domain
21, 41, 79, 141, 151, 174, 187, 229: New York, The Metropolitan Museum of Art, public domain
24: Museum für Franken – Staatliches Museum für Kunst- und Kulturgeschichte in Würzburg
26, 28, 37, 50, 207: Bayerische Staatsgemäldesammlungen
29, 30, 40, 69, 74, 93, 117, 186, 209, 210: National Gallery of Arts, Washington D.C., public domain
31, 33, 34: Theo Noll
32: Kunstmuseum Basel, public domain
35: The British Museum, London
36, 205: Szépművészeti Múzeum, Budapest
39, 43a-b, 56, 58, 60, 64, 65, 66, 70, 96, 125, 142, 143, 173, 185, 203, 211, 228, 230: Staatliche Museen zu Berlin, Kupferstichkabinett / Jörg P. Anders, Public Domain
42: Mainz, Landesmuseum
44a-b, 47, 72, 119, 154, 156: Staatliche Kunsthalle, Karlsruhe/ Wolfgang Pankoke, public domain
44c-d, 52, 53a-b, 54, 162, 163, 169: Städel Museum, Frankfurt am Main
45, 49a-b: Historisches Museum Frankfurt, photo: Horst Ziegenfusz
51: The Chicago Art Institue, public domain
57: Nationalmuseum, Rotterdam
61: Kunsthistorisches Museum, Vienna
62, 63, 124, 128: Kupferstich-Kabinett, Staatliche Kunstsammlungen Dresden, Photo: Herbert Boswank
71: Collection Guy Ladrière, Paris
73: Smith College Museum of Art, Northampton (Mass.)
76: Klassik Stiftung Weimar, Museen, Inv.-Nr.: KK 118
78, 221: Musei Civici del Castello Visconteo, Pavia
80: Photo: Cecilia Heisser / Nationalmuseum, Stockholm, public domain
82, 83, 84, 85, 86, 88, 89, 90, 91, 92, 95, 100, 101, 102, 103, 104, 105, 106, 109, 110, 111, 113, 115, 120, 121, 126, 129, 130, 132, 133, 134, 135, 136. 137. 138. 139, 145, 147, 148, 149, 150, 153 : Musée Unterlinden Colmar, RMN-Grand Palais / Stéphane Maréchalle / Mathieu Rabeau
94: College Episcopal Saint Etienne, Strasbourg
97, 98, 123: C2RMF, Paris, Elsa Lambert
107: Oskar Reinhart Collection "Am Römerholz", Winterthur
108, 168: Museo Nacional Thyssen-Bornemisza, Madrid
112: RMN-Grand Palais / René-Gabriel Ojeda
114: Archivio Fotografico Fondazione Adriano Bernareggi, Bergamo/ Photo Marco Mazzoleni
118: Musée Unterlinden Colmar, photo Christian Kempf
127, 204, 207: Staatliche Museen zu Berlin, Kupferstichkabinett / Volker H. Schneider, public domain
131: Friedrich-Alexander-Universität Universitätsbibliothek, public domain
140, 161: Staatliche Museen zu Berlin, Gemäldegalerie / Jörg P. Anders, public domain
144: Augustinermuseum, Freiburg im Breisgau
146, 183, 184, 192, 215, 216: Mauro Magliani
157: Roma, Galleria Doria Pamphilj © 2024 Amministrazione Doria Pamphilj s.r.l. Tutti i diritti riservati
158: photo © RMN-Grand Palais (musée du Louvre) / Michel Urtado
164: Spencer Art Museum, the University of Kansas, Lawrence
165: Ville de Grenoble /Musée de Grenoble –J.L. Lacroix
166: Photography courtesy Denver Art Museum
167, 170, 194: Ministero della Cultura, Pinacoteca di Brera, Milan
171: Su concessione del Ministero della Cultura – Direzione regionale Musei dell'Emilia-Romagna
172: Comune di Como, Civico, Pinacoteca di Palazzo Volpi
176, 177: Vienna, Albertina
178: Liebieghaus Skulpturensammlung, Frankfurt am Main
179, 180: Akg images
182: The State Hermitage Museum/photo by Vladimir Terebenin
188: Musée du Louvre, Dist. RMN-Grand Palais / Philippe Fuzeau
189, 190, 193: Augustinermuseum-Städische Museen Freiburg, photo H.-P. Vieser
195: RMN-Grand Palais (musée du Louvre) / Jean-Gilles Berizzi
196: Ashmolean Museum, University of Oxford
197: Würth Collection, Inv. 6576 (photoHorst Ziegenfusz, Frankfurt am Main)
198: Wikipedia Commons, public domain
199, 225: The Trustees of the British Museum
200: Accademia Carrara, Bergamo
201, 202: Staatliche Graphische Sammlung, Munich
212: Zentralbibliothek, Zürich, public domain
213, 214, 218, 220, 222, 224, 227: Staatliche Kunsthalle, Karlsruhe
219: The Devonshire Collections, Chatsworth. Reproduced by permission of Chatsworth Settlement Trustees
223: Royal Collection Enterprises Limited 2025 | Royal Collection Trust
226: Staatliche Museen zu Berlin, Skulpturensammlung und Museum für Byzantinische Kunst / Antje Voigt, Public Domain
231, 232: Staatsgalerie Stuttgartstadt
233: Institut für Stadtgeschichte, Frankfurt am Main
236: St. Martin Pfarreiengemeinschaft, Aschaffenburg
237: Alessandro Alganon, Arona (private archive)

Printed on the presses of Intergrafica, Verona, in the month of August 2025

Ex Officina Libraria
Jellinek et Gallerani